HISTORY OF THE PARISH OF WALLSEND

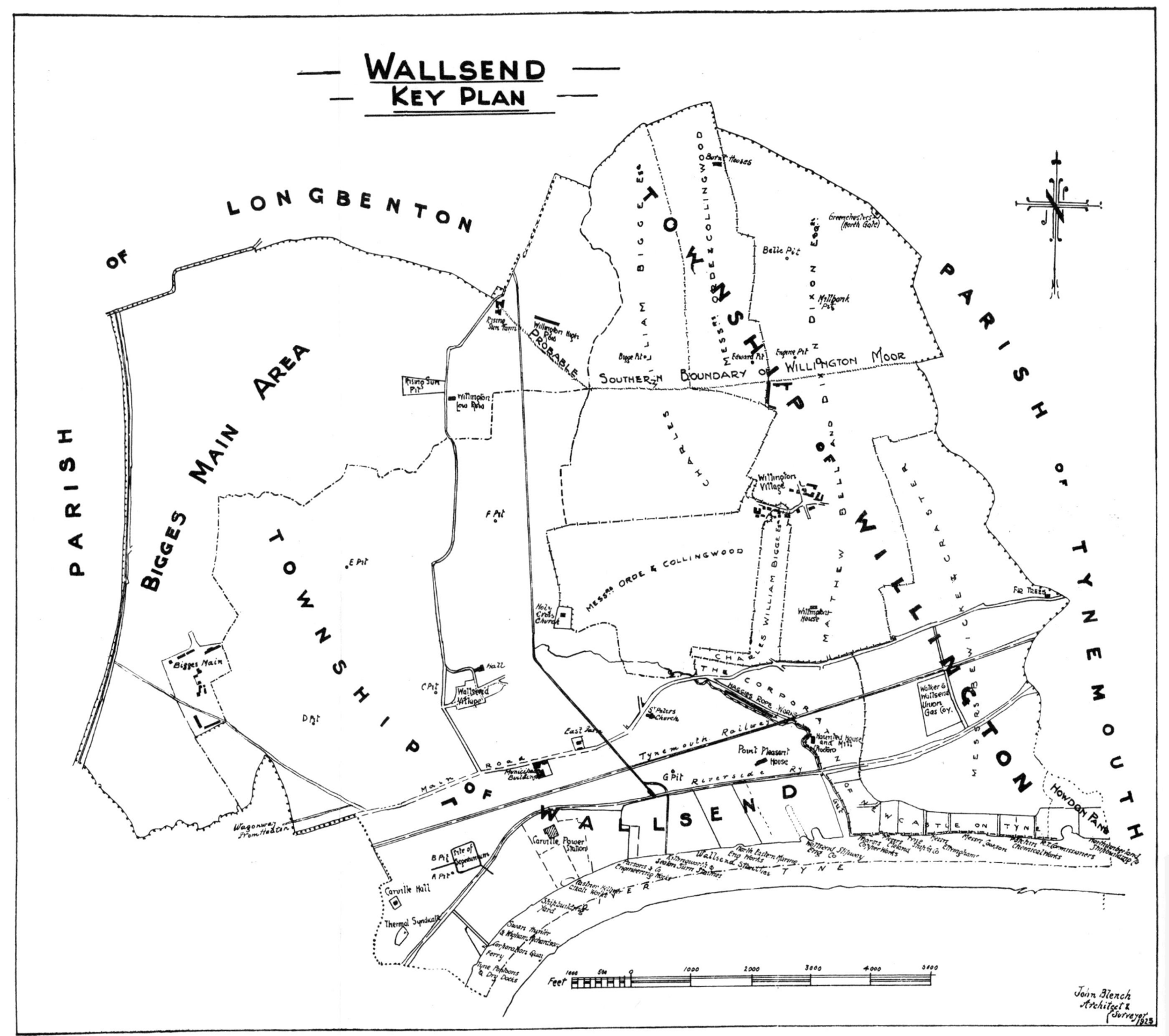

This shows the situation of the principal places mentioned in the History.

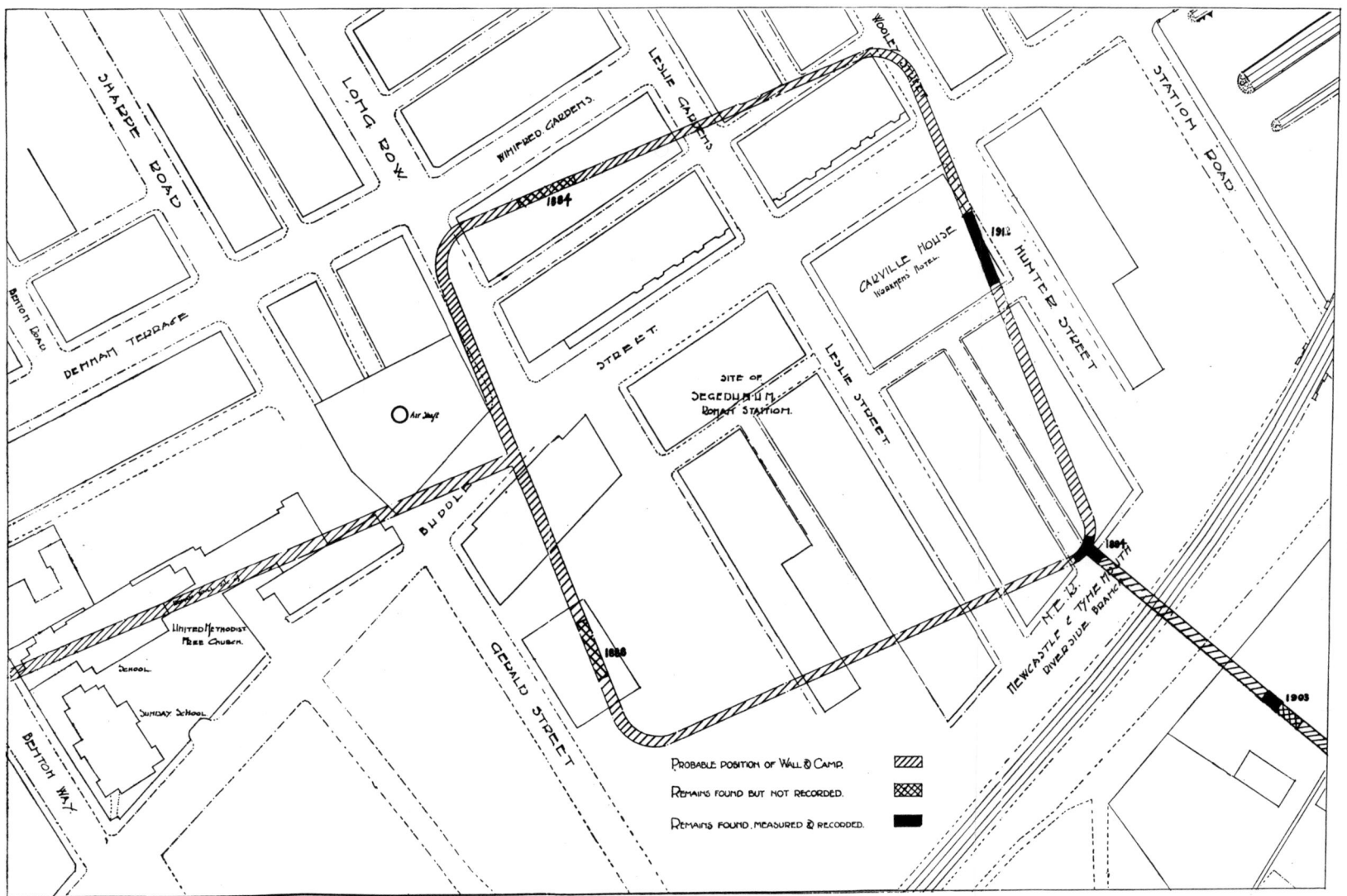

Plan showing the end of the Roman Wall and the site of Segedunum. Scale $\frac{1}{1500}$ [Facing page 22.

HISTORY OF THE PARISH OF
WALLSEND

THE ANCIENT TOWNSHIPS OF
WALLSEND AND WILLINGTON

GENERAL, ECCLESIASTICAL, INDUSTRIAL AND
BIOGRAPHICAL

BY

WILLIAM RICHARDSON

PIONEERS

A.D. 81

Hadrian	Buddles
Durhams	Procters
Anderson	Haggies
Henzells	Allens
Tyzacks	Coutts
Hurrys	Potters
Bells &	Boyd
Brown	Hunter
Russells	Parsons

A.D. 1923

THE NORTHUMBERLAND PRESS LTD.
NEWCASTLE-UPON-TYNE
1923

First published by the Northumberland Press, Newcastle upon Tyne, 1923

This edition published by
City of Newcastle upon Tyne
Education & Libraries Directorate
Newcastle Libraries & Information Service,
and North Tyneside Libraries, 1998, reprinted 1999

ISBN: 1 85795 034 8

Facsimile edition printed by Athenaeum Press, Gateshead

THIS BOOK IS DEDICATED TO THE MEMORY OF MARIA ISABEL RICHARDSON, WITHOUT WHOSE CONSTANT ASSISTANCE AND ENCOURAGEMENT IT WOULD NOT HAVE BEEN WRITTEN

MARIA ISABEL SPIVEY, the daughter of Mr William S. Spivey, solicitor, was born at Carmarthen on December 27th, 1868. She was educated at Carmarthen High School and Whitelands College, Chelsea, and she came to Newcastle in January, 1895, to join the teaching staff of the Durham College of Science, as teacher of the Methods of Education.

On May 23rd, 1900, she married the writer of this note and began her married life at Field Head, Willington-on-Tyne. She soon interested herself in the public work of the district, and there were few good causes she did not help. In the work of the Willington and Howdon Nursing Association, the Northumberland County Education Committee, the Borough of Wallsend Education Committee, and the Governing Board of the Secondary Schools she took special interest.

When the war broke out, the wives of the men "called up" were directed by the War Authorities to apply to the nearest town hall, or to the local Soldiers' and Sailors' Families Association, for financial assistance until their pay could be arranged by the Army Paymaster. There was no S. and S.F.A. in Wallsend, and for a few days the authorities at the town hall met the increasing applications. But the need for some proper organisation became imperative, and at the request of the Borough Treasurer Mrs Richardson took in hand the formation of a branch of the S. and S.F.A. for the Borough. In five days she had made the necessary inquiries, received the official authority from the

Central Association, and on August 18th she entirely took over the work, assisted by Mrs A. J. Haggie, Miss Thompson, and Miss Carrie McIlvenna.

The number of families requiring assistance very rapidly increased, and although more helpers flocked in, the pressure upon her was such as to occupy her all day and for a time Sundays also. It was when she had to deal with and assist the newly made widows and orphans, and when, at the request of the War Office, she undertook the guardianship of several motherless children that the strain told most heavily upon her. However, unlike the majority of the helpers, she held on to the end, though it was done only with an effort and a sacrifice of health.

When the Local War Pensions Committee was formed she was appointed the Hon. Secretary, and held this position until its work was properly organised and in working order.

For her war work she was appointed a Member of the Order of the British Empire,[1] and she was also especially commended by the London authorities of the S. and S.F.A., but her real reward came when men wrote from the front thanking her for what she had done for their wives or their children, and in the knowledge that the trials and troubles of the families of our Wallsend men were lightened as much as sympathy and effort and money could lighten such dark days. She was always proud of Wallsend's effort in this direction.

It is more than possible that the stress and strain of this strenuous time laid the foundation of her fatal illness. In any event she never regretted her efforts nor murmured over the cost.

After making every arrangement for the transfer of her public work, she passed away after eight months' illness on 5th July, 1920, clear-minded and thinking of others to the end.

---

[1] Only two such honours were given in Wallsend for honorary services. The other was allotted to Mr David West.

PREFACE

WITH regard to this history, sixteen years ago I was released from other work and I began to collect the history of our district. At first, beyond what the " oldest inhabitants " could remember, there seemed very little history available, but gradually many sources were discovered. Progress, apart from the war time, has been very slow, and I often had long delays in special directions. For example, for three years I failed to discover how Lord Howard de Walden got possession of the whole of Willington. However, steady search brought success, and now, had printing been less costly, I could have filled two volumes instead of one.

I found that our parish not only had an interesting history, but one that our town may well be proud of. I have been greatly assisted by many friends; all I appealed to did what they could to help. I owe special thanks to the Dean and Chapter of Durham, the Rector of Wallsend, the late Richard Welford, Mr T. A. Thorp of Alnwick, Dr F. W. Dendy, Mr Robert I. Dees, Mr John Henry Burn, Mr John Blench, Mr Robert Calvert, Mr Geo. R. Baston, my sister Anne I. Richardson, and my nephew Wm. Leslie Richardson; also to Mr Geo. D. Charlton of Dundee, an old Tynesider, for contributing the plate for the title page in memory of our pleasant days together on the Gareloch; to the Society of Antiquaries, the Borough Corporation, Mr Henry Giles, the Wallsend Slipway Co., the North-Eastern Marine Engineering Co., " Parsons " and " Swan & Hunters " for the loan of blocks, and to Mr Walter S. Corder, Mr Gideon S. Forster and Mr George Hill for the use of photographs. Then finally I gladly record my debt to Mr W. T. Mayne and his staff at the Northumberland Press Limited for guiding my inexperienced steps through the worries and troubles of book printing and publishing.

The Table of Contents will show the arrangement of the work (a perplexing thing to settle). Generally, the persons spoken of are mentioned in connection with the church, works, or property they were associated with, but the Index will clear up doubts. It is unfortunate the word " Wallsend " sometimes means Wallsend township and sometimes Wallsend parish, which includes Willington and Howdon. Wherever possible I have made clear which area is meant.

I trust my readers will find the history interesting and also reliable. The work of collecting the material has been a pleasant hobby, and for its faults, omissions, and failures, I bespeak a lenient verdict.

WM. RICHARDSON.

Field Head,
    Willington-on-Tyne,
        January, 1923.

CONTENTS

CHAPTER I

GENERAL HISTORY UP TO THE RESTORATION OF CHARLES II.

Introduction — Geological — Roman period — Pre-conquest — Norman—The townships under the Prior and Convent of Durham—In Feudal days—King v. Parliament—Act of Uniformity (1662) 17

CHAPTER II

LANDOWNERS AND LEASEHOLDERS FROM THE DISSOLUTION OF THE MONASTERY OF DURHAM IN 1540

Willington township : The estates and owners under the Crown and in private hands up to 1921—Wallsend township under the Dean and Chapter : Owners and tenants at Wallsend village; Carville Hall; Point Pleasant; Wallsend House and Carville House 50

CHAPTER III

ECCLESIASTICAL HISTORY

A history of each church and chapel with notes relating to many of those prominently connected therewith. Begins with Holy Cross in A.D. 1145 and finishes with the New Mission at Willington Square 110

CHAPTER IV

INDUSTRIAL HISTORY

Howdon Panns from the days of Queen Elizabeth : Its origin —The Andersons (salt pans)—Henzell and Tyzack (glass-makers)—Hurrys—Strakers and Love and others . 187

CONTENTS

CHAPTER V

INDUSTRIAL HISTORY—COAL MINING

Willington : In A.D. 1580 — In modern days; Bells and Brown; Matthew Bell — Wallsend : The Chapmans; the Russell era; disasters; the mid-Tyne pits overwhelmed; the Russell family; John Buddle—Social conditions near the end of the eighteenth century : Land enclosures; conditions of labour in the mines; ballot for the Militia; Navy hated; Wallsend Vestry as a recruiting agency; the press gangs; Parliamentary franchise; Jacobites club at Howdon; first Friendly Societies—Present-day collieries : The Tyne Coal Co., The Wallsend and Hebburn Coal Co. 210

CHAPTER VI

INDUSTRIAL HISTORY—CHEMICAL PERIOD

Pioneers in alkali manufacture : Wm. Losh, Allen's chemical works, John Glover and the Carville Chemical Co., John Lomas & Company—The decline of the trade on Tyneside and its cause—The Allen family; John Glover—The beauty of the district as the result of this period . . 271

CHAPTER VII

INDUSTRIAL HISTORY—(continued)

Early works :—Willington Ropery (established 1785) : The Chapmans, Washington Potts, The Haggies, Frank Dean; Willington Mill (established 1806) : The Unthanks, The Procters and the Ghost, Sampson Langdale; Willington Slipway (established 1835) : The founders, The Adamsons, Wm. Cleland (Clelands Limited); Willington Lead Works (established 1844) : Richardson & Currie, The Cooksons; Wallsend coke ovens and furnaces (established 1848) : John Carr, Palmers, Royal Greek Iron Co.—Iron and Steel Shipbuilding :—John H. S. Coutts, Parkinson, Muntsey & Jansen, Palmers; Schlesinger Davis & Co.; C. S. Swan & Co., Swan & Hunter and successors; Marshall, Cole Bros.,

CONTENTS

                                                                PAGE
Tyne Iron Shipbuilding Co.; Northumberland Shipbuilding Co.; Eltringhams Ltd. — Marine Engineering :— Wallsend Slipway & Engineering Co., North-Eastern Marine Engineering Co., Parsons Marine Steam Turbine Co.—Sundry Works :—Walker and Wallsend Gas Co., Tharsis Sulphur and Copper Co., H. D. Pochin & Co., Willington Foundry, Tyne Pontoon and Dry Dock Co., M. W. Swinburne & Sons, Newcastle Electric Supply Co., Castner Kellner Alkali Co., Thermal Syndicate Ltd., Wm. Thomas Weir, John Smith's Forge, Tyneside Tramways and Tramroads Co., Co-operative Societies . . . 282

CHAPTER VIII

LOCAL GOVERNMENT

The local records—The Select Vestry : " The Four and Twenty "—The reformed Vestry—Poor Law Union—Local Boards of Health : Wallsend (formed 1867); Willington Quay (formed 1863); Howdon (formed 1864)—The County Council—The Local Government Act of 1894—District Councils—Parish Council—Wallsend Burial Board—The Incorporation of Wallsend township—The Borough Arms —The Town Hall—The enlarged Borough—The Mayors of the Borough—Education : Early schools and schoolmasters; the School Board; Education Committee; The Café Technical classes—The Commission of the Peace—Rates and Rating, A.D. 1531-1922—" Farms "—Detailed valuation lists 360

CHAPTER IX

ADDITIONAL BIOGRAPHICAL NOTES

The ancient family of Durhams—The Surtees family—Billy Martin—George and Robert Stephenson and the Memorial Schools—The Weatherleys of Howdon—Dora Russell, novelist—Andrew Leslie—Wm. Thos. Stead—Dr Ernest Woodhouse—Wm. S. Daglish—Sir James Knott and others—The eighteen Mayors of the Borough . . 416

CHAPTER X

MISCELLANEOUS

River, roads, railways and wagonways — Bigges Main — Freemasonry—Wallsend Nursing Association—Willington Quay and District Nursing Association—The Wallsend Golf Club—Subscriptions for French War (A.D. 1798)—In the days of the cholera (A.D. 1831)—The " booming " years of housebuilding (A.D. 1898-1902)—Wallsend newspapers—Various events—Population Statistics . . 463

APPENDIX

Story of the Great Colliery Disaster in 1835—Epitaphs in the churchyard of Holy Cross Church—Extracts from deeds relating to Howdon Quay—Coal miners' wages in 1829 . 498

INDEX 521

LIST OF ILLUSTRATIONS

	PAGE
Roman Altar found in May, 1892	23
Wallsend as it appeared in 1850 ⎱ *between* ... ... ⎰	24
Wallsend in 1903 ... ⎰	25
Wallsend Hall in 1890	72
Wallsend Village School and House	82
The Grange, Wallsend Village. (Two views)	87
Part of the Village Green in 1890	93
The Red House, Wallsend Village. (Two views)	97
Carville Hall, Wallsend	101
Carville Shore about 1830	103
Point Pleasant House, Wallsend, in 1911	107
Ruins of Holy Cross Church in 1900	117
Ruins of Holy Cross Church in 1910. (Two views) ...	118
St Peter's Church in 1823	130
St Peter's Church in 1893	135
17th Century Communion Plate	140
The Colliery Chapel, Wallsend (*Wesleyan Methodist*) ...	144
"Zion" Methodist New Connexion Church, Wallsend, in 1900	166
Willington House in 1911	221
The original Wallsend Colliery ("*A*" *pit*)	226
The Haunted House and Mill, Willington, in 1895	290
Swan, Hunter and Wigham Richardson, Ltd., 1922. Shipyard—Building Berths and *Mauretania* at Quay ...	303

LIST OF ILLUSTRATIONS

	PAGE
Bird's Eye View of Wallsend Slipway, 1920	316
The Wallsend Slipway and Engineering Co., Ltd. The s.s. *Giulio Cesare* under the 180 ton crane	321
North-Eastern Marine Engineering Co., Ltd. View of Works from Airship, May, 1920	322
The Parsons Marine Steam Turbine Co. Ltd. The epoch-making *Turbinia* steaming at 34 knots	327
The Coach and Horses Inn, Wallsend	364
The "Arms" of the Borough	392
Stephenson's Cottage	422
Wm. Thomas Stead	434
The first six Aldermen of the Wallsend Borough Council	444
Views of Wallsend in 1900	472

MAPS AND PLANS

Key Map of District	*In front*
Plan showing the end of the Roman Wall and the site of Segedunum	22
Plan of Wallsend Village in 1840	70
Ground Plan of Holy Cross Church made 1910	111
Plan of Howdon Panns in 1836	199
Plan of Wallsend Township in 1800	*At Conclusion*

HISTORY OF THE PARISH OF WALLSEND

CHAPTER I

GENERAL HISTORY UP TO THE RESTORATION OF CHARLES II.

Introduction—Geological—Roman period—Pre-conquest—Norman—The townships under the Prior and Convent of Durham—In Feudal days—King v. Parliament—Act of Uniformity (1662).

THE parish of Wallsend is situated on the north bank of the River Tyne between Newcastle and North Shields. It consists of the two old townships of Wallsend and Willington (including Howdon) together with part of the parish of Long Benton, which was added in 1910 (see key map), and it is conterminous with the Borough of Wallsend.

The area of the parish, excluding the river, is:

	Acres.
Willington old township (including Howdon)	1433·618
Wallsend township	1096·546
Area taken from Long Benton . . .	819·625
	3349·789

The Roman Wall, stretching from the Solway to the Tyne, terminated within the western township and hence the name of Wall's end. As regards the name of Willington, " ing " was an Anglo-Saxon patronymic akin to the Scottish " Mac " and the Irish " O," " ton " denoted an enclosure, or fortified homestead, and hence we may have the enclosure or homestead of Willing. Further, Professor Allen Mawer, of Liverpool University, has kindly pointed out that a still earlier form of Willing is Wivling, or Wiveling, possibly from the Old English " Wifel." Confirming this, in the first entry we quote from the Halmote Rolls for A.D. 1296, Willington is called " Wyvel."

Geological

Wallsend is founded in more senses than one on the " coal measures," and the nature of these foundations has been of such importance to its history that they merit special mention. These coal measures lie under some 150 feet of boulder clay, or glacial drift, and they consist of 14 or 15 bands or seams of coal, separated by beds of sandstone and thin layers of fire clay.

The seam of coal of workable thickness nearest the surface is $6\frac{1}{2}$ feet thick (the High Main). It is at a depth of 600 feet at the south side of Wallsend, and it rises nearly 200 feet towards the northern boundary. The lowest seam (the Beaumont) is $2\frac{1}{2}$ feet thick, and lies about 500 feet below the High Main.

In geological times these foundations were laid towards the close of the Primary period. For vast ages the future site of our parish had been beneath a deep pure sea, and had slowly risen until it was barely above water level, and if we imagine ourselves taking a walk in the future Wallsend, while the coal measures were being formed, we should find ourselves in a dense, swampy, tropical forest.

The trees surrounding us on every hand would especially attract our attention; they are not the trees of to-day, but belong to the lower divisions of the plant kingdom and resemble the tree-ferns, horse-tails, and club mosses of the present age. In size, however, they greatly exceed their descendants of modern times, for, instead of the three or four feet attained by the tallest of the tropical club mosses of to-day, these tower to a height of even a hundred feet. Amid all this luxuriant foliage we look in vain for the bright colours and delicate forms of the flowers that characterise our present vegetation; here and there we may see tall forms, suggestive of our familiar pine trees —the forerunners of our present flowering plants—but flowers, as we know them, were ages later.

As we walk wonderingly along the edge of the sluggish streams, if we look carefully we may find tiny air-breathing shell-fish, and gliding in and out of the water we see that amphibia abound, and upon closer investigation we realise that the day of pure land animals is yet afar off.

As we grow accustomed to the giant ferns and mosses, and to the strange fish-like reptiles, we discover that beyond the splash made by these half-water, half-land animals, as they dive into the lagoons, the woods are strangely silent. This is due to the entire absence of bird life; indeed, untold ages have yet to pass before even that precursor of birds, the winged reptile, is developed. It would seem a strange world to us, and yet this is what would have been found in the beginnings of Wallsend.

After generations of this early plant life had grown and died, the land again slowly sank beneath the sea not far from a large river, and the old forest was covered up by sand, and as it sank deeper still, by mud, then it rose again, and the process was repeated, until after long intervals we have the remains of four thick forest growths, in four valuable coal seams. Immediately above the coal measures lies the glacial drift, for, of all the sedimentary deposits between the carboniferous age and those of recent times, not a vestige remains in Wallsend.

We have, however, within our borders, one or two legacies of the immensely long interval which intervened between the Coal Measures and the Boulder Clay. Long before the formation of these coal measures the Cheviots had been blazing volcanoes which had died out. Then after our carboniferous strata had been laid down and denuded and then covered up by the Permian rocks, old Cheviot blazed up again, and its volcanic energy caused the whole of the thick coal measures, and probably thousands of feet of other strata, to be torn through again and again. One of these breaks or " faults " runs from east to west through Wallsend—a little to the south of Willington House and of the Church Pit, and to the south of the " A " Pit—and along this line the whole stratum is dropped down thirty to fifty feet on the south side. Another rent runs across the south side of Wallsend village, the strata being thirteen feet " down cast " on the south side. There is a third " fault " on the east side of our district running from north to south and increasing from a few feet in depth to over seventy feet, and there are several smaller " troubles," to use a miner's expression. These " faults " are the only signs to be found of the enormous changes which occurred here during the Secondary and Tertiary ages.

Coming to the comparatively recent glacial periods, these are much in evidence all round. Our mother earth in her slow climatic changes was then imposing an arctic climate upon the first Wallsender, who probably reached Tyneside at this time. Vast glaciers were slowly grinding their way over our area from two directions, one ice drift coming from the north, and another from the direction of Norway. These, after planing down our land surfaces, left behind an immense quantity of boulder clay.

Prior to this period, the surface of the land was much higher than at present, and the Tyne was a much larger river. From borings made from time to time in our parish, it is seen that the old bed of the river was forty to fifty feet below its present level; furthermore, it was much wider, and had much more water flowing through its channel. The Wear originally ran into the Tyne through the Team valley; another large tributary came in from Greenhead, and an old pre-glacial stream entered just above Newcastle. During the glacial period the Team valley was choked up and the Wear diverted towards Sunderland; the other valleys were also filled up, and the bed of the river itself partly filled, and somewhat altered by the all-pervading glacial clay " drift." As the climate grew warmer, and the arctic conditions disappeared, the land surface was finally left pretty much as we know it to-day, although, even in comparatively recent times, the Tyne entered the sea through two channels in addition to the present one: one through the depression west of the Prior's Haven, and another through that near the Milldam, South Shields, and along the site of Ocean Road.

As we have already said, man probably found his way to the north of England during one of the intervals between the later glacial periods.

Roman

Little is known of Tyneside in pre-Roman times, but although the larger part of Northumberland was given up to forests, bogs, and wastes, it is probable that our part of the county was more or less inhabited by the native Britons.

Those on the north of the Tyne were the Ottodini, a tribe of the Brigantes—tall, active, war-loving men and fair, finely-shaped women. Usually both men and women had long reddish hair; they were clothed with skins, and lived in the most primitive kind of huts. They reared cattle, and probably tilled the land.

The Romans first landed on the south shores of Britain in 55 B.C., but it was over a hundred and thirty years before they had forced their way northward under Agricola and conquered the fierce tribe on the north banks of the Tyne.

The ebb and flow of the Romans farther north is outside

our scope—sufficient to say that they became firmly settled on Tyneside about A.D. 81.

Probably Agricola established camps and an earthen rampart from the Tyne to the Solway; and the Emperor Hadrian, who arrived on the Tyne towards the close of A.D. 119, began the Great Wall.

Hadrian made for Britain, in which country he set many things right, and was the first to draw a line of wall for 80 miles (73 English miles), so as to divide the Barbarians from the Romans.[1]

The eastern terminus of the Wall was the military city named by the Romans, Segedunum. The Great Wall joined the west side of the camp, which was about three and a half acres in extent, and from the south-east corner a flanking wall went down to the edge of the river.[2]

According to a Roman notitia, or army list, the Fourth Cohort of the Lingones was stationed here. This would comprise about six hundred foot and horse soldiers, but having regard to the fact that this city was the one on the line of the Wall most accessible to shipping, and that a good road ran the whole way alongside the rampart, doubtless Segedunum, with its quays and sea-borne traffic, would be the busiest place on the Wall, and the centre of a large civil population. A considerable proportion of the officers, traders, and others would live outside the walls of the city near the river on the south-west.

Segedunum would also be the headquarters of the outlying camps at Tynemouth and Chirton, and it is probable that another outpost was within our parish, half a mile to the north of Willington Square, although this camp is not mentioned by Dr Bruce, the historian of the Roman Wall.

About the year 1600 there were some cottages on the boundary of the north moor of Willington called Green-

[1] Spartianus Vita Hadriani.
[2] See plan.

ROMAN ALTAR FOUND IN MAY, 1892. *[Facing page 23.*
It is dedicated to Jupiter by the Fourth Cohort of Lingones.

chesters,[1] which retained this name for some considerable time after the moorland was enclosed.[2] Furthermore, the two fields to the north-west of Greenchester, on an old plan of the Milbank estate, are named East Greenchester and West Greenchester.[3]

From West Greenchester could be clearly seen the great camp of Segedunum, and it is the nearest point from which a wide view to the north could be obtained, from which direction the Picts would come. From here can be seen Penshaw Hill, Cleadon, the sea, the high land to the west, and as far north as the Cheviots and Simonside Hills. Hence the commanding position of Greenchester confirms the probability of the existence in this place of such an outlying camp.

We need not go into the details of the Roman occupation of Wallsend, as these are well known; sufficient to say that it lasted for about three hundred and thirty years, from about A.D. 81 until about A.D. 410. The arrival of these invaders had been strenuously opposed, but they had secured peace for the inhabitants around, and brought a much higher standard of civilisation to Tyneside. During these three hundred years the natives and the foreign element had so mingled, that, when the Roman Government recalled their forces, the departure was viewed with dismay and greatly lamented.

Many relics—altars, pottery, and coins—have been unearthed from time to time, and the most interesting of these still get-at-able are preserved by the Newcastle Society of Antiquaries. One particularly fine and important altar was found at Philiphaugh in May, 1892 (see illustration). It is 35 inches high, 16 inches wide, 16 inches deep, and was dedicated to Jupiter by the Segedunum garrison, the

[1] See page 212.
[2] On August 27th, 1724, there was buried in the churchyard of Earsdon " David Richardson herd of a place called Greene Chester belonging to Willington in the Parish of Wallsend "— Earsdon registers.
[3] Watson papers, Mining Institute.

Fourth Cohort of the Lingones. It proves that Wallsend was the Segedunum of the Romans, which was somewhat uncertain before this.[1]

An important find was uncovered in 1903 when Messrs Swan & Hunter were extending their shipyard towards the riverside railway. In digging into the hillside about seventy yards south of the camp, the Roman angle wall running down to the river was unearthed (see illustrations). It was five to six courses high and six and a half feet thick. Many stones were taken away as curiosities, and the remainder re-erected in Wallsend park. When Mr Robt. Casson built Camp House, at the foot of Hunter Street, in 1894, fourteen silver denarii were found.

Wallsend, however, in 1887 missed its last opportunity of retaining a priceless possession. In that year the land on which the Roman Camp stood was for sale. The southeast angle of the station was partly excavated, and the Roman bulidings and walls partly traced. Mr Boyd endeavoured to purchase the one and a half acres needed to preserve the ruins. The owners, Buddle Atkinson's trustees, asked £680 for the land. The Local Board undertook to look after the ruins if the purchase money could be raised. Mr Boyd endeavoured to raise the amount necessary, but failed, and the site was given over to the house builder, and what remained of the city, nearly two thousand years old, which would have attracted visitors from all parts, was broken up for road-making.

The plan shows where in June, 1912, there was opened up what was probably the last piece of Roman work which will be found in Wallsend. The old Carville House and grounds, once occupied by John Reay, were pulled down to make way for Simpson's Hotel. That house was situated between Hunter Street and Leslie Street, with its back to Buddle Road. It had large grounds in front, and had stood undisturbed probably one hundred and twenty

---

[1] See " Arch. Aeliana," 2nd Series, Vol. xvi., p. 76.

WALLSEND AS IT APPEARED IN 1850.

Drawn by John Storey from where the middle of Gerald Street now is. Note the mound on the left covering the south wall of the Camp and also the long jetties carried over the river foreshore to the deeper water.

WALLSEND IN 1903.

From a photograph taken by Mr. Walter S. Corder from a point a little south-east of Storey's drawing. The X in each picture indicates the position of the **Roman Wall discovered** in 1903.

years or so. During the excavations a considerable portion of the foundations of the Roman Walls and the eastern gate of the camp were discovered.

Beyond the remains of the walls the only " finds " which were unearthed were fragments of pottery, the bones of deer, and six coins. The earliest coin was one of Trajan's and the latest one of Gratian's, thus covering a period of nearly three hundred years. The foundations of the gateway were taken and laid down in the park, and the coins, pottery, and some other Wallsend Roman relics were presented to the town in 1919 by Mr W. S. Corder, and to these Mrs Robt. Casson added twelve of the coins found when building Camp House.

Pre-Conquest

The withdrawal of the soldiers from the Wall immediately brought the Picts from the north, and the Brigantes held their own with great difficulty for less than fifty years. Then the Angles, sailing from near the mouth of the Elbe, added to the troubles of the natives, and time after time spread ruin along Tyneside.

While the Picts were raiding our district from the north, the Wallsenders' stronghold would continue to be behind the Wall and within the strongly walled camp itself, and it would be here that they would store all their possessions. But when the sea rovers swarmed up the river again and again, anything of value in the old Roman station would be a standing temptation to the plunderers, and the riverside would cease to be a desirable place of abode. It was probably at this time that the Roman encampment was abandoned, the inhabitants removing out of sight from the river and making their homes where the village now stands. This settlement was possibly called Valeshead.

Ida the Saxon, by flame and sword laid waste the whole of the north in 547, and Wallsend would doubtless suffer in the general devastation. But presently the golden age of Northumbria came. Edwin established order and peace all over his kingdom, and when he married Ethelburga she brought the first Christian missionary—Paulinus—to the north with her. The consequent adoption of Christianity by large numbers was only a temporary one, and we are indebted to King Oswald (635-642) and to Aidan, who came from the monastery of Iona in 635, for the first permanent conversion of our district to the Christian faith.

Aidan, and afterwards Cuthbert, proclaimed Christianity in every corner of the north. Presently Bede (673-735) made Jarrow one of the famous centres of learning in Western Europe, and tradition says that the highway from the north for students and visitors, to the important monastery at Jarrow, was through our parish, and that a ferry was kept by the monks at Howdon, and a hospitium, or guest house, was also maintained there for travellers who could not, at once, cross the river.

This happy time of peace and progress came to an end at the close of the eighth century when the plundering Danes—heathen and unlettered—swarmed up the Tyne in 794, and once again devastating war and intellectual darkness descended upon the north.

The years preceding the coming of William of Normandy show only a changing picture of struggles and invasions, Danes and Saxons striving for the mastery, and both Danes and Saxons were successful in ruling for a time.

The Roman camp near the north-east boundary, being outside the Great Wall, would be a purely military outpost, and wholly abandoned when the Romans left, but the name Willington implies that the eastern side of our parish was settled again in Saxon days, and moreover we know that in the year 894 the owner was one Bernard. This person became a priest, and joined the community of monks of Lindisfarne, then settled at Chester-le-Street, and on being admitted to the household of St Cuthbert he gave them his estate at Willington.

NORMAN CONQUEST

In this old Northumbrian order men were permitted to marry. The monks were religious men, living with their families, forming one religious community, and holding all their goods in common. At this time they had fled from Lindisfarne in fear of the Danes, bearing with them the body of their patron saint, and they were presently to find a final resting-place at Durham.

About this period, or soon afterwards, Wallsend also seems to have passed into possession of the monks of St Cuthbert, and thus both Willington and Wallsend were owned by the bishop and congregation of St Cuthbert in pre-conquest days.

NORMAN CONQUEST

The conquest of the north by William of Normandy was a ruthless one. Before he felt assured that his victory was complete, he had swept over Tyneside with relentless force, and when he stayed his hand most of the towns, villages, and homesteads between the Humber and the Tweed were smoking ruins. Houses, cattle, everything of value, all were alike destroyed, and for years the north was a desert.

Generally speaking, William conditionally gave the lands thus conquered to his followers, and in pursuance of this policy he made Walcher, a nobleman of Lorraine, Bishop of Durham, and also Earl of Northumberland. It will be remembered that the agent of this Norman bishop aroused the ire of the people on Tyneside, who on May 14th, 1080, after burning the Church of Gateshead over the bishop's head, murdered him as he tried to escape from the burning building. His successor was another Norman, William de St Carileph.

Among the many changes made at this time was the disbanding of the monks of St Cuthbert. In this old religious order, men, as we have already said, lived with their wives and families, having all their goods in common. This in the eyes of the Normans was quite unorthodox, and hence the establishment in their place of a community of Benedictine monks at Durham.

The idea of this change seems to have arisen with Bishop Walcher, but it was carried out by Bishop de Carileph.

UNDER THE PRIOR AND CONVENT OF DURHAM

A.D. 1083-1540

With the express consent of the Pope and the King, Wallsend and Willington were transferred to the new order of monks to sustain and strengthen their monastery. Some historians quote a charter at Durham, dated 1082, as the authority for the transfer of our area to the Benedictine monks, but this is undoubtedly a forgery.

From this time onward until the dissolution of the Durham monastery on 31st December, 1540, the Prior and Convent were the owners of the two townships.

As Willington, and probably also Wallsend, was given to the " Household of St Cuthbert " while they were at Jarrow, both townships were included, for ecclesiastical purposes, in the parish of Jarrow, and so they remained until after the Durham monastery was dissolved.

The successive Bishops Palatine were, for all practical purposes, kings. The law courts of the people were the courts of the bishop, and all writs ran in his name. He appointed justices, coroners, and sheriffs. He could pardon any crime, and granted charters for markets and fairs, and had the right to coin money at his own mint.

While the bishops were the heads of the Church, yielding these powers, the priors of the Convent were the lords of the manor and feudal owners of the lands and other temporal possessions of the Convent. They administered each township within their jurisdiction separately, for the township is the oldest of all the territorial divisions into which England has been divided. Mr F. W. Dendy, who has gone into this very thoroughly, says:

> As a landmark of past history it (the township) has more value than either the manor, or the parish ... the present boundary line of the township is still in most cases identical with the original metes and bounds of the rural colony who peopled it from pre-historic times.[1]

As we shall see, Wallsend township and Willington township were treated as separate units for many centuries, and this continued long after Wallsend and Willington were formed into the parish of Wallsend. From a land-owning point of view the unit was the manor, and the two townships, together with Heworth, St Hilda's (South Shields), and other contiguous estates, were grouped, and formed the Manor of Westoe. (Wallsend still belongs to this manor, but Willington became a separate manor when Henry VIII. took possession.)

For years after the conquest our area was doubtless a waste, but by the middle of the twelfth century it was again inhabited and the Holy Cross Church was built for the benefit of the residents.

We have no records concerning the next hundred years, but before the close of the thirteenth century, and during the fourteenth, we have most interesting notes from the Convent rolls giving us a fairly clear picture of Wallsend and Willington six hundred years ago.

During the thirteenth and fourteenth centuries there were four classes of tenants in the townships : (a) The free tenants, who had certain rights of inheritance to their lands, who paid a " fine " on entry and sometimes a yearly rent, but they owed homage and fealty to the lord. This class had most freedom. (b) The tenants who rented the

[1] "Arch. Aeli.," Vol. xvi., N.S.

demesne lands. These were the lands in each township which the lord reserved for his own profit, and the next two classes were obliged to provide the labour to cultivate these. As the Convent had demesne lands in every township, they were farmed out and the tenant who took them held them for a term of years, or for life, and paid an agreed rent to the prior. (c) The third class were niefs who held at the will of the lord. They were, to a considerable degree, serfs. They were attached to the land and could not leave it without the licence of the lord. When they obtained such permission they made a payment for it. (d) The fourth class were the " villeins," who had the least freedom of all. They had some land and a cot provided for their own subsistence, but they had to work on behalf of their lord, or the tenant of the lord's land, and, generally speaking, they were the " hewers of wood and the drawers of water " for the vill to which they belonged, and were part and parcel of the lord's property.

The inhabitants had cots or houses which they were bound to keep in repair, though the prior supplied the timber needed. Each dwelling was surrounded by a garden, but both townships, as a whole, were unenclosed—part was in cultivation on the open field system and part was in commons and wastes.

Every tenant had his proportion of cultivated land which must be sown and worked in accordance with a prescribed rotation. There was also some land cultivated jointly for the common good. On the commons and wastes a certain number of cattle, pigs, and geese grazed, guarded by a common herd who must not allow them to trespass upon the cultivated lands, or meadows, or stray beyond the boundary of the vill. The two townships had a joint mill, owned by the lord. This mill was at Wallsend, where all grain had to be ground.

Wallsend and Willington had a reeve who acted for both townships and was elected by the tenants.

In Feudal Days

As we have already said, both Wallsend and Willington were in the manor of Westoe. Three times a year—in early spring, in summer, and in autumn—the representatives from Durham held court at the Manor House at Westoe, to which they summoned their tenants. The court received reports from each vill, " let " or relet lands, collected fines and rents, and generally ordered and administered the affairs of the several communities. Disputes or doubtful matters were often referred to a jury of tenants.

The proceedings relating to each township were entered upon skins of parchment, twelve inches wide and generally about eight feet long. Sometimes the proceedings were fully described, but generally the bare results were very briefly recorded.

The earliest Manor Court Roll extant begins in 1296, and in the extracts we give[1] the numeral I, II, or III which follows the year, denotes whether the record given relates to the first, second, or third court held in that year. Remembering that the old English year began on March 25th and that Lady Day was New Year's Day, the first court was in the summer.

Further, to the casual reader the fines, rents, etc., may seem odd amounts, e.g., 40d., 13s. 4d., £3 13s. 4d. The reason is that the unit of value at this time was the mark, equal to 13s. 4d., so that 40d. was quarter of a mark, 13s. 4d. one mark, 20s. one and a half marks, £3 13s. 4d. four and a half marks.

Another point to remember is that while for the sake of simplicity in translating the records the numerals are nearly always given in what are now our ordinary figures (Arabic) (or Indian?). these were not even known in England until the beginning of the seventeenth century and did not supersede the Roman numerals for some time after that.

[1] Translated from Vol. lxxxii, Surtees Society.

A.D. 1296 II

WYVEL. Patrick de Staneryar for the merchet of his daughter 10/-.[1] Hugo de Wyston because he unjustly took the ground corn of Christiana Gervais 6d.

WALISEND. The land of Henry Yole of Walisend is taken into the hand of the Lord on account of his lack of strength.

WYVELINGTON III. Ralph de Pitingd', because he ploughed the land of Alan de Heberine without licence, in mercy, 6d. And it is judged that the said Ralph shall recover from the aforesaid Alan the expenses that he can.

A.D. 1345 I

WALLESEND. All persons in the township are ordered to keep the peace in the corn meadows, pastures, and ways, and that none of them shall be hostile or rebellious to their neighbours, and that none of them may implead elsewhere than in the Court of the Prior. And if anyone shall be convicted of this he shall give the Lord Prior 20/-.

There is a gap in the records of the Halmote Court for nine years, from A.D. 1347 to 1356. These years were years of fear, death, and confusion, due to the Black Death from which England suffered so much.

This great pestilence had its origin in the far east, in the year 1333, and made its way rapidly along the trade routes from Cathay, as China was then called, spreading terror on every hand. In the summer of 1348 it made its appearance in England, and by the autumn of 1349 Tyneside was panic-stricken, and the whole district in terror.

In the rent rolls of the Convent, there is an entry:

Concerning the Tenants of the Prior who died in the first pestilence, who held at will, or were not free tenants.

Walisend 9 deaths, including Richard the Reeve, who held 23 acres, and Robert the Pinder with a cottage and 2 acres.

Wylington, 7 deaths.

It is probable that this bare and brief record of the

[1] The merchet for which 10s. was paid was a fine payable by a villein on the estate (who held his tenement for life) for licence to give his daughter in marriage.

death of these sixteen landholders covers the fact that two-thirds of the inhabitants of our district were swept away by this loathsome scourge.[1]

One of the results of this awful visitation was that it very considerably hastened the extinction of serfdom, and worked a revolution in the economic conditions of the labouring classes. With one half of the labourers of the north swept away, the demand for tillers of the soil was extreme. If a serf could escape from his lord, and remain untraced and out of his reach for a year and a day, he could not be reclaimed, and in spite of legal enactments, bailiffs and stewards, whose land was going out of cultivation owing to the death of their labourers, did not inquire very closely whether men who offered themselves for hire were free men or belonged to another distant landowner.

At the commencement of the fifteenth century, it is recorded that serfs were escaping from Durham across the Tyne to Wallsend and Earsdon.

A.D. 1358 I.

William de Munkton and Andrew de Wilyngton came and took the mill of Wylyngton and Wallisend for a term of years, yearly rent £6.

A.D. 1361 II.

Wyllyngton. John Ponder is elected to be reeve by the assent of Wyllyngton and Walleshend, and is sworn in Court.[2]

A.D. 1364 II.

[Wallsend and Willington]. From John son of John and John Yoill because they did not, for their shares, make the lanes, whereby the corn of John de Harton is depastured to the damage of half a sheaf. ... It is enjoined upon all the tenants of the vills of Wyllyngton and Walleshend that they

---

[1] Some townships suffered worse than ours. The entry concerning West Thickley is also brief and bare: "No tenants come from this vill for they are dead."
[2] Tenants of a vill were obliged to meet when summoned by the bailiff or other officer to assist to settle certain matters concerning the township, and here a reeve was elected for the two vills.

shall have a fold built before the next court, under a penalty of 6s. 8d. John Yoill is enjoined to come to the land in Wyllyngton under a penalty of losing the aforesaid land.

A.D. 1368 II

WALLESHEND. It is enjoined upon all the tenants of the vill that each of them shall come at the warning of the reeve to treat concerning the common business touching the profit of the vill.

John de Durham came in to the court and took one bondage tenement which Richard Aruas first held, and surrendered on account of lack of strength, to have and to hold for the term of his life : paying and doing the ancient services as the same Richard paid and did. And he gives for a fine 6s. 8d.

A.D. 1369 I

WALLESHEND. From William Belt because he did not repair 1 grange and 1 cottage upon the demesne lands 12d.

A.D. 1369 II

WILLYNGTON. Richard, son of William Watson came in Court and took all the holding which the same William first held : to have and to hold for the term of his life : paying and doing as the same William his father paid and did, and doing to the Lord and to the neighbours the things that are incumbent upon him. Pledges of the farm and of all other things incumbent . . . And he gives for a fine 20s. : reduced to 12d. From Roger Luttre of West Chirton because he did not come to answer to the Commonalty of the township, pledge William Paule. And it is ordered that he shall be distrained at the next court, 3d.

A.D. 1369 II

WALLESHEND. The jury is enjoined to enquire to what extent the land and tenement which belonged to John Tyngring, deceased, have deteriorated, and to cause all the goods and chattels which belonged to the same John to be seized into the hand of the Lord until he shall be satisfied. Robert Ponder took one tenement 24 acres of land which John Tynryng first held—for the term of his life, he found 6 acres twice ploughed, price of 1 acre 20d. . . . he shall give up the tenement and land in a sufficient state at the end of his term—he gives for a fine 40d. and he took for the repairing of the houses, 40 thraves of straw and 8s. of money—John son of John de Yarow—took one tenement and 16 acres of land which were in the tenure of 1 Caterina del Stayn and she surrendered to the use of the same John : to have and to hold for the term of his life : paying and doing in all things as the same Caterina first paid and did. And the aforesaid John shall satisfy the Lord concerning all the debts of the same Caterina and also he shall give the aforesaid Caterina half a quarter of corn and

2 bushels of peas. He shall give up in a sufficient state at the end of his term—he gives for a fine 40d.

A.D. 1369 III

WILLYNGTON. The jury of this vill and of the village of Walleshend are enjoined to view the water course running next the boundary of John de Monkton, and to order the right course to flow where it shall be the least source of damage. John de Monkton came in court and took one messuage and 30 acres of land which John Ponchon first held and surrendered to the use of the same John de Monkton : to have and to hold for the term of his life : paying the old rent, and doing to the Lord and to the neighbours the things encumbent upon him. Payment to begin at the feast of Martin 1371 and not before because a moiety of the rent of the term of Pentecost of the same year is pardoned, and the aforesaid John Ponchon shall pay the other moiety of the same term of Pentecost by agreement. And he gives for a fine 2s.

A.D. 1370 II

WALLESHEND. From Robert Punder for breaking the peace with his beasts, 6d. All are enjoined to make a gate within the tenement of John Punder where they have common passage. All the tenants of the vill are enjoined, and it is arranged between them that each of them shall come to treat concerning the common businesses as often as they shall be warned by the reeve. All the tenants of the vill are enjoined to have a common pigstye—It is arranged by common consent that each tenant shall come to make the hay of the common meadow when he shall be warned, under the penalty of losing his share and also under the penalty of a heavy fine.

A.D. 1370 II

WILYNGTON. John son of Andrew de Wilington, John de Houghton, John de Houghton, John de Dunelm, and William del Eawe his pledges, are ordered to cause to be repaired one house of a tenant upon the holding which the same John son of Alexander took in the year of the Lord 1365 because five years have elapsed and he had 6 years to build in.

A.D. 1371 I

WILLINGTON. John de Houghton is enjoined as in the last Halmote that he shall cause to be arrested the corn and beasts of John de Monkton so that he come and abide upon the Lord's land : and the same John de Houghton, the reeve, testifies that he arrested 2 horses, 3 oxen worth 5 marks and 7 acres of corn, 3 acres of oats. From the same, because he sowed the land with oats when he ought to have sown it with beans and peas, to the loss of the Lord as it is proved, 40d.

The jury of this vill and of the village of Walleshend are enjoined to view the tenements of John de Monkton to see to what extent they have deteriorated.[1]

WALLESHEND II. John Arnas, nief of the Lord dwells in Horton as is known.[2]

A.D. 1372 I

WALLESEND. It is proved in Court that William Alan shall recover against the tenants of the vill 1 sheaf of arrows worth 18d.[3] A day is given to Robert Ponder to wage his law that he does not owe to Adam, the servant of John de Dunelm', 1 rood of beans and peas from the time when he dwelt with him, for his kindness.[4]

A.D. 1372 II

WALLESHEND. It is enjoined upon all the tenants that each of them shall cause their tenements to be repaired before the feast of the Purification of the Blessed Mary, as in many Halmotes, under a penalty of half a mark : And also that they shall cause the timber to be replaced in their houses, of the gift of the Terrar.[5]

A.D. 1372 III

WALLESHEND. It is enjoined upon all the tenants of the vill that they shall have a common shepherd to guard the sheep. From this vill and the vill of Willyngton, because they have not had a common smith, and because they have not repaired the common forge 2s.[6]

---

[1] We have seen that John of Monkton only took the land in the spring of 1369 and was very generously treated. Now his stock and corn are arrested because he has not come to live on his land. He is fined a quarter of a mark because he did not follow the proper rotation of the crops, and finally a jury from the two villages was to see how much John's land had been damaged.

[2] A nief was bound to the land, but could leave his vill and reside elsewhere provided he obtained the licence of the lord and paid him a fixed sum. Hence at the Halmote Courts frequent notes are found as to where an absent nief lived.

[3] In the second statutes of Robert I., King of Scotland, Cap. 27, S. 4, a sheaf of arrows is said to consist of twenty-four arrows.

[4] When one tenant had a claim against another, or a dispute, a day was set apart for him to place his case before the Lords' Court and have it settled.

[5] Apparently the timber is the gift of the Terrar, who was one of the officials who looked after the property of the Convent.

[6] At a later court the tenants of both townships were again fined because "they did not have a common smith as was enjoined upon them in many Halmotes."

A.D. 1372 III

WILLYNGTON. It is enjoined upon all the tenants of the vill and of the vill of Walleshend that none of them shall permit geese (etc.) to leave the vill without being guarded. Thomas son of John Watson took all the holdings last in the tenure of the aforesaid John to have for the term of his life; paying for the first three years for each year 53s. 4d. and afterwards for each year 66s. 8d. payment beginning at the feast of Pentecost A.D. etc. 74 to. . . . And it is known that he finds the aforesaid tenements and land in a sufficient state, and he shall thus give it up. . . . Fine 40s. and it is reduced by the Terrar to 6s. 8d.

A.D. 1373 II

WALLESHEND. The jury of this vill and the vill of Willyngton. It is enjoined upon all the tenants of the vill that they shall sufficiently enclose the park. The fishery of Walleshend is taken into the hand of the Lord, because the tenant sublet that fishery without the Lord's licence.

A.D. 1375 I

WALLESHEND. From Alan de Dunelm' and John del Rawe for breaking the peace collecting peascods 2s. It is enjoined upon all the tenants of the vill that none of them shall collect peascods except for their own use, and not to sell at Newcastle, but in the place appointed by the reeve.[1]

A.D. 1376 III.

WALLESEND. It is proved by the oath of the jury that Richard Arnas, nief of the lord, is married and dwells in Horton and John Arnas is his brother and is of the same condition and dwells in Ylayton (?) as is believed John Watson (is) nief of the lord and dwells in Northumberland. Jon son of Henry Egill is of the same condition and dwells in Newcastle in Pampden with Walter Kaa.

A.D. 1377 I

WYLLYNGTON. Cristiana who was the wife (i.e. the widow) of John de Houghton came in Court and took 1 messuage 30 acres

---

[1] Peascods, i.e., peas in the shell. These must have been grown on common land, and the other tenants appear to have objected to Alan selling the peas at Newcastle—hence the breaking of the peace.

of land last in the tenure of her husband formerly in the tenure of William de Riton : to have and to hold for the term of her life : paying the old rent. Fine 26s. 8d. John son of John de Houghton came in Court and took 3 messuage 46 acres of land and also 1 messuage 30 acres of land which are called Whitmalland last in the tenure of John de Houghton father of the aforesaid John : to have and to hold for the term of his life : paying the old rent. Fine £4 13s. 8d. a moiety to be paid before the next court, and the other moiety within a year then next following. And it is known that the aforesaid Cristiana mainprised the aforesaid pledges, to keep them from loss.

A.D. 1378 II

WALLESHEND. It is enjoined upon all the tenants of the vill, that each of them shall cause to be ploughed all fallow land as well barren as otherwise, in future, under the penalty of half a mark. The mill—William del Rawe the elder and William del Rawe the younger came and took the wind mill of Walleshend from the feast of St. Mark 1378 for a term of three years paying therefor yearly 60s., and they shall maintain the aforesaid mill as other farmers before them were accustomed to do, pledge one of the other.

A.D. 1379 I

WALLESHEND. It is arranged by common consent that each of them shall make the enclosures of the demesne grounds there before the feast of S. Michael next coming, under a penalty of 12d. Thomas Benet made a rescue of beasts about to be impounded there. William Clerk of Tynemouth and the common huntsman took hares there. It is enjoined upon all the tenants of the vill on the one part and upon William the chaplain that none shall abuse the other in words or deeds henceforth under a penalty of half a mark to be paid.

It is enjoined upon all the tenants of the vill that they shall cause the common fold to be repaired before the next court under a penalty of paying 40d., and also that they shall not put the common beasts of the vill in the aforesaid fold under a penalty of half a mark. John de Yarow (with seven others among them Richard Tubb) took the demesne lands of Walleshend with the buildings belonging to the demesnes aforesaid; to have for a term of 9 years, paying £10 16s. 8d. and they shall give up the aforesaid demesne lands at the end of the term in a sufficient state. John de Dunelm' has licence to sublet 1 cottage and 4 acres of land to a sufficient tenant. John de Dunelm' afterwards came and surrendered the aforesaid cottage and 4 acres of land to Robert Letani in the presence of the lord Prior to the use of the same Robert; to have at the will of the lord Prior, because he is a nief of the lord, paying yearly 3s. 6d. at the exchequer of the lord Prior as the aforesaid John paid, and for the works of the manor 15d. and all other services belonging to the manor aforesaid.

A.D. 1379 I

WYLLYNGTON. From all the tenants of the vill, for the arrears of the rent of Williamsmor[1] for 13 years past, for each year 10s. Robert son of Andrew took 1 messuage 46 acres and also 1 messuage and 30 acres of land called Witmallands : to have for the term of his life, paying the old rent and service, and he finds 20 acres twice ploughed which he shall thus give up; pledges William del Raw the younger (and others). And if it shall happen that the aforesaid Robert shall die within 3 years, the lord Prior wills and grants that William del Raw the younger if he shall live, shall have the aforesaid messuage and land for a term of three years.

A.D. 1379 II

WALLESHEND. From Agnes who was the wife (i.e. the widow) of John Ponder for demesne lands twice ploughed, whereof John de Yarow satisfied her, which the lord Prior ought to have received because her husband thus found it, 5s. From the same Agnes for two ploughings of the same lands which she took of William the chaplain belonging to the Prior, for the same cause 4s. William the chaplain came and took the herbage of the wood of Walleshend from the feast of S. Mark for a term of 7 years, paying for the first three years for each year 24s. and for the four years following 26s. 8d. And the aforesaid William shall maintain the wood in enclosures and all other appurtenances and also he shall have rods for measuring and other necessaries and appurtenances for his plough. And if anyone shall be convicted of trespass done there at the complaint of the aforesaid William, the aforesaid William shall have a moiety of the profits taken or damages obtained for the same.

---

[1] With regard to Williamsmor (Willington moor). If we took the footpath which enters our parish at the " Blue Houses," then runs westward to the Willington Square, then continues as a bridle road to Battle Hill, we believe we should follow the southern boundary of the moor and the track which would naturally be made over the " common " between Long Benton and North Shields. The moor was almost certainly all the land in the township lying north of this line (see key map). It seems to have remained unenclosed for over three hundred and fifty years after the date mentioned here, as when Isobel and Julian Dent had their joint lands divided into two, the West Farm estate had to take one hundred and twenty acres north of these public roads. This land is quite isolated from the rest of the land grouped into the West Farm, and it appears that the sole season for this inconvenient division was that each of the three estates (the Milbank, the North Farm, and the West Farm) might take their proportion of the moorland. Confirming this is the fact that on an old plan the fields on the Orde estate, immediately north of the Square, are named North moor field, Middle moor field, and South moor field.

A.D. 1380 III

WALLESHEND. It is enjoined upon all the tenants of the vill that none of them shall keep grey hounds for taking hares.[1]

A.D. 1381 III

WILLYNGTON. William Edward took the mill of Walleshend for a term of 6 years paying 40s. and the lord shall find the great timber and millstones, and the aforesaid William shall find sails and cogges.

A.D. 1382 I

WALLESHEND. For a certain fray in the field of Walleshend by the men of Tynemouth when blood was spilt, and they were arrested there by John del Raw, and William Wessy became the pledge of John del Raw for the damage aforesaid, therefore John del Raw shall answer for 40d. It is enjoined upon all the tenants of the vill and the village of Willyngton that they shall cause to be repaired the way in the high road under the wood sufficiently, before the feast of S. Michael next coming, under a penalty of half a mark.

A day is given to John Schephird to wage his law that he did not break the agreement with Simon Yardolf and that he faithfully served him and did not withdraw himself from his service, with the 6th hand at the next court, under a penalty of half a mark. Robert Smith found pledges of peace towards John Schephird that he shall not do any damage by himself, or by another, under a penalty of £10. Pledges William del Raw and John del Raw. Item, John Schephird found pledges of peace towards John Smith in the same manner and under the same penalty. Pledges John de Yarow and Roger de Saxton. A day is given to John de Dunelm' to wage his law at the next court that he did not promise William, son of Stephen, 2 oxen for 1 year to plough the land newly taken, last in the tenure of John de Dunelm' and also that he should plough the land of the aforesaid William before

---

[1] In the first court of the year preceding this, William, the clerk, is noted as taking hares, and now we have all the tenants prohibited from keeping greyhounds for this purpose. It is not quite clear why the tenants of the vills were forbidden to take hares, but in 1363 Edward III. had ordered the general practice of archery on Sundays and holidays, in lieu of other rural pastimes, which were forbidden under pain of imprisonment. It is probable coursing hares for amusement was preferred to practising archery for the good of the realm, and the Lord of the Manor was in this way helping the Royal edict.

the feast of S. Peter in chains[1] (" S. Petri ad Vincula ") next coming under a penalty of 40d.

A.D. 1382 I

WILLYNGTON. It is enjoined upon all the tenants of the vill and the village of Walleshend, that they shall not grind elsewhere than at the mill of Walleshend, under a penalty of half a mark.

A.D. 1382 II

WALLESHEND. From John del Raw, because he took 1 horse belonging to Peter del Redhough in the field of Walleshend, and put it in the fold at Benton, to the loss to the said Peter of 2d. for a fine 6d.

A.D. 1382 III

WALLESHEND. A day is given to Henry Diconson to wage his law with the 6th hand, because the beasts of the vill, whilst he was in charge, did damage depasturing the herbage at Walkerborn, to the value of 12d.

A.D. 1383 II

WALLESHEND. It is enjoined upon all the tenants of the vill that each of them shall cause his land to be ploughed before the feast of Easter, under a penalty of paying 40d. etc. From William Schephird, the common shepherd because he put sheep in the Frithfeld,[2] against the penalty appointed, of mercy a fine 12d.

A.D. 1384

WILLYNGTON. It is enjoined upon all the tenants of the vill that they shall place their timber given by the lord, in their houses, before the feast of S. Cuthbert next coming. It is enjoined upon all the tenants of this vill and the village of Walleshend

---

[1] " St Peter in chains " is an obsolete expression referring to the day he was sent to prison. This feast was kept on August 1st, and it was customary on that day to make offerings of the firstfruits of the harvest. A loaf became the symbol of these, and the day was known as Loafmas, which became corrupted into Lammas. In the north of England and in Scotland, occupiers of lands paid their dues in kind on this day, but now when we pay our rents in cash on August 1st few of us associate the day with " Saint Peter in chains."

[2] Probably an unused pasture field set apart for hay.

that none of them shall go to law nor implead others in any other court than in the court of the lord Prior, under a penalty of paying 20s. From Sir William the chaplain, because he removed 1 servant of Robert de Heryngton, as is proved, outside the lordship, to the damage of 4s. fine 6d. It is enjoined upon William Dromond the miller, that he shall grind the neighbours' corn at convenient days and times, each according to his turn, under a penalty of 40d. and also that all the tenants of either vill shall grind their corn at the mill of Walleshend, and not elsewhere under a penalty of half a mark. It is presented by the jury that corn growing upon the land of the priest is bound to be ground at the lords' mill there, to wit, at the "lossoken" to wit at 16 vessels, and not otherwise.

Thus we have pictured to us from the Court rolls the agricultural life of the tenants in our district under the Convent during the fourteenth century, but important changes were meanwhile going on all over England.

Serfdom was giving place to free tenancies, services due from the freemen were being commuted for money payments, and beyond these changes connected with the land England was beginning to develop a manufacturing industry and a foreign trade. In the reign of Edward III. we have a very early glimpse of local shipowning and foreign trading. In the Calendar of Patent Rolls of the 34th Edward III. there is recorded under date of

1360, April 17th. Whereas a ship called le Rodecogg of Newcastle-on-Tyne,[1] whereof Nicholas de Wylyngton is Master, was arrested in Flanders. . . .

The cause of his arrest was he had not joined the King's fleet when called upon.

Nicholas of Willington pleaded that his seamen were taken for other ships, and his was "left empty," and therefore he was unable to offer his services. It is satisfactory to find that the first Wallsend shipowner we know of was speedily released and that the King granted him a licence "to go to his own parts or else where as shall be most to his advantage during the King's pleasure."

[1] All the Tyne was then in the port of Newcastle

On the north-west boundary of the township there is an area of land which for about seven hundred years has been known as Threap Moor. " Threap " in the olden days, in the north country, meant "debatable," and the dispute concerning this particular land began in the days we are now dealing with.

Early in the thirteenth century Little Benton was held by Eustace de Benton under the barony of Heron, whose tenants were in continual disagreement with the Wallsend tenants of the Prior and Convent of Durham. In order to put an end to this state of affairs, an arrangement was made between the two owners. The agreement is of considerable interest, although most of the landmarks mentioned are untraceable, and the meaning of the arrangement is not always clear.

The following is from the Records of the Priory of Durham for the year 1464 :

In the year 1246, an agreement was made between the Prior and Convent of Durham, of the one part, and John of Little Benton, with the consent of his master, W. Heyrun, of the other part, to wit, that the whole moor—from the boundary of Adam Barat[1] (which was settled between Thomas, a former Prior, and the Convent of Durham, and Adam), towards the N.W., near the path which lies between the said moor and the land of Adam Barat, and so ascending through another path which goes between the moor of Wallsend and the aforesaid moor towards the N., as far as the boundary between the land of Little Benton and of Wallsend —is to remain common to the said Prior and Convent and their

---

[1] Adam Barat's land was on the Walker side of the moor, and a Subsidy Roll made in the twenty-fourth year of Edward I. shows that he owned or leased more than half of the township of Walker. Subsequently the land thus set aside to be held in common by both townships was divided between Little Benton and Wallsend, and the area which was allotted to Wallsend was still to be held in common among the Wallsend tenants. In 1800 this area amounted to 19 acres 1 rood and 23 perches, and although originally divided into seven shares, when the land of the Dean and Chapter began to be enfranchised, and re-sold with restricted rights, the common was, for convenience sake, held in twenty-eighths. In 1892 owing to various sales the Dean and Chapter held eight twenty-eighths, Wm. Allen and Mrs Allen eight twenty-eighths, Robt. R. Dees seven twenty-eighths, Dame Allan's Charity four twenty-eighths, and Wigham Richardson one twenty-eighth.

men of Wallsend, and to the said John and his heirs or assignees of Little Benton. So that neither the Prior nor the said Convent nor their men, nor the said John nor his heirs or assignees nor their men of Little Benton may for the future cultivate or strip the said moor, but it is to remain for ever common pasturage to both parties, with due regard, however, to what was examined by the said Prior and Convent on their own behalf and on that of their successors, that that part of the moor which lies to the N.W. from the old ditch towards the arable land of Benton and the ground of the aforesaid John of Little Benton and of the estate of W. Heyrun, which part of the moor the said John claimed as his own separate property, appertaining to the aforesaid house of Little Benton, shall nevertheless lie for ever as common pasture to the aforesaid houses of Little Benton and of Wallsend, as is aforesaid.

Witnessed by Hugo de Bolebek, R. de Kamboe, R. de Cressewell, and others.[1]

By the time we reach the stormy years of the conflict between Henry VIII. and the Pope, the old feudal conditions had passed away. Wallsend township was divided into seven farms, and all the tenants were occupying their leaseholds on payment of a rental. In the rent rolls of the Bursar of the Convent for the year 1539, the year preceding the dissolution of the monasteries, we have the names of the tenants.

Those for Wallsend township were: Richard Chicken, Gawan Hyndmers (afterwards Hindmarsh), Richard Stott, Agnes Ponchon, William Ponchon, William Preston, and John Hall. Each of these paid a rental of 34s. 7d. per annum, while the widow of John Durham paid 5s. 4d. per annum for a cottage.

Those for Willington were: John Punchon, Roger Morton, Robert Unthank, John Robinson senior, Wm. Robinson, Wm. Robinson junior, John Hunter, and John Herryson. Each of these held his land at a rental of 33s. 4d. per annum. There was also "Thomas Bell, for land for one salt pann," who paid 3s. 4d. per annum. Here we see that the township of Willington was divided into eight leaseholds or "farms."

[1] Surtees Society, Vol. lviii

Of these leaseholders, one of the Durham family and one of the Ponchons had already been landholders under the Convent for one hundred and seventy years. We will, however, deal with the leaseholders and landowners in our next chapter.

WITCHCRAFT

In the depositions of ecclesiastical proceedings in the courts of Durham from 1565 to 1573, there is a case showing that the craze for accusing people of witchcraft was as rampant in our district three hundred and fifty years ago as it was then in other parts of the country, and the evidence given shows what vague gossip was accepted by the courts.

This particular trouble began when Robert Thompson, who was vicar of Benton, lost his mare. He suspected a man named Jenkyn Pereson of the theft. The neighbours also blamed Pereson for the absence of the " mayr," and bad feeling was engendered in consequence. However, the missing animal was presently returned to its stable mysteriously, but the vicar was not content. It was a case of giving a dog a bad name, and in those days we shall see it was an easy matter to raise a cry of witchcraft against unpopular neighbours, so both Pereson and his wife were accused. Hence we have

Robert Durham of Walshend, farmer, aged 72, deposes he is sure, that Jenkyn Pereson was in troble for a mayr, and he haithe herd saye that Jennet Pereson uses wytchecraft in measuringe of belts to preserve folks frome the faryes.

Catherine Fenwick, daughter of Constance Fenwacke, generos. aged about 20 years.

She saithe she doithe knowe that William Pereson, Jenkyn son staill a mayre, but whether Jenkyn was privy thereto or no she wote not.

She saithe she haithe herd that Jenkyn Pereson was a forsworn man, but wherein she knoweth not.

She saithe that about 2 yeres ago hir cosyn, Edward Wyddrington had a childe seke, and Jenkyn Pereson wyfe axed of Thomas Blackberd, then this deponentn mother servannte, how

Byngemen (Benjamin) the child did, and bad the said Blackberd byd the childe's mother comme and speke with hir. And upon the same this deponent went unto hir; and the said Pereson wyfe said the child was taken with the farye, and bad hir sent 2 southrowninge (south-running) water, and theis 2 shull not speke by the waye, and that the child shuld be washed in that water, and dib the shirt in the water, and so hang it upon a hedge all that night, and that on the morowe the shirt shuld be gone and the child shuld recover health : but the shirt was not gone, as she said. And this deponent paid to Pereson wyfe 3d for hir paynes, otherwais she knoweth not whether she is a wytche or not.

Robert Thompson, vicar of Benton, aged fifty-two years, gave evidence as follows :

He herd wido Archer's doughter, called Elizabeth Gibson saye that Jenkyn Pereson's wyfe heled hir mother who was taken with the farye, and gave hir 6d. for hir paynes.

The vicar adds that he owned the " mayr " that " was stowen frome hym but afterwards the matter was stayed he cannot tell how."

Unfortunately we are unable to trace what fate befell either Jenkyn or his " wyfe."

From the will of Thomas Loren (Lorraine), who was a younger son of Robert Lorraine of Kirkharle, we get some interesting information concerning the stock of a farmer, over three hundred years ago, and of prices then prevailing in Wallsend.

Thomas Loren was a very large agriculturalist, who had land and stock not only in Wallsend, but also at Flatworth, Benton, Prestwick, Kirkharle, and other places.

The date of the will is November 4th, 1594, and it begins :

Thomas Lorens of Walsend, gentleman. . . . My bodye to be buryed in the parishe churche of Walsend.

The Inventory shows that he had

at Walsend—40 ewes £9, 3 nags £6, nyne oxen £20, 12 Kie £18, 5 gelde nolte £3-15-0, twentie boules of wheat £10-10-0, 40 boules of otes £10, 8 boules of peese 53s. 4d., waines and plewes with the appurtenances 53s. 4d., all the Household stuff £10, 10 boules of corne sowen £10.

KING v. PARLIAMENT

During the years of struggle between the Royalists and the Puritans the evidence available appears to show that upon the whole the landlords of Wallsend and Willington sided with the Royalists and the people with the Puritans.

John Cosyn, who built what was afterwards Carville, was strongly on the side of the Puritans, and was one of the local Sequestration Committee, but he appears to be the only local man of his class who was an active supporter of the Commonwealth.

Soon after the Long Parliament met, the government began to treat those opposed to their policy as "delinquents," and these they called to account.

A news sheet of December, 1646, mentions that there are some "malignants on the south side of the Tyne and on the north side," "some are towards Walker, Willington, and so towards Tynemouth," "that way lie the great ones that came from Oxford," and the "Records of the Committees for Compounding, etc., with delinquent Royalists in Durham and Northumberland "[1] show that Royalists scattered from the headquarters of Charles at Oxford might have many powerful friends in our district.

Many well-known local Royalists surrendered to the Committees, compounded for their "delinquency," and paid their fine. Those who did so early escaped easily, as in the stress of finding money for the Army, more and more stringent measures were taken against the estates of the Royalists.

Sir Francis Bowes, a Wallsend landholder, was a conspicuous supporter of Charles. An order for the sequestration of his estate was issued on August 23rd, 1644. He surrendered himself two months later. On March 30th,

[1] Surtees Society, Vol. cxi.

1646, on oath, before the Committee appointed to deal with delinquents, he declared that since his surrender, he had conformed to all the orders of Parliament, and he gave particulars as to his possessions. These included " a farm in Wallsend, held of the Dean and Chapter, of the yearly value of £30 clear." On 28th April he was fined £544, and the fine was paid on May 21st, 1646, and the estate was discharged. Sir Francis Bowes held his land in Wallsend at a rental of 37s. plus 4s. for wood rent.

His father was Henry Bowes of Newcastle, and his mother was Anne, daughter of Sir Francis Anderson, who was also a Royalist.

Sir Nicholas Tempest, as we shall presently note, at this period held the manor and township of Willington. He neglected to surrender and to compound, and on the 5th May, 1647, he petitioned the Compounding Committee, to be allowed to do so. This was not granted at once, but he was allowed a fifth part of his rents. He declared he was never in actual service against the Parliament.

He must have recovered possession of his lands at Willington soon afterwards, because he mortgaged these estates in 1655.

Sir Francis Anderson, of Anderson Place, Newcastle, was a landowner in Willington, but not until after he had been in arms on behalf of Charles I., and imprisoned at York, and his estates impounded. On June 18th, 1646, he recanted and subscribed to the National League and Covenant, and took the oath renouncing his belief in the Pope's supremacy, in transubstantiation, in purgatory, and in images, and the same day his fine was fixed at £1,200.

Another local family involved in sequestered estates was that of Timothy Tyzack of the Howdon Glass Houses. He, on behalf of himself and his wife Elizabeth, on November 18th, 1652, petitioned for the release of a family estate in Yorkshire, in which the said Elizabeth had an interest. Elizabeth confessed she was a papist, but her share of the estate was released.

The Act of Uniformity

When the Restoration took place, however, and when Charles II., in spite of his promises and pledges, assented to the Act of Uniformity on August 24th, 1662, the result showed that the majority of the people in this district were Puritan. The curate at Wallsend was Joseph Craddock, and he, as might be expected, was on the side of his patron, Bishop John Cosin, but almost all the independent vicars around refused to confirm, and were ejected from their livings, and forced to abandon their homes. These Nonconformists were Alexander White, vicar of Benton Magna, William Henderson, vicar of Earsdon, Alexander Gourdon, vicar of Tynemouth, Francis Batty of Jarrow, Thos. Weld of St Mary's, Gateshead, Samuel Hammond, vicar of Newcastle, Wm. Durant, lecturer at All Saints, and Henry Leaver, lecturer at St John's.

We can only faintly realise to-day, the pain, hardship, and cruelty inflicted upon the district by this Act, as the ministers thus driven out of their churches and vicarages were forbidden to preach or to teach, and it was a crime for their congregations to organise contributions for their support. They were not permitted even to act as private tutors. Hitherto, the Puritans had been members of the Established Church, now they were driven out, and, as Nonconformists, began a new chapter in our religious history.

CHAPTER II

LANDOWNERS AND LEASEHOLDERS FROM THE DISSOLUTION OF THE MONASTERY OF DURHAM IN 1540

Willington township: The estates and owners under the Crown and in private hands up to 1921—Wallsend township under the Dean and Chapter: Owners and tenants at Wallsend village; Carville Hall; Point Pleasant; Wallsend House and Carville House.

IN the previous chapter we barely mentioned the great conflict between Henry VIII. and the Pope, but the result of this brought great changes to our two townships, and especially to that of Willington.

In the year 1536, two years after throwing off the power of the Pope, Henry VIII. swept away the most important privileges of the princely bishops of Durham, and those living in the Palatine came much more directly under the laws common to the whole country.

Then followed four years of uncertainty and doubt concerning the fate of the greater abbeys. This was settled, so far as our district was concerned, on the last day of December, 1540, when Hugh W. Whitehead, who was then prior of Durham, quietly surrendered the convent and its possessions to the representatives of the King, and the landholders of Wallsend and Willington became the tenants of the Crown.

The King, however, treated the monks of Durham gently, for in the following May (1541), he appointed Hugh Whitehead, the late prior, to be the first Dean, and twelve of the monks, including one of the Hindmarshs, to be

THE DEAN AND CHAPTER

the first prebendaries, and he incorporated them with a common seal as the " Dean and Chapter of the Cathedral Church of Christ and Blessed Mary the Virgin," and he restored to the Dean and Chapter thus created a large proportion of the lands of the old monastery.

This grant to the newly created Dean and Chapter was made by the King at Westminster on 16th May, 1541, and it is an extensive one. But the part which concerns us is that it includes all manors, lands, waters, fishings, etc., in " Wallesende in the parish of Jerro " and " the tithes of corn of the Townships of Wallesende, Willington " and other places which " formerly belonged to the said late monastery of St Cuthbert of Durham."

It also grants certain knights' fees, tithes, etc., in both Wallsend and Willington and " the nominations of all curates, chanters, and chaplains in the Church of Wallesende."[1]

We need especially to note that the township of Willington was not regranted to Durham, though the tithes of both Wallsend and Willington were. The ownership of Willington was retained by the King, and the whole of it thus became the property of the Crown.

WILLINGTON TOWNSHIP

Willington Tenants

By statute Henry VIII., c. 27, a special Court was created for the management of the vast revenues arising from the possessions of the dissolved monasteries. This Court was " The Court of the Augmentation of the Revenues of the Crown," and all the farmers, reeves, bailiffs, collectors, and other Ministers of the Crown, rendered their accounts to this Court.

In these accounts, for the first year after the dissolution,

[1] Patent Roll, 33 Henry VIII., Part 9, m. 15-20 (709).

the account of John Robynson, bailiff and collector to the King, shows:

> Wyllyngton—He renders account of £13 6s. 8d. of the farm of eight farm tenements in the tenure of John Robynson, the elder, William Robynson, John Robynson, the younger, John Hunter, George Wylkynson, John Punchon, Roger Morton aed Robert Vunthank each of them paying yearly 33s. 4d.
> (Farm of the Salt pans)—And of 6s. 8d. of the farm of the site of two salt pans.
> Multure[1] of the tenants, with the Salmon fishery.—He does not answer here for 26s. 8d. of the farm of the multure of the tenants there, because the said multure is demised to the same tenants in Wyllyngton, with the farm and rent of the same.
> There is no profit from the salmon fishery in the Tyne, adjoining the land of the said lordship.

It is to be noted here that the tenants of Willington are the same as those who occupied under the monastery in 1339, except John Harryson has dropped out and a George Wylkynson and John Robynson, junior, have become tenants. The rent each tenant pays is the same as while under the Convent. The salt pan has changed hands, but there are now two and the rent is doubled.

In 1550 by Letters Patent dated 15th April, 4th Edward VI., the King granted to Robert Darknall, Esquire, the lands in Willington in the several tenancies of the same tenants as above. In 1566 this lease was marked "surrendered," and Queen Elizabeth granted the same premises to Sir Robert Brandlinge, Knight, at a yearly rental of £13 6s. 8d. for twenty-one years, and a note says: "These farms are distant about twenty miles from the Borders and are very good things of the Rent."[2]

This lease having been also surrendered, by Letters Patent dated 16th May, 1576, Elizabeth granted the said messuages to Robert Dudley, Esquire, for twenty-one years for £13 6s. 8d. rent and on payment of a fine of £26 13s. 4d.[3]

[1] The share due to the lord from the tenants.
[2] Augmentation office, Leases 109, No. 26.
[3] Patent Roll 1149, 18 Elizabeth, part 13.

WILLINGTON TOWNSHIP

In 1585 Queen Elizabeth gave directions " to make eighte several leases to the tenants in possession for three specified lives yelding to the Queens Mag^{tie} the yerely rente and fyne," and on one very large sheet the details are given in three columns.

The heading is as usual—" County of Northumberland, Parcel of the possessions of the late Monastery of Durham in the County aforesaid."

In column one are the names of the tenants (three lives). Column two gives the particulars of the tenements, and column three the rents payable.

As to the tenants:

The first parcell to Ri : Robinson, Agnes Robinson and Willm Robinson, brother of the said Richarde.
The seconde parcell to Georg Robinson, Margarett his wief and Georg Robinson there sonne.
The 3 parcell to Robt. Robinson, Alice his wief and Robert Robinson the younger.
The 4 parcell to Willm Hunter, Willm Hunter his sonne, and Henry Hunter his brother.
The fifte parcell to Wyllm Wylkenson, Robert his sonne and Margarett his dawghter.
The sixte parcell to Agnes Puncheon, Jenett Reye and Nicholas Peirson.
The 7 parcell to Roger Moreton, John his sonne and Robte his sonne.
The 8 parcell to Robt Bayly, Jenett his wief and Gerrarde his brother.

The particulars in column two are all worded alike and are:

Willington township in the county aforesaid.
Farm of one tenement and certain arable lands, meadows, feedings and pastures with the appurtenances situate, lying and being in Willington in the county aforesaid, now or late in the tenure or occupation of (tenant's name) or his assigns.

The rents in column three are also alike for the eight tenements, viz., " xxxiijs iiijd " (i.e., two and a half marks).

Conditions were, on each change of tenant, a " fyne of

one yere's rent, and a covenant of service vppon the borders."

Which all and singular premises are thus let to farm to Robert Dudley gentleman by letters patents of the present Queen Elizabeth, bearing date at Westminster xvjth day of May in the xviijth year of her reign for a term of xxj years. Paying therefor yearly as above as is more fully contained in the same letters patent

xvth November 1585
Examined by Willm Spencer, Auditor.

The cleare yerelie value of the premises is xiij li vjs viiijd.[1]

The tenants were bound to the Queen by bonds, deposited in the Exchequer to pay their rents and observe their agreements.

We fail to see what profit Robert Dudley gets out of his lease under which he pays to the Queen's Majesty as much rent as the tenants pay.

Grants by James I.

When James I. came from Scotland (A.D. 1603) he brought a good many of his fellow-countrymen with him, and it was in favour of one of these that Willington ceased to be held by short leases direct from the Crown.

In the second year of his reign he cancels or allows the lease to Robert Dudley to lapse, and by Letter Patent dated December 8th (1604)[2] he grants

to James Elphenston, Lord Balmermouth, Chief Secretary of Scotland and to his heirs and assigns the Manor and Castle of Harbottle, Walkwood Forrest the Manor of Wark, and eight tenements in Willington, co. Northumberland, formerly parcel of the possessions of the late Monastery of Durham.
To hold the castle and manor of Harebottle and Walkwood Forest of the king in chief, by the service of 1/40 part of a knight's fee, paying therefor a yearly rent of £72 12s. 4d.
To hold the lordship and manor of Wark and the tenements in Willington of the king, as of his manor of East Greenwich co.

---

[1] Particulars for Leases, Northumberland, File 107, No. 64.
[2] Patent Roll, 1633, part 3.

GRANTS BY JAMES I. 55

Kent, by fealty only, in free and common socage, and not in chief, or by knight's service; paying yearly for the lordship and manor of Wark £29 17s. 1d., and for the tenements in Willington £13 6s. 8d.

He was to pay a rent for Willington and hold it by "fealty only in free and common socage." Land might be held by tenants ploughing their lord's land with their own plough. This was a servile tenure, called villain socage, but where a rent was taken instead, which James would naturally do, and here does, this was common, or free socage.

"By fealty" an oath was taken at the admittance of every tenant to be true to the lord (or king) of whom he holds the land. These conditions—an oath and a payment of rent to the King—made the holding of the land as free as it could be in those days.

Lord Balmermouth no sooner received the above grant than on 29th January (1604-5) by Letters Patent he had the whole of it transferred to George, Lord Howme of Berwick, Chancellor and Sub-Treasurer of the Court of Exchequer, to hold on the same tenure.[1]

The next steps in the history of the township are that George, Lord Howme of Berwick, who was one of the favourites of King James, is made Earl of Dunbar and presently dies, and his daughter and co-heiress, Elizabeth, marries Lord Howard de Walden, who was the son and heir of the first Earl of Suffolk.

The following extract continues the history of Willington.

By indenture dated 4th March, 19 James I., A.D. 1621-2.

Theophilus, Lord Howard de Walden and Lady Elizabeth, his wife, bargain and sell to Sir Nicholas Tempest of Newcastle upon Tyne, Knight, their Manor and Township of Willington, co. Northumberland, and eight tenements in Willington, now, or late in the several tenures of Robert Robinson, William Hunter, John

---

[1] Patent Roll, 1636, 2 James I., part 6.

Murton, Robert Wilkinson, John Robinson, John Baily, Mary Robinson and Robert, her son, and Ralph Robinson; and all the estate and right which they have in the said manor or other premises, by force of Letters Patent dated 29 January, 2 James I. which granted to the late George, Lord Howme of Berwick, and his heirs the said manor and other premises before mentioned. A yearly payment of £13 6s. 8d. is to be paid to the King for the premises aforesaid.[1]

In the later days of the Convent (1539) the number of tenements in Willington were eight, and we have traced these eight tenements down to this transfer, hence it is clear that the " eight tenements in Willington " which were thus sold to Sir Nicholas Tempest,[2] comprised the whole of the township.

The deeds of the Orde estate show that Sir Nicholas Tempest and Sir Francis Anderson[3] mortgaged the estate in 1655.

In 1663 the County Authorities made an assessment, and the owners of Willington then were "Sir Francis Anderson, Richard Stote Esq., and Mr James Methem."

Sir Francis Anderson was selling his land, and presently he disposed of the whole of it and the township became split up into five estates.

With regard to that part owned by James Methem. Prior to this date, Julian Methem, widow of James Methem, senior, purchased the land lying at the western side of Willington from Sir Francis Anderson. This widow married Thos. Dent of Newcastle. They had two daughters, Isabel and Julian, and Thos. Dent and his wife settled their estate upon these two, and made James Methem

---

[1] Extract taken from the Close Rolls, 2521, 20 James I., pt. 33, No. 31, which consist of enrolments in Chancery of deeds of bargain and sales, conveyances, etc.
[2] Sir Nicholas is described in the records of the Newcastle Merchant Adventurers (where his son Richard is enrolled) as " Nicholas Tempest of Wyllington, Northumberland Knight." He died in 1656, and was buried in St Nicholas Church on September 16th.
[3] Sir Francis Anderson represented Newcastle in Parliament in the reign of Charles II. In 1665 he secured a lease of the foreshore of Willington as mentioned in dealing with Howdon.

(2), the son of Mrs Julian Dent by her first marriage, the trustee for his half-sisters. Hence in 1663 James Methem appears as an owner in Willington, although he was only holding the land as trustee.

Meanwhile, in 1666, Isabel Dent had married Wm. Bigge, attorney-at-law of Newcastle and Hawkhurst, Kent, and in 1679 the other sister, Julian, had married John Hindmarsh of Little Benton, late of Wallsend Hall.

James Methem, the trustee for the estate, died on 23rd April, 1684, and was buried in All Saints.

In 1727 it was agreed that the Dent estate, thus held jointly, be divided, and John Harris and John Carr were appointed to make the award.

Thomas Bigge represented Isabel's portion, and Thomas Hindmarsh that of Julian. The award is dated 1st February, 1728, and recites that the owners were

seized as Tenants in Common of a Farmhold with the appurtenances situate in Willington and being desirous of making Partition of same did by mutual Bonds agree to abide by such division as sd Harris & Carr should by Award make.

They the sd Arbitrators had surveyed the premises which by such survey contained 550 a. 3 r. 36 p. exclusive of Towngate & the high part of Borewell Dean Did make award as follows—

Then the details are set forth, from which we see that the Willington moor was still undivided, as the new line dividing the properties was to run from the north hedge

of the high pasture northwards, close by a well or spring in the middle of the moor and from thence northward to Kellingwood Moor.

The net result of the award was that the present West Farm, containing 275 acres 1 rood 3 perches, plus an area to be held in common, was allotted to Thos. Hindmarsh and his heirs in full settlement of his half, and the remainder, the North Farm, went to Thos. Bigge and his heirs.

The Willington dene was then known as the " Borewell dean," and the bore well was somewhere above the West Farm portion. On the West Farm lands there was a wood containing 10 acres 1 rood 3 perches. The award gives to the West Farm owners 114 acres 1 rood 30 perches of the moor, which was quite isolated from the other portion of their lands. There was then no Willington Square, and no public cart road in that direction. The roads northward from Willington vill were only bridle roads over the moors towards Benton and towards Earsdon, and the latter was over the Milbank lands, hence the award provides that the Bigges, holding the North Farm, must give a right of way to the moorlands to the West Farm owners " in case the way through the Milbanks land is stopt."[1]

North Farm Estate

The succession of the North Farm estate is as follows: Isabel Bigge's eldest son was Thomas Bigge, who married Elizabeth Hindmarsh. They had two sons: William Bigge, born 25th March, 1707, who inherited the North Farm, and Thomas Bigge, a mercer in Ludgate Hill, who built the White Hall at Little Benton, where he died in 1791.

William Bigge, the heir, married Mary, the daughter and sole heir of Charles Clarke of Ovingham, on 29th January, 1736. They had several children, the eldest of whom was Thomas Charles Bigge, born 24th January, 1739, who married Jemima, daughter of William Ord of Fenham, at St Andrew's Church, Newcastle, on 6th November, 1772. (The fourth son was John Bigge of Carville Hall.)

Thomas Charles Bigge died at Bath on October 10th,

---

[1] Mr T. A. Thorp's MSS. relating to the Orde and Collingwood estates.

THE NORTH FARM ESTATE

1794, and his eldest son, Charles Wm. Bigge, who built Linden House, near Longhorsley, succeeded. He was for over fifty years the leader of the Liberal party in the north, and one of the most popular men of his day. In 1814, he moved from Benton to his new house at Linden. He was offered a Baronetcy, but preferred to remain without a title. He was a banker, having become a partner in " The Old Bank " on August 17th, 1806. On January 1st, 1825, Charles John Bigge, his eldest son and heir to the Willington estate, joined the banking firm. In 1836, the death of Sir Matthew White Ridley, and the withdrawal of his capital, left a gap in the firm, and finally on 20th March, 1839, the Old Bank (founded in 1755) amalgamated with the Northumberland and Durham District Bank, which had been established in 1836. Mr Bigge remained a partner, and it was a disastrous investment. We may note in passing that Wm. Boyd, the grandfather of Mr Wm. Boyd of the Wallsend Slipway Company, was one of the partners of the Old Bank, but he disposed of his interest and retired when this amalgamation took place. Mr Boyd died on 18th February, 1855, aged eighty-two. Thus he did not live to see the disaster which overtook the business he had been connected with for half a century.

Charles Wm. Bigge died at Linden on December 8th, 1849, aged seventy-six years. Eight years later, on 26th November, 1857, the District Bank stopped payment, and this spread tragic failure and distress all over Tyneside. Few works could pay any wages; trade and employment suddenly stopped. This slowly righted itself, but to the shareholders the ruin was irremediable.

The executors of Charles Wm. Bigge found they were saddled with 3,375 shares, and were faced with a first call of £35 per share—£118,125 at a time when money and credit were unobtainable.

Under these circumstances, the Willington North Farm estate was sold by the executors to Riddell Robson, a wealthy Newcastle builder and property owner, who left it to his daughter, Mrs Thos. Bell, of Whorlton, with reversion to her eldest son. On Mrs Bell's death in 1904, the son, Riddell Robson Bell, came into possession, and he sold it to the present owners, the Wallsend and Hebburn Coal Company, in 1912. The area of the estate bought was two hundred and sixty-one acres. Mr R. R. Bell (now Mr Riddell Robson Humble) retained the twenty-two acres attached to the Middle Farm.

West Farm Estate

With regard to the other half of Mrs Julian Dent's Willington estate, which, under the agreement for division, fell to the share of her daughter Julian in 1728. It is to be remembered she had married John Hindmarsh, who was born at Wallsend Hall in 1649, but who moved to Little Benton.

Mrs Julian Hindmarsh left the estate to her son, Thomas Hindmarsh, who on his death left it to the three daughters of his sister Ann, the wife of the Rev. Leonard Shafto. Hence the estate was in the hands of Sarah Shafto (wife of Thomas Orde, vicar of Kirknewton), Ann Shafto, and Julian Shafto.

Sarah left her third share to her son, John Orde, of Weetwood. Ann left five-eighteenths to him, and one-eighteenth to Thos. Shadford (the husband of Elizabeth Orde, who presently sold it to Cadwallader Bates). The other sister, Julian, left her third to Edward Collingwood of Chirton.

The succession in the next generation becomes still more complicated, but we need only add that John Orde willed his one-third to the Rev. Leonard Shafto Orde, who on his death on 9th February, 1895, passed on his share to his grandson, Leonard Shafto Horace Charles Orde, who was born on 15th July, 1864. Shortly after, Mr L. S. H. C. Orde arranged to buy out the other co-owners, and thus he became the possessor of the whole of the West Farm estate.

On 4th July, 1901, Mr Orde sold about thirty acres to Messrs Geo. B. Hunter, Wm. Boyd, and John Wigham Richardson, twenty acres of which (the Burn Closes) was offered to the Borough of Wallsend as a park, and then to Willington Quay Urban Council. Both authorities declined the gift, but it was afterwards accepted by the enlarged Borough Council. In 1909 Mr Orde sold the northern portion of the estate (one hundred and twenty-two acres) to the Wallsend and Hebburn Coal Company. In 1909 the West Dene (seventeen acres) was sold to Mr Hunter and given by him to trustees for a recreation ground, and in 1910 thirty-three acres were sold to the Corporation for a cemetery.

Bewicke Estate

The estate of two hundred and ninety-six acres situated at the south-east side of Willington is that which was sold by Sir Francis Anderson to Richard Stote.

A Richard Stote was holding one-seventh of the township of Wallsend under the monks and prior of Durham in 1539, which lease was renewed by the Dean and Chapter by an indenture dated July 18th, 1564, which we will presently quote. Therefore when Richard Stote purchased this land at Willington it was not a case of strangers coming into the parish. The date of the sale was probably 1658, at which time Richard Stote of Lincolns Inn purchased other lands from Sir Francis Anderson at Jesmond, and made Stote's Hall his family residence.

Sir Richard Stote died on 25th December, 1682, aged sixty-one, and his property descended to his only surviving son, Bertram Stote, a merchant adventurer and a hostman. He died unmarried in 1707, and his heirs were his three sisters—Margaret, Frances, and Dorothy.

Dorothy married the Hon. Dixie Windsor, and she

presently became the sole owner on the death of her sisters, the other co-heirs. On 26th December, 1756, she died in London at the age of eighty-four, without having made a will and without direct heirs.

Sir Robert Bewicke of Close House, and John Craster of Craster, claimed to be the rightful heirs as descendants of Dorothy Windsor's great-great-grandfather. This remote claim was contested by the Crown, and by several others, but the chief claimant was Stote-Manby of Louth, who put forward his claim as the great-grandson of Dorothy Windsor's uncle. He was a poor man, and although he won his first trial in 1781, he finally compromised the law proceedings in consideration of receiving £1,500 for costs and £300 a year, one-third of which he assigned to his attorney-at-law.

He died in 1790, and his grandson, Wm. Stote-Manby, a gardener at Louth, re-opened the matter at the Northumberland Assizes in 1855, but was non-suited. The case was afterwards carried into the Court of Chancery on the ground that the estates had been obtained by fraudulent means, but the plaintiff's case was dismissed on 22nd April, 1857. After this Messrs Bewicke and Craster remained in undisputed possession.

Samuel Warren, Q.C., was the leading counsel for the last claimant, Wm. Stote-Manby, and it is said that the romance "Ten Thousand a Year," of which he was the author, was founded on the story of this estate. It is also stated that Warren undertook the case gratuitously.

Newcastle Corporation Estate

In 1671 Sir Francis Anderson and Robert Tempest of Thornby and two others disposed of another part of the township, lying at the south-west side, to Edward Carr, master and mariner, of Newcastle.

In January, 1717, Edward Carr as mortgager, and

Robert Rymer as mortgagee, conveyed this land and the Halfway House to the Corporation of Newcastle-upon-Tyne. This "Halfway House" farm and the strip of old river foreshore covered by ballast under the lease granted in 1665 to Sir Francis Anderson constitutes the Willington estate of the Corporation which they still hold.

Milbank Estate

We have been unable to trace the early history of the Milbank estate, which lies on the north-east side of the township.

A Milbank is said to have been a cupbearer to Mary Queen of Scots, and on account of a duel he fled over the borders and first bought an estate in Chirton.

On September 21st, 1596, Edmund Milbank made his will:

> Will of Edmund Milbancks of the parishe of Tynemouth sick in bodie : to be buried in the chancell of St Oswold's church at Tynemouth . . . to my fourth sonne Edmond Milbancke my land at Willington and one close in Merchut called Askue and 20 marks, half a dussen silver sponnes, my lesser silver peace, and my greate Bible. . . . Bryan Walker of Willington to be tutor to my sonne.[1]

But we have traced the owners of Willington down to 1621, when the whole of the township was transferred to Sir Nicholas Tempest, and neither as owner nor tenant does the name of Milbank appear. Furthermore, no Milbank is mentioned among the owners given in 1663, sixty-seven years after Edmund Milbank made his will. We have searched the official records, and Mr John H. Burn has carefully examined his old deeds relating to the estate, and no reference to the original grant, or sale, can be found.[2]

[1] County History, Vol. viii., p. 327.
[2] The Patent roll and the Close roll calendars. The Feet of Fines for Northumberland and also those for Mixed Counties have been searched and no grant or indenture or transfer can we discover.

We must leave this puzzle to be solved by others, but as a matter of fact the Milbanks from an early date did own the estate of four hundred and fourteen acres in Willington for many generations.

The family held a prominent position in the north, but they are not particularly associated with our district. Marke Milbanke, the nephew of Edmund, was Sheriff of Newcastle in 1638, and Mayor in 1658 and 1672. He supplied the exiled Charles II. with large sums of money, and on the Restoration, Charles proposed to make his generous supporter a Baronet, but he declined the honour, and asked that it might be conferred upon his eldest son and namesake. This was done, and the Milbank Baronetcy was created on August 7th, 1661.

The sixth Baronet—Sir Ralph Noel Milbank—sold the estate in December, 1818, for £24,500, to Matthew Bell of Woolsington and Dixon Brown of Long Benton, who were then the co-partners in the Willington Colliery.

At the time of the District Bank disaster, Dixon Dixon, the son of Dixon Brown, appears to have advanced money to his partner, and in the year following (1858) Matthew Bell transferred his interest in the estate to him. In November, 1865, the Rev. Dixon Brown, the heir of Dixon Dixon, sold the estate to David Burn, who three years prior to this had bought the Little Benton estate. From Mr Burn it passed to his son, John Henry Burn, of Tynemouth, and in 1898 to his sons, Messrs John Henry and Frank Hawthorn Burn, who in 1919 sold the whole estate of four hundred and fourteen acres to the Battle Hill Estate Company, an offshoot of the Wallsend and Hebburn Coal Company.

Ancient Boundary

To one of the Hindmarshs we owe an ancient document which describes the boundaries of the township of Willington as they were originally. It is as follows:

ANCIENT BOUNDARIES

WILLINGTON TOWN. The Bounder of Willington beginneth at ye seite of Walsend Dean, And up ye same till that come to the Moares between them, and Benton to the Haggerstones; And then to the Moares between Benton, Willington and West-Shirton and then down ye Burne called Greene Chesters burne, till it come to ye Moare-stones, at ye North-East-Nooke of Rawes Moore; And then down ye Dyke and Dean called Howdon between Flatworth, and Willington, till it come to ye Wator of Tine And so up to the Wator of Tine, till it come to ye Mouth of Walsend Deane where it began.

. . . .

I copied this Boundary from a paper I found in my Father's study and which is now put (with some others) in the Map safe. As witness my hand October 15 1720.

THO : HINDMARTH.[1]

Note that the township is still the " town " and also that this is probably the first time the name Howdon is mentioned. Greenchester became North Gate some time after the moor was enclosed, and the landowner had placed a gate across the bridle road to restrict the wheeled traffic. Greenchester burn is, even to-day, clearly a boundary and not merely an ordinary watercourse, for at its very commencement at Greenchester it is three feet deep and six feet wide. The " North East Nook " of " Rawes Moore " was apparently at the Fir Trees.

As to the date of this interesting record, all we have to guide us is that when Thomas Hindmarsh copied it, over two hundred years ago, the spelling was already antiquated and the name Howdon had come into use.

The moor on the Milbank estate was partly enclosed about 1680, for in an award soon after that date, in the Tynemouth Manor Court, the boundary of the shire moor is traced up a " letch to a place in Willington *New Close* called Greenchester."[2]

The date of the Hindmarsh document might therefore be between the years 1600 and 1660.

---

[1] Mr T. A. Thorp's MSS. relating to the Orde and Collingwood estates.
[2] County History, Vol. viii., p. 413.

Wallsend Township

Leaseholders under the Dean and Chapter of Durham

We have quoted the material parts of the grant whereby the township of Wallsend was given to the newly established Dean and Chapter. The mode of government and the letting of the lands under this new authority was substantially the same as it had recently been under the Prior and Convent.

The manor house was still at Westoe and the leaseholders were still summoned to attend. That the tenants did not always appear when summoned to South Shields is evidenced by the following entry of the Court Leet held at South Shields on 10th October, 1671, before John Jefferson as Seneschal. Under the heading for " Fines for not appearing at the Court " :

WALLSEND. Jo Punshon for the like ...	...	00.01.00
Jo Hindmers „ „ „ ...	...	00.01.00

Of the landholders who held under the Convent, generally speaking, all continued their holdings upon the same tenure and at the same rent as before.

Dean and Chapter Leases

As, for example, we see by an indenture dated July 18th, 1564, a lease is secured to :

Richard Stott, son of Robert Stott of Wallsend, yeoman, and Edmond, Robert and William, sons of the same Robert Stott, and the longer liver of them all that their farmhold or seventh part of the Township of Wallsend with its appurtenances (one parcel of ground called Wallsend Wood now in the tenure of the said Robert except and reserved) to hold to the said Richard for 21 years from Michaelmas next ensuing, and if he die before the end of the term, then to Edmond, Robert, and William or the longer liver of them. Paying yearly 34s. 7d. at two terms Martinmas and Pentecost, and all other by rents, customs, fruits, and duties, which of antiquity have been accustomed to be paid.[1]

---

[1] Deeds N.S.A. A.A., Series 3, Vol. v., p. 121.

A daughter of a later Richard Stott married George Raine, the minister of Holy Cross Church 1620-28. She and her husband were buried in the chancel, and fortunately the grave cover still survives.

"Edward Stott of Wallsend Gentleman," is returned as a freeholder in 1638-39, and in 1663, exactly one hundred years after the date of the lease quoted above, a still later Richard Stott, Esq., is returned as holding property of £120 rental value in Willington.

In a "Book of Surveigh and an abstract out of the Rentale of all the Lands, Tenements and Revenews that belonge to the Cathedrall Church of Durism," made in A.D. 1580, we have again a list of the leaseholders, rents, etc.

WALLESEND.
(1) Anthony Rey for one tenement for the year, 33s. 4d. (2½ marks).
   A lease dated July 18th in the 6th year of the Queen (A.D. 1564).
(2) Wedow Hinemers for one tenement for the year, as above.
   A lease dated 22nd January in the 14th year of the Queen (A.D. 1572) in the name of Xpofer (Christopher) Goodbarn.
(3) Ric. Punshion for one tenement for the year as above.
   A lease dated 1st Sept. in the 4th year of the Queen (A.D. 1562).
(4) Ricardus Stot for one tenement for the year as above.
   A lease dated 10th December in the 14th year of the Queen (A.D. 1571) in the name of John Wildon.
(5) Richard Rey for one tenement for the year as above.
   Hennie Stott is to have a lease hereof and pay fyne.
(6) Xpofer Preston for one tenement for the year as above.
   A lease dated 10th January in the 14th year of the Queen (Dec. 10th 14th year from Martymas followinge, in margine) in the name of Thomas Wood, gentleman.
   Ricardus Rey for a cottage for the year 5s. 4d.
(7) Valentine Durham for one tenement for the year as above.
   He is to have a newe lease and to pay for the same to the House use at Michaelmas and Candelmas next £5.
The tenants there (at Wallsend) for the rent of a wood for the year 26s. 8d.
For money to the Terrar[1] there yearly 16s.
For Gellicorne[2] there yearly 2s. 2d.
The sum of this vill £14 12s. 3d.

---

[1] Terrarius means landholder.
[2] Probably small corn given to the poor.

There is some slight error in the above abstract of rents. Seven tenements at 33s. 4d., one cottage 5s. 4d. The wood 26s. 8d. plus 16s. for the Terrar and 2s. 2d. for Gellicorne make the total £14 3s. 6d. as " the sum of this vill," not £14 12s. 3d.

The number of tenants are the same as in 1539, but two families have changed and the rents have been reduced to 33s. 4d., the same as the Crown tenants at Willington were paying.

The next list of leaseholders we have is shown in the county rate assessment made in 1663, and this assessment gives the assessed yearly rental value, not the rent paid to the Dean and Chapter.

These leaseholders were:

Mr John Cossens	Rental	£60
,, Richard Hindmers	,,	£50
,, Robt. Durham	,,	£50
Sir Francis Bowes	,,	£50
Mr John Hindmers	,,	£50
,, Henry Burfield	,,	£50
,, John Punchon	,,	£50

This list is a little out of date, as John Cosyn, the builder of Cosyn's House at Carville, had died two years previous to this. The Hindmers and the Burfields we deal with when we speak of Wallsend Village, and the Durham family in connection with Howdon Hall. Sir Francis Bowes, as we have already seen, was fined for delinquency seventeen years before this, and it is to be noted that he then, in view of a fine, declared the yearly value of this farm to be £30, i.e., sixty-six per cent less than it is here assessed.

The Punchon family had held land in Wallsend in the days of the Convent, and John Punchon was one of a well-known Killingworth family. The will of Timothy Punchon of Killingworth, described as a " Preacher of the Gospel," was proved at Durham in 1717, and therein he mentions his farm at Wallsend.

Of the later estate holders and owners it will be simpler if we deal with them and their families, as far as possible, under the mansion houses which were attached to their estates at the Village, at Carville and at Point Pleasant.

The Dean and Chapter continued to be the owners of the whole township until 1851. Rents paid in the earlier days of the Dean and Chapter varied from sixpence to one shilling per acre. Leases for land were granted for forty years and for house property twenty-one years, and the twenty-one year leases were renewable every seven years, on payment of a fine of one and a half year's rent. Under this system there arose a recognised " tenant right " which was valuable and saleable.

In 1700 the township was still divided into seven leaseholds, and the holders in that year were: George Hewbank, Jacob Burfield, Robert Broude (?), Robert Durham, William Punchon—who each held one farm from the Dean and Chapter at a rent of 34s. 7d., and Richard Hindmarsh held two farms at 69s. 2d.

The " farms " were still described as " all that farmhold or husbandry or seventh part of the township of Wallsend."

Until the middle of the century this division continued, but apparently when the Hewbanks sold their estate, Robert Carr did not take the whole of the leasehold, and it was divided into two.

In May, 1800, the Dean and Chapter had the township accurately surveyed by John Bell, and this is the earliest map of Wallsend we know of. We give a copy of his plan and his abstract of each holding (page 520), and if we add the land held by Mrs Harrison to that held by John T. Bigge we will see how the township had been divided into " sevenths " from the early days when the lands were first enclosed.

An Act of Parliament was passed on August 8th, 1851 (14 and 15 Vict., c. 104), which permitted ecclesiastical corporations to sell, enfranchise, and exchange church lands. On the passing of this Act, far-seeing holders began to enfranchise their holdings, and Wallsend drifted largely into private hands.

Wallsend Village

We have already said that it is probable the inhabitants who were left after the departure of the Romans were driven from the old Roman encampment by the incursion of the sea rovers who pillaged the river banks, and that they took up their abode in what is still known as " the village," where they were out of sight of the raiders. In any case the Anglian settlers would make their village in the centre of the township for convenience of their " common field " system of cultivation.

Although none of the present erections are really old, in form it is still a typical old English village (see plan). One hundred and twenty years ago this was more true than it is to-day. Then the village school-house, the vicarage, four farm steadings, four large mansion houses, with other less important houses and cottages, clustered round the village green, which had an area of over six acres. The occupiers had a right of stintage on the green during certain times of the year, but the parish authorities regulated the grazing, and the fines for breaking the regulations went to the poor. The village smithy was on the south side of the road, a little to the west of the green, and the stocks were nearer the village, on the opposite side of the road.

The village green has now dwindled to 3·6 acres, and the story of the spasmodic and therefore futile resistance to the encroachments can be traced in the parish records.

In the Autobiography of the Rev. Dr Alex. Carlyle of Inveresk (" Jupiter Carlyle ") Wallsend is thus mentioned :

PLAN OF WALLSEND VILLAGE.
A.D. 1840.

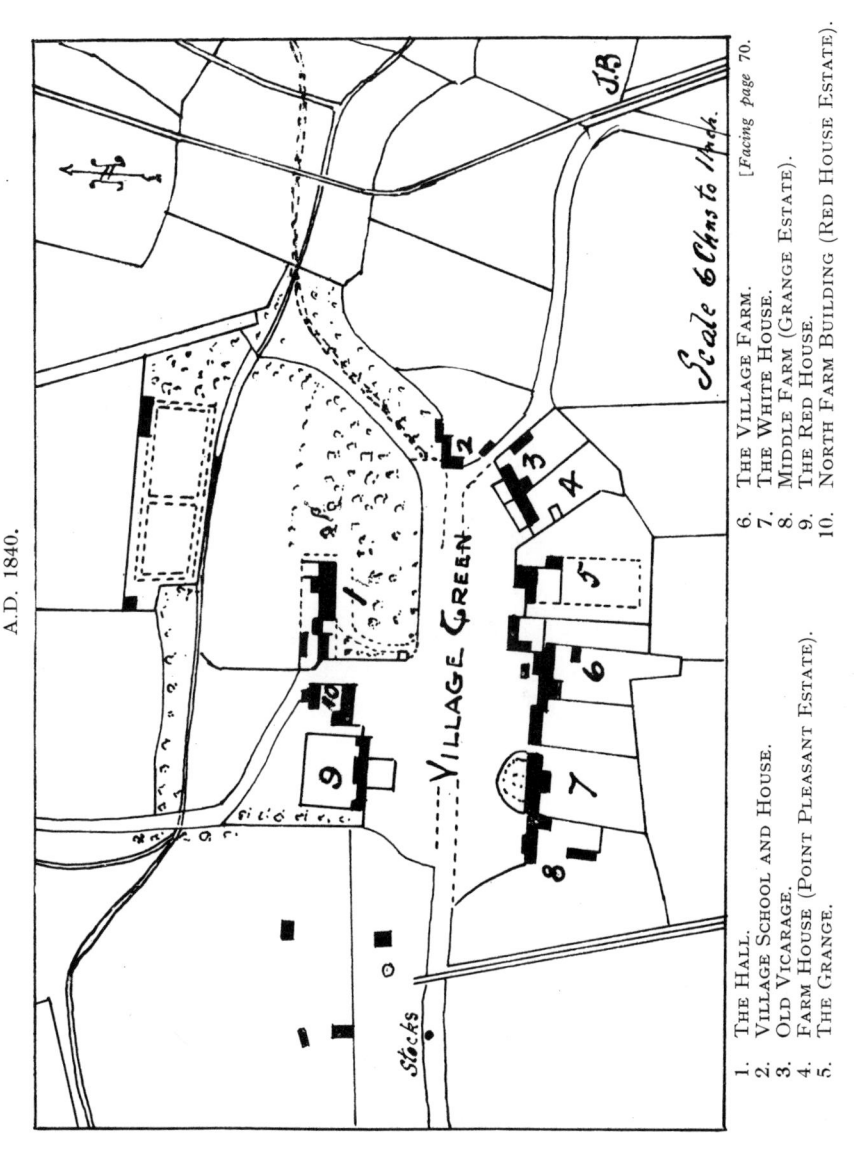

[Facing page 70.

Scale 6 Chns to 1 Inch.

1. THE HALL.
2. VILLAGE SCHOOL AND HOUSE.
3. OLD VICARAGE.
4. FARM HOUSE (POINT PLEASANT ESTATE).
5. THE GRANGE.
6. THE VILLAGE FARM.
7. THE WHITE HOUSE.
8. MIDDLE FARM (GRANGE ESTATE).
9. THE RED HOUSE.
10. NORTH FARM BUILDING (RED HOUSE ESTATE).

We arrived at Wallsend (April 1769) a very delightful Village about 4 miles below Newcastle, on the road to Shields, where Mr Blackett had a very agreeable house for the summer.

There were other two gentlemen's houses of good fortune in the Village, with a church and a parsonage-house. Next day tho' 1st May, was so very warm that I with difficulty was able to walk down to the church in the bottom of the village, not more than two hundred yards distant.

Mary Home, a cousin-german of Mrs Blackett's and my Wife's was residing here at this time, and had been for several months at Newcastle.

We stayed here for eight or ten days, and visited all the neighbours, who were all very agreeable, even the clergyman's wife, who was a little lightsome; but as her head ran on fine clothes, which she could not purchase to please her, but only could imitate in the most tawdry manner, she was rather amusing to Mrs Blackett, who had a good deal of humour—more than her sister, who had a sharper wit and more discernment. The husband was a very good sort of man, and very worthy of his office, but oppressed with family cares. Mr Potter, I think, was an Oxonian.

We did not fail to visit our good friend Mr Collingwood of Chirton, and his lady, Mary Roddam, of both of whom my wife was a favourite. . . .

[John Erasmus Blackett, who had his country residence in the village over a hundred and fifty years ago, had his town house near the top of Pilgrim Street. He was a coal fitter and a useful and popular man. He was four times Mayor of Newcastle, and Richard Grainger named Blackett Street out of compliment to him. His daughter, Sarah, on 18th June, 1791, married " Captain Collingwood " of H.M. frigate *Mermaid*, afterward the distinguished Lord Collingwood. Mr Blackett died on June 11th, 1814.

Mr Collingwood, visited by Dr Carlyle, was Edward Collingwood who had married Mary Roddam of Roddam, and she had inherited Chirton House (pulled down in 1900) from her father. Mr Collingwood was part owner of the Willington West Farm estate and was one of the Wallsend " Four and Twenty."]

The Hall

The most important residence in the township for a long period has been the Hall, or the buildings which preceded it.

We are unable to trace with absolute certainty the occupiers further back than two hundred years, but it is almost certain that nearly four hundred years ago it was in possession of the Hyndmers, or Hindmarshs, who were then the chief family in Wallsend. They bore arms—three hinds' heads couped argent on a field vert.

The town house of the family was opposite the end of the High Bridge in Pilgrim Street. For two hundred years we have some records of the births, marriages, deaths, and other events connected with the family.

One of the family, Edward Hyndmers, was a Benedictine monk who advanced to high office in the Durham Monastery. He took his B.A. degree at Oxford in 1513. He was appointed warden of Durham College at Oxford in 1527, became a D.D. in 1553, and he held the office of Spiritual Chancellor to Bishop Tunstall. He continued warden of the Durham College, Oxford, until the monastery was surrendered on December 31st, 1540, and as the College at Oxford was not regranted to Durham, Henry VIII. made him the First Prebendary of the first stall in the Cathedral.

In 1539 Gawan Hyndmers was holding one-seventh of the township under the Prior and Convent of Durham at a rental of 34s. 7d.

In 1628 " Richard Hindmarsh of Wallsend, Gent," was taking legal proceedings against a neighbour, " John Butler of Greys Inn and Wallsend," for outlawry for debt. Incidentally we may add that a jury, making an inquest into Butler's estate on Mr Hindmarsh's behalf, reported on oath " that the said John Butler was possessed on 1st May last (1628) of one tenement and appurtenances at Wallsend of £3 6s. 8d. (5 marks) clear annual value and also two stacks of Hay standing on the premises, value £4 6s. 8d. (6¼ marks) and nothing more."

In a record made in 12 Charles II. (1660) of " Proprietors of lands in Wallsend " we find Richard Hindmarsh and his son John Hindmarsh, each holding one farm and

WALLSEND HALL IN 1890.

fine to the Dean and Chapter of Durham, of the value of £140. Richard died on 12th November, 1667, and was buried in the chancel of the church of the Holy Cross. Six years later, in 1673-4, John had taken over the holding of his father, and increased his own, for he is recorded as holding two farms and six-fourteenths of the value of £400. Thus he became by far the largest leaseholder in Wallsend. He died on 1st November, 1707, aged " ninetie yeeres," and was also buried in the chancel of Holy Cross Church, near other members of his family. The grave cover is still *in situ* in excellent state of preservation.

This appears to have been the last of the Hindmarsh family who resided in Wallsend.

His son, Richard, predeceased him, and his son John, who matriculated at Christ's College, Cambridge, on 5th July, 1665, was married at All Saints' Church, Newcastle, on 4th October, 1679, to Julian Dent, daughter and co-heiress of Thomas Dent, whose possessions in Willington we have already traced.

John Hindmarsh and his wife lived at Little Benton. They had two daughters, one of whom, Elizabeth, married Thos. Bigge in 1706, and through this marriage the Benton property came into the hands of the Bigge family, and the Wallsend branch of the Hindmarsh family died out.

After the removal of the Hindmarsh family from Wallsend, the Hall was owned and occupied for more than three-quarters of a century by a family of the name of Moncaster or Muncaster,[1] who held about one half of the land in the township, and took a constant and prominent interest in its affairs.

From the details we know of their business and history, we obtain some idea of the nature of the trade of those who belonged to the Guild of " Merchant Adventurers " who, in conjunction with the " Masters and Mariners," did so

[1] The Wallsend family always signed their name Moncaster.

much to make England "a nation of shopkeepers," whose customers were in every part of the known world.

James Moncaster the elder, son of Wm. Moncaster of Arnaby in Cumberland, came to Newcastle to be apprenticed to John Whitfield, a Merchant Adventurer. His indentures were dated 11th November, 1699, and he was duly admitted to the Guild on 7th December, 1709. His warehouse was under the Netherdean bridge, which crossed what is now Dean Street, at which place river craft could then load and unload. Although he was entered in the books of the Merchant Adventurers as a draper, he did not confine his attention to cloth.

Alderman John Whinfield, Mayor of Newcastle, died during his Mayoralty in June, 1710, and by his will dated 14th June, he left his estate in trust to his kinsman James Moncaster and to George Blenkinsop, and three others. This trusteeship was continued for over thirty-five years, James Moncaster the younger taking the place of his father on his father's death, and it ended in a lawsuit in the Court of Chancery, against the trustees.

From the pleadings in this case we learn many details concerning trade which these Merchant Adventurers carried on, in addition to their trade in cloth.[1] The heirs asserted fraud and mismanagement, and more especially against James Moncaster and George Blenkinsop, which the trustees denied.

It appeared that the deceased Mayor had a shop in Newcastle, and carried on a retail trade in iron goods, and that a few days after the testator's death, James Moncaster, in accordance, it was alleged, with an arrangement with the testator, took over the shop and stock at a valuation, and carried on the business. In the accounts we note that the trustee was a debtor to the estate for years, to the extent of £800, for which he paid interest at the rate of five per cent. In addition to this retail iron trade, and possibly by virtue of it, Mr Moncaster entered into partnership with

[1] Richard Welford's MSS.

George Blenkinsop (his co-trustee), Thomas Wasse, and Ralph Harle, and carried on an extensive trade of buying and selling iron and steel and nails. They had a forge at Derwent Coats, in the Derwent valley, and the firm appears to have had a large trade not only with dealers in the north of England, but also in Yorkshire, the Midlands, London, and Aberdeen.

Thus James Moncaster, Merchant Adventurer of Wallsend, dealer in cloth goods, iron forgings, nails, and the requirements of country smiths, became a wealthy man, and was Sheriff of Newcastle in 1724.

He died 8th June, 1739, aged fifty-seven years, and his wife Isabel died twenty-five years later, on 29th February, 1764, aged sixty-eight, and both are buried in the nave of St Nicholas Church, Newcastle. He had one son, James, and two daughters.

His Wallsend estates appear to have been divided between his son and daughters. The elder daughter, Mrs Stewart, became the owner of an estate of one hundred and twenty-seven acres on the east side of the township, which included Mount Pleasant House and the Coach and Horses Inn, and four acres of land attached thereto. She earned a title to a place in our records by giving to the parish, in 1748, a school and schoolmaster's house at the east end of the village green, and at the same time her mother, Mrs Isabel Moncaster, gave the garden and land behind.

The younger daughter, Frances, received an estate of one hundred and twenty-four acres. It included one field to the west of the village, eight fields extending to the north boundary, five fields on the east side of what is now Station Road, and three fields near the eastern boundary. Also a mansion house, " The Grange," and the farmstead at the west end of the village. The lands lay almost entirely in the centre of the township, and hence the name " Middle Farm."

James Moncaster the younger, following in the footsteps of his father, was admitted by patrimony into the Newcastle Guild of Merchant Adventurers on 12th December, 1739. He inherited from his father an estate of one hundred and forty-six acres, including the Hall, ten fields and a farm-house (the West Farm) near the west boundary, the farm near the fourth milestone, and six fields near the east boundary, and he purchased the estates in Wallsend held by his sister, Mrs Stewart.

In 1753, for the sum of £10,500, he became by purchase Lay Rector of Felton, and by deed dated 17th September, 1767, he settled the rectory upon his marriage with Elizabeth Dale of Howdon Panns, to secure her a jointure of £300 a year.

His will is dated 31st October, 1776, and amended by a codicil dated 8th July, 1791. He left, in addition to other bequests : to his sister, Frances Atkinson, £1,000; to his nephew, James M. Atkinson, £500; to his niece, Isabel Atkinson, £500; to his niece, Isabel Ward, £2,000; to Miss Shepherd of Howdon Panns, £100. The rectory of Felton, and his other estates, he left to his wife.[1]

Like his father, he took a constant interest in Wallsend parish affairs. He was one of the " Four and Twenty," and for three or four years held the office of grieve. His last attendance at a Vestry Meeting was on 30th September, 1796. He died on the 19th of the April following, aged eighty-one, and was buried at Felton. The monumental tablet, " Sacred to the memory of James Moncaster late of Wallsend," shows the family arms—Barry of six argent and azure, a bend gules Moncaster; impaling gules, a Swan wings expanded, argent Dale.

Before his death he sold Wallsend Hall and lands to William Clark, son of William Clark of Dockwray Square, North Shields.

Mr Clark moved into the Hall about 1790. On September 23rd, 1793, he married his first wife, Ann, daughter of James Hutchinson; and two years later, Miss

[1] County History, Vol. vii., p. 290.

Lydia Clark, who resided with her brother at the Hall, was married on 10th June, 1795, to John Wright of North Shields. Mrs Ann Clark died on 23rd September, 1802, aged thirty-two years, and a mural tablet to her memory will be found in St Peter's Church.

Although Mr Wm. Clark did not stay long in the village, he looms largely in the history of Holy Cross Church, as, probably with the best intentions, he ensured its final destruction.

In an old manuscript book containing facts, comments, and illustrations relating to Wallsend, in possession of Mr Robert I. Dees, we have:

> William Clark Esq. on his coming to Wallsend, encroached considerably upon the Town Green for his Garden etc. and conceived an idea of repairing the Old Church, (which would in all human probability have stood a number of years) he took off the roof, but selling his estate to Alderman Anthony Hood, he left the Church in a dilapidated state.

While Mr Clark was interesting himself in the affairs of the parish, he acquired the distinction of being the first recorded Mayor of Wallsend. He was elected to that office by the Vestry, which was then the controlling representative of the parish, on Easter Monday, 1802, and he was re-elected the two following years.

Mr Clark moved from Wallsend to Little Benton House, and died there on June 10th, 1837, aged seventy-one. He had purchased an estate at Belford in 1811 which became the family residence of the next generation—the Atkinson-Clarks.

The next owner and occupier was Anthony Hood, the founder of a well-known timber business. He was an Alderman in Newcastle Town Council, a Deputy-Lieutenant of the County, and a Lieutenant-Colonel of the Loyal Newcastle Associated Volunteer Infantry. He was elected to be the second Mayor of Wallsend. The resolution passed at the Vestry held on Easter Tuesday, 1808, was as follows—" The resolve of the present aldermen and common council is, that Anthony Hood Esq. be appointed Mayor in the room of Wm. Clark Esq. and Mr John Walker, be Grieve for the present year." This is the only occasion we have found where the " Four and Twenty " of Wallsend refer to themselves as the aldermen and common council.

While Alderman Hood was at the laying of the foundation stone of the Moot Hall in the Castle Garth on 23rd July, 1810, he was taken ill, and died at Wallsend early next morning.

The owner and tenant who followed Mrs Hood in 1812 was Mr John Wright, who had married Miss Lydia Clark of the Hall on 10th June, 1795, as already mentioned. He was appointed Mayor of Wallsend on 19th April, 1812, and was re-appointed year by year until 1829. He took an interest in St Peter's Church, and presented to it two silver collection plates in 1835.

Next followed Edward Grace, who moved to Wallsend from Byker Hill. His ancestors were Irish and belonged to one of the oldest families in Ireland. By profession he was a land agent and a civil engineer, but he owned the quarries at Byker, and also, like many men of his day who had capital, he was considerably interested in coal mining.

He had three brothers: John, who lived at Carville and afterwards at Point Pleasant; Nathaniel, owner of the Scotswood Paper Mills; and William, of Old Durham, the grandfather of Mr Herbert W. Grace of Hallgarth Hall, Winlaton.

Mr Edward Grace, who was born in 1782, died at the Hall on the 23rd June, 1853. He left no family, and by his will dated December 4th, 1840, he bequeathed to Sarah, his wife, all his real and personal estate, and appointed her and his three brothers executors. His business as land agent was carried on in Drury Lane, Newcastle, by his nephew, Edward Nathaniel Grace, who was Mayor of Newcastle in 1856, and who died of heart failure in the train at Seghill on 4th August, 1865.

Wallsend Hall

On 23rd August, 1853, the Wallsend property of Mr Grace was put up for sale at the Turk's Head, Newcastle, but was not sold. The Hall and grounds were thereupon " let " to Mr John Carr, whose tenancy was a short one. On 24th October, 1856, he sold most of the furniture, wines, etc., and left Wallsend for Ebchester.

Meanwhile, the Hall was again advertised " to let," and Mr Robt. Richardson Dees, finding it was also for sale, agreed in 1856 with Mr E. N. Grace, acting on behalf of the executors, to purchase the place, and to have possession on November 11th. He moved from St Mary's Place, Newcastle, into the Hall on the 16th December, 1856, and this was, for more than fifty years, his home. The area bought at this time was 11 acres 1 rood 25 perches, but immediately afterwards he bought a further 2 acres 1 rood 29 perches. To this new resident we must give more than a passing note.

Mr Robt. Richardson Dees was the son of Mr Robert Dees of H.M. Customs, who was married at All Saints' Church on 15th November, 1813, to Miss Martha Richardson, third daughter of Robert Richardson, corn merchant.

Mr Robt. R. Dees was the eldest of a family of ten, and was born in Westgate in 1814, and was named after his father and the family of his mother. He was educated at Dr Bruce's School, Newcastle, and Glasgow University. He was articled to Mr Ingledew of Newcastle, then in 1835 went to a London firm for a time. After he was admitted a solicitor in 1836, he returned to Newcastle, and for some time was a partner with Mr George Bates, and finally joined the firm, which until then had been carried on as Donkin, Stable & Armstrong. This firm was then reconstructed and Mr Armorer Donkin retired from business. Mr Wm. Armstrong preferred gun-making to law, and the business was carried on as Stable & Dees until 1861, when Mr Stable retired on account of age. For the next ten years Mr Dees carried it on himself. In 1871 Mr Thos.

Wm. Thompson joined him, and the firm became Dees & Thompson. A sound lawyer, Mr Dees attained to many positions of honour in his profession. He was a keen student in antiquarian and historical matters.

When the first Local Board of Health for Wallsend was formed, he was one of the thirty-six candidates, but failed to secure a seat.

In 1897 he gave fourteen acres of land for a public park. He was a Conservative in politics. He was not married, and for the last thirty years he lived a quiet, studious, and retired life. He died on November 30th, 1908, at the age of ninety-five, after several years of feeble health, and his will, dated November 3rd, 1901, was proved at £95,667 16s. 8d. After leaving sundry legacies to relations and others, including £20 to the Rector of Wallsend for the benefit of the poor, the residue of his estate was left to his nephew, Robert Irwin Dees.

Mr Robert Irwin Dees, who thus succeeded to the estate, was the son of Mr James W. Dees, an engineer, brother to Robt. R. Dees, who in many ways took an active part in church and civic affairs.

Mr Robert I. Dees, after his schooldays, served his apprenticeship as an engineer at the North-Eastern Marine Engineering works, and then after he had obtained further experience at sea, he retired from engineering and took over the management of his uncle's property.

In January, 1899, he married Miss Edith Henderson, daughter of Canon Henderson, the Rector of Wallsend, and after the death of his uncle he spent over £2,000 in modernising the Hall. In 1909 he and his family moved from Highfield (built by Mr Dees in 1901) and took up their residence at the Hall.

Mr R. I. Dees was an energetic worker in the affairs of the parish. He was a Poor Law guardian, a town councillor, an active chairman of the Borough Education Committee, and a useful supporter of St Peter's Church. He was Mayor of the town for the year 1908-1909. He

WALLSEND VILLAGE SCHOOL AND HOUSE.

[*Facing page* 82.

He had brick and tile works near the Wallsend Quay, and a brewery on the north-east side of the village school. He and John Reay were in partnership as lime burners, and had lime kilns near Lime Street, and these two jointly purchased part of the Moncaster land situated between the Burn Closes and the Tyne, including the East Farm. Mr Mordue had a ballast crane from which he deposited ballast on the foreshore of the river, part of which was his own. The land thus reclaimed from the river later became of great value as sites for works. He died on November 25th, 1872, aged seventy-nine, his wife, Phillis, (*née* Fisher) having predeceased him on April 26th, 1871, at the age of seventy years.

He left three sons—Joseph (4), Francis John, and Thomas—and six daughters—Amelia, Phillis, Mary, Elizabeth, Harriet, and Isabella.

Although Mr Francis Mordue won a seat on the first Local Board of Health, neither he nor his brothers took a prominent part in public matters. They managed the brewery until it was closed in 1879, and the tile works and lime kilns until they were also closed.

Mr Joseph died at Wallsend on January 8th, 1874; Mr Thomas died at Wallsend on October 8th, 1894; Mr Frank died at Harrogate on 8th November, 1901, and was buried there; and Miss Isabella Mordue, the last of the name, died at Dene House, Wallsend, on June 12th, 1921, aged eighty-four, and was buried in St Peter's churchyard.

From time to time considerable controversy has taken place concerning the ownership of this property as this was schoolroom and schoolmaster's house and land which was given to the parish by the Moncaster family. The facts on which these discussions have been based are briefly as follow:—

The Vestry minute books show that as long as the school was open, it was owned and managed by the " Four and Twenty " on behalf of the parishioners. The following outlines the course of events:

On January 4th, 1805, Mr Jos. Mordue, the schoolmaster, was instructed not to exceed sixty children of the parishioners at five shillings per quarter for teaching to read, and six shillings per quarter for teaching arithmetic, and " should any dispute arise as to the number of children to be taught, or to the quarterage, or the management it shall be settled by the Overseers of the Poor for the time being, or the four and twenty of the Parish every Easter Monday."

On June 2nd, 1818, Joseph Mordue was appointed to succeed his father as schoolmaster.

On April 12th, 1819, a Vestry Meeting was held on the ground and planned some alterations in the buildings.

On March 31st, 1834, Mr Mordue's assistant was suspended, as the number of scholars had gone down.

April 20th, 1835—" Resolved that Mr Joseph Mordue having discontinued the Parish School in consequence of the same having considerably diminished, he be permitted to occupy the School-house as a dwelling house until the same shall be again required by the Parish as a School."

On Easter Monday, April 20th, 1840—" Resolved that Mr Mordue pay 10/- per annum as an acknowledgement for the School and appurtenances belonging to the Parish in his occupation, such rent to be appropriated to educate a poor child in the National School of Wallsend on the clergyman's appointment."

April 12th, 1841—" Resolved that Mr Mordue be requested to place the stone with the inscription describing the purpose for which the House was built in a conspicuous place in front of the building."

It will be seen that the permission given in 1835 was a fateful error, which was not mended by the resolution of 1840, because no record can be found that any acknowledgement for the use of the land and buildings was ever paid.

The last time the claims of the township were publicly discussed was in 1893, when crowded Vestry Meetings were held and much public interest was manifested. A small committee was appointed to investigate and report concerning (1) the encroachments upon the village green, (2) the unauthorised enclosure of Threap Moor, and (3) the ownership of the village school property. The report of this committee can be seen in the Vestry minute book, but as the writer is the only survivor of the small sub-committee appointed to investigate the matter, we may as well record the final result, to save any recurrence of these claims. The theory on which the parish claims were based was the axiom " Once a public right always a public right—Time does not run against the public." The committee consulted the best legal authority on land tenure in Newcastle, and while he was very sympathetic and would make no charge for his opinion and his investigations, the whole claims were squashed when he pointed out that the residents of the township of Wallsend were not synonymous with " the public "—that time did run against claims made on behalf of a particular township and that all the enclosures and encroachments upon the village rights had been completely lost owing to the lapse of time.

Standing somewhat outside the old village, on the south side of the school and school-house, are two large semi-detached houses, built by Mr Frank Mordue on what had been the school-house garden. Opposite to these facing south is Nelson Villa. This was built in 1854 by Mr Edward Nelson, a traveller for Palmer, Hall & Co., timber merchants.

On the south side, at the east end of the green, was the old vicarage, a long, low, two-storied house with a small garden in front and a large orchard behind.

The vicar, the Rev. John Armstrong, moved into the new vicarage in 1853, and John Nelson, who had been a master corver for the collieries, came from Walker to live here, and his only sister Isabella kept house for him. He took a good deal of interest in local affairs, and in 1859 he was appointed a trustee for the annuitants in the

Church Tontine Scheme. He was selected as "returning officer" for the first Local Board election, and he was a churchwarden of St Peter's Church for fifteen years (1858-1873). Miss Nelson died in the old vicarage on 20th March, 1879, aged seventy-six, and he died on 12th November following in his eighty-second year.

With the Nelsons resided John Crosse Brooks, who came to Tyneside from the south in 1830, and in 1840 became book-keeper and cashier at Mr Coutt's yard at Low Walker.

In the same office were Charles Mitchell and William Swan.

Mr Brooks became a considerable shipowner, and one of his ships, the *Sally Gale,* under Captain Bishop, had her name spread far and wide. In January, 1871, during the Franco-Prussian War, she was carrying coals from the Tyne to Rouen. She had delivered her cargo at the gas works and was returning down the Seine when the Prussians boarded her and five other north county traders. They put the crews ashore without money and without clothes, except what they stood in, and sunk the ships. Immediately an immense outcry was raised from one end of Britain to the other against this "Prussian outrage," this "astounding insult," and to "vindicate the honour of England," and Prussia nearly had Great Britain to fight as well as France.

When Mr Brooks left Wallsend he settled at No. 14 Lovaine Place, Newcastle, where he died on 13th March, 1897, aged eighty-five.

He was an enthusiastic collector of coins, tokens, and autographs, and his collection of the latter in twenty-six royal octavo volumes may be seen in the library at the Black Gate.

The old vicarage and grounds, in all 2,500 square yards, were put up for sale on 24th November, 1880, and were sold to Mr George Auburn Allan for £455. Mr Allan and his family lived here until he built a more modern house in the

THE GRANGE, WALLSEND VILLAGE.
North Front in 1890.

THE GRANGE, WALLSEND VILLAGE.
South Front in 1890. [*Facing page* 87.

orchard; he then had the old vicarage pulled down, and the site cleared.

Next to the vicarage was a farm-house and buildings. These were demolished in 1875, and the land added to the new " Hall Farm." On the site, two semi-detached villas were erected by Mr R. R. Dees.

The Grange

Next came the Grange, with its grounds two acres in extent. It was a large house of fourteen rooms (with dairy, laundry, byres, etc.), fronting south, with the main entrance on the north. This was the mansion house of the Middle Farm estate consisting of one hundred and twenty-four acres.

The Grange mansion house and lands were part of the property acquired by James Moncaster the elder, and on his death they passed to his youngest daughter, Frances. On 4th October, 1757, she married Charles Atkinson, a coal owner and hostman. The marriage was by special licence at St Nicholas Church, and although both the bride and groom were widely known, we may assume it was a very quiet wedding. The only witnesses who signed the register were James Moncaster, the father of the bride, and Tim Phillipson, who was evidently the verger judging from the number of other weddings he witnessed. Charles Atkinson was an Alderman of Newcastle and Mayor of that town in 1775 and 1783, and not only was he interested in collieries and coal exports, but he was a sugar boiler in the Close and a partner in the Commercial Bank.

Yet, notwithstanding his many activities, his attendance as one of the " Four and Twenty " of Wallsend was most regular. From the time he came to the Grange, until 1786, he only missed one meeting. In 1786 we have the signature " James Moncaster for C. Atkinson," and thereafterwards his presence is less regular.

Mrs Atkinson died in September, 1793, aged sixty-seven, and her husband was killed at Dunfermline on

12th February, 1797, by stepping upon an unsafe plank and falling down the pit shaft. They left a son and a daughter. The daughter, Isabel, married Shafto Craster. The son, James Moncaster Atkinson, inherited the estate from his mother and resided in the Grange until about 1811.

The next owner was Nicholas Fenwick of North Shields, a solicitor, who married Elizabeth, daughter of Samuel Hurry of Howdon dock, on 27th February, 1812.

Mr Fenwick was appointed grieve for the township from 1818 to 1823. He died in February, 1848, aged seventy-one, and on June 6th following this leasehold was put up for sale by auction in four lots at the Turf Hotel.

Lot 1 consisted of the High Farm, Lot 2 the Grange and two acres of ground, Lot 3 the Swan Inn and the houses on each side of it (west end of High Street East), and Lot 4 the village smithy with dwelling-house attached (opposite the Park Gate).

When this estate was sold, the Grange was occupied by Mr Ralph Walters, a solicitor, who, prior to his living in the district, took a good deal of interest in local affairs, especially at Howdon. He was agent for Sir Wm. Alex. Maxwell of Edinburgh, the mortgagee in possession of the Hurry estate. He assisted to build the Howdon Temperance Hall in Main Street, and he laid the foundation stone of the Howdon Independent Church in 1835.

At Wallsend he established a lending library at the north end of Long Row, for the benefit of the inhabitants, and he asserted the rights of all the villagers to a share in the village green. This he did by putting a cow to graze upon it, although his neighbour, Mr W. R. Swan, had rented all the grazing rights from the landholders. The landholders objected to mere occupiers sharing in their privileges, but in the end Mr Walters made good his claim.

In later life he became very well known in the north. In 1852, as a Radical parliamentary candidate he unsuccessfully contested Gateshead, and five years later Sunderland, but in 1859 he was elected for Beverley. However, his chief activities centred round Newcastle, and particulars of these may be read in Mr Welford's " Men of Mark."

In 1853 Mr Ralph Walters was succeeded by Mr Wm. J. Grey, a shipowner and insurance broker, as owner and occupier of the Grange. Next in 1859 came Mr Bennett Pell, a colonial agent, as tenant for two years, then in 1862 the house was bought by Mr George Angus, a Newcastle leather merchant, who founded the firm of George Angus & Co. After several years' residence he sold the property on 15th June, 1869, to Mr Martin Schlesinger.

Mr Schlesinger, senior, was a retired teacher of languages who came to the Grange from Rye Hill, Newcastle. He settled at Wallsend in order that his son, Charles Albert Schlesinger, who lived with him, might be near his shipyard. Mr Martin Schlesinger died at the Grange on 12th January, 1882, aged eighty-one years, and was buried in St Peter's churchyard.

In March, 1883, Wm. and John Russell took possession; both were unmarried. Their father was Mr Wm. Russell, who came to Wallsend in 1848 as manager for Mr John Allen, and who, in 1856, began copper smelting at Walker. He died on August 18th, 1868, and the two sons continued the copper works.

On July 22nd, 1883, John put an end to his life in the Grange garden, and shortly afterwards his brother William left Wallsend. He died on November 22nd, 1893, in the Isle of Wight, but he was buried in St Peter's churchyard beside his father and brother. A few years afterwards, Mr Russell's executors sold the house and gardens for £900 to Mr John Ross, a Gateshead auctioneer and estate agent, who sold the site to Mr Dees, and in 1913 Grange Villas were erected upon it.

Village Farm

Next to the Grange was the Village Farm-house, with its buildings, attached to an estate of 131 acres 1 rood 33 perches.

The earliest exact reference to this estate is that in the years 1628-9 and 1630 Henry Burghill of Wallsend is returned as one of the grand jurors for Northumberland, and in 1660, in a list of landholders of Wallsend, Henry Burfield is given as holding one farm and fine from the Dean and Chapter, value of £140. In 1663 he was holding one-seventh of the township.

He died in 1677, and on July 5th was buried in Holy Cross churchyard. His estate descended to his son, James Burfield. The last reference we have to this family in Wallsend is when " Jane, daughter of James Burfield of Wallsend," was married to Philip Spearman of Preston, on 26th August, 1703.

Three years before this date James Burfield had sold the leasehold to Eleanor Allan of Newcastle and her son Francis. This Eleanor Allan was the founder of Dame Allan's School. The history of this good lady has all the elements of a romance; sufficient here to say that her father was a Wm. Luck, a goldsmith in Newcastle. She married John Allan, a merchant who could not make his tobacco shop successful, and he died in poor circumstances. After his death, his widow and his son, by their frugality and their energy, converted the business into a sound paying concern, and laid up considerable wealth. They purchased the leasehold of the Wallsend Village Farm and held the lease at a rental of £61 19s. 5d. Francis died unmarried and left his share of the business and the leasehold to his mother, and on the 20th February, 1705, she assigned her tenant rights to trustees to found a school for forty poor boys and twenty poor girls belonging to the parishes of St Nicholas and St John. Dame Allan died on January 21st, 1708-9, and the school was opened in 1709. The funds were added to, so that the scholars were clothed as well as educated. It is interesting to note that the boys' clothing included leather breeches.

The history of the school is outside our limits, but one of its masters, as the grandfather of Mr Robt. R. Dees, has some local interest for us. In 1785, Ralph Dees succeeded to the head mastership, and in a note concerning the epitaphs of the Dees' family, in St John's churchyard, we have the following : " Died, March 27th, 1828, aged seventy-two years, highly respected, Mr Ralph Dees, who had held the situation of master of St Nicholas and All Saints' Free-schools in succession for forty-two years, and had been secretary to the Schoolmasters' Association for above thirty years. He was an unassuming and upright man, an excellent penman, and a good teacher."

Amongst the tenants of this leasehold was a family which for several generations were farmers in Wallsend. Thomas Swan entered into occupation of this farm in 1735 at a rental of £80 per annum. He died on the 23rd November, 1744, aged sixty-one, and was buried in Holy Cross churchyard. His grandson, Wm. Swan of Wallsend, farmer, died 4th August, 1825, aged sixty-eight years. He was succeeded by his son, Wm. Robert, and his daughter Mary.

Mary Swan married Mr John Allan, the chemical manufacturer. Wm. Robert Swan increased his leaseholds and became the largest leaseholder in Wallsend. He also studied law, and was in middle life a well-known lawyer on Tyneside. He was born at Wallsend in 1799 and lived all his life at the Village Farm, the house of which he rebuilt. He began to practise as an attorney about 1826 in the Blue Post Yard in Newcastle. A year or so later he entered into partnership with Mr Edward Helmsley, who, however, died soon afterwards. Thereupon Mr Thomas Burnip, of Jesmond Terrace, joined Mr Swan, and the firm became Swan & Burnip, which continued until 1872, when Mr Burnip retired and Mr Thomas Arnott took his place. As " Swan & Arnott " the business was continued until the death of Mr Swan in 1880. The name of Swan, however, was still retained in the firm, as Mr Henry Charles Swan, a nephew, joined it and it became Arnott & Swan. This continued until 1886, when Mr John

Duguid Walker entered the business, which then became known as Arnott, Swan & Walker, and now as J. D. Walker & Son.

Thus we see that Mr Wm. R. Swan was head of this firm for nearly fifty years, and in Wallsend was generally known as " Turney " Swan. He was a shrewd, careful, far-seeing man whose advice and assistance was much sought for in local affairs. He was an active helper in collecting contributions for the relief of those who suffered by the great colliery disaster in 1835, and he was treasurer to the fund. He was an overseer and a member of the first Wallsend Local Board. Although keenly interested in the cultivation of his lands he was more a lawyer than a farmer.

He died at Wallsend on 8th May, 1880, at the age of eighty-one, and he left his estates to his nephew, Mr William Allan, and his nieces, Mrs Elizabeth Jane Lee and Mrs Margaret McCallum, the son and the two daughters of his only sister, Mary Allen (Mr Charles Sheridan Swan of the Wallsend Slipway and of Messrs C. S. Swan & Hunter was his half-cousin). His executors gave up the farm in May, 1881, and his farming stock and " Implements of Husbandry " were sold on May 4th, and Mr Wm. Hall, junior, became the tenant.

Meanwhile the trustees of Dame Allan's Charity had, from time to time, sold part of the land, and finally in December, 1921, they sold the remainder, consisting of seventy-two acres, to the Battle Hill Estate Co., for £8,500, and a few months later they disposed of the farm-house and buildings to Mr Stephen J. Long of High Street East.

White House

The next large house was the White House (on the right hand side of photograph), which contained three reception-rooms, two kitchens, five bedrooms, two attics, wine cellars, larders, etc. Attached were large stables and coach-house, large pleasure grounds on the south side with a fish pond and kitchen garden, and a shrubbery on the north. There

PART OF THE VILLAGE GREEN IN 1890.
Showing "The Villa," and on the right, "The White House."

[*Facing page* 93.

The White House

were also two cottages (afterwards altered into a seven-roomed house) and buildings for kennels. This was the mansion house of one of the old seven leaseholds into which the township was divided. The estate consisted of one hundred and twenty-nine acres, and in 1750 it was in the possession of Lewis Hicks, a hostman, whose wife was Anne, daughter of William Lake of Long Benton.

On the death of her husband, the estate passed to her, and on May 18th, 1772, she married Alderman William Cramlington. However, before she married Mr Cramlington, a settlement was made giving her full power to dispose of the estate which she had inherited from her first husband. In the survey made by John Bell in 1800 Wm. Cramlington is given as the owner of the White House and estate, but it will be seen that this was correct only to a limited extent. He was Sheriff of Newcastle for the year 1775 (the year Charles Atkinson of the Wallsend Grange was Mayor), and he occupied the position of Mayor of Newcastle in 1787 and 1796, and was succeeded by Alderman Anthony Hood, also of Wallsend. He served his time as a ropemaker and carried on business in the Broad Chare, and he was also a hostman. He was one of the Wallsend " Four and Twenty," but not a very regular attender. The first meeting he attended was at Easter, 1777, and the last in 1796.

He kept an account of his expenses as Mayor of Newcastle, and during his first term of office he spent £2,051 13s. 9d.; deducting the allowances received from the town, the net cost was £718 6s. 3½d. During the second year of his Mayoralty he only spent £1,083 2s. 10d.; and his net outlay was £214 5s. 4½d.

Mrs Ann Cramlington made her will on November 1st, 1800, and by it she left the White House property to Miss Alice Hicks and to Mrs Elizabeth Hedley (wife of Robert Shafto Hedley), who were her daughters by her first marriage. She died on March 23rd, 1804, aged seventy, and her two daughters succeeded to her Wallsend estate.

So far as Mr Cramlington is concerned when he made his will three months after the death of his wife, he had a town house in Pilgrim Street and a country house at Walbottle. He left his property to his only child Anne and to his nephew Henry Cramlington.[1] He died on 12th May, 1810, at the age of eighty-five years, and was buried beside his wife in the family vault in All Saints' churchyard. The tombstone shows the arms of the Cramlington family quartered with that of Scott.

The new owners held the leasehold jointly, and in 1809, when the seats in St Peter's Church were allotted to the various proprietors, Pews No. 4 and 5 " were set out " to Mrs Hedley and Miss Hicks as landowners, and their tenants were Wm. Swan and Humphrey Curry. (It may be presumed that Wm. Swan was the tenant of the land and Humphrey Curry of the White House.)

About the year 1820 the leasehold was disposed of. Part was secured by John Buddle and others, but the White House and its adjacent grounds and eleven acres of land to the west of Shiney Row were bought by Captain John Potts, J.P., whose wife was Miss Sarah A. Henderson, daughter of Mr Edward Henderson, an occupier of the Red House.

Captain Potts was one of the leading factors in the social life of the village for years, and was keenly interested in all that concerned the Army. He kept a pack of hounds and hunted the district, and for fifty years he was an officer in the Northumberland Light Infantry. He was commissioned an Ensign in 1814, received his Captaincy on 29th April, 1831, and was promoted to Major on 27th August, 1862. He resigned from the Army in 1864.

When the late William Clark's Benton estate was offered for sale on 23rd October, 1837, Captain Potts bought it for £9,100, and he moved from Wallsend into the Red Hall, Little Benton.

Mrs Potts died in London on 14th August, 1867, and

[1] " Arch. Aeli.," Vol. xix., p. 9.

Major Potts also died there on 24th April, 1870, but both are buried in St Peter's churchyard.

On the south wall of the church there is a white marble memorial stone to the memory of Major and Mrs Potts, and below this a " brass " commemorates the memory of their five sons and daughter. Furthermore, the east window of the church was erected by Mr John Potts, junior, in 1893.

After Captain Potts left Wallsend in 1837 for Benton, he sold this mansion house and the eleven acres of land to the west of Shiney Row to Mr Thos. Chater, who " let " the White House to Mr Wm. Bainbridge, a barrister, who was his son-in-law.

The succeeding tenant who entered in April, 1857, was Mr George Hunter, a Newcastle coal merchant. Meanwhile Mr Thos. Chater had built " The Villa," on the east side of the White House. On 18th March, 1868, the whole of the Chater property was put up to auction at the Queen's Head Hotel, Newcastle.

From some notes of the sale made by Mr R. R. Dees, we see that the White House, occupied by Mr Geo. Hunter at a rent of £52 10s., did not reach the reserve price, but was sold a few days later to Mrs Mary Allen, widow of Mr John Allen, for £1,100, and she became the occupier. The small dwelling-house adjoining, occupied by Mrs McAllum (rent £20), was sold to Mr Shaw for £320. The new villa, occupied by Mrs Allen at a rent of £40, was withdrawn, as the reserve of £900 was not reached, but Mrs Townsend of Hope Villas and Newcastle, bought it later for £850, and the eleven acres of land were bought for the Wallsend Co-operative Society by Mr John Smith for £1,210.

After this, the house for a while was in the hands of Mr Henry Wilson of the cement works, father-in-law of Mr W. T. Stead the journalist, and the last owner and occupier was Mrs Thomas Stewart, who moved to Tynemouth in 1903.

Then the house was pulled down and a skating rink was erected by Mr W. Ridley, a builder of Consett. This was opened on November 16th, 1910, by Alderman James Allan, but it was not a success. During the war it was used as a factory in which to build aeroplanes, and after this, in 1919-20, it had a brief and unsuccessful career as a boxing hall.

In 1922 the land and buildings on the west side of the large hall was bought by the Daimler Company Ltd., who moved their motor business here from St Mary's Place, Newcastle.

Middle Farm

Westward of the White House, and at the south-western end of the green, is the Middle Farm. It derives its name from the fact that the greater part of its land lay in the middle of the township, running from the north boundary to the river. The mansion house, which formed part of this leasehold of one hundred and twenty-four acres, was the Grange, and this we have already dealt with.

Red House

The house at the west end, on the north side of the village green, was the Red House, a large red-bricked mansion house of three stories (see illustrations), containing over twenty rooms, with stabling, gardens, etc., in all over two acres. Prior to the death of Mr Buddle in 1844, only a narrow strip of flower border separated the front of the house from the green. Following the example of others, the owner attempted to extend his boundaries, but Mr Buddle defended the public rights.

His pitmen demolished the objectionable railing, and he rode on horseback over and over the enclosed ground. To impress this event upon the memory of the public, he had ale, bread and cheese and cakes provided on the green for all and sundry, and this obvious hint sufficed to

THE RED HOUSE, WALLSEND VILLAGE.
South Front in 1895.

THE RED HOUSE, WALLSEND VILLAGE.
North Front in 1895.

[*Facing page* 97.

delay the re-enclosure until the upholder of the village rights had passed away, when a lawn and flower garden were filched from the green.

Long before this, for many years, the house was the residence of the Waters family. From 1722 to 1737 the Vestry minute book shows that Henry Waters was one of the Wallsend "Four and Twenty." He was, like several other Wallsenders, a hostman. In 1404 it was enacted "that in everie citie, towne and porte of the sea in England, where marchants, aliens or strangers be or shall be repairing, sufficient hoostes shall be assigned to the said marchants by the Maior, sheriffes or bailiffes of the said cities," and the merchants and strangers were to dwell in no other place.

The majority of the foreign merchants who came to Newcastle, came to buy coals, and the "hosts" of these merchants made the most of their opportunities. The coal trade of the river soon passed completely into their hands. Queen Elizabeth, for a consideration, incorporated them and they became a wealthy and powerful Company.

In 1749 (May 16th) the enrolments of the Clerk of the Peace shows that "William Waters of Wallsend, gentleman," held a mortgage on the estate of Mark Swinburn and Eleanor his wife for £2,500.

In 1759 Thomas Waters, a merchant adventurer, is one of the local "Four and Twenty."

In 1766 his son, Matthew Waters, Esq., was appointed grieve for the parish, and was yearly reappointed for the following nineteen years. He was a barrister-at-law, and his wife was Mary Walker, third daughter of Henry Walker, a master and mariner residing at Tynemouth, who came from Whitby in 1724 and acquired a considerable amount of property near North Shields.

Matthew Waters died at Wallsend on December 17th, 1785, aged sixty-six, and was buried in the family vault at All Saints' Church, Newcastle. For several years prior to his death he had retired from his profession. His book plate shows a shield with arms: Argent a fesse dancette between three cross crosslets fitché gules and below, "Matt. Waters Esq. Walls End." His widow inherited one-third of her father's property, and we note that when Tynemouth Shiremoor was divided she and her sister claimed 5⅓ acres of the 448 stints.

She sold the Red House and grounds and the lands attached thereto, in all 175 acres 2 roods, to her cousin, John Walker, of Dockwray Square, in the year 1799.

The new owner moved from Dockwray Square to the Red House and became an active worker in Wallsend. He was one of the pioneers in opening up at Backworth the coal seams on the north side of the ninety fathom dyke, and among his co-partners were John Buddle of Wallsend, and Humble Lamb of the Howdon collieries.

John Walker, who was one of the "Four and Twenty," was appointed grieve at the Vestry in 1802 and was reappointed annually until 1817. He died at the Red House on January 18th, 1822, aged seventy-six years. He left £50 to the poor of the township of Wallsend. His daughter and heir was Elizabeth, who married John Kerrich of Harleston. She sold the estate, and Mr Francis Peacock, a retired rope manufacturer and one of the owners of the Walker Colliery, bought the mansion house and one hundred and twelve acres of the land.

As Mr Peacock did not require the house immediately, he "let" it to Edward Henderson of Newton-by-the-Sea, who came to Wallsend when he was eighty years of age to be near his daughter, Mrs John Potts, who was at the White House. He had purchased Bilton Banks estate near Alnmouth on 12th May, 1800, for £1,550, and his sister-in-law, Miss Taylor, had left him the estates of Newton-by-the-Sea under her will dated 3rd December, 1807. Mr Henderson died at Wallsend on 18th April, 1826, aged eighty-three years, and was buried in the Potts' burial ground near the door of St Peter's Church.

Both the Newton estate, which had a rental of £992, and that of Bilton Banks came into the possession of Mr Potts, of the White House, the Newton property being transferred to him the year after Mr Henderson's death and Bilton Banks under the terms of the will of his brother-in-law, Edward Henderson the younger.[1]

After the death of Mr Henderson, Mr Francis Peacock took up his residence in the Red House, and in 1828 he was elected Mayor of Wallsend in succession to Mr John Wright, and he was re-elected to this office until 1832. He died on 29th October, 1833, aged seventy-seven. His son, Francis Edward Werge Peacock, succeeded to the mansion house and estate bought by his father. Sixteen years later, in 1849, his estate passed into the hands of trustees, and he left Wallsend. At a sale of his household goods the valuable silver plate (200 ounces) and the Louis XV. furniture attracted many buyers.

The trustees " let " the house to Mr Thomas Aynsley Cook, and finally put the whole estate up for sale by auction at the Queen's Head Inn, Newcastle, on 28th September, 1858. Mr John Allen, the chemical manufacturer, bought the Red House and gardens, etc., of over two acres. He also bought thirty-three acres at the west end of the parish between the main road and the North Road. Of the Allen family, who thus came into possession, we have spoken elsewhere. After Mr Wm. Allen, Mr Jos. E. Lee, his nephew, became tenant. He moved from Wallsend to Osborne Road, Newcastle, in 1882, and on August 15th the house and grounds were again offered for sale, and Mr R. R. Dees became the owner.

The house was next used as a Cripples' Home for children, who were moved from Whickham. Fifty beds were provided, and on 27th September, 1889, the Mayor of Newcastle welcomed them to Wallsend. A new

[1] County History, Vol. ii., p. 461.

"Home" for the children (fifty-five boys and twenty-five girls) was built at Gosforth, and they left Wallsend in September, 1897. A stained glass window in St Peter's Church testifies to the kindness they received during their sojourn at Wallsend.

The old Red House was then pulled down, and the four semi-detached villas (Hawthorn Villas) built on the site, and Park Villas erected on part of the garden.

On the east of the Red House stood the Village North Farm buildings, and land attached thereto; in all, eighty acres. These were part of the Peacock estate, and were offered for sale at the same time as the Red House. Mr R. R. Dees bought this property together with Bridge Row Cottages (the north-east of the park covers the site, and the bridge brought the coals from the north, and joined with the wagonways from the gas pit).

In 1870 to 1871, the farm buildings were pulled down, and Elm Terrace built on the site. Mr Dees combined the land attached to this farm, and the land belonging to the farm on the south-east side of the village, and built the Hall Farm buildings, three-quarters of a mile to the north.

Replacing these two farmyards and buildings by good residential houses considerably added to the amenities of the village. The next property eastwards is the Hall and grounds, with which we have fully dealt.

CARVILLE HALL

This house was originally built by John Cosyn, about 1635. He was a well-known woollen cloth merchant, who married Miss Jane Horsley in All Saints' Church on October 20th, 1632. He was an Alderman of Newcastle, and when the North was swaying between Royalist and Puritan, he took an active part on the side of the Commonwealth.

He was appointed Comptroller of Customs, and while

CARVILLE HALL, WALLSEND.

[*Facing page* 101.

he had a splendid town house at the west end of Newcastle Quay (which remained in excellent condition as Nos. 1 and 2 Quayside until a few years ago), he built his country house close to the Wall's end.

The house had extensive grounds surrounding it, and one old souvenir of Cosyn's house may now be seen on the top of the old Castle at Newcastle. This is the sun dial, given by the late Mr Wigham Richardson to the Society of Antiquaries before the Carville garden was built upon. It bears the Cosyn Arms, and the date of 1667. The words are—

> "Time, tide
> doth haste
> Therefore
> Make haste
> We shall"

and the dial itself completes the rhyme—"Die all."

When the Restoration of the Stuarts took place in 1660, the worthy Comptroller of the Customs lost his office, but he was a lover of books, and had considerable wealth, and probably during the few remaining months of his life he would often escape the political and social re-action in his quiet country retreat.

He died on 21st March, 1661, and was buried in the north aisle of the old All Saints' Church. He left no sons, and it appears that within a few years the property passed to the Lawson family.

"Ralph Lawson, Gentleman," died here, and was buried in Holy Cross churchyard on 11th September, 1679.

Sir William Lawson sold the property to the Hewbanks, but the family kept up some connection with Wallsend afterwards, for there is an entry in the registers of Holy Cross Church on October 26th, 1706—"Richard Lawson of All Saints' Parish—Scrivener, buried."

The Hewbanks were in possession of Cosyn's house in the opening years of the eighteenth century, and occupied a prominent position in Wallsend. The arms of the family were—Sable three chevrons interlaced gold on a chief gold three annulets sable; and for crest : on a wreath a dragon's head. The head of the Wallsend branch was then George Hewbanks, a master and mariner.

On 24th September, 1710, Elizabeth, wife of George Hewbanks, died, and George died eight years later. Both are buried in the family vault in the chancel of Holy Cross Church, and the grave cover is still in an excellent state of preservation.

He was succeeded by his eldest son, George, who had married Sarah Hambleton of North Shields at Wallsend on January 9th, 1709-10, but he only survived his father two years, for he died at Cosyn's house and was buried on October 7th, 1720. His second son, John, married a neighbour, Margery Hindmarsh, in the parish church on September 23rd, 1703. The Hindmarshs, as we have seen, were one of the oldest families connected with the district. John Hewbanks was one of the Elder Brethren of Newcastle Trinity House in 1721.

The Hewbanks sold the property to Robert Carr, one of the Carrs of Etal, but nevertheless a draper in London in partnership with Thomas Bigge of Byker, who built the White Hall at Little Benton, where he died in 1791.

Robert Carr married his partner's daughter, Grace Bigge, and he rebuilt Cosyn's house and renamed it Carville. In 1777, on the death of his brother, he assumed the title of Sir Robert Carr, and he died on 6th March, 1791, aged eighty-five.

In the *Newcastle Journal* of May 13th, 1758, the Hall was advertised to be let or sold, and it was forthwith let to Mrs Elizabeth Montague, well known for her beauty and her exceptional literary talents. She occupied it while Denton Hall was being repaired, and found the house and surroundings both interesting and pleasant. Very shortly after Mrs Montague left, Carville was sold to Mrs

Carville Shore about 1830.
Showing the Pilot Track and Benton and Heaton Coal Spouts.

[Facing page 103.

Dorothy Proctor. She made her will on 29th March, 1768, and she is described as Dorothy Proctor of Carville, Northumberland—widow. She bequeaths " Carvill otherwise called Cousens House to my cousin George Lisle of Newcastle Esq."

George Lisle died at Carville in March, 1776. His will, dated 2nd March, 1772, gives " an annuity of £200 to the Rev. Wilfred Lawson, my friend . . . my mansion house at Carville and the use of my furniture for his life." The Rev. Wilfred Lawson was the vicar of Warkworth, a grandson of the first Sir Wilfred Lawson. Mr Lawson retained his living, but retired to Carville in 1771, and died there on 27th November, 1777, aged seventy-one. He was buried at Warkworth, and in his will dated 2nd January, 1776, he leaves to " the Rev. George Bowe of Warkworth, my best gown and cassock and my father's sermons and my own, which, if he does not make use of himself, I request it of him that he would not hack them, or lend them to others."[1]

John Bigge, a younger brother of Thomas Charles Bigge of Benton, purchased the property. Born in Newcastle on 14th January, 1742, in early life he entered the business house of his uncles in Ludgate Hill and became a silk mercer and presently succeeded to the business.

John Bigge resided at Carville several years, and then returned south to chambers in the Temple, London, where he died on March 11th, 1797. He left his estate of Carville to his nephew, John Thomas Bigge.

The next occupier was John Surtees, then followed William Redhead, a Newcastle corn merchant, who added two lodges on the turnpike road in 1810.

John Grace, brother of Edward Grace of Wallsend Hall, was the next tenant. He was a shareholder in the Walker colliery and the principal owner of the Felling

[1] County History, Vol. v., p. 187.

colliery. In 1826 he left Wallsend for a time and moved to Felling Hall.

Anthony Easterby then became both occupier and owner. He and his partner, George Doubleday, began the manufacture of soap on the Tyne, and built up a large business. He was one of the many prominent men in Newcastle affairs who made Wallsend their country residence, and when the first election of town councillors for Newcastle took place, on December 26th, 1835, under the Corporation Reform Act, he was elected for All Saints' ward, and was also elected one of the first Aldermen. He left Wallsend in 1840 when he was over eighty years of age, and was retiring from active life. He died at Heworth on 16th February, 1844, aged eighty-seven.

Charles Rayne, of the Walker Linseed Oil and Cake Mills, bought the estate for £5,900, which at this time consisted of the Hall and sixty-eight acres of land. He took up his residence in the Hall soon after Mr Easterby removed, and remained in occupation until 1863.

In May, 1863, Mr John Ormston succeeded Mr Rayne, but he only rented the Hall and four acres of the land. He was interested in the Low Lights Brewery, and also in the Tyne Steam Shipping Company. The next tenant in 1866 was Captain James Gordon, a tar distiller, who failed in business in 1868 and soon after left Wallsend.

In December, 1873, Mr Wigham Richardson bought the Hall and the sixty-eight acres from Charles Rayne. His first idea was to live there, but finally, for family reasons, he decided to remain in Newcastle and devote the land to works and workmen's houses. He was always keenly alive to the need of housing his men in airy, comfortable homes, and on the Carville estate the cottage type in the south-east part of " The Avenue," Carville Gardens, and Wilberforce Street are types of working men's houses far in advance of their day.

Mr Thos. Stewart was the last tenant in the Hall, which was pulled down in 1898, and the site was built upon and mainly occupied by the north end of George Road. The estate cost Mr Richardson about £30,000.

John Wigham Richardson, while he was a Walker man, and only to a smaller extent a Wallsend man, had a considerable influence in our district. In addition to his house building operations, he was a director of the Gas Company, and it was due to him that their profit-sharing scheme was adopted. He was also a director of the Tyne Pontoons and Dry Dock Company.

His father was Edward Richardson, leather manufacturer of Newcastle, and his mother was Miss Jane Wigham of Edinburgh. He was born on the 7th January, 1837, and was trained as a ship designer and engineer. In 1860 he began shipbuilding at Walker with John D. Christie as his assistant, and afterwards as his partner.

After a successful business career, he died on 15th April, 1908, in London, after an operation. He had a deep love of nature, and especially of trees, a genial kindness of heart, and an amount of perseverance which overrode all opposition to his plans.

Point Pleasant House

This house and pleasure grounds were attached to an estate of 127 acres 22 perches. It was one of the three estates in the possession of James Moncaster the elder, of Wallsend Hall. On his death it passed to his daughter, Mrs Stewart, who sold it to her brother, James Moncaster, junior. Wm. Clark bought it, together with other Moncaster estates, and then after he left Wallsend he sold them to Mr Wm. Losh (of Messrs Losh, Wilson & Bell), who became both owner and occupier.

During the year 1822, Point Pleasant House was the scene of two fashionable weddings. On 2nd March, Margaret, the youngest daughter of Wm. Losh, was married to Spencer Boyd, of Penkell Castle, Ayrshire, and on 1st August, Alice, the eldest daughter, was married to James Crosby Anderson, the third son of John Anderson of North Shields, who had bought the manor house and certain lands in Jesmond in 1805, and settled there.

Mr and Mrs Anderson took up their abode at Point Pleasant, and Mr Wm. Losh removed to the White Hall, Benton.

James Crosby Anderson was in business in Newcastle as a wine merchant, and took little part in the general affairs of the parish. He became owner of the leasehold of Point Pleasant in 1822, and continued to live there until his death on 1st April, 1837.

He left a widow, three sons, and two daughters. His will was made on October 4th, 1833. His executors were to pay to his wife an annual sum equivalent to the interest of £7,500 at the current rate for the time being. By a codicil dated 26th February, 1834, he appointed as his executors his brothers John and Matthew, his friend, James Losh of Newcastle, barrister, and his partner, John Fairbairn, and they jointly administered the Point Pleasant estate. Mrs Anderson left Wallsend soon after her husband's death, and on 23rd September, 1839, was married to Henry Player at the British Embassy, Paris.

In 1838 John Grace, brother of Edward Grace of Wallsend Hall, moved from Felling Hall to Point Pleasant, and thus for a second time became a resident in Wallsend. He was followed in 1842 by John Straker, who was a churchwarden and an overseer for the years 1843 and 1844. On his book plate he displays a simple faith—" John Straker, Point Pleasant, Deus est super domam " (God is stronger than the devil).

The next tenant was John H. Coutts, the shipbuilder, followed by Thomas William Jobling.

Mr Jobling came from Jarrow on his marriage in 1857. He was a mining engineer with an extensive practice in the north of England, and also in Yorkshire and Wales. He was manager and part owner of Jarrow Colliery, and also

POINT PLEASANT HOUSE, WALLSEND, IN 1911.

[*Facing page* 107.

of Walker. He founded the Bebside and Choppington coal companies, for which he was the viewer.

His brother, Alderman George Jobling, of Tynemouth, connected with the Hartley Bottle Works and the coal and shipping trade, met a tragic death while on a visit to Point Pleasant. On the 8th December, 1867, he left his brother's house about nine o'clock, and, as was his usual custom, got on to the railway and walked across the viaduct on his way to Howdon station. Unobserved, the train overtook him and struck him when about two hundred yards east of the bridge, and he was killed instantaneously. His body was discovered about twenty minutes later by some passengers coming along the railway side from Howdon station toward the mill.

Thos. Wm. Jobling lived at Point Pleasant all his married life, and died there on 25th March, 1869, and was buried in St Peter's churchyard.

His son, Thos. Edgar Jobling, followed his father's profession as a mining engineer, but left Wallsend and settled at Bebside. He was well known in the coal mining world, and a valuable steady worker in Local Government affairs. He was a county alderman, vice-chairman of the County Education Committee, and chairman of its elementary sub-committee. He was for years a member of the Tynemouth Board of Guardians, and at the time of his death was chairman of the Assessment Committee.

He took a deep interest in the home defence movement, at first as one of the Tynemouth Artillery Volunteers, where he rose to the position of Colonel, and later he worked hard to ensure the success of the " Territorials." In all matters he took a wide, all-round view of things, and his reasonableness and his willingness to hear both sides could always be relied upon. He died at Bebside Hall on 7th October, 1916, aged fifty-seven years, and was buried at Horton.

Mrs Thomas William Jobling only remained at Point Pleasant a few months after her husband's death, and near the close of 1869 Wm. Glover, son of John Glover the chemical manufacturer, married Miss Louise Wilson, daughter of Captain Charles Wilson of Church Street, Howdon, and they became the tenants for nearly two years.

In 1870 Messrs George Elliott, Hylton, Philipson, and others bought the leasehold from the trustees of the Crosby Anderson estates, and on the foreshore and part of the riverside grounds the Wallsend Slipway Company started their works. In 1871 Mr Charles S. Swan, the managing director, took up his residence at the Hall, but left in 1874, and it was divided and at present it is occupied by Mr Robert Wallis, the works manager, and Mr Jos. W. Tocher, the manager of the dry dock.

In April, 1879, the Wallsend Slipway Company bought the leasehold from Messrs Elliott, Philipson, and partners.

Wallsend House and Carville House

There were two other mansion houses in Wallsend of pre-colliery date, smaller than those already spoken of. Both were on the Grange estate. Wallsend House, facing west, occupied the south-west corner of the Roman Camp (half-way up the west side of Davis Street). The pleasure grounds, however, extended beyond the camp, and the " A " shaft of the colliery was just in front.

After the colliery started the tenants were the Buddles, father and son, then John Allen, the chemical manufacturer, who moved to the Red House in 1858. He was followed in 1859 by Andrew Leslie, shipbuilder, who removed to Coxlodge in 1880. The tenancy was then divided, and on April 1st, 1890, the house was destroyed by fire, and soon after the land was sold for building sites.

The other house, Carville House, was also within the site of the camp, near the east gateway. (Simpson's Hotel now occupies the north part of the ground.) This was the home of John Reay, the colliery cashier for many years, and its hospitality was well known to those interested in the colliery chapel. Mr Reay moved to East Farm and resided there for some years, and meanwhile Carville House was occupied by Joseph Heatherington, a coal owner, who failed in 1845 and soon after left Wallsend. In 1856 Mr Reay returned to his old residence, where he died in 1867. Then Frank Robinson (a partner of Robinson and Allan, cement manufacturers, Point Pleasant) was in possession for a short time, and he was followed in 1874 by Dr Thomas Wilson, who moved from a small detached villa on the east side of Station Road. After residing in Carville House for nine years, the doctor built himself a villa at the corner of Station Road and Buddle Street. Mr Wm. Norman was the next occupier of Carville House in 1883. Then followed Mr John A. Ryrie, who was the last tenant. After an existence of about a hundred and twenty years the house was demolished and the land was laid out for building, Simpson's Hotel being built on part of it.

CHAPTER III

ECCLESIASTICAL HISTORY

A history of each church and chapel with notes relating to many of those prominently connected therewith. Begins with Holy Cross in A.D. 1145 and finishes with the New Mission at Willington Square.

HOLY CROSS CHURCH

WE have already seen how the Prior and Convent of the Benedictine House at Durham became the owners of the townships of Wallsend and Willington.

The Pope had sanctioned and blessed William's invasion of England, and in return all the Norman bishops were eager to put the " Holy Catholic Church " on a proper basis in the newly conquered country. Hence as soon as the country had settled down under the Norman rule an era of church building and rebuilding began all over England.

It is not possible to say exactly when the church of the Holy Cross was built, but Alan, priest of " Valeshead," is a witness in some charters dated 1153. In a charter of King Henry II. (1154-89), relating to the possessions of the church at Durham, there is mentioned : " In Northumbria, Walleshende with its chapel, and Wiuelinton, with their appurtenances, and the land which they have in Cramlington." From this and other evidence it is fairly safe to say that the church was built about the year 1150; that is to say, after the Norman church at Tynemouth (A.D. 1110) and before the " Old Castle " in Newcastle (A.D. 1177).

GROUND PLAN OF HOLY CROSS CHURCH MADE 1910.

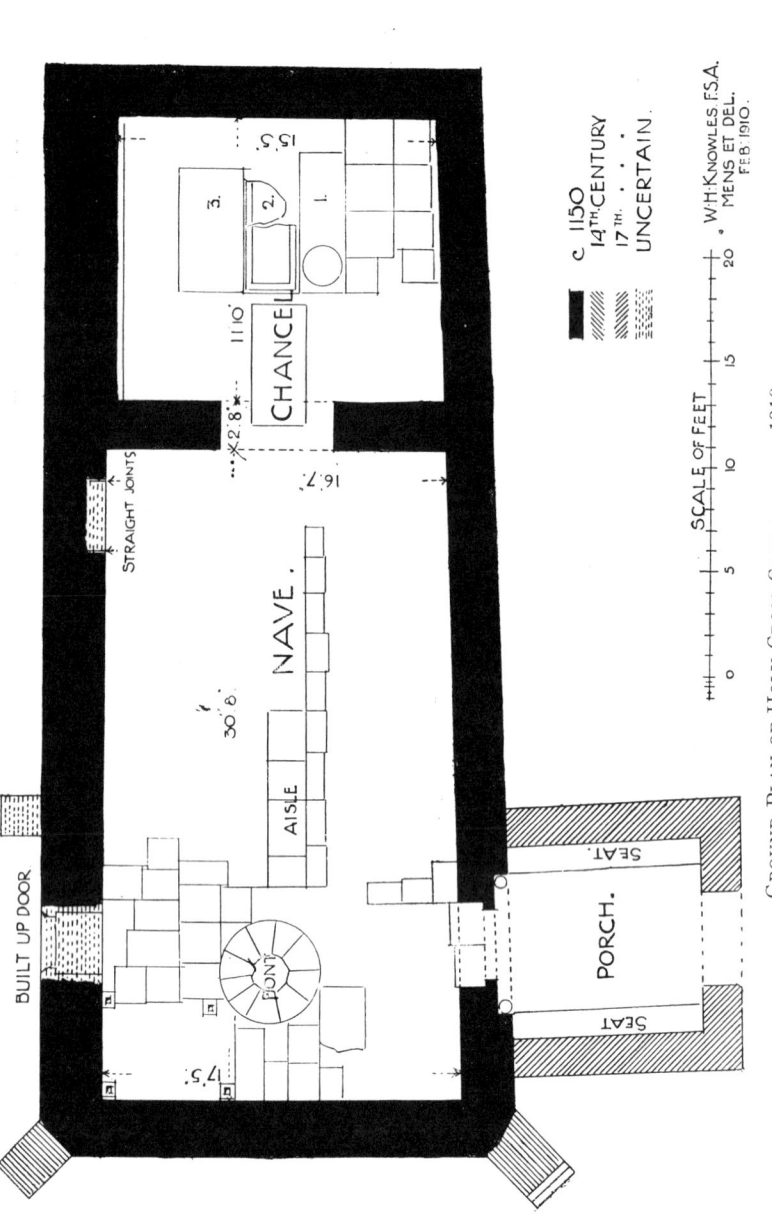

(1) Grave cover of the Hewbanks. (2) Grave cover of George Raine. (3) Grave cover of the Hindmarshs.

As to the church building, on the outside it is 52 feet long by 22½ feet broad. The interior of the chancel measures 11 feet 10 inches by 15 feet 5 inches across, the nave 30 feet 8 inches by 17 feet. (See ground plan.) There was a door on the north side, afterwards built up. The main entrance, on the south side, is by a semi-circular headed doorway, the arch of two orders, the outer moulding and impost being carried on single detached shafts. The porch was added in the seventeenth century.

The church was a small one and served a large area, but it is to be remembered that it was built for private prayer, baptisms, and marriages, rather than regular services such as are held to-day. Probably a parishioner who attended Mass once or twice a year would be considered to have fulfilled his religious duties.

From Wallsend village there was a paved "church way" to the bottom of the steps leading to the churchyard. From Willington village, a hearse road began at the West Farm, led down the dene to the stream which it followed for about fifty yards, then went up the west side of the hill to the gate near the iron well. (The old route from here was diverted from the middle of the field to the present road by order of the Spring Quarter Sessions of 1910. At no point was the new road to be less than twenty-one feet wide.)

Ecclesiastically, Wallsend was at first under the Benedictine cell at Jarrow and was part of the large parish of Jarrow. Jarrow, in turn, was dependent upon the Monastery of Durham.

In the Rent Roll of the House of Jarrow for the year 1303 we have the following entry:

The day after the day of St Oswyn, King and Martyr. Item Gilbert Fleminge for the lesser tithes of Alterage of Wallsend de VIj terminis LXXS.

In 1343, John, prior of the church at Durham, sent a citatory letter to the parish chaplain of "Jarowe," commanding him to summon the chaplains, ministers, and lay delegates of the " chapels on the parish church of Jarowe dependant," and those of " Wylington " and " Walleshend " were among those directed to go to the chapel of " Heword."

In 1347 Brother Thomas of Greystanes, Master of the House of Jarrow, reports having received £4 from William of Tynemouth, chaplain, as a " fine " for a lease of ten years for the chapel of Wallsend, and he also enters having paid William of Tynemouth 60s. as his stipend for the chapel of " Walleshend."

In 1369 the tithe was commuted to 13s. 4d. per annum.

In 1370 the successor of Thomas of Greystanes, " John of Lumley, Master of Jarrow, Received 13s. 4d. from the chapel of Wallsend," but in 1376 he only received " Vjs VIIjd for rent of the chapel of Walleshend." Two years later the rent rises again to VIIjs IIIjd., and at this amount (one mark) it remains for several years.

In 1408 an entry records that " nothing is received from the Altarage and profits of the Chapel of Wallsend, because the chaplain has received them in place of his stipend."

In 1432 the tithes on the fishery—the small tithes, etc. —were permanently assigned for the support of the chaplain, and many such entries relating to Wallsend and Willington are found in the Rent Rolls of the House of Jarrow.

In the Manor Rolls of the Monastery of Durham, in the notes of the first visitation for 1379 we have:

Walleshend—It is enjoined upon all the tenants of the vill on the one part and upon William the chaplain, that none shall abuse the other in words or deeds henceforth, under a penalty of half a mark.

The year before the monastery of Durham was dissolved we find in the bursar's rent returns: " From the chaplain at Wallsend for a cottage and garden, nil, because they are waste."

HOLY CROSS CHURCH

The cell at Jarrow and the monastery at Durham were both " dissolved " in 1540, but the township of Wallsend and the tithes of both Wallsend and Willington, each of the value of 73s. 4d., were regranted to the newly established Dean and Chapter, as we have already noted.

The church thus came directly under the jurisdiction of the new Bishop of Durham. Wallsend and Willington, however, still remained in the parish of Jarrow, and in the " Ministers' Accounts," Henry VIII. 708, we find the first account of Hugh Whytehed, dean of the cathedral church of Durham for the year

from Michalmas 32 Henry VIII. to Mich. 33 Henry VIII. (1540-41).
Arrears—none, because this is the first account.
He does not account for £1,829 11s. 0d. of the farm of the site of the late Monastery, nor of the tithes of grain of the parish of Jarrow, to wit, the vills of Wallsend 73s. 4d., of Wyllyngton 73s. 4d., of Wardley 10s., etc., because they were granted by the King to the said Dean and Chapter of Durham for a yearly payment of £218.

In a grant dated 26th January, 1544-45, Henry VIII. gives to Lord Eure very considerable possessions of the late cell of Jarrow, including " the site of the late house or cell," but he adds " except nevertheless and entirely reserved to us, and our heirs and successors . . . all tithes of grain of the Townships of Willyngton, Wallesende, formerly belonging to the late Monastery of Durham and being parcel of the possession of the cell of Jarrowe."

Sir Wm. de Eure was deputy warden of the East-marches, and the son of Sir Ralph de Eure, the lord warden whose power and authority kept the borders in peace and quiet for many years. Henry in this grant reserves the tithes of Willington and Wallsend to himself and his heirs, whereas he had already regranted these tithes to Durham, but we think the fact that the grants to the Dean and Chapter, including these tithes, were subject to an annual payment of £218 to the King, explains the matter.

On 20th July, 1567, it was agreed by the Chapter of

Durham that every prebend should have allocated to him certain revenues in order to augment his present income. There was allotted:

To the Seventh Prebend
    The corn tithe of Harton in the Parish of Jarrow   £9 10 0
    The tithes of Wallsend in the same parish   £3 13 4
To the Twelfth Prebend
    The tithes of Westoe in the Parish of Jarrow   £6 18 6
    The tithes of Willington in the Parish of Jarrow   £3 13 4

In a summary of the Revenues of the cathedral church of Durham made in 1580, the lessees of these tithes are given and the history of those for Wallsend. Under the heading of the Rectory of Jarrow we have:

    James Dodes for the tithe of sheaves of Wallsend per annum £3 13s. 4d. To the VIIth Prebend.
    Dated XIXth June 2 and 3 of Philip and Mary (A.D. 1556).
    Lease to Thomas and Janet his wiff for a term of XXI years following, a lease to Ja Rokeby dated XXIX January in the XXXVI year of Henry (A.D. 1545) for a term of 21 years for both Wallsend and Willington.
    Richard Marshall for the tithe of sheaves of Willington per annum £3 13s. 4d. To the XII Prebend.[1]

In Bishop Barnes's record of churches (1577-87) Wallsend is returned among the parish churches without incumbents and served by stipendiary priests.[2]

On Sunday, 1st February, 1577, on the occasion of the Chancellor's visitation, Richard Raye, the vicar, was cited to appear at St Nicholas Church, but Roger Norton, the clerk, was not called. At a similar visitation held in Newcastle, Richard Raye was again called, this time to give evidence of his "progresse in learninge and studinge of the scriptures." The test was to give an account of the Gospel of St Matthew, in Latin if he could, but if not, in English. However, it was found that our vicar had not completed his task, and he was given until Michaelmas to do so.[3]

[1] Surtees Society, Vol. lxxxii., p. 208.
[2] Ibid., Vol. xxii., p. 8.
[3] Ibid., p. 71.

HOLY CROSS CHURCH

The bishop appointed " Mr Doctour Pilkingtone " to preach " XIj " sermons during the year 1578-79 in certain churches, and in the list of those we find " Wallsend j."[1]

This Mr Doctour Pilkingtone was Leonard, brother of the bishop, the first Protestant bishop of Durham, and as he was a prebendary of the seventh stall, his visit was to a place from which he derived part of his income.

The first minister we have many details about is Thomas Dockwray, who matriculated at St John's, Cambridge, on 14th April, 1673, when he was sixteen years of age. His father was Dr Thos. Dockwray, who was the vicar of Newcastle, then of Whitburn, and then of Tynemouth.

Shortly before Thomas Dockwray went up to Cambridge his father was killed in a naval battle against the Dutch, while he was serving on board one of our fleet as chaplain to the Earl of Sandwich. When the news reached the north, his elder son, Stephen, was appointed to the vicarage of Tynemouth, and when he died on 29th September, 1681, his younger brother, Thomas Dockwray, was appointed to the vacancy, and twenty-two years later, on 29th January, 1703, he was also appointed curate of Wallsend.

He resigned the living of Wallsend in 1718, and six years later he died, and was buried at Tynemouth on 24th February, 1724-25. When he resigned the curacy of Wallsend, his son, Thomas Dockwray, junior, M.A., succeeded him. He, like his father, was a graduate at St John's College, Cambridge, having matriculated on 3rd May, 1706, when he was sixteen. He was appointed to Wallsend on 28th November, 1718, and held the appointment until 17th October, 1759.

He was an afternoon lecturer at St Nicholas' Church from 1726 to 1752. He died, aged seventy, on 15th May, 1760, and was buried two days later in St Nicholas', where a monumental slab records his services and death.

[1] Surtees Society, Vol. xxii., p. 82.

The minister who followed was Emanuel Potter, who matriculated at Queen's College, Oxford, on 5th July, 1733, and was appointed to Tynemouth in 1749, and after the death of Thomas Dockwray he was appointed on 27th September, 1760, to the parish of Wallsend. He also took the services on Sunday afternoons at the Bridge End Chapel (Saint Thomas') under an arrangement with the Newcastle Corporation.[1]

Mr Potter records the area of the glebe land as measured on 8th June, 1765. The memo is as follows:

Wallsend Glebe, measured June 8th, 1765.

	A.	R.	P.
West Close	3	2	31
Home Close	7	3	17
East Close	4	3	15
North Close, adjoining the dene	4	2	21
Dene Close	5	0	20
Churchyard	2	0	00
Pow Close and Waterside Pasture	9	0	26
	37	1	10

Garden and Stackyard of Em. Potter, minister, not measured.

The last vestry Mr Potter attended was that of Easter Monday, 13th April, 1789, and the last resolution he put to the meeting was:

> That the steps leading from Wallsend to the church be new laid at the expense of Wallsend in particular, and Mr Moncaster (he was the grieve) be requested to employ proper persons for doing the same in the best manner and at the easiest expense, and he, the said Mr Moncaster, is desired to set forward a Subscription among the landlords and private inhabitants in order to lessen the rate.

His signature to the Minutes, " Em. Potter, Minister," is extremely shaky, and he died on 18th November following, at the age of seventy-four. He was buried at Cramlington on November 21st, 1789. We may add that

---

[1] A note in the *Newcastle Chronicle* of February 23rd, 1782, reports that " on October 30th last, Mr John Potter, son of the Rev. Mr Potter of Wallsend, was unfortunately drowned in going off in a boat at St Helena."

Ruins of Holy Cross Church in 1900.

both the steps and the rails were repaired at a cost of £3 18s. 5d., but, as might be expected from " the Landlords and private Inhabitants " of that day, Mr Moncaster failed to collect the amount, which was presently paid out of the rates.

On the death of Mr Potter, Mr Robert Blacket was appointed to Wallsend. It was during his term of office that the church of the Holy Cross was closed for lack of adequate repairs, and fell into ruin.

After surviving the storms of over seven hundred years the building was allowed to fall gradually into decay, and at last the roof was so bad that it was necessary to hold the services in the village school-house. Mr Wm. Clarke, son of Mr Wm. Clarke of Dockwray Square, North Shields, who lived in the Hall and who concerned himself a good deal in the affairs of Wallsend, undertook to put on a new roof, and about the year 1797 took off the old one. He, however, sold his estates to Alderman Anthony Hood, and left Wallsend for Little Benton, and left the church roofless.

During the next hundred years both the church and churchyard were neglected, walls were pulled down (see illustration), gravestones were taken away or destroyed, and iron railings around graves broken up. The font fortunately was found in the stream and taken to Carville Hall, and was given to St Peter's Church by Mr Wigham Richardson in 1891. In 1909 the churchwardens and overseers, in order to preserve what remained of the ruin, had the interior of the church cleared of debris (see illustrations), and the walls protected by cement. An iron fence was erected, enclosing the majority of the stones, and those visible outside this area were removed within it.

The removal of the rubbish which had accumulated inside the church revealed four gravestones in good preservation in the floor of the chancel; one was without any inscription, and another was broken and part of it missing.

The oldest stone,[1] not quite complete, is the middle one. The inscription reads:

George Raine, Clarke and Cumtime, Minister of this Church, with (his) wife Margaret and . . . September 1625. Francis ther daughter depted the 25 of July 1626. His wife was daughter to Richard Stotte, Marchant.

This George Raine was elected perpetual curate of Wallsend in succession to John Todd on 4th October, 1620, but his curacy was a short one, as he was succeeded on May 13th, 1628, by Joseph Cradock, A.B. As regards his wife's family, her father, Richard Stott, was one of the "Merchant Adventurers" of Newcastle, and her mother was Eleanor, daughter of Edward Bertram, who also belonged to the Newcastle Guild of Merchant Adventurers.

Prior to the dissolution of the monasteries the Stotts were holding lands in Wallsend as tenants of the Monastery of Durham, and they continued to do so for many generations.

The next stone in the chancel,[2] in point of age, commemorates one of the oldest and most important families in Wallsend. The inscription is:

Richard Hindmarsh, who dyed ye 12th day of November 1667. Elizabeth his wife dyed ye 6th day of January 1675. Elizabeth, ye wife of John Hindmarsh, who departed this life the 16th day of April, Anno D'M, 1702. John Hindmarsh, he dyed ye 1st November, 1707, aged ninetie yeeres.[3] Richard Hindmarsh Esq., who departed this life ye 15th April, Anno Domini, 1703, aged 58 years.

The Hindmarshs had been landowners in Wallsend for at least one hundred and twenty-eight years prior to the earliest date mentioned on the stone, and we have traced some of their history as residents of the Hall.

It is somewhat curious that there is no mention on the stone of Ann, the wife of Richard, the grandson, as we

[1] Number 2 on plan, page 111.
[2] Number 3 on plan, page 111.
[3] John Hindmarsh and Elizabeth Bainbridge were married at Earsdon on 17th July, 1645 (Earsdon Register).

RUINS OF HOLY CROSS CHURCH IN 1910 FROM S.W.

RUINS OF HOLY CROSS CHURCH IN 1910 FROM N.E.   [*Facing page* 118.

know she died in May, 1682, twenty years before the date of the last inscription.

The third stone in the chancel[1] is surmounted by a shield and the family coat of arms, and marks

> The Burial Place of George Hewebanke, Master and Mariner, and Elizabeth, his wife. She departed this life, September ye 24th, 1710, in the 57th year of her age. He had issue by her, seven children, three whereof survived her, viz., John, George and Sarah.

This family lived in Cosyn's house (afterwards Carville Hall), and they owned it and the adjoining estate. Particulars concerning the history of this family will be found in the pages dealing with Carville Hall.

Before passing on let us endeavour to realise how far back in history the church and these tombstones take us. This church was an old building—over four hundred years old—when the Spanish Armada threatened our shores. George Raine lived in the days of Queen Elizabeth, when England was pulsating with new energy and ideas. He was a contemporary of Sir Walter Raleigh. He was the minister of this church when the Pilgrim Fathers sailed away to the newly discovered America and founded a New England beyond the seas. John Hindmarsh was a boy eight years old when Charles I. came to the throne. When a youth, he would see the King as he made a Royal progress down the river to Tynemouth amid great joy and acclamation on June 5th, 1633. He lived all through the Civil War and also through the days of the short-lived Commonwealth. He saw the high hopes entertained at the restoration of Charles II., and he saw these hopes bitterly disappointed. He saw the flight of the next King, James II., and he was an old man of seventy-two when William of Orange was elected King. He lived eighteen years after this, and saw the death of Mary and of William, the accession of Queen Anne, and died just after the Union of England and Scottish Parliaments. This old land-

[1] Number 1 on plan, page 111.

owner, whose remains rest here, lived through a period unparalleled in our history either before or since. His life extended into seven reigns, and through such a time of storm and sunshine, of changes and settlements, as we hope no man in England need ever see again.

The Churchyard

Outside the church there are fifty-one tombstones more or less complete. Prior to 1909 the only known record of the epitaphs in Wallsend old churchyard was that made by the Rev. John Hodgson and checked and corrected by Mr J. C. Hodgson in 1907.[1] However, in 1909 Mr Robert Irwin Dees found a list of "Gravestones in the old churchyard copied November 28th, 1813," which had been preserved by the late Mr Robt. R. Dees.

Mr Dee's list gives the inscriptions of fifty stones and two tablets. Of these thirty-four are given in Mr Hodgson's list, which includes five not given in the record of Mr Dees. In 1910 the two lists were carefully compared with the stones which still survive, and the inscriptions recorded here and in the Appendix may be taken to be as nearly correct as possible.

The order for closing "Forthwith and entirely the old churchyard of the Holy Cross, or Chantry churchyard in Wallsend in the County of Northumberland" is dated 19th February, 1889.

Outside the church the oldest stone is that lying flat to the south-east of the church. The inscription is round the border and is now almost entirely worn away, but some kindly hand, a few years ago, recut the year, that of 1675. The Dees' manuscript gives the full lettering, which read :

Here lyeth the body of Thomas Spours. He departed the 29th March, 1675.

The next oldest stone is to the east of the church, and it is also lying flat and in good condition. It tells us:

[1] Antiq. Proceedings, 3rd series, Vol. iii., p. 58.

Here lyeth the body of | Edward Henzil senior | broad glas maker of | Houldinpans who departed | this life the 24th day of | January, Anno Domini | 1686 aged 64 years. | Here lyeth the body of Edward Henzell broad | glas maker of Houdown-pands | who departed February ye 19th | 1734-5 aged 62 years.

Edward Henzel, senior, was born in 1622, and no doubt his father was one of the first continental emigrants who settled at Howdon. Two other stones of this old family remain; on one only the first four lines are decipherable, but the inscription read:

The burrial place of | Mr. Edward Henz | ell brod glassmaker | at Houdown and Ann | his wife who had | issue 7 children viz: | Edward, Margaret, George . . . their | daughter, Barbara, | departed this life ye | 10 of July '98 aged | 24 years, | George departed | ye first day of Feb | ruary 1702 aged 17, | Ann his wife departed the 3 of October 1715 | aged 73 years. | He departed the 30 | day of November 1721 | aged 75 years.

Next, on the south side of this is

The burial place of | Moses Henzell, | broad glass maker of | Howdon Pans and Elizabeth | his wife. Barbara their daughter, | departed July the 23 1739 aged | 11 years. | Joshua Henzell, | son of the above, M. and E. | principal agent to the Northumberland Glass Co. |, Lemington obt. 4 July 1788 | aet 63 years. | He lived truly respected and died deservingly lamented | Catherine, daughter of the above | obt. 3 July 1781: aet 20 years.

A little to the east of the pathway to the church is the burial ground of the Bonners and the Mortons, who were ancestors of Lord Northbourne. The Bonner stone is surmounted by a coat of arms: gules, a lion passant between two escallops; and a crest: a hand holding a sword. The stone reads:

In Memory of Joseph Bonner who died February the 12th 1757 aged 62 years. Also Elizabeth his wife who died August the 4th 1762 aged 60 years. Also Elizabeth their daughter who died June 5th 1740, aged 19 years. And likewise is interred here the remains of Isabella Swan, granddaughter of the above Joseph Bonner, who departed this life the 22nd of June 1780 aged 15 years.

Joseph Bonner was born at Ponteland on 12th March, 1694-95. He was admitted a Merchant Adventurer by patrimony on 5th October, 1724. He married and lived at Howdon Panns. One of his daughters, Margaret, married Thomas Swan of Howdon, shipwright; another daughter, Sarah, married Andrew Morton, master mariner, at Wallsend in 1755.

The stone of the Mortons adjoins that of the Bonners and is:

> Sacred to the memory of Andrew Morton of Ouseburn late of St Anthonys, who departed this life the 27th August 1798[1] aged 66. Margaret Lewen Morton, daughter of the above Andrew Morton died January 12th 1823 aged 59 years. Ann Ward Morton, wife of Joseph Morton, son of the above Andrew Morton, died June 8th 1825 aged 47 years. Joseph Morton, son of Andrew Morton and husband of the above Ann Ward Morton, died December 6th 1838 aged 70 years. Sarah, widow of Andrew Morton daughter of Joseph Bonner, died at Durham August here buried August 12th 1828 aged 96 years. The name of the Lord is a strong tower.

Joseph, the eldest son of Andrew Morton, born in 1768, married Ann Ward Shadforth, and their daughter, Ann Ward Morton, went out to the Crimea as a nurse with Florence Nightingale, a very exceptional undertaking for a woman in those days. The oldest daughter of Andrew Morton, Grace Ord, born 1756, married Henry Ibbotson.

The descent of the Northbournes is through Grace Ord Morton and her husband Henry Ibbotson. Their daughter, Isabelle Grace, married Cuthbert Ellison of Hebburn, and their daughter, Sarah Caroline Ellison, married Sir Walter C. James, afterwards the first Lord Northbourne.

Several years ago the stones of the Bonners and the Mortons were repaired under the direction of the Rev. J. W. Carr of Barming, near Maidston, who was also a descendant, the late Lady Northbourne meeting most of the expense. With regard to the arms and crest on the stone, Mr Carr informed us that he had seen these nowhere else except on the seal of the Warwicks of High Callerton.

A list of the other stones will be found in the Appendix.

[1] Church Register gives date as 17th August, 1798, and date of burial 19th.

St Peter's Church

Towards the end of the eighteenth century the general interest in the only church in the district had fallen to a very low ebb. As we have already related, during the last decade the ancient church dedicated to the Holy Cross had fallen into such decay that the village schoolroom had to be used for the few religious services which were held.

The district had grown; pitmen had flocked in to the new pits at Carville, Willington, and Howdon. The influence of Wesley and Whitefield was beginning to be felt on Tyneside, and yet here we have the only church building between North Shields and Newcastle closed and falling into ruin. Apparently the "Four and Twenty," upon whom the local government of the parish rested, did not feel quite easy at this state of affairs, because at their meeting held on Easter Monday, 1791, they agreed to call together the proprietors and parishioners to consider the enlargement or rebuilding of the church. At the meeting held on June 13th it was resolved that the church should be rebuilt so as to hold five hundred persons.

From this date onwards, numerous meetings were held and resolutions passed. Sometimes it was agreed to build a church on a new site, and sometimes to rebuild the church on the old site. Plans were prepared and abandoned, and fresh ones were made.

This went on for years, and at last when a sufficient majority had agreed to take definite steps, the plan decided upon was to build a new church on a field called the Three Nooked Close, belonging to Mrs Waters. The cost of the whole scheme was to be met out of the rates, and a Parliamentary Bill was prepared to carry this into effect.

When this Bill came before the House of Commons, it was "blocked" by the Dean and Chapter of Durham, and on the 18th January, 1804, a representative attended a meeting at Wallsend to explain their opposition. It was pointed out that, under such an Act of Parliament, the occupiers and householders alone would be liable for the cost, and they thought the owners should pay a share, and promised that if the owners of the collieries and other properties would subscribe a sufficient amount towards " the proper relief of the occupiers " the passing of the Bill through Parliament would be greatly facilitated.

They promised £200 towards the cost, but the owners showed no eagerness to adopt the hint of the Dean and Chapter and subscribe. The solicitor called in, however, hit upon a solution, and on 17th April, 1804, he laid before a meeting of the owners and the principal inhabitants a scheme for raising the money by a tontine. This was accepted, and it was agreed that the Bill as drafted be altered and the tontine plan inserted.

The estimate now was:

Cost of church, etc.		£2,900
To be raised by tontine	£2,745	
Promised by Dean and Chapter ...	200	
	£2,945	

There were present at this meeting: Mr Henry Ulrick Reay, of Killingworth, in the chair, Rev. R. G. Green representing the Dean and Chapter, Mr William Russell of Brancepeth Castle (of Wallsend Collieries), Mr William Clarke of Wallsend Hall, landowner, Mr Thomas Bigge of Carville Hall, Mr Edward Hurry of Howdon dockyard, Mr John Buddle of Wallsend, and six others.

After this decision it was hoped that the period of delay was at an end, but the matter still hung fire. Two years later, on January 7th, 1806, an appeal was sent by some churchmen to the authorities at Durham, " to request them to aid and devise a plan, or use such authority as may be vested in them, to obtain a church for the due celebration of public worship, and for the spiritual welfare of the parishioners," and the petitioners added " there have been many plans but no unity among the proprietors at the different meetings."

The bishop and Dean and Chapter began to threaten to take legal proceedings against the churchwardens to compel them to repair their church, but the scheme still hung fire until an appalling discovery was made. The schoolroom in the village, which had been used as the church, was an unconsecrated building and not licensed; the banns published, and the marriages celebrated there were illegal. The marriages were of no effect, the children of such marriages were illegitimate, and finally the curates who performed the services were liable to very serious penalties. This discovery spread consternation in many circles, and roused widespread distress and anger, and hence at last the Act was pushed rapidly forward, and passed on August 8th, 1807.

It is difficult to understand why sixteen years were spent, and forty-four meetings were held, preparing plans and altering decisions. It was not owing to any lack of ability on the part of those who met so often. At all the meetings, some of the best business men to be found anywhere attended. For example, at a meeting held on 30th October, 1794, there was present: Francis Johnson, Mayor of Newcastle, in the chair; James Moncaster of the Hall; Henry Ridley, representing the Bigge family; Wm. Cramlington of the White House, an Alderman of Newcastle; Francis Hurry, head of Howdon dockyard establishment; Richard Bell, one of the owners of Willington Collieries; Edward Collingwood of Chirton House; Shafto Craster of Craster Hall; Thomas Shadforth, for himself, and the Orde family; and Calverley Bewicke of Close House. The last four were all landowners in Willington, and there were ten other gentlemen, some holding proxies, all representing leasehold or freehold lands in the parish. The Minutes record is: " Resolved that it is the unanimous opinion of the meeting that a new church must be built," and all present sign their names immediately underneath this resolution. " Upon the question of whether the church be built upon the old site, or on a new site, the same being put to the vote, it was carried for building upon the old site, nine being for the new site, and fifteen for the old site, with all proper carriage and foot roads, if to be accomplished." But nothing further was done to carry out the decision.

Ten years later, a committee meeting to push on the tontine scheme was held on July 12th, 1804. There were present: Wm. Russell (of Brancepeth Castle), Wm. Clarke (of Wallsend Hall), Edward Hurry (of Howdon Dock), John Buddle (of Wallsend Colliery), and Mr Thomas (Bewicke & Craster's agent). This was one of the strongest committees for its size which could be formed, and yet the whole outcome was: " Resolved (after doing no other business than merely taking down a few names as subscribers to the new tontine scheme) to order a general meeting for next Tuesday by Public Advertisement."

There must always have been an important and active minority sufficient to paralyse the majority, and, as we have shown, this went on for sixteen years.

The Act of Parliament which was passed on 8th August, 1807, authorised the disuse of the church of the Holy Cross, sanctioned the erection of the new church on the site near the Turnpike, and also the raising of money by a tontine. It legalised the banns which had been published and the marriages which had taken place in the schoolroom, and granted an indemnity to the ministers concerned.

The fee simple and inheritance of the ground for the new church was transferred from the Dean and Chapter, and vested ex officio in half a dozen public officials, including the Mayor of Newcastle for the time being, and nearly thirty gentlemen, chiefly the landowners and leaseholders of the parish. The coal seams underneath were reserved. No one was to be buried in the church, or within twelve feet of the outside wall.

Pews in the new church were to be " set out " for the curate, the churchwardens, and the poor of the parish, also for the owners and proprietors of seats in the old church. A number of common seats were to be provided, and the residue were to be divided amongst " the owners and proprietors of Messuages, Lands and Tenements in the said parish in right of their said Messuages," which right was to be " for ever there-after held and enjoyed " as appurtenant to the said messuages. The Act authorised the raising of a sum not exceeding £3,294 by a tontine, and the trustees of the church could take a further sum of £500 from the rates if the tontine limit proved too small.

The tontine was a system of granting an annuity to the purchaser during the life of the person nominated by him. When one nominee died, that annuity was divided among the remaining nominators or their heirs, and so on, until the nominator of the final survivor was receiving the whole amount.

These speculations in the lives of other people are sufficiently novel to justify our referring to this one in detail. There were four classes: In the first class those nominated must be under twenty years of age; in the second between twenty and forty; in the third between forty and sixty, and in the fourth above sixty.

The price of a first class annuity was £60, second class £51, third class £42, and the purchaser received an increasing yearly sum, beginning at five per cent., so long as his nominee survived.

The tontine began on 13th October, 1807. The first purchaser was William Russell of Brancepeth Castle, who bought two annuities in each class. For the first class he nominated: Wm. Fenwick of Burmigell, then aged seventeen; John Brown of Sedgefield, then aged fifteen.

We find Fenwick died on 29th May, 1814, so his life was a bad investment, but Brown, living until 10th April,

1859, proved to be a fairly good one. Mr Russell lost sight of one of his nominees for the second class altogether, and as he could not produce a certificate proving he was alive, the name was written off as " missing," and the annuity was stopped.

John Jobling, of Howdon Panns, nominated in the second class Charles Weatherly of Willington Quay. Mr Weatherly was then twenty-eight years old, and as he lived until he was over eighty-one, Mr Jobling had a good deal to thank him for.

As further showing the speculative nature of the system, we see Mr Wm. Bell of Newcastle (builder) took up three third class annuities, and nominated himself and two others. Wm. Bell died on 17th January, 1810, only two and a quarter years afterwards. One of his nominees lived for thirty years after, and the other was the last survivor of his class, living for over forty-two years after being selected. Thus Mr Bell made an unfortunate guess at his own length of days, but a most profitable one for his heirs so far as the other two nominees were concerned.

Among those whose lives were entered in this novel competition, we find persons of every rank: labourers, sons of labourers, schoolmasters, innkeepers, merchants, ladies and gentlemen. There was one knight, Sir Wm. Scott (afterwards Lord Stowell), who was nominated by the Rev. Wm. Haigh of Wooler,[1] and there was a baronet, Sir Matthew White Ridley, who was nominated by Chas. W. Bigge of Eslington Hall. Sir Matthew, however, died on 16th April, 1813, only six years after the tontine began.

The advantage of this scheme to the borrowers of the money, was that they paid an annual, prearranged interest on the amount, until the last nominee of each class died, then the payments stopped. There was no repayment of capital. The interest paid to the lenders was raised by a special rate (authorised by the Act) on the Poor Rate

[1] Lord Stowell died on 28th January, 1836, aged 93, and was the last survivor of his class (IV).

St Peter's Church

assessments, which rate was limited to 1s. in the £, and the churchwardens had the same powers to enforce payment as in the case of the Poor Rate. To the lenders, the scheme was almost a pure gamble, based upon selecting a person who, they hoped, would out-live his fellows.

To finish the history of the tontine scheme, in 1874 there were still two of the first class annuities surviving. One was owned by the Rev. John Frederick Bigge of Stamfordham on the life of Thomas Edward Bigge, then aged seventy-three. The other was owned by Mr Wm. A. Clarke on the life of Jane Margaret Atkinson (*née* Clarke), then aged sixty-eight. Each owner was then receiving £27 a year on his £60, and this amount, of course, would be doubled to the survivor when one nominee died.

As all the nominees of the second, third, and fourth class had died out, the expense of collecting the tontine rate levied upon the parish was out of proportion to the amount which required to be raised, so it was suggested that the claims upon the fund should be bought out and extinguished. It was found that Mr Bigge was willing to sell his claim for £150, and Mr Clarke for £225 10s., and finally Mr Robert R. Dees undertook to purchase these claims on behalf of the ratepayers, and at a special Vestry Meeting held on 27th June, 1875, it was agreed to raise a rate of 1¾d. in the £ to repay Mr Dees for his outlay. Mr Dees bought out the last of the Wallsend tontines, but we see by a memorandum he made that he lost £11 on the transaction, owing to the rate collected being short of the required amount.

Returning to the history of the church, the foundation stone was laid on 10th November, 1807. The church was dedicated to St Peter, and the burial ground was consecrated on 27th April, 1809, by Thos. Burgess, D.D., Lord Bishop of St David's.[1]

---

[1] A fuller account of these two events will be found in Sykes' "Local Records" under date of November 10th, 1807.

The cost was:

	£	s.	d.
Building the Church	1985	0	0
Expenses of ground	200	0	0
Interest on ground	11	4	0
Sexton's house and walling	442	19	11
Law expenses, interest, etc.	1435	10	0
	£4074	13	11

The very large proportion spent in legal charges, etc., was the result of the numerous alterations of the plans.

The church was a plain building, the east end was semi-circular, and at the west end there was a square tower surmounted by a " candle extinguisher " shaped spire. (See illustration.)

The ground floor was taken up by roomy square pews which were allotted to the principal estates and mansion houses in the parish, and which were sold or transferred when the estates changed hands.

At the Easter Vestry (15th April), 1816, the evil of Sabbath breaking perturbed the church officials. It was resolved that a pair of stocks be built and placed in the churchyard, and that another pair be built and placed near Mr Buddle's house, and the constables were requested " to give more than ordinary attention to prevent Sabbath breaking." In the next accounts is an item: " For the Iron Stocks £2 9s. 7d.," and one pair still stands in the churchyard and reminds non-churchgoers of to-day what might have been their fate one hundred years ago.

At the Easter Vestry, 1818, it was agreed to " engage a person to teach Psalmody in our parish church in unison with the organ," the cost, not to exceed £10 per annum, to be paid out of the church rate. (The " Four and Twenty " arranged for the Psalmody to be taught for £5.)

In 1830, Robert Blackett, the curate-in-charge, resigned, and on 7th March, 1830, he was succeeded by Rev. John Armstrong, who was born on 31st October, 1794, at Dockwray, in Cumberland.

St. Peter's Church in 1823. [*Facing page* 130.

The original church had a gallery at the west end, and owing to the allotted seats, there was not much room for the ordinary inhabitant. Hence, two additional side galleries were erected in 1830 " to be free and unappropriated forever for the use of the poor." The cost was about £150, and was raised by subscriptions, the Dean and Chapter giving £40, and the Durham Diocese and Church Building Society, £30.

A new organ was opened on Sunday, May 12th, 1833, and in the same year a school-house, costing £200 and accommodating one hundred and eighty children, was built on the north side of the churchyard. The money was raised by voluntary subscription, the Dean and Chapter giving £25, the Diocesan Church Building Society £50, and the executors of Bishop Barrington £75. The master and mistress were in the appointment of the Incumbent of Wallsend, who also had the sole superintendence, subject to the Bishop and the official of the Chapter of Durham. The dedication stone, " Deo et Pauperibus 1833 " (For God and the Poor), originally placed above the fireplace in the school-room, may now be seen built into the west wall of the school-yard.

In 1835, Mr John Wright of Wallsend Hall presented a pair of silver salvers for collecting the alms. The £5 paid for teaching the Sunday School was transferred to the Day School.

The inconvenience of paying tithes in " kind " is obvious, and after some preliminary discussion, an agreement was come to on 24th March, 1838, at a meeting of the owners and leaseholders of the lands in Wallsend held in the Vestry. The agreement was between the said owners and the

Rev. Henry Douglas, Prebend of the Seventh canon or stall of the Cathedral Church of Durham, the owner of the Tithe of corn and grain and
Rev. John Armstrong, curate of the Parish of Wallsend and owner of the Tithe of Hay and all the small Tithes, agreed that—

£193 10s. 6d. be paid instead of the Tithe of corn and grain.
£27 0s. 0d. be paid instead of the Tithe of Hay and all the small tithes.

This agreement for the commutation of the tithes in Wallsend was confirmed by the Tithe Commissioners on the 26th June, 1839.

A turret clock was placed in the tower in 1838, at a cost of £40. £31 16s. 7d. was raised by public subscription, and the balance was contributed by the vicar.

On 6th December, 1840, there was ordained to the curacy of Wallsend Edward H. Adamson, who became a prominent and popular representative of the intellectual life of Tyneside in the middle of the last century. Most of the learned societies of the north owe a great deal to him, and it is worth while to note that it was in Wallsend he began his work as a clergyman.

Mr Armstrong's High Church practices and his indifference to the feelings of his congregation alienated the great majority of Church of England members in Wallsend, and in 1850 a strong effort was made to force his resignation. On 26th December a public Vestry Meeting was called by the churchwardens,

for the purpose of considering the general conduct of the Incumbent, as the Minister of the Parish, the Manner in which the Services of the Church are conducted and the Propriety of any interference with the Ornaments or articles of the Chancel or with Alms collected for the Poor.

The church was nearly filled, and the following are some of the matters they strongly complained of: that the Incumbent was not attached to the Protestant faith; that he was intolerant and overbearing, particularly towards the poor; that he had an exaggerated notion of the priesthood; that he neglected his duties; that he had more zeal for ceremonies than for vital religion, and that his conduct provoked painful feelings of indignation among his parishioners.

They appealed to the bishop and they instructed the

churchwardens to have the large candlesticks removed from the Communion Table.

The resolution setting forth their outspoken complaints was carried with only one dissentient. Among those who signed the protest in the church minute book were many of the most influential men in the parish.

The candlesticks were not removed by the Incumbent and so the churchwarden removed them (" stole " them, the vicar said), sold them, and gave the proceeds to the poor.

Below the resolution, Mr Armstrong adds:

N.B.—The Bishop ordered the Candlesticks to be replaced upon the Altar which the above Churchwarden had sacrilegiously removed, and begged of him and the rest of the parishioners to pay respect unto the teaching and ministry of their pastor.
JOHN ARMSTRONG, Vicar.

A new vicarage was built in 1852, as the old vicarage in the village was out of date and too far from the church.

Mr Armstrong's attitude tended to make the collection of a rate for the upkeep of his church difficult, and towards the end of " the fifties," the number of ratepayers who refused to pay the church rates was increasing. In 1857 there is noted in the church rate book: " Joseph Procter's rate, due March 1856, received per Clarkson, police-officer, 6th May, 1857, 17s. 6d." A year or two later only about one-third of the rate was paid. Opposition increased, and the last church rate made was for 1860 at 1s. 1d. in the pound, and it only brought in £29 8s. 6d. The following year the church expenses were met by voluntary subscription, which amounted to £37 17s.

In 1859 the ecclesiastical parish was divided. The township of Willington was severed from that of Wallsend and divided into two new parishes—Howdon Panns and Willington-on-Tyne.

Up to the year 1866 the living of Wallsend was a perpetual curacy. During this year Mr Armstrong took the necessary steps under a recent Act of Parliament, and the benefice was constituted a titular Rectory by the Ecclesiastical Commissioners, and the living was gazetted as such in the *London Gazette* of 20th November, 1866.

On 7th December, 1871, Mr John Armstrong died, after holding the living for over forty years. He was a High Churchman when such were very rare, and, as we have seen, this created great friction. He, however, continued to disregard and ignore the desertion of his congregation. All dissenters were anathema to him, and often out of sheer perverseness he insisted upon the burial of leading Nonconformists taking place at night. He carried through several improvements connected with his parish, but he never attained to popularity even in his later years when his aggressive attitude softened down. When he died he was seventy-seven years of age; and a small stone cross marks the place of his interment near the vestry door.

The Rev. Richard Jenkyns was instituted into the living of Wallsend in February, 1872. He was the son of the Rev. H. Jenkyns, a canon of Durham Cathedral, and professor in the university there. He was educated at Eton and Oxford, and married Miss Rose Isabel Ilderton, daughter of Thomas Ilderton, of Ilderton.

In February, 1874, a stained glass window was placed in the east end of the church. It was supplied by the stained glass works of G. J. Baguley of Newcastle, and the subject depicted was the Good Shepherd. The cost was £62 16s. 6d., of which the Jenkyns family subscribed £12 7s., and Robt. R. Dees, Wm. Allen, Martin Schlesinger, and John Lomas gave £5 each. In 1874 also, the National School was enlarged to accommodate two hundred and fifty children, the sexton's house was incorporated in the school, and other alterations were made at a cost of £1,500. The reopening took place on December 1st.

Another alteration Mr Jenkyns made was to hold a service in the evenings. Up to this time the church had been lit by candles and services only held in the mornings

St. Peter's Church in 1893. [*Facing page* 135.

and afternoons. Mr Jenkyns had gas laid into the building and changed the second service to the evening.

Mr Jenkyns headed the poll when the first members of the Burial Board were elected, and he was the first chairman, but he did not take a large share in general public affairs. He went to Bournemouth on account of his health, and died there unexpectedly on the 6th June, 1886. The ground floor of the church tower was converted into a baptistry in 1892 and dedicated to his memory.

The next rector, the Rev. James Henderson, was the son of Dr A. Henderson, and was born at Berwick on 16th September, 1840. He was a graduate and Fellow of the University of Durham, and was ordained in 1863. For two years—from October, 1863—he was a curate at St Nicholas' Church, Newcastle-on-Tyne, and for eighteen months at Hurworth-on-Tees. In 1866 he was appointed vicar of Ancroft, where he remained nineteen years, and while there he married (in 1867) the daughter of A. R. Lowrey, J.P., of Berwick. He was rector of Shadforth for fifteen months, then on 10th July, 1886, he was collated rector of Wallsend, and here Mr and Mrs Henderson for twenty years were in the forefront of the religious and social life of the parish, with special emphasis on the side of temperance.

Mrs Henderson was chiefly instrumental in founding the Wallsend Nursing Association in 1894, and was President of the Wallsend Ladies' Committee of the Society for the Prevention of Cruelty to Children.

By the year 1887 the township had grown very considerably, and in that year the parish of Wallsend was again divided, and the west side was formed into a new parish, that of St Luke's.

In 1892 a very considerable alteration was made in the church. The interior was gutted, the windows taken out, the roof removed, and the top of the tower taken down. Then at a cost of £4,676 it was changed into a " perpendicular " style of building (see illustration) with modern seat-ings. All the galleries were removed, the church clock was not replaced, as it was worn out, and the stained glass in the east end window, put in in 1874, fell to the lot of the contractor, as it was too wide for any of the new windows. While the alterations were going on the congregation united with the congregation at St Luke's. Part of the money necessary for this alteration was raised at the time; the balance was advanced by the bank until June, 1897.

With regard to the new east end window, this was filled with stained glass by Mr John Potts, the son of Major John Potts, in memory of his brothers and sisters. We have related how this family once filled an important place in Wallsend, when their home was in the White House. (See also the Hendersons at the Red House.)

On September 10th, 1903, the corner-stone of a parochial hall and institute was laid by Lord Armstrong in Charlotte Street. Though it was a very wet day a very representative gathering of friends of St Peter's were present, including the Mayor of Wallsend (Alderman Geo. B. Hunter) and Mr Crawford Smith, M.P. for "Tyneside." A public tea and meeting was held afterwards in the Co-operative Hall, at which Bishop Lloyd, the new bishop, was welcomed. The site was given by Mr R. R. Dees and the buildings were estimated to cost £2,600.

In 1905 extensive alterations were made in the "national" school, including the provision of a new infant school and a caretaker's house. These brought the number of school places up to three hundred and fifty.

Mr Henderson was appointed Archdeacon of Northumberland, the fifty-fourth line of succession, on 1st November, 1905, and residentiary canon on 6th March, 1906. His appointment to the Archdeaconry involved his removal from Wallsend, but before this took place Mrs Henderson died suddenly on January 18th, 1906. She was buried in Wallsend cemetery on January 20th.

At a large public meeting held in the Masonic Hall on April 11th, 1906, a presentation to the departing rector was made on behalf of every section of the community. That this testimonial, consisting of a piece of plate and a cheque for £320, was not a denominational one is evidenced by the fact that the preliminary meeting was called by the Mayor, that the Chairman of the Testimonial Committee was a Presbyterian (Mr G. A. Allen), and the two secretaries were Congregationalists (Mr Wm. Richardson and Mr Wm. Pyle).

Mr Henderson preached his farewell sermon to his parish on the Sunday following (April 22nd) and removed to Clifton Terrace, Newcastle.

The next rector of St Peter's was the Rev. Charles Edward Osborne, M.A. He is a native of Dublin and a graduate of Trinity College, Dublin. He was a curate at Landport, Portsmouth, under Father Dolling, whose " Life " he subsequently wrote. He came to Wallsend from Seghill, where he had been vicar for twelve years, and was inducted into the living by Archdeacon Henderson on 19th May, 1906.

On June 16th, 1912, he had a very narrow escape from a dreadful death. He was travelling between Copenhagen and Stockholm *en route* for Russia and was in the sleeping car of the night express near Malmslätt (Sweden) when it crashed into a stationary train. The Rev. Geo. Clibburn of Cricklewood, Mr Osborne's fellow-traveller, who was in the berth above him, was killed, as were also twenty-one other passengers. Mr Osborne was seriously injured, but after two operations and a month spent in hospital he was able to be moved to a sanatorium, where he slowly recovered.

As soon as the news of the disaster reached Wallsend, Mr H. W. Clothier went out to see that everything possible was done for the rector, but the Swedish authorities were already doing everything that could be done. The Queen visited him after he was able to see visitors, and sent him flowers every day, and presently the Swedish government, on behalf of the railway management, sent him a thousand pounds as some sort of compensation. A window, with St Patrick as the central figure, was inserted in the west wall of St Peter's Church by Mr Osborne to commemorate "God's great mercy on June 16th, 1912."

He is a broad-minded High Churchman and takes a general interest in local affairs, especially education and socialistic movements. In politics he favours the Labour party point of view and nominated the first "Labour" Member of Parliament for the Wallsend Division.

The income of the living is returned in Crockford's Clerical Directory of 1922 as £1,289 gross and £986 net and a house.

The following is as complete a list as we can give of the succession of Incumbents attached to the Church of the Holy Cross and to St Peter's:

1153	Allanus, presbiter de Waleshead.
1269	Rogerium, chaplain of Wallsend.
1347—1382	"William, clerk of Tynemouth."
. . . . . .
	(Dissolution of Durham Monastery 1540).
1541—1565	George Winter (resigned).
1565—1598	Richard Raye, appointed 12th March, 1565.
1598—1599	John Philpot, appointed 26th January, 1598.
1599—1603	Richard Dearham, appointed 8th May, 1599.
1603—1605	Richard Chambers, A.M., appointed 2nd March, 1603.
1605—1620	John Todd, appointed 20th July, 1605.
1620—1628	George Rayne, appointed 4th October, 1620.
1628 —	Joseph Cradock, A.B., appointed 13th May, 1628.
	(Period of the Commonwealth.)
— 1683	"Mr Anthony Proctor, Minister." (Died 30th October, 1683.)
1685—1703	Thomas Teasdale, A.M., appointed 28th May, 1685.
1703—1718	Thomas Dockwray, A.M., appointed 29th January, 1703.
1718—1759	Thomas Dockwray, A.M., appointed 28th November, 1718.
1760—1789	Emmanuel Potter, B.A., appointed 27th September, 1760.
1789—1830	Robert Blackett, transferred from Holy Cross to St Peter's (resigned).

St Peter's Church

1830—1871 John Armstrong. (See page 130.)
1872—1886 Richard Jenkyns. (See page 134.)
1886—1906 James Henderson. (See pages 135-7.)
1906—   Charles E. Osborne. (See pages 137-8.)

Within the church are memorials relating to the Potts and Henderson family, to Christopher Stephenson, to the escape from death of Rev. C. E. Osborne, to Ann Clark, Joseph Mordue, Wm. R. Swan, Rev. John and Mrs Armstrong, Rev. Richard Jenkyns, John and Isabella Nelson, and the Cripples' Home. Notes concerning these will be found elsewhere.

On the north side the window of three lights is to commemorate the recovery to health in 1918 of Annie Flora Clothier, wife of Mr Henry Wm. Clothier of Hawthorn Villas, an earnest church worker. The window of two lights, in memory of George Walton Wallace and Eleanor his wife, is to two old church members who resided in the now out of date Glover's Row. Mr George W. Wallace was foreman cooper in Glover's Chemical Factory.

The brass plate in memory of John Taylor of the Northumberland Fusiliers, who lived in Richardson Street and who was killed in 1916 while saving a comrade, speaks for itself.

The window of three lights, nearest the chancel, was inserted in 1922 by Mrs Stephenson, widow of the late Christopher Stephenson. It is in memory of

(a) Her daughter, Sylvia, who went out to Egypt early in the war as a Red Cross nurse and died in Cairo on November 9th, 1915, aged twenty-three.

(b) Her son, Second-Lieutenant Robert Brewis Stephenson, who joined the Northumberland Yeomanry when the war broke out and in February, 1917, received his commission in the Northumberland Fusiliers. He won the Military Cross, but died of wounds in France on 23rd October, 1917, aged twenty years.

(His elder brother, Christopher, who reached the rank

of Captain in the Northumberland Fusiliers, also won the Military Cross.)

Amongst the church plate at Wallsend is an exquisitely wrought seventeenth century silver salver (see illustration). As described by the late E. H. Adamson, who was at one time curate at St Peter's, it is $10\frac{3}{4}$ inches in diameter. The centre of the salver is sunk about half an inch, around it is engraved wreaths of flowers and leaves tied to the top and bottom with knots of riband. On the outer rim, which is $2\frac{5}{8}$ inches in diameter, are four oblong medallions representing the four seasons. Spring is represented by the figure of a boy crowned with roses reclining with the left hand resting on a basket of roses by his side, and holding in the right hand, which is crossed over his breast, a bunch of the same flowers. The background is filled up with a landscape of trees, etc., beautifully executed but much worn. Summer, on the right hand of the salver, is represented by the upright figure of a boy, crowned with ears of corn, sitting on a bank overshadowed by the boughs of a tree, having a sheaf of corn in his left arm, and a sickle in his right hand. Autumn, at the bottom of the salver, is represented by a boy crowned with vine leaves and grapes, with his right hand raised to his head and his left hand resting on fruit. Here, as in the opposite compartment, is a landscape with trunks of trees in the foreground. Winter is represented by the upright figure of a boy, with a curious old-fashioned cap on his head, sitting and warming his hands at a fire, the flames of which ascend from the ground and curl up in front of him. Behind him are the boughs of a leafless tree. At the top of the dish is the old silver mark, a three towered castle, and I.H. surmounted by a star.

There is also a cup with an engraved band "Sacra Sacris 1684," and two collection plates " Presented to Wallsend Church by Mr John Wright 1835."

Sometimes our area is spoken of as the " ancient parish of Wallsend," but we see its history hardly justifies this

17TH CENTURY COMMUNION PLATE.
St. Peter's Church.

[*Facing page* 140.

St Peter's Church

description. In the earliest days both townships were attached to the Northumbrian Religious House of St Cuthbert, and dependent upon Jarrow; then from the Norman Conquest until the dissoluion of the monasteries, both townships remained in the parish of Jarrow, and this continued until some time after 1567. In that year part of the tithes of Wallsend and Willington were allocated to two of the prebends of the new bishopric of Durham, and both these townships are recorded as being in the parish of Jarrow, and we have been unable to discover exactly when Wallsend (and Willington) became an independent parish.

The records of the Dean and Chapter at Durham are very misleading. The payments of moneys from our district are set forth with exactness and clearness and we have traced them for nearly three hundred years, and all the payments from Wallsend and Willington are entered under the heading of the Rectory of Jarrow until we come to 1858 when Wallsend for the first time has a separate heading. This is certainly wrong, for Wallsend was an independent parish long before this.

We think it most probable that the townships of Willington and Wallsend were formed into a separate independent parish between the year 1567 (see above) and the year 1577 when Richard Raye the " vicar " was cited to appear at St Nicholas's Church (see page 114). The immediate cause for this severance from Jarrow was, we think, that in the middle of the sixteenth century all over England definite areas were made responsible for the repair of the highways, and generally speaking the ecclesiastical areas were fixed upon. It would, however, have been most inconvenient for our two townships to have been joined with Jarrow for this purpose, so that Wallsend and Willington townships would together become an independent civil and ecclesiastical parish.

WESLEYANISM, HOWDON

It is uncertain whether John Wesley preached in our parish during his early visits to Tyneside. However, towards the end of his life he certainly was at Howdon, for it is on record that on Wednesday, June 1st, 1784, he preached at Howdon Panns at nine o'clock in the morning, and as a result of the influence he then exercised a society was formed during the following year. The members were not able to erect a meeting-place of their own until twenty years later, when a comfortable chapel, holding about two hundred and fifty persons, was built at the top of Chapel Street in 1805. It and the Wallsend Village school-room were at that time the only places of worship between North Shields and Newcastle.

For nearly eighty years the Wesleyans worshipped in this building, and then the growing membership, and the movement of the Howdon population westward, led to a suggestion to build a large church at the west end of Norman Terrace.

This idea was adopted in 1878, while the Rev. Wm. Slack was Superintendent, and a scheme drawn up. In 1884 a site was bought on the Calverley Bewicke estate for £339 9s., and the following year a school-chapel and vestries (part of the larger scheme) were built at a cost of £891 14s. 11d. These premises were opened on 6th February, 1886, by the Rev. Jos. Dyson. The debt entailed by this effort was all paid off within twelve months of the opening, and the members began to look towards the completion of their plans.

On May 17th, 1899, no less than thirty-four foundation stones were laid, and on May 20th, 1900, the present church, seating about four hundred persons, and costing £2,260, was opened by Mrs Walter Robinson, of North Shields. In August of the following year a very fine organ was presented to the church in memory of the late

Mr and Mrs Wm. Bowman by Mr Wm. W. Bowman and Mrs T. Johnston, their son and daughter.

The old chapel in Chapel Street was sold in 1887 to the Salvation Army, who did good work in it for many years, until they too moved westward to new barracks in Bewicke Street, the foundation stones of which were laid in February, 1901.

Associated with the Wesleyan Church at its foundation was one of the most brilliant men of his day. This was Wm. Anthony Hails, the son of a shipwright who was employed at Howdon dockyard. Owing to ill health he was unable to attend school until he was eleven years of age, and when he was fifteen he was apprenticed to Messrs Hurry to follow the trade of his father. However, his ambitions extended beyond his work at Howdon dock, and he secured for himself a considerable knowledge of algebra, trigonometry, and natural history. When he was eighteen, John Wesley came to Howdon, and from then until his death he was a fervent Methodist. Assisted by the Wesleyan preachers, he became a diligent student of the Bible and an able and well-known local preacher. He studied with success Latin, Hebrew, and Greek, and became one of the best Hebrew scholars in the north of England.

Had he remained at Howdon, there is little doubt that the ability and zeal of the young shipwright would have speedily secured a meeting-place for the infant society, but unfortunately Hails left Howdon for South Shields as soon as his apprenticeship was finished. In 1798 he became a schoolmaster in Newcastle, and as the years went by, for science, oriental languages, and general scholarship he became one of the "Men of Mark 'twixt Tyne and Tweed," and died on August 30th, 1845, aged seventy-nine years.

In later years the main supporters of the denomination were Robert Marshall, shipbuilder; Henry Salkeld, agent for the Newcastle Corporation; John Elliott from Wallsend, provision dealer; Joseph Ward, Secretary to the Wallsend Slipway Company; Wm. Bowman, works manager for Cookson & Co.; and George Joplin, staithman, whose younger brother, Hopper Joplin, was also, in his early life, a very active member of this church. As a local preacher and as a lecturer he was well known beyond the bounds of Howdon. He decided to join the Congregationalists, and in 1878 became the pastor of their church at Amble. Then in 1881 he accepted a " call " to Jarrow, afterwards he was at Hull, Sunderland, Maryborough in Queensland (1891-93), then he returned to Jarrow and was for some time the editor of the *Jarrow Guardian* and *Wallsend Herald*. He died on March 9th, 1915, and his wife four days later.

METHODISM, WALLSEND

It seems probable that Wesleyanism was established in Wallsend about the year 1800; certainly in 1802 Carville was a preaching station in the plan of the Newcastle circuit. The first meetings of the cause were held in a cottage in the Long Row, which stood on the east side of the present Carville Road, and afterwards a place was secured at the east end of the Swan Buildings (corner of Chestnut Street and High Street). For ordinary purposes this small building sufficed; on special occasions, however, the timber lying near the saw pit was utilised both by preacher and congregation, and it afforded both pulpit and seating accommodation.

In 1805 Mr John Reay came from Washington, and settled at Carville. He was an earnest, energetic Methodist, and with his help and under his guidance the cause increased, and a better meeting-place became urgently needed. A chapel seating four to five hundred persons was built near to the oldest pit shaft at Carville at a cost of £1,500. It was opened on January 12th, 1812, and became the centre of still further increasing effort.

The Colliery Chapel, Wallsend (*Wesleyan Methodist*).

[*Facing page* 144.

In 1838 Mr Reay's house in Carville, on the south side of Buddle Street, became the rallying place of Wallsend Wesleyanism.

In the stirring years of 1849 and 1850 Mr Reay and most of the Carville chapel leaders took a prominent part in the movement for reform, and the climax was reached when, after the conference of 1850, Mr and Mrs Reay were excluded from church membership, as they were considered, rightly enough, to be the centre of the local revolt. Thereupon the other six class leaders, and upwards of one hundred members of the church, followed them into religious exile, and the majority of those left behind were in more or less sympathy with the reformers.

Unfortunately for the conference party, shortly after these exciting events the Dean and Chapter lease of the premises expired. This the conference party neglected to renew, and Mr John Reay secured a new lease in his own name. As soon as this was legally completed, the Wesleyans were surprised at finding themselves treated as trespassers, and shortly afterwards the "reformers" returned to their old chapel, which has remained in the possession of the Free Methodists ever since. The few real Wesleyan anti-reformers were now the homeless ones, and for many years travelled to Walker Chapel.

The high-water mark of the old chapel was in the pre-reform days. Mr Charles Adams is said to have told Mr Geo. Luckley that the society had at one time over four hundred members, which seems a remarkable figure for the size of the meeting-place. The low-water mark was in the early "seventies" when the membership dropped below forty, but it will be seen that even with a small membership the cause did not stand still.

When Mr John Reay died in 1867 there was still a debt of £250 upon the building. This Mr Reay had promised to pay off, and in accordance with his wishes the executors of his estate in 1870 paid over this sum to the trustees. Hence after fifty-eight years the church was free from debt.

In 1871 the freehold of the site was purchased for £250, the interior of the building was remodelled, and the roof was altered. This cost £1,350, and when the church was reopened on October 10th, 1871, only £454 of this sum had been raised. In 1878 some cottages and the land in front of the chapel were bought, and new schools costing £1,100 were opened on September 23rd, 1888.

In 1900 the debts had all been cleared off, and a fresh scheme for a new church was drawn up. One thousand one hundred and forty-five square yards of land were added, at a cost of £450, to that already purchased, and the foundation stones of a large Carville chapel were laid on May 24th, 1905. No fewer than fourteen stones were "well and truly laid." The stone layers included the Mayoress of Wallsend (Mrs S. T. Harrison); Mrs Roland Philipson of Tynemouth; Miss Alice Hall, daughter of Mr J. Percy Hall of Sydenham; Mr W. S. Daglish, town clerk of Wallsend; Mr John Gibson Youll, Clerk of the Peace, Newcastle, who was born at Bigges Main and was an old member. At the public meeting held in the evening Mr H. Crawford Smith, M.P. for the Tyneside Division, occupied the chair. The new church was to seat eight hundred persons, and the cost was estimated at £5,000.

The last service in the old chapel was held on Sunday, May 13th, 1906, Mr Alf. Fletcher of Gosforth preaching the last sermon. The new building was opened on May 16th, 1906, by Alderman G. B. Hunter, J.P., and on the following Sunday, the 20th, the morning service was attended by the Mayor (Councillor M. Murray) and the members and officials of the Corporation. The preacher was the Rev. Henry Hooks of Manchester.

When the Centenary Services were held in 1912 the membership was two hundred and six, there were eighty teachers, and over seven hundred Sunday school scholars.

On Sunday, 26th October, 1919, a memorial window was unveiled by Miss Stephenson of Elswick House, and a commemorative tablet was uncovered by Mr Summers Hunter, to those of the 1st Wallsend Company of the Boys' Life Brigade who had served and fallen in the Great War. Sir George Lunn was the preacher and the Mayor was present.

JOHN REAY.—It will be seen that Mr John Reay was the leader and chief supporter of the Methodist Church in Wallsend in the early years of its existence. He was born in 1784 after his father had been killed in a colliery accident, and Mr Wm. Russell, the coal owner, sent him to school until he was fourteen years of age and then found him a place in the Washington colliery office. When he was twenty-one years old he was transferred to Wallsend and presently promoted to the position of cashier and commercial agent for the collieries there.

He married Miss Dorothy Simpson for his first wife, and after her death he married Miss Dorothea C. Brown, in 1838.

His name often occurs in the record of events connected with colliery affairs, and he was a straightforward, reliable, and trusted official, but it is in connection with Methodism that his name and work is best known in Wallsend. For years a class meeting was held in his house every Sunday at nine a.m., and for over sixty years he occupied a prominent position as a local preacher on the Methodist plan and was widely known in the district around Tyneside.

After the colliery closed he moved from the colliery house, and occupied the East Farm as leaseholder, under the Dean and Chapter of Durham, but farming did not suit him, and in the spring of 1857 he returned to his old home at Carville and put a tenant into the farm, of which he still held the lease. On April 11th, 1865, he and Mr Joseph Mordue bought the freehold from the Dean and Chapter, and divided the estate between them—Joseph Mordue taking the land nearest the river, and John Reay the part more inland which included the East Farm buildings. The indenture made on this date shows that John Reay, with the approval of the Ecclesiastical Commissioners, enfranchised his seventy-one acres eleven perches on the payment of £2,500 (a little over £35 per acre), the minerals being reserved.

Mr Reay died on December 12th, 1867, at his old home, aged eighty-three, and his second wife only survived him two months. There is a memorial window in the present Carville Chapel to his memory.

The succeeding owners of his East Farm estate were as follows: Mrs Dorothea Cradock Reay, the widow; James Brown, brother of Mrs Dorothea Reay; Mrs Margaret Kirk, sister of Mrs Dorothea Reay; Margaret Kirk, daughter of Mrs Kirk; Wilhelmina J. Brown Kirk, another daughter of Mrs Kirk; David Kirk, of Edinburgh, son of Mrs Kirk and brother to the previous two owners.

Another well-known family connected with Carville Chapel was that of the Giles.

Mr Wm. Giles was born in the county of Durham in 1802, and came to Wallsend in his boyhood. For forty-seven years he was a staunch member of the church, and for many years a class leader. He was a miner, and in the great explosion of 1835 he lost three brothers. He died on March 19th, 1870, aged sixty-eight, leaving three sons—William, Robert, and John—and one daughter, Miss Margaret Giles.

Mr John Giles was born in Gas Pit Row, on March 5th, 1835, and was christened at St Peter's Church on the Sunday on which most of the funerals of those killed in the great explosion took place. He began work in the pits when only eleven years old, but shortly after he served his time as a grocer with Mr Edward Moor in Shiney Row. When he was only about twenty-one he started business on his own account in the Swan Row, then he moved to Dr Milne's chemist's shop in High Street, on the west side of the passage into Clyde Street, and finally settled a few yards farther east, in the shop just then vacated by Mr Robert Hann, who was leaving the village. Here, greatly assisted by his sister, he built up a thriving grocery and provision business.

He married Miss Susanna Watson of Burnopfield, at Howard Street Chapel, North Shields, on August 9th, 1864.

His interests were not confined to the Carville Chapel. Although he was one of the prominent members there for over fifty years, he also devoted much of his time to general public work. In 1871 he became a member of the Local Board of Health, but retired in 1885. On the formation of the Urban District Council in 1894, he was elected a member, and remained a councillor until he was chosen as one of the first Aldermen[1] on the Incorporation of the Borough, in 1901. He was an Overseer of the Poor, and also a Poor Law Guardian and a County Magistrate.

He was kindly, straight-dealing, and a hard worker to the end. When he died on September 18th, 1907, the town lost one of its most painstaking and reliable helpers.

Another Carville Chapel member who exercised considerable influence in Wallsend was Charles Adams, who was born in the year 1808. In early life he was a miner, but meeting with an accident in the pit, he opened a school.

He was chapel steward, a trustee, and for thirty years the superintendent of the Sunday school. Although he was almost entirely self-educated, he was an efficient teacher. Among his older pupils were Mr John Giles, Mr Philip A. Berkley of Jarrow, Mr R. C. Forster of Willington Quay, Mr J. Gibson Youll of Newcastle, and Mr Robert Reay of Gosforth. Among those of later date were Mr John Nixon of Blyth, Mr Matthew Murray of Tynemouth, Mr Percy Hall of London, and Mr Matthew Hall of Walker and Hexham. He died at Wallsend on May 30th, 1877.

[1] For photograph see p. 444.

Two more members, William Crister and Joseph Lawson, are mentioned in connection with the colliery disaster in 1835, and space alone limits our mentioning other members of this church who have rendered good service to the town.

Presbyterianism, Wallsend

The second Nonconformist Church in Wallsend township was established by the Independents. When the Colliery Chapel was opened in 1812 it was felt that the Wesleyan methods were not satisfactory to all the Nonconformists in the district, and presently the idea of starting an Independent Congregational Church was developed, and in 1815 a minister, the Rev. Robert Neil, who had previously been in charge of a church in Burton-on-Trent, was duly invited and took charge of this new cause.

The new church soon found that to support a minister unaided was a difficult task, even though the other churches of the denomination rendered such help as was possible.

The Independent Churches in the north federated as the " Durham and Northumberland Association of Congregational Ministers and Churches," on 26th February, 1822. Mr Neil and the Wallsend Church were among the first members, and as their financial burden was so heavy, at the December meeting the Wallsend members appealed to the new Association for monetary help. The urgency of the appeal was recognised, but the Association then had not sufficient funds, and could only " defer " attending to the case until the annual meeting at which it was recorded that " the claims of Wallsend will be considered first." However, this did not satisfy the Wallsend members, and after an existence of eight years as Independents, they seceded from the Congregationalists, and in 1823 were admitted by the " Associate Presbytery of Newcastle."

The books of the Congregational Association note an instruction to their Secretary

> to write to Mr Neil and the Church separately, stating plainly what the Independents have done for Wallsend, and regret that a step of that kind should have been taken in so hasty a manner without correspondence with the officials.

No reply was made to these letters, and the Wallsend minister and church were taken off the Association books.

In 1823 a church was built on the south side of High Street West on what are now Nos. 132, 134, and 136 High Street West. It had galleries round three sides, and was fitted with square pews, to seat altogether about two hundred and fifty persons. Mr Neil continued his ministry under Presbyterianism until 1833, when he resigned, and he died the following year.

The second minister—the Rev. John Robertson, M.A.—was ordained in May, 1832. He came to Wallsend in 1834, and was inducted to his charge on October 8th. The church was not in a prosperous condition when he came, and the whole income for the year of 1834 was only £36. Under Mr Robertson the church began to make progress, and presently he took a prominent part in establishing a Presbyterian Church at Walker, where he regularly preached on Sunday evenings.

When a separate congregation was formed at Walker in April, 1846, he was transferred there, and the Rev. David Wilson, a native of Hawick, took charge of Wallsend. Mr Wilson was minister of the church for thirty-one years, and one of the monuments of his term of office is the Manse. Mr Andrew Leslie undertook to carry out the scheme for building this, and the house at Western Villas nearest the main road was erected, but the majority of the church members objected to it, as too large and too expensive, so Mr Leslie retained it for himself, and the present Manse was built, under a committee appointed by the church members. Mr David Wilson died on October 15th, 1877, aged sixty-four years, and was buried in St Peter's churchyard.

The fourth minister of the church was the Rev. Wm. Stuart, M.A., of Glasgow, who was ordained at Wallsend in July, 1879. During his ministry of nearly thirty years Wallsend grew from a village to a town, and by his energy and his faithful service his congregation more than kept pace with the increase of the population.

The foundation stone of a new church in Border Road was laid by Sir Edward Grey on July 31st, 1886. This building was completed at a cost of £2,152 16s. 3d., and opened on October 5th, 1887, by the Rev. J. B. Meherry, D.D., of Newcastle. In 1905, £670 was spent on the Sunday school and £400 on an organ.

On April 5th, 1909, Mr Stuart died, aged fifty-seven, and was buried in Wallsend cemetery on April 9th. He took little part in public affairs, but rendered notable service to his church. He began his ministry with eighty-six church members, and at his death the membership was four hundred and twenty-five. His successor, the Rev. A. T. Ogilvie, was inducted into the pastorate on July 14th, 1909.

In 1912 a memorial window was dedicated to the memory of Mr Stuart.

Primitive Methodist Society, Howdon

On Monday, February 11th, 1822, the Rev. Wm. Clowes, one of the founders of the connexion, visited the neighbourhood and amongst other places preached at the Crane at Howdon Panns. Mr Clowes had a large audience, and afterwards paid other visits to Howdon.

The first indoor meeting was held in a dwelling-house adjoining the pit heap, opposite Dr Huntley's residence at East Howdon, and from about 1830 to 1840 the society met

Primitive Methodists, Howdon

in Martindale's school-room in Glass House Lane. In 1840 the Temperance Hall in Main Street was built, after which the meetings were held there.

When Mr Joseph Salkeld came to Howdon as ballast assessor for the Newcastle Corporation in 1841, he joined the society, and from that time it made more headway, and on March 25th, 1844, a site was secured in Church Street (then named East Terrace) on lease from the Newcastle Corporation, at a ground rent of thirty shillings per annum, and a chapel was erected at a cost of £150. There were then eighty-eight members on the church roll.

It was not until the Good Friday of 1850 that the debt on this building was cleared off. From the founding of the society, temperance work occupied a considerable share of its attention, and this was notable, as in those early days of the teetotal movement many of the churches would have nothing to do with it.

In 1860 it was felt that the chapel should be enlarged, but as the managers could not come to terms with the owners of the adjoining property, the scheme was abandoned. In June, 1874, the matter was revived, and from this time an entirely new church was part of their definite programme.

It was not, however, until 1880 that a site near the east end of Howdon Lane was secured, and the new church and schools were built. These were opened on Easter Sunday, April, 1881, and the special sermons were preached by the Rev. Thos. Southron and the Rev. Wm. Stead. At this time only £100 had been raised for the building fund, and a debt of £1,200 was still owing.

This debt was a burden for twenty years, until a bazaar, held in October, 1901, cleared £220; this with the proceeds of the Easter services in the following year enabled the trustees to extinguish the debt which had been hampering them for so long.

The men who were the leaders in the second half of the nineteenth century were Thomas Hudson, a coal trimmer, whose thoughts found expression in poetical imagery and couplets; William Crow, who died on 8th February, 1894, aged eighty-four, and was for fifty years a fluent and forcible local preacher; Benjamin Hall, the argumentative village shoemaker. There was also John H. Joplin, who in his boyhood came to Howdon with his parents from Bell's Close, Newcastle. As a young man he was engaged as a " travelling preacher," but on account of ill-health this had to be given up and he presently entered the office of Messrs Cookson & Co., at their Hayhole works. He was with this firm forty-seven years, retiring about 1910. His great interest was temperance reform, and he was one of the founders of the Howdon Sons of Temperance Society in the year 1865. A life-size portrait of him hangs among the notable temperance men in the North of England Temperance League Hall, Newcastle. In the church, he served as a local preacher, Band of Hope worker, and church choir-master. He died at Norman Terrace on March 16th, 1915, aged seventy-seven years.

Adam Rutherford, the village baker, joined the church in 1858. He was also widely known throughout the circuit, and was for many years the chairman of the School Board, and a member of the Howdon Local Board.

Primitive Methodists, Wallsend

The first idea of organising a settled church took shape about the year 1826 with some Methodists who met regularly in a cottage adjoining the Swan Inn (opposite the café). The result was the building of a small stone chapel in 1829, or 1830, abutting the Heaton and Benton Colliery wagon-way (near Portugal Place), and here they remained for over forty years.

We can only trace two records of this period. When a fund was raised for the sufferers in the great pit disaster of 1835, the church and congregation gave " £2 6s. 3d. per the Rev. R. Chester and Mr B. Pyle." This was a small amount compared with other churches, but is large enough to show that they were not doing badly. Then on March 17th, 1844, their Sunday school had fifty scholars and twelve teachers, which is also quite a fair school.

Prior to 1870 Wallsend was increasing in population and the old building became too small, and hence on Whit Monday, 1871, a chapel, costing £1,350, was opened at the south end of Blenkinsop Street, with a Temperance Hall on the ground floor. There was no day school accommodation in this part of Wallsend, therefore the Co-operative Society arranged to rent this hall and fitted it out as an elementary school. This was formally opened by Mr John Glover on July 1st, 1872, and about one hundred and thirty children joined immediately. The school was an expensive item for the originators, but was continued until 6th August, 1875, by which date the School Board had been formed and commenced its work. In July, 1902, the Rev. John Learmouth came from Sunderland and became the first resident minister. A building fund had been established some time before this, and on 28th May, 1903, the foundation stone of a school-chapel was laid by Mrs G. B. Hunter (the Mayoress) on a site in Station Road. The opening services were held on January 29th, 1904. Mr Edward Liddle, the oldest member, officially opened the door, and a special sermon was preached by the Rev. T. H. Hunt, President of the Conference, and this was followed by a public tea and meeting.

STEAD MEMORIAL CONGREGATIONAL CHURCH

Prior to 1830 the Rev. Alex. Reid of Newcastle, the Rev. W. H. Stowell of North Shields, and others had for years occasionally preached in Howdon; and so when the Durham and Northumberland Association petitioned the Home Missionary Society to appoint a preacher for the village, the Rev. Robert Caldwell, who had been thirty years with the Congregational Union of Scotland, was engaged.

On March 30th, 1834, in the forenoon, the Rev. Alex. Reid opened a room in the Carpenters' Houses, Howdon, for regular services, while Mr Caldwell, the minister-elect, preached at Jarrow. In the evening the new pastor himself took charge of the cause.

The room could hold barely one hundred persons, and in two or three weeks proved too small for those attending. A move was made to the long-room of the "Seven Stars" public-house, which stood half-way up Chapel Street on the right hand side.

This also proved too small, and moreover, one or two earnest souls were troubled at the trade carried on in the other part of the house. As one of them put it, "They objected to preaching salvation and selling damnation in the same house at the same time," and a committee was appointed to secure a site and build a church. At a cost of £48, payable to Sir Wm. Maxwell, Bart., of Edinburgh, they secured a site on Cinder Hill, Main Street, the place where in olden times the glass-workers deposited the ashes from the glass-houses.

The foundation stone was laid on Wednesday, 24th February, 1835, by Ralph Walters of Newcastle, and " a much enjoyed dinner " followed. Mr Ralph Walters was a Newcastle solicitor, who at one time lived in the Grange, Wallsend. He was the estate agent for the mortgagee of the Hurry estates. He materially assisted in the building of the Temperance Hall in Main Street and in several other ways showed considerable interest in the welfare of the village. On Whit Monday, June 8th, 1835, the building was opened. Rev. A. Jack, of North Shields, preached in the forenoon; Rev. Samuel Blair, of South Shields, in the afternoon; and Rev. J. W. Richardson, of Sunderland, in the evening. For some time Mr Caldwell on Sunday mornings preached at Jarrow, Monkton, or Willington Square, then at Howdon, both afternoons and evenings.

On Sunday evening, November 8th, the Howdon Independent Church was formed with a membership of twenty-six. The pioneers of the church were Robert Elliott, the principal grocer and tallow chandler in the place—his shop was in Main Street, and was afterwards converted into the "Royal Oak" public-house; Robert Golightly, a staithmaster, who kept a public-house at the head of the dock; Edward Elliott, manager and clerk at Procter's mill, who acted as clerk to the church on Sundays—he sat in a little pulpit immediately below the minister, and gave out the hymns; Dr William Moffit, who came to Howdon as assistant to Dr Huntley, and presently began on his own account; John Robinson, a trimmer, who emigrated to Australia; William Weir, the local joiner (grandfather to the present W. T. Weir), and David Mitford, a keelman.

In 1842 Mr Caldwell resigned his charge on Sunday, 9th January, on account of age. He had admitted eighty members into church fellowship, and when he left the membership was sixty-two.

The Rev. Wm. Hall Jackson, from Rotherham, accepted an invitation and began his ministry on November 13th, 1842. His best friends could not say that Mr Jackson was a satisfactory minister, and church matters did not run smoothly. Some of the members were strong temperance men and objected to certain practices, which they regarded as throwing discredit on the church. Mr R. Hood Haggie led those who wished for a better state of things, while the senior deacon sided with the minister. Matters grew strained, and at last one Sunday evening the climax was reached when in the prayer meeting Mr Haggie courageously prayed for "their ungodly minister." This was carrying the war into the enemy's camp with a vengeance, and at a memorable church meeting held on 27th February, 1848, it was found that the minister's party had a majority and Mr Haggie was forthwith expelled from church membership for "railing schism."

The section which undoubtedly had right on their side seemed defeated, and Mr Haggie preached in his own Ropery Mission Chapel on the following Sunday, from the text " And they cast him out." However, he had the support of the many friends he had left behind, and until Mr Stead was settled, when he rejoined the church, he regularly held a service and Bible-class at the Ropery, and preached often at Willington stables.

On July 1st, 1849, Mr Jackson resigned, and on October 5th a unanimous call was given to the Rev. Wm. Stead, then minister at Embleton, who began his work at Howdon on November 18th, 1849. £80 per annum was the salary, and in the early years it was seldom that even the £80 was forthcoming. However, a new era was opening and a lasting steady improvement was begun.

In 1860 Mr William Deans, one of the brightest members of the church, entered Airedale College. Also in 1860 a harmonium was installed and the string band was superseded. Many people even now look back to the fiddles with regret. However, harmoniums were the fashion of the day, and so a harmonium was got.

1865 saw a school-room added, the old " two-decker " pulpit removed and replaced by a modern pulpit and platform. In the November the Rev. Wm. Deans, broken down in health, sailed for Port Philip. The doctors there said a stay would be useless and he sailed on his homeward voyage on the 3rd May, 1866, on board the *General Grant*. It was not until early in 1868 that news reached Howdon from New Zealand that the *General Grant* had been wrecked on the Auckland Islands, and that ten survivors had been rescued after a residence of eighteen months on a desolate shore, while seventy-three souls, including the young Howdon minister, had perished.

In 1870 the financial state of the church was such that the minister's salary was raised from £120 to £150.

In 1871 Tyneside was greatly agitated over the great "Nine Hours Strike." The strikers wished to hold meetings in the chapel, and some objected, and this dispute lost the church two good members, as Mr Malcolm Cowen, afterwards of Tyne Dock, and Mr Thomas Spence, of Wallsend, championed the cause of the workmen and resigned their membership.

On Good Friday, 1872, a notable novelty was presented to the Howdonians in a dramatic representation of the "Pilgrim's Progress." This was a mere shadow of the succeeding Good Friday dramas and it was not until Miss Stead wrote "Moses" for the year 1875 that the novel, instructive, and profitable "dramatic entertainments" were fully carried out.

Tuesday, June 10th, 1873, was a red-letter day in Howdon. Flags and streamers waved across Main Street, and the chapel was decorated and crowded. It was the wedding-day of Mr Wm. T. Stead and Miss Emma L. Wilson. Special hymns were written by the bridegroom's brother, Herbert, and a special marriage service by the bridegroom himself, from which the autocratic word "obey" was omitted.

On July 28th, 1875, Mrs Stead, the wife of the pastor, died at the age of fifty-one years. Her willingness to help or advise everyone in the village who needed help and her gentle loving sympathy with everyone's troubles had endeared her to all who came in contact with her. A monument in Preston cemetery, erected by the congregation and friends, testifies to the affectionate remembrance in which she was held.

In 1876 the Dock Mission to Sailors was started, and in October Mr F. H. Stead (late warden of Browning Hall, London) entered Airedale College to study for the ministry.

On the 6th April, 1881, a movement was started to build a new chapel and school, and a "Five Years Guarantee Fund" was commenced.

On 27th November, 1883, Mr Stead resigned his pastorate owing to ill-health, and on February 13th, 1884, he died at the age of sixty-nine.

His ministry of thirty-four years was an exceptional one; aided by his wife and family the years between 1864 and 1884 were the " golden age " of Congregationalism in Howdon. The church did real, earnest, aggressive work. New residents were visited. Educational lectures were given. Temperance was pushed. Bible classes and house-to-house prayer meetings were held. Every ship in the dock was boarded on the Sunday mornings and books and tracts distributed, and sailors became regular visitors. Non-churchgoers were called upon week after week, and, in fact, an astonishing amount of missionary work was carefully and habitually got through.

In addition to his church work, Mr Stead occupied a prominent position in the public affairs of the district. He was a member of the School Board and for some time its chairman. He lectured at the Mechanics' Institute, and almost as a matter of course was put upon all committees formed to carry out local schemes for the common weal. He was a strenuous, systematic worker, regularly beginning his day at six o'clock. His broad-mindedness, his patience, and his kindness of heart caused him to be trusted by all classes.

The year before his death the number of church members was ninety-five; the average attendance at the Sunday services was one hundred and twenty-three in the mornings and two hundred and eighteen in the evenings. In the Sunday school the average attendance was: teachers, nineteen; scholars, seventy three boys, ninety girls.

Of Mr Stead's brilliant son, Wm. Thomas, we speak elsewhere, but to appreciate fully Mr Stead's work for the village and for his family it should be remembered that his salary never exceeded £150 a year.

The minister who followed Mr Stead was the Rev.

Geo. Wood from Newburgh (Fife), who accepted a "call" in April, 1884. His ministry did not turn out to be a success, and his resignation was accepted and his pastorate was concluded on 31st March, 1885.

Mr Wood began another church and held services in the Stephenson schools, which, however, only lasted seven weeks. Fourteen members resigned and followed Mr Wood, but the greatest injury done to the church was owing to the troublesome times preceding Mr Wood's resignation. In two and a half years the average attendance on Sunday morning services fell from one hundred and two to forty, and the average at the evening service from one hundred and sixty-three to sixty-five.

The next pastor was the Rev. B. P. Senior, who came from Oldham on 16th December, 1888. Land had been bought for a new church in 1885, but the difficulties during Mr Wood's pastorate had delayed the plans for building and it was not until October 1st, 1890, that the foundation stones were laid. One was laid by Miss Stead, one by Mr Andrew Leslie, late of Wallsend, and one by Mr Frank C. Marshall of Tynemouth. At the stone laying Mr Leslie suggested that the new building might be fitly dedicated to the memory of the Rev. Wm. Stead, and this idea was cordially adopted by the church.

On 26th April, 1891, Mr B. P. Senior concluded his ministry at Howdon, and returned to Oldham. Mr James Brighting from Nottingham Institute took over the pastorate on July 19th, and on November 15th the last ordinary services of the church were held in the Main Street building.

On Tuesday, November 17th, 1891, the Stead Memorial Church was opened, the special sermon being preached by Rev. F. H. Stead, M.A.; the Revs. Metcalf Gray of South Shields, J. H. Jowett, M.A., of St James, Newcastle, John Hughes, the vicar of Howdon, Miss M. I. Stead, Mr Frank C. Marshall, and others taking part. The cost of the land (including the site for a school), buildings, furnishings, and general expenses was £2,336. The membership then was fifty-one and the average attendance in the morning sixty-one, and evening ninety-eight.

On January 20th, 1892, Mr James Brighting was ordained, and in the same year an organ was given to the church by Miss Stead in memory of her father. This was built by Messrs Nicholson & Son of Newcastle and was opened on September 25th by Mr Wm. J. Ions, the organist at the Cathedral, Newcastle, who had superintended its building,

Mr Brighting having accepted a call to Denton preached his farewell sermon on June 11th, 1893. During his ministry the membership increased by seventeen.

The next minister was the Rev. Edward H. Steel, who began his pastorate on November 26th, 1893. In 1899 the membership stood at eighty, which was higher than it had been for over ten years. There were one hundred and ten scholars in the Main Street School and one hundred and thirty-four at Bewicke Street, and the balance of £575 debt upon the new church was paid off.

In 1901 the church lost one of its old standards, Mr Luke Richardson, who died on July 5th. He had joined the church in August, 1850, and had been Sunday school teacher, church treasurer, and for thirty years a deacon—a steady, unobtrusive worker. He was a link with old Howdon when its graving dock was still in existence and the tide washed the sandy shore where the Northumberland Shipbuilding Company now has their yard.

After 1899 progress seemed to lag, and on March 6th, 1904, Mr Steel resigned the pastorate and took a post under the newly formed Yorkshire West Riding Education Committee.

In May, 1904, individual Communion cups were first used, having been presented to the church by Mr W. T. Weir and Mr Wm. Richardson.

On 7th August, 1904, Mr Arthur Jones began his ministry and he was ordained on September 7th. The year following the Bewicke Street buildings were extended by enlarging the small hall and adding two class-rooms. This extension was opened on December 27th, 1905, by Mr Robert Strachan of Gateshead, an old scholar. The cost of the buildings was £571 and the furnishings £47.

On 27th February, 1906, Mr W. T. Weir, who had been treasurer fifteen years, and Mr Wm. Richardson, who had been secretary for twenty-four years, resigned their offices.

Mr Jones remained at Howdon nine months after this, and on November 21st, 1906, delivered his farewell address (with the late secretary in the chair), and he left for Newport, Isle of Wight.

The next minister, Mr S. Ivan Bell, came from Edinburgh and began his pastorate in November, 1907, and remained until July 4th, 1909. Then followed the Rev. A. S. Rogers, who had been in South Africa. His recognition took place on 30th November, 1910, and he left Howdon on 24th September, 1911, to become a curate at North Shields. The membership at this time stood at sixty-one.

On 18th October, 1913, the church lost another of its old standards by the death of Mr John Crowthers at the age of sixty-seven. He joined the church in July, 1869, and had filled the post of treasurer, secretary, deacon, and Sunday school superintendent—one who was always at his post.

In the nine years since Mr Steel left Howdon, the church had had three ministers. However, the members were more fortunate in their next selection, and on 26th October, 1913, the Rev. John M. McGaulay began his ministry. He came from Dunoon, where he had a salary of £150, and came to Howdon for £120 because there were better opportunities for work on Tyneside. He was an M.A. of Glasgow and a real student, a sincere worker, a man with fresh ideas and of transparent honesty.

When he began his ministry at Howdon the church had sixty-one members, and when he resigned in January, 1919, to return to his first church in Ayrshire, the membership stood at eighty-four and the church was in a very efficient state.

The next minister was the Rev. T. Emmett Kaye, a native of Manchester, who came from Alnwick, where he had been eleven years. His recognition services were held on June 9th, 1920. The public meeting was presided over by Mr Wm. Richardson, ex-chairman of the County Union. It was necessary to secure a house for Mr Kaye, and the officers bought one in Tynemouth Road, the cost of which was about £650.

The present church secretary is Mr George B. Moyes, who has held this office since March, 1907.

METHODIST NEW CONNEXION, WALLSEND

In 1835, when the arbitrary acts of the Methodist Conference roused the strong opposition of many members, a number left the parent church at Wallsend and formed a Methodist New Connexion Church.

The first meeting-place was the long-room of the " Greenland Fishery " public-house in the North Road. Then two rooms in the house next door to the inn were made into one and the services were held there.

In 1841 this new church, together with a large proportion of their circuit members, followed the fortunes of the somewhat unstable Rev. Joseph Barker, but this wandering in the wilderness was of short duration and the little Wallsend society soon returned to the " New Connexion."

The society, however, did not make headway and the Conference statistics for 1855 show that the church had only six members and one on trial.

The man who kept the " New Connexion " cause alive in Wallsend during the early days of its history was

Edward Moore. He was a man of strong character and great energy and one of the outstanding Wallsenders among the tradesmen and the churches of his day. He was born at Willington Square in 1788, his father being a pitman. In his early years he was brought up in the Roman Catholic faith, which was the faith of his mother. She died in 1801 and his father the year following, and Edward moved to Wallsend with his two younger brothers and two young sisters.

He was brought under the influence of Methodism, and in 1813 married the daughter of Robert Thompson, a Wallsend Wesleyan local preacher. A marvellous cure by faith is related in the Wesleyan Methodist Protestant Magazine for 1835. His wife, after eleven years of serious disease affecting her foot, which was pronounced incurable, was, however, cured by prayer; her hand gig was discarded and she regained her power of walking. About 1831 Edward Moore ceased working at Wallsend Pit and began business as a grocer in Shiney Row, and it was with him that the late Alderman John Giles served his apprenticeship.

When he and the other members left the Colliery Chapel, he threw still more vigour into his religious work, and was the pivot upon which the New Connexion turned for nearly twenty years.

An honest business man, a well-known local preacher, and a devoted Methodist, Mr Edward Moore continued to the end. Five weeks before his death he preached at Willington, and on Thursday, 30th May, 1867, he died. At his funeral on the Sunday all classes were represented from far and near. It had to be held in the evening on account of the prejudice of the vicar, who had little love for the aggressive Nonconformist and who ineffectually endeavoured to exclude from the churchyard all but the family.

The year 1855 was the low-water mark of the church, and henceforth they began to gather strength, and two years later the membership had increased to twenty, and a Sunday school had been started.

This improvement was largely due to the work and influence of Mr John Allen, who had transferred his membership from the Felling Church to Wallsend. He thought the prospect so hopeful that he urged the erection of a more suitable place of worship, and it was his offer of a " site " and a handsome subscription towards the building that simulated the members to erect their " Zion " at the north-east corner of where the present Station Road crosses the High Street.

The foundation stone of this chapel was laid on 25th June, 1857, by Mrs Love of Willington Hall (County Durham), the wife of Mr Joseph Love, lately of Howdon Dry Dock. At the stone laying Mr Love gave £50, and Mr Allen (in addition to the land) gave £100 and promised another £100 as soon as the building was finished. Mrs Love when laying the stone gave £25. The cost of the building was estimated to be between £700 and £750. (See illustration.)

The proceedings commenced at three o'clock, with Mr John Allen acting as chairman. After the stone laying and the speeches, the company adjourned to the " Wesleyan Reform Chapel " for tea, at which over five hundred friends assembled. A public meeting was held in the evening at the same place, presided over by Mr Joseph Love, and among the speakers were the Rev. G. Hallatt of North Shields, and Mr John Allen.

An important addition was made to the Zion Church when Mrs Townsend, a widow, moved from Pilgrim Street, Newcastle, where she had a china business, to Wallsend. Her daughter, Isabella, was threatened with consumption and the mother was so struck with the healthiness of Wallsend that she bought the " Greenland Fishery," cancelled the licence, and built a villa alongside and named it Hope Villa, and it may be added that Mrs Townsend's hopes were duly realised. In 1868 she

"Zion" Methodist New Connexion Church, Wallsend, in 1900.
(North-east corner of junction of High Street and Station Road).

[*Facing page* 166.

bought the villa on the south side of the green, but continued to reside at Hope Villa.

The "Zion" served its purpose for over forty-six years, when the building and site were sold and a more modern building was contracted for to take its place. The last Sunday the "Zion" was used was 2nd August, 1903, and the chief foundation stone of the new church was laid in North Road on September 12th, 1903, by the second Mayoress of Wallsend, Mrs G. B. Hunter. Meanwhile the services were held in the Café Hall until 27th April, 1904, when the new building, which cost over £6,500 and planned to seat five hundred persons, was opened.

In order to commemorate the great services which the late Mr and Mrs John Allen rendered to the church, it was decided to name it the Allen Memorial Church.

United Methodist Church, Willington Quay

In the early years of the nineteenth century there was a group of colliery cottages clustered near the east end of the Keelman's Row. They formed almost a square and here lived many of the workers at Procter's mill and the Ropery, and it was here this church was located for nearly half a century.

About 1836 some Wesleyan services began in a house behind the Dun Cow Inn. Presently, in 1840, Solomon Mease of North Shields laid the foundation of a stone building to hold one hundred persons. This was built near the centre of the square on the north side of what is now Western Road, and became known as the "Little Chapel." The leading members were John Richardson and John Ridley, millers, and Thos. Davidson, who lived at Prospect Hill.

Thos. Davidson had been a schoolmaster at Benton Square and then at the Bigge pit and began business as a grocer in 1842 next door to the Kettle Inn. At this time two public-houses existed at Prospect Hill, the Northumberland Arms at the west end of the houses facing north, and the Kettle Inn at the east corner. The post office was between them, having been moved from the isolated Paddock Hall four hundred or five hundred yards farther east, which was pulled down in 1915.

In 1854 Mr Davidson built a commodious shop and house next the two colliery cottages on the east side of the road leading down the Millers' Bank, and this was the beginning of the modern Ravensworth Street.

It was in the " Little Chapel " that the Rev. Robert Cooke, who became one of the noted Wesleyan ministers, and the Rev. John Trotter, who became a bishop of Sierra Leone, both began their public careers. In 1849 the church sided with the " reformers " and continued its even course for eighteen years. When the " Little Chapel " was built it had only a small population near it. The Millers' Field, where Headlam Street, Hodgson Street, and Philipson Street stand, was still occupied by cattle and not by houses, but Nelson Street was in the process of being built, and Potter Street was developing. Furthermore, the " Little Chapel " was becoming too small for the congregation, and, therefore, a movement towards a larger building was inaugurated. Philip Augustus Berkley, manager of Palmer's Wallsend Rolling Mills and Blast Furnaces at Jarrow, came from Yorkshire in 1864 and took up his abode in the house built by the late Dr Anderson near the top of Rose Hill. He was the treasurer of the building fund, and even after he removed to Jarrow in 1872 (where he was twice Mayor) he continued to assist the church he helped to build. He died in Newcastle in May, 1909, aged seventy-six.

Mr Robt. Davidson, son of Thomas Davidson, the grocer and postmaster of Prospect Hill, was secretary to the building fund. On the committee were John Davidson of Potter Street, who was also a grocer and a postmaster, and the partner and brother of Thos. Davidson, George

Clavering of Howdon Farm, and Thos. Davidson, junior.

The site chosen for the new church was a plot of waste land at the junction of the old Willington wagon-way (Rosehill Road) and Ropery Road (Western Road). The foundation stones were laid on Whit Monday, 1866, by the Mayoress of Tynemouth (Mrs Joseph Green) and the Mayoress of South Shields (Mrs James).

The church was opened on November 31st, 1866, by the Rev. John Hurst, and at an evening lecture Mr George Luckley occupied the chair.

On the Sunday following Mr Thos. Cuthbertson of London preached morning and evening and Dr Bruce of Newcastle took the service in the afternoon.

Three years later Sunday school buildings were erected at a cost of £450 and a day school was established. The best-known teacher connected with this was Mr Michael Parker, who took over the school in June, 1870, and was master here for over thirty-five years. On January 31st, 1906, he retired from the teaching profession and the day school was closed. He died at Willington House on 31st May, 1912, aged sixty-five years.

Among the later members of the church were Robt. C. Forster, draper and grocer, who died at Rosehill villas on 26th November, 1892, aged fifty-eight, and George Clavering, spoken of elsewhere.

WILLINGTON CHURCH

One parish church had sufficed for the whole parish until the shipbuilding trade caused a large influx of population, and it was then decreed that the eastern part of the parish should be severed from the western part, and the eastern part divided into two. Hence in the year 1859 under Orders in Council 3 & 4 Vict., ch. 113, and 6 & 7 Vict., ch. 37, and published in the *London Gazette* for 30th September, 1859, Willington township north of the railway was created an ecclesiastical parish, and Howdon and the south part of Willington was made into another parish named Howdon Panns.

The first vicar appointed for the new parish of Willington was the Rev. E. H. Augustine Geake, who held his first public services in Mr John Oliver's kitchen, Willington Square, in 1859. After a few services held in cottages, the long-room of the Engine Inn was utilised, then three cottages were converted into a mission room on the north side of Willington stables.

Meanwhile a building scheme was set on foot, Mr John H. Burn of Tynemouth giving half an acre of land for a church, and a similar piece of land on the opposite side of Copperas Lane for a vicarage. On July 29th, 1874, Mr John H. Burn, junior, laid the foundation stone of the new church, which was dedicated to Saint Mary the Virgin, and consecrated by Bishop Baring of Durham, on 6th July, 1876. Mr Geake died in 1875, and on 18th July, 1875, the Rev. H. Robinson, from Nenthead, Cumberland, took up the duties.

Mr Robinson held the living for forty-one years, and on account of his health he retired at the end of November, 1916, and took up his residence at Wylam. His elder son, Harry, was at this time vicar of Hartlepool. His younger son, Frank, was a consulting marine engineer. He enlisted as a private into the Quayside Battalion, the 9th Northumberland Fusiliers, when the war began, and won his commission on the field. Before removing from Willington he was compelled to retire from the army on account of shell shock.

The successor of Mr Robinson was the Rev. Wm. John Watson, B.A., who is a native of Dromore, County Down. Prior to coming to Willington he was chaplain to the Leeds Union Workhouse and Infirmary, and previous to that he was for some time Assistant Chaplain to Lord Allendale at Bretton West. He began his duties at Willington on 22nd February, 1917. In Crockford's

ST PAUL'S CHURCH, HOWDON 171

Directory for 1921 the net income of the living is returned as £243 and a house.

HOWDEN PANNS CHURCH

The new ecclesiastical parish created in 1859 was named Howden Panns owing to a clerical error made in London. Many attempts were made to have this corrected, but red tape was too strong, and Howden Panns it remains.

This new parish was put in charge of the Rev. T. E. Lord, who came to Howdon in 1860 as perpetual curate. Mr Lord proposed that a church with a churchyard should be built near the west end of his new area, and induced the Newcastle Corporation to agree to sell three acres of land for this purpose at £90 per acre, which was only half its value. However, he found this scheme was quite beyond his resources, and furthermore it was desirable that the church should be nearer the centre of the population. Hence in 1866 the Corporation gave £100 to the revised church building scheme in consideration of the claim upon the three acres being relinquished. The first services were held in the old school-room at the west end of the East Terrace, Willington Quay, and then an iron church was erected a little lower down, and the street was renamed Church Street

Mr Lord was transferred to Escombe in 1867 and was succeeded by the Rev. John Hughes, who came from Annfield Plain.

After the scheme for a church and churchyard at the west end of Willington Quay was abandoned, Mr Calverley Bewicke gave an acre of land in Howdon Lane, on which a house for a vicarage was built. The North-Eastern Railway Company, however, soon afterwards bought the land and house, on account of their riverside line, and another site of half an acre was obtained a little farther east in Norman Terrace. The foundation stone of the church was laid by Mrs Addison Potter, the Mayoress of

Newcastle, on August 11th, 1874, and the collection taken amounted to £48 16s. Then a public tea was held in the Drill Shed, followed by a concert presided over by Mr Charles Tully of Tynemouth. The church, which cost about £2,600, was consecrated by Bishop Baring in February, 1876, and dedicated to St Paul.

In 1884 a mission room was opened in Rosehill Road, and a commodious parish hall and institute was opened in Bewicke Road by Bishop Lloyd on May 15th, 1906.

On September 30th, 1916, Mr John Hughes retired after nearly fifty years' service,[1] and the Rev. Wm. Dawson Totten was instituted by the Bishop of Newcastle on Thursday, November 9th. Mr Totten had been chaplain to the bishop prior to this appointment.

On August 1st, 1922, a faculty was decreed authorising the completion of the church by the addition of a chancel.

The net living is returned in Crockford's Directory for 1921 as worth £300 and £45 for a house.

ROMAN CATHOLICS

In the year 1857 the first attempt to establish a school at Willington Quay was made by the Rev. Thos. Gillow. By means of subscriptions a school was opened in the Red Lion Inn, but owing to the lack of sufficient support, and to removals from the district on account of the serious depression of trade at that time, the effort was abandoned for a while.

In 1865 a Mission was begun with the Rev. Father Riley in charge. The services were held in the Rose Inn from the beginning of October, 1865, until the end of May, 1866. These services were intended for the Roman Catholics residing in the whole of the parish of Wallsend.

On the 8th December, 1865, the foundation stone of a

---

[1] Mr Hughes died in Wales on 18th August, 1922, aged eighty-three.

school-chapel was laid by the Rev. Antoninus Williams, on a site on the east of Rosehill Road. A tea and concert were held in a large tent, in the field adjoining, where Argyle Street now stands. During the building of the school, children were taught in a temporary erection. In May, 1866, the school-chapel, dedicated to St Aidan, was completed, and the building of the presbytery was begun. Father Riley left Willington Quay the following August, then followed in quick succession the Rev. James Farrell, the Rev R. J. Franklin (January, 1867), the Rev. Lawrence Boland (March, 1867, who was the first occupier of the presbytery). The Rev. Robert S. Sharples came in May, 1867, and remained until November, 1871, then the Rev. W. Perrin had charge until October of the following year, being followed by the Rev. John McNerney.

Meanwhile the foundation stone of a school-chapel was laid in Wallsend on July 25th, 1875, by Dr Chadwick, the Bishop of Hexham and Newcastle, which was completed, and opened by Father McNerney on June 5th, 1876. He left Willington Quay in February, 1878, and the Rev. Michael O'Brien succeeded. In 1882 Father Lennon was appointed as curate to serve the Wallsend congregation, and he was succeeded by the Rev. Michael Lonergan, who remained at Wallsend until it was established as a separate Mission at the end of the year 1885, under the care of the Rev. Michael Devane.

In September, 1886, the Rev. Father O'Brien was replaced at Willington Quay by the Rev. G. Van Kippersluis, who remained until May, 1899. During his term of office he added an infant school, and built a new sacristy. In 1899 Father Van Kippersluis was removed to Hartlepool, and his place was taken by the Rev. Frederick W. Savory. During his pastorate the new church was opened by the Right Rev. Richard Collins, Bishop of Selinus, on 6th February, 1907. Father Savory left the district for Bishop Auckland in October, 1907, and was succeeded by the Rev. Charles Hayes from St Mary's

Cathedral, Newcastle, and the new infant school was opened by him in 1913.

Father Hayes was transferred to Crook in June, 1915, and in the same month Dr George Wheatley took charge of the parish. Before coming to Willington Quay Father Wheatley was Professor of Sacred Scripture at Ushaw College, Durham.

Roman Catholic Church, Wallsend

The Mission chapel at Wallsend became an independent unit in 1885 under the Rev. Michael Devane, but prior to this the foundation stone of the present Wallsend school was laid on July 25th, 1875, by Dr Chadwick, the Bishop of Hexham and Newcastle, and the building was opened on June 5th, 1876, as already mentioned.

Father Devane left Wallsend in 1889, and on the 6th November the Rev. Edward Walsh from Trimdon took charge. During his pastorate the present church was opened on Trinity Sunday, May 29th, 1904, by the Right Rev. Richard Preston, D.D. It cost rather over £1,000 and seats seven hundred persons. Father Walsh was transferred to New Tunstall on December 16th, 1904, and was succeeded by the Rev. Wilfred Downey from Gateshead. He remained until January 29th, 1912, when he went to Sacriston, and on February 4th, 1912, the Rev. Wm. Toner from Thornley took over the duties.

Presbyterianism, Willington Quay

Owing to the development of shipbuilding, a great many families came to Howdon from Scotland about the year 1860, the majority of whom were Presbyterians, and they for some time attended Sunday services either at the Howdon " Independent " Church or at the Scotch Church at Jarrow. Presently a movement to secure a Presbyterian Church was made, and the most active promoters of this were Mr Wm. Cleland and Mr Geo. A. Allan. They induced the Newcastle United Presbyterian Synod to send supplies in 1865, and services began in Mr Robinson's school-room at the south-west end of Church Street.

The mission grew considerably. A church was formed in May, 1865, and on March 25th, 1867, a piece of land one thousand square yards was secured under a lease for seventy-five years from the Newcastle Corporation at a rental of £10, which was reduced in 1881 to £3 10s. The plans showed a building with a tower, in which a clock was to be placed surmounted by a spire ninety-two feet high. The cost was estimated at £1,600, and the church was intended to accommodate four hundred and seventy-eight persons.

Tuesday, July 17th, 1866, was a great day for the new cause. The proceedings began at midday with a public dinner at Martin Clarks of the Ship Inn. Councillor Beck of Newcastle occupied the chair, and Mr Geo. A. Allan the vice-chair.

After feastings and toasts and complimentary speeches, the company adjourned to the site of the proposed building. Mr Wm. Cleland acted as chairman, Mrs Addison Potter with a silver trowel laid the foundation stone, and the Rev. Dr J. Collingwood Bruce of Newcastle was one of the speakers, who wished the enterprise and the adherents, who now numbered nearly two hundred, every blessing.

This part of the programme having been completed, more than a thousand friends made their way to Mr Potter's brick works, where the drying shed had been swept and garnished and tea provided. After the tea a soirée was held, over which Mr Chas. M. Palmer should have presided; he, however, was unable to attend, and Mr A. Potter took his place.

In the spring of 1867 Mr Thos. S. Trench from Hamilton presbytery became pastor of the new church, and on Tuesday, 19th November, the new building was opened. Mr Trench was ordained at the opening services. The Rev. Robert Brown presided and the Rev. Richard Leitch gave the charge to the minister. This service was followed by a public tea in Mr Potter's works and a meeting in the church was held at night. Mr Trench left Willington Quay on July 1st, 1875, and after a vacancy of two years Mr James Craig was ordained in the church in 1877 and continued in charge until his death on 21st April, 1904. During his pastorate a manse was built in Churchill Street.

His successor was the Rev. J. L. Ainslie, M.A., who came first as a probationer and remained as minister from December 21st, 1904, until 1908, when he left for Liverpool. He was followed by the Rev. J. D. S. McCubbin, M.A., who was inducted on February 3rd, 1909.

Mr McCubbin is a native of Glasgow and was educated for the ministry at Glasgow University and the Edinburgh Theological College. He came to Willington Quay from Chollerford and soon proved a steady, useful worker for the public welfare of the district. He was elected a Poor Law Guardian in 1917 and was Moderator in the Newcastle Presbytery for the year 1919-20.

The history of this church has hardly fulfilled its early promise. The men who have been its best-known leaders were Mr Wm. Cleland (of Clelands' Slipway), Mr Geo. A. Allan (Water Company's agent), and Dr Thos. Aitchison, and these were greatly aided by Mr Addison Potter (firebrick and cement manufacturer).

WESLEYANISM, WALLSEND

The early history of Wesleyanism is noted under the record of the Colliery Chapel.

When the " reformers " re-entered into possession of this building, the adherents to the orthodox side were few and lost all cohesion. No movement was made to form another church until about 1861, when David Stone, a shoemaker and a local preacher, came to reside at Bigges Main. He was the means of starting a class meeting at

Shiney Row (North Road). In 1866 regular services were held in what had been two rooms of a house in High Street, a little west of the old Presbyterian Chapel, now No. 144 High Street West. The friends of Wesleyanism were enabled to make this venture largely owing to the assistance of Miss Barbara Hunter (daughter of Mr Cuthbert Hunter) of Walker, and to Mr Robt. Hann, who owned the property. Robert Hann, who did a good deal to re-establish Wesleyanism in Wallsend, had a grocer's business in Carville (High Street West).

Following this, an iron building was secured at a cost of £256, for land and building, and erected behind the Anchor Inn, near Hepple's Cottages. This was opened on 28th September, 1871, by the Rev. Peter McKenzie, one of the most quaint and popular preachers of his day. However, the membership did not make headway. In a report for 1874, the number of members is given as twenty, and the iron building had to be sold, and for five or six years services were held in a room in the Co-operative Society's premises.

In 1882 the church had thirty-four members and over fifty Sunday school scholars. A few men such as David Stone, Andrew Spoor, John Cheeseman, James Stimpson, and Alexander Carlow, kept the flag flying, and presently the tide turned and the numbers increased. Owing to the growing importance of Wallsend, the Wesleyans from outside gave their assistance, and the foundation stone of a new chapel, estimated to cost £1,000, was laid on the south side of High Street East, on the 26th June, 1883, by Mrs John Robson of Newcastle. The south end of the building was used as a Sunday school, and in the church there was seating accommodation for about two hundred and fifty. This was opened on the 14th November of the same year, and served for seventeen years.

On the 14th November, 1900, the foundations of a larger and more modern church were laid on the opposite side of the street. There were several " foundation stones," but the chief layers were Mrs Wm. Thompson of Heaton, George Alderson of Wallsend, James W. Munby of North Shields, and Wm. H. Storey, also of North Shields.

In the building, which cost £7,084, there was seating accommodation for eight hundred persons in the church, and for five hundred scholars in the school-room. The church was opened on Easter Monday, March 31st, 1902, by the Rev. Marshall Hartley, the secretary of the Conference.

The first resident minister was the Rev. Geo. H. Bainbridge, who came to Wallsend in 1901.

The older building was used, first as sale-rooms, and then was bought by Mr Jas. MacHarg and converted into the Royal Picture Hall.

Rosehill Wesleyan Church

In the sixties a son of Edward Moore of Wallsend moved to Willington Low Pit and there began brickmaking on the old pit heap. He and his wife (Miss Townsend of Newcastle) were both fervent New Connexion Methodists, and they formed a small society, using the old Corving House at the Low Pit as a meeting-place. The cause languished, and in the early part of 1873 it was abandoned by the New Connexion Society on Mr Moore's removal to Newcastle.

Mr Robert Davidson, then a Methodist Free Churchman, and some friends took over the old building and began a Sunday school in the forenoon and a preaching service in the evening. There was also a Good Templar Lodge, the " Robert Nicholson," and Mr Davidson had a singing class during the week. All the meetings were going well, and there were forty scholars in the Sunday school, hence as the room was a very unsubstantial one and the walls had to be " shored up," it was proposed to secure a site and a new building. This scheme was not approved of by the local Free Methodist Church. A mission service at the Low Pit was considered to be all right, but they would not sanction a new independent church so near to their own at Willington Quay. The result of this was that in 1876 Mr Davidson and his friends united with the North Shields Wesleyan Circuit.

With a great effort some land for a chapel was secured in Willington Terrace, and contributions collected, and on 16th July, 1879, the foundation stones were laid by Mr James A. Game of Ryton, Mrs John Elliott of Howdon, Mr James Hunter on behalf of the local preachers of the district, and Mrs Robert Davidson on behalf of four hundred British phonographers. The church was opened on Thursday, the 6th November, 1879, and the Rev. Wm. Hirst, chairman of the district, preached the opening sermon. The building cost £800 and the land two shillings per square yard.

The name of Robert Davidson is inseparably bound up with the history of this church. To it, for over forty years, Mr Davidson gave his time and his money. He was a well-known native of the district. His father we have already mentioned as a founder of the United Methodist Free Church at Willington Quay. He was a grocer at Prospect Place, now known as Ravensworth Street, and it was here Mr Robert Davidson was born on 3rd September, 1848. He carried on the business established by his father, and began a branch at Willington Terrace in 1870 (one of the first houses to be built), and he acted as postmaster at Rosehill until about twenty years ago, when his duties as Income Tax Collector and Registrar of Births and Deaths required all his attention. However, his chief interests lay outside his daily business.

He was a Poor Law Guardian, a member of the School Board, Surveyor and Collector for Howdon Local Board of Health, but what he had most at heart were the temperance movement and his church. He was one of the pioneers of Good Templarism, a founder of the " Robt. Nicholson " Lodge, and he passed through all the offices in the Northumberland and District Lodge.

We have just related how he took over the derelict mission room at Willington Low Pit, and although brought up as a Free Methodist, how he and his fellow-workers joined the Wesleyans. To his persistent efforts and his years of steadfast work is due the beginning and the continuance of the church.

On the 1st September, 1872, he married Miss Margaret Murray of Wallsend, and until her death on 15th October, 1915, she took her full share in church and temperance work.

Mr Davidson's willingness to assist anyone he could, and the fact that he was well known to all, made him the guide, philosopher, and friend of scores living in Rosehill. He died on the 22nd September, 1917.

St Luke's Church

Owing to the increase of population, the ecclesiastical parish of St Peter's was divided in 1887 and the western portion was made into the parish of St Luke.

Mr Geo. B. Hunter gave the land for the new church and also he gave £1,000 anonymously towards the building fund. The foundation stone was laid on 23rd July, 1885, by Ernest Roland, Lord Bishop of Newcastle. The church was consecrated and the new vicar instituted by the bishop at the evening service on Sunday, 31st July, 1887. At that time only the nave and north aisle was finished, though the south aisle was in course of erection. Mr Wrenford, the first vicar, had been for thirteen years curate at Rothbury, but he did not remain long at Wallsend. He left in 1892 for Matfin and was succeeded by the Rev. W. M. O'Brady Jones.

At Eastertide, 1894, a tragic accident cast a shadow over the whole parish. There was to be an entertainment organised by the church, and at a rehearsal in the Co-operative Store Hall a boy was playing with a revolver and shot Kathleen Jones, the vicar's eldest daughter (aged eleven). The vestries at the west end of the church were erected in her memory.

In 1903 the vicarage house, costing £2,000, was completed, Mr Geo. B. Hunter again giving the land, and Mr J. Gibson Youll of Newcastle, who was once a schoolboy at the Carville Chapel School, adding a fine Spanish mahogany suite of library bookcases and cupboard for the use of the vicar and his successors in the benefice.

In 1906 the chancel, lady chapel, and tower were completed. It was intended to have a spire above the tower, but a quicksand below the site prevented the full plan being carried out.

Mr Jones died at the vicarage on January 14th, 1908, aged fifty-two, and was buried in Wallsend cemetery, but no headstone marks his grave. Although he lived in Wallsend for sixteen years he never attained much influence in the town outside his own congregation. This was partly because he was a very High Churchman of the type which does not easily harmonise with those who differ in opinion from him.

Canon Ralph Nicholson, who had been secretary for the Church Missionary Society for the diocese, followed Mr Jones as vicar, and began his duties on May 13th, 1908. On September 4th, 1909, Mr R. Irwin Dees laid the foundation stone of a block of parochial buildings in Frank Street which cost £1,900. Mr Frank Buddle Atkinson gave the land, Mr Geo. B. Hunter gave £250 cash, and an anonymous donor contributed £500. These buildings were opened by the bishop, Dr Norman D. J. Stratton, on 12th February, 1910. Canon Nicholson left St Luke's for Newton Hall (Stocksfield) and held his farewell service on May 12th, 1912.

On August 1st the Rev. Thos. Wm. Allen, late of St James's Church, Morpeth, was inducted to the living.

In 1894 two paintings were fixed upon two of the arch spandrels; one was to the memory of Kathleen Alice O'Brady-Jones, and the other was to the memory of the father of Mrs Jones. He was Wm. Ash Gaussen of Londonderry and was " a great-great-grandson of Louis Gaussen of Languedoc, who for conscience sake was exiled at the Revocation of the Edict of Nantes." Brass plates on the pillars mark the place where these paintings were. The paintings themselves were taken down a few years ago as they had deteriorated, and placed over the entrance.

In 1908 three memorial windows were added to the lady chapel, one representing four women—Ruth with corn sheaves, Dorcas with needlework, Monica praying, and Hilda carrying a picture of Whitby Abbey of which she was the founder. This is dedicated to the memory of Mrs Alice Marian Annie Pinkney, who died on the 14th of May, 1905, aged thirty-one years. She was the daughter of Mr and Mrs Geo. B. Hunter and the wife of Mr Edmund R. Pinkney.

The other two windows, representing Moses and Solomon and the Virgin Mary and St Luke, are in memory of Mr Robt. Hudson, and were inserted by Freemasons of the Carville Lodge of which he was one of the founders in 1893 and its first Master. Mr Hudson was a brother of Mrs Geo. B. Hunter, who came to the Wallsend shipyard from Sunderland in 1882. He resided at Tynemouth, but took an active interest in local Freemasonry and in the building of St Luke's Church. He died on 3rd May, 1905, aged seventy years.

Nearly all the churches have War Memorial windows, and these we have not mentioned, but the east window in St Luke's is said by experts to be one of the finest in the whole Tyneside area.

The church carries on a mission in an iron building near West Street. This is dedicated to St Aidan and is erected on land given by the late Wm. Allen of Evenly

Hall. A site for a church at Philiphaugh was given in 1898 by the partners of Messrs Wigham Richardson & Co., i.e., Messrs John Wigham Richardson, C. J. D. Christie, John Tweedy, Philip W. Richardson, and J. Denham Christie.

It was intended that a new parish, to be named St Patrick's, should be created for the south-west area of Wallsend, and the scheme was sanctioned by the authorities and a considerable sum towards the building was subscribed. Difficulties arose, however, and in consequence the plans for the new parish and church have been lying in abeyance.

CONGREGATIONALISM IN WALLSEND

The second Nonconformist church to be formed in Wallsend township was that founded by the Independents in 1815, and we have related how they left the Congregational organisation and attached themselves to that of the Presbyterians.

The next movement towards forming a Congregational Church in Wallsend was initiated by the Newcastle Churches in the year 1898 when services, arranged by Mr John C. Drury of Tynemouth, were begun in the café. For some time the Rev. Hopper Joplin was in charge, and he was followed in 1899 by the Rev. Edwin Charles Rattray, who came from Bishop Auckland. On May 8th, 1901, the foundation stone of a school-chapel and classrooms was laid in Park Road by Miss Hunter on behalf of Mr G. B. Hunter.

The opening ceremony was performed by the Mayor, Ald. Wm. Boyd, on Wednesday, 5th February, 1902. After the opening, a sermon was preached by the Rev. G. H. R. Garcia, B.A., of Sunderland, chairman of the Durham and Northumberland Congregational Association, and among those present were Revs. D. L. Ritchie of St James's, David Young, B.A., of Morpeth, Jas. Groat of Gateshead, and Ed. H. Steele, M.A., of Howdon.

A public tea meeting was held in the Co-operative Store Hall. At the evening meeting, Ald. J. Beattie, ex-Mayor of Newcastle, presided, and the Revs. Ebenezer Rees of Sunderland and D. L. Ritchie of Newcastle were the principal speakers. The site and buildings cost about £2,200, the hall seating three hundred adults.

Soon after the opening of the church Mr Rattray left for Haydon Bridge. He was followed by the Rev. Francis Adams, who left for London in 1906. In June, 1908, the Rev. A. Glover Green from Glasgow was appointed minister, and his recognition service was held on September 9th.

In 1921, in order to provide better facilities for Sunday school and social work, a large wood building was erected on the unused site adjoining. The older building was reseated with pews and the portable seats were moved into the new hall. This scheme, including the lighting and the heating of the hall, cost between ten and eleven hundred pounds.

Baptists

Immediately the Presbyterians vacated the school-room in Church Street, Howdon, the Jarrow Baptists secured it and opened a branch church there on Sunday, December 22nd, 1867. Services were held in the afternoon and evening for some time, but the effort was presently abandoned.

Afterwards a few cottage meetings were organised from time to time, but it was not until forty years later that the next serious attempt was made to establish the Baptist cause in the parish.

On 16th September, 1906, Mr W. R. Galloway, who came from Jarrow, began regular services in the Co-operative Society's Hall, Carville Road, Wallsend, removing from there to 37 High Street West on March 16th, 1907. The numbers increased, and the result was that a comfortable iron building, costing over £200, which holds one hundred and fifty persons, was publicly opened in North View, Wallsend, on March 29th, 1911. The proceedings were presided over by Mr Edwin W. de Russett of Tynemouth, and the Mayor, Mr M. W. Swinburne, formally opened the building.

There was then attached to the church thirty-four members, five teachers, and eighty Sunday school scholars. Mr Galloway was an honorary minister, and after his death the pastorate remained vacant.

WILLINGTON SQUARE MISSIONS

When the " Edward Colliery " was reopened many workmen were transferred from the " G " pit, and amongst these were Mr W. S. Kirkley (checkweighman, a Justice of the Peace, and a member of the Town Council) and Mr John C. Thompson (master shifter), both active Primitive Methodists.

In the spring of 1914 the Coal Company started to erect houses for their workmen, and the first to be built were those in Embleton Avenue. These were an exceedingly good type of dwelling, but were too costly. The next houses were those on the east side of Gibson Street (the streets being named after directors of the company). As there was no Nonconformist church near, the Newcastle Primitive Methodist Quarterly Meeting in March, 1915, requested Mr Kirkley and Mr Thompson to start a Mission at Willington Square.

An old cottage at the south-west corner was secured and altered, and a Sunday school and ordinary services were begun on May 9th, 1915, and for sixteen months this mission was carried on with increasing success as a Primitive Methodist Mission.

For several years prior to this the United Methodists had a mission-room at Willington High Row, and as the Edward pit developed they also wished to establish their cause at Willington Square, and on March 17th, 1915, a site for a church was secured from the Coal Company. Then they appealed to the Primitive Methodists to leave the place to them.

As the Primitive Methodist Mission was going on well this request was declined. The matter was taken to the "Joint Concerted Action Committee," and the workers of the Mission were surprised to receive orders to close their place. This was done and the last Primitive Methodist sermon was preached on 27th August, 1916, by the Rev. Walter Duffield, and next day all the possessions of the first mission in Willington Square were given up.

At this time the workers of the Mission, in addition to Messrs Kirkley and Thompson, included Mr J. W. Purdy, overman; Mr Douglas Bell, deputy overman; Mr Thos. Mason, winding engineman; Mr James Dunn, banksman; Mr R. Peart, blacksmith; Mr James Ramshaw, hewer; and P.C. Thos. Wilson. These resolved that they would continue their religious work in the district as an independent cause.

In 1918 the Committee of the Independent Mission were given 1,076 square yards of land by the Battle Hill Estate Company for the nominal price of one shilling per yard, and Mr R. S. Anderson, the agent for the Battle Hill estate, who had already proved a substantial friend to the effort, made himself responsible for the two thousand pounds necessary for the erection of a church building and its furnishings. This chapel was opened on Saturday, September 3rd, 1921, by Mr W. S. Kirkley. There was a service, public tea and public meeting, and the following day services were held morning and evening, and a Sunday school in the afternoon.

Meanwhile the North Shields circuit of United Methodists had erected a wooden building upon their site in Gibson Street, and held their first service there in June, 1920.

CHAPTER IV

INDUSTRIAL HISTORY

Howdon Panns from the days of Queen Elizabeth : Its origin—The Andersons (salt pans)—Henzell and Tyzack (glass-makers)—Hurrys—Strakers and Love and others.

THE earliest signs of industrial enterprise began at the east side of our area, and no doubt it developed here because the coal seams were nearest the surface at this part of our district.

The first industry established was that of salt making, and the first salt pan was already working in the year 1539, for in that year Thomas Bell was paying a rental of 3s. 4d. to the Convent of Durham for a salt pan at Willington, and opening a coal pit at Willington, under Robert Dudley's lease of 1581, would facilitate such enterprises.

However, up to this period the name of Howdon, or Howdon Panns, had not emerged. In the Halmote Rolls of the Convent there is no mention of Howdon, and when the Dean and Chapter leased the salt pans to Oswald Chapman in 1561, they were still considered as part of Willington.

After the dissolution of the Convent, Willington was not, as we have seen, restored to the new Dean and Chapter, however, as the land where the salt pans were had been recovered from the river and was not traditionally part of the township of Willington; the authorities at Durham in 1540 ventured, when surrendering their estates, to withhold the salt pans. However, soon after Elizabeth came to the throne her keen business instinct induced her to appoint commissioners to see that she was getting all the property of the surrendered monastery, which she was entitled to. The Queen's commissioners were sent to Willington and found this " concealment " out. Their report concerning the salt pans and the village speaks for itself.

Parcel of the possessions of the late Monastery of Durham Northumberland.

Two Salt pits in Willington, co. Northumberland worth 63s. 4d. The farm of a salt pit in Willington on the north of the Tyne, with houses, gardens, and a salt pan late in the tenure of John Coke, leased to Oswald Chapman by indenture under the Common seal of the Dean and Chapter of Durham, dated 14th April 3 Elizabeth, for 21 years. Repairs to be at the cost of the farmer, except great timber and the hempscottes and balkes made of iron, at a yearly rent of 53s. 4d.

The farm of another salt pit built there, and a house in which the salt maker lives, and a salt garner, abutting on the aforesaid salt pit, late in the tenure of John Coke, and demised to Oswald Chapman; at a yearly rent of 10s., to wit, for the salt pit and land upon which the house etc., is built, 3s. 4d. and for the tithe thereof belonging to the vicar of Wallesend, 6s. 8d.

The tithe doth not belong to the Queen, but to the vicar of Wallesend.

The Dean and Chapter of Durham hath always taken the profits of these Salt pannes until of late that I and other Commissioners appointed to enquire of concealments did stay the same to the Queen's uses as rents witholden wrongfully from Her Majesty.

The said pannes are no annoyance to the tenants nor much hurtful saving that the tenants do allege that Carriers of Salt who repaireth thither to buy salt for the Country do hurt the meadows and grounds in their passage and therefore they require that either the salt there made may be sold to ships and delivered by water as it hath been, or else that such way may be used for that purpose as may be without damage to the said tenants.[1]

There is no signature to this document, but W. Burghley and J. Fortescue were probably the commissioners.

This interesting report shows that the lands around Howdon were still unenclosed and that " salters roads " were not yet set out.

The payment of the rents to the new Dean and Chapter

[1] Augmentation Office Leases 110, No. 23.

were thus stopped, but Oswald Chapman retained the "farm" under Letters Patent dated 11th February, 5th Elizabeth (1562) for twenty-one years.[1]

Oswald Chapman had been both Sheriff and Mayor of Newcastle, and by his will dated October 6th, 1566, he left to his wife, Marion Chapman (one of the important Anderson family), "bothe my salte panne at Willington Fieldes," and we find in the Records office a "lease of the two salt pits at Willington for a yearly rent of 63s. 4d. to be paid to the Queen," was made out in her name.[2]

There was still no name of "Howdon Panns," but shortly after this it appears likely that, as the place grew in importance, the general name of Willington was too vague and the south-east corner of the township then became known as Howdon Panns.

Several explanations have been offered as to the meaning of the name of Howdon, none of which we think satisfactory, and so we offer another solution, remembering that we have a settlement of houses on a peninsula, formed by the junction of the Howdon Burn and the Tyne—a piece of land which was almost certainly reclaimed from the river, for it was not part of the adjoining estates owned by the monks of Durham—and also remembering that the Anglo-Saxon word "hof," meaning an enclosure, became later "how," and the Celtic word "dun," a hill, became also "dune," meaning a sandhill; therefore we suggest we may have Howdon, meaning an enclosure on the sand-banks. This name covered a small area of six or seven acres, until the foreshore of the Howdon burn was covered with ballast, which increased its size to a little over nine acres. It has always been a commercial area, and its history is bound up inextricably with its manufactures and its trade.

The next landmark in the history of the place was the

---

[1] Leases 112, No. 23.
[2] Leases 112, No. 49.

settlement of the glass-makers. Forty or fifty years prior to this time, glass-makers from the Continent had been induced to settle in Sussex, in the hope that English workmen would learn the secret of the manufacture, but when a Royal Proclamation was issued forbidding wood to be used as fuel, the trade was driven into the coal districts, and especially to Tyneside.

Once glass-making was established in England, the bitter religious persecutions on the Continent drove many of the Huguenots oversea, and some of these settled at the mouth of the stream which joins the Tyne at Howdon. They came here only as to a place of temporary refuge, and several of their children born on Tyneside received the Christian name of Peregrine (i.e., a wanderer or a pilgrim), a pathetic indication that the earlier settlers—strangers in a strange land—keenly felt their exile, and looked with wistful eyes towards their old homes across the North Sea.

Glass-making was one of the few crafts in which nobles on the Continent could engage, and two of the families who settled here—the Henzells and the Tyzacks—were both of this class, and were landowners in the Vosges in Lorraine. Their coats-of-arms were the same: Three acorns slipped two billets in chief impaling a fesse inter three lambs passant, no colours. The crest was a fire bolt and fire ball, and in the motto " Seigneur je te prie guarde ma Vie " (Lord, I beseech Thee protect my life) we see reflected the dangers which threatened to overwhelm these two families on the Continent. No doubt the Henzells and the Tyzacks were closely related to each other.

Thus some time soon after the year 1600 we have glass-making in addition to that of salt-making established at Howdon Panns—salt-making in the hands of the Anderson family, and glass-making just established by the two families from Lorraine. The glass made was chiefly flat, or window glass, for which there was an increasing demand, although at that time only the mansion houses of the rich had glass in their windows.

For making their furnaces the glass-makers required a special kind of clay capable of standing great heat, and this was brought chiefly by ships, as ballast. Some of the special clay, however, was carted to Howdon Panns from clay pits at West Thurston, near Felton, these having been leased in 1625 to Sir Robert Mansel, who held the glass monopoly. In 1695 the output of the pits was a hundred and six tons.[1] The sand used for the glass was chiefly brought from France, also as ballasting for ships.

The County Assessment made in the year 1663 shows that Howdon was doing well, for " Holdon Glass Houses " were separately assessed and charged three shillings, and " Holdon Pans " is also charged at three shillings, while all the remaining part of Willington was rated as one item at thirty shillings.

About a hundred years after the founding of glass-making at Howdon this centre of industry had so increased as to become more populous than all the rest of the two townships put together.

During the three years 1700 to 1703 the Wallsend registers show that forty children were baptised. Of these: nine were born at Wallsend, three at Willington, twenty-five at Howdon, and three at places not stated. Howdon thus accounts for sixty-two and a half per cent. of the total, and of the twenty-five children born there, the fathers of twelve of them were in the glass trade.

After being established at Howdon Panns for nearly two hundred years, the glass-houses were approaching their end. The works were old and out of date, and broad glass (window glass) was being made by better processes. Hence about the year 1780 a company was formed to take over the Howdon broad glass-houses, also the old high and low glass works at Newcastle.

[1] County History, VII, p. 318.

The new company built four large glass-houses with offices, warehouses, etc., at Lemington. This new establishment was, at that time, said to be the most complete glass manufactory in England, and Joshua Henzell of Howdon was put at the head of the concern. The partners in this new adventure included Sir Matthew White Ridley, Bart., George Lakes, Esq., Paul Henzell, Gent., Ann Shaftoe, Ann Ord, Hannah Ord, spinsters, Thos. Shadforth, master mariner, Jonathan Tyzack, mariner, Sarah Tyzack, spinster, Wm. Hargrave, Esq., Alex Adams, Esq., Martha Rawlinson, widow, John Hays, Gent., John Robson, merchant, and Anthony Hall, Esq. They traded as the Northumberland Glass Company, and it was under their direction that the Howdon glass-houses were closed. For about one hundred and eighty years the Henzell family had carried on the glass-houses. They had resided in the village and had been intimately concerned with the progress of the place, the people, and of Howdon.

The happy chance that one Priscilla Bainbridge applied to Mr Edward Henzell for poor relief causes a letter to be written to the churchwardens and overseers dated "Howdon Panns, September 20th, 1762." From it we find that Mr Edward Henzell, as the owner of the glass-houses, and Mr Edward Anderson, as the owner of the salt pans, were keeping the poor of Howdon, as well as paying to the general poor rate.[1] Remembering that both of these manufactures were then declining, it speaks well for the characters of the representatives of the Howdon glass trade, and of the salt pans.

Three stones marking the burial places of some of the Henzell family still exist in Holy Cross churchyard, and copies of the inscriptions are given when dealing with this church. One stone records the death of "Edward Henzell, senior, broad glass-maker of Houlden Pans, who departed this life the 24th day of January Anno Domini 1686, aged sixty-four years." This broad glass-maker was

[1] Vestry Minute Book.

born in 1621 or 1622, so his father was almost certainly one of those first immigrants who introduced the art of glass-making into the north of England. Their family history can be broadly traced in the church records of births, marriages, and burials.

We are not certain in what year the Henzells left Howdon, but the following are the latest entries as to burials of this family in the Holy Cross records, and they show that they ceased to live within our area between 1754 and 1760, and became closely connected with the glass works at the Ouseburn, and lastly with the new works at Lemington.

1754, Dec. 11. John, son of Moses Henzell of Howdon Panns.
1760, Feb. 20. Joshua, son of Joshua Henzell of the Low Glass Houses, buried.
1761, Jan. 21. James, son of Joshua Henzell of the High Glass Houses, buried.
1765, Aug. 4. Catherine, daughter of Mr Joshua Henzell of Chapelry of All Saints, Glass-maker.
1774, Sep. 15. Martha, wife of Joshua Henzell of the High Glass Houses, Glass-maker.
1780, Feb. 22. Mr Edward Henzell of Jesmond, Gentleman.

Our last record of all the Henzells buried in the churchyard of Holy Cross is:

1788, July 12. Joshua Henzell of the Low Glass House, Glassmaker.

He was the son of Moses and Elizabeth Henzell, and was sixty-three years of age when he died. His tombstone is still readable and tells us that he was "the principal agent to the Northumberland Glass Co., Lemington."

The old Howdon glass-houses were not closed for some little time after they were taken over by the new company, they were still separately rated in the year 1790, after which the new system of rating began.

With regard to the Tyzacks, the other founders of the Howdon glass trade, the best known man of the family was Timothy Tyzack, who was not only a glass-maker at

Howdon Panns, but also a merchant adventurer at Gateshead, where he was an overseer and a churchwarden.

The following entry in the records of the Gateshead Guild of the Drapers, Mercers, and Hardwaremen's Company show us that he was a man of impetuous temperament:

January 6th, 1622, Memorandum. That at a meeting as above, Tim. Tizacke, a member of the Company did in ye presence of the major pt of ye compa, then Assembled reproachfully and ignominiously tearme the 2 Stewards wh the rest of ye company that meet ye 30 of December 1661 wth the names of fools and knaves with many other bitter words and imperiously deserted the meeting house, encouraging severall others to goe wth him whout leave from the Stewards or Corpn.

His wife was Elizabeth Metcalf, a Yorkshire lady who was treated as a " delinquent " in 1652, as we have already noted. Timothy " Depted this life ye 6th day of February, 1684," and a fine tombstone in the chancel of St Mary's Church, Gateshead, records his death. The arms and motto on the stone are the same as those of the Henzells.

Some of the Tyzacks became followers of Fox, who rejected the Ordinance of Baptism, hence they did not attend Holy Cross Church to have their children baptised. The incumbent, however, did not always lose his fee, for we have the following note in the Wallsend registers:

About March 1st, 2nd, 3rd, or 4th, 1701-2, a child was born to John Tisack, Quaker, Broad Glass Maker, of Howdon as I understand by the information of others. No notice thereof from John Tisack, nor none of his family, till I told collectors of it the latter end of March, and ordered them to call for his birth.

Then we have a later entry on April 2nd, 1702:

Michael Carr and . . . say yesterday they received for the Birth of Tisack's child . . . (indecipherable) they had then orders to tell me John Tisack's child was born March 1st 1701-2.

In 1758 the family mansion house at Howdon was still

of importance, and it was either owned or occupied by a later Timothy Tyzack. In that year the cess was eight shillings and eightpence upon each "farm," and the only property in the parish separately rated was: " and Mr Timothy Tyzack's house one shilling and fourpence halfpenny."

The following entries of burials would show that the Tyzacks left Howdon between the years 1761 and 1787:

1761, Oct. 24. Dorothy, daughter of Joseph Tyzack of Howdon Panns, Glass-maker.
1787, Apr. 16. Hannah, wife of Joseph Tyzack of the Parish of All Saints, Glass-maker.

And the last member of this family to be laid to rest in our parish was Joseph:

1789, Mar. 30. Joseph Tyzack of the Parish of All Saints, Glass-maker.

The Tyzacks' glass-houses were taken over by the Northumberland Glass Co.; as we have seen, two of the family were partners in the firm.

Salt-making had also done well during the seventeenth century. Marion Chapman, who had possession of the pans in the days of Queen Elizabeth, was the daughter of Henry Anderson of Newcastle, and from the time of her death the salt pans at Howdon remained in the Anderson family for two hundred years.

The best known member of this family was Sir Francis Anderson of Jesmond Manor. During the civil war he was the leader of the Royalist party in the north, and as a "delinquent" we have spoken of him in Chapter I. He was a Mayor of the town more than once, and represented Newcastle in Parliament from 1661 until his death, in 1679. He was the owner of Willington township, and his lands were bounded by the river high water mark, from the Willington Gut to Howdon, the Corporation of Newcastle claiming the river and the land between high and low water mark. At this time and for long afterwards it was a most profitable business to discharge vessels, which came to the Tyne for coals, of their " ballast," but a place must be available where the ballast could be deposited, and Sir Francis Anderson proposed to use the foreshore of his estate for this.

At this date, westward of the ancient Howdon, the edge of the river was much farther north than at present. The high tide came close to the front of Mr Clavering's garden, and if we wish to picture the old foreshore of the river we must clear off all the houses and ballast from West Street, Howdon, up to the Railway Inn bank, at the end of Keelman's Row. From Howdon farmhouse the shore line was to the north of Church Street, south of Bewicke Street, north of Boundary Street, behind Potter Street, leaving Low Willington House and Western Road, close to the river bank, that is to say from West Street, Howdon, to Potter Street, the north boundary of the Newcastle Corporation land was the high water mark of the river up to 1665.

The riverside old pilot track passed on the landward side of Low Willington House, and thence direct to Howdon on the north side of the Howdon farm buildings. Of course none of the houses now standing had been built in the middle of the seventeenth century.

Sir Francis Anderson saw his way to establishing a long stretch of ballast shore along the margin of Willington, and on September 9th, 1665, he obtained a lease for a thousand years from the Newcastle Corporation of " all that parcel of ground within the territories of Willington between high and low water mark, in length from east to west, 1,274 yards, and in breadth from low water mark, 120 yards, with liberty to build Keys, and cast ballast upon paying 2d. per ton for all ballast cast thereon."

He at once made his first " ballast shoare " close to the west end of Howdon, and the earliest deposits seem to have been made where Church Street, Chapel Street, and Brunton Street now stand, and hence it was under his lease that the new river shore line was made on the south side of Stephenson Street, and he it was who laid the foundations of a good part of Willington Quay, including Church Street, Stephenson Street, Palmers Terrace, Boundary Street, Potter Street, and Nelson Street, and all Howdon on the north side of Main Street.

In 1685 a later Francis Anderson addressed a petition to the Mayor and Aldermen of Newcastle setting forth that his grandfather, Henry Anderson, was a free merchant of Newcastle, and that his father, Francis Anderson, then of Howdon Panns, had taken his freedom of the town, but not of the Merchants' Company, and praying that he might be admitted to his freedom in some society or other, and that he might take apprentices for the management of his calling and employment of a confectioner. Accordingly at a meeting of the Common Council held 31st March, 1685, he was given leave to join any society he liked, and on April 15th he joined the Goldsmiths. He was required to give a bond " that neither he nor his servants would exercise the trade of a Goldsmith but only the trade or art of a confectioner."

The Holy Cross Church Registers for the year 1695 notes: " August 16th, ffrancis Anderson of Howdon panns buried."

From time to time we come across records of the continued connection of this family with Howdon, but these are not very numerous as, except for a short time, they resided in Newcastle.

In 1702 the Government began to impose a tax on salt, and we learn from the following memo that twenty years later this tax had grown seriously. Lord Harley in the year 1725 made a journey down the river to Tynemouth, and on his return he visited Howdon and makes some interesting notes. They are as follow:

May 7th.—When this (their dinner) was over we came back again up the river, and landed at Willington Stairs on the north side to see the salt pans, which I think are called Howdon pans.

Each pan makes one tun and a quarter of salt at eight boilings, which lasts three days and a half. Each consumes fourteen chaldrons of coals in seven days; in which time it makes two tuns and half of salt.

The wages for Pumpers, i.e., those people who pump the salt water out of the river into the pans is fivepence per diem. The Watchers, i.e., those who continually have an eye to the pans and the fire stoves, have sixpence a day.

What salt is here sold for twenty five shillings, produces to the Government six pounds and six shillings.[1]

In his records of this visit Lord Harley calls the coal spouts, not staiths, but " steathes," the name the trimmers still use.

The Excise Returns for the eight years 1739-46 show that the output of the Howdon Panns averaged then ninety-four tons per annum, which indicates a falling off of the output, and as the duty finally increased to over thirty times the manufacturing cost, the trade was slowly strangled.

Returning to the Anderson family. In February, 1747-8, Francis Anderson voted for his freehold at Howdon Panns, but his residence was at Newcastle. In 1762 we have seen Edward Anderson, in conjunction with Mr Edward Henzell, undertook to support his own poor tenants and workmen at Howdon Panns, and he was a very regular attender at the meetings of the " Four and Twenty " until 1786. When he voted in the 1774 election his residence is described in the poll book merely as Newcastle.

The Howdon salt pans were in a bad way in 1775, and soon after his last attendance at the Wallsend Vestry Mr Edward Anderson's affairs went into bankruptcy, and his Howdon property was assigned to Timothy Featherstonhaugh of Kirkoswald, Esq., and Jasper Harrison of Newcastle, Gentleman. Thus ended the first recorded manufacturing concern started in our parish.

In its early days the village of Howdon, with its salt

[1] Duke of Portland's MSS., Hist. MSS., Vol. vi., p. 105.

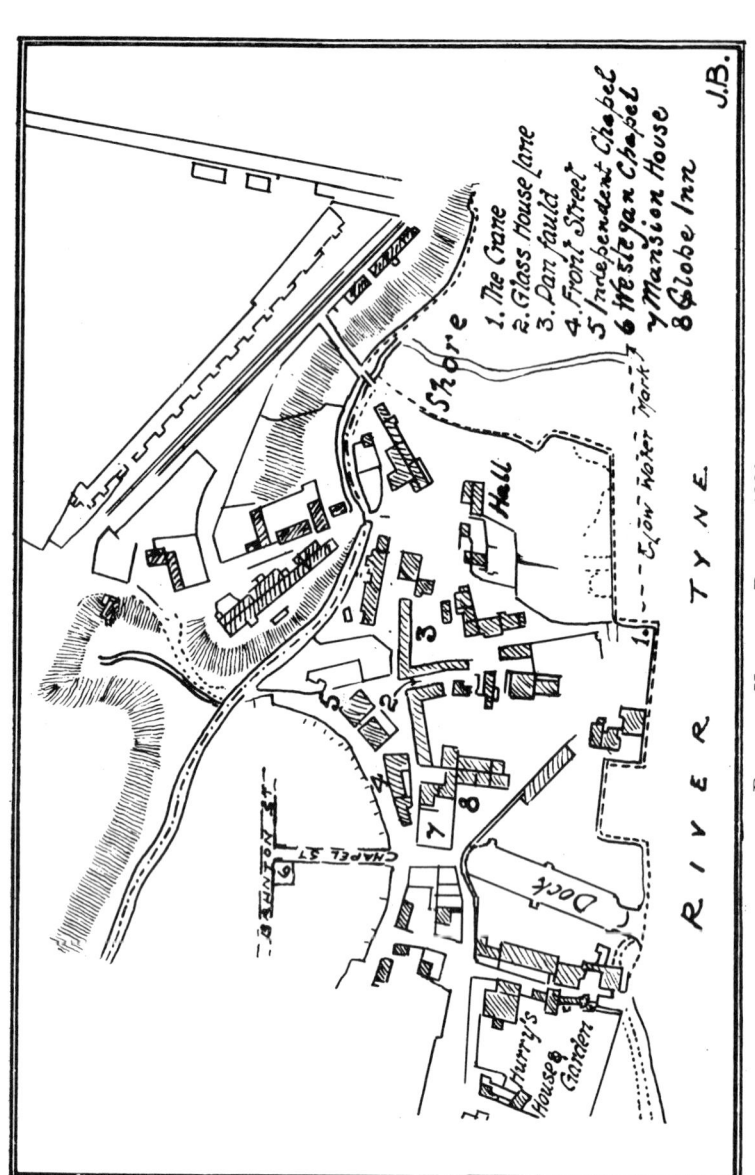

PLAN OF HOWDON PANNS, 1836.

pans and glass works, stood on the small peninsula bounded by the river on the south, and the Howdon burn on the east and north. This stream, which was the boundary of the township, had low banks, and at high tide boats and keels were able to float up to the site of the Primitive Methodist Church. Tradition adds that in still earlier days the tide flowed up into the bog field, and even at times made an island of the land lying east of what is now Byron Avenue. Near the mouth of the stream, in line of Tyne View Terrace, there was a wood bridge for general traffic, and at the east end of Main Street there was a foot-bridge and a ford.

The general level of the village was about eight feet below the present level, and the position of the salt works and the glass-houses is indicated by the " Pann Fauld " and " Glass House Lane," on the accompanying plan. The older houses on the south side of Main Street formed the north boundary of the village. The roadway was then named Front Street; it faced the flat shore of the Howdon burn until the ballast was deposited on the foreshore and the hill formed, which was presently to become the site of Chapel Street and Brunton Street.

While the trade of the salt pans and the glass-houses were declining, the first shipbuilding yard in our area was being started within a few yards of the glass-works.

The Hurry family, who were shipowners, came from Great Yarmouth and commenced building ships at Howdon, and they also made a large graving dock which was completed by January, 1759. This was capable of taking the largest ship afloat, and between the years 1770 and 1805 Howdon dockyard was one of the best known in England.

In those days our navy consisted of those " wooden walls of old England " we used to hear so much about, and many of our largest " wooden walls " were built here. The Howdon establishment was a very extensive one for its day, consisting of a double dry dock, building slips for four vessels, a quay nearly eight hundred feet long, facing the river, a ropery, sail-making lofts, warehouses, etc., so that not only were the hulls of ships built, but the ropes, cordage, and sails were made on the premises.

Mr Francis Hurry was the resident managing partner, and on 17th May, 1758, he was married at All Saints' Church to Miss Peggy Airey, third daughter of Mr Thomas Airey, a Newcastle shipbuilder. The newspapers of the day describe the young lady as " of great merit and accomplishment and with a fortune of £1,500." They lived in the large house which faced the river immediately to the west of the present Tyne Commissioner's offices, the garden stretched to the waterside, and the " Coach Open " indicates the entrance on that side of the grounds.

One of Mr Francis Hurry's sons, Thomas, was in the course of years taken into partnership, and he spent most of his time in London, keeping the works well supplied with orders. The firm, however, not only did work for the government, but built many ordinary merchant ships, and large East Indiamen. In short, our present Wallsend dock owners and shipbuilders have every reason to be proud of the first of their line.

For many years a small fleet belonging to the firm sailed from Howdon to the Greenland fisheries, and on the foreshore of the east side of the Howdon burn were facilities for bone cleaning and blubber boiling. Tradition says that the Hurry partners were kindly and thrifty employers, and the huge business they built up testifies to their skill and energy.

The houses of the village and the ships lying at the yard quay were in very close proximity, and this closeness nearly resulted in a great disaster in the year 1766. At two o'clock in the morning of February 4th, one of the dockyard watchmen discovered that the vessel *Greenlandman* of Newcastle was on fire. The alarm bell was rung, but the whole ship was ablaze. A strong wind from the south was blowing, scattering flaming embers over the houses. Another vessel, a brig belonging to Scarborough, took fire and added to the danger.

The whole village was engaged in protecting their property against the fiery onslaught, and at last they succeeded, but, as one chronicler records, " it was with great difficulty the village was saved." Some thatched roofs suffered, and the two vessels were burnt down to their keels, although some of their ropes and cables were rescued.

1779, July 29th.—Was launched at Howdon-dock, on the River Tyne near North Shields, His Majesty's frigate, the *Syren*, of 28 guns, commanded by Captain Dodds, and supposed to be one of the finest frigates in the navy.

1781, June 7th.—The *Argo* a 44 gun line of battleship launched at Howdon. The largest ship that had been built on the Tyne.

1782, October 9th.—A fine new frigate, called the *Madona*, was launched at Howdon docks upon the River Tyne, which was capable of mounting above 30 guns.

1789, May 26th.—A large and elegant new house, at Howdon Panns, on the River Tyne, belonging to Mr Lionel Robson, of the Broad Chare, Newcastle, was entirely consumed by fire. The flames were communicated to the bowsprit of a ship then building, which was immediately cut off to prevent their spreading farther.[1]

[Lionel Robson was a wealthy freeman in Newcastle who in 1778, and for ten years after, had an inn near the head of the Broad Chare. He was one of the Guild of Shipwrights, and probably had a shipbuilding or repairing yard at Howdon. The burning of his " elegant new house " did not cause him to leave Howdon, because in the years 1794, 1795, and 1796 he often attended the numerous meetings concerning Holy Cross Church. The rebuilt mansion house is that which faces " The Black Bull," and it still shows sufficient evidence of its former " elegance."]

The long naval war with France, which brought great trade and large profits to the Howdon shipbuilders, was practically closed by Nelson's victory at Trafalgar on

[1] Sykes' " Local Records."

October 21st, 1805. This was a great gain for England, but the reaction in shipbuilding and shipping which followed involved the Hurry firm in financial difficulties, and by the end of the following year there was " A commission of Bankruptcy awarded and issued against Francis Hurry, and Thomas Hurry, of Howdon Dock, in the Parish of Wallsend, Shipbuilders and Co-partners, Dealers and Chapmen."

Mr Francis Hurry survived the downfall of his business only about eighteen months; he died on 8th October, 1808, aged seventy-nine years, and was buried in St John's churchyard, Newcastle.

The estate was assigned to trustees, but owing to its huge ramifications they had a difficulty in winding it up, and therefore the assignees carried on the business for some considerable time. It was not until January 31st, 1815, that they were able to put the dock and shipbuilding yard up to public auction, but no satisfactory bid was made.

Unable to sell the Hurry estate, the assignees split it up. The sail lofts near the dockyard gates were occupied for many years by Joseph Salkeld, the father of the late Mr Henry Salkeld. The ropeworks were " let " to John and Matthew Knott, then to Isaac Knott, and finally to Mr Robert Robson.

The dock and part of the shipyard were continued by the trustees of the estate for ten years, then for some time they were occupied by Messrs Wharton & Weatherley, and finally Messrs Straker & Love became the tenants. Had it been possible for this firm to have continued their Howdon business, judging from the success which they afterwards attained in Durham, they might have made the dockyard the nucleus of a vast Tyneside shipping and shipbuilding concern, but the plans made in order to effect a much-needed improvement of the river put an end to the dock as a workable business.

The River Committee of the Newcastle Corporation in

1839 began to build a groyne to the westward of the dock—this was run from the old quay wall opposite George Stephenson's cottage into the river about three hundred feet, then turned westward. By this means a considerable amount of foreshore was reclaimed which was afterwards the site of Messrs Pochin's and Messrs Cookson's works, but this " improvement " altered the current and caused the river to silt up in front of the dock and very seriously interfered with the docking of the ships. Messrs Straker & Love, tenants of the dock and dockyard, sent in a claim for damages to the Newcastle Corporation, who were then the river authority. The ownership of the dock and a considerable portion of Howdon village before this date had passed out of the hands of Hurry's trustees into the possession of the mortgagee, Sir William Maxwell, of Calderwood and Edinburgh, who died in 1837. His property passed to his eldest son, Sir Wm. Alex. Maxwell, hence the claim upon the Corporation for damages to the dock was a joint one, made by the owner and the tenant. The entrance became so silted up that we find Messrs Straker & Love ceased to pay rent for the dock in 1846, though they remained in occupation of it and the building yard.

Meanwhile the Howdon Colliery Company had worked under the village, and a subsidence broke the dock walls, and a part of the floor of the dock was forced up. For this damage the Colliery Company had to pay, but the dock was not repaired at the time as it was useless to spend money on the concern until it was seen what the river authority would do regarding the entrance.

In the end, the Newcastle Corporation agreed to buy out Sir W. A. Maxwell and Messrs Straker & Love for £12,000, and when the River Tyne Improvement Act was passed on July 15th, 1850, it provided that this £12,000 should be chargeable to the new authority, and that they should take over the property. In this way the derelict dock and the adjacent land and buildings passed into the possession of the River Tyne Commissioners, and Messrs Straker & Love left Howdon and turned their exceptional talents to the Durham coal field.

Both the members of this firm became men of note in the north. Mr Joseph Straker was the third son of Mr George Straker of Walker, a mariner and shipowner, and for some years a resident and timber exporter in Memel. Like his father, Joseph was also a mariner, and after spending a good part of his life at sea, he retired, and in partnership with Mr Jos. Love became a timber merchant at the Low Lights, North Shields. He was, however, still interested in ships, and hence he and his partner took Howdon dock and building yard, and there carried on ship repairing, etc. Their business office was in Newcastle Chare, Newcastle.

Mr Joseph Love, the junior partner in this Howdon firm, was born at New York, near North Shields, and began his eventful working life at a very early age as a pit boy. The family next moved to West Moor, and then to Percy Main. The youth was firmly resolved to improve his position, and with his intelligence and unflinching industry and perseverance he succeeded, and in 1839 he and Mr Straker entered into a partnership which was one of continuous progress. He was not only a good business man, but also a devoted member of the Methodist New Connexion Church and a popular local preacher, and the church at Wallsend was only one of a large number which he aided with both money and personal service. A resolution passed by the annual conference at Hanley in 1874 records the debt the whole of the Methodist New Connexion owed to their active, wealthy, and generous supporter. He died at Mount Beulah near Durham on 22nd February, 1875, at the age of seventy-eight, and left his widow, Sarah Love, his sole heiress. His personal estate was sworn to on March 25th as under one million pounds.

Mr Joseph Straker was not so widely known as his partner, although he devoted a large part of his mature years to the public affairs of North Shields, in which town he resided nearly all his life. He was one of the first River Tyne Improvement Commissioners. In the general parliamentary election in 1852 he was the chief nominator of Mr Ralph Wm. Gray, who was opposed by Mr Hugh Taylor. He and Mr Joseph Cowen headed the procession when the foundation stone of the Tynemouth pier was laid on June 15th, 1854, and he frequently took a prominent part in matters concerning the borough of Tynemouth. After he moved to Newcastle, we still find him taking a generous interest in the old seamen of Shields, and personally presiding over their annual dinner. He died at Benwell House, Newcastle, on 13th October, 1867, aged eighty-three. Just a few weeks before his death he had contracted to purchase Stagshaw House and estate.

Both Mr Straker and Mr Love acquired great wealth, and died noted for their integrity and their generosity.

The failure of the Hurry firm with its large and varied enterprises in 1806 was a serious matter for Howdon, as they employed a large number of men, but the misfortune was mitigated by the dockyard being used to some extent, and by the expansion of the new coal mining industry.

The Howdon Panns colliery was completed in 1799, when the High Main seam was reached at a depth of one hundred and twenty fathoms. The shafts of the Howdon, Percy Main, and Flatworth collieries are outside our parish and beyond the scope of our history, and I need only record that while Humble Lamb was the principal owner, two of the partners, John Walker and Joseph Hetherington, were Wallsend residents. Furthermore, the viewers were John Watson of Willington House and afterwards John Buddle, and Robert Johnson of Willington assisted in the new winning of Percy Main. The coal under Bewicke and Craster's Willington estates, two hundred and ninety-seven acres in extent, was worked by the Percy Main Company and not by the Willington Company.

Before closing this section of the history of Howdon we should add that the land and property towards the close of the eighteenth century was almost entirely in the hands of two owners: (1) The Hurry family, (2) the assignees of Edward Anderson. The former had acquired some houses and land from the owners or trustees of the salt works and glass-houses, and they had also reclaimed some land from the river. Eventually some of these lands and houses were sold by the mortgagees of the Hurry estate in small parcels, but a large portion went into the hands of the River Improvement Commissioners as a result of the law proceedings we have already related.

The other owners were Messrs Timothy Featherstonhaugh and Jasper Harrison, the assignees of Edward Anderson. They disposed of some of their property on 30th September, 1788, and a large portion of the estate on 8th May, 1789, by sale to " George Dickinson, without the West Gate, Newcastle, Gentleman."[1] Mary Ellison of Newcastle, widow, was the only sister and heiress-at-law of George Dickinson, and on 12th March, 1806, she sold her Howdon property to Benjamin Brunton of Newcastle and Alexander Crighton of North Shields.

Benjamin Brunton in early life was a cordwainer in the Side, and afterwards a brewer living in the Forth in Newcastle. In the property he and Mr Crighton purchased at Howdon he appears to have had the larger share, as when land was sold the mineral rights were reserved, three-fourths to the Bruntons and one-fourth to Mr Crighton.

All the Ballast hill in front of Front Street (Main Street), upon which Chapel Street and Brunton Street was built, was part of the Brunton and Crighton estate, and they established the Howdon Brewery in 1802. Mr Brunton was a member of the Wallsend " Four and Twenty." He died on December 29th, 1816, aged eighty-

[1] See Appendix, p. 516.

six. He had two daughters: Ann, who was a spinster, died on 6th March, 1832, aged seventy-four; Mary, who married Alexander Falconer, a schoolmaster of Newcastle, died on 17th July, 1819, aged fifty-nine years, and she left a son, John Brunton Falconer, who was born in 1798, and a daughter, Mary, who married John Blackwell, an alderman of Newcastle.

With regard to the Crightons, Alexander Crighton was a shipowner and resided in Northumberland Square, North Shields. He did not appear to take much part in the affairs of our parish, and he disposed of his share of the brewery and the Howdon property to John Brunton Falconer. On the death of his aunt in 1832 Mr J. B. Falconer acquired her share of the estate, too.

We have to record one more alteration in the physical features of Howdon. In the early sixties, probably partly owing to the river improvement and partly to the sewers laid down, the old part of Howdon was often flooded at spring tides. We have seen over a foot of water in Glass House Lane, and the flooding was becoming increasingly serious. The matter was solved by clearing away the old low-lying village and covering the site with six feet or so of ballast, which was discharged from the ships in the Northumberland dock. In this way the river shore east of the Howdon burn was levelled up and nearly all the ancient village disappeared. Only a part of Globe Terrace, whose lower story was buried, and the east side of Dock Street, which was already on a higher level, remained. The ground floor of the houses on the south side of Main Street had already been partly buried when Main Street was formed and Chapel Street was built in 1830. The Independent Chapel and the Temperance Hall, which had been erected on the " Cinder hill " (the cinders from the glass-houses), were on the new level of Main Street.

The burial of the ancient village of Howdon Panns was part of an improvement as the streets and dwelling-houses were out of date and unfitted for modern use, but sentimental regret was felt at the disappearance of the old Hall and the old quay.

After the Hall ceased to belong to the Durham family in 1746, the next time the house is specially mentioned in a rate was in 1758, and it is "Mr Timothy Tyzack's house." Then from 1766 to 1779 " Mr Henzell's house."

In 1830 it had been empty for years, and it was reputed to be haunted. In that year part of it was dismantled and the house made smaller, and it was occupied by Mr Charles Wilson, a master mariner and shipowner, and his family. In 1842, the Wilsons left the old Hall and went into Hurry's house on the south-east side of Church Street, and Mr Thomas Davison, the block and mast maker, became the tenant, and he used part of the old Hurry shipyard for his business. The Davisons were the last occupiers of the Hall, and they remained until May, 1865, when the site of both house and mast-making yard was, as we have said, doomed to be buried with the ballast. They removed to Philipson Street, where they had built a house, and a site for the mast-making yard was found on land alongside "the Gut," which is now part of the Willington Foundry.

The old Howdon quay and crane had been used by river craft in connection with the salt works and glass trade for ages, and also as the landing-place for the ferry which had plied between Jarrow and Howdon probably from the days of Bede's Monastery. It was also the common meeting ground for the itinerant preachers and the " gossips " of the village.

When the property so long attached to the salt pans and the glass-houses began to be sold by the assignees of Edward Anderson and the successor to the Henzells (the newly formed Glass Company), there was transferred to each purchaser the right to the use of Howdon Panns Quay, and in the Appendix we give a copy of part of the deeds which shows us the owners of the quay in 1788 and the rights transferred. It will be seen that each salt pan had a name, " Newcastle Pans," " Wallsend Pans," and " Howdon Pans."

The River Tyne Commissioners moved the public access to the river and the public crane eastward to the Howdon burn, which they covered in, and they incorporated the site in their repairing yard.

CHAPTER V

INDUSTRIAL HISTORY—COAL MINING

Willington : In A.D. 1580—In modern days; Bells and Brown; Matthew Bell—Wallsend : The Chapmans; the Russell era; disasters; the mid-Tyne pits overwhelmed; the Russell family; John Buddle—Social conditions near the end of the eighteenth century : Land enclosures; conditions of labour in the mines; ballot for the Militia; Navy hated; Wallsend Vestry as a recruiting agency; the press gangs; Parliamentary franchise; Jacobites club at Howdon; first Friendly Societies—Present-day collieries : The Tyne Coal Co., The Wallsend and Hebburn Coal Co.

WILLINGTON

THE first records we have concerning coal mining in our area dates from the twenty-third year of the reign of Elizabeth (A.D. 1580). At that time Willington belonged to the Crown, and, by virtue of a royal commission,

Thos. Bates, Charles Hall, and Alan Kynge went to the vill of Willington, co. Northumberland, and examined by themselves and by experts in all the fields and territories there, if there were any coal mines and could not hear of any.

The report shows that :

Edward Bulmer of Newcastle upon Tyne, yeoman, viewer of the queen's mines in and about Newcastle, aged 65, says he knows Willington, and no coals have been wrought there in his remembrance. He thinks there is some kind of coals in the fields and territories of Willington, but cannot tell what it would cost to work them with a profit. He thinks for £100, proof could be had whether they can be won or not. He cannot estimate what it would cost to win them as the ground is very dangerous to win for want of good roof of stone and good conveyance of water. If they can be won he thinks each pit should be worth a yearly rent of £3 6s. 8d.

Edmond Mealebancke of North Shields, yeoman, and Henry Sheill of Newcastle, smith, say like the previous deponent.[1]

In spite of this report the prospect must have appeared hopeful, for directions are given for a lease to be made to Robert Dudley for twenty-one years at a yearly rental of one hundred shillings to be paid to the Queen, the lease to begin on the 25th March, 1581. Robert Dudley was at that time holding the " vill of Willington " under lease from the Crown, and there is little doubt that coal mining began soon after this date. A well-built culvert to the east of Ravensworth Street was cut into when a sewer was laid down Rosehill Road, and again near the east end of Keelman's Row, when another sewer was being laid. Assuming it ran in a somewhat straight line, it would lead from the " Willington Gut " to a point to the east or south-east of Willington Village. The old culvert is between four and five feet high, it was certainly used to drain some ancient coal workings, and it is safe to say that it was unknown to the Willington Colliery owners in 1775, or they would have utilised part of it when they made a similar one almost parallel to it, for a considerable distance.

Fifty hundredweights of coal were required to extract twenty hundredweights of salt, hence there was a steady demand for coals at Howdon, but whether the coal seams near the surface dipped too deep for their primitive methods of ventilation, or turned out to be too " fiery," can only be surmised. The mines were stopped and even their site forgotten.

In the early part of the eighteenth century steam engines began to be used, by 1750 the art of coal mining was making considerable strides, and hence in 1772, one hundred and ninety-one years after the date of the lease granted by the Crown to Robert Dudley, another lease of some coal seams in Willington was signed, and the working of these modern pits so altered the district that it will

[1] Leases 112, No. 46, Augmentation Office.

be of interest to sketch what the inland part of Willington was like just prior to this period.

The houses to the north of Willington village were: (*a*) the North Farm and cottages (Battle Hill). The farmstead probably dates from the time when Isabel and Julian Dent divided their joint estate in 1728. (*b*) The outlying group of cottages originally known as Greenchesters, then Willington Out Farm, then Moor Gate, then North Gate, and now that the gate is removed, it is called Middle Engine. When the Willington Collieries began in 1772 the moor gate was on the edge of the vast expanse of the Shire and the Killingworth moors. At the moor gate, in addition to the cottages there was a wayside inn—under the sign of the Plough. It was only a small house consisting of a large room and an offshoot on the ground floor with a cellar and an attic. Its customers would be those who crossed the moor from Benton to Tynemouth, or from the north to Howdon. The inn was closed about 1835. (*c*) About half a mile north-west of the moor gate there were two cottages and a byre or stable, probably dating from the days when Willington moor needed a cow herd: these were burnt down about 1850.

The village of Willington consisted chiefly of the farm-houses and buildings connected with the West Farm, the Middle Farm, and the Willington Farm, with a wide, oval-shaped village green. This extended from the dene eastwards some three hundred and sixty yards, and had a breadth of about seventy yards, making about five and a half acres.

All the houses of the West Farm and the Middle Farm (several of which are now demolished) were on the south side of the green, or "Town Street," and those of the Willington Farm were on the north side. There was a pond at each end, and the village smithy was between the West Farm and the Middle Farm. At the west end of the green where the old public road to Holy Cross Church descended into the dene, stood the West Farmhouse and buildings. The north walls of the house still remain (the present West Farmhouse was built about 1845).

There was the Rose Inn (Halfway House Farm) which supplied refreshment to man and beast who travelled between Newcastle and North Shields on the main road which was reported in an official memo in 1747 to be " so deep and ruinous that Travellers cannot pass without great danger." There was the Padock Hall a hundred yards east of the Bewicke school, where the first Willington post office was established, and there was the Willington Low or East Farm. This farmstead was probably built when the east side of the township (Raws moor) was enclosed, and it appears that this was the last land in the township to be enclosed, except the great moor on the north side.

This rural condition of the township had probably existed for hundreds of years, except for the early coal mining in the sixteenth century. The first to break in upon this state of affairs were the owners of the Killingworth Colliery, who in 1762 built their earliest wagon-way over Killingworth moor, and through Willington, turning southward at what is now Milbanke Square, down through the east end of Willington Town Street, over the Turnpike a few yards west of the Bewicke schools, over the site of the Roman Catholic schools, thence to their staiths where Messrs Cleland's offices now are.

This wagon-way is one of historic importance. The width between the rails was four feet eight inches, and this fixed the standard gauge for the Killingworth wagons, and for the Willington Colliery owners when they came to use the same line of rails.

When George Stephenson moved from Willington Quay to Killingworth in 1804, the gauge was thus already a settled matter for these collieries. An award dated December 15th, 1810, shows that the rails were then wood, for the owners of the Kenton and Coxlodge Collieries were adjudged to " pay the Willington owners 3s. 4d. per ten of 440 Bolls per mile for the upkeep of the present Wood Railway, and 2s. 6d. per ten per mile if metal rails be laid." The step between wood rails and iron ones was made when thin plates of iron were nailed on to the top of the wood. These plates greatly protected the wood, and it is owing to this old type of rail that we still use the term railway plate layer.

In 1813, when Stephenson designed and built his engine, he built it for this four feet eight gauge and tried his first locomotive on it on July 25th, 1814. His later engines followed on similar lines, and naturally he planned the Stockton and Darlington line for the same width, so that his engines could run on it.

It is difficult to find the reason why the Killingworth Colliery owners laid down their first wagon-way with the rails four feet eight inches apart; there were then several other gauges in use in the district. Mr Tomlinson in his history of the North-Eastern Railway goes fully into this matter, without being able to arrive at any decided conclusion, however. Doubtless railway engineers, cramped as they now are for lack of width and height for engines and carriages, often wish this Willington wagon-way had been built on more generous lines.

In 1772 Wm. Gibson of Westgate Street, Attorney-at-Law, and Town Clerk of Newcastle, Matthew Bell of Westgate and afterwards of Woolsington, and William Brown of Heddon and later of Long Benton, arranged to take a lease of the coal seams under the estate of Sir Ralph Milbank for thirty-one years from 12th May, 1773. A few months later they also took a lease dated 5th November of the Willington Farm, the Backwell Farm, and part of the Milbank estates for thirty years from old May Day, 1774.

They sunk a shaft to the north-east of where Willington Square now stands, as this gave them easy access to the Killingworth wagon-way running to Willington Quay. The first notes entered into the minute book of the partners are :

Willington Colliery 27 January 1774. The Engine pit is now sunk to 40 faths.

A meeting held at Mr Wm. Browns, Westgate street, Newcastle 29th January 1774. Present, Wm. Gibson Esq., Matt. Bell Esq., Senr., Matt. Bell Esq., Junr., and Mr Wm. Brown.

And the partners thus so carefully graded as to rank proceed to arrange about the purchase of an engine. One year and nine months later a minute records " Willington Colliery 28th October 1775. The main coal is now through and is 6 feet 4 inches thick." This was the " Engine " pit, and the winning of the coal was celebrated five days later, on November 2nd, 1775, amid great local rejoicings. The owners' contribution to the festivities were a fat ox roasted, a large quantity of ale, and a wagon load of punch.

The following is the account of this event as recorded by the viewer under the date of November 4th, 1775:

On Thursday a treat was given to celebrate the winning of the Colliery which was done with the greatest decency, 262 people were at the dinner at the same time in the granary, and 150 more partook of the liquor, and what ale was left, was yesterday drank out and the same good order observed, so that upon the whole it was a complete thing of the kind.

Raising large quantities of water from the pits to the surface was very difficult in those early days, and to save this as much as possible, the owners tunnelled a " drift " from the pit down through Willington to the Gut. This " Tyne Level Drift " is 2,030 yards long, and must have cost a large sum to construct. Leases provided a water course rent for its use of two shillings per ton on the coal wrought on the Collingwood, Orde, Bigge, and Bewicke (Benton) estates.

The rents payable to Sir Ralph Milbank were " certain rent " £400 per annum, for 533 tons. For the Balkwell and Willington Farms, £750, to be raised to £850 after ten years. To the Corporation of Newcastle for wagon-way leaves to their staiths at Willington Quay, £100 per annum per 800 tons; for staith room, for quay, and " ground behind the ballast hills," £24. Rent for Tyne level water drift, £20. For the Quay Farm £60, and the lease provides " 2 keels of coals for the use of the Mayor to be delivered yearly."

Other extracts from the viewers' reports show the course of events:

May 4th, 1776.—The Colliery is now working for the London trade.
May 18th, 1776.—The New pit called the Edward Pit is now broke in Mr Collingwood's grounds and sunk 3 fathoms.

It will be seen that Messrs Bells and Brown had leased the coal under the Collingwood and Orde estate in addition to that belonging to Sir Ralph Milbank. They next took a lease, dated 22nd June, 1782, of the coal under the land of Thos. Charles Bigge, and the first shaft sunk on the Bigge estate was half a mile north of the present Bigge pit at Battle Hill. The later shaft was not sunk until the " high main " in the more northerly area was worked out. The third shaft sunk by the company seems to have been the " Milbank " pit, three hundred and twenty-five yards north of the " Engine " pit, but the records left us are not clear. The " Venture " pit, marked on some old mining maps, two hundred and fifty yards north of Willington stables, was only partly sunk, then abandoned. The " Belle " pit, two hundred and sixty yards north-west of the " Milbank," was the only other pit on the Milbank estate.

Soon after the partners got possession of the land they built the south and west side of Milbank Square for their men, and also a large number of stables near the farmstead at Willington for the horses necessary to haul the coals to their staiths. One horse took two wagons, and the Killingworth wagon-way then in use was also used by the Willington owners as far as the site of the Catholic schools, then the Willington wagons diverged to staiths near the entrance to the Gut which are still used by the Tharsis Sulphur and Copper Company.

On April 3rd, 1782, William Gibson assigned his share of the undertaking to Matthew Bell, and on the death of Mr Bell on 3rd September, 1786, the firm became " Bells and Brown," with Matthew Bell the younger, of Woolsington, half share; Richard Bell, of Sellaby Hall, quarter share; William Brown, of Long Benton, quarter share.

The coal seams under the Willington lands of Messrs Bewicke and Craster were worked by the Percy Main Company, and the Newcastle Corporation seams under their Willington estate was the occasion of considerable local feeling, mainly directed against Alderman Anthony Hood, then residing at Wallsend Hall. In 1802 the Corporation of Newcastle proposed to let the High Main coal under their " Half-way House Farm " containing about one hundred and fifty acres. Messrs Bells and Brown gave in a tender dated 28th February, 1802, and Mr Simon Temple of Jarrow Colliery also gave in a tender. When the Corporation Committee opened these it was found that the Willington offer was the higher one. However, Alderman Hood stated he had an authority from Mr Temple to add two shillings per " ten " to the terms of his offer, and after some discussion Mr Temple got the lease. It was felt, however, that the working of these coals should have come to Willington and not gone to Jarrow, and hard things were said about the alderman by his neighbours. If the Willington coal owners had obtained this lease, they proposed to put down a new shaft on the Corporation land instead of near the south side of Orde's land (Willington Low Pit). The Newcastle Corporation was often reminded afterwards that had the Willington owners got the lease, the Corporation would have got the " shaft rent " on the coals, both from their own land and also from the Orde and Milbank estates, whereas in giving the lease unfairly to Jarrow they got no shaft rent whatever.

On 13th May, 1809, Messrs Bells and Brown became

the tenants of Willington West Farm under a twelve years lease from John Orde and others.

In the year 1820 a new wagon-way for the Benton and High Willington coals was laid from Battle Hill to the Low Pit, crossing Willington dene by a wood bridge on stone pillars, thence down the present Rosehill Road. This route was worked on the inclined plane system, and dispensed with the old line, and also with the horses necessary for this route. The Willington stables were therefore converted into dwelling-houses in 1821 or 1822, and the first tenant to occupy one of the cottages was Wm. Bowran, father of the late Thomas Bowran of Middle Farm.

On 31st May, 1815, Richard Bell the elder, owner of one-fourth of the colliery, died at Bath, and a valuation of the whole property was made. This shows:

	£	s.	d.
Coal remaining sufficient to supply an annual vend of 60,000 chaldrons for twelve years, and this was valued at	100,000	0	0
Live stock, timber, etc. ...	15,000	0	0
Stock on the farms—			
Willington Farm £1,824 7 11			
Long Benton Farm 1,358 16 6			
East Benton Farm 356 10 1			
Willington West Farm 1,385 19 0			
	4,925	13	6
Latimers premises, house at Howdon, and Skinnerburn wharf	381	0	0
	120,306	13	6
Deduct amount of dead stock such as Engines, Wagons, Wagon-ways, etc., employed in making the estimated revenue	39,355	8	7
	£80,951	4	11

The share of Richard Bell of Sellaby Hall passed to Richard Bell of Pensey Castle, Wilts.

The high water mark of the colliery was, we think, the

period between the year 1808, when the vend was 52,651 chaldrons, and the year 1816, when it was 52,588 chaldrons. During these busy times the wages of the workmen were raised. In August, 1810, wages were increased and the amount of the advance given varies from twopence per day to engine wrights and joiners, to eightpence per day to wastemen.

The wages after this increase were as follow: labourers and cartmen, 2s. 6d. per day; firemen, 2s. 7d. per day; engine wrights and joiners, 3s. per day; men working engines, 3s. 2d. per day; wastemen, 3s. 4d. per day; smiths, 3s. 8d. per day; and the viewer, who leaves a note of this increase of wages, adds a valuable memo saying that at the time these wages were fixed the average price of wheat sold at Newcastle market was twenty-six shillings per boll.

The actual amount of money spent in working the colliery for one year, that of 1821, is given by Mr John Watson, and was £47,683 14s. 8d. They worked three shifts, and that year vended 36,000 chaldrons of coals.

As showing the amount and fluctuations of the profits: In the year 1816 the coals—52,588 chaldrons—were sold for £83,799 16s. 2d., the expenses totalled £64,584 15s. 0½d., leaving an excellent profit of £19,215 1s. 1½d.

In a year soon after this the profit available for division was only £6,256 3s. 11d., and the partners wrote a curt letter calling for an explanation.

In December, 1818, Messrs Bell and Brown bought the Willington Milbank estate for £24,500, which was then owned by Sir Richard Milbank. The property consisted of the coal seams, two good houses occupied by colliery agents, eighty-six other houses, stables, granaries, etc. Also the farm and four hundred and fourteen acres thirty-three perches of land for which Messrs Bell and Brown were paying a rental of £525.

There were also the Copperas works with an area of

three roods thirty-six perches, situated on the north side of Willington House, at that time leased to Mr Joseph Lamb for £150 per year, and also sundry wayleaves which included £300 from the Killingworth owners. In the property offered were two pews, Nos. 30 and 43 in the new parish church at Wallsend.

The plan of the estate issued with the conditions of sale show that only the west and south side of Milbank Square was then built. The road from the stables westward beyond the Engine Inn and Middle Farm was named Willington Town Street. The Copperas works had two Copperas houses, a dwelling-house, a yard, and large Copperas beds.

In 1831 a serious explosion occurred at the Low pit. This was sunk in 1806 as far as the High Main seam, and was the last pit opened by the Willington Company. In 1831 a staple was being sunk from the High Main to the Bensham seam, which was thirty-seven fathoms lower. At nine a.m. on September 20th, while all the shift was at work, the gas from this new seam fired and three men and eight horses were killed outright. Other fourteen men were very seriously burnt, of whom four died in a few days. So much gas came up this staple that presently it was arched over and the gas conveyed by a pipe to bank, where it was lit and burnt in the same way as was done at the Wallsend gas pit.

Prior to this, on 3rd December, 1829, four men were lost, and on 30th March, 1840, three men and five boys were burnt, one of the men soon afterwards dying. It will be seen, however, that the Willington collieries, although working the same seams, and at the same time, were much freer from accidents than those at Wallsend.

The worst accident in the history of the colliery occurred on Monday, 19th April, 1841, at the Bigge pit, where thirty-eight men and boys were working underground when the pit exploded and only three escaped with their lives. It was proved that Richard Cooper, one of

WILLINGTON HOUSE IN 1911.

[*Facing page* 221.

the victims, was the immediate cause of this disaster, and he came in for the whole of the blame. He was a trapper boy, and his duty was to sit hour after hour behind a door, and open and shut it when any coals passed his way. The little fellow, who was only nine years of age, tired of the darkness and loneliness, had propped open his door, and gone some little way off to play with two other small boys, and destruction was the result. What could he realise about air courses, gas accumulation, and mine ventilation?

On the death of Wm. Brown, his son, Dixon Brown, succeeded to his father's quarter share of the collieries. In 1837 the partnership was as follows: Matthew Bell, thirty-two sixty-fourths; Dixon Dixon, sixteen sixty-fourths; George Johnson, four sixty-fourths; Rev. Wm. Ramsden, nine sixty-fourths; Mrs Mary Bell, one sixty-fourth; Rev. J. Bell, two sixty-fourths.

With regard to the above, when Dixon Brown succeeded through his mother, Margaret Dixon, to the estates of Wm. Dixon, he assumed the name of Dixon Dixon. Richard Bell's quarter share, it will be seen, was split up— twelve sixty-fourths fell to his heirs, and George Johnson, the viewer, bought his four sixty-fourths from the executors.

The Willington collieries continued on their even and successful way. Mr John Watson, the viewer, seems to have been an exceptionally capable man. Mr John Buddle frequently consulted him officially in serious difficulties, and it is a patent fact that, compared with Wallsend, the number of accidents at Willington was exceptionally small.

Mr Watson lived in Willington House (see illustration). Like many other men when the coal trade was in its infancy, he widened his interests. In 1805 he bought West Chirton farm. In 1806 he sold out his interest in Heaton colliery and bought into Collingwood Main. In 1812 he was a viewer for Willington, Collingwood Main,

Kenton, Fawdon, and Denton, and was check viewer for the Newcastle Corporation and others.

In 1826 he retired from active work at the colliery, and removed to Newcastle, where he continued business as a consulting mining engineer and agent. His letters concerning the colliery are in 1826 dated from Northumberland Street and in 1831 from Picton Place. He was succeeded at Willington by Mr George Johnson, who became owner of a four sixty-fourth share of the colliery, and he was already part owner of Benton collieries. He also lived at Willington House.

He brought up two of his nephews—John Johnson, who became his assistant at Willington, and Walter Johnson, who became land steward at Trench Hall under Lord Ravensworth. John presently married Miss Robson of West Chirton Hall and took up his residence at the Villa, Willington Village. On the death of Mr George Johnson he succeeded his uncle as viewer. The widow of Mr Johnson, senior, changed houses with her nephew and went to the Villa, and Mr John Johnson resided in Willington House until after the colliery closed, when he moved to Ferryhill.

THE FIRM OF BELLS & BROWN owned the Willington collieries, and a large part of the Willington township. They also farmed the Balkwell farm at Flatworth, the Willington farm, and the Willington West farm. Thus their names were household words in the parish for a long period, but Willington was only one of their business centres, for they developed their firm into one carrying on an immense land-owning and coal-mining business. They began at Heddon, then extended to Willington, Long Benton, and elsewhere.

It is related that this partnership came about in the most casual way.[1] Mr Wm. Brown, a remarkably able man, was an overman for Lord Carlisle's collieries, and Mr

[1] "Arch. Aeliana," N.S., Vol. xi.

Matthew Bell was a well-to-do draper in Newcastle, residing in the Westgate. One day Mr Wm. Brown went into Mr Bell's shop to buy some flannel for his pit clothes. He happened to mention to Mr Bell that he thought it was a pity that Heddon pit should be " laid in." After going carefully into the matter, the capable colliery overman and the shrewd wealthy draper entered into a coal-mining partnership which became well known throughout the whole of the coal trade.

The chief partner, Matthew Bell, married Jane, daughter of Richard Ridley of Heaton Hall, and at the time the Willington colliery was opened he still resided in Westgate Street. He died on 3rd September, 1786. His eldest son, Matthew (2), had predeceased him, and hence his grandson, Matthew (3), succeeded to the ownership of his estate. He, when he came of age in 1791, like his father and grandfather, became a partner in the Old Bank in Newcastle, the firm being Ridley, Cookson, Widdrington, Bell & Company. In 1806, fortunately for the Bell family, Mr Bell retired from the partnership, his place being taken, as we have already seen, by Chas. Wm. Bigge. Matthew Bell's wife was Sarah Frances Brandling of Gosforth, and their eldest son, Matthew (4), born in 1793, was for half a century one of the prominent men in the northern counties. When he was twenty-three he was high sheriff of Northumberland, and in the same year, on 10th October, 1816, he married Elizabeth Anne, only child and heiress of Henry Utrick Reay of Hunwick Hall. Ten years later he won one of the most notable parliamentary contests ever fought in the north. The Tory party was losing ground after long years of success. Mr Beaumont had been converted to the side of Reform; the other representative, Chas. J. Brandling, kept to the Conservative faith.

In 1826, Mr Brandling died, and the Hon. H. T. Liddell, afterwards first Earl of Ravensworth, endeavoured to hold the seat for the Government, but Matthew Bell entered the lists and won it. This contest was barely over when Parliament was dissolved, and the famous general election fight of 1826 took place. For Northumberland the candidates were Thos. W. Beaumont, who threw over both parties and stood as an independent Reformer; Matthew Bell, a good Tory; H. T. Liddell, also a Tory, but willing to make concession to the Catholics; and Lord Howick, a Whig. Each fought for his own hand, and when the poll opened at Alnwick on 20th June, to elect the two members, the county was at fever heat. From our district the voters could either be driven by coach with flags flying and horns blowing, or they could embark at Shields, land at Alnmouth, and drive to Alnwick. There was free conveyance, free dinners, free lodgings, free drinks, free everything. We can imagine what Alnwick was like during this time.

Every man, whether he had a vote or not, took sides. In every village the party agents kept an "open house" at their headquarters, which was always an inn. Bands paraded with the different colours, and each candidate had a "gathering tune," Mr Bell's being "The Bonny Pit Lad," an old tune, and Mr Liddell's "Northumberland's Choice," which was composed for this election. Work was neglected and nothing talked of but the latest news as to the state of the poll at Alnwick, where every afternoon the result of the open voting was declared, and the candidates addressed the free and honest electors. This went on for fifteen days, excluding Sundays, and at the end the figures were: Liddell 1,562, Bell 1,380, Beaumont 1,335, Howick 977.

Willington went more or less delirious over the result, and Wallsend helped them to rejoice. This election cost Mr Bell £30,000, but Mr Beaumont spent no less than £80,000, and, it is said, seriously crippled the family fortunes for some time. He paid for inns at Alnwick £11,050, at Newcastle £5,620, and lesser amounts all over the county.

Going over the poll books gives us a practical illustration of the state of the franchise at that time. No resident in Wallsend township had a qualification for Wallsend, because all the district was leasehold. John Buddle (who split his vote between Bell and Beaumont) voted on account of a qualification in Benwell, and four other Wallsenders voted by virtue of having freeholds elsewhere. Fifteen residents of Howdon had votes by virtue of Howdon freeholds, and three had votes for Willington. Of the Willington voters, two plumped for Bell, one split between Bell and Howick, but upon the whole the local votes show that Liddell was their favourite, while Bell stood next.

Before leaving the old coal-mining period of Willington, we may say that the colliery owners were responsible for the reduced area of the village green, and the only active opponent to the enclosure was, strange to say, Billy Purvis. This popular entertainer and his company regularly visited all the fairs and almost all the villages in Northumberland and Durham.

About the year 1825, Messrs Bell & Brown reduced the green and Town Street very nearly to its present dimensions, but the enterprising showman had been used to set up his booth on the east side of the green near the site of the present church. On finding his old standing ground walled off, he and his assistants forthwith pulled the wall down, and erected his tent in the customary place.

The owners took no immediate notice, but rebuilt the walls. On his next visit, the walls were again taken down and the show again opened, but now, instead of crowded houses, a mere sprinkling of patrons attended. Billy learned that the colliery owners had banned his visits, and that the pitmen dare not patronise their inimitable merrymaker.

WALLSEND

We have seen that modern coal mining in our district, apart from that which began in the days of Queen Elizabeth, commenced at Willington six years earlier than at Wallsend.

During the summer of 1756 the seams of coal in the parish of Wallsend, under the lands owned by the Dean and Chapter of Durham, were advertised in the *Newcastle Journal* " to be let on lease, on or before 28th September next." These royalties, however, remained unlet, until a family of Quakers in Newcastle, named Chapman, took them, and in 1778 began sinking a shaft a little to the east of Carville Hall. When they began, they expected they had ample funds to " win " the coal, but unfortunately, like scores of other coal seekers, they encountered innumerable difficulties, in the shape of water and quicksands, and they had to borrow money to carry on their undertaking.

There is preserved one of Chapman's pay sheets, for three weeks in October, 1780, during which time they were sinking the first shaft of the original Wallsend colliery.

The total amounts to £115 14s. 8¼d. The details are only given for a few of the items, but they tell us something of the wages and prices a hundred and forty years ago.

No. 21. An Acct. of the Expenses for Sundry Sorts of Work and Incident Charges at Walls End Colliery for the use of the Owners of the Said Colliery from Oct. 4th to 10th and 18th 1780.

[The men's wages for erecting buildings, leading bricks and coals, and general work varied greatly. One was paid at 2s. 8d. per day, nineteen at 1s. 6d., and eleven at 1s. Engine-men, sinkers, etc., are not set out in detail.]

THE ORIGINAL WALLSEND COLLIERY ("A" pit).
Wallsend House (*John Buddle's*) on the right.

INCIDENT CHARGES :

	£	s.	d.
Paid Jam⁸ Harper and others 9 tides (Viz) 7 wth. small coals and 2 with sand at 12s.	5	8	0
Paid Wm. Dodds 7 weeks lodging as p. agreement at 6d.	0	3	6
Paid Boatman for bringing glass over water	0	1	0
Paid Wm. Young 1 Quarter Window cess for both Houses	0	11	0
Paid Geo. Johnson ¼ years Salary due Sept 30th last Past	25	0	0
Paid Wm. Redhead 10 thrave straws at 16d.	0	13	4
Paid John English 31 Boles Beans at 3s. 5d.	8	7	11
	£40	4	9

[Geo. Johnson, Senior, was probably the viewer in charge of the work.]

At the end of the sheet is the note :

	fath.	ft.	
Sinking New pit this pay p. shift	2	4	0
do. formerly	40	5	0
Total	43	3	0

Messrs Chapman obtained a loan from a Sunderland firm, that of Messrs Russell, Allan & Wade, but before the coal seam was reached the money advanced was called in, and as the Chapmans could not find the cash, the mortgagees foreclosed, and in 1781 took possession of the works.

Hence we have William Russell, Robert Allan (his brother-in-law), and Thomas Wade owners of the machinery shaft and leases.

There seems to have been a widespread impression that calling in their money at this juncture was a piece of sharp practice on the part of the mortgagees, but we find that, after the foreclosure, and before the coal was actually found, one of the mortgagees, Robert Allan, withdrew from the adventure, so that we may fairly assume that there was then still considerable uncertainty as to how the enterprise would turn out.

The coal was, however, reached almost immediately, by the new partners, at a depth of six hundred and sixty-six feet. The seam proved six and a half feet thick, it was a house coal of the highest quality, nine-tenths of the whole output was large coal, and it soon spread the name of Wallsend far and wide.

The first shaft was completed to the High Main seam in 1781, and almost simultaneously the " B " shaft was sunk ninety-five yards to the north of the " A " shaft. In 1786 the third or " C " pit was put down near the west end of the village, where the park now is. In sinking this shaft, when one hundred and eighty feet below the surface, a very large feeder of water was encountered, giving off one thousand seven hundred gallons per minute. This was stemmed back by oak cribs, nine inches thick, with half inch fir sheeting between, the use of cast iron tubing for this purpose not being known then. In the same year (1786) the " D " shaft, or West pit (north-west of Industrial Terrace) was commenced. Next followed the " E " pit in 1791-93 (near the High Farm).

In 1796 a " coal machine " to raise coals from the pit was erected at the " C " shaft. It cost £615 and it was counted as equal to twenty horse-power. Steam engines had been used to draw water for many years prior to this, but for raising coals the horse gin had been employed.

In 1802 the " F " shaft (south-west of the hospital) was opened, and last of all the " G," or Church pit, was sunk as a separate winning, and at first was not connected with the other workings. The need for so many shafts was due to the great difficulty in ventilating the workings, when they were any considerable distance " in-bye."

The first lease, granted to William and John Chapman by the Dean and Chapter of Durham, was for twenty-one years. This was renewed in the name of the Russells on 20th November, 1799, for a further twenty-one years, and afterwards renewed for another twenty-one years, and finally for a seven years' term. The rent paid on the 1799 and 1820 leases was £500 10s. per year " certain rent " for 572 " tens " with overworkings. A Dean and Chapter " ten " was equal to 47 tons 14 cwts., therefore this rent equals a royalty of 4½d. per ton, exclusive of any " fine " which would be paid on each renewal of the lease.

Taking the sales of the Tyneside collieries in the year 1808, Wallsend heads the list with 64,683 chaldrons, Willington comes second with 52,651 chaldrons, and Bigges Main comes ninth with 18,768 chaldrons.

The Minute Book of Mr George Johnson, viewer of Benton and later of Willington collieries, records that the number of bound hewers in 1805 were: at Willington 98, Bigges Main 80, Wallsend 110, Walker 109, and Percy Main 125. " The total number of hewers bound in all the collieries on the north side of the Tyne from Walbottle to Percy Main—1,279."

It is of interest to note that the North of England Coal Trade endeavoured more than once to maintain a huge coal trust. The first in which Wallsend and Willington were concerned was that in force in 1790, but the best organised combination was that arranged in 1809 and put into operation on 31st March, 1810. Sales, prices, and output were controlled by a joint committee. All direct selling was to cease. If the output of a colliery exceeded its agreed quantity, it returned five shillings per chaldron to the pool; if its output was less than its quantity, it received three shillings per chaldron out of the pool. The committee fixed the prices for sales.

Matters did not work quite smoothly, and there is an interesting letter from Mr Buddle to Mr John Watson of Willington, dated Wallsend Colliery, 17th September, 1810.

Mr Buddle says : " It is to be regretted that the exceedings are so great," and he laments " the baneful effects of a bad example, at the same time we may console ourselves with the idea that it is never too late to mend."

The humour comes in when we see in the returns that these two, he and Watson, are by far the greatest transgressors, Wallsend having an over-production of 2,700 chaldrons over the agreed quantity, and Willington and Percy Main following closely behind with 2,600 chaldrons each, and only three other collieries showing an insignificant amount. Is Mr Buddle arguing that his friend and neighbour, Watson, set him a bad example by exceeding with both his collieries, or is Mr Buddle " owning up " himself, and excusing his fellow mining engineer and suggesting that they amend their ways?

This agreement was to last seven years, and it continued with increasing friction for that period, but towards the close each owner scrambled for a bigger output, bribed buyers and ship captains by rebates, etc., and the arrangement collapsed.

The basis of the agreement shows what the northern coal trade was at that time, the shipments for 1808 being: from the Tyne, 615,293 chaldrons; from the Wear, 330,144; from Blyth, 28,191; from Hartley 18,655; total, 993,283 chaldrons.

The quality of the High Main coals at Wallsend secured for them the premier place in the coal markets of the world, and they commanded the highest prices. In 1813 Wallsend coal was selling at 34s. per chaldron f.o.b., Willington was a shade below at 33s. and 34s., while Elswick coals brought only 20s.

As to the profits made from this flourishing business, few records are available. However, an authority on the coal trade[1] says that for the year 1813 the profits at Wallsend was 12s. 6d. per chaldron. On a " vend " of 60,000 chaldrons this would leave a profit for the year of £37,500.

In 1813 a statement was printed which gives us some interesting information concerning the coal trade of that day. A vessel of twenty-two keels loaded Russell

[1] Notes on Northern Industries (Jas. S. Jeans).

WALLSEND COLLIERY

Wallsend coals for the London market, and the following is the detailed account:

	£ s. d.	£ s. d.
176 chas. of Wallsend Coals at 34s. per Newcastle chal.		299 4 0
Spoutage on 112 chals. at 6d.	2 16 0	
Keel dues on 64 chals. at 13s. 4d. per keel	5 6 8	
Beer and bread money to keelman 3s. 10d.	1 10 8	
		9 13 4
Coast duty and certificate 1s. per chal. ...		8 16 6
Lighthouses		6 16 8
Newcastle Corporation dues, at 3d. per chal.		2 4 0
Insurance on £326 14s. 6d. at 1½ guinea per cent., and 2s. 6d. per cent. duty ...		5 3 0
		331 17 6
CHARGES IN LONDON RIVER		
Sundry dues	4 1 6	
Metage and Orphan dues 1s. 2d. per London chal. on 343 chals.	20 0 2	
King's duty, 12s. 6d. on 343 chals.	214 7 6	
Discount, etc.	9 18 0	
Factor's commission ¼ per cent. on £876 11s. 1d.	4 7 7	
		252 14 9
Freight		291 18 10
		£876 11 1

This gives per ton about the following figures:

	£ s. d.	£ s. d.
Coal owner for coals at spout	0 12 9	
Expenses in the Tyne, etc.	0 1 1½	
Coast Duty	0 0 4½	
		0 14 3
DUES IN THAMES DISTRICT, ETC.		
Freight	0 1 8	
King's duty	0 11 1	
		0 12 9
Freight (sea)		0 12 7
		£1 19 7[1]

It will be seen even this small vessel could not load all her cargo, 466 tons, at the spouts, and over one-third of it

[1] Edington on the Coal Trade.

was loaded at Shields from keels. The coals were sold at 34s. per chaldron at the spout, and if the estimate of 12s. 6d. profit be correct then the cost of winning the coals was 21s. 6d. per chaldron.

We come across few notes of Mr Russell visiting the village from which he was drawing so much wealth, but one of the few notes is the following entry in the Diary for the year 1812 kept by Matthias Dunn, Mr Buddle's assistant: " June 18th.—Mr Russell here all day examining the Bills."

The coals were raised from the pits in wicker-work baskets, or corves, and the corving house at Wallsend, where these were made, was at the south end of Park Road, on the east side. They were supplied by a contractor for a fixed sum per ton of coal raised by the colliery. There were no cages—when coals were drawn, the corves were hung on to a chain at the end of the winding rope, three at a time. When the men and boys went up and down, the corves were taken off and the men hung on to the chain; there ought to be foot loops attached, but these were often not used, and many sad accidents took place.

A well-known Percy Main poet-pitman used to relate a pathetic story of what he saw. A boy was returning up the shaft clinging to the chain, with his older brother just below him. The youngster felt the chain slowly slipping through his hands. He called out, " A'm gannen to fall, Jimmy." " Slide down to me, hinny," his brother replied. But when the boy slid down, his brother could not hold him. In spite of an agonising struggle the chain slowly slipped through his fingers, and together they went to their death.

At first all the coals were loaded into keels as near the colliery as possible (a keel holding $21\frac{1}{5}$ tons) and discharged into ships at Shields. We have just seen in the accounts quoted, this was a costly method, and when staiths and spouts came into use they roused the keelman's bitter resentment.

During the strikes of 1794 and 1822 they did all the damage they could to the spouts, and finally they had recourse to the law. In 1824 Wm. Russell was indicted for obstructing the river, and the case came before the York Assizes on 11th August. As the spouts all projected some distance into the river the keelmen alleged they were an obstruction and a nuisance. The owners replied that they facilitated the loading of vessels and thereby increased the commerce of the port and so could not be a nuisance. The case lasted twelve hours and the special jury returned a verdict of " not guilty " in three minutes.

The same matter was again tried on 14th and 15th August, 1828, at Carlisle, and this time after four hours' deliberation the special jury returned the following singular verdict: " We find that the navigable channel of the River Tyne opposite Wallsend has been straitened, narrowed, lessened, and obstructed by the gears described in the indictment, but we find nevertheless that the trade of the town of Newcastle and the harbour of the Tyne has at the same time greatly improved." Both sides claimed the verdict, and the question as to who was to pay the costs was settled in London.

As showing the custom of the trade, the householders of Newcastle would get Wallsend best screened coals at 5s. 6d. per load of 15 cwts., bean coals for 3s. 8d., and small coals for 3s. Orders could be given at the bar of the Royal Exchange Hotel, Hood Street, to Mr G. R. Turnbull, hosier, Westgate, or to Mr Pape, Collingwood Street.

Two interesting visitors came to Wallsend on 9th December, 1815; these were their Imperial Highnesses the Archdukes John and Louis of Austria. They were shown round by Mr Buddle, and took great interest in the work above ground, but no persuasion could induce them to venture down the shaft.

The first accident took place on 21st October, 1782,

about four hundred yards from the " B " shaft. A small blower of gas from the roof fired at a hewer's candle. The man was not hurt, but was greatly frightened; and instead of at once beating out the jet of flame with his jacket, he ran to the shaft and called to the other men near to get away also. John Johnson, an overman, realised the situation, and after vainly asking some of the others to go back with him, went " in-bye " alone. A little while after, when the viewer and his assistants arrived at the place, they found poor Johnson lying suffocated by the after-damp and smoke coming from the fire, which had extended to some bratticing and to the coal, and it was already serious. To get this extinguished, the pit had to be laid in and " drowned out."

This was the forerunner of the following explosions: 6th November, 1784, three lives lost; 12th December, 1784, two lives lost; 9th June, 1785, one life lost; 4th December, 1785, two lives lost; 9th April, 1786, six lives lost; 4th October, 1790, seven lives lost; 25th September, 1803, thirteen lives lost.

The reports of each of these accidents threw the whole village into a panic until the particulars were forthcoming, and in all cases they cast a gloom over the life of the village.

In the early days a meagre light was obtained in dangerous places by sparks from a flint mill—an arrangement worked by a boy, whereby a toothed wheel struck a stream of sparks off a piece of flint. This was thought at first to be a safe way of obtaining a little light, but several explosions took place which cast a doubt upon this method of illumination, and the explosion on 9th June, 1785, was proved conclusively to have originated at one of these light producers. All sorts of expedients were tried, even fish in a phosphorescent state, but the light from this was of little use.

When the Davy lamp was introduced in 1815, it was hoped that it would put an end to these recurring disasters, but unfortunately the tale of loss was still far from complete.

Another sad colliery disaster befell the village in May, 1815. The scene of the accident was not at Wallsend pit but at Heaton. However, the connection between these two places was very close in those days. All the Heaton coals came down by a wagon-way, which passed over the site of Albert Villa, joining the Benton wagon-way near West Street, and were shipped at Wallsend. Many of the miners lived at Wallsend, and hence it came that as a result of this Heaton accident, thirty-nine bodies lie buried at the south-east corner of St Peter's churchyard. Their end was a tragedy indeed.

The old Heaton and Jesmond collieries were abandoned nearly half a century before the date we speak of, and their workings were flooded. The new Heaton shaft was sunk at the lowest point of the seam, and on 3rd May, 1815, two men extending a drift unexpectedly bored into some of the old workings filled with water. The two drifters saw the possibility of danger, and after an earnest discussion they told a boy who was with them to run and tell the other miners to leave work and hasten to the shaft. The lad started off, but the talk of the men and the spouting of the water had frightened him. He was alone and in darkness, and he had not the courage to go away from safety upon his dangerous errand. Instead, he hurried to the shaft and was drawn up to bank. Meanwhile the flood burst in. One of the engineers, Wm. Miller, heard of or saw the threatening water, and sacrificed his life in attempting to do what the boy was too terror-stricken to try. Rapidly the water filled the mine near the bottom of the shaft, and sealed up the only way of escape for the forty-one men and thirty-four boys still in the pit.

The officials at the surface knew from the depth of the water that the men in the pit were higher than the level of the water, and that a large part of the workings were still clear of water. Horses were available in cases of extreme hunger, and at first there seemed every hope of getting the men out alive, but in spite of the greatest efforts the water could not be cleared. Old shafts were tried (one being in front of Heaton Hall), the best advisers were called in, scores of schemes were discussed, but every plan failed and the heartbreaking days slipped by. Hope darkened into despair, and nine weary months passed before the bodies of the seventy-five men and lads were reached. They were high above the water level, and had fixed sticks to act as a water gauge, and they had been forced to kill a horse for food, but in the course of time the lack of fresh air had put an end to their anxieties and miseries.

On 20th February, 1816, the remains of fifty-one men and boys were laid to rest at Wallsend, and sixteen days later eight more bodies were added, and, as I have said, the south-east corner of St Peter's churchyard became a reminder of one of the most tragic stories in the annals of our district. Three of the boys were only seven years of age.

The next Wallsend casualty was an explosion on 5th August, 1818, in which four lives were lost. Then there was freedom from accident until Tuesday, 23rd October, 1821, when about eight o'clock in the morning the pit once more fired. The force of the explosion was terrific; it shook the ground above, and made the furniture and crockery in the houses " dance." Fifty-six men and boys were in the pit, and of these only four survived. Two of the four were Edward Comby, who afterwards took part in an attempted rescue in the 1835 explosion, and William Johnson, who was killed in the great explosion.

Four of the killed were buried at the Ballast Hills, Newcastle, two in the Holy Cross churchyard, and forty-six at St Peter's, fourteen of whom were buried in one grave as they were all related to each other.

In 1831 the High Main seam, which had been the source of so much wealth, was closed, although it was not quite exhausted. The yearly bonds of the pitmen in the north were due to expire on 5th April, and the men belonging to forty-seven collieries on the Tyne and Wear refused to renew them except on better terms.

The matter was not so much one of wages as of objectionable conditions. The first mass meeting of the men was on 21st March, when twenty thousand pitmen assembled on Newcastle town moor.

In the first part of April there was much excitement and agitation, and on the 18th over a thousand strikers marched to Blyth and Bedlington, and forced the men there to lay the pits idle. The strikers did a good deal of damage to property, both on this day and at other times. Several mass meetings were held without disturbances, but all over the affected area detachments of troops were on duty. Wallsend was one of the centres where disorder was feared, and during the strike both cavalry and foot soldiers were stationed here, and constantly patrolled the area. The strike, generally speaking, failed in its purpose, and in June the men gradually returned to their work.

At the end of this section we deal with some of the conditions of pit employment at this period.

The strikers would not allow the shifters to go down to keep the rolley ways open, and when the strike was over the ways in the High Main seam had "crept" so close that it was not worth while to re-open them.

Ten years prior to this the Bensham seam, which lay two hundred and four feet below the High Main, had been opened out, and at the time of the strike it was reached by shafts at the " A," " C," and " G " pits, and hence from 1831 until the colliery was laid in all the coal won was taken from this seam. This coal, however, was a gas coal, and not a house coal. Gas making was then in its infancy and the market for this class of fuel was restricted; furthermore, its fiery nature in the mine increased the difficulties of ventilation and the risks to life and property. All this tended considerably to lessen the profits of the enterprise.

Of the dangerous nature of this seam many illustrations were given, but the most serious of all was the explosion of 1835.

This occurred in the afternoon of Thursday, 18th June, 1835, and involved the death of a hundred and two men and boys. It plunged the whole of our district into distress and mourning, and awakened an intense feeling of sympathy and pity all over Tyneside. It was the greatest disaster known in the history of Wallsend.

Several fragmentary accounts have been published, of which Mr John Buddle's is the most complete, but his report was written largely for mining experts, and furthermore he represented the owners concerned.

After carefully examining the daily newspapers, the special news sheets issued, the official accounts and all the material available, we have compiled and printed in the Appendix a detailed story of the tragic event which will always form an interesting page in our local history.

This great disaster caused the owners seriously to consider the position of the collieries. For some time past these had not been paying as they used to do, and while profits were getting smaller, working expenses were increasing owing to the methods of coal mining at that time being still crude and costly. Furthermore, the question of dealing with the quantity of water coming from the High Main was becoming more and more serious, not only to Wallsend, but to all the collieries in the neighbourhood, and so as soon as the colliery had been put once more into order as a going concern, William Russell advertised in the Newcastle newspapers of September, 1836:

> To Let by proposal as from 2nd November next, all the Wallsend Colliery as a going concern for the remainder of the Lease, which expires on November 20th, 1848. At the staiths vessels of 20 Keels burden may load.

No suitable offer was made, and the colliery went on for the time being as before. Two years later a mysterious occurrence took place on Wednesday evening, 19th December, 1838, between six and seven o'clock. Eleven shifters went down the pit, and so far as those at bank could see, things went on as usual, but about ten o'clock a messenger arrived at the " C " shaft, sent by the furnacemen at the bottom of the " B " pit nearly a mile away, to say that foul air was coming in large quantities from the east, and they wanted to know if there was anything wrong. Those on the surface told the messenger that all was right, but on going below to where the shifters were supposed to be working, they found that every man had been killed. Strange to say, all the horses except one were found unharmed. The cause of this accident was never discovered.

As the termination of the current lease drew near, Mr Wm. Russell intimated to the leasers that he would not ask for a renewal, and so once more, after an interval of ninety-one years, the Dean and Chapter of Durham advertised the Wallsend royalties to " let."

The Bensham seam was supplying all the " vend," and although the Low Main and Beaumont seams had been bored to, they had not been worked.

No applicants appeared at the time, and hence the famous colliery was closed on Saturday, 20th November, 1847, and the machinery, plant, and staiths were put up to auction on Monday and Tuesday, 15th and 16th May, 1848.

Part of the plant, etc., was bought by Messrs Wm. Archbold (the well-to-do owner of the Queen's Head Hotel, Newcastle), David Burn (of Ridley Villas, Newcastle, whom we have mentioned in connection with Bigges Main), and George Clarke of Walker, and in 1848 they took a lease of both the coal seams and the colliery houses.

It is said that owing to the water trouble they made no profit, but they managed to " carry on " until June, 1854, when their workings were hopelessly flooded out and abandoned. A few months afterwards the colliery, pit cottages, etc., were taken over by Messrs Losh, Wilson & Bell of the Low Walker iron works. They had an idea that the Low Main seam might be worked, and Mr T. E. Forster began to direct preliminary operations, but there were no means of keeping the water at bay, or confining it within bounds, and the attempt was given up. Messrs Losh, Wilson & Bell, however, continued to hold the cottage property and other colliery buildings for several years.

The events which brought about the flooding of this celebrated colliery are worth recording. The same disaster closed Wallsend, Willington, Bigge Pit, Bigges Main, and Hebburn. It brought serious and unexpected loss to owners and workmen alike, and a little later we outline the main facts of this mid-Tyne calamity.

THE RUSSELL FAMILY.—The name of Russell must always be closely associated with this era of the mining history of Wallsend. For three-quarters of a century the fortunes of the vast majority of the inhabitants of the village were directly, or indirectly, bound up with the interests and enterprises of this family, therefore they deserve more than merely a passing mention.

The Russells belonged to Cumberland, but in the year 1700 Matthew Russell went to Sunderland, and established himself there as a timber merchant. About fifty years later he took his nephew William into the business, and when he died in 1760 he left him half his considerable fortune.

The firm then consisted of William Russell, Robert Allan, John Maling, and Thomas Wade. To their merchant business they had gradually added bill broking and money lending. Presently, they developed into the earliest bankers in Sunderland; thence it came that when the Chapmans were in need of money it was lent them by this firm.

The Russells

William Russell married Mary Harrison, daughter of Robert Harrison, a Wearside merchant, and Wm. Russell's two partners, Allen and Maling, married Mr Harrison's other daughters, Elizabeth and Anne.

For some reason Maling did not participate in the advance of money to the Chapmans, and as we have already said, Allan withdrew immediately after the foreclosure of the mortgage.

William Russell had been a well-to-do merchant and trader up to the year 1781, when the Wallsend colliery began to make him, who was the principal partner, an exceedingly wealthy man.

He now aspired to take a leading position in the county, and as a first step, in 1796 he bought Brancepeth Castle and estates from Sir Henry Vane Tempest, Bart., for £75,000, and lived there in great state.

The older county families resented his pretensions, and especially when in 1800 he put up his son, Matthew, to contest a parliamentary election in the city of Durham, against the son-in-law of Sir Henry Vane.

Feeling ran high,[1] and Matthew Russell was not elected, but his father bought him a pocket borough, and he entered Parliament as member for Saltash in Cornwall in the following year.

William Russell, the elder, did not do much for the place which brought him so much wealth. He helped to equip a Wallsend Corps of Riflemen, which was commanded by Mr John Buddle, but that seems to have been the extent of his interest. For his second wife, he married Anne, granddaughter of Sir Ralph Milbank, Bart., who was part owner of Willington township. He died at Brancepeth Castle on 8th June, 1817, in his eighty-third year, a wealthy but a disappointed man.

He was succeeded by Matthew Russell, his son, who on his father's death was accounted one of the richest commoners in England. He died only five years after his

[1] See Mining Institute papers (Wallsend).

father, on 8th May, 1822, aged fifty-seven years, leaving a daughter, Emma Mary, and one son, William, who succeeded to the estates and the Wallsend royalties.

William Russell the younger was elected Member of Parliament for Durham, in 1830, without a contest, where his father had failed thirty years before. He was a straightforward man, and a good consistent Whig, who voted for the Reform Bill, although it swept away three of his own " pocket " seats. He it was who decided to allow the Wallsend leases to lapse, because the profits had sunk to nothing. He died, unmarried, at Brancepeth Castle, on 30th January, 1850, at the age of fifty-two, and left his great wealth to his sister.

This sister had on 9th September, 1828, married Gustavus Hamilton, only son of Viscount Boyne, and on her accession to the Russell estates, the Boynes added Russell after their family name, which became Hamilton-Russell. We need not pursue the history of this family further, as its connection with Wallsend ceased soon after 1850.

JOHN BUDDLE.—Another name almost as prominent in this period of our history is that of Mr John Buddle, one of the foremost mining engineers of his day.

His father, John Buddle, senior, in early life was a schoolmaster at Chester-le-Street, whence he removed to Kyo, near Tanfield, and there his son John was born in the year 1773.

John received nearly the whole of his education at his father's school, and at an early age showed a special liking for scientific studies. Mr Buddle, senior, was more than a schoolmaster, for in his leisure hours he took great interest in the problems connected with coal mining and kindred subjects, and corresponded with Hutton and other well-known men of his time. Owing to his known abilities in this direction he was appointed manager of the Russell coal mines.

Mr Buddle, senior, at Wallsend was the first to use cast iron tubing for damming back water in shafts, and in many other ways fully justified his appointment to the management of the mine.

John Buddle the younger at an early age began to assist his father in matters connected with the pits, and he too showed special aptitude for mine management. In 1806 Mr Buddle, senior, died, and his son, then aged thirty-three, was put in charge of the Russell collieries.

From this time onwards John Buddle steadily rose in his profession, until his name was known wherever the art of coal mining was pursued, and locally his designation " King of the Coal Trade " showed that his attention and study were directed not only to the engineering problems involved, but also to the commercial side of coal mining.

It had been customary to allow large pillars of coal to remain untouched in order to support the roof and permit the ventilation of the pit, and under this method of working about forty-five per cent. of the coal was lost. In the years 1809 and 1810 Mr Buddle instituted an improved system: he divided the area into districts, separated from each other by a barrier of solid coal to prevent " creeps," then after reaching the boundary of the coal royalty, he worked back towards the shaft and took out the pillars or " broken." By this system he got out almost the whole of the coal available.

His experience and skill was not confined to the enterprises of Messrs Russell and partners, but his advice and assistance was sought from far and near.

When the Marquis of Londonderry began his scheme at Seaham, which he confidently threatened would cause the streets of Sunderland to be covered with grass, he entrusted his great work to John Buddle. The making of Seaham Harbour was an immense undertaking for a private individual, and the foundation stone of the north pier has a plate commemorating the fact that:

In this undertaking the founder has been chiefly advised by the tried experience and indefatigable industry of his valued friend and agent John Buddle Esq. of Wallsend.

At Wynyard Park there is a large oil painting depicting the laying of the foundation stone of Seaham Harbour on 28th November, 1828. The principal figures are portraits, and No. 1 is John Buddle handing a silver trowel to the Marquis of Londonderry.

He was one of the chief promoters of the Natural History Society of Newcastle. He urged upon the coal-mining world the need of making and keeping in an accessible place complete records of the plans, etc., of all coal workings, and as an example he published a model record with plans and sections of Wallsend pit. He did excellent work as a member of the Dean Forest Mining Commission, and in many other ways took a foremost place in his profession.

As the Russells rarely visited Wallsend, and as Mr Buddle represented the owners in all things, the position he occupied in the village was a good deal more than that of colliery viewer and manager. He acquired the lease of a considerable area of land at Carville, upon which many of the colliery houses were built. He organised a Volunteer Rifle Corps, of which he was the captain. It began on 1st June, 1803, and within twelve months it had one hundred and forty-five efficient members. This corps was well maintained, for a muster roll dated 28th April, 1812, shows one hundred and forty-seven members.

His house was the centre of much hospitality, and he was one of a group of enthusiastic local musicians which usually met at his house. It included Dr Huntley of Howdon, and Thos. Haswell of North Shields.

As an employer of labour he was liked and respected. He always paid the highest current wages to his men and he invariably looked after the widows and orphans of the all too many men who lost their lives in his pits.

Both he and his sister, Miss Buddle, were ever ready

to listen to the wrongs and complaints and troubles of those around them, and in the more serious disputes it was a common practice to lay the matter before Mr Buddle, whose wise and often humorous decision would be cheerfully accepted.

Among the work people of Wallsend he always spoke in the vernacular, and many stories could be told of his kindly ways. There was a half-witted lad whose father had been killed down the pit, and who was enabled, as an act of charity, to support his widowed mother by his earnings. Mr Buddle kept him employed on the corving heap at the West pit as a corf " dadder," to clean and dry the corves after they had been emptied, previous to their being sent below to be refilled. For this light job he had eighteen pence a day with free house and firing. Some of the other lads vexed him one day by telling him he had too little pay; for So-and-so, naming another " dadder," had a shilling and sixpence for the same work.

Next time Mr Buddle passed he intercepted him, and complained of this gross injustice in his own artless way, begging that he would speak to the master corver (Mr Coulthard) about it. Mr Buddle heard him to an end, and then said to him very gravely, " Aye, hinny, we'll see to that. Aw'll speak to the maister corver aboot it. Elways come to me when thou's put upon, and aw'll see thee rightit." The lad was quite contented, and he was in future always paid by one shilling and one sixpence and often a few coppers over.

In religion Mr Buddle was a Unitarian and one of the Rev. Wm. Turner's congregation. In politics he was a Liberal and supported the " Reform " party. On 10th October, 1843, after a distinguished and useful career, he died at Wallsend in his seventieth year. On Monday, 16th, he was buried at Benwell, and the funeral was one of the most impressive ever witnessed at Wallsend. Sixty gentlemen from a distance breakfasted at Mr Buddle's house, and at noon an immense procession started for

Benwell. In front were fifty gentlemen on horseback, then followed a band of mutes, then the hearse drawn by four horses, next nine mourning coaches with relatives, thirty-seven private carriages, and hundreds of friends, neighbours, and the workmen from the collieries with which he was connected. Thirty more private carriages, including those of the Coal Trade Committee, joined at Eldon Square. Among the local gentlemen noted as present were Wm. Losh, John Grace, Edward Grace, John H. Coutts, Jos. Hetherington, John Redhead, George Johnson, John Reay, and the Rev. John Armstrong.

Mr Buddle's household furniture at Carville was sold by public auction on 19th March, 1844, and the following days. He never married, and he bequeathed his estates at Wallsend and Benwell, and his colliery property at Stella, Backworth, and elsewhere, to the value of over £150,000, to Robert Thos. Atkinson, the son of his sister. Mr Atkinson had been trained as a mining engineer under Mr Buddle, but on inheriting this estate he retired and lived at High Cross House, Benwell. He died on 9th March, 1845, leaving two daughters and one son. His daughter, Ellen, married Wm. Robson of Hoyle, Robson & Co. Annie married Benjamin C. Browne, afterwards Sir Benjamin C. Browne. The son, Buddle Atkinson, inherited the bulk of the Buddle property, and as he was a minor, the trustees, Lord Armstrong, Amorer Donkin, Thos. Sopwith, administered the estate, which considerably increased in value before 1862, when the heir came of age.

Mr Buddle Atkinson was for some years in the Royal Artillery. He married Miss Clara Draper in 1863, and had four children. He died on 7th December, 1880. His eldest son, Mr Frank Buddle Atkinson, succeeded to the estates. He chose the Army as his profession and had retired from it when the war began in 1914. He offered for service, and he served in the Durham Light Infantry at home and overseas. At the Armistice he retired with the rank of Captain. He resides at Gallowhill, near Morpeth.

The Mid-Tyne Coal Basin Overwhelmed

In 1850 the mid-Tyne collieries seemed still to have a lengthy and prosperous future before them, yet all unseen a disastrous end was near at hand.

For some little time the coal owners of the district had been pursuing a policy which was to bring overwhelming ruin upon their properties. That this policy was adopted from absolutely selfish motives and to save their own pockets regardless of other owners, makes the subsequent destruction of their pits one of the most dramatic chapters in the history of coal mining.

All the pits in the mid-Tyne area had to deal with very considerable quantities of water coming through the small layers of sand found in the overlying boulder clay. The first Wallsend shaft was abandoned owing to this, and the " A " shaft nearly shared the same fate. In sinking the " C " pit, a feeder giving off one thousand seven hundred gallons a minute had to be wedged back by oak boards or " cribs " nine inches thick, and all the collieries had similar difficulties.

As the High Main seam became worked out, little effort was made by any of the owners to keep it clear of water, which followed the " dip " of the seam, and presently flooded out the " Tyne Main," one of its lowest points. The other owners then realised that by and bye the water would reach them, and would pour down their shafts from the High Main into their lower seams, and hence the owners of Willington, Wallsend, Walker, Heaton, Felling, and the Tyne Main arranged in 1843 to subsidise the owners of the Friars Goose pit, near the Tyne Main colliery, to maintain sufficient pumping power going to keep the water level down.

However, after this arrangement was made several of

these owners inserted "tubing" into their shafts to prevent water from the High Main entering their own lower seams, and as soon as they thought they had made themselves individually safe, they gave notice to withdraw from the joint pumping agreement, regardless of the others.

In consequence of these withdrawals the Friars Goose engine stopped pumping in September, 1851, and the result was appalling. Gradually the water rose, and only the Walker pit stood the strain. The water pressure was far beyond expectation. Jarrow, which had no "tubing," suffered first. At Wallsend the "tubing," which had been put in by Mr Buddle, proved unequal to the test, and the mine was inundated and stopped in June, 1854.

When the Willington owners saw destruction flooding towards them, they hoped they might yet save their mine. They built a large massive stone engine house at the Low pit and ordered a very powerful pumping plant, but before the machinery could be put into the engine house the water "drowned out" the low-lying seams. The work was stopped at Low Willington in February, 1855, and the owners realised that the control of the water was beyond them, and gave up the effort. The Bigge pit held out a year longer, but was "drowned out" and obliged to close on 13th February, 1856. Bigges Main was abandoned in August, 1857. Hebburn held on for a little while longer, their shafts had been tubed off, but under the increasing pressure of the water the tubing in their "C" pit began to leak in 1858, and while the engineers were viewing this with intense anxiety, the barrier in their "A" shaft collapsed in May, 1859, and Hebburn colliery also speedily filled with water.

As we have said, Walker alone withstood the general disaster and their tubing alone proved equal to the pressure.

It was in this way that the earlier part of our coal mining period closed.

This stoppage of the collieries affected the Bigge pit village, Battle Hill, more than the other colliery villages in our parish. Before the pit closed Battle Hill was a populous place. There was a school in which Thomas Davidson, afterwards grocer and postmaster at Willington Quay, was assistant master. There was a Wesleyan Methodist chapel which held over four hundred people. Although at the Scar Hall there was a large provision shop, now occupied by the successors of Mr Stafford and the late Mr George Dixon, one colliery cart went every week to Newcastle for groceries for all and sundry, and two extra carts were needed on the pay week. One of these went via Benton and called at the Willington High Row, and the other went via the Rose hill and called at the Low pit.

Of the busy village at Battle Hill hardly a vestige remains.

SOCIAL CONDITIONS NEAR THE END OF THE EIGHTEENTH CENTURY

It is impossible to deal with the social conditions of the people at every period we have written about, but we have endeavoured to give some idea of our two townships during the fourteenth century and, as one hundred and fifty years ago the whole of England was passing through a very serious industrial revolution, we will try to show how this affected our district. The period embracing the later years of the eighteenth century and the early years of the nineteenth was that during which the social severance between the employers and the employed greatly widened.

In the days of Elizabeth every cottage had to have four acres of land allotted to it, and every inhabitant had his rights in the common lands. This commendable state of affairs had greatly altered before the end of the eighteenth century, but it was during these years and the early years of the nineteenth century that the small freeholders and yeomen were finally elbowed off the land.

From time immemorial the small householder had kept a cow and one or two pigs and a few geese which fed by right upon the common lands guarded by the village herd. Their allotments provided a large proportion of their food, and the moors and woods a large portion of their firing.

The close of the eighteenth century saw nearly all these rights wiped out owing to Enclosure Acts, promoted by men who saw the increasing value of land and the growing prospects of coal mining.

In our parish the amount of land taken from the commons at this period was insignificant as the townships were already enclosed, but we have two glaring examples just over our northern boundary.

Until after the middle of the eighteenth century, immediately to the north of our parish there was a wide expanse of open unenclosed common. The area was over three thousand two hundred acres in extent and stretched from Earsdon westward to North Gosforth, with a few clusters of houses like Long Benton lying at the side of the main tracks which crossed the great moorland. There were few trees, several wide ponds, and a good deal of brushwood. The tenants living in the townships and the owners had rights of pasturage, etc. Brand quotes from the Priory deeds dated 1378: " Every cottager in the township of Tynemouth shall have common for his animals on the common moor, viz., Shire moor at all seasons of the year and not elsewhere." The eastern portion of this was the Tynemouth Shire moor, which had an area of one thousand three hundred and five acres.

In 1788 an Act of Parliament to enclose the moor was obtained on behalf of thirty-six persons. The small occupiers who had " rights " on the moor were bought out for small sums (the fact that they had no power to barter away the rights of the next generation was ignored). Roads were set off for the public use and the rest of the moor was " awarded " to the promoters of the Act of Parliament which authorised the enclosure.

Social Conditions

The Duke of Northumberland received two hundred and seventeen acres, Ralph Milbank ninety-five acres, John Lawson seventy-two acres, Edward Collingwood eighteen acres, and the remainder was distributed among the other promoters of the Act of Parliament.

Immediately after this the owners of lands on the west side of the moor followed suit, hence two years afterwards a similar Act of Parliament was passed to enclose Killingworth moor, which consisted of one thousand nine hundred acres. The rights of the small occupiers were, as usual, "bought out," and the whole area was awarded to twelve neighbouring landowners, Calverley Bewicke and Shaftoe Craster receiving three hundred and nineteen acres. The award was signed on 1st July, 1793, and is deposited at the Moot Hall.

The rapid introduction of machinery superseding home industries did not cause distress in our district as it did elsewhere, but other legal enactments, in addition to the Enclosure Acts, did a great deal to lower the social position of the industrial class on Tyneside near the end of the eighteenth century. Corn laws for the protection of the landlords and farmers forced up the price of wheat so that in 1800 and 1801 it was 128s. per quarter, and the only bread of the working people in Wallsend was rye bread. Furthermore, laws were passed and put in force which in effect tied the labourers hand and foot to their employers.

It was under these circumstances that the poorer people were driven into the mines, where they worked under conditions which are hardly conceivable to-day.

Wages were so low that children had to be sent to work as soon as ever they could earn a shilling or two, and in this district nearly all the boys had to go into the pits.

Boys seven and eight years old were employed underground for twelve hours a day, this involving thirteen to fifteen hours from their homes. A report published as late as 1842 by a government inspector who visited our district, says there were one hundred and seventeen boys in the Willington mines under the age of eighteen, and he gives instances of children aged five being sent underground. We have recorded an accident at the Bigge Pit, where at the inquest a child nine years of age was held to be responsible for the disaster. These boys were dependent upon Sunday Schools for any education they received, and it is surprising to learn from the inspector's report that one hundred and two out of the one hundred and seventeen boys at Willington could read.

At Howdon, the salt workers, the glass-makers, and the men engaged at the Howdon dockyard were working for kindly, reasonable employers, and so far as their daily work was concerned, no complaints were made, but at the mines the men were working under really servile conditions.

Here is an announcement published—a hue and cry raised to secure two men:

GENERAL HUE AND CRY
PITMEN ABSCONDED—MAY 16TH, 1799

Whereas about five Weeks ago Robert Simpson and about five days ago Ra. Boggan Bound servants to Messrs. Bell Brown & Co. at Bigge's Main Colliery have left their employment without leave. It is particularly desired that no Person will employ the said Robert Simpson and Ra. Boggan otherwise Prosecutions will be entered against any Person so doing and whosoever will give Information where either of the said Pitmen are shall be rewarded for their trouble.

Here is another from a Newcastle newspaper in May, 1786:

PITMEN DESERTED
FROM WILLINGTON COLLIERY

Martin Shipley, Thos. Calley, Luke Robson, Joseph Anderson, James Tindell, Matthew Purdy, John Miller, Wm. Frame and John Frame.

It is desired by Matthew Bell Esq. & Co. that no Coal Owner or their Agents, or any other person whatever, may employ the above Pitmen after this notice, otherwise they will be prosecuted as the Law directs.

The pitmen were obliged to sign yearly bonds of

employment, and the laws made by Parliament held the men down under most unrighteous terms. " If any artificer, miner, collier, keelman, pitman, putter or labourer, shall contract with any person for any time, or term, and shall absent himself from his service before the time of his contract is completed " he might be apprehended, and any one Justice of the Peace might sentence him " for any time not exceeding three months nor less than one."[1]

When a man left his work without permission he was a fugitive, and a reward was upon his head. Any Justice of the Peace could sentence him, there was no need to bring him before a Court, and he could not merely fine him, he must send him to prison for at least one month.

It will be seen by these notices that anyone who employs the missing men " will be prosecuted as the law directs " and 9 Anne, c. 28, s. 9 provides that any coal owner or his agent who hires, retains, or employs anyone employed by another owner incurs a penalty of £5.

It, however, did not pay the coal owners to imprison their men. What really happened was that they got him back to work with the threat of gaol and fined him themselves. If a man lay off a day, they usually fined him two shillings and sixpence so that he had to work nearly another day for nothing.

While the men were bound hand and foot to the colliery for a year, there was no guarantee that wages would be given him when pits were slack. In 1812 the coal trade was very bad, and the coal owners held a meeting in the Assembly Rooms, Newcastle, on 26th June, to consider what should be done regarding the men who were starving. It was " Agreed that when wheat is from 35s. to 45s. per boll, ninepence per week be allowed each child or individual unemployed when the weekly earnings of the family shall be under 5s. per week per head. When wheat

[1] 6 George III, c. 25, s. 4.

is from 28s. to 35s. per boll, sixpence per head per week be allowed." (Bread corn was then 44s. per boll.)

Needless to say that no trade unions of workmen were permitted, although the colliery owners formed huge combinations to limit the sales and fix prices.

In 1793 social friendly societies were permitted, but any association to influence wages involved transportation. As late as 1834, six Dorset men who formed a society of agricultural labourers were arrested. There was no evidence even offered that they proposed to ask for higher wages, or thought about a strike. The farmers took alarm as to what they might do, and they were sentenced on 18th March to seven years' transportation, and actually sent to Botany Bay.

Another great hardship which our workmen and tradesmen had to endure at this period was the way the press gang was used, and it was at Howdon where this was most felt.

In February, 1793, war broke out between France and England, and since neither our Army nor our Navy was popular, men between eighteen and thirty were called up by ballot through the militia for the Army, and many were unwilling to go. Tradesmen, mechanics, farmers, who were not classed as yeomen (who were free), and others formed clubs, and when one of their members was "balloted" a substitute was bought and the cost was paid out of the club funds. The cost of a substitute for the Army varied from £5 to £15.

With these offers there does not appear to have been much difficulty in obtaining men for the Army, but with regard to men for the Navy, the matter was very different. The Navy at that time was hated with the bitterest hatred. It is only when you go back to contemporary records that such bitterness and dread is comprehensible. The cruel brutal flogging, for the most trivial offences, the general harsh ill-treatment, and gross injustices inflicted upon the men were infamous.

The officers on board were responsible for the brutal treatment of the men. The officers ashore were responsible for the financial injustices inflicted, e.g., a man after being impressed could only look forward to buying his release. He and his family would save and beg and scrape for two or three years until enough was raised. Then he would get a discharge and a " protection " against further impressment. However, in perhaps a month or two the authorities would issue orders for a special impressment and suspend all " protections," and the unfortunate man would again be dragged off from his family. This was done repeatedly. Furthermore, dearly earned prize money was kept back for years, often until the man was dead, oftener until the man had deserted.

A few captains stand out above this sea of brutality. Nelson and Collingwood had no trouble about men, and we see one young fellow asks his people to see Sir Tom Swinburn to get him into a Captain Bennet's ship.

Our English merchant seamen had no fear of the Frenchmen at sea, and fought their ships whenever the conditions were anything like equal, but if during the course of a battle with a Frenchman, an English war-ship came upon the scene, the contest was abandoned, and the English ship made off as quickly as possible. They dreaded an English war-ship far more than a French privateer.

One result of this hatred of service in the Navy was that the Admiralty had to resort to extraordinary means to secure men for their ships. One method was to make every district supply a fixed number of men. As every parish was included, the number asked from each was not large. In 1796 " the Justices of the Peace, at a General Sessions for the County of Northumberland, fixed three men to be raised for the service of His Majesty's Navy by the townships of Wallsend, Willington, and Howdon Panns and the township of Byker."

How could three men out of this large area be induced

to offer to enter this detested service? This was really a serious question.

A meeting representing the four areas was held at Wallsend on 6th December, 1796, when it was resolved that a wide appeal must be made by handbills and advertisements in the three Newcastle newspapers, and that thirty guineas be offered for each man and that a reward of one guinea be given to anyone who could bring up a man willing to go at this price. But the meeting realised that three men might not be obtainable even for £94 10s., so they empowered the overseers " to go the length of five guineas more to each."

Even thirty-five guineas appears to have been too small an inducement, because at the next meeting the three men had not been obtained, and the " Four and Twenty " agreed to levy a special rate " for the purpose of finding the three men ordered by the justices."

Inducing men by the offer of rewards to enter the Navy was quite fair, but from the ratepayers' point of view it was too costly, and from the Navy point it was too slow. The other method adopted of securing men was cheap to everyone except the unfortunate victims and their families.

The press gang with its system of spies and informers had been employed on Tyneside during the war with our American colonies, especially in the years 1776 and 1777, and now the obnoxious system was revived.

The shipwrights, ropemakers, and other workmen at Messrs Hurry's dockyard could not be touched. They were all building ships or making ropes, etc., for the Government, but there were many seamen, keelmen, tradesmen, and others who were not " protected." Hence Howdon was again and again invaded. Inns and houses were searched and streets swept clean of men, and those caught were taken as they stood and hustled on board the tender lying at Shields.

If, by chance, notice was received that the " press "

was coming they found only women, and these always gave them a warm reception—dirty water played a great part—and a band of small boys and vengeful women with tin cans followed them through the village until they departed. Hiding-places were contrived. Many attics had a false end wall, holes under the flooring were arranged. One place of refuge was the village oven. Two men could get in and lie at the far end, then a fire would be made at the other end. Once the men were discovered, as the woman supposed to be making bread made the fire smoky, and the smoke made one of the men cough just as a " press " man was passing. Often the men and the " press " came to open warfare, although the odds were all in favour of the " press."

In March, 1793, the tender *Eleanor* had a very large number of pressed men on board, and on the 18th it was agreed to try and seize her and rescue them. Five hundred men collected at North Shields armed with swords and pistols, but they found the war-ship fully guarded, so next day the armed party resolved to march to Newcastle to release the men from the collecting place there.

When the rescuers reached Howdon, they came across one of the press gang, George Forster, and they ill-treated him to such an extent that they nearly made an end of him, to the joy and delight of everyone else in the village. Then the party marched on, but meanwhile Newcastle had taken the alarm, the drums beat to arms, the North York Militia and the Dragoons were called out, and with the Earl of Fauconburg at their head a large force marched to the house in the Broad Chare, where the imprisoned seamen were held. When the five hundred found their adventure hopeless they gave up their quest.

For ten or twelve years no family in Howdon where the man was not a dockyard worker went to bed at night without the dread of the press gang pouncing upon him before the morning.

The unjust laws relating to land enclosures and employees, and the equally unjust laws legalising the press gangs, were the outcome of the fact that the " masses " had no voice in the making of the laws or in the government of their country.

In counties, the qualification for a vote was the ownership of a freehold estate in land, worth at least forty shillings a year. A man who merely rented a farm, however large it might be, or a house, had no vote. The voting power lay with the owners alone. Hence no one had a vote in Wallsend township except the curate, who had the glebe land as his freehold, and the owner of the corn tithes.

In boroughs the franchise lay with all sorts of holders. Often it was the owner of the land on which the town was built. In the House of Commons in 1793, there were ninety-seven members elected for " pocket boroughs." (Mr Wm. Russell owned three.) Including the above, three hundred and six of the members were elected by one hundred and sixty persons. Many of the other members bought their seats by almost open bribery.

Such were the social conditions at the close of the eighteenth century; the power was in the hands of the landowners and employers, who used it to its utmost in their own interests. However, there were two movements, one at Howdon and one at Wallsend, which foreshadowed an improved state of affairs.

In Howdon the seafaring men, the shipwrights, and those attached to the dockyard were fully alive to the injustices imposed upon the masses, and they were bent upon having their wrongs righted. In the early days of the French Revolution, when the French people succeeded in throwing off the tyranny of their nobles, a new hope and a new courage sprang up in men's hearts, and an active Jacobin Club was formed at Howdon to help the cause. Its headquarters was at the Half Moon Inn, and all the ardent spirits in the village enrolled as members. When the Bastille fell, great was their enthusiasm and hope, and many in Howdon thought, as Wordsworth later expressed it:

> Bliss was it in that dawn to be alive,
> But to be young was very heaven.

The days of redemption and emancipation seemed at hand.

The leaders of the Howdon Club were John Hench, who built and owned the houses on Henches Hill, and Duncan McLeod, a shoemaker, who, like many of his trade, was a shrewd, well-read man.

When the excesses of the Reign of Terror had shattered the hopes of nearly all, and alienated the sympathy of England, the Jacobin Clubs dissolved, except those few aggressive associations which supported the ideals of the French " through good and through evil report," and one of these few was the Howdon Club. Even when Pitt was forced into war with France in February, 1793, Howdon was still on the side of France, and they must have had some considerable influence beyond our area, for once while Mr Thomas Hurry was in London, the Prime Minister sent for him and began questioning him about Howdon and the Howdonians. Pitt revealed an astonishing knowledge of Howdon and of Howdon men, and finally he produced two miniature portraits which Mr Hurry recognised as his neighbours—John Hench and Duncan McLeod. Pitt's system of espionage was evidently widespread, and Mr Hurry had to undertake to damp down the zeal of his fellow-townsmen, and of the Howdon Jacobin Club, or lose the Government orders. For years afterwards this special interest of England's great statesman in a Howdon Club was a matter of great local pride.

Hence when the eighteenth century closed, although the employee was unfairly treated a spirit of resistance was already aroused and a determination to insist upon reform was already fairly widespread.

The other promise of better days was to be found at Wallsend and was the establishment of the first Friendly Society to be formed in the district.

Until 1793 any kind of banding together of workmen was impossible, but in that year Friendly Societies were made lawful. Wallsend was one of the first established. We have examined the Rules of over thirty Societies formed between Morpeth and Sunderland, and only two of these were begun before that of Wallsend.

This first " Walls End Friendly Society " " held at the house of Nicholas Thornton, Walls End (" The Coach and Horses ") in the County of Northumberland " commenced to enrol members on the first day of January, 1800. The society's aim was to help members in times of illness, distress, or old age; to stop fellow-members quarrelling with each other, not only in the club room, but also outside; to stop the members gambling, or bragging, or taking too much drink (especially on Sundays), and to ensure that they should go to church, although they were not very exacting as to the frequency of this.

In these good old days total abstainers were rare and must have had a hard time of it if they enrolled themselves in a Friendly Society; the rules show that temperance was promoted, but our readers will see that it was promoted in a quaint fashion. I give extracts from the rules which speak for themselves:

> Each member is to appear at the Club House at six o'clock by the clock in the Club House, and from that time until eight shall be in the Club House. . . . If any come after seven, or be absent, shall be fined twopence.
> Every member shall pay one shilling to the box, and threepence for ale every six weeks. If any members send their money, the person who brings it shall have a gill of ale for each man's money, and if any member brings another's money he shall have a gill of ale for each man's money.
> If any member shall drink out of his turn without leave of the stewards, shall pay twopence for each offence except on the head meeting day.

The money was to be kept in a box, two stewards each

had a key, and a " middle key " was kept by the landlord. Also

the Landlord to keep a good fire in the club room from St Michael's day into Lady day next and there shall be an almanack and an hour glass in the Club room.

If the stewards allowed any extra supplies to come into the room they were responsible for the payment. Rule 5 says:

If the stewards shall suffer any more liquor to come in than each man's club it shall be at their charge.

We can imagine that this rule might be a source of great worry and expense to the stewards on a warm summer night, but there were compensations, for we also find:

When they (the stewards) draw any sick money they shall have a quart of ale for each five shillings, and a quart of ale for every member, widow or child's funeral, to be paid out of the next six weeks drinking money.
If any member come into the Club disguised in liquor he is fined sixpence.

One more rule there is concerning this aspect of the society. Rule 13 seems as if it might encourage disputes, for it provides that each member attending a meeting to " settle anything the articles do not clearly decide," is to have a pint of ale.

Members did not come into benefit until they had been in the society a year and a half; after that any

afflicted or seized with sickness or soreness, whereby they are disabled to go about their lawful business, shall have five shillings per week for twenty-six weeks, and two and sixpence per week during the remaining weeks they shall continue their said illness, or during life, or if they be reduced to want through old age or other unavoidable accidents.

If a member died his widow or executors got three pounds out of the " box " and sixpence from each member; this was two pounds more after five years' membership.

If a member's wife died he got thirty shillings plus sixpence from each member and ten shillings extra after five years' membership.

Members got threepence from each fellow-member if their child died " that shall have got church, or private baptism," but if no baptism then no benefit money. In addition to these grants, on a death they got " the loan of the gloves belonging to the box."

As no man on Tyneside knew when he might be hurried away by force into the Navy, naturally they deal gently with members who are " impressed," but they can only take up their membership provided they come back " safe from wounds or lameness."

To curse or swear, or to offer to lay any wager, or " challenge anyone to work at his trade or calling," involved a fine of sixpence. Any member striking at another was fined five shillings if in the Club or two shillings and sixpence if outside. If a member got " drunk on the Sabbath day " he was fined sixpence. " Neglecting public worship once a month," also cost him sixpence.

On 28th January, 1810, a society was formed at Howdon Panns chiefly for shipwrights, which still continues under modern rules; and a women's society, started at the sign of the Rose (Rosehill) on 7th January, 1828, still flourishes.

Two societies for women were also started, one at the " Coach and Horses " and one " at Mr Thos. Swans, innkeeper, Shields Road " (on the west side of Geo. Hill's shop), and their rules were even more sensible than the men's.

The rules of both women's societies are alike and are more stringent regarding order; in fact, so admirable is Rule 8 that no society, nay, not even a Town Council of to-day could improve upon it, and its enforcement would save much misspent time.

It enacts that

Every member of this Society at their entrance into the meeting-room shall pay their respects to the stewardess (chairman) and while they are therein, give them the title of Mistress, or pay two pence fine for each offence, and when the Society is sat, and the Stewardess has called for silence, she who speaks while business is doing shall pay the same. No member shall be allowed to speak while another is speaking, or without leave of the Stewardess, and when any member is speaking all the rest shall be silent under the penalty of two pence for each offence.

The following are some of their other rules:

At the paying of any sister's legacy, they are to take six shillings in ale from the house the Box is kept in, if not in ale, to the same amount of spirits.[1]

The toll for ale or spirits is somewhat heavy, but at almost all funerals in those days it was customary to serve ale or spirits all round, with a piece of cake, before the procession left the house.

She who promotes any discourse about religion, or lays a wager in the meeting room, sixpence fine.[2]

She who puts a period to her own days shall forfeit both funeral charges and legacy to the Box.[3]

Every member who comes into the meeting room disguised in liquor and she who disguiseth herself therewith, shall pay two pence fine.

"Disguised in liquor" is a most happy expression, and is much more exact and expressive than our present equivalent. The respect in which Sunday was then universally held is illustrated by the following rule:

Every member that is disguised with liquor upon the Sabbath day (commonly called Sunday) shall pay sixpence fine, and she who is found drinking in time of Divine Service, one shilling.

These societies or "boxes" served as a useful purpose for over thirty years. They were good first attempts to teach mutual help and self-restraint, and their rules give us a fair idea of the habits and ideals of social reformers in that day. Political clubs like that at Howdon, which sought a wider liberty for the masses, and the establish-

[1] Article 22.   [2] Article 16.   [3] Article 7.

ment of "boxes" at both Wallsend and Howdon for mutual help and discussion, were the first signs that brighter days were to come.

Present-day Collieries

We have seen that the early period of coal mining closed at Wallsend in June, 1854; at Willington, February, 1856; at Bigges Main in August, 1857.

The local mining engineers presently consulted together as to how all the great coal area now lying derelict could be recovered, and they planned a "Tyne Coal Drainage scheme for the drainage of the Coal Basin eastward of Newcastle."

A preliminary meeting was held in the coal trade office, Newcastle, on 24th October, 1860. There were present Messrs Tom John Taylor, T. E. Forster, Edward Boyd, M. Liddle, and John Johnson. It was estimated that a capital of £60,000 would be required; that the coal area to be drained was at least 13,000 acres; that the cost of pumping would be £7,800 per annum, and the interest on the capital £3,000. The coals raised would be 350,000 chaldrons and 8½d. per chaldron would cover all the pumping expenses.

This scheme involved a large undertaking, and it was felt by those at the meeting that the proposed company must be organised under an Act of Parliament.

The matter was further considered, but the difficulties proved too great and the scheme was after a while given up.

The next attempt to open up the flooded collieries was made in 1863, when the prospectus of the Tyne Coal Company Limited was issued. This company was to be formed for the purpose of draining and working the Wallsend, Willington and Hebburn collieries. The shares were £2,500 each and no subscriber was to hold less than two shares. The chief promotors of this scheme were

Messrs James Easton, George Anderson, Joseph Anderson, R. Burdon Sanderson, John Spencer, John Harvey, and J. D. Lambton.

The sinking of a new pit at Wallsend, about thirty yards south-east of the " G " pit, was commenced on 9th August, 1866. This is known as the " H " pit, and is seventeen feet diameter.

Mr James Easton, who was a mining engineer, had, so far, directed the work; but he retired from the active management in August, 1867, and Mr John B. Simpson took charge.

At the " G " pit, two high pressure horizontal pumping engines by Barclay of Kilmarnock were erected. Both engines had forty-four inch cylinders and six feet stroke; one was put under steam on the 30th November, 1867, and the second on 22nd February, 1868. The capacity of the two engines was five thousand gallons per minute. The " puff " of the exhaust of these was heard day and night beyond the parish boundaries for some years. By means of these engines the water in the " G " pit was lowered to a point fifty-five fathoms from the surface in May, 1868, and it was interesting to note that these pumps had considerably lowered the water at Willington and Heaton and, to a smaller extent, at Percy Main, Flatworth, Lawson Main, and Friars Goose.

A large engine-house, a boiler-house and two high chimneys were also erected in order to meet the requirements of two Cornish pumps with cylinders of one hundred inch diameter and with eleven feet stroke.

One of the contemplated Cornish pumps, purchased September, 1868, was erected at the " H " shaft; this was put under steam on 4th June, 1873, when it took the place of the " G " pit Kilmarnock engines, the latter being retained for use in case of emergency.

In March, 1869, it had been decided to defer the completion of the work in progress for a time and continue only to keep the water in the " G " pit at a point fifty-five fathoms from the surface by the drawing of the feeders with the two forty-four inch horizontal engines. This decision was arrived at in consequence of the operations at Hebburn colliery, which clearly proved that there was no connection as regards water between Hebburn and Wallsend. The water at Hebburn was so reduced that in May, 1870, the pit was drained as far as the Low Main seam (one hundred and seventy fathoms), and the company began the shipment of coal from the Hebburn pit. To mark this event the directors gave a dinner in one of their workshops on 10th September to all their workmen and agents. Mr J. B. Simpson, the viewer (under whose direction the Hebburn colliery had thus been reopened), was in the chair, and the principal toast was—" The health of Mr R. Burdon Sanderson, the chairman of the company, the other directors, and the success of the Tyne Coal Company."

By 1873—the " H " pit being three hundred and twenty-eight feet down, one Cornish engine working, and the water in the " G " pit three hundred and thirty feet from the surface—the amount of money already spent deterred the company from carrying their original plans further and they contented themselves with drawing coals from the Hebburn pit only.

In August, 1873, Mr John B. Simpson retired, and in September Mr Chas. Ashley Shute took over the duties of viewer. He was followed in November, 1888, by Mr Ralph T. Swallow.

In 1891 the present company, the Wallsend and Hebburn Coal Company, was formed and took over the Tyne Coal Company as from 22nd February, 1892. This new company was supported by Messrs Norman and George J. Cookson, Geo. Baker Forster, the Strakers of Hexham, the Spencers of Newburn, Wm. Gibson, J. B. Simpson, C. W. C. Henderson, and Geo. Anderson of Little Harle Tower, and their aim was to continue the sinking of the " H " pit and re-open the " G " pit for coal drawing and complete the unwatering of the whole of their royalties. The operations were carried out under the supervision of Mr G. B. Forster.

In December, 1893, Mr Henry Ayton followed Mr Swallow as viewer.

A second Cornish engine was put under steam on 21st May, 1894, and the water being further lowered, the " H " shaft was sunk to the High Main seam by February, 1895, six hundred and seventy-two feet from the surface.

This new company had ample money, skill, and energy at their command, and they proposed to carry out completely the original plans of the Tyne Coal Company. The task they undertook proved to be very difficult, and any company with less wealth and determination would have given it up.

After great difficulties had been overcome the " H " pit passed through the Yard seam and reached a depth of seventy-two feet below the Bensham seam, and the first coals were brought to bank from the Yard seam up the " H " shaft, on 16th August, 1897.

On 16th July, 1898, the Low Main coals, which had for some years been worked from the Hebburn shafts, were drawn from the " G " pit, and on 15th July, 1901, the Bensham seam coal was also worked from the " G " shaft.

In re-opening these shafts, when passing through the old famous High Main seam, to which the Russell family owe so much, it was found that the floor of the seam was squeezed up to the roof in a compact mass.

Mr Ayton died 19th August, 1900, and was succeeded by Mr Robert Simpson Anderson of Elswick colliery on 3rd October, 1900. He later removed to Highfield, Wallsend, and was the first resident viewer since the days of John Buddle.

The output at Wallsend in 1901 was 168,000 tons, and the cost of pumping alone was £16,000 a year, and hence a large output was essential to secure a lower cost per ton.

However, it was found that the pumping operations did not, as expected, drain the water from the old workings at the northern portions of the royalties owing to creeps and stoppages, and so drifts were driven up from the Low Main seam at Wallsend to the Bensham seam near the old Bigge pit workings, and bore holes were put through. Then it was found that the water was at a very high pressure—180 pounds to the square inch. After anxious care, eventually two ranges of pipes were coupled to the bore holes and the water conveyed to the pumps at Wallsend and Hebburn,—night and day, for eighteen months, about 1,700 gallons per minute being run off. In 1904 for every ton of coal raised $8\frac{1}{2}$ tons of water was pumped 1,100 feet to the surface. The drainage of this area liberated over five million tons of coal in the Bensham seam.

Dealing with the gas from these old workings was another trouble, as the ventilating fan was over a mile away at the " G " pit. It was also necessary that the men should not have to travel so far underground to their work.

A new shaft was, therefore, sunk near the Rising Sun Farm. It was commenced on 21st February, 1906, and the Bensham seam was reached, at a depth of 128 fathoms, on 18th February, 1908. A winding engine and screens were erected and coal-drawing was started on 30th September, 1908.

In 1913 the old Edward pit was re-opened and coals were drawn again on 20th October.

On 19th June, 1912, Mr Charles A. Nelson came to Wallsend as assistant to Mr Anderson. Mr Nelson had been a mining engineer under the Var Mines Ltd., in the south of France, for three years, residing at Saint Raphael. After being assistant viewer at Wallsend until 1914 he took full charge of the technical work and a house was built for him at Battle Hill within easy reach of the three Wallsend pits.

In order to insure improved ventilation and make the Rising Sun independent of the " G " pit, a second shaft was put down near the same place and finished on 27th August, 1915.

In January, 1916, Mr Anderson began business on his own account as a consulting mining engineer in Newcastle: he, however, remained estate agent and consulting engineer for the company.

Mr Anderson had installed electric plant to a considerable extent, but Mr Nelson decided on the complete adoption of electric power throughout the collieries, thus superseding the use of steam for winding, ventilating, pumping, and underground work. This he found to be necessary to secure the best output and decrease the costs.

The cost of pumping water (whether the pit worked or not) in 1913 amounted to £8,000, as compared with £16,000 in 1901; but on the other hand in 1914 the output rose to 2,600 tons per day. Then came the war, and 1,173 men enlisted for services and 742 went into the shipyards. As this was fifty per cent. of the whole workmen, in 1916 the year's " vend " dropped to 386,933 tons.

With regard to the coal under the Newcastle Corporation's land at Willington, it was, in the old days, worked by the Temples from Jarrow, until it was drowned out by the general flood. On 4th July, 1883, the Newcastle Corporation signed a lease of the Low Main seam for forty-two years as from 1st January, 1881, to the Tyne Coal Company. There was a certain rent of £225 and a tentale of sevenpence per ton. Coals were worked from this Royalty, under this lease, and brought to bank at Hebburn colliery, but after 1882 these " workings " were a decreasing quantity and the lease was cancelled from 1st January, 1894. After the Wallsend and Hebburn Coal Company got into full working order, the Bensham seam coal was leased to them as from 1st July, 1916, for twenty-one years at a certain rent of £200; coals were first drawn at " G " pit from this district in 1916.

Industrial History—Coal Mining

In October, 1915, in order to facilitate dealing with land and other property, The Battle Hill Estate Company, Ltd., was formed with Mr Robt. S. Anderson as manager and secretary. The company did not come into active operation until 1919.

The " fault " which runs north-east beneath the Rising Sun Farm has a " down-throw " to the north of eighty-four feet at the " Burnt Houses," and as the Backworth Coal Company could reach the Bensham seam north of this fault easiest they arranged with the Wallsend Company to work it, and they worked out these coals between the years 1911 and 1920; the Wallsend Company working the Backworth coal—lying to the south of the fault—in exchange.

In 1920 the " vend " from the Wallsend and Willington pits rose to 524,715 tons. Then came the National strike from 1st April to 30th June, 1921, and the " vend " for this year fell to 474,727 tons. After the pits started working again on 1st July, 1921, the daily output increased, with the result that for the year 1922 the output was: 318,940 tons from " G " pit, 432,392 from the Rising Sun, and 123,260 from the Edward pit, a total of 874,592 tons; the highest day's record being 4,117 tons on Thursday, 14th December, 1922.

A forgotten tunnel.—In 1864 when preparing to re-open the Wallsend colliery, it was proposed to pump fresh water from the Willington Gut into ponds at the " G " pit. An underlevel drift was made from the stream at a point fifty yards south of the main road bridge and a pumping engine actually fixed close to the side of the burn. Neither engine nor culvert were ever used, as objections were made to the water being taken. The boiler house, engine, etc., were removed, and the tunnel under the Cemetery and North Terrace was left to puzzle some future generation.

CHAPTER VI

INDUSTRIAL HISTORY—CHEMICAL PERIOD

Pioneers in alkali manufacture: Wm. Losh, Allen's chemical works, John Glover and the Carville Chemical Co., John Lomas & Company—The decline of the trade on Tyneside and its cause—The Allen family; John Glover—The beauty of the district as the result of this period.

IN the year 1847, when Wallsend was anticipating a gloomy future owing to the closing of the Russell collieries, a new and unlooked-for chapter of our commercial history was opening almost unheeded.

The rise, development, and decline of the alkali trade on Tyneside is an interesting story which has not yet been told, but here I can only tell it sufficiently to make its place clear in the industrial history of Wallsend.

The base of the industry is common salt (chloride of sodium) and the object is to separate the soda from the chlorine. In Le Blanc's process the salt was treated with sulphuric acid, the soda then combined with the sulphur and formed sulphate of soda; next the sulphate of soda was burned with chalk and coal, and the resultant material, after cooling, was broken up and covered with water, the alkali then dissolved out, and it was run off in solution. This alkali liquor was evaporated, and pure alkali (soda ash) was left. The residue, after the alkali liquor was run off, was known as " tank waste " and its accumulations were, until recently, prominent features on the landscapes of Tyneside.

Alkali is used in many industries, but a considerable proportion was re-dissolved in water, then left to crystallise in shallow pans and form soda crystals—the washing soda of our households. The chlorine which was given off from the salt in the first process, after the soda had been extracted, was passed over ordinary lime, which absorbed it and formed chloride of lime, more commonly known as bleaching powder.

The manufacture of these three products—alkali (soda ash), soda crystals (washing soda), chloride of lime (bleaching powder), and their by-products—was for many years our leading industry, and it owes its establishment on Tyneside very largely to two men who were residents of Wallsend: William Losh and John Allen.

Wm. Losh received a considerable part of his education abroad, and was studying chemistry in Paris when the Revolution broke out, and he stayed there until it was no longer safe to do so.

During the French Revolution, a French chemist discovered a new process of making alkali, and after France had finally settled down into normal conditions, Wm. Losh in 1816 returned to Paris to study the new discoveries. As a result he introduced Le Blanc's process into the Walker alkali works as a great advance on their old methods. He began this process at Walker in 1821. Two years earlier Mr Chas. Tennant had started the same process at Glasgow, and these were the first alkali works erected in Great Britain to utilise the French discovery.

After Mr Losh returned from Paris the first time, he married Alice Wilkinson of Carlisle, and for many years lived at Point Pleasant House. While living there, although he greatly extended his Walker works, he was keenly interested in mechanical inventions as well as improvements in chemical processes.

George Stephenson, who was eleven years his junior, was greatly helped by Mr Losh. The budding railway engineer very often spent a large portion of Sunday at Point Pleasant, where the enginewright and the chemical manufacturer used to plan out improvements and experiments, while the draughtsman of the Walker iron works (brought down to Wallsend by Mr Losh) would draw their rough sketches to scale, and put them into workable shape.

Mr Losh himself invented many improvements in furnaces, boilers, tramways, etc. He was a very careful and thrifty man, no one would guess his position in life by his dress, and several humorous stories are told of mistakes made by strangers because of this. In many ways he showed his thrifty habits; he almost always wore a waterproof cover over his high hat to preserve its freshness, and often he would be seen passing through Wallsend with pieces of old iron in his hand, which he had picked up by the wayside, and which would be carefully added to the heap of " scrap " at the iron works.

The other Wallsend man of note in the early history of the chemical trade on Tyneside was one who took a much more active interest in the life of the village.

John Allen was born in the year 1791, and was in early life a chemist and druggist at South Shields. Realising the possibilities of the infant trade, in 1828 he started the third factory on the Tyne for making alkali by the Le Blanc process. This was at Heworth Shore; at first it was on a small scale, and he was in partnership with Mr Thos. Coulterd. His special contribution to the success and growth of the chemical trade was in 1840, when he relieved the infant industry of a danger which threatened to strangle it. It will be seen the chief materials used were salt, sulphur, chalk, and coals. The salt was brought into the Tyne chiefly from Cheshire by sailing ships, coals were close at hand, and chalk came from the south of England. However, as regards the sulphur, in the early days it came from Sicily, and at first it was delivered in the river for £6 to £8 per ton, but in 1838 the King of Sicily gave Messrs Faix and Company, of Marseilles, a monopoly of all his sulphur mines, and this immediately raised the price on Tyneside to £13 or £14 per ton, with every prospect of it going much higher. Under these adverse conditions the very existence of the new manufacture was in danger. Fortunately Mr Allen arrived at the conclusion that the required sulphur could be extracted from pyrites, and in June, 1840, he imported a trial cargo into the Tyne. His experiment proved a success and showed that the French monopoly could be ignored.

When the lease of the premises at Heworth expired, the partnership with Mr Coulterd was dissolved, and Mr Allen decided to open another place on his own account, and he selected a site in Wallsend which had a good river front, just east of the present road leading down into Swan & Hunter's shipyard, on land held by Dame Allan's Charity.

He began to erect his works in 1847 and the unusually high chimney then put up was a local landmark for years. He invited Mr Wm. Russell, who had been his foreman at the Felling Shore, to return from St Helens to be his works manager, and this gentleman (who afterwards turned his attention to copper smelting at Walker) arrived at Wallsend on 28th October, 1848, and took up his abode in the house in High Street East, which had been the Swan Inn (opposite the present café).

The site of the chemical factory is now occupied by the Carville goods yard and the north-east side of the present shipyard. Although it was built out fifty yards beyond high water mark, the state of the river then was such that a trolley way over two hundred yards long had to be constructed over the sand and foreshore to the jetty, where deeper water was available. (See illustration, page 24.)

The alkali works thus started in 1848 grew and flourished, and in 1854 Mr Allen took his son into the business and the firm became Messrs John & Wm. Allen. Mr Allen built the houses on the High Street, eastward of the Old Swan Inn (westward of Sycamore Street), for some of his workmen. In 1857 the alkali works of Messrs John & Wm. Allen were rated at £350, which was higher than any other works in the whole parish. The next highest rated were the iron works of Chas. Palmer & Company, at Wallsend Quay, assessed at £300, Mr Addison Potter's "Coak Gas and Brick works" at Willington Quay, and Messrs Wm. Cookson & Company's Howdon lead works stood at the same figure.

In 1868 the land on which the factory stood was bought from Dame Allan's Charity by Wm. Robt. Swan, the area acquired was bounded by the Station Road, the old railway line, and what is now the south end of Park Road and the river.

In 1862 a second chemical works began working in Wallsend. This was erected by Mr John Glover, and carried on as John Glover & Company until 1868, when it was converted into a limited liability company under the name of the Carville Chemical Company. The site of these works is now occupied by Messrs Parsons' Marine Turbine Company.

The third alkali works was that of Messrs John Lomas & Company. It occupied seven acres between the river and a point a little north of where Point Pleasant railway station stands; it was not begun until the early part of 1871. Mr John Lomas already had works at Jarrow, and when he opened his Wallsend works the chemical trade was booming. Twelve months after beginning operations, the rateable value of the place was £334, but the buildings and plant were so increased that four years later, in 1875, this had risen to £1,723.

The high water mark of success of the Wallsend firms was reached about this year. The rateable value (i.e., the net estimated annual rental value of the land, buildings and fixed plant, after "upkeep" had been allowed for) of the other two works in 1875 were John and William Allen, £2,436; the Carville Chemical Company, £1,335.

The manufacture of alkali and other chemicals constituted for many years our chief industry. The factories were successful in affording employment to a large proportion of our work people and were the means of making considerable profit for the manufacturers, but alas! they were also the means of blighting almost every tree and hedgerow within a mile of the riverside. The hydrochloric acid gas, which was given off during the formation of sulphate of soda, was allowed to escape with deadly effect upon our rural beauty.

The many stately, well-grown trees, chiefly of elm and ash, and the thickets of briar in the Burn Closes, Willington Dene, and other places were almost all destroyed.

The decline of the chemical trade was brought about in two ways. First, as we have seen, the Le Blanc process of making alkali was long and complicated. Presently it was discovered that by passing a stream of carbon dioxide through brine saturated with ammonia, bicarbonate of soda is obtained, and this when calcined yielded alkali. This was a simpler and more direct process than that of Le Blanc, and was destined to supersede it.

In the year 1872 Mr Ludwig Mond visited Ernest Solvay's factory at Charleroi, to examine his ammonia-soda process, with the result that three years later, he, a brilliant chemist, and Mr John T. Brunner, a thorough business man, erected works at Northwich in 1875 for making alkali by a method of their own, which was an improvement on Slovay's.

The ammoniacal process of soda manufacture did not displace that of Le Blanc at once, because an economical method of conserving the ammonia was not quickly discovered, but presently Messrs Brunner Mond & Company made this process a practical success, and hence in England their name has always been associated with it. The Tyneside was not a suitable place at which to carry on the newer method as compared with places in Cheshire, where the brine could be pumped direct from the salt beds into the alkali works.

The other factor in the decline of our Tyneside chemical trade was that the large export of soda crystals almost ceased owing to a very simple cause. Our alkali works all made soda crystals as we have already explained, and they consisted of about sixty-three per cent. of water and thirty-seven per cent. of alkali, i.e., of every ton of washing soda sent from the Tyne to London, Hamburg, or Berlin, about seven and a half hundredweights was alkali, and about twelve and a half hundredweights was ordinary water. Presently some thoughtful wholesale buyer in London, or Hamburg, asked himself why he paid heavy sea freight and railway charges for bringing very ordinary water from the Tyne. Why did he not buy the alkali only, and mix it with Thames or Elbe water himself? Once such a simple question was asked, the doom of the large Tyne export trade in soda crystals was sealed.

However, one considerable product of the Tyneside chemical works still held its own, for in the Brunner process the chlorine from the salt was lost, and therefore chloride of lime would not be made by it, but so far as Wallsend was concerned the new process of making alkali resulted in the closing of all our chemical works.

Of the men connected with this chemical period we have spoken of Wm. Losh of Point Pleasant, but the Allen family and John Glover requires more than a passing mention.

Mr John Allen's first residence in the parish was at Wallsend House, near the original shaft of the colliery, which Mr John Buddle had occupied five years previously. The settlement of Mr Allen at Carville, as the west and south-west side of the township was then called, was not only a gain because his factory was the forerunner of a new industry, but also because he and his family were a distinct acquisition to the religious and civic life of the village.

When he came to Wallsend, he was fifty-seven years of age, and his mature experience and his earnest religious character were soon appreciated by his neighbours.

At the Felling Shore he was a leader of the Methodist New Connexion Church, and was as long as he lived one of of the official trustees for the whole Connexion. He was a widely known local preacher and a man with great influence in his denomination. He retained his membership with the Felling Church for some time after his removal.

Mrs John Allen was the sister of Mr Wm. R. Swan, farmer and lawyer of Wallsend, and she too was an earnest Methodist and did a good deal for their cause. The Wallsend Church was very weak in the "early fifties," and, as we have seen, it was due to Mr and Mrs Allen that the Zion chapel was built in 1857 at the north-east corner of the junction of Station Road and High Street.

On 28th September, 1858, the executors of F. W. E. Peacock offered for sale by public auction the Red House and grounds. This was a mansion house of over twenty rooms, with stabling, etc., and two acres fourteen perches of gardens and grounds, facing the Green where Hawthorn Villas now stand. It was then in the occupation of Mr Thos. Ainsley Cook, a partner in the Walker Alkali Company. This fine old house (see page 97) was bought by Mr John Allen, and he shortly moved there. In less than two years after this, on 10th August, 1860, he died at the age of sixty-nine, and was buried in St Peter's churchyard.

Mrs Mary Allen survived her husband for nearly thirty years, and died at the exceptional age of ninety-three, on 8th December, 1889. Although she left Wallsend fourteen or fifteen years before her death she kept up her interest in her Wallsend church, and every quarter sent two pounds as her "quarterage" until the end of her life. The names of these two worthies are perpetuated in the Allen Memorial Methodist Church, which was built in 1903.

Mr Wm. Allen, who on the death of his father became the head of the firm, also took a keen interest in the life of the village, especially when it was proposed to form a Local Board. He married the eldest sister of Dr James R. Lownds of Walker, and in 1875 he retired from the personal control of the alkali works and he and his family left the Red House and went to live at Bournemouth.

He became a wealthy man after the death of his uncle, " Turney " Swan, and in July, 1887, he bought the Evenley Hall estate at Brackley and went to reside there shortly afterwards.

He died on 10th January, 1905, aged eighty-one years, and his two sons, Major John Allen of Brackley House and Major Wm. Henry Allen of Evenley Hall, now own the Wallsend property.

Mr John Glover, who was the founder of the second chemical factory in Wallsend, was born in Newcastle on 2nd February, 1817, and he was trained as a plumber. Between 1831 and 1845 he had charge of the old Pants which supplied the inhabitants of Newcastle with water in those days. Then for some time he was at John Lee's chemical works at the Felling Shore, and, as we have seen, in 1862 he began a factory on his own account at Wallsend. He built " Glover's Row " in order to provide houses for his workmen, and this was the earliest row of " flats " built in the parish.

When the first Wallsend Local Board was elected in February, 1867, Mr Glover with two hundred and five votes tied with Mr Wm. R. Swan for third place. He was chosen chairman of the Board, and this position, with the exception of one month, he held until July, 1881, when he resigned. He was by no means a progressive member of the authority, but did good work for the district during his fourteen years' chairmanship.

He was well known in the chemical world, and after long study and careful experiment he invented the " Glover Tower," which still holds its own. He declined to patent the idea, although the Tower effected a saving of nitrogenous compounds to the estimated value of £300,000 a year. The Chemical Society, as a slight recognition of his disinterested services, presented him with a gold medal on 15th July, 1896. He never used his talents merely to make money, and died a comparatively poor man on 1st May, 1905, aged eighty-five.

As we have already said, the decay of the chemical industry was a gradual process. There was a serious fire at the factory of Messrs John Lomas & Company on 5th April, 1877, when everything was burnt out except the offices, three hundred men were thrown out of employment, and £20,000 worth of damage was done. The fire began at seven p.m., and the blaze of a building fifty feet high and sixty yards square was seen for miles around. This hastened the closing of these works.

The Tyneside chemical trade in 1881 and 1882 was in a most depressed condition, and both the Carville Chemical Company and Messrs John & William Allen had practically ceased working in 1883.

The complete closing down at "Allen's," however, was still a little way off, as the dying trade showed symptoms of a revival in 1883, and Mr Jos. Edward Lee (the nephew of Mr Wm. Allen), Mr Walter Scott, the contractor, and Mr John Spencer of Newcastle, re-started the works under the title of the Wallsend Chemical Company. In addition to the limited manufacture of alkali, bleaching powder, and soda crystals, this firm also made pale and fancy soaps. The Wallsend Chemical Company continued until the whole of the chemical works on Tyneside were pooled and taken over by the United Alkali Company, which was formed in 1890 with a capital of over £8,000,000. The directors of the new company decided to close "Allen's," and the works were dismantled. The lease of the land expiring on the 31st March, 1894, Messrs Swan & Hunter secured the ground, and erected their east yard upon it.

Here are two descriptions of the beauty of the district, largely the result of the chemical period:

> There's chemicals, copper, coals, clarts, coke an' stone,
> Iron ships, wooden tugs, salt an' sawdust an' bone,
> Keels, an' steam ingins, bar iron an' vitrol,
> Grunstans an' puddlers (aa like to be litt'ral),
> At " Howdon for Jarrow," " Howdon for Jarrow,"
> " Howdon for Jarrow,"[1] maa hinnies, loup out.[2]

For a number of years it was my hap to live at Willington Quay, on Tyneside. That is a most dingy place, of many smells and few beauties. The unloveliness of this region oppressed me at first. Its grime, its noise, its squalor, suggested a suburban hell, tempered with smoky sunlight. In these circumstances, I found it necessary to track down the natural beauty of the neighbourhood, lay snares for it in the twilight, stalk it at dawn—with most fascinating results. Gradually I came to know where this beauty lurked, to trace its swift and secret ways, to wait the happy turn of its times and seasons. There was an expanding sense of freshness and colour when the sea-tide brimmed up from the bar at Shields with a salt sparkle where the winter sun hit the coloured sides of the ships; there was fine appeal in the grey glaze of the river as it slid in the twilight between the black wharfs with their overhanging staiths; there was suggestion of mystery in the midnight fires of Jarrow furnaces as they shot out in palpitant crimson on the black river, where haply a phantom ship passed seaward twinkling with fire on spar and mast.[3]

---

[1] From 1839 until 1872 Howdon was the nearest railway station for Jarrow for passengers from the north and west, and the board at the station proclaimed it was " Howdon for Jarrow."
[2] Tyneside song, Harry Haldane.
[3] Hamish Hendry, in *The Review of Reviews*, 1890.

CHAPTER VII

INDUSTRIAL HISTORY—(*continued*)

Early works—Willington Ropery (established 1785) : The Chapmans, Washington Potts, The Haggies, Frank Dean; Willington Mill (established 1806) : The Unthanks, The Procters and the Ghost, Sampson Langdale; Willington Slipway (established 1835) : The founders, The Adamsons, Wm. Cleland (Clelands Ltd.); Willington Lead Works (established 1844) : Richardson & Currie, The Cooksons; Wallsend coke ovens and furnaces (established 1848) : John Carr, Palmers, Royal Greek Iron Co.—Iron and Steel Shipbuilding :—John H. S. Coutts, Parkinson, Muntsey & Jansen, Palmers; Schlesinger Davis & Co.; C. S. Swan & Co., Swan & Hunter and successors; Marshall, Cole Bros., Tyne Iron Shipbuilding Co.; Northumberland Shipbuilding Co.; Eltringhams Ltd.—Marine Engineering :—Wallsend Slipway & Engineering Co., North-Eastern Marine Engineering Co., Parsons Marine Steam Turbine Co.—Sundry Works :—Walker and Wallsend Gas Co., Tharsis Sulphur and Copper Co., H. D. Pochin & Co., Willington Foundry, Tyne Pontoon and Dry Dock Co., M W. Swinburne & Sons, Newcastle Electric Supply Co., Castner Kellner Alkali Co., Thermal Syndicate Ltd., Wm. Thomas Weir, John Smith's Forge, Tyneside Tramways and Tramroads Co., Co-operative Societies.

EARLY WORKS

The Willington Ropery

THESE works were commenced about the year 1789 by Wm. Chapman of Whitby, a merchant ship captain and owner, who, before he settled down on Tyneside, traded chiefly between the Tyne and the Baltic. He was a shrewd and enterprising man, and when he left the sea began rope-making at Willington.

He died at Saville Row, Newcastle, on 15th October, 1793, and left two sons, William and Edward Walton, who carried on and extended the Willington rope-works.

The elder brother was born at Whitby in 1750, and spent his early youth at sea. Seamanship, however, did not appeal to him, and he started, with the help of James Watt and Matthew Boulton, as a civil engineer. He came to Newcastle in 1794 in order to report upon the proposed Solway to Tyne canal, and, remaining there, he attained considerable success on Tyneside in his profession. He was made a Freeman of the town, and died on 28th May, 1832.

The younger brother, Edward Walton Chapman, was the practical rope-maker, and managed the Willington works. He lived on the spot, in a house on the south side of the road immediately to the west of the present gateway office. He and Robert Oxen were overseers for Willington township in 1804, and he was reappointed for the year following. In 1814 he and Joseph Unthank were the Willington overseers, and they were the last overseers to be appointed especially for Willington until 1894. In 1815 instead of two overseers being appointed for each of the three townships, three were appointed for the whole of the parish, and Edward Walton Chapman was one of the three.

Several useful inventions were patented by the two brothers. One of these was a method of insuring that there should be an equal strain upon each and all of the separate strands of the rope. This was a great advance upon previous methods and was the beginning of modern hemp rope-making. Another invention was a machine for making a rope of endless length. This created more than local interest, and after a long life of one hundred years it is still at the Ropery in good going order.

Mr William Chapman died on 29th May, 1832, aged eighty-two years, but he had retired from partnership in the Ropery some ten years before his death, for although the lease of the rope works was renewed in his name on 25th March, 1820, at a rental of £40 a year, Edward was regarded at that date as the sole owner.[1]

[1] Parson & White's Directory, pub. in 1828

Probably because of his brother's retirement Edward W. Chapman took another partner into the business about 1829, and the firm became Chapman & Potts.

In "Men of Mark" it is doubtingly suggested that William Chapman, one of the partners who began to sink the Wallsend colliery and failed before the coal was reached, was the same as the William Chapman who started the Ropery. We can find no evidence to support this theory, and the indirect evidence against it is very strong. William Chapman, who founded the Ropery, was for a large part of his life a Whitby man, and the Wallsend colliery Chapmans were a Newcastle family. Furthermore, the colliery Chapmans had reached the end of their financial resources by 1781, and in the Mining Institute papers relating to Wallsend colliery there is a copy of the following notice:

A meeting of the Creditors is called for 26th October, 1790, by the Commissioners in a Commission of Bankruptcy awarded and issued forth against Wm. Chapman and John Chapman of the Town and County of Newcastle-upon-Tyne, Dealers, Chapman & Co-partners in Trade.

This shows that their financial affairs were still unsettled in 1790 and hence they could not have established the Willington rope-works in 1789 while their affairs were in the Bankruptcy Court.

The new junior partner in the Ropery was Mr Washington Potts, who quickly settled down into the public life of the district, for on 4th April, 1831, he was appointed by the "Four and Twenty," together with Mr John Reay, as Collector of Assessed Taxes. This post was not one sought after, and Mr Potts was not present when he was appointed, but the holders were changed every year and therefore it did not fall heavily on any one person. However, on 23rd April, 1832, Mr Potts was elected a churchwarden, which was a much more desirable position. He built for himself Low Willington Villa, which afterwards became the family residence of Mr Robt. Hood Haggie, then of Mr Arthur J. Haggie, and lastly of Mr Frank Dean.

In the closing years of the eighteenth century, the rope-making business in Newcastle area was in the hands of four firms. The heads of two of them, William Cramlington and Francis Peacock, were residents in Wallsend.

About the year 1800 a new firm was established at the South Shore, Gateshead—Messrs Pollard, Haggie & Co. The senior partner was James Pollard, who lived in Westgate Street, and the junior partner was David Haggie, who resided in Oakwell Gate, Gateshead, which was then a fashionable residential quarter.

This David Haggie came from the north of Scotland and was the first of a long succession of Haggies who have made the name widely known throughout the ropemaking world.

Mr Haggie had three sons, Robert Hood (born 1810), David, and Peter. When these sons had grown up, the firm of Pollard, Haggie & Co. dissolved and the younger generation launched out on their own account.

Their mother was a Miss Sinclair whose sister married one of the Hoods, well known in the timber trade, and it may have been owing to this family connection that the Haggies went into the business of selling timber as well as the business of making ropes. At all events we find that in 1843 David Haggie, junior, Peter Haggie, and their father were in partnership under the style of Haggie Bros. as ropemakers, timber merchants, and chain manufacturers, with their business place on the South Shore, Gateshead.

Mr Robert Hood Haggie married Miss Elizabeth Knox of Newcastle at St Nicholas' Church in August, 1832, and in 1843 he was trading on his own account as Robert Hood Haggie & Co., timber merchants, with a yard at the South Shore, and he was also carrying on under his own name only the Willington Ropery which he had acquired from Mr Washington Potts about three years before this. The office for both businesses was 61 The Close, but he himself resided at that time in Mulgrave Terrace, Gateshead, where his father, David Haggie, senior, was also living. Some time after this Mr David Haggie, senior, died, and David, junior, left Peter at Gateshead and began rope-works at Sunderland.

Mr Robert Hood Haggie gave up the timber trade, came down to reside at Low Willington Villa, and devoted himself entirely (so far as business was concerned) to rope-making. He made for himself a position in local affairs apart from his business, and was keenly interested in the moral welfare of the district. Mr Haggie, who was a Congregationalist, and Mr Joseph Procter, who was a Quaker, were the local leaders in all the social movements of the day in Willington and Howdon.

One of the questions was that of prohibiting slavery in British possessions, and, as we shall see, Mr Procter took the more active share in that.

Another prominent matter was the anti-church rate protest, and in this Mr Haggie was the leader. The Wallsend churchwardens rated all the parish in order to support St Peter's Church, and this many of the non-churchgoers and Nonconformists passively resisted, and none more sturdily than Mr Haggie.

The churchwardens of Tynemouth also rated him for his warehouse at North Shields. But he resisted to the uttermost, by pen in the local press, by denouncing the injustice of the rate before the Law Courts, and by vigorous protests when his goods were taken and sold. Mr Jos. Procter's goods were also seized and sold, but he suffered quietly. The opposition gradually won their cause, and so far as Wallsend was concerned, the church rates were given up in 1860.

About the year 1849 Mr Haggie and Mr Jos. Procter opened a school under the British and Foreign School Society, intended chiefly for the children of their workmen. Mr Haggie built the school-room, which had a large raised preaching platform and desk at the south end, and a gallery at the opposite end. (The school was afterwards transformed into the gatehouse office for the Ropery.) The working arrangement was that Mr Haggie should provide the school-room and the coals for heating, and Mr Procter the books and £12 per year towards the teacher's salary, and the teacher might charge the scholars not more than twopence per week. The number of the scholars varied from thirty to forty.

It will be seen that the school-room was well fitted for religious services, and this was arranged so because Mr Haggie was carrying on an aggressive temperance mission work, which was not very popular with the church dignitaries of that day, and which led to a serious crisis in the Howdon Independent Church, of which he was a member (see page 157). On Sunday afternoons he had a regular attendance at his Bible class at the Mission room of from twenty to forty adults, and in addition to this he usually preached at Willington village, and other places not reached by the churches.

Mr Haggie was an especial favourite with the local children. He gave them many a pleasant outing and treat, and to many of the older people he acted as guide and friend. When he died in March, 1866, the district lost a useful, kindly worker.

On 3rd June, 1873 (Whit Tuesday), the old rope-works were almost entirely burnt down. The main rope-making works consisted of a large four-story building packed with wood fittings and wooden reels, and on the south-west side of this was the boiler-house and engine-room. West of the main building was a two-story spinning loft, and still farther west was the present long rope walk. On the south of the spinning loft was the tar-house, a detached building one hundred feet by eighteen feet.

About four o'clock a girl discovered a quantity of hemp ablaze at the western end of the spinning loft, and within a few minutes the fire had a good hold. No buckets or fire appliances were near at hand, and when the local firemen arrived their hose was not sufficient, and the Newcastle and North Shields fire brigades were sent for. Meanwhile a strong west wind was sweeping the fire toward the main building and had set the tar-house ablaze.

A little after five the North Shields firemen arrived, and, almost at the same time, the fire engine from Newcastle, but the tide was low and the water in the Gut was of little account. When the flames reached the four-story building the conflagration was immense. The railway bridge above the works was in course of being altered from wood to iron, and the flames leaped the ninety-eight feet and stopped the traffic. The railway fire engines were hurried down, and although their supply of water was small, with the help of wet sheets they prevented the bridge from taking fire.

The rising tide presently gave the fire brigades a good water supply. At eight o'clock the walls of the large building fell in and the climax was over. The long rope walk and the detached house occupied by the " waltzer "—the endless rope-making machine—were saved; all the other works and buildings were in absolute ruins, the damage being estimated at £25,000 to £30,000.

The rope-works were re-erected with modern improvements, and continued by Mr Robert Hood Haggie (the eldest son of Mr Haggie), Mr Stevenson Haggie, and Mr Arthur Jamieson Haggie, until the year 1900, when the firm was converted into a limited liability company with a capital of £160,000, since increased to £320,000.

In 1903 Mr Frank Dean, from Messrs Craven & Speedings, Sunderland, was appointed works manager, and he initiated several changes. Messrs Haggie & Sons had in 1885 taken over the buildings used by Sampson Langdale (see page 292) and were making wire rope in part of the building. Mr Dean started the making of binder twine in the old mill, he also reorganised the works generally, and by 1912 Hood Haggie's had steadily grown and prospered, until it was in the first rank as a prosperous commercial concern.

Of Mr Haggie's three surviving sons, Mr Robt. Hood Haggie, junior, on the death of his father became the senior partner, and later, the senior managing director of the works, to which he gave his closest attention until his death at Jesmond in 1908 at the age of seventy-one years. Unlike his father, he took little part in outside affairs. He was quiet and retiring, and his interests, apart from the business, were in music and local history.

Mr Stevenson Haggie, the present chairman of directors, was the second surviving son. The youngest was Mr Arthur Jamieson Haggie, who took a more active part in public life than either of his brothers. In May, 1884, he married Miss Kate Stewart of Newcastle, and they began their wedded life at Low Willington Villa. In June, 1904, Mr and Mrs Haggie moved to Manor House, Benton, which they had built, and Mr and Mrs Frank Dean became the occupiers of the Villa.

Both Mr and Mrs A. J. Haggie took an outstanding part in local affairs. Mr Haggie was for some time a member of the Willington Quay Local Board and one of the Tynemouth Guardians, and also an overseer. He was appointed a Justice of the Peace for the county in 1899, in 1901 he was elected to represent Willington Quay on the County Council, and in 1910 he was made a county alderman. Mrs Haggie also did excellent work for local causes, part of which was the founding of the Willington Quay Nursing Association, and the starting of the Tipperary Clubs in Wallsend and Howdon during the Great War. After the peace she greatly helped in the establishment of the Wallsend Young Women's Christian Association at Salisbury House, Station Road, which opened on 7th May, 1919.

After Mr and Mrs Dean moved to Low Willington Villa they both became well known in the district, and Mrs Rosa Dean became an active Poor Law guardian and also worked for the Society for the Prevention of Cruelty to Children. In 1912 the Deans removed to Jesmond, and the Villa and grounds were attached to spacious diningrooms built for the Ropery workers.

Mr Frank Dean resigned his post as managing director of the works on 31st December, 1919, and although he remained an ordinary director of the company he left Tyneside and retired to the healthy quietness of Burgess Hill in Sussex. Mr Ernest Frail, who had been Mr Dean's assistant, was appointed works' manager, and in 1922 was elected upon the Board of Directors.

The commercial offices of the firm are at Akenside House, Newcastle, and at the head of the company, in addition to the directors already mentioned, there are Mr Robert J. Nichol, who has been with the firm since 1882, and is now deputy-chairman, and Mr Stanley S. Haggie, son of the late Mr Robert Hood Haggie. The secretary is Mr B. Fenwick Smith, who has been with the firm since 1904. The fact that the company last year paid a dividend of ten per cent. free of tax in spite of the loss of their extensive Russian and mid-Europe trade, speaks volumes for the resource and energy of those in charge.

Willington Mill

This mill, together with the house which adjoined it, was far more famed for its " spirit " than its flour. It was started in 1806, and was the first steam flour mill in the north of England.

The mill for its day was a large one, being seven stories high, and intended for seven pairs of stones. The house on the north side of the mill yard was also spacious, having three stories and containing twelve or thirteen rooms and attics. The mill, house, and garden occupied a semi-circular promontory pointing westwards, with the Willington Gut sweeping half round it.

THE HAUNTED HOUSE AND MILL, WILLINGTON, IN 1895. [*Facing page* 290.

In the early days, the mill was owned by George Unthank, and in the year 1829 Mr Joseph Procter joined him in partnership. Mr Procter took up his residence in the mill house, and Mr Unthank removed to Battle Hill Farm.

Presently the partnership was dissolved, and Procter's Mill was well known for many years on Tyneside. A detailed story of the Willington Mill ghost hardly comes under the heading of history. This ghost, however, was widely known by repute, and from the years 1835 to 1856 many serious attempts were made to solve the mystery. The " spirit " was of the " family ghost " type. It greatly troubled the Procters, but did not annoy the Unthanks, and it left the house when Mr Joseph Procter moved from it and went to Benton in 1847.

The evidence by absolutely sane, unimpeachable witnesses, in support of the fact that there was something supernatural at the mill and mill house, is overwhelming, but we must refer our readers to " Real Ghost Stories," by W. T. Stead (Grant Richards, 1897), and the *Newcastle Monthly Chronicle* for 1887 for fuller information.

Mr Joseph Procter came to Willington from North Shields. About two years after he entered into partnership with Mr Unthank, he married in 1831 Miss Elizabeth Carr of Kendal, sister of Mr Jonathan D. Carr, the founder of the biscuit factory at Carlisle.

The Procters were " Friends," and in a quiet way they always assisted any movement for the betterment of the people. We have mentioned his share in establishing a school at the Ropery. He was one of the first to join the temperance movement. He and Mrs Procter were strong anti-slavery advocates, and through their influence many thoughtful families in Willington and Willington Quay refused to buy slave cultivated sugar.

After he started milling at the Ouseburn and removed to Benton, he still continued his interest in the district. He arranged for his book-keeper and cashier, Mr Edward

Elliott, to distribute regularly papers such as the *British Workman* and *The Band of Hope*. After an excellent reputation for its flour and an exciting record for its ghost, the mill was closed in 1865.

The mill remained empty until 1871, when Mr Sampson Langdale (the founder of the Langdale Chemical Manure Works) bought the buildings and built an annex on the opposite side of the road.

It is reported that when this transaction was arranged, Mr Procter said to Mr Langdale, " Now, Sampson, I sell thee the mill with the ghost," and Mr Langdale replied, " All right, see that you deliver the ghost." The new owner was evidently a humorist, because some time afterwards he sent his solicitor to Mr Procter to demand a specific performance of his contract, and to produce the ghost.

The ghost, however, followed the family, and Mr Wigham Richardson tells the story he heard relating to the cousin of one of his servants, who was engaged by the Procters who then lived at Gosforth. She sent her box securely corded and locked, and when she went to her room she found her box still locked and corded, but the contents scattered about the room. The old cook told her that the ghost did this to every new arrival, and that three girls that term had already left the place terrified.

Mr Joseph Procter died at his residence, Fairfield, Gosforth, on 6th November, 1875, aged seventy-five years.

Mr Langdale spent some £20,000 here in an endeavour to make soap out of partly crushed olives. The process was a most inflammable one, and the building had to be lit by lamps fixed outside the windows. Mr Wm. S. Daglish was one of Mr Langdale's supporters in this experiment, but it did not prove a commercial success, and was given up. Once more the old mill was untenanted until 1885, when Messrs R. Hood Haggie & Son took it.

The Willington Slipway (now Clelands (Shiprepairers) Limited)

This ship repairing yard and slipway was founded by Thompson Smith about 1835 on a piece of land behind the Ship Hotel, and it was carried on successfully by him and his brother Charles. He built the workmen's cottages which were afterwards known as Potter's Square, and of which a fragment is incorporated in the wall west of the Ship Hotel. In 1851 Thos. Brown became the tenant, and he extended the place westward and added a sawmill, and the rateable value was raised from £40 to £200. But within twelve months, as a floating dock from Howdon was being moored at the Quay, he unfortunately fell into the river and was drowned.

His successor was Wm. Adamson, a Dundee man who had married Miss Emma Weatherley, daughter of Mr Robert Weatherley of Church Street. At first Mr Adamson lived in the White House, a large house opposite the Slipway, standing about fifty yards north of Potter Street (the Picture Palace occupies part of the front garden).

The firm continued as Messrs Thomas Adamson & Son from 1851 until 1857, during which period, in addition to repairing ships, they built tugboats and one composite ship, the *Minnie,* which had iron keel and frames and wood sheathing.

In 1857 Mr Thos. Adamson's son, Mr Wm. Adamson, took over the business and extended it. In 1864 Mr Wm. Adamson took into partnership Mr Thomas Pringle, one of Hawks Crawshay & Company's officials, but this was not a success.

The Adamson family did not take much part in local affairs, except that Mr Wm. Adamson raised a corps of Riflemen of which he was the Colonel, and, as he was a Scotsman, he dressed them in Highland costume, and they were formally incorporated on 15th May, 1860. This was before Mr Addison Potter and Mr G. A. Allen began to form their company. A few years later he built Rosehill House, the large house facing west overlooking the Burn Closes. The large attic was arranged as a rat pit. It was the first modern house in what is now known as the Rosehill district.

In 1866 Mr Wm. Cleland, who had been manager of Palmer's shipbuilding yard, took the Willington Patent Slipway from the assignees of Messrs Adamson and Pringle. In January and February, 1867, he advertised in the newspapers that he had taken the Slipway, Gridirons, and Shipbuilding Yard, that he could undertake repairs on iron and wood ships and furnish plans and specifications for iron steamers and sailing ships, and added: "The Slipway is the best in the north of England, being six hundred feet long, and, with the present alterations, capable of taking a ship of one thousand tons."

For many years these patent slipways earned a good revenue, and by an agreement dated 26th July, 1872, Mr Cleland, together with Mr Richard Welford, of the Tyne Steam Shipping Company, and Alderman W. D. Stephens of Newcastle, converted the business into a limited company under the title of Wm. Cleland & Co. Ltd. Mr Cleland died at Rosehill House on 31st March, 1876, aged fifty-four years, and was buried at Preston cemetery.

In 1890 in order to raise more capital, and with a view to constructing a dry dock on the site of one of the slipways, which had been seriously damaged in 1889, the company was reconstructed and its title altered to Cleland's Graving Dock & Slipway Co. Ltd. The proposed dry dock was not proceeded with, but the damaged slipway was reconstructed at a cost of about £15,000.

In the course of years, owing to the increased size and length of steamers, "Cleland's" drifted from its place in the front rank of ship repairers, and now specialise in repairs to steamers up to 300 feet in length, and they also have an extensive trade in forgings.

The dry dock proposed to be made in 1890 was never constructed, and in 1920 the title of the firm was amended to Clelands (Repairers) Limited. Mr Thomas H. Leathart is the chairman of the directors, Mr Joseph Dunn is managing director, and Mr Henry Jervis Ward is the secretary of the company.

Cookson's Willington Lead Works

Thos. Richardson and George Currie took a lease from the Newcastle Corporation of 10,195 square yards on the west side of Tyne Street on 29th September, 1847, and started lead works. In 1852 Mr Currie retired and the firm became Thos. Richardson & Co.; at this time the rateable value had risen to £300. Two years later the title of the firm changed again and became the Howdon Smelting Co. In 1856 the works passed into the hands of Mr Wm. I. Cookson, one of a family which was already of note in Northumberland and Durham.

Isaac Cookson, who came to Newcastle from Penrith about 1700, may be regarded as the founder of the Tyneside branch of the family. He was a merchant of Newcastle, and after a prosperous career he died in 1744 at the age of sixty-four. His wife Hannah (*née* Bolton) died in 1760, and both were buried in St Nicholas' Church, Newcastle.

Wm. Isaac Cookson, who became associated with the lead industry in our district, was the son of Isaac Cookson of Meldon, who in turn was the great-grandson of Isaac Cookson of Penrith.

Mr Wm. I. Cookson's first wife was Miss Jane Ann Cuthbert, sister of Mr Wm. Cuthbert of Beaufront Castle, the marriage taking place in 1839.

When the Willington Quay Lead Works were taken over by Mr Wm. I. Cookson in 1856, the firm of W. I. Cookson was already established at Gateshead and at the Hayhole at East Howdon in 1850. The partnership consisted of Messrs Wm. Isaac and John Cookson and their brother-in-law, Mr Wm. Cuthbert. Eight years later the firm also acquired a lease of 21,810 square yards of recently reclaimed land, on the east side of Tyne Street, for seventy-five years as from 29th September, 1864. In 1870 they commenced, and completed in 1871, the erection and equipment of works for the manufacture of Antimony and Venetian red.

Mr W. I. Cookson's two eldest sons, Mr Norman Charles Cookson and Mr George John Cookson, took an increasingly active part in the business from 1865, and soon the older partners retired and left the management in the hands of the younger men.

Mr Wm. I. Cookson removed from Eslington Park to Denton Park, Otley, in 1867, where he resided three years, and sixteen years later, on 1st November, 1888, he died at Worksop Manor, Nottingham, at the age of seventy-six.

Mr Norman and Mr George raised the works from a comparatively small place to one in the front rank. Owing to changes made in the tariffs of other countries and to fresh discoveries in science, they had often to adapt their works to meet new conditions—for example, in 1890 the production of Venetian red was entirely given up and the works used for more profitable products. However, the courage, resourcefulness, and energy of the partners were always equal to the emergency.

In our district, in addition to the lead works, Mr Norman Cookson took a considerable share in supporting the Wallsend & Hebburn Coal Co. in its trying years, and he was also a large shareholder in Messrs Parsons' Turbine works. For some fifty years the names of Mr Norman and Mr George Cookson were a synonym for all that was upright, straightforward, and fair-dealing; their word was literally as good as their bond. Mr George Cookson retired in 1889 and removed to the south. He died in London on 27th February, 1913, aged sixty-eight.

The firm of Cookson & Company was converted into a

private limited company in 1904, and Mr Norman C. Cookson became its chairman and remained so until his death on 15th May, 1909, at Oakwood Hall, Wylam, at the age of sixty-seven. His son, Mr Clive Cookson, then became chairman, the controlling interest in the company being still held by him and other members of the Cookson family.

Apart from his varied business interests, Mr Norman Cookson took a great practical interest in orchid growing, and his scientific orchid hybridisation made his name as widely known in the horticultural world as was the name of the firm in the commercial world.

Of late years the operations of the company have been very considerably extended in many directions, a number of new articles being added to those previously manufactured, and numerous branch offices and subsidiary businesses being conducted both in the United Kingdom and many other parts of the world; and the output of silver, antimony, and various descriptions of alloys of metallic lead has been very large.

Wallsend Coke Ovens and Blast Furnaces

In 1848 a considerable number of coke ovens were started at Wallsend Quay, near the present Davy Inn. These were erected and worked by Mr John Carr, who then resided at High Villa Place, Newcastle. He was interested in several concerns. He made firebricks at Scotswood, lampblack at Gateshead, and had other coke ovens at Jarrow.

In 1854 he removed from Newcastle, and became the occupier of Wallsend Hall, in succession to Edward Grace. The following year he built two large blast furnaces near the coke ovens. These were not a success, and twelve months later he was obliged to give up both iron smelting and coke making.

These undertakings came into the possession of

C. M. Palmer & Company. At this time the rateable value of the coke ovens was £250, and that of the iron works £300.

On 13th May, 1864, great consternation was caused over the whole district by a serious explosion which occurred at the blast furnaces, where five boilers were in use. In 1866 both furnaces and coke ovens were closed, and they remained unworked until 1874, when the Royal Greek Iron Company restarted them with Mr F. M. Bragiotti as manager.

Messrs Palmer & Company's connection with Wallsend had one good permanent result. They secured a considerable parcel of land and drew up an excellent " hire purchase " scheme for small self-contained houses for workmen. The houses were in advance of almost any of their class, and after the rent had been paid for a certain period, the houses became the property of the tenants. Under this scheme, First Street to Seventh Streets were built, and some sixty working men became owners of their own houses.

Iron and Steel Shipbuilding

The staple industry of the district which followed the first modern coal mining period was that of iron shipbuilding. The idea of superseding wood ships by iron ones only slowly won approval, and the early iron shipbuilders met with great difficulties. One of the foremost pioneers was Mr John H. S. Coutts, who came from Aberdeen and in 1840 began at Walker the first iron shipbuilding yard on Tyneside.

Here he turned out the paddle steamer *Prince Albert,* measuring 155 feet long by 19 feet 6 inches broad, and her iron plates were ⅜ and ¼ inch. She was the first iron ship of any size built on the Tyne, and was built for passenger service on the Thames.

Mr Charles Mitchell was in Mr Coutts' drawing office,

Mr Wm. Grey was yard manager, Mr Wm. Swan was in the commercial office, and Mr John C. Brooks was cashier.

Several vessels were built, including the *Q.E.D.*, an auxiliary screw collier of 271 tons which was the first ship to carry water ballast in a double bottom. Unfortunately this early iron shipbuilding yard at Walker was not a financial success, and was closed in 1848. However, Mr Coutts had great faith in the future of iron ships, and, with the aid of a partner, on 25th March, 1849, he secured a lease of about two and a half acres of land to the west of Messrs Potter's Brick and Coke works at Willington Quay, and he and his partner began shipbuilding as **Coutts & Parkinson**.

The prospects and business seemed good, and the largest iron vessel hitherto built was launched here on 28th August, 1851. She was named the *Thomas Hamlin* and her registered tonnage was 1,350 tons.

On 3rd September of the year following, the iron East Indiaman *W. S. Lindsay* was also launched. This event was celebrated by a dinner given by the builders to four hundred guests. Mr W. S. Lindsay was in the chair, and Sir John Fife of Newcastle and the Mayor of both North and South Shields took part in the proceeding. This large function, which was somewhat unusual, was partly to advertise iron ships, but chiefly to promote emigration to Australia.

In the autumn of 1852 the firm extended their yard westward, by leasing an additional two and a quarter acres.

Mr Coutts built himself a house at the west end of Church Street, Howdon, and took considerable interest in local affairs, and in the year 1855 was an Overseer of the Poor.

The success of the yard did not continue. Mr Parkinson retired in 1853, and after carrying on the business for about two years on his own account, Mr Coutts also gave it up. In 1856 Messrs Muntsey & Jansen took over the yard and nominally held it for over three years, but during that time Messrs Charles Mitchell & Co., by arrangement, built a number of iron barges here in 1857 for India. The next occupiers were Messrs Palmer Bros. Mr Charles Mark Palmer and his brother George had begun to build ships at Jarrow in 1852, and at this time the business was rapidly increasing, so at the end of 1859 they took over the Willington shipbuilding yard, and the increased usefulness of the place can be judged by the fact that its rateable value was raised in a few months from £127 to £250, and then in 1862 to £375. The first vessel they built here was the *Port Mulgrave*, which was launched on 24th June, 1860.

Mr Wm. Cleland, who had come from the Clyde to be manager for Messrs Thos. & Wm. Smith of North Shields, left this firm and came and took charge of the yard for Messrs Palmer & Co., and for several years the place did good work.

A most striking event and an exciting spectacle, probably unique in the shipbuilding trade, was planned by Mr Charles M. Palmer to take place on Saturday, 15th August, 1863. He arranged for two steamers to be launched from each side of the river, and the four to be started simultaneously. The two to be launched from the Willington yard were the s.s. *John M'Intyre*—227 feet long and 100 h.p.—and the s.s. *The No. 1*—200 feet long and 150 h.p. The two to be launched from the Jarrow yard, which was directly opposite, were the s.s. *Europa* and the s.s. *Latona*. The total tonnage of the four steamers was 4,100 tons, fairly large vessels for their day. Mr Wm. Cleland was in charge at the Willington yard, and Mr John M'Intyre at the Jarrow yard, while Mr Palmer looked after the general arrangements.

Great crowds gathered on both sides of the river. At four o'clock a gun was fired as the signal to start the four steamers, and when the last ship was clear of the ways, and completely afloat, a second gun announced the success of the interesting event. This sort of " criss-cross " launch of four vessels is probably unparalleled. At this time the firm employed 6,000 men in the iron works at Jarrow and Wallsend, and the two shipbuilding yards at Jarrow and Willington.

The following year saw a strike of workmen at Jarrow, Willington, and Wallsend, and a considerable amount of angry feeling was aroused. Mr Palmer brought large numbers of outsiders to fill the places of the local men, including one hundred men from Lynn, and local excitement was at times intense, and the whole district threatened with riots.

Mr George Palmer had retired from the firm in 1862, and Mr Charles M. Palmer, who was actively interested in a great many other enterprises, felt that the shipyards, blast furnaces, rolling mills, iron stone mines, etc., should be placed upon a broader basis than that depending upon one individual. On 2nd June, 1865, the whole of Messrs Palmers' works were disposed of to a limited company—with a capital of £2,000,000. A Manchester firm who had bought Bolckow, Vaughan's business the previous summer, carried through the operation, and although Mr C. M. Palmer took a large interest in the new firm, and was the chairman of it, the shares of the company were not very freely taken up at first by local investors.

One of the results of this change in the firm was that the iron works and coke ovens at Wallsend were closed in 1866, and towards the end of 1867 Mr Wm. Cleland left Palmer's and began business on his own account.

Messrs Schlesinger, Davis & Co.

The first shipbuilding yard opened at the western side of the parish was started in 1863 by Messrs Schlesinger, Davis & Co., on a piece of land now occupied by the west part of the Wallsend shipyard.

Mr Charles Albert Schlesinger was the son of Mr

Martin Schlesinger, who resided at Rye Hill, Newcastle, and then at the Grange, Wallsend village. The head of the new firm had served his apprenticeship as an engineer at Stephenson's engine works, Newcastle, which in those days was considered to be *the* place for a lad who wished to secure the best training in engineering.

The other partner was Mr Frederick Blake Davis, son of Mr E. D. Davis, the well-known lessee of the Theatre Royal, Newcastle. He had been trained as a shipbuilder under Mr Chas. Mitchell, and had spent four or five years in India, carrying out some contracts for Mr Mitchell's firm.

Mr Henry Raincock, who came from Messrs Mitchell's yard and afterwards became associated with Mr C. S. Swan at the neighbouring yard, was manager for Messrs Schlesinger, Davis & Co.

The first two vessels built by Schlesinger, Davis & Co. were sailing ships. The first steamship was laid down in 1864. She was bought by Mr Chas. E. Stallybrass of Cardiff, who some years prior to this was on Newcastle Quay and was one of the founders of the steam shipping trade of South Wales. This vessel was 411 tons gross register, was named the *Llandaff*, and was the first steamer registered at the port of Cardiff. The firm of Schlesinger, Davis & Co. prospered, and as house accommodation could not be obtained for their workmen, they bought some forty-four tenements in Clyde Street for them.

Mr Schlesinger and Mr Davis both took some interest in local affairs, and when the election of the first Wallsend Local Board of Health took place in 1867, Mr Schlesinger was sixth at the poll out of thirty-six candidates, with one hundred and ninety-one votes, but Mr Davis was much lower and was not elected. Mr Schlesinger retained his seat on the Board until 1881, though his last attendance was on 1st March, 1880.

Mr Schlesinger was of a nervous, anxious temperament, and his health completely broke down. Mr Davis bought

SWAN, HUNTER & WIGHAM RICHARDSON, LTD., 1922.

SHIPYARD, BUILDING BERTHS AND "MAURETANIA" AT QUAY

[*Facing page* 303.

out his partner's interest in 1880, and continued the yard under the old name.

In 1882 the post of chief draughtsman to this firm was occupied by Mr M. C. James, who had been an apprentice of Mr Chas. Mitchell, but had been trained in the associated yard of Coulson, Cooke & Co. and C. S. Swan & Co.

Mr James has for many years been well known as head of the Mercantile Dry Docks at Jarrow, and a prominent public man in that busy borough.

For the year 1880 the shipbuilding returns show:

Schlesinger, Davis & Co. ...	10 vessels,	11,932 tons
Tyne Iron Shipbuilding Co. ...	7 ,,	12,481 ,,
Wigham Richardson & Co. ...	6 ,,	10,757 ,,
C. S. Swan & Hunter ...	6 ,,	8,532 ,,

It is of interest to note that the price of iron ship plates at the beginning of this year was about £8 10s. per ton, and at the close of the year about £6 10s. At this time steel had scarcely become a competitor of iron, which, however, it was soon destined completely to displace.

In 1883 the late Mr Wm. Wood, who had been cashier to Messrs Schlesinger, Davis & Co. for many years, left them to form the firm of Messrs Wood, Skinner & Co.

In its earlier days the firm of Schlesinger, Davis & Co. was a most successful one, but after the depression in shipbuilding which occurred in 1884 Messrs Schlesinger, Davis & Co. for some reason did not recover their trade, and gradually the business went down until in 1893 the first shipbuilding yard in Wallsend township was closed.

Messrs Swan & Hunter

The firm of C. S. Swan & Hunter (afterwards merged in the company now known throughout the shipping world as Swan, Hunter, & Wigham Richardson Ltd.) owed its origin to three gentlemen who were all connected with

Messrs Charles Mitchell & Co., shipbuilders, of Walker, which firm was merged in the Armstrong company in 1882. In 1871 Messrs Chas. Mitchell & Co. could obtain more orders for iron steamers than they could build, and on the suggestion of Mr Mitchell, Mr John Coulson (who was yard manager under Mr Wm. Dobson at "Mitchell's") and Mr Richard Cooke (Mr Mitchell's brother-in-law, who was in the commercial department of his shipbuilding yard) began business at St Peter's as Coulson, Cooke & Co. The site there available soon proved too cramped, and after they had built their ninth vessel, in October, 1873, the young firm moved to a more commodious site of six and a half acres at Wallsend, on the east side of the yard of Messrs Schlesinger, Davis & Co. Things went well for a time, but, strange to say, while they were building their *No. 13*, ill luck stepped in. They found themselves in financial difficulties owing to a bad contract, and other causes, and it was arranged for Mr Chas. Mitchell to take over the whole enterprise as it stood. He put the place into the hands of Mr Charles Sheridan Swan (another brother-in-law), who then retired from the managing directorship of the Wallsend Slipway Co. Ltd., and took over this shipbuilding business, which thus became known as C. S. Swan & Co.

A sad event five years later made another change in the firm necessary. On 26th April, 1879, Mr Swan was returning from a business visit to Russia, via Calais, and, while crossing towards Dover, fell over the bow of the steamer, was struck by one of the paddles, and when picked up was quite dead. He was buried at Long Benton four days later.

A managing partner for the yard was shortly afterwards advertised for. After brief negotiations with Mr Mitchell and Mr Henry Frederick Swan, Mr George Burton Hunter left the firm of S. P. Austin & Hunter of Sunderland, and in partnership with Mrs C. S. Swan (a daughter of Mr John Glover, the chemical manufacturer), became the managing partner of the firm of C. S. Swan & Hunter, from the 1st January, 1880.[1]

When Mr Hunter came to Wallsend the business was a comparatively small one. The number of men and boys employed was 717, the area of the shipyard was six and three-quarter acres, the river frontage 270 feet and the output for 1880 was 8,532 tons. In the Valuation List of the parish, the then estimated rental value of the land, buildings, and fixed plant was only £640, whereas the shipyard adjoining was valued at £1,112 per annum.

The change in the partnership just mentioned proved the beginning of a new era in the development of the present famous Wallsend shipyard. There was a boom in shipbuilding in the autumn of 1879, and in the next three years Swan & Hunter's business increased rapidly and more room was required. Accordingly early in 1883 the land belonging to Messrs J. & W. Allen, the chemical manufacturers, comprising sixteen acres, was bought, and the portion lying between Messrs Allen's works and the River Tyne was laid out as an additional shipyard, being separated from the original yard only by a road forty feet wide leading to the public quay of Wallsend, which was of the same width as the road. In course of time, this, Messrs Swan & Hunter's east shipyard, was enlarged until it comprised the whole sixteen acres bought from Messrs Allen, their works having in the meantime being discontinued and dismantled, owing, as we have already noted, to the changes in the fortunes of the soda making industry.

The year that Mr Hunter came to Wallsend, Mr Geo. S. Scorer (afterwards of Smith's Dock Co.) was brought from Messrs W. Gray & Co.'s shipyard at West Hartlepool and became yard manager, and the late Mr Christopher Stephenson came from the same place as chief

[1] See the " Eighteen Mayors of the Borough " for further biographical notes.

draughtsman.[1] Early in 1882 Mr Hunter brought his brother-in-law, the late Mr Robert Hudson, from Sunderland, where he held an appointment under the River Wear Commission, to assist him in the commercial side of the business, and in July, 1882, Mr F. J. Culley from the office of Messrs Edward Withy & Co., West Hartlepool, succeeded Mr R. Farbridge as cashier and chief clerk. In 1884-85 the first vessels built of steel in Wallsend, the s.s. *Burrumbeet* and the s.s. *Corangamite*, were launched by the firm to the order of an Australian company—Messrs Huddart Parker & Co. In 1893 they built nine vessels with a tonnage of 31,088 tons and thus headed the list of Tyne shipbuilders for output for the first time.

In 1895 it was resolved to turn the partnership into a limited liability company. In September of that year Mr Thos. H. Bainbridge of Newcastle; Mr John Price, formerly general manager of Messrs Palmer of Jarrow; his nephew, Mr Wm. Denton, also from Jarrow, who had at one time been the agent of Messrs Palmer at Cardiff; together with Mr G. B. Hunter and Mr Charles Sheriton Swan (son of the late Mr C. S. Swan) became the first directors of the new company of C. S. Swan & Hunter Ltd., with Mr Hunter at its head.

The business and output of the firm continued to increase, and still more ground was needed. Therefore in January, 1897, the lease of the yard, formerly occupied by Messrs Schlesinger, Davis & Co., was acquired from Messrs Lambton & Co., bankers, of Newcastle. This new ground comprised about seven acres and was used primarily for the construction of floating dry docks. The first to be constructed on the newly acquired ground (to which other three acres were subsequently added) was one for the port of Havana, Cuba, built to the order of the Spanish Government, and towed out in the autumn of the same year. The following year another large dock was built and towed to Stettin, in Germany.

[1] See the "Eighteen Mayors of the Borough" for further biographical notes.

A few years later, in June 1903, a large combination was effected, C. S. Swan & Hunter Ltd. and Wigham Richardson & Co. Ltd., of the Neptune shipyard and works at Walker, being amalgamated as Swan, Hunter & Wigham Richardson Ltd., with a nominal capital of £1,500,000, of which 994,297 shares were issued. Seven shares were paid for in cash, and fully paid shares in the new company were allotted to the vendors as follows: 225,900 five per cent. preference shares and 338,850 ordinary shares to the shareholders of C. S. Swan & Hunter Ltd; 158,025 five per cent. preference shares and 206,225 ordinary shares to the shareholders of Wigham Richardson & Co. Ltd., and in accordance with certain agreements entered into, and with a view to secure community of interests, 65,290 preference shares were allotted to certain shareholders of the Wallsend Slipway and Engineering Co. in exchange for shares in that Company.

Towards the end of the same year the new firm purchased the business and assets of the Tyne Pontoons & Dry Docks Co. Ltd., at Wallsend, by the issue to that Company's shareholders of 89,630 preference shares, and 89,650 ordinary shares of Swan, Hunter & Wigham Richardson, Ltd. This made the river frontage of the enlarged Company continuous for nearly 1,400 yards. The area of the works in Wallsend parish is 39.5 acres, and the remainder, almost an equal amount, is in Walker, now a portion of the city of Newcastle-on-Tyne.

The next considerable event in the history of the shipyard was one in which thousands who knew little of shipbuilding took great interest. Were the German shipowners going to put us into a back seat in our shipping trade?

In 1900 the Blue Ribbon of the Atlantic steamers for speed, was held by the *Deutschland* built at Stettin. She had reciprocating engines of 36,000 i.h.p. and a speed of 23.5 knots. In 1901 the same builders launched the

Kronpinz Wilhelm, and in 1903 the *Kaiser Wilhelm II.*, equally speedy vessels.

It was felt that British ships were dropping behind, and the Government presently encouraged the Cunard Company to build two steamships " capable of maintaining during a voyage across the Atlantic a minimum average speed of from 24 to 25 knots (say 27 to 29 miles) in moderate weather," and other very strict requirements were laid down by the Admiralty. The two vessels were to act, if required, as auxiliary cruisers, and in exchange the Government would give an annual subsidy of £150,000 and also provide not exceeding £2,600,000 at 2¾ per cent. interest.

It was at first proposed that these two special ships be driven by three sets of tandem quadruple expansion five cylinder reciprocating engines, developing together 60,000 i.h.p., but in August, 1903, the type and design of the engines were referred to a strong committee, and in 1904 this committee reported in favour of the Parsons steam turbine principle.

The result was the building of the sister ships, the *Lusitania*, built at Clyde bank, and the *Mauretania*, built at the Wallsend shipyard and engined by the Wallsend Slipway & Engineering Co. These vessels opened up a new chapter in shipbuilding and marine engineering. They exceeded by 75 per cent. the greatest power installation previously fitted on board any merchant ship. They were 790 feet long overall and 88 feet broad. Engines 70,000 horse-power. Gross tonnage of the Wallsend ship 31,938 tons (500 tons more than the *Lusitania*.)

All Tyneside became interested in the building of the *Mauretania* and took a holiday when she was christened by the Dowager Duchess of Roxburghe and launched on 20th September, 1906, and half Tyneside bid her " Good Luck " when she left the Tyne for Liverpool, on the afternoon of 22nd October, 1907.

She was a floating palace with ample accommodation

for 2,335 passengers and a crew of 812. The upper bridge was as high as the roadway on the " High Level Bridge," the tops of the funnels were 154 feet above her keel, and the masts were 56 feet higher still.

From the year 1897 the firm had specialised in the building of floating docks, and on 4th January, 1912, they launched the largest floating dock in the world, which covers two and a half acres. It was built for the British Admiralty, was 680 feet long by 144 feet broad, the inside width being 113 feet. Its lifting power was 33,000 tons.

It was intended to be stationed in the Medway, and was there until after the war broke out, when it was brought back to the Tyne and moored at Jarrow Slake. Here it was kept busy, day and night, repairing battle ships and cruisers, and no ship was too large or too heavy.

In the same year as this dock was started on her useful career, the firm was further enlarged by acquiring the assets and business of Messrs Barclay, Curle & Co. Ltd. This firm was founded on the Clyde in 1818 to build wooden ships. In 1912 they had a shipyard with six building berths at Whiteinch, engine and boiler works at Stobcross, and had recently acquired a graving dock 525 feet long, and a shipyard at Elderslie. The interests of the shareholders in the Clyde firm were bought by Swan, Hunter & Wigham Richardson Ltd., and paid for by the issue of new shares of the latter company. The management of the Clyde works continued as before, but to secure co-operation in working, three of Swan, Hunter & Wigham Richardson's directors joined the board of management of Barclay, Curle & Co. Ltd. and three of Barclay, Curle's directors became also directors of Swan, Hunter & Wigham Richardson Ltd. Also in 1912 a yard was opened on eleven acres of new ground, at Southwick-on-Wear for building floating docks, caissons, etc.

At present Sir Geo. B. Hunter, K.B.E., D.Sc., is the chairman of the directors. The yard manager is Mr Norman M. Hunter, who came to Wallsend from the

Clyde, and Messrs F. J. Culley and R. H. Winstanley are the joint secretaries.

Tyne Iron Ship-Building Co. Ltd.

This yard was started by Robt. J. Marshall, the son of Thomas Dunn Marshall, of South Shields, who had a small iron shipbuilding yard near the Lawe. It is claimed that the iron paddle steamer *Star*, which Mr Marshall, senior, built in 1839, was the first iron ship launched into the Tyne.

When his father retired from business in 1859, Robt. Marshall, who had been trained as an enginewright and had worked for some time with his father, came to Howdon and opened a shipbuilding yard on a strip of land recovered from the river. This he took from Thomas Adamson, who had in 1852 leased from the Newcastle Corporation more land than he required for his slipway.

The first year the name of the firm was called Marshall & Co., which in 1862 was changed Marshall Bros. The head of the firm was not an experienced shipbuilder, and he had as managers John Redhead and John Softley.

After carrying on the work for six years, the enterprise failed, and for two years Wm. B. Hornsby from Sunderland was the owner.

Then two brothers, Henry Aylwin Bevan Cole and Robt. Ernest Cole, from the south of England, undertook the business, and from 1871 to 1876 they built a good type of vessel. They had for their manager Mr Wm. John Bone, a first-class man, who began his professional career at the Royal Dockyard at Devonport and was a trusted surveyor for Lloyd's Register, and whilst in that position assisted in a thorough revision of Lloyd's Rules.

However, ill fortune still haunted the premises, and Cole Bros. were obliged to give up their efforts and retire with a serious loss. The principals are said to have been excellent men and good masters, and they afterwards paid all their creditors in full. After this occurred, Mr Bone still believed the place might have a successful future. He secured the support of several personal friends, and organised the Tyne Iron Ship-Building Co. Ltd., with himself as managing director, in 1876.

His skill, energy, and manifest ability turned the tide, and solid success rewarded his efforts. The " Tyne Iron " since its formation has had a considerable share of orders and established a reputation for good work. Mr Bone retired in 1901 and died at his residence at Linskill Terrace, North Shields, on 30th November, 1909, at the age of sixty-six.

Mr G. F. Mulherion, who was formerly secretary to the company, succeeded Mr Bone as managing director. He had been with the company since its incorporation, and had had a valuable training under Mr Bone.

In August, 1901, Mr John Bourn, from Messrs Armstrong Mitchell & Co., Low Walker, was appointed works manager and was later appointed general manager. He remained with the company until 1918. In August of that year he took the position of shipyard manager with Messrs Earle's Shipbuilding and Engineering Co., Hull.

The first Isherwood framed vessel built on the Tyne was built by the Tyne Iron Ship-Building Co. She was the s.s. *Leucadia*, 6,500 tons d.w., and was launched on the 8th June, 1910. The firm has another similar record to its credit for on 26th February, 1914, they launched the s.s. *Elbruz*, an oil tanker, 6,700 tons d.w., which was the first twin screw Diesel engined vessel launched on the Tyne.

During the Great War the company was responsible for design of the " C " type of standard ship, and became the parent shipbuilders of the type, of which the company built seven vessels and supplied particulars to over twenty other shipbuilders in the United Kingdom, about one hundred vessels of this type being ordered by the Shipping Controller. On 16th June, 1917, the " Tyne Iron " was honoured by a visit from Their Majesties King George V.

and Queen Mary while on their tour round the north-east coast shipyards, and for services rendered during the war Mr Mulherion was given the O.B.E.

On 1st October, 1919, Mr Albert Briggs, O.B.E., was appointed secretary. He is a solicitor, and during the war, after serving in the Royal Engineers, he was acting secretary of the department which controlled Merchant Shipbuilding.

On 14th April, 1920, Mr Alexander Thomson became general manager. He was born in Wallsend and served his apprenticeship on Tyneside, but he came to the " Tyne Iron " from Montrose, where he was general manager for the London and Montrose Shipbuilding and Repairing Co. The chief draughtsman is Mr George Oxley, who has been with the company since its formation.

The establishment has three building berths capable of taking vessels up to nearly 400 feet long, an excellent deep water frontage, and when fully employed they have about 700 employees. The annual output in normal years is about 20,000 tons gross.

Owing to the tact and sympathetic qualities of Mr Bone and later Mr Mulherion, there have never been any serious labour troubles in the yard, and the men regard it as a satisfactory place where, if grievances arise, they are promptly dealt with and fairly settled.

The chairmen of the company since its formation have been: Mr Geo. Clough of North Shields 1876 to 1888; Mr Jos. Robinson of North Shields 1888 to 1904; Mr Chas. S. Hunting of Newcastle was appointed in 1905 and held the position until his death on 16th September, 1921, after which Mr James Wm. Ellis of Gosforth was chosen.

The Northumberland Shipbuilding Company, Ltd.

The site of this yard was the foreshore of the river and the Howdon burn. After the Northumberland dock was opened and the river training wall laid down by the

Northumberland Shipbuilding Co.

River Tyne Commissioners, ballast discharged from the ships was deposited to level up the ground which became cricket pitches for the youths of Howdon.

Then Messrs H. S. Edwards, of South Shields, leased the land from the Duke of Northumberland, on which they built small craft. On 26th May, 1898, "The Northumberland Shipbuilding Co." was registered as a private company, and they took over Messrs Edwards's land and plant. The first managing director of this concern was Mr Rowland Hodge.

The shipyard up to 1900 had been wholly within the borough of Tynemouth, but owing to the need for more room the yard was extended over the Howdon burn into the parish of Wallsend. In July, 1918, the firm became a public company under the management of Sir Alexander Kennedy, and they acquired nearly all the shares of Wm. Doxford & Sons Ltd., of Sunderland. In December, 1919, they secured eighty-five per cent. of the ordinary shares of the Fairfield Shipbuilding and Engineering Co. on the Clyde. Next they bought the whole of the ordinary share capital of Messrs Workman Clark & Co., Belfast, and they also purchased one of the National Shipyards at Chepstow, now known as the Monmouth Shipbuilding Co.

At present their ordinary share capital stands at one and a half millions in one shilling shares. The chairman of the company is Mr R. A. Workman, and the managing director is Sir Alexander M. Kennedy.

The Howdon yard covers 15 acres and has a river frontage of 750 feet. The recent extension, however, involved the closing of the public roadway to the river, which was made by the River Tyne Commissioners in exchange for the ancient quay.

Eltringhams Ltd.

In 1912 Messrs Addison Potter & Son transferred their business to the British Portland Cement Manufacturers Co. Ltd, and Mr Charles J. Potter became a director of the larger company. At the end of the year the works so long associated with the name of Potter were closed and the land, etc., became open for sale.

On 24th July of the same year Messrs Palmer's Shipbuilding and Iron Co. Ltd. completely closed their Howdon yard, and hence as a result a long stretch of land, with river frontage, lay unoccupied between Messrs Cookson's and Marshall Street.

At this time the business established at South Shields in 1846 by Mr Joseph T. Eltringham, who died in 1897, had grown to such proportions that the firm there were seriously cramped for room, and it was arranged that the concern should be formed into a public company as Jos. T. Eltringham & Co. Ltd., with an authorised capital of £50,000 consisting of 25,000 six per cent. cum preference shares and 25,000 ordinary shares all of £1 each.

The promoters of this new company were Mr Durham W. Fitzgerald of South Shields and Mr George Renwick, M.P., of Newcastle. These two acquired, on behalf of the firm, the whole of the land vacated by Messrs Palmer & Co., and part of the site recently occupied by Messrs Potter & Sons, in all, rather more than four acres, with 460 feet of river frontage.

They secured the land from the Newcastle Corporation on a ninety-nine years' lease as from 29th September, 1912. In consideration of these two gentlemen securing the lease, financing the equipment of the new works, etc., they received 2,500 ordinary shares in equal proportions, and the good will of the old South Shields firm. and their running contracts were transferred to the new firm for the sum of £1, surely one of the most generous transfers in modern " company promotion."

As originally planned, the east side of the ground was laid out for building berths, the centre for engineering, joiners, frame and other shops, and at the west end 120 feet was reserved as a site for a dry dock 355 feet long.

ELTRINGHAMS LTD.

This ground was afterwards utilised for an additional shipbuilding berth. The offices and stores were on the north side and the whole establishment was thoroughly up to date.

This new shipbuilding and marine engineering works was formally opened on 5th February, 1914, by Mr Durham Walker Fitzgerald, chairman of the company, in the presence of a distinguished gathering.

When the transfer from South Shields to Willington Quay was duly effected, and the new company formed, the directors of the company were Messrs D. W. Fitzgerald of South Shields (chairman), Geo. Renwick, M.P., of Newcastle, Harry Eltringham of Westoe, Henry M. Grayson of Liverpool, and Arthur F. Fitzgerald (managing director), the secretary being Mr D. W. Fitzgerald, junior.

At South Shields the speciality of the firm had been boiler making, the building of tug boats and steam trawlers, and the docking and repairing of steamers. During the war the output of the works was largely controlled by H.M. Admiralty, for whom the company built a large number of war vessels, including $21\frac{1}{2}$ knot twin screw patrol vessels driven by geared turbines, some of these vessels being disguised as merchant steamers with concealed armament. They also built and engined several cargo steamers of from 4,000 to 5,500 tons deadweight, the Willington Quay Works being specially laid out and equipped for this class of work.

During 1917 the company came under new control. The original directors retired, and a new Board was formed under the chairmanship of Mr Rowland Hodge, the other members being Messrs Clarence C. Hatry, H. Pelham-Clinton, P. Haig-Thomas, and A. F. Fitzgerald, managing director.

In 1919 the company was reconstructed under the name of Eltringham's Limited, the registered office address being 37/41 Gracechurch Street, London, E.C.3, and the secretary Mr J. G. Dixon. As a capital of the new company, 160,000 eight per cent. cum part. preference shares of £1 each and 200,000 ordinary shares of 10s. each were issued.

Mr Stanley J. Passmore joined the Board shortly after the reconstruction.

In March, 1921, Mr A. F. Fitzgerald retired from the managing directorship and Mr James G. Scott was appointed general manager and a director. In the same year the company invested £127,000 in the United Brass-founders & Engineers Limited, of Manchester, thereby securing 142,000 nine per cent. cum part. preference shares and 160,000 ordinary shares fully paid up. Sir Rowland Hodge and Mr James G. Scott became directors of this company. During 1922 the " slump " was so bad that the shipbuilding yard was closed.

MARINE ENGINEERING

Wallsend Slipway & Engineering Co., Ltd.

The making of marine engines in Wallsend began in a most modest way, and was at first quite subsidiary to another business.

The history of the genesis of this important industry in Wallsend is really the history of the Wallsend Slipway & Engineering Company.

Three large firms, Messrs C. Mitchell & Co. of Walker, Messrs Watts, Milburn & Co. of Blyth and Newcastle, and Messrs Nelson, Donkin & Co. of North Shields and Newcastle, who owned and were interested in a number of steamers, decided to establish a slipway and repairing yard, primarily for the purpose of repairing their own vessels.

As a result of this, the Wallsend Slipway Company Limited came into existence on 18th November, 1871, with

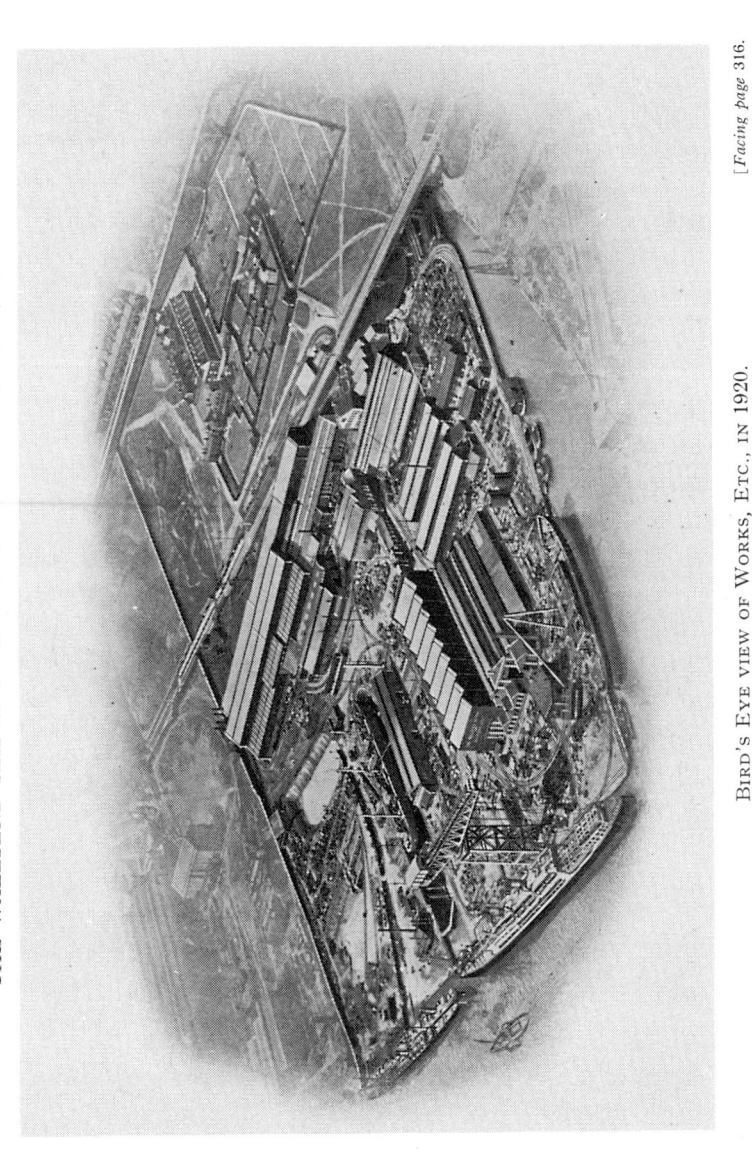

THE WALLSEND SLIPWAY AND ENGINEERING COMPANY, LTD.

BIRD'S EYE VIEW OF WORKS, ETC., IN 1920.

an authorised capital of £45,000, of which only £8,250 was at first required and paid up.

The site of the new undertaking was the foreshore between high-water mark and the river training walls, which had been put down by the Tyne Commissioners, under their improvement scheme. The old " Pilot Track " ran between the grounds of Point Pleasant House and the shore, on which up to 1870 was a margin of white sand and pebbles, although towards the centre of the river it degenerated into slake.

On this site two slipways, each one thousand feet long, were laid down by the late Mr William Jackson of Tynemouth, a well-known contractor, and the oldest brother of the present Sir John Jackson.

Each of the three firms mentioned nominated three directors. These were: Charles Mitchell, C. S. Swan, Henry F. Swan, representing C. Mitchell & Co.; Wm. Milburn, E. H. Watts, Edward Stout, representing Watts, Milburn & Co.; Henry Nelson, Robt. S. Donkin, Thomas Nelson, representing Nelson, Donkin & Co.

The first chairman of the company was Mr Charles Mitchell. While Walker was the centre of Mr Mitchell's activities, yet he did a good deal for the industries of Wallsend. He was the means of starting Messrs Swan & Hunter's shipyard. He took a leading part in the formation of the Slipway Co., and during a slack time he kept Palmer's Howdon shipyard going.

He was born at Aberdeen on 22nd May, 1820. When serving his apprenticeship the policeman called him at four o'clock every morning to give him more time for study. He was for some time assistant draughtsman to Mr John H. S. Coutts, both at Aberdeen and at Walker. On 9th May, 1854, he married Anne, the eldest daughter of Mr Wm. Swan of Walker, one of a family for many years closely associated with both Walker and Wallsend. The two other directors, Mr C. S. Swan and Mr H. F. Swan, representing Messrs Charles Mitchell & Co. on the Board of the Slipway Co. were his brothers-in-law. He retained the chairmanship until his death on 22nd August, 1895.

The chairmen who followed Mr Mitchell were Mr Henry F. Swan, March 1896 to June 1903; he was succeeded by Mr Thomas Bell, who died on 19th September, 1914. Then followed Sir Walter Plummer, one of the Members of Parliament for Newcastle, whose death took place on 10th December, 1917, and the chairmanship remained open until April, 1920, when Mr Alfred Bonnin was appointed.

The first managing director was Mr Chas. S. Swan, whose wife was a daughter of John Glover of the Carville Chemical Works.

The first secretary was Mr Thomas Crawford, cashier for Messrs Mitchell & Co. He acted until 1874, when the post was given to Mr Joseph Ward. He retired on 23rd November, 1891, and Mr Matthew Murray from Messrs Wigham Richardson & Co. succeeded him on 1st January, 1892. He resigned in 1912 owing to ill-health, and Mr James C. Henderson, the present secretary, was appointed. He had been with the company since 30th June, 1890, and is the son of the ex-Rector of Wallsend (afterwards Archdeacon of Northumberland, and still a Canon of Newcastle).

The first vessel to be taken on the slipway was one belonging to the Tyne Steam Shipping Co., the *Earl Percy*, which was berthed on 5th November, 1873.

In 1874 Mr C. S. Swan wished to be released from the slipway in order to take over Messrs Coulson, Cooke & Co.'s Wallsend shipyard, which was working in conjunction with Mr Chas. Mitchell. Mr Wm. Boyd of Messrs Thompson, Boyd & Co. of Newcastle was therefore invited to become the managing director, and the following extract from Mr Boyd's Memoranda gives a vivid picture of what the place was then like. He says:

I well remember my first visit to the works on March 11th, 1874. Mr C. S. Swan was then living at Point Pleasant House, and he and I and Mr H. F. Swan went all over the site of the new works.

WALLSEND SLIPWAY CO.

The first vessel had been taken on the slipway in November, 1873, and up to the time of my visit some thirty-five vessels had been dealt with.

It was rather a dreary looking place in these days. There was a small shop at the head of the slipways, containing the hydraulic machinery for hauling up the vessels, and a limited number of machine tools for executing repair work. At the western end was the boiler shop with a few tools. The whole being about 140 feet long by 70 feet wide overall.

Stretching down to the river were gaunt looking lines of railway—two for each slipway—with the line of rack plates between each, and these terminated in two jetties, one on each side, but outside the ground covered by the slipways, and by a line of railway to the wharf, the original slake had not then been filled up.

The riverside railway was not then in existence, and in front of Mr C. S. Swan's residence at Point Pleasant there was a large garden, with trees and shrubberies reaching down to the northern boundary of the works.

On 9th May, 1874, Mr Boyd was provisionally appointed managing director. On 22nd June this was confirmed at a Board meeting, and he entered upon his duties at once. Mr Boyd's appointment proved a turning point in the history of the company. Up to this time the business of the company centred round the slipways, and the only engineering work done was repairing work of a very limited description.

Mr Swan's interest was in ships, and fifteen months before he left, extension of the works in the shape of a graving dock was considered, but not proceeded with. Mr Boyd was, on the other hand, more interested in engines than in shipbuilding, and it was due to his initiative and foresight that the slipway branched off into marine engineering, and it was under his management that the foundations of the present huge engineering works were laid and then built up.

It is worth while noting that at this time—1874—the number of men employed was about three hundred, and the wages paid in the year were about £22,000.

The earliest movement towards engine building was made as soon as Mr Boyd got fairly settled down, for in

September, 1874, the question was raised of undertaking the manufacture of marine engines and boilers, mainly with a view of keeping the workmen together when there was a slackness in ship-repairing.

Accordingly, a set of engines and a boiler partly constructed were bought in Sunderland, and, after being completed, were fitted on board the s.s. *Castor of Hamburg*, and tried at sea on 4th April, 1876. About the same time a set of castings for engines of 100 i.h.p. were purchased from Messrs Thompson & Co. of Newcastle, and after completion were fitted into the s.s. *Maud*, belonging to Messrs Henry Clapham & Co., and successfully tried at sea on 6th November, 1875.

The boilermaking and engineering side of the works prospered, and Mr Boyd soon adventured further. In 1878 the first steel boiler made on the Tyne was built by the company for a vessel called the *Ethel*, built by C. Mitchell and Co. for Messrs Henry Clapham & Co. The plates were of Siemens mild steel, and rolled at Landore, in South Wales. The price, it is interesting to note, was on the basis of £14 per ton.

On 7th September of the same year the word "Engineering" was added to the title of the firm, and it became the Wallsend Slipway & Engineering Company Limited.

Another notable event in the history of marine engineering was that in April, 1882, the Slipway Company made a contract for the first triple expansion engines built on Tyneside. They were designed by Mr Alex. Taylor, and successfully fitted into the *Isle of Dursey*, owned by Messrs Dixon, Robson & Co. of Newcastle.

The next important landmark in the company's development was the opening of a dry dock, 540 feet long, on 12th January, 1895, and in October of the following year Mr Andrew Laing came from the Fairfield works, near Glasgow, as engineering manager, in order to relieve Mr Boyd of some of the rapidly increasing responsibility of the growing concern.

THE WALLSEND SLIPWAY AND ENGINEERING COMPANY, LTD.

THE S.S. "GIULIO CESARE" UNDER THE 180 TON CRANE.

[*Facing page* 321.

WALLSEND SLIPWAY & ENGINEERING CO.

In January, 1902, Mr Laing undertook the responsibilities of general manager, and in 1903 became a director of the company.

Mr Laing is an engineer of great experience and initiative, and under his guidance the enterprise begun by Mr Boyd has been fully developed. He re-organised the works and fitted them with the latest appliances for the largest kind of work.

In January, 1897, the company bought the site of the old cement works for £4,400 with a view to extensions westward.

In May and June, 1903, an arrangement was effected whereby the interests of the company and those of Messrs C. S. Swan & Hunter became closely allied. The shipbuilding firm were allotted fifty thousand unissued one pound preference shares, and they arranged to secure a large holding of the ordinary one pound shares. In this way the two firms became closely associated, with considerable interests in common. On the other hand, it will be noted that when the shares in Swan, Hunter & Wigham Richardson Company were allotted, certain shares were allotted to shareholders in the Slipway Company.

In 1905 the making of marine steam turbine engines was begun, and the first steamer the company engined with turbines was the s.s. *Immingham* of 6,500 h.p.; the 68,000 h.p. turbine engines of the *Mauretania*, finished the following year, show the rapid progress made in this direction.

Meanwhile the slipways became of less and less importance, and finally they were discarded in October, 1909, the last vessel taken on being the s.s. *Jet*.

July, 1910, saw in use the large electric crane, the second of its kind on Tyneside. It is capable of lifting 180 tons, and has a maximum reach of 140 feet.

On 31st December, 1911, Mr Wm. Boyd[1] retired from

---

[1] See the "Eighteen Mayors of the Borough" for further biographical notes.

the active management of the company, after nearly thirty-eight years of service. How greatly the works grew under his charge may be gauged by this brief sketch of its history.

The works under Mr Laing continued to prosper. During the war, like all other similar firms, they were working at full pressure, under difficult conditions, as eight hundred and thirty-four of their men, sooner or later, joined H.M. Forces. To replace these as far as possible, they engaged two hundred and twenty girls and trained them for their special jobs in the engineering shop, boiler works, foundry, pattern shop, and turbine blade-making department.

In the five years (1914-1918) sixty-eight ships were engined with a total i.h.p. of 1,346,290. These included the first class battle-ships, the *Queen Elizabeth* and the *Malaya*, both of which were fitted with four screw direct driven engines, with Parsons' geared cruising turbines. They also engined the "mystery" ship, *Furious*, and others, and twenty-six T.B.D.'s. The engines of the earlier boats were geared turbines of Parsons' type, but the later ones were all of the Brown-Curtis type.

The firm further constructed one hundred and eighty-eight oil burning installations of 522,100 i.h.p. for various vessels, and their hands were always full with repairs, overhauling, and dry dock work.

The North-Eastern Marine Engineering Co.

The North-Eastern Marine Engineering Company commenced business as marine engine builders, etc., in 1865 at South Dock, Sunderland. Some time previously the promoters acquired land at Wallsend, where their engineering works were built, and manufacturing operations commenced in 1882. The Wallsend works were known as the Northumberland engine works.

The first chairman of the company was Alderman

NORTH EASTERN MARINE ENGINEERING COMPANY, LTD.

VIEW OF WORKS FROM AIRSHIP, MAY, 1920.

NORTH-EASTERN MARINE ENGINEERING CO.

William Hunter of Newcastle-upon-Tyne, and the first managing director was Mr John Frederick Spencer. Other directors were Mr Hilton Philipson, Sir George Elliott, Mr William Black, and Mr John Jonassohn. At a later date Mr Hugh Morton of Biddick, Sir Lindsay Wood, Bart., and Mr Michael Havelock joined the company and eventually became directors.

Mr William Stobart succeeded Mr William Hunter as chairman in 1883, and at this time Mr Roland Philipson was serving his apprenticeship in the works, and in the course of the next few years acquired a large interest in the company. Mr Roland Philipson became a director in 1890, followed Mr Stobart as chairman in 1905, and continued to fill the position until he was killed in the deplorable railway accident at Grantham on the 19th September, 1906. He was the son of Mr Hilton Philipson of Tynemouth, one of the founders, and a nephew of Mr W. S. Daglish. He took especial interest in this district and was a director of the North-Eastern Railway Co. He was a generous supporter of every good cause, and his death at the age of forty-three was a great loss to Tyneside.

As a mark of the regard in which he was held, the workmen and apprentices of the North-Eastern Marine Engineering works decided to endow a cot for children at the Newcastle Infirmary at a cost of £500, and levied themselves until the amount was raised. The bed was handed over on 13th April, 1907. His brother, Mr Hylton Philipson, succeeded him as chairman of the company.

When Mr Spencer resigned his post as managing director in 1869, owing to advancing years, Mr P. D. Nichol succeeded him, and on Mr Nichol's death, caused by the bursting of a steam pipe in January, 1871, Mr William Allan was appointed general manager, and Mr Kelsey works manager. Mr Allan retained the position of general manager until he left the company in 1887.

It was he who planned the first buildings at Wallsend, and the houses for the foremen at Northumberland Villas, for the mechanics at North Terrace, and for lower paid employees at South Terrace—over one hundred houses in all. Mr William Allan was an adventurous Scotsman who was born at Dundee on 29th November, 1837. He was chief engineer in a blockade runner during the American Civil War, and for some time a prisoner in the hands of the Federal Navy, and he was a poet as well as an engineer. He ultimately went into the House of Commons as parliamentary representative of Gateshead in 1895. There he did good work for the engine room staff in the Navy, and with great effort assisted in securing for the engineers a status corresponding to the rank held by deck officers.

After he left the Wallsend firm in 1887 he established the Scotia engine works at Sunderland, where he inaugurated an eight-hour working day. This experiment was at first such a success and its results appeared so convincing and satisfactory, that Mr Allan succeeded in inducing the Government to adopt the eight-hour day for their dockyards.

This experiment was based on the theory that a man would do as much work during an eight-hour day as in nine hours. Labour leaders inspired the men to prove that their contention for shorter hours, without reduction of pay, was right, but the workmen soon fell back, with the result that the firm, to get the same output, had to pay an extra hour's work as overtime. Recently the same theory was advanced by the miners, with the same unsatisfactory result.

Although the Scotia works and the dockyards continue this shortened day, no yard on the Tyne has followed this example.

Mr Allan was a genial, energetic, and useful Member of Parliament, and in 1902 received the honour of Knighthood. He died on 28th December, 1903.

NORTH-EASTERN MARINE ENGINEERING CO.

Mr J. H. Irwin became general manager for the company in 1887, with Mr William Kilvington manager of the Wallsend works. In 1892 Mr Summers Hunter was appointed assistant manager.

In 1895 Mr Kilvington died somewhat suddenly, and Mr Hunter was appointed general manager of the Wallsend works and a director of the company. In 1900 Mr Irwin retired and Mr Hunter was appointed managing director of both Wallsend and Sunderland works.

Mr Walter Beattie, who had joined the company at its inception in 1865 as chief accountant, was appointed secretary in 1870, which position he held until 1912. During this year Mr S. T. Harrison,[1] who for some years was joint secretary with Mr Beattie, was appointed secretary on the retirement of Mr Beattie, and in April of the same year the head office of the firm was moved from Sunderland to Wallsend.

The gradual growth of the company has been remarkable, and especially during the last twenty years. In 1901, when the Newcastle Electric Supply Co. commenced active operations, the North-Eastern Marine Co. was one of the first to take advantage of the electric supply, and the Wallsend works were completely equipped with electric driving. They were the first large works in the country to purchase electric power in bulk, and for some years they were the largest purchasers of electricity in the country.

This firm erected the first electric cantilever crane on the north-east coast. It was tested and in working order in July, 1909. Its height above the wharf level is 154 feet, and it is capable of lifting 150 tons at a radius of 80 feet.

Mr Hylton Philipson succeeded his brother (Mr Roland Philipson) as chairman of the company in 1906, and on Mr Philipson's retirement Mr Hunter was appointed chairman on 30th June, 1920.

[1] See the "Eighteen Mayors of the Borough" for further biographical notes.

Mr Summers Hunter, who is now at the head of the company, was born at Inverness on 12th July, 1856, and received his early education at the Inverness Royal Academy. His family came south in 1869, and in 1870 Mr Hunter commenced to serve his apprenticeship as an engineer at Kidsgrove in Staffordshire. During his apprenticeship he was brought into close touch with some well-known engineers, such as Mr George Bidder (who was known as the "calculating" boy), Mr Sam Bidder (his brother), and Mr George Elliott (afterwards Sir George Elliott, Bart.). These men had an influence upon young Hunter's life, and we find him attending science classes at the Wedgwood Institute, Burslem, for some years; he often had to walk some five or six miles to these classes, and for a few years he was a teacher in science subjects. In 1880 Mr Hunter came to the North-Eastern Marine Engineering Works at Sunderland. He spent two years at sea as a guarantee engineer, was shipwrecked twice, and in 1883 he accepted a junior appointment at the Wallsend works. It is worthy of note that he has passed through every grade in engineering in the works which he now controls, and his close association with workmen of all classes has made him a fair-minded and sympathetic employer, and he is known as a hard worker. He took a great interest in our local Volunteers, and helped greatly to secure the Drill Hall in Wallsend for the 5th Northumberland Fusiliers. He was also for a time on the Urban District Council.

In recognition of his work during the war, he was made a Commander of the Order of the British Empire. Mr Hunter is a past President of the North-East Coast Institution of Engineers and Shipbuilders, and also of the Institute of Marine Engineers; he is a member of Council of the Institution of Civil Engineers, and the Institution of Naval Architects.

THE PARSONS MARINE STEAM TURBINE COMPANY, LTD.

THE EPOCH-MAKING "TURBINIA" STEAMING AT 34 KNOTS.

[*Facing page* 327.

The Parsons' Marine Steam Turbine Co. Ltd.

Messrs The Parsons' Marine Steam Turbine Co. Ltd.

This is one of the important works on Tyneside. The founder was the Hon. Charles Algernon Parsons, the fourth son of Earl Rosse, of Birr Castle, King's County, whose studies in astronomy are well known. Mr Parsons was born on 13th June, 1854, at Connaught Place, London, and was educated at St John's College, Cambridge, and was eleventh wrangler in 1877. Soon after leaving Cambridge he went into the Elswick works, where he served his time as a practical engineer.

In 1876 he patented an epicycloidal engine which may be considered the forerunner of his turbine. Nine years later the first steam turbine was successfully used on land to generate electric current. This was a great achievement.

A steam turbine differs from an ordinary engine by the substitution of a rotary for a reciprocating action. In the one case, steam forces a piston forward, then it is stopped, then forced back again, and so on, backwards and forwards, entailing great loss of energy and great strain in the stopping and starting of each stroke. In the turbine there is simply one continuous motion always in one direction, with few working parts and little loss by friction.

At this time Mr Parsons was a partner in the firm of Clarke, Chapman, Parson & Co., of Gateshead. In 1889 he retired from this firm and built the Heaton turbine works.

In order to explore the practical possibilities of the turbine propelling ships and to test thoroughly Mr Parsons' theories, a syndicate was formed under the title of the Marine Steam Turbine Co. Ltd., with its registered office at 57 Westgate Road, Newcastle. Those chiefly associated with the company were the Earl of Rosse, Christopher J. Leyland, John B. Simpson, A. A. Campbell Swinton, George Clayton, Norman C. Cookson, H. C. Harvey, and Gerald Stoney. In January, 1894, this company agreed to take over and work Sir Charles Parsons' inventions and pay him a royalty on every engine sold. A licence in pursuance of this agreement was granted by Mr Parsons to the company, dated 4th December, 1894.

The epoch-making *Turbinia* was built by this pioneer firm, and she ran a trial off the Tyne on 16th December, 1896, when a speed of 29·6 knots was obtained. The *Turbinia* was a steel vessel 100 feet long, 9 feet beam, 3 feet draught, and 44 tons displacement. (See illustration.)

She was sent to the naval review in the following June, and her speed of thirty-one knots was the wonder of the day, and created immense interest in marine engineering circles.

The success of this trial vessel was such that the builders felt assured of their future prospects and decided to wind up the syndicate and form a new company. Hence in 1897 The Parsons' Marine Steam Turbine Co. Ltd. was registered. This company had a capital of £500,000 in £100 shares. There were issued 800 fully paid and 1,641 shares £80 paid. By an agreement dated 22nd September, 1897, all the original company's rights under the licence of 4th December, 1894, and all its other assets were transferred to the new company.

Land for the new works was secured at Wallsend Quay on the site previously occupied by the Carville Chemical Co., and afterwards the land to the west, given up by Mason & Barry, copper smelters, was also secured.

The directors were the same as those in the pioneer company, with the Hon. Charles A. Parsons as managing director.

In spite of the success of the *Turbinia*, steam turbines only very slowly won their way into our naval marine.

The first torpedo boat destroyer built for the Navy, the *Viper*, was unfortunately wrecked during a fog on the Channel Islands, and the second vessel, the *Cobra*, had an even more disastrous history. This torpedo boat destroyer was a twin screw boat 223 feet long and 350 tons displacement, built by Sir W. G. Armstrong & Co., and fitted with turbine engines at the Wallsend works. On her trials she had run thirty-five knots an hour. She left the Tyne on Tuesday forenoon, 17th September, 1901, in charge of Lieutenant Alan W. Bosworth Smith, with seventy-nine men on board. Over twenty-nine of these were from Messrs Parsons' yard. On Thursday, news reached Wallsend that the *Cobra* was lost and that nearly all of those on board were drowned.

The affair was a tragedy; she had run upon a sandbank near the Dowsing Lightship at seven-thirty a.m. on Wednesday, and in the rough sea only twelve men, including two of Messrs Parsons' fitters, escaped. The lost included Mr Robert Barnard, manager of Messrs Parsons' works, and Mr Sanderson of the Elswick shipyard.

In 1911, in recognition of the great value of his work as a discoverer and engineer, the Honourable C. A. Parsons was created a Knight Commander of the Bath. He has served on many National Committees and has been awarded many degrees and positions of honour, and what his inventions have done for science and for commerce have been especially recognised in America, France and Germany.

As we have already said, the turbine type of engine was only slowly adopted, and for some years they only used them for fast war ships, cross channel steamers, etc. Then the large liners tried them, and afterwards their adoption became general. During the war "Parsons" had their hands more than full, and turned out engines over 700,000 horse-power.

With regard to the early direct driven turbines they were found not to be economical for the ordinary tramp vessels, and the primary reason why direct driven turbines (turbines connected directly to the propeller shafting) are unsuitable for slow speed steamers, i.e., ordinary cargo ships, from nine to twelve knots speed, is because it is necessary to have a high rate of revolutions to obtain economy of steam in the turbines, and that ships of the cargo boat type are most efficiently driven by a propeller of large diameter, working at a comparatively low number of revolutions. To utilise direct driven turbines, therefore, meant a compromise and sacrificing both the efficiency of the turbine itself and of the propeller to such an extent that ordinary slow running reciprocating engines were the more economical of the two. The only means of reducing the rate of revolutions for direct driven turbines is to increase the diameter of the rotors, at a very much increased cost of manufacture. However, by the adoption of mechanical gearing between the turbines and the propeller shaft, the foregoing sacrifices are almost entirely eliminated. At first single geared turbines were tried, i.e., the turbine was run at about 1,650 revolutions per minute and geared down so that the propeller ran at about eighty-three. This compromise, however, was hardly quite satisfactory, and eventually double reduction gearing was introduced so that the turbines might be run even as high as four thousand revolutions and the propeller at about sixty-five. This solution is a great improvement as further economy is obtained and at present holds the field for slow speed ships. By choosing a suitable ratio of gearing, the turbine and propeller can each be run at their respective speeds of maximum efficiency.

At present Sir Charles A. Parsons, K.C.B., is chairman, he and Mr Robert J. Walker, C.B.E., are joint managing directors of the Parsons' Steam Turbine Co. Ltd., and Mr W. H. Pilmour is the secretary.

As regards the Marine Steam Turbine Co. Ltd., it was found impractical to wind it up, and it still continues with its registered office at the Turbinia works, Wallsend. In April, 1922, there were twenty-three shareholders; the Hon. Sir C. A. Parsons held one hundred and eighty vendor's shares, and there were three hundred ordinary shares issued, all at £50 each, and of these Mr Parsons

holds eight. The largest ordinary shareholders were
Mr C. J. Leyland, The Meade, Beal, who held forty-
four shares; Messrs Clayton and Gibson, 7 Grey Street,
held forty; Sir J. P. Griffiths, Rathmines Castle, Dublin,
had thirty, and the Hon. G. L. Parsons, Worthing
House, Basingstoke, held twenty-two shares. The
present directors are: Sir C. A. Parsons, Messrs C. J.
Leyland, A. A. C. Swinton, civil engineer, London,
S.W., and J. B. Simpson. Mr W. H. Pilmour was the
secretary.

The Shipbuilding and Engineering " Slump "

The years 1921 and 1922 were years of acute general
depression in trade all over the country. After a period
of artificial and feverish prosperity the " after the war
slump " came with unexpected suddenness, precipitated by
the miners' strike, which shut down many furnaces and
works for lack of coals.

How this depression affected our town can be estimated
by the following comparisons between the output of six of
our shipbuilding and engineering works for 1922, as compared with the year 1911, which was a year of general good
trade.

Shipbuilding—Tonnage Launched on the Tyne

	In 1911	In 1922
Swan, Hunter & Wigham Richardson, Ltd.	125,050 tons	71,853 tons
Northumberland Shipbuilding Co. Ltd.	66,400 ,,	18,054 ,,
Tyne Iron Shipbuilding Co. Ltd.	19,459 ,,	—
Totals	210,909 ,,	89,907 ,,

Marine Engineering—Indicated Horse-power Fitted.

	In 1911	In 1922
Wallsend Slipway & Engineering Co. Ltd.	72,800 tons	20,300 tons
North Eastern Marine Eng. Co. Ltd. (at Wallsend)	55,080 ,,	32,110 ,,
Parsons Marine Steam Turbine Co. Ltd.	68,500 ,,	17,500 ,,
Totals	196,380 ,,	69,910 ,,

Taking the Tyne as a whole, the tonnage launched in 1922 was 240,129 tons, as compared with 436,466 tons in 1911.

Sundry Works

Walker and Wallsend Union Gas Co.

To Mr Addison Potter we owe the first gas supplied to the district. He was a Newcastle man whose father, Addison Langhorn Potter, resided at Heaton Hall (having bought the Heaton estate from Sir Matthew White Ridley in 1840).

He began to manufacture fire bricks, gas retorts, and fire clay goods at Willington Quay in 1846 on land recovered from the foreshore of the river. Two years later he started a gas-making plant. At first it was a very small concern and the purifier was in a downstairs room of a dwelling-house.

Howdon, unlike Willington and Wallsend, was then a compact village, and for many years Mr Potter supplied twelve street lamps with gas free of charge.

In 1855 Mr George Auburn Allan came from Earsdon to act as manager of the growing gas works, and shortly after this the first gas pipe was laid to Wallsend, crossing the Gut near the present slipway bridge. As the use of gas increased, Mr Potter required a larger place, and on 25th March, 1863, started new works near the Willington Gut on a piece of land having an area of 3,116 square yards.

On 7th December, 1868, the village of Carville was illuminated by nine lamps, and gradually gas lighting spread in streets and works, but less quickly in private houses.

In the meanwhile the Walker & St Anthony's Gas Company, which was formed in 1861 to take over the gas supply commenced by Messrs Losh, Wilson and Bell in 1840, had established itself to the westward, but neither

The Gas Company

firm had obtained statutory powers under an Act of Parliament; hence when, in 1864, the Newcastle Gas Company got their Act passed, they ousted the Walker Company from St Anthony's without compensation, merely buying the pipes already laid. This insecure position as a private Gas Company, and the fact that both companies were supplying gas to Wallsend, led the Walker Company to make overtures to Mr Addison Potter to join them in obtaining an Act of Parliament, and the Act of 1866 incorporating the Walker & Wallsend Union Gas Company, with a capital of £19,000, was the result.

The industrial works, which had hitherto made their own gas, discontinued their own gas plant and obtained their requirements from the new statutory company, whose area comprised the mid-Tyne district between Newcastle and North Shields.

In 1866 the gas made by the united company was eighteen million feet, and the price to the ordinary consumer was 4s. 6d. per thousand cubic feet.

Mr Thos. Forrest was at this time the manager for the Walker Company, and Mr G. A. Allan the manager for Mr Potter. On the amalgamation it was arranged that Mr Forrest should be the manager for the united company and that Mr Allan's services should be retained as a director. Mr Forrest continued (except for an interval of four years) as manager until January, 1896, and Mr Allan continued his directorship until his death. He was for fifteen years deputy chairman, and for one year chairman.

The united company occupied the gas works at Willington Quay in conjunction with the old works at Walker until 1908, when the large modern works near Howdon station were erected. This new place, built under the supervision of the company's own engineer, Mr Alex. B. Walker, covers an area of twelve and a half acres, and can produce one and a half million cubic feet per twenty-four hours. It was opened on 9th October, 1908, by the chairman of the company, Colonel Crawford.

The output increased to over three hundred million cubic feet, and the pre-war price was 2s. 5d. per thousand cubic feet less five per cent.

The authorised capital of £19,000, with which the company commenced in 1866, has been augmented to £319,255.

The following are the chief officials associated with the history of this prosperous concern:

Chairmen of Directors.
>   Mr Addison Potter from commencement until July, 1878.
>   Richard Cail from July, 1878, until October, 1893.
>   Thomas Crawford from November, 1893, until December, 1908.
>   George A. Allan from January, 1908, until January, 1909.
>   Charles J. Potter (son of the first chairman) from January, 1909—

Managers.
>   Thomas Forrest from the commencement until September, 1885.
>   Hugh McGillivray, September, 1885, until August, 1887.
>   R. J. McMillan, August, 1887, until January, 1890.
>   Thomas Forrest, January, 1890, until January, 1896.
>   A. B. Walker, January, 1896—

Secretaries.
>   R. Calvert Clapham, commencement to December, 1881.
>   Frank Carr, January, 1882, to May, 1894.
>   Chas. H. Armstrong, June, 1894—

Tharsis Sulphur & Copper Co. Ltd.

The copper works at Willington were started by Wm. Herbert Gossage, one of a family widely known for some eighty years as inventors and manufacturing chemists.

Wm. Gossage of Widnes was a man whose services in the realm of practical chemistry have rarely been surpassed. The new processes he introduced were numerous and covered a wide field, and among these were soap-making and copper-smelting.

As to soap-making, he founded the widely known firm of Wm. Gossage & Sons, which his younger son, Mr Frederick Herbert, carried on after Mr Wm. Gossage's death in April, 1877.

As to copper-smelting, the eldest son, Mr Wm. Herbert, elected to come to Tyneside to erect works to carry out his father's methods, discovered and tested at Runcorn.

Wm. Herbert Gossage secured a lease of 17,270 square yards from the Newcastle Corporation commencing from 29th September, 1853, and started copper-smelting at Willington, and he also, for a short time, was interested in soap-making at the Ouseburn.

While he resided in our district he was chosen an overseer for our parish and took an active interest in our local affairs. He was, however, a martyr to rheumatism, and after about three years' work at Willington, hoping that a drier and a more sunny climate would effect a cure, he emigrated to Australia, where he founded the Apollo Soap Works.

Mr Gossage transferred the copper works in 1856 to Mr Cornelius F. Clements, a merchant of Liverpool, and he disposed of them in 1858 to John Williamson, James C. Stevenson (the owners of Tyne Dock, Jarrow, and Friars Goose Alkali Works), and Charles Tennant of the Hebburn Alkali Works. These three gentlemen traded at

Willington Copper Works as John Williamson & Co., and five years later they took a lease of about half an acre additional land for sixty-five years as from Michaelmas Day, 1863. In 1867 the works were transferred to the newly formed Tharsis Sulphur & Copper Co. Ltd., of which prosperous concern the three partners in the Willington Company were the chief founders.

The connection between alkali making and copper extraction will be obvious if we remember that pyrites is of vital importance for the manufacture of sulphuric acid (see page 273), and that the Spanish ores, from the Tharsis mines, contain about fifty per cent. of sulphur and about one per cent. of copper.

The ore is brought from the mines and is first shipped to the alkali works, where the sulphur is extracted; then it is handed over to the copper works, where the copper and a small amount of silver is taken out. The residue is an iron ore of which sixty-five per cent. is pure iron.

As at first erected, and up to about the year 1870, only furnaces for the smelting of copper ores and precipitates were worked at Willington Quay. In that year, however, some of the smelting furnaces were demolished, and others, for the calcining of poor ores, by what is known as the " wet process," were erected.

About the year 1891 the smelting furnaces were entirely dismantled, and the copper precipitates produced by the " wet process " at Willington Quay are now sent to the company's works at Hebburn to be smelted and refined. In 1913 two mechanical furnaces were erected which took the place of the twelve calcining furnaces worked by hand; and a small briquetting plant was added in 1918 to transform the by-product of iron ore ("Blue Billy") into briquettes, so as to be more adaptable for iron and steel making. About a hundred and thirty men are employed at the Willington works, and Mr Wm. T. Holt is the works manager.

Messrs Henry D. Pochin & Co. Ltd.

This firm was established in Lancashire many years before they came into our district. It was founded by Mr Henry Davis Pochin, who resided in Leicestershire, but whose business office was in Salford.

The firm makes various grades of sulphate of alumina, which is used in paper-making and in the purification of water. The raw material is china clay, which is the felspar resulting from the decomposition of granite rocks. Cornwall is the great source of supply.

The site of the Willington Quay works was recovered from the river as part of the River Improvement scheme, and from 1864 to 1867 Messrs Bainbridge and Wilson built small vessels on the land.

However, in 1867 Messrs H. D. Pochin & Co. began the present works. The object of having these works on the Tyne was to supply the paper makers in Scotland, and on the Tyne, and as far south as London, as the freight on their products to these districts was much less from the Tyne than from Liverpool, and furthermore the freight on the china clay from Cornwall to the Tyne, where coal cargoes home were available, was cheaper than to the Mersey.

Hence the establishment of this Lancashire firm upon the banks of the Tyne.

In June, 1867, the rental value of the place was £250, but in the year 1870 Mr H. D. Pochin discovered and patented a process of making an improved form of aluminous cake, and this was the means of greatly extending their business, and involved an extension of their Willington works. In 1874 the rateable value rose to £1,000.

The company is now the second largest owner of china clay mines in Britain, and the second largest producers of sulphates of alumina in the country, and the only company which can supply all the various materials used in the potteries.

The resident managers have been : Mr J. Broughton until 1871, Mr John Johnson 1871-1876, Mr John Bowker 1876-1903, and Mr Edwin B. Andrews 1903—

The Willington Foundry Co. Ltd.

Mr Thomas Davison, who carried on the business of block and mast-maker on part of Messrs Hurry's dockyard, at the south-east side of Howdon, was obliged to vacate his premises owing to the contemplated deposit of ballast over the larger part of the old village of Howdon Panns. Hence in 1865 he moved his mast-making yard to a site near the mouth of the Willington Gut, recently occupied by James Clark.

Mr Thos. Davison died on 24th March, 1871, aged fifty-seven years, and the business was carried on by his sons, Thomas and Matthew, under the title of Davison Brothers. However, owing to the decreasing demand for wooden masts, the works were gradually converted into a foundry for the manufacture of metal goods, used by chemical works and shipyards.

In 1890 the place was transferred to Thos. E. Brigham of South Shields, and it was carried on as R. F. Brigham & Co. until 1908, when Mr James W. Ellis of Gosforth (who is interested in several other firms on Tyneside) and Robert Ellis, his son, took over the works and continued the business under the title of the Willington Foundry Co. They greatly enlarged the area of the premises, and increased the capacity of the foundry so as to deal with a larger class of work. In 1916 the concern was converted into a limited liability company with Mr Robert Ellis as the managing director. The foundry now turns out castings up to fifteen tons weight for marine engines, turbines, and shipwork generally.

The Tyne Pontoons & Dry Dock Co.

In 1883 Mr Geo. Renwick (of Messrs Fisher and Renwick, shipbrokers and shipowners, Newcastle) and Mr Alex. Taylor promoted a dry dock company with the idea of using pontoons of Mr Taylor's own special design, rather than the old form of graving dock. On 26th August, 1884, the Tyne Pontoons & Dry Dock Co. was formed, and twenty acres of land were secured at the extreme south-west of the parish. Mr Geo. Renwick was the chairman, Mr Alex. Taylor was works manager, and Mr Sidney Old was the secretary.

The first pontoon was finished and the workshops ready by 4th May, 1887, on which date the place was formally opened by docking the Chinese cruiser, *Cheh Yuan*.

It was found that a manager who could devote his whole time to the docks was necessary. Therefore Mr Alex. Taylor, who was a consulting marine engineer in practice in Newcastle, retired from his position at the dock, and Mr Jas. G. McIlvenna, of Messrs Edwards' Dry Docks, South Shields, was invited to become general manager, and took entire charge in July, 1887.

After the works were put into complete working order, the company became very successful. A graving dock and a second pontoon were added.

The firm continued its course until 1903, when it was incorporated with the new firm of Messrs Swan, Hunter & Wigham Richardson. Three years after this Mr McIlvenna retired from the docks and began on his own account as a consulting naval architect.[1]

M. W. Swinburne & Sons

The founder of this business was Mark Wm. Swin-

[1] See the "Eighteen Mayors of the Borough" for further biographical notes.

burne, who was a native of Newcastle and served his apprenticeship as an engineer at Elswick works. Before commencing business at Wallsend, he had been twenty-five years with Henry Watson & Co., of the High Bridge, Newcastle.

In 1892 he and his son, Charles, built and equipped a brass foundry and began business on an acre of land which had once been the site of Gair's Ropery. The business prospered and both Mr Swinburne and his son took an active interest in the public affairs of the town.

In November, 1908, he was elected to represent the Holy Cross Ward on the Borough Council, and on 10th December his name was added to the Commission of the Peace. When Mr S. T. Harrison left Wallsend Mr Swinburne was chosen to take his place on the Aldermanic Bench. On 11th November, 1910, he was chosen as the first Mayor of the extended borough, and twelve months later he was again elected for a second term of service.

He founded a boot club for Wallsend, and he was careful to arrange that the poorer people had an opportunity of joining in the general festivities when King George V. was crowned.

He was a consistent Wesleyan, took an active interest in temperance work, and in all his dealings showed an old-world courtesy and a gentleness and kindness of manner that won for him the regard of everyone who came in contact with him.

He died at the age of seventy-six at Jesmond Park East after a brief illness, on 23rd May, 1912, and was buried on 25th at Jesmond old cemetery. His estate was valued at £26,460 6s. 6d. gross, and was left to his widow, his two sons, his daughter, and his son-in-law.

The business was continued by his younger son and partner, Mr Charles Curry Swinburne, who had taken a less prominent part in civic affairs. On 1st November, 1912, when there was a casual vacancy in the Hadrian Ward, he was elected upon the Town Council, and on the

November following he changed to the Carville Ward. He became a Justice of Peace in December, 1912.

The pressure of business prevented his giving much time to other matters, and in order to lessen his burden he retired from the Town Council on 1st November, 1920. This retirement unfortunately did not sufficiently lighten the load. Overwork and overstrain unhinged his mind, and he ended his days by stepping in front of an approaching train at Heaton station on 12th October, 1922.

The Newcastle-upon-Tyne Electric Supply Co. Ltd.

The science of gas lighting in the " eighties " was in a very crude state compared with what it was twenty years later, and when the usefulness of electricity began to be recognised it was looked upon as a source of illumination rather than a source of power.

John T. Merz, Ph.D., a well-known manufacturing chemist and chemical works organiser; Robert Spence Watson, a solicitor, the leader of the Liberal party in the north of England, and a literary man who earned his degree of LL.D.; and Thomas George Gibson, a solicitor, an alderman of the city of Newcastle, and a wealthy city property owner, promoted the formation of an electric lighting company, and as a result the Newcastle-upon-Tyne Electric Supply Company was incorporated in 1889, mainly with the object of supplying electric light in the city of Newcastle. Before a provisional order was obtained, the Newcastle & District Electric Lighting Company also was formed. Instead of fighting each other, these two companies agreed to divide the prospective spoils, the District Company taking the western part of Newcastle, and the Supply Company taking the east part of the town.

The original directors of the company were Messrs T. G. Gibson (chairman), John T. Merz, F. R. Goddard,

M. W. Lambert, James Tennant, Dr R. Spence Watson, and Mr Lindsay Wood.

The first generating station was erected at Pandon Dene, to the north-east of Ellison Place, and the plant consisted of two 200 horse-power slow speed engines, each driving an alternator of 100 horse-power capacity by means of ropes.

During the first few years the energies of the company were devoted to showing how superior the electric light was to gas, and this put the gas companies on their mettle, and we had a very healthy, and, from a consumer's point of view, a very profitable competition. The Newcastle Corporation Street Lighting Committee gave both systems an opportunity to display their merits, and as a result the public got the choice of electric lighting or vastly improved gas lighting.

Meanwhile the value of electric power for works and factories was recognised, and the directors of the Supply Company saw a wider field of opportunity before them. The action of the Walker & Wallsend Union Gas Company, however, in securing parliamentary powers to supply electricity in Wallsend, Willington, and Howdon, brought the Newcastle Electric Supply Company face to face with the loss of a large and very important area which they had hoped to secure for themselves. The result of this was that terms were arranged in 1900 with the Gas Company, and their contemplated power station at Neptune Bank was taken over by the Supply Company and electricity in bulk was to be sold to the Gas Company, at cost price, plus six per cent. on capital expenditure.

The banks of Pandon Dene had not proved a bed of roses to the Supply Company. The residents of that part of Newcastle would not be convinced that the smoke and grit which issued from the generating station chimneys were quite harmless and healthy, nor was the spray of condensed steam, which was freely distributed upon passers-by, considered as merely a harmless shower-bath.

Hence an unsympathetic City Corporation was often interfering and unfeelingly complaining about nuisances.

When the acquisition of the Neptune Bank power station and the limited site at Pandon Dene came before the directors, they faced the matter boldly, and with sanguine visions of a very wide extension of area before them, they resolved to equip an entirely new power station at Wallsend. This policy necessitated the scrapping of plant which had cost over £100,000, but events, as will be seen, in a very short time fully justified this course.

Hence the generating power station was established at Wallsend, where the company had more room to grow, and where the Newcastle officials would cease from troubling, and those weary of " injunctions ". might have rest.

The Neptune Bank power station was opened in 1901 by the Right Hon. Lord Kelvin, and Pandon Dene was converted into a sub-station where the current was transformed to a pressure of 240 volts direct current for lighting, and 480 volts for power. The equipment at Neptune Bank was designed to supply three phase current at a pressure of 6,000 volts, and the generators were driven by three marine engines, one made by the Wallsend Slipway Company, and two by Wigham Richardson & Company.

Not content with the mid-Tyne possibilities, the company in the same year secured rights to supply electricity to Gosforth and Long Benton. In 1902 authority was obtained to supply a large coal-mining area of 375 square miles to the north of Wallsend, and also to supply the County of Durham Electric Power Supply Company. In the year following, the company obtained an Act enabling them to take over the whole of the Walker & Wallsend Gas Company's electricity undertaking, and all their electric cables, etc. The same Act authorised the transfer of the powers possessed by the Walker Urban District Council for forty-two years, and it also gave permission to supply the North-Eastern Railway Company in any part of Northumberland and Durham, and to lay cables under the River Tyne.

Within three years the area of the company's operations had grown from a small district to one of about 600 square miles.

In 1900, before the company left Pandon, the horse-power connected with the company's system was 2,800. In 1903 this had increased to 15,500 horse-power. The Neptune Bank works, although considerably enlarged, had become inadequate, and in 1901 14½ acres of unoccupied land was secured from Allen's trustees, and the Carville power station was established. It was equipped with two 3,000 horse-power and two 7,000 horse-power turbo-alternators, and all the boilers, switch gear, and plant were of the latest type. This station was put into commercial operation in June, 1904, and it was at that date the largest generating station in Great Britain.

The works on Tyneside soon realised the advantage of buying their power from the Supply Company, and gave up their own electric generating plant, and largely scrapped their boilers and steam engines. To the shipyards and factories, this resulted in a saving in cost, and to the public and residents it meant less smoke and grime and a purer atmosphere.

In 1904 the North-Eastern Railway adopted electric traction on their Newcastle to Tynemouth lines, and the current was taken from the Carville power station. In 1906 the deputy chairman of the Railway Company stated that " the running cost, including all repairs of rolling stock and full depreciation, had been with electric traction 6¾d. per train mile as compared with 14½d. under steam; by running smaller trains and more of them, they were able to serve the public better, and make a larger profit."

Certainly the travelling public, as well as the manufacturers, have been the gainers by there being cheap electric power available.

Furthermore, two new industries were induced to start

Newcastle Electric Supply Co. 345

at Wallsend on account of the cheap current obtainable: the Thermal Syndicate Ltd. in 1903, and the Castner Kellner Alkali Company in 1906.

The Carville power station grew until it reached a size beyond which further extension under one roof was deemed inadvisable. Therefore, a second station (Station B) was erected in 1916 on the adjoining land entirely independent of the other. The capacity of Station A is 56,000 h.p., and that of Station B 73,700 h.p.

In 1920 the original Wallsend power station at Neptune Bank was entirely superseded as a generating station. The three marine engines and the old turbine were scrapped and the engine house and boiler shed were converted into storage houses and part of the land at the west end was transferred to the Thermal Syndicate.

Dr John T. Merz, who had been chairman since 1905, retired from the chairmanship in 1915 and was succeeded by Mr John H. Armstrong. He, in turn, retired from the post in 1921, and Mr Robert P. Sloan, who had, as the retiring chairman said, " nursed " the company for over sixteen years, was made chairman as well as managing director of the still growing enterprise.

We are not dealing with the general history of the company except so far as it concerns Wallsend. Sufficient, therefore, to say that on 31st December, 1921, its share and debenture capital was £7,692,755. The power connected to its system amounted to over 500,000 horsepower, and it supplied users as far north as Shilbottle in Northumberland, and as far south as Malton in Yorkshire. The consulting engineers are Messrs Merz and McLellan, the chief operating engineer Mr James Cusworth, and the secretary to the company Mr Matthew Short.

The Castner Kellner Alkali Co. Ltd.

The early days of this company have an interesting history.

In 1886 Mr Hamilton Young Castner came from New

York to London to introduce his invention for making metallic sodium. This metal was required for making aluminium by the reduction of the double chloride of aluminium and sodium. It was the only method known at that time of obtaining aluminium, and was being carried out then in a small works near Birmingham.

The high cost of materials made the price of aluminium 60s. per lb., and this prohibited its general use, but Mr Castner's invention promised, if successful, to make a large reduction in cost possible. Mr Wm. Hart Cullen, who was then acting as consulting mechanical engineer in London, designed and erected experimental furnaces in London on such a scale that the invention of Mr Castner was proved commercially practical. The result of this was the formation of " The Aluminium Co. Ltd. " in 1887, with Mr Castner as managing director, and Mr Cullen as resident engineer.

The chairman was the Right Hon. G. W. Balfour, and among other influential members of the Board of Directors were the late Sir Henry Roscoe of Owen's College, and the late Sir Wm. Anderson, Director-General of H.M. Ordnance Factories, Woolwich.

Ground was taken at Oldbury, near Birmingham, on which works were erected for the manufacture of sodium and aluminium and its alloys.

By means of the improved process aluminium was sold at 20s. per lb. instead of 60s., and later this price was further reduced. This was the result of cheaper sodium, and the lower cost opened up new uses for both products.

At that time chemical knowledge was making rapid strides, especially in electro-chemistry, and P. Héroult of Switzerland, and C. M. Hall of Pittsburg, U.S.A., brought out simultaneously their inventions for producing aluminium by direct electrolysis of alumina (bauxite) in a bath of molten cryolite. These two methods were practically alike, and both so effective that the price of aluminium was reduced to about 1s. 6d. per lb.

This great reduction was a deadly blow to the Aluminium Co., so that they had to abandon the manufacture of aluminium altogether. But Mr Castner was convinced that there was a field for sodium. He had already done a considerable amount of research work in its production, and had been perfecting a new method of producing sodium by the electrolysis of molten caustic soda. This gave the company a new start, and the old works were altered, new plant erected, and the demand for sodium increased rapidly, necessitating frequent additions to the plant, and producing increased profits for the company.

The old Le Blanc process of making caustic soda gave a product with many impurities which were detrimental to the manufacture of sodium. Mr Castner thereupon next turned his attention to obtaining a purer article. This he did by direct electrolysis of common salt without any intermediate chemical processes.

At this time another person entered upon the scene: Mr C. Kellner was an Austrian and held a patent for making caustic soda by a method similar to that used by Mr Castner, and the result was that a new firm was started by the Aluminium Co. on 19th October, 1895— that of the Castner Kellner Alkali Co. which erected works at Weston Point, near Runcorn, where the necessary brine was easily obtained.

At this time Mr Castner's health was much impaired, and although he passed several winters in Florida, his health did not improve, and in 1899 he died in the Adirondacks deeply regretted by all who knew him.

The Aluminium Co. continued working at Oldbury under its old name, which had become a misnomer as the firm was then making only sodium and sodium peroxide. This was continued until 1900, when the Aluminium Co. was merged into the Castner Kellner Co. and the Oldbury works closed and transferred to Weston Point.

In time the works at Weston Point became too small, and as cheap electric power was available at Wallsend, it was decided to erect there the sodium department on much improved and extended lines, and again Mr Cullen was entrusted with the design and erection of the new works, on land leased from the Newcastle Electric Supply Co.

The works were begun in March, 1906, and the first unit commenced operation in August of the same year, other sections being started in quick succession. The works were enlarged in 1912, in consequence of a larger demand for the products.

The process is not of a nature requiring a very large number of workmen, but it does require a very steady attendance on the part of the men, as three eight-hour shifts per day are worked continuously throughout the year.

To induce good timekeeping, the company in 1908 introduced a holiday scheme by which all the men could obtain up to ten days holiday per year on full pay. By a graduated scale the most regular men obtained the full time, and those who lost time by their own fault lost a portion of their holiday. Illness, of course, did not count as lost time.

The directors started a profit-sharing scheme by giving each man a percentage on his earnings, which percentage varied with the dividend paid to the shareholders. This rose from about twelve per cent. to twenty per cent., and it was an incentive to the men to do their best. The profit bonus was paid monthly, but the scheme was given up in 1918.

The Castner Memorial Institute was built in Park Road at a cost of £4,000 by Sir G. T. Beilby, LL.D., F.R.S., of Glasgow, a director of the company, and given to the firm for the use of the employees on payment of a small fee for membership It was opened in 1910 by the Right Hon. Gerald W. Balfour, the chairman of the company.

Mr Wm. H. Cullen, who had been so closely identified with the beginning and growth of the company, retired from active management in 1919, and Mr Alex. Fleck,

D.Sc., of Glasgow, who had been the works chemist at Wallsend, became manager.

In May, 1916, there had been an exchange of shares with Brunner, Mond & Co. in order to effect an alliance between the two firms, and in February, 1920, Brunner, Mond purchased seventy-five per cent. of the Castner Kellner Co.'s shares not already owned by them, and hence at the present time the works and business are almost entirely owned by that company.

The registered offices of the company are at Weston Point, Runcorn.

The Thermal Syndicate Ltd.

Fused silica, or fused quartz, is a material which excited a considerable amount of interest among scientific workers during the latter part of the nineteenth century. It is one of the most refractory of materials, melting at about the same temperature as platinum (about 1750° C.), and on account of its low co-efficient of expansion, it has the property of resisting sudden changes of temperature, without cracking, in the most remarkable way. It is also acid resistant to a very high degree.

Hence to be able to manufacture suitable vessels of this material would be of great assistance to many industries, e.g., in the electrical industry as an insulator (especially in cases where high temperatures are involved), in the gas lighting for heat-resisting globes and chimneys, and in the chemical industry generally.

Up to 1902 the only fused quartz available was made by fusing together very small pieces of rock crystal with an oxyhydrogen blowpipe, and working these up into small pieces of apparatus for chemical laboratory use.

About this time a London barrister, Mr R. A. S. Paget (now Sir Richard Paget), was in the laboratory of the late Lord Rayleigh, where the Hon. R. Strutt (the present Lord Rayleigh) was working quartz with the oxyhydrogen blowpipe, and he was struck with the possibilities of the material, provided it could be manufactured cheaply into articles of a larger size for the chemical and other industries.

One of the requirements for fusing quartz on a large scale was ample electric power, and Sir Richard Paget discussed the matter with Messrs Merz & McLellan, the consulting engineers for the Newcastle Electric Supply Co., and also Lord Armstrong. As a result a small syndicate was formed in 1903 under the name of The Thermal Syndicate, to carry out experiments in fusing quartz, or silica, electrically. Land was secured at Neptune Bank from the Newcastle Electric Supply Co., and the work was put in charge of Dr James Francis Bottomley, who was then engaged in research work for Messrs Merz & McLellan.

Dr Bottomley was the son of Dr J. Thomson Bottomley, F.R.S., Professor of Science at Glasgow University. He was educated at Glasgow University, took his Ph.D. at Heidelburg, and worked under Sir Wm. Ramsay at University College, London. He was an ideal man for the work now before him.

The problem presented considerable difficulties, but after three years, during which Dr Bottomley was ably assisted by Mr R. W. Clark from Messrs Merz & McLellan's staff and who is still with the company, the experiments were sufficiently advanced to commence working on a commercial basis, and the syndicate was formed into a small private company in 1906 with a capital of £7,000, Sir Richard Paget being chairman and Dr Bottomley manager.

The raw material used in the manufacture is a very pure sand obtained from France. It contains over ninety-nine and a half per cent. of silica, and is first fused in an electric resistance furnace, afterwards being worked into the finished product by grinding, or re-fusing. The material made from the sand is not transparent, but can be produced highly translucent, or with a bright reflecting surface. A transparent material is produced from rock crystal.

The first articles to be manufactured were small pieces of apparatus for the chemical laboratory. Later, the scope of the manufacture was increased, and much larger vessels, for the larger chemical industry, were put on the market.

At the outbreak of war, there was a very serious shortage of refractory and acid proof material in the country, and The Thermal Syndicate were able to make good a great deal of this deficiency by a rapid increase in the output from their factory. They played a considerable part in equipping the numerous factories which were erected in this country and by the Allies for the manufacture of explosives, especially in connection with the concentration of sulphuric acid and the condensation of nitric acid.

During the war, Sir Richard Paget went to the Admiralty to serve in the Board of Invention and Research, and Lord Armstrong took his place as chairman of directors. Meanwhile, the works of the company were entirely rebuilt on modern lines to meet the urgent demands made upon them. After the war, the demand for the explosive factories of course fell off, and the company had to turn its attention to reconstruction to meet peace time requirements.

The largest field which seemed open was the manufacture of globes and chimneys for incandescent gas lighting, oil lighting, etc. These articles, prior to the war, were very largely imported from Germany and Austria, and, as is well known to most users, give a great deal of trouble through breakage. Fused silica offers many advantages for this purpose, but the methods of manufacture were too costly, and it was necessary to make large alterations in the works, and introduce special labour-saving machinery.

The Silica Syndicate Ltd. in London had developed a different process for manufacturing articles of transparent quartz, and in 1917 the Wallsend firm made arrangements to acquire the whole of the shares of this company, and the manufacture was transferred to Wallsend, where advantage could be taken of the relatively cheap electric power which is available in the district.

At the present time the company's manufactures include plant and apparatus of various descriptions for use in the chemical industry, globes and cylinders for gas and electric lighting, insulators for electric heating, etc. Their goods are sold under the trade name " Vitreosil " and they can be subject to a continuous heat of over 1100° C. and to very much higher temperatures for short periods. (Glass will melt at 500-700°.)

Gradually the authorised capital of the concern has risen to £100,000 as the plant and sales increased. They have branches in America and France, and in 1911 an affiliated German company was formed.

In 1922 the company sustained a great loss by the sudden death of Dr Bottomley. During the influenza epidemic which swept over Tyneside during January, 1922, he took the prevailing " flu," pneumonia followed, and he died on the 16th at the age of forty-seven. He was of an essentially modest disposition. He established and for fifteen years managed an important industry in our midst, yet Wallsend heard little of him, and few Wallsenders knew him even by sight, but as one ever ready to help others he was one of the best.

On 25th October, 1922, a granite slab erected in the factory to his memory was unveiled by Sir Richard Paget. It records that " To his scientific skill and perseverance the development of these works is due."

The present directors of the company are: The Right Hon. Lord Armstrong (chairman), the Right Hon. Lord Rayleigh, F.R.S., Sir Richard Paget, Bart., Mr W. McLellan, Mr Percy St Clair Matthey, and Mr H. A. Couves.

The general manager of the company is Mr R. H. Houstoun, A.M.Inst.C.E., A.M.I.E.E., who succeeded Dr Bottomley. Mr Houstoun received his early engineering training at the Scotswood works of Messrs Sir W. G.

Armstrong Whitworth & Co. Ltd. The secretary of the company is Mr Norbert Merz, and the secretary of the Silica Syndicate Ltd. is Mr Thomas Graham.

Wm. T. Weir of Howdon-on-Tyne

The founder of this business was William Weir, who came to Howdon in 1824 from Reaveley Green, near Ingram, and started as a joiner and cartwright on a piece of ground at the west end of Main Street. He built up a good local trade and retired in 1864. He lived in Church Street until he was ninety years of age, and died in 1876.

In 1864 his second son, John, took over the business and continued it until his death on 12th July, 1880, when the business was transferred to his eldest son, Wm. Thomas. It was still that of a local village joiner. Mr Wm. Thos. Weir, however, saw that Howdon was extending and the trade growing. He started brick-making in the bog field, and in conjunction with his brother-in-law, Mr John Gilling Williams, built a number of houses on part of the Bewicke estate, which was then just opened out as building land. They built some houses in George Street, then Bewicke Street, and then Norman Terrace.

After house-building he began contracting for schools and extended his work to that of a general contractor, and as such became widely known.

Locally he built the Richardson-Dees schools in the year 1900, the Western schools in 1905, and the Central schools in 1913. He also widened the County Bridge over the Willington Gut in 1902, and built the Ferro Concrete Bridge over the Burn Closes in 1912.

On 22nd May, 1890, he married Miss Sarah J. Shippen, and for fifteen years they resided in Norman Terrace. In 1905 they moved to Monkseaton. Mr Weir was a member of both the Howdon and Willington Quay Local Boards when they were dissolved in 1894.

John Smith's Forge

The founder of this company was John Smith, who started on a small scale in 1848 in a workshop behind what is now the Station Hotel. He began by making shovels and small goods, but he was so successful that in 1863 he moved to Wallsend Quay and made a much larger type of forgings.

He had three steam hammers—one of forty hundredweights, one of twenty hundredweights, and one of ten hundredweights—with four large furnaces. This was considered a large plant sixty years ago, and enabled him to make most of the forgings required for shipbuilding, engineering and colliery work.

He resided at Hope Villas, which was formerly known as the Greenland Fisheries public house, then in 1873 he moved to Rose Hill Villa, Willington, vacated by Mr John J. Christie. After he removed to Willington he took an active interest in St Mary's Church, where a stained glass window perpetuates his memory. He died on 16th February, 1890, aged seventy years, and was buried at Preston Cemetery, North Shields.

The forge was continued by his executors under the management of his brother, Thomas Smith. Mr Thos. Smith made several improvements in the works and added to the success of the business. He died in November, 1900.

After the death of Mrs John Smith of Rose Hill Villa, the firm was converted into a private limited company in 1907, and the business is now carried on by Mr Surtees Smith (a son of Mr Thomas Smith), who is the managing director of Smith's Wallsend Forge Co. Ltd.

The Tyneside Tramways & Tramroads Co.

The Act authorising the formation of this company was passed on 9th August, 1901. The local supporters

The Tyneside Tramways Co.

who were among the first subscribers were Messrs Wm. Boyd, Geo. B. Hunter, J. Wigham Richardson, John and C. D. Christie, John Tweedy, Summers Hunter, Matt. Murray, Roland Philipson, and Chas. John Potter.

The qualification of a director is the possession of not less than fifty shares, and the first directors were Messrs William Armstrong Watson Armstrong (chairman), John Hobart Armstrong, Geo. Edward Henderson, Summers Hunter, John Theodore Merz, John Henry Brunel Noble, and James Tennant.

The authorised capital was £180,000 in £10 shares. The Act provides a maximum fare of one penny per mile, and bars the raising of the fares on Sundays or holidays. Passengers may take twenty-eight pounds of personal hand luggage. The company may carry small parcels, and must provide cars at convenient times for artisans, mechanics, and "daily labourers" (note, not merely men) at halfpenny per mile. The local authority may use the tramlines between midnight and five a.m. for the removal of house refuse, etc.; and they may purchase the undertaking at the end of twenty-five years.

The formal opening took place on 29th September, 1902, when Mrs W. A. Watson Armstrong started a car with a large party at Gosforth on its way to North Shields.

The Wallsend and North Shields section was opened on 4th September, 1902; the Wallsend to Gosforth section on 18th October, 1902; the Gosforth to Gosforth Park section on 18th June, 1904; the Park Road to Newcastle, via Riverside, in November, 1906.

When the Newcastle Corporation laid their tramlines to the boundary at Western Villas in July, 1903, the passengers for Wallsend and Shields were obliged to change cars, but a joint running agreement was made, and on 29th August, 1904, Newcastle cars continued to Park Road, and every twenty minutes a Tyneside car ran through from North Shields to Stanhope Street, Newcastle.

Owing to the general increase of wages and prices, the company obtained another Act of Parliament which was passed on 2nd July, 1920. The main points are, the company is empowered: (*a*) To issue mortgages up to one-third of their paid-up capital, instead of one-third of each £60,000 issued. (*b*) To increase all the fares fifty per cent. over the previous maximum. (*c*) To run motor omnibuses in connection with the tramways, but not over roads upon which the Newcastle or Tynemouth tramcars run, and not upon roads maintained by the Northumberland County Council unless they give their permission in writing.

Clause 12 stipulates that when the cheap fares for the labouring class works out at less than one penny for the single journey they may charge one penny, but they shall, on demand, issue a ticket for the double journey at the right fare, e.g., the halfpenny tickets are now one penny, but, on demand, a ticket for the double journey must be issued for three-halfpence.

Mr M. Short (Newcastle Electric Supply Co.) was the secretary and manager up to 1902, when Mr John C. Little, its present secretary, was appointed. Mr F. C. Kidman was resident engineer up to 1906, when he was succeeded by Mr Francis H. Briggs, the present engineer.

Co-operative Societies

The pioneers of the co-operative movement in Wallsend were Thomas Smith (a brother of John Smith of the Forge), who was an engineman at the Walker Oil Mills; Thomas Blenkinsop, a presser at the Oil Mills; Robert Douglass, an engineman at Southern's ballast-crane (where Swan & Hunter's yard is now); Wm. Reaveley, who was also employed at the Oil Mills. They formed the nucleus of those who resolved to adopt the principles of co-operation as far as possible, and who began the Wallsend Industrial Co-operative Society.

The actual start was made in 1862, and the end colliery cottage in Long Row, now Carville Road, was rented from J. B. Atkinson, the two rooms were converted into one, and a window was made in the end overlooking the High Street. These alterations were effected, and the store was put into order almost entirely by the members—the total cost of the hired work being only £3 10s. The premises were rated at £8 gross and £7 rateable value, and were opened on Saturday, 26th April, the membership being eighty-six.

The spirit which actuated the originators was "Each for all," and this was shown in many ways. Two or three of those who had the means, more especially Mr Douglass, Mr Smith, and Mr Blenkinsop, went to Newcastle weekly to buy the needed goods, and they advanced the money for them until the week-ends, when the members made their purchases. One week the buyers advanced £40 for supplies. Mr Smith usually undertook to obtain the flour from Procter's Mill at Willington Quay, and in default of enlisting the assistance of some friendly carter often wheeled the sacks up to Wallsend in a barrow.

Under the economical and devoted management of the committee, the co-operative idea spread, until at the end of the first year they had one hundred and twenty-eight members. The business continued to grow, and the stores gradually extended down the Long Row.

After five years' success the committee struck out in a different direction. On 18th March, 1868, the White House in the village, together with some other property and land, was put up for sale by auction. Lot No. 4 consisted of 11 acres 3 roods of freehold land on the north side of North Road, producing a rental of £35.

After serious deliberation, Mr John Smith was authorised by the committee to attend the sale and buy this lot if it could be obtained at a reasonable price. At the sale it was knocked down to him for £1,210 (equal to fivepence per yard) and the Society presented him with a ham as an acknowledgment of his successful mission.

The first houses erected on the land were those in Douglas Street and Alpha Terrace, next some in Artizan Terrace, then followed Industrial Terrace, Provident Terrace, Hopper Street, and the adjoining property.

These working men's houses were so superior to the average house available that the doubting members realised that this extension of their movement had far more than justified itself.

In 1912 the Society celebrated its Jubilee and published a history of its early struggles and final success. The introduction is by the writer of this memo. There are brief biographical notes by Mr Alfred Fletcher (a former secretary) of Mr Robert Douglass and Mr Thos. Blenkinsop, two of the chief pioneers. There is a detailed history of the Society from 1862 to 1867 written by Mr Robert Douglass, and from 1867 to 1912 by Mr Fred Robertson. We therefore refer our readers to this publication for further information relating to this period.

In 1921-22 there was a considerable agitation concerning the administration and management of the Society. A "Committee of Inquiry" was appointed and reported. Excited meetings were held, and only the Skating Rink was large enough to hold the members eager to attend. All sorts of accusations were made, but in the end a new committee was appointed. Several of the employees and members left, and a new Society, The Wallsend Progressive Co-operative Society Ltd., was opened in Atkinson Street on 14th August, 1922.

Mr Wm. Forrest is now secretary and manager of the old Society.

The Willington Quay & Howdon Co-operative Society Ltd. began business in 1861. The premises they occupied were the corner of Stephenson Street opposite the Alma

Inn, and Mr Wm. D. Ford was the manager. They moved to new buildings in Bewicke Road in 1891, which were extended in 1899. In 1902 they began a branch at Rosehill, which was opened by Mr Peter Rutherford.

The present officials are: Mr John P. Simpson, president, and Mr William Rutherford, secretary.

The Co-operative Laundries Ltd. built their first laundry in 1909 in David Street at a cost of £7,736 for land, buildings, and machinery, and it was opened by Mr Edward J. Graham, of the Wholesale Society, on 22nd August.

The first half-year's turnover was nearly £4,000, and the concern has had to be enlarged from time to time to keep pace with the trade. Up to December, 1922, there had been spent on the premises £13,285 in addition to the original outlay. The progress of the business is shown by the following—for the year ending 30th June, 1922, the income amounted to £31,543 0s. 11d., and the expenditure to £27,110 13s. 7d., leaving a net surplus of £4,432 7s. 4d.

The manager and secretary is Mr G. Hodgson, and Mr Wm. Forrest is the local representative upon the Committee of Management.

CHAPTER VIII

LOCAL GOVERNMENT

The local records—The Select Vestry: The "Four and Twenty"—The reformed Vestry—Poor Law Union—Local Boards of Health: Wallsend (formed 1867); Willington Quay (formed 1863); Howdon (formed 1864)—The County Council—The Local Government Act of 1894—District Councils—Parish Council—Wallsend Burial Board—The Incorporation of Wallsend township—The Borough Arms—The Town Hall—The enlarged Borough—The Mayors of the Borough—Education: Early schools and schoolmasters; the School Board; Education Committee; The Café Technical classes—The Commission of the Peace—Rates and Rating, A.D. 1531-1922—" Farms "—Detailed valuation lists.

LOCAL RECORDS

THE oldest local records are those of the church, and the earliest are in a leather-bound book with parchment pages. The entries are in separate parts of the book and not in the order of date. They begin with baptisms in May, 1669, and the first entry is: " May 8th. Ann, daughter to Francis Lawson, baptised." During the year 1669 there were nine baptisms. The next year, beginning, of course, on the 25th March, there were eight, and the record of baptisms continue until 1st May, 1692. After these baptisms follow minutes of the Vestry meetings, the first of which is dated the 25th April, 1709, and is as follows:

Agree on (at the Usual meeting upon Easter Monday) by the Ministr, Church Wardens and four and twenty of the Parish of Walls End that a cess at five shillings and three pence p. Farme be forthwith Collected, for discharging the Parish debt for the year

1708 and likewise for clearing the Ensueing Court at Durham as wittness our hands this 25th Aprile, Anno Domini 1709.

The next Vestry entries are for 1716, 1717, and 1718. After the Vestry minutes is a list of the poor of the parish for 1749, showing that ten persons were in receipt of poor relief, then follow baptisms again as from 1st May, 1695, but these are headed "The Register of the Parish of Wallsend in the County of Northumberland. Since May 1st, 1695, when the Act of Parliament Commenced for Granting to His Majesty William Third, King, etc., upon Burials, etc.," and the first entry here is made on 12th May, 1695: "a son, born of Robert Durham and Mary his wife, of Wallsend, and baptised George, June 5th, 1695."

A break again occurs in October, 1697, and the next entries are marriages, beginning in 1669, the first record being made on 28th December: "John Bilbo, and Barbara Anderson was married." The next year (1670) two marriages were performed, both on 22nd December. "Ralph harison and Sushany hensey was married." "Georg horsly, and Joan Anderson."

In July, 1686, the record of marriages came to an end for the time being and began again as from 1st May, 1695, with the same heading regarding the Act of Parliament as is given concerning the baptisms. The only marriage recorded that year is as follows: "About Martinmas 1695 John Ratcliffe and Mary Elder, married, I know not where, pd. King's duty."

In 1696 there were six marriages, including: "September 20th as I am informed, Francis Gatenby and Ann Lyddll of Howdon Panns married at Gateside by a Paptist Priest." In September, 1697, the marriages once more stop, and the Vestry minutes begin again and continue until the Easter Monday of 1759.

The last three pages contain a register of births, and they go back again to 1st May, 1695, and the first entry here is: "The child of Thomas Wood and Alice, of

Howdon, born dead in May as I am informed, was buried about their house," and on the same page another burial is recorded as having taken place " near their house."

After the irregularly kept, patchwork records, contained in the first volume, the books are improved, and the Vestry minutes are kept in separate volumes, larger and better bound.

The oldest Poor Rate Book is for a Poor Rate made in February, 1857, at sixpence in the pound, and the Overseers Minute Book begins in May, 1853, and at first was not well kept.

THE SELECT VESTRY

The " Four and Twenty "

The two townships of Wallsend and Willington were the unit for local government for many centuries although they did not lose their separate identities.

The parish was one of those which was governed in its early days by a Select Vestry. The origin of these bodies is untraceable, but as a matter of fact, certain persons established the right in many parishes to represent the rest of the inhabitants. They were usually known as " The Twelve " or " The Four and Twenty," and in Wallsend parish the " Four and Twenty " consisted of the owners and leaseholders of the two townships who met yearly on Easter Monday.

They elected the grieve, the constable, the surveyor of highways, and the overseers. They assessed the annual valuations of the property and levied the Poor Rate. They decided upon who was to receive poor relief, and generally looked after the affairs of the parish. During one period they elected a Mayor year after year.

Although the records of the " Four and Twenty " do not go far back, they contain several interesting entries. After the meetings the Select Vestry dined together at the

"THE FOUR AND TWENTY"

expense of the rates, and one of the outstanding features is how the cost of these grew and how much wine was consumed at dinner one hundred years ago.

For the year 1774 to Easter 1775, we have:

To Dinner and Ale this day being Easter Monday	£1 10 0
To cooking s^d dinner	2 6

Odd items in this year's accounts are:

To making Bag for Velvet Cushion	3 10½
To bringing home Velvet Cushion	10 0

and the same charge for bringing home the cushion is made in the following year. There is a recurring charge:

To old and new churchwardens at Easter	16 0

A reward was given for the destruction of Pole cats:

1774-1775 To 1 Pole cat head	4
1775-1776 To 3 Pole cats' heads	1 0

Wages for these years were low:

To 3½ days, Thos Twizel Labouring in the churchyard	4 0
To 1 day, Henry Scott, Walling the Bridge	1 8
To 3 days John Cutter, sholling the snow of the Church stairs	2 0

At the 1776 Vestry, "the Rev. Mr Potter and the Four and Twenty" remove William Gill from his post as clerk, on account of his infirmity and incapacity, and appoint Mr Swinbank. The clerk for the parish does not appear to have any regular salary, he received certain fees, though his charges are not heavy, for in the well-written yearly accounts there is the item:

To making up this Bill	1 0

Then the cost of the dinner mounts up surprisingly. Here we have the details for the Easter of 1816:

Wines and Spirits for dinner 1816	£6 18 0
Butcher Meat	2 12 1
Bread	12 0
Flour and Groceries	16 5
Ale	1 16 0
A total of	£12 14 6

At this meeting there were present: George Jackson, minister; Wm. Falconer and Wm. Swan, churchwardens; John Wright, of the Hall; John Buddle, agent for the Wallsend Colliery; Wm. Stawpert, Willington agent for Matt. Bell & Co.; Charles Weatherly, of Low Willington House; John Watson, viewer of Willington; and nine other important ratepayers.

The year before this, the dinner cost £10 8s. 1d., plus "half a dozen wine from Thornton's by order of the Four and Twenty of the parish, £6 18s. 0d." (Mr Thornton was the owner and occupier of the Coach and Horses Inn.) Seventeen ratepayers were present. The heaviest item for wines was that for 1832, when the cost was £15 4s.

Among the other items in the accounts are the following:

1817 June 24.—County Cess for Wallsend and Willington as p. precept	£3 16 0
Aug. 13th.—County Cess for Wallsend and Willington as p. precept	£11 14 7

[The poor rate for this quarter was 4d. in the £ and the following quarter 3d., but the usual rate for years at this time was 1s. to 1s. 3d., and the County cess for the year was £44 to £46.]

1818 June 20th.—Expenses clothing Eliz. Wanless to go to service	£1 5 5½
Aug. 4.—Expenses burying one of Mary Crosby's children	7 0
Sept. 11.—Extra relief to Mary Parkinson's family ill of Typhus Fever	1 0 0
Nov. 2.—Pair of shoes for Thomas Sowerby	6 0
Nov. 14.—2 shifts for Crozier and Lowther	5 0
1819 March 27.—Expenses at the examination of the Poor at Wallsend	4 7 5[1]

[1] This was a yearly custom and continued until twenty-five years ago. The poor were given ale and beef and bread, and ratepayers might attend and see who were getting relief. In the writer's time it was a feast day for the poor at the Rose Inn until a hard-hearted Local Government auditor intervened and threatened to surcharge the cost upon the overseers personally.

THE COACH AND HORSES INN, WALLSEND.

[*Facing page* 364.

			£	s.	d.
1820	April 11.—Cash paid for eggs and heads of sparrows		6	0	0[1]
1821	March 23rd.—122 dozen sparrows at 3d. p. doz. ...		1	10	6
1822	Oct. 5.—Cash paid as premium for binding for nine years as a Tinsmith and Brazier Wm. Henderson a pauper belonging to this parish		5	0	0
1823	January 31.—Cash paid for 5,054 sparrows' heads and eggs		5	5	3½

The "Four and Twenty" continued to manage the affairs of the parish until the Easter of 1835, when they gave place to a Vestry consisting of the rated inhabitants as at present. As soon as the old type of Vestry ceased, the following resolution, passed on 4th April, 1836, put an end to dinner expenses: "Resolved that in future every parishioner attending the Easter Monday dinner shall provide himself with a ticket to be supplied by the acting Overseer at 6s. each."

It does not inform us what wines were included for the 6s.; but as 6s. is less than one-third of the old cost, we may assume under this system that every parishioner paid for his own drinks.

The Poor Law Union

The first movement to relieve the old Vestries of part of their work was the Poor Law Act of 1782, which gave authority to parishes to group themselves into Unions, the controlling members being Poor Law Guardians. These Guardians were at first appointed by the Justices of the Peace. This law, however, was rarely adopted until the Poor Law Amendment Act of 1834, which abolished many evils, made the union of parishes general, by making the Boards of Guardians mainly elective. This Act also created a central Poor Law Board of Control in London.

It was not until 10th August, 1836, after the reign of the "Four and Twenty" was superseded by the ordinary

[1] The "Four and Twenty" had offered 1s. 3d. per dozen for sparrows destroyed or eggs, but this proving too much, the reward was reduced to 3d. and this was continued for five years.

Vestry, that Wallsend parish joined the neighbouring parishes in forming a Poor Law Union.

This was composed of eight townships of Tynemouth old parish, eight townships of Earsdon Chapelry, and eight other parishes or townships, including Wallsend. These were as follows:—Tynemouth, North Shields, Chirton, Monkseaton, Murton, Whitley, Cullercoats, Preston, Earsdon, Backworth, Burradon, Holywell, Newsham and South Blyth, Hartley, Seaton Delaval, Seghill, Cramlington, Long Benton, Wallsend, Horton, Hartford West, Hartford East, Cowpen, Bebside.

The first meeting of the Board of Guardians was held at the " George " Tavern, North Shields, on Wednesday, 7th September, 1836. The Wallsend representatives were Wm. Robt. Swan (solicitor, Wallsend), Thompson Smith (dock owner, Howdon), Peter Russell (farmer), and Joseph Mordue (schoolmaster and parish clerk). For the purposes of poor relief, rating, registration of births and deaths, the Union was divided into districts. Wallsend, with a population of 5,510, and Long Benton (which then included Walker) with 6,613, were grouped to form one district.

The rateable value of the Union was £13,140, and Wallsend, with a rateable amount of £1,440, stood fourth in order of valuation. The first precept was made on 15th September, and the rate levied was one-tenth, Wallsend's first contribution being £144.

At the third meeting Mr John Fawcus was appointed relieving officer for Wallsend and Long Benton, at a salary of £90, and at the following meeting Mr Edward Lamb was appointed collector of rates. Mr James Anderson, the Willington colliery doctor, was appointed medical officer.

Some of the prices of goods accepted by the Guardians on 27th October, 1836, are interesting: Wheat flour (whole meal) 43s. per sack, sugar 7½d. per lb., tea 4s. 8d., coffee 1s. 10d., soap 5d., treacle 30s. cwt., candles 5s. 6d. per dozen, prime ox beef or mutton 39s. per cwt., blankets 15s. 10d. per pair.

The following year the Wallsend representatives were Joseph Mordue, Washington Potts (of Chapman & Potts, Willington Ropery), John Reay (colliery cashier), and Thomas Davison (farmer).

Boards of Health

Wallsend

After Poor Law Unions had been started, the next important advance in Local Government was the passing of the first Public Health Act in 1848, and the amending Acts, which provided for the formation of Local Boards of Health in populous places. But Wallsend township was very slow in taking advantage of these new powers; both Willington and Howdon had Boards before Wallsend.

Mr Andrew Leslie, Dr Jas. Aitchison, Dr James Milne, Mr John Brooks, and a few others assisted by Mr W. S. Daglish, began an agitation to secure a Board of Health, and as a result, in July, 1864, a Government Inspector was sent down to Wallsend and held an inquiry. The granting of the application was opposed, but the need was proved, and the Inspector reported in its favour. Notwithstanding this, however, the opposition, which came chiefly from the manufacturers, was so powerful that two years elapsed before those in favour of progress succeeded in inducing a Vestry meeting of the rated inhabitants to sanction the scheme.

This meeting of the ratepayers was held on 26th September, 1866, when a motion was carried resolving to establish a Local Board under the provisions of the Local Government Act of 1858. This resolution was by no means unanimous, and a poll was demanded by the minority. The poll was taken, and at a meeting held to hear the result on 27th October, in Mr Adam's schoolroom, Carville, the chairman, Mr Andrew Leslie, announced the result. Fortunately the opposition was not very active and the voting papers showed that one hundred and fifty-five rated inhabitants were in favour of the adoption of the Act, and only twenty-seven against it. At this meeting Dr Jas. Aitchison and Mr W. S. Daglish were among the speakers. Dr Aitchison reminded his audience that the inhabitants had had a long tussle for the Act, and now they had surmounted the difficulties, he therefore called for "three cheers for the intellectual and social improvement and the domestic happiness of the residents of Wallsend." These were heartily given, then three cheers were given for Mr Andrew Leslie, who had taken a very active part in the matter.

The first election for the New Board was held on the 2nd February, 1867, when there were no fewer than thirty-six candidates for the twelve places. Those elected were: William Allen, chemical manufacturer, who was at the head of the poll with 251 votes; Joseph Harbit, butcher, had 242 votes; Wm. Robt. Swan, solicitor and landowner, 205; John Glover, chemical manufacturer, 205; John Warwick, lead smelter, 197; Chas. Albert Schlesinger, shipbuilder, 191; Francis Mordue, lime burner, brewer and innkeeper, 187; Thomas Wanless, grocer, 181; John Smith, forgeman, 164; Wardle Shaw, joiner, 159; John Turner, butcher, 157.

Rev. John Armstrong, with 140 votes, was at the bottom of those elected. These were all considerable property owners except two. The highest of those who were not elected were Dr Jas. Aitchison, who received 125 votes; Robert Richardson Dees with 120; Andrew Leslie with 113—all "progressive" candidates. The lowest candidate received only two votes. The Returning Officer was Mr John Nelson.

The progressive ratepayers held a dinner on 11th February, at the Queen's Head, to commemorate their success in securing the actual establishment of a Local Board. Dr Jas. Milne was in the chair, and over thirty ratepayers were present. Although it will be seen that those who had opposed the scheme had secured nearly all the seats on the new Board, yet those assembled were full of glowing hopes concerning the coming improvement of the district. They did not yet realise that the majority upon the Board still intended effectually to hinder progress and prevent the increase of rates.

A preliminary meeting of the new Board took place on the 7th February, 1867; the first two meetings were held in the Zion Chapel, but subsequent meetings were held in the Vestry. On 12th February Mr John Glover was chosen as chairman; Mr W. S. Daglish was appointed clerk, at a salary of £30 per annum; Mr Jos. Thompson of Walker Gate, surveyor; and Mr Wm. Rookey, Inspector of Nuisances and Sanitary Inspector, at £5 per year. The seal adopted was a reproduction of the River God Tyne. See page 394.

Twelve months later, in January, 1868, a deputation consisting of the Rev. David Wilson, Presbyterian minister, Dr Jas. Aitchison, Mr Hepple, shipbuilder, Mr Marley, chemist, and other gentlemen attended the Board Meeting, and said that at a public meeting held on 2nd January, it had been unanimously declared that the ratepayers and owners of property in the township of Wallsend were out of all patience, disappointed, and thoroughly dissatisfied with the sanitary condition of Wallsend, and Dr Aitchison declared Wallsend was the dirtiest place in Northumberland. In wet weather the mud in the roadways was over the boot tops. They further stated that the meeting deemed it most important that the village of Carville and other places be properly lighted with gas, and that sundry improvements ought to be taken in hand at once. It was a lively meeting and the deputation spoke their minds very freely, but without much result.

The accounts for the first year of the Board's proceedings, ending 8th April, 1868, show how much, or rather how little, was being done.

2A

Scavenging cost	...	...	...	...	...	£2	14	0
Rent of board room and cleaning	...	...	...			6	9	4
Sundries amounted to	...	...	...	...			13	7

This, and the amounts spent on cartage and laying a sewer and securing a loan for it, was the total expenditure for a year, and the whole balance sheet is shown in eight lines.

On 2nd November, 1868, it was arranged that Carville village be lighted, and that the lamps be lit thirty-six weeks in the year, and that they be extinguished seven days each full moon occurring during the currency of the first thirty-six weeks. The total cost was to be £24 per annum, and on 7th December the nine lamps arranged for were duly lighted.

At the election on 1st February, 1869, Mr Andrew Leslie and Dr Jas. Aitchison secured seats on the Board, but the following incidents show how difficult it was to get any improvements agreed to. On 6th September, 1869, Mr Jos. Harbit proposed that each side of the Turnpike Road from the post office (now Bank of Liverpool) to the Coxlodge and Benton Wagon-way be flagged and channelled; this was seconded by Dr Aitchison, and only those two voted for the motion. Six voted against it.

After Andrew Leslie secured a seat on the Board, he wished to have the road lighted from the railway station to the High Street. The chairman, Mr John Glover, expressed the ideas of the majority at the meeting on 6th December, 1869, when he laid down " that such as were compelled to be in the place after dark might provide themselves, as their fathers had to do, with lanterns." (Mr Leslie lived in the place and Mr Glover did not.)

The High Street was still like a quagmire in wet weather, and two and a half years after the first attempt to have part of it flagged, a more modest scheme was suggested, when on 4th March, 1872, Mr John Giles proposed, and Dr Aitchison seconded, that the Board put in a curbstone and channel in front of the houses in High Street, and leave the owners to do any further repairs or flagging they think proper. Mr Shaw proposed and Mr Mordue seconded an amendment " That the motion be not entertained," and five voted for the amendment and only four for the motion.

These incidents show us the difficulties encountered by those who desired to improve the village fifty years ago. It is to be remembered that in those days the electors were the rated occupiers and inhabitants, and that the Rate Books then took no account of indirect ratepayers. Furthermore, persons whose total assessments were below £50 had one vote, £50 to £75 two votes, and so on, until those assessed upon £150 had six votes, and finally any company rated could give their legal number of votes through their secretary or manager in addition to the number of votes he was entitled to otherwise.

Within the next few years the more progressive party in the township gradually strengthened their hold upon the Board, and more progress was made.

1874. Mr Charles Adams and Mr John Wigham Richardson became members. The Board declined a suggestion from Howdon to appoint a medical officer for Wallsend, Howdon, and Willington Quay. Dr Jas. Aitchison was appointed for Wallsend at a salary of £30. Mr Chas. S. Swan was elected in place of Dr Milne, deceased. The well pumps in the Burn Closes broke down, and Abbott & Co. were engaged to put them into order at once. The total establishment charges for the year ending 25th March, excluding interest, was £173 6s. 1d.

1875. It was agreed to ask the Gas and Water Companies the cost of extending their pipes to the west end of the township on the Turnpike Road.

1876. 7th February. Mr Wm. Allan resigned the chairmanship and was succeeded by Mr C. S. Swan. The surveyor was ordered to "make a good and efficient footpath in Station Road."

1877. Mr Joseph Ogilvie (Whiting Works, Wallsend Quay) was elected upon the Board in place of Mr Braggiotti (managing director of the Royal Greek Iron Works), who had left the district. Dr Aitchison applied for an increase of salary, and the salary for the post was raised from £30 to £50, but it was advertised and Dr Thomas Wilson obtained the appointment.

1878. 4th March was the date of the last attendance of Mr Andrew Leslie, who resigned.

6th May. First attendance of Mr William Boyd.

1879. This year Dr Aitchison was again appointed medical officer. Mr Boyd was elected chairman, in succession to Mr C. S. Swan, who was drowned. Mr James Wm. Dees (father of Mr R. I. Dees) was elected in place of Mr C. S. Swan. The opposition to the stoppage of an ancient path alongside the river (the "Pilot Track") became acute in Wallsend, and from this time onwards the matter was over and over again before the Board, and the chief member who pressed for the road being reopened was Mr John Giles. He encountered great opposition, passive rather than active, from most of his fellow-members. Mr Wigham Richardson and other west-end owners met the public demands reasonably, by planning Neptune, Buddle and Hadrian Roads, but at the east end no solution could be arrived at.

1880. Local rates raised to 7d. in the £ after being 6d. for some years.

1881. 7th March. Invitation was received from Willington Quay Local Board asking for a conference with the Wallsend and Howdon Local Boards to consider the amalgamation of the three districts. The invitation was declined. Only Mr Boyd, Mr James Dees, and Mr Jos. Lee voted in its favour.

1881. 4th July. Mr John Glover resigned.
1882. 9th January. Mr Thompson appointed surveyor at £52, and he was to take no private practice in the district.
   1st May. Rate 8d. in the £.
   4th September. Rate 9d. in the £.
1883. 7th May. Mr Geo. Hollings of Jarrow was appointed Inspector of Nuisances at £40 per year and Road Inspector at £40. Mr Thompson was retained at £52. Mr George A. Allan's first attendance.
   5th June. A Joint Hospital sanctioned.
   16th October. The clerk was instructed to file indictments against the Wallsend Slipway Co., the Union Cement Co., and the North-Eastern Marine Engineering Co. for the stoppage of the Pilot Track.
1884. Rosehill House, built by Mr Wm. Adamson, was for sale and the vendors' price was £1,200. The clerk suggested it as an Infectious Diseases Hospital, and a committee reported in its favour, but the residents near raised a storm of protest and the idea was abandoned on 17th June. On 21st October Dr Henry Aitchison was appointed medical officer on the death of his father, at £50 per annum. On 16th December a committee was appointed to investigate the encroachments on the village green.
1886. Mr Jos. Davidson (farmer) and Mr Samuel T. Harrison (cashier) elected. Mr John Giles resigned.
1886. Mr Thomas Hedderly and Mr Sidney Old, secretary, elected.
1887. Dr Thomas Wilson appointed medical officer at £50 per annum. The land on which the Roman Camp stood was for sale and the Board undertook to look after the ruins if the land was purchased.
1890. The Joint Hospital Committee was held and selected a site at Willington Dene.

The trial concerning the closing of the " Pilot Track "

was adjourned from time to time, and negotiations took place with no satisfactory result. At last on 17th March, 1890, the matter was tried at the Quarter Sessions and the result was that the District Council lost the case. This was not quite the end of the matter, for in 1892 a new scheme to carry a road from Hadrian Road to Potter Street was put before the landowners, but when Mr Charles Mitchell, the chairman of the Slipway Co., stipulated that the bridge across the Gut must be twenty-two feet above high water at spring tides, the idea was abandoned.

1891. Agreed to substitute a site on Dame Allan's land for the hospital in place of the site which the " provisional order " mentioned. Mr Wm. Hope appointed architect and a tender of Mr Nicholas Ritchie for £6,495 8s. was accepted.

In 1893, the last year of the Local Board, the members were: Wm. Boyd, chairman, Geo. A. Allan (agent), Jos. Davidson (farmer), Robt. Douglas (store secretary), Jos. Duffy (builder, etc.), Thos. Forrest (gas works manager), Thos. Hedderly (plumber), Geo. B. Hunter (shipbuilder), Wm. Kilvington (engineering draughtsman), Francis Murphy (draper, etc.), John Alex. Ryrie (paint manufacturer), and Geo. Thorpe Scott (Queen's Head Inn).

The assessable value for the district rate purposes was £39,645. The district rate for the last two years averaged 9d. in the £.

Willington Quay

This area is quite modern, and in 1830 the only houses between Mr Robt. Weatherley's, Howdon, and what is now Nelson Street were: Five cottages close to the shore where the Stephenson schools stand. A cottage on the side of the hill below the east end of where Palmer's Terrace now is. A group of houses including the Ship Inn, afterwards " Potter's Square." (These were built for the men connected with the Killingworth spouts, which were just to the west of them.) Then beyond, was the White House, a mansion with coach house, stables, gardens, etc. Close to the Red Lion public house was the Willington Colliery staiths and a few cottages. Next, on the west of the Willington colliery wagon-ways, and just beyond them, was a row of colliery houses on the site of the west side of Nelson Street. Then we have Low Willington House, then an irregular square of cottages in front of the " Dun Cow," and a few mill cottages behind it. At the top of the Miller's Bank was another group of houses named Prospect Place, but sometimes Hill Top, or the " Doctors' Houses " (Dr Huntley of Seaton Delaval having built part of them). At Prospect Place, facing north, were two public houses, the " Northumberland Arms " and the " Kettle Inn," the post office being between them. There was also the Keelman's Row, the Ropery Houses, and at the west end of the long Rope Walk a fair-sized house with a garden facing west in which Dr Anderson lived until he built himself a house on the Rose Hill (now Mr Mullen's). Two cottages where the wagon-ways crossed the Turnpike (where Hill Crest and the Bewicke school caretaker's house now stand) complete the list of all the houses on the south side of the Main Road in the Willington township.

It will be remembered that all the older part of Willington Quay, near the river, stood on the old foreshore, and that after the change of the shore-line made under the Anderson lease a later lot of ballast was piled up in hills. The last ballast hill was finished in 1838 at the west end of Palmer's Terrace, and the quay where the vessels discharged this, was behind the Ship Inn. When the ballast was deposited upon the shore, it was tipped so as not to encroach upon the land which had previously sloped down to the river, hence all along to the north was a valley which was afterwards utilised in order to level down some of the hills.

By 1850 a good part of Stephenson Street was built, and the ballast was being levelled and Potter Street and the first row of Palmer's Terrace begun. Then followed some houses in Tyne Street, and in 1864 Thomas Davidson built a house and shop at Prospect Place and started Ravensworth Street. In the early sixties Nelson Street was begun, and thus we arrive at the period when new streets were being formed and a new village rapidly springing up.

  The men interested in this development realised the value of Local Government, and as a result the first " Local Board " on the riverside was formed on 12th May, 1863. The area was taken from the rural township of Willington, and although the older works still retain the name of Willington only, yet the formation of this local area established officially the name of " Willington Quay " as distinct from that of Willington.

  The first meeting of the Local Board was on 10th June, when Mr Addison Potter was chosen chairman, and one of the first matters arranged was for the laying of pipes, etc., for the lighting of their area, and the public gas lamps were first lit in November, 1863. The seal of the Board had a shield in the centre on which was one of Stephenson's " Puffing Billies."

  The two men who did most to establish this local authority were Colonel Addison Potter and Mr W. S. Daglish, the latter being appointed clerk to the Board at their first regular meeting on 10th June, 1863, and an extended note of his work in the district will be found in another section.

  Mr Addison Potter, who was elected the first chairman, was already well known and had shown his practical interest in the village ever since he established his fire-brick works at Willington Quay in 1846, as described in our note concerning the Walker & Wallsend Union Gas Co. He took the chief part in establishing the local 3rd Northumberland Artillery Volunteers in 1860, and he provided headquarters for them at his gas works until 1867.

In that year, mainly owing to Mr Potter's efforts, a drill hall, 80 feet long by 35 feet broad, was built in Potter Street on the ground which was once part of the Killingworth wagon-way. The land on the east of the hall was secured as an exercise ground. Both were opened on 25th November, 1867, by Mrs Potter in the presence of a large company, which included Corps from Newcastle and Tynemouth.

Mr Potter remained chairman of the Local Board of Health until his death, and always took wide views, e.g., on 19th November, 1879, at the monthly meeting, he proposed a scheme for uniting Wallsend, Howdon, and Willington Quay Boards. Mr Henry Salkeld suggested that Walker might be added, and the four townships incorporated, and the proposal was unanimously approved, but the idea proved thirty years too far ahead for the other areas.

Mr Potter was the acting trustee for the Stephenson Memorial schools and for the Savings Bank. He was the first chairman of the School Board, and both he and Mrs Potter took a keen interest in the district. That they did not confine their activities to Willington Quay and Howdon is shown by the fact that Mr Potter was twice Mayor of Newcastle, and held many other offices. He was promoted to be Lieutenant-Colonel and then a C.B. He died at Heaton Hall on 23rd February, 1894, and Mrs Potter in September, 1904.

The firm of Messrs Addison Potter & Son, which had gradually become cement manufacturers rather than firebrick makers, was continued after Mr Potter's death by his son, Mr Charles J. Potter, until February, 1912. It was then taken over by the British Portland Cement Manufacturers Ltd., who closed the works. This ended the connection of the Potter family with Willington Quay, which had lasted over sixty years and had been of the most friendly description.

Mr Charles J. Potter in May, 1904, presented a large

life-like portrait of his father to the Willington Quay Urban District Council, which now hangs in the town hall, Wallsend.

Another man who was one of the influential men on the new Local Board was George Clavering, at that time a farmer occupying the Howdon Farm.

His great interest was the advance of the temperance movement. He was tireless in speaking and singing on behalf of temperance efforts. His " Sandy's a Templar noo," " Dare to be a Daniel," " Teetotal for ever, teetotal hurrah," were known in all the villages around. In the early days of the teetotal movement on Tyneside there were the well-known " Four Georges " : George Dodds of Newcastle, George Charlton of Gateshead, George Tomlinson, and George Clavering. Next to aggressive temperance work came his interest in the Free Methodist Church. He was one of the four guardians for the parish, also one of the School Board, and he continued his Local Board work to its end. He died on 5th November, 1895, aged eighty-four, and a good portrait of him now hangs near that of Mr Potter in the town hall.

A third member of the first Local Board of Health in our area was Mr Henry Salkeld. He was resident agent for the Newcastle Corporation and built himself a house and laid out a pleasant garden on what was then an eminence looking northward, with its back to the east end of Palmer's Terrace.

Better known as Harry than Henry, he was keenly interested in local affairs and a " shining light " among the Wesleyans. He published a lecture on " Howdon and its associations," delivered at the Stephenson Memorial Institute on 18th October, 1865. Mr W. S. Daglish was in the chair. The lecture is largely founded on the reminiscences of the old people; two or three errors are made, but the publication is well worth acquiring. He died on 20th September, 1890.

These three pioneers in Local Government were all

popular, worked sincerely for the people's good, were thoroughly trusted by all who knew them, but all vastly different types of men.

Another member associated with both Howdon and the Willington Quay Local Board was Mr John Wesley Clavering, the eldest son of Mr George Clavering, who was born at Fiddlers Green in 1841 and came to Howdon with his family when he was six years of age.

After he grew up he worked side by side with his father in public affairs. He succeeded his father on the Tynemouth Board of Guardians and was a member for over fifteen years. From the years 1889 to 1896 he was chairman of the School Board. He represented the district for six years on the County Council and was a Justice of the Peace for the County and also for the Borough. He was for many years the recognised leader of the Liberal party, and along with Mr Nicholas Woodman and Mr Thos. Bolam fought many a tough battle. In his youth he was secretary to the Independent Church Sunday school, but latterly, like his father and mother, he was an adherent of the Methodist Free Church. In his later life he drifted more into the background, and died after a short illness on 5th January, 1913, aged seventy-one.

When Local Boards were dissolved in 1894 the Willington Quay members were: Messrs George Clavering, John W. Clavering, Nicholas Woodman, Benjamin Swan, Peter Rutherford, James Ed. Wilkinson, Wm. Thos. Weir, Michael Parker, and Adam Rutherford.

Colonel A. Potter, C.B., who had been chairman of the Board since its beginning, did not see its close, for, as we have already mentioned, his death took place in the preceding February. Mr W. S. Daglish was still clerk, and Mr Wm. Hope had been surveyor for some time.

Howdon

As soon as the Willington Local Board was established the people at Howdon also wished to have one. An application was made to " the powers that be," and in April, 1864, an inspector held a public inquiry into the matter. There was no opposition, and a representative from the Willington area promised to work in co-operation. The boundaries were forthwith defined, and were from the river along the centre of the West Street of Howdon, a little way along the road towards the station, then northward in front of the " Shipwrights Arms " to the Howdon Burn, then along the Burn to its entrance into the river.

Sanction for the formation of a Local Board of Health was given. It was to consist of six members, and the election was held in the Black Bull Inn on 16th August, 1864. The following were the candidates with their occupations taken from the voting papers:

Wm. Linsley Thompson	Offputter and occupier of the Black Bull.
Wm. John Clavering	Butcher.
Robert White Falconar Res. Newcastle	Ironfounder.
Matt. Robson	Druggist and Grocer.
Henry Salkeld Res. Willington Quay	Agent for Newcastle Corporation.
Thos. Davidson	Block and Mast Maker.

Wm. Stead, Minister of the Gospel; Joseph Salkeld, sailmaker; Wm. Turnbull, ship repairer; Luke Reay, post-master; John Porteous, innkeeper; John Ridley, butcher. The first six mentioned above were elected. The Board met on 19th August, and Henry Salkeld was chosen chairman, John Brunton Falconar, junior, solicitor and clerk, Mr Hodgkin treasurer, and John Weir surveyor, collector, and inspector.

The history of the Board was not an eventful one. It, however, had one distinction—it was the smallest local Board of Health district in England. Its total area was only 9·451 acres. Howdon was also the first part of the parish to have street lamps, and this was due to the public spirit of Mr Addison Potter, who supplied twelve lamps free of cost for some years. In 1867 Howdon and

THE COUNTY COUNCIL

Willington Quay united to resist a proposed union with the Borough of North Shields, but generally speaking little that was exciting arose.

The County Council Order of 24th June, 1894, made under the Local Government Act of that year, terminated its existence and united the ancient and historic village of Howdon with the very modern and unromantic Willington Quay.

The last members of the Howdon Board were Edward Green (the managing partner in the Brewery), who was chairman, John W. Clavering (farmer), Rev. John Hughes (vicar), John Rutter (blacksmith), Adam Rutherford (baker), and Wm. T. Weir (joiner and contractor). Dr C. T. U. Babst was the medical officer, Robert Davidson the surveyor and collector, and J. Montgomery of Newcastle was the clerk.

THE COUNTY COUNCIL

The Local Government Act of 1888 established County Councils in England and Wales. They took over the civil administration of the Quarter Sessions. From the highway authorities they took over the responsibility of the main roads, and they had a multitude of other duties delegated to them. Boroughs which had on 1st June, 1888, a population of not less than 50,000 were constituted County Boroughs.

The first election for the Northumberland County Council was held on 16th January, 1889. Dr Henry Aitchison and Mr Wm. Boyd were the candidates for Wallsend. The result was Dr Aitchison received 650 votes and Mr Boyd 379.

Willington Quay, Willington, Howdon, Long Benton, and Weetslade were grouped together, and allotted three representatives, and those elected for this area were: Michael Dodd, Lemington House, mining engineer; Robert Simmons, Dudley, builder; Joseph Snowball, Seaton Burn House, recently retired from the Commissionship of the Duke of Northumberland.

The first meeting of the Council was held on 24th January, 1889, and they took over their duties as from 31st March.

The districts were re-arranged before the second election, and when this took place on 3rd March, 1895, Dr Henry H. Aitchison was re-elected for Wallsend, and Michael Dodd for Howdon and Willington Quay, without a contest. Robert Simmons was elected for Weetslade, and there was a keen contest for Long Benton and Willington, which were grouped together. The result was: Jas. G. McIlvenna, dock manager, Rose Hill House, 291; J. R. Dransfield, solicitor, Killingworth, 257.

Mr Michael Dodd was made an alderman on 14th March, 1895, and Mr John Clavering was elected in Mr Dodd's place for Willington Quay in April. In 1901 Mr Clavering retired, and his seat was contested for on 7th March. The voting showed: Arthur J. Haggie, rope manufacturer, 480; Benjamin Swan, foreman plumber, 288.

The county was again re-divided for election purposes in 1903, and four seats were allotted to Wallsend. Dr Aitchison was elected for Northumberland and Wallsend wards; Robert I. Dees was elected for Holy Cross ward; George A. Allan was elected for Carville ward; Garforth Drury for the old Buddle and the Hadrian wards.

Mr A. J. Haggie was re-elected for Willington Quay, and as Mr James G. McIlvenna did not offer himself for re-election, Mr Daniel E. Stanford was elected for Long Benton and Willington.

At the elections on 3rd March, 1910, the Wallsend representatives were re-elected, except that Mr Wm. Giles took the place of Mr George A. Allan for Carville ward. On 17th March Mr Haggie was chosen an alderman, and in April Mr Benjamin Swan again contested the seat for

Willington Quay, which this time he won, although Mr John T. Watson entered the lists in opposition.

The first general County Council election after the termination of the war took place in March, 1919, and the Labour Party of Wallsend prepared to contest every seat. Mr Garforth Drury did not seek re-election, and Mr John Reid offered himself for Buddle ward instead of Carville.

The voting took place on 8th March, 1919, and the result was as follows: Northumberland and Wallsend wards, James Adams, checkweighman, in place of Joseph Davidson, farmer; Buddle ward, William Forrest, store manager, re-elected; Holy Cross, Geo. Ellis, boilermaker, in place of Charles C. Swinburne, brass founder; Carville, Jos. Harrison, shipwright, in place of John Reid, retired boot and shoe dealer; Hadrian, John James Heron, caulker, in place of Garforth Drury, solicitor; Willington and Willington Quay, Benjamin Swan, foreman plumber, re-elected; Howdon, Jos. Mullen, monumental stone mason, in place of Geo. Reid, who had removed from the district.

The Labour Party thus secured all the seats in the west portion of the Borough.

Dr Henry H. Aitchison, Mr Robert Irwin Dees, and Mr Arthur J. Haggie were re-elected aldermen.

THE PARISH COUNCILS ACT

The passing of the Local Government Act of 1894, widely known as the Parish Councils Act, made a considerable difference to our district. Under this Act the two Local Board areas of Howdon and Willington Quay were united to form the Urban District Council of Willington Quay. The Wallsend Local Board of Health was changed into the Wallsend Urban District Council, and a Parish Council was established for the rural area of Willington.

The Urban District Councils had a little more power

given to them, taken from the Vestries. It was in the rural districts, with their parish meetings and Parish Councils, where the great value of the Act was felt. Further, an important reform was the creation of a Parochial Electors' List for all local elections.

Before this, in every election for Local Boards each voting paper was written out from the rate books. It showed how many votes the elector was entitled to, and was delivered to the voter and collected afterwards. In the case of an election for Guardians the voters' list was written out after the last date specified for withdrawals. This system meant day and night work for the assistant overseer just prior to an election, and on the day of the contest he had an equally difficult task in deciding the claims of those who said they were entitled to vote, but had not been entered into the rate book. Printed parochial registers swept this kind of election into ancient history.

The 1894 Act ordained that "unless the County Council for special reasons otherwise direct," every urban district should be a separate civil parish. A strong effort was made to show to the County Council that it was a serious retrograde step to divide our compact parish into three, but they declined to "otherwise direct," and so on Michaelmas Day, 29th September, 1894, three parishes —Wallsend, Willington Quay, and Willington—were started, each complete, with separate overseers, rates, and accounts. Under this new law the first overseers for Willington Quay were: Arthur J. Haggie, rope manufacturer; Nicholas Woodman, foreman pattern maker; Peter Rutherford, trimmer. First overseers for Willington were: Andrew Halliday, foreman joiner; Wm. Dodd, farmer; James Bickerton, timekeeper. First overseers for Wallsend were: George A. Allan, agent; Wm. Forrest, store manager; John Giles, grocer; Samuel T. Harrison, cashier.

For sixteen years the old parish was thus split up. This was a wasteful and inconvenient division, yet when the Wallsend Borough Council drew up their "Representation" to the Local Government Board regarding the extension of the Borough, it was proposed that the three areas should remain three separate parishes. However, the assistant overseer saw that the opportunity was too good to be missed, and fortunately the position was not complicated by having three sets of officials, as Mr Wm. Richardson still held that post for the whole of the area. Hence, when the Provisional Order was issued, Article 26 set forth, " the Parishes of Willington and Willington Quay shall be amalgamated with the existing parish of Wallsend." Thus the old civil parish was once more quietly united, with the part of Long Benton taken over and added thereto.

Under the Local Government of 1894 the first Wallsend Urban District Council election was held on 17th December, 1894, and the Wallsend Urban councillors elected were: Messrs Geo. A. Allan, Wm. Boyd, Wm. Cawthorn, Jos. Davidson, Robert Douglas, Thos. Forrest, John Giles, Thos. Hedderly, Geo. B. Hunter, John O'Hanlon, Thos. Richardson, and Thos. Snaith, and at the first meeting of the new Council held on 7th January, 1895, Mr Wm. Boyd was elected chairman.

The new Urban District Council of Willington Quay held their first meeting on the last day of 1894, and the first members were: Messrs Nicholas Woodman, Benjamin Swan, Peter Rutherford, Adam Rutherford (members from the old Local Board), Arthur J. Haggie, George Bagnall, Thos. Bolam, Dr Thos. Aitchison and James Heads. The Willington Quay Local Board officials were retained and the Howdon ones compensated.

WILLINGTON PARISH COUNCIL

The Parish Council of Willington was, according to the County Council order, to have ten councillors, and the first parish meeting was called by the overseers, and held in the Bewicke schools, on the 4th December, 1894. Dr George B. Craig, of Rose Hill, was elected chairman, and Mr Wm. Richardson acted as clerk *pro tem.* Twenty-four candidates were nominated.

When the chairman declared those having the ten highest votes were elected, a poll was demanded, and this was taken on 15th December. (One of the candidates, Mr Joseph Ward, the secretary of the Wallsend Slipway Co., died suddenly the day before.)

The result of the poll was: Jas. G. McIlvenna (dock manager) was elected with 114 votes; then followed Wm. Jas. Watson (boilermaker), Jas. Bickerton (timekeeper), Wm. Rossiter (chargeman), Wm. Oliver (joiner), And. Halliday (foreman joiner), John Appleby (fitter), Allen Blakey (postman), Thos. Watson, and Robt. Holmes (labourer).

Those not elected were: Robt. Davidson (registrar), Wm. Dodd (farmer), Wm. Cooke (builder), Thos. Aitchison (M.B.), Wm. D. Ford (grocer), Geo. G. Richardson (importer), Henry Robinson (vicar), Thos. Thompson (foreman fitter), and Michael Parker (schoolmaster).

The first meeting of the Parish Council was held on 3rd January, 1895, at which Mr Jas. G. McIlvenna was elected chairman, and Mr Wm. Richardson undertook the work of clerk, for the time being, without salary.

The rateable value of the new rural parish of Willington was £3,745. The population in 1891 was 1,511, the number of houses 217, and the number of householders 305. The number of voters of the Parochial Register was 262.

While the Parish Council had not much power itself to enforce sanitary and road amendments, it had sufficient driving power to insist upon the needed improvements being carried out by the District or County Authorities.

In 1895 none of the streets of the parish were paved, and it was absolutely impossible at times to get a cart down

Willington Parish Council

the back street between Rosehill Terrace and Willington Terrace. There were no public gas lamps in the district and no fire plugs. On 9th September, 1895, fifteen street lamps were lighted for the first time; they were fixed at Rosehill, Burn Terrace, and up the Copperas Lane. The back street of Rosehill Terrace was paved before the first winter was over. A committee of the Council found that several public footpaths had been blocked up, some of them for years. Most of these were forthwith re-opened, either with the landlord's consent or without it.

One landowner stopped the path from the bridge over the Gut, leading through Willington Dene to the Square. The owner strongly denied the public right to the footpath, and after the District Council had failed to assert the public rights effectually, the Parish Council took the matter in hand.

The obstruction was at first a simple rail across the path and rubbish tipped by carts over the pathway. This was removed at night by willing workers and replaced by day by the owner. Then a large stretch of road was strongly barred off and the local excitement increased. To show the strength of the public feeling, the inhabitants were invited to muster in the Burn Closes at a fixed time and bring crowbars, saws, shovels, etc. On 30th May, 1902, about three hundred men and lads assembled, with many ladies as onlookers. On the pit heap overlooking the fencing and other obstructions, barring the path, was the landowner on horseback and thirty police constables he had brought. Mr Wm. Richardson and Mr N. Woodman first interviewed the officer in charge of the police and assured him that no unnecessary damage would be done and there would be no disorder on their side. Then the eager defenders of the public rights made short work of the posts and fences, and the shovel brigade levelled the pathway, and hundreds of men, women, and children, cheering the cause and hooting the landowner, swarmed up and down the disputed road, the police, of course, being mere spectators. This demonstration settled the matter for the time being, and the obstructions were not again replaced, though two years later another attempt to obstruct the path was made and defeated.

Another red-letter day was the freeing of the bridle road between Milbank Square and New York for vehicular traffic. A toll had been charged for all wheeled conveyances and the road kept in repair by the farmer. The Parish Council arranged with the landowner and the Tynemouth District Council that the toll should be abolished and the Rural District Council would keep the road in repair. On 9th September, 1907, at six-thirty p.m., in the presence of a large gathering, the toll gate was removed and speeches were made by Mr J. G. McIlvenna, chairman of the Parish Council, and by Mr Thos. Anderson, who represented Mr John H. Burn, the owner, for whom hearty cheers were given.

Other items of general interest were:

On 1st September, 1897, Willington was invited to consider a scheme for the incorporation of Wallsend, Willington, and Willington Quay. The Parish Council approved of the proposals, and on 21st December, at a public meeting held in the Rosehill Lecture Hall, the scheme was approved by thirty-two votes against four.

Wallsend Council afterwards decided to proceed alone, because Willington Quay declined to join in the scheme—a mistaken policy as Wallsend afterwards found.

From time immemorial Willington and Willington Square had depended upon the wells in the dene for their water supply, and in a dry season the best well, three hundred and thirty yards below the Square, had a "waiting list" almost the whole night through. The Parish Council arranged with the Water Company to carry their pipes to High Willington, and the wells in the dene lost their importance.

In 1896 a letter box near the vicarage was added to the conveniences of Willington village. In 1907 gas was laid up to Willington Square after the Parish Council had secured certain guarantees. In 1909 a letter box was arranged for the Square also.

On 1st November, 1905, a proposal to appoint a committee to confer with a Willington Quay Committee, with a view to uniting these two areas, was lost. Eleven months later the same proposal was again rejected.

In December, 1909, Wallsend again invited Willington to agree to a proposal to incorporate the three districts. On the other hand Willington Quay Urban District Council wished Willington to unite with them and jointly oppose the Wallsend scheme. The Parish Council declined the Willington Quay proposal and made terms with Wallsend. The principal conditions being: (a) that for ten years the maximum rate levied was to be 5s. 5d. in the £; (b) the Wallsend Council to accept Mr Hunter's offer of the Burn Closes as a recreation ground, which they had declined two years before this.

This decision to unite with Wallsend was arrived at, not because Willington expected to be better, or more economically managed, but because they were faced with the breaking up of the Tynemouth Rural District Council. Furthermore, for years the Council saw that if there was to be an amalgamation the old parish ought to be united for Local Government purposes, and finally they did not think the opposition of Willington Quay to Wallsend would succeed as the heads of several of the Willington Quay works were in favour of joining Wallsend.

The last meeting of the Parish Council was held on 2nd November, 1910, when the chairman, Mr James G. McIlvenna, and the clerk, Mr Wm. Richardson, were empowered to wind up its affairs. Out of the original ten members elected in December, 1894, five were still in office when the Council ceased to exist on 8th November, 1910.

One of the matters which Willington was not able to end satisfactorily was the encroachment of a house and garden on the road-side, which was part of the highway at the Fir Trees. The Fir Trees house was one of the old gate houses which was sold by the road trustees when the toll ceased. One of the conditions of sale was that they had to be removed forthwith, but instead of doing this the purchaser got some of the road trustees to give him a title deed to the house and garden. This title, the Parish Council was assured, was absolutely without proper authority, and they appealed, through the District Council, to the County Council for the removal of the encroachment.

The County Council induced the landlord to offer to return part of the land on condition that all claims to the remainder would be withdrawn. This the Parish Council refused and preferred to allow the house and garden to remain until such time as the County Authority was prepared to enforce the public rights.

WALLSEND BURIAL BOARD

A Vestry Meeting for the election of a Burial Board was held on 28th February, 1876, at which seventy-six ratepayers were present. There were seventeen candidates, and as a result of the voting the following were chosen: Rev. Richard Jenkyns, rector; Rev. David Wilson, Presbyterian minister; Andrew Leslie, shipbuilder; Geo. Clavering, farmer; Dr Jas. Aitchison; James W. Dees, engineer; Chas. S. Swan, Wallsend Slipway Co.; Mr R. C. Forster, draper, Willington Quay; Wardle Shaw, joiner, Church Bank.

Among those not elected were John Turner, butcher; John Glover, chemical manufacturer; Rev. John Hughes, vicar of Howdon; George Dixon, grocer, Willington; John Smith, Wallsend Forge.

The first meeting of the Board was held on 29th March, and the Rev. R. Jenkyns was appointed chairman, and on 12th April, 1876, Mr Chris. Scott, clerk to the Tynemouth Guardians, was appointed clerk.

In the same year nine and a quarter acres of land for a cemetery were bought from Dame Allan's Charity and the Dean and Chapter of Durham, at a cost of £3,350.

The first interment took place on 2nd April, 1879, and on 10th July a chapel and a portion of the ground was consecrated by Bishop Lightfoot, of Durham, in the first year of his episcopate.

When the Local Government Act of 1894 came into force, and the old parish was divided into three, the Burial Board became a Joint Committee. On 21st April, 1910, the Vestry sanctioned an agreement to buy from Mr L. S. H. C. Orde thirty-three acres of land to the north-east of Holy Cross churchyard at £375 per acre. On 12th October, 1916, the Bishop of the diocese consecrated the Anglican portion of this ground, and the first interment took place on 12th November, 1918. The last meeting of the Burial Joint Committee for Wallsend, Willington, and Willington Quay was held on 7th November, 1910, and on 9th November the newly-elected Town Council for the enlarged borough of Wallsend became the Burial Board. The clerks were as follows: Christopher Scott, 12th April, 1876—10th January, 1883, resigned; John Henry Mussel, 14th February, 1883—21st January, 1889, suspended and dismissed; George H. Cameron, 21st January, 1889—(continued under new authority).

The Borough of Wallsend

For several years prior to 1901 the idea of incorporating Wallsend, Willington, and Willington Quay was discussed, but nothing definite was done until 1897, when the Wallsend Urban District Council asked the other two authorities to hold conferences to discuss the matter. In the end, Willington was decidedly in favour of the incorporation scheme as outlined, and Willington Quay elected to stay out. Wallsend decided not to take Willington without Willington Quay, and proceeded to petition for the incorporation of the Wallsend township alone. This they obtained under a Charter dated 6th February, 1901. The new Borough was divided into six wards, and the number of electors was 3,706. The first election took place on 1st November, and thirty-one candidates offered themselves for the eighteen seats. Of the old District Councillors, Mr Wm. Boyd, Mr Geo. B. Hunter, and Mr Summers Hunter did not enter the contest. It was understood that Mr Boyd and Mr Hunter would be elected Aldermen, and that Mr Summers Hunter wished to devote his time to other matters.

We, however, need not enlarge upon the incorporation, as full details of the scheme for the Charter, the report of the first election, and all other matters relating to the event was compiled by Mr Matt. Murray and published in an interesting illustrated history, " The Incorporation of the Borough of Wallsend." There are a few slight errors, e.g., the Mayor is reported as saying that " the patronage of the Church remained with the Dean and Chapter of Durham from 1082 to 1881 " (page 48), whereas there was no Dean and Chapter of Durham until 1541, and the date of the incorporation of Jarrow is given as 1825 instead of 1875, and hence this did not precede the incorporation of " South Shields and Tynemouth by twenty-five years " as stated (page 46).

The Mayor's gold chain was presented to the Corporation by Alderman Wm. Boyd and Alderman Geo. B. Hunter, and Alderman Boyd also gave a robe for the use of the Mayor. With regard to the Borough Arms, the eagle copied from a Roman sculptured stone found at Bremium in Redesdale is shown as standing on what was intended as a Roman wall (see illustration), but the wall is manifestly a " perpendicular " wall, hence we have a Roman eagle sitting upon a wall built about one thousand years after the Romans had left Britain, which suggests an exceedingly aged bird. We have been unable to trace who was responsible for such a manifest anachronism. Mr Cad-

THE "ARMS" OF THE BOROUGH. [*Facing page* 392.

walleder J. Bates was one of those consulted by Mr Boyd, and he suggested the general idea of the design, but as regards making the Roman wall into an embattled one, the correspondence with Mr Wm. Boyd shows that although Mr Bates agreed to the final design, he anticipated that the anomaly would be criticised.

The motto was also the subject of considerable discussion; the words finally adopted were those suggested by Canon James Henderson, the rector.

The first meetings of the Town Council were held in the Masonic Hall, but a site for a block of municipal buildings had already been secured.

THE TOWN HALL

A lease of 7,300 square yards of land, owned by the Ecclesiastical Commissioners, had been obtained. The lease is for 999 years, as from Lady Day, 1899, and the rental is £75 12s. 10d. per annum.

The foundation-stone of the town hall was laid on 19th June, 1907, by Mr Wm. Boyd, the first Mayor, and the buildings were opened by Alderman George A. Allan, the chairman of the Building Committee, on 16th September, 1908. The total cost of the building and fittings was £15,657 12s. 11d. Immediately after the opening ceremony Miss Sylvia Stephenson, daughter of the Mayor, started the public clock which was presented to the town by Mr Boyd.

THE COUNCIL CHAMBER

The Council Chamber is lit by nine stained-glass windows, and on each there are two shields, or other devices. Beginning at the south-east end we have shields representing:

1 (*a*) Boyd. (Mr Boyd was the first Mayor of the Borough.)

(b) Grey. (Lord Grey was Lord-Lieutenant of the County when Wallsend was incorporated.)

2 (a) Northumberland. (The Duke was Lord-Lieutenant when the municipal buildings were opened.)

(b) Newcastle Bishopric. (In whom is vested the patronage of the episcopal church livings in Wallsend.)

3 (a) Wallsend. (Arms of the Mayor and Aldermen and burgesses of the town.)

(b) Northumberland County. (Of which Wallsend forms a part.)

4 (a) Tynemouth. (Wallsend is in Tynemouth Poor Law Union.)

(b) Durham Bishopric. (At one time patrons of the church living at Wallsend.)

The fifth window contains the most interesting device in the series. It is a copy of the " Mask " of the river god Tyne. The front of Somerset House, which faces the Strand, is adorned by eight " Masks " emblematical of eight English rivers, including the Tyne, and this is a representation of what was designed by Sir Wm. Chambers and carved in stone by a Royal Academician, Carlini, when Somerset House was built about the year 1785. It will be seen that the head of the Tyne-god is surmounted by a basket of coal on fire, and in his hair are entwined shovels, pick, fish, and grain. The Rev. John Brand made the design familiar in the north when he published it in his history of Newcastle, and it was adopted as the seal of the Wallsend Local Board of Health. On the other division of the window is a ship sailing.

In the sixth window (north side) we have : (a) A picture of the Gas or " C " pit. (b) A duplicate of the god Tyne.

7th window: (a) St Andrew. (b) Scotland.

8th window: (a) St George. (b) England.

9th window: (a) St Patrick. (b) Ireland.

These last require no explanation. It has always seemed to the writer disappointing that of the many men fully entitled to bear Arms, who in olden days lived and worked and died within the two townships, and who at home and abroad helped to make England what she is, not one of them except Mr Boyd is represented among these heraldic reproductions.

On the walls of the Council Chamber there are three oil paintings. That of Mr Wm. Boyd, the first Mayor of the Borough, is a " speaking likeness." That of Mr W. S. Daglish, the first town clerk, is not quite so good. Both are by Ralph Hedley, and were presented to the two gentlemen by subscribing friends, and they presented them to the town. The third is of Dr Henry H. Aitchison, who was the hospital medical superintendent for Wallsend. This is by Frank S. Ogilvie, and was presented to the Borough Council by the Aitchison family and some personal friends in 1922.

In the Committee Room there are large photographs of Colonel Addison Potter, C.B., presented by his son; of Mr George Clavering, presented by his son John; and of W. S. Daglish, who was for thirty-nine years clerk to the Willington Quay Local Authorities, presented by members of the Local Board. These originally were in the District Council Board Room at Willington Quay. There are also photographs of the members and officials of the Willington Quay District Council, of the first Borough Council, and of the first enlarged Borough Council, and the laying of the foundation stone of the town hall.

In the corridor a case contains a number of Roman coins, pieces of Roman pottery, antlers of red deer, etc., found in Wallsend between 1884 and 1913 and presented by Mr Walter S. Corder and Mrs Robert Casson.

The Enlarged Borough of Wallsend

When the question of incorporating Wallsend, Willington, and Willington Quay arose, not only was the Willington Parish Council faced with the breaking up of the Tynemouth Rural District Council of which Willington formed a part, but Long Benton was also in the same position. Matters were brought to a crisis on 28th September, 1909, when Willington Quay applied to the County Council for an order to include Willington in their district, and the City of Newcastle decided to apply to the Local Government Board for power to include part of Wallsend and part of Long Benton in Newcastle.

Long Benton wished to remain outside the City and preferred to be converted into an Urban District, and they petitioned the County Council for urban powers, but they knew that when the Local Government Board held an inquiry, Newcastle would face them with the fact that Long Benton had no outfall for their ever-increasing sewerage except through Newcastle sewers, and therefore Newcastle would urge that their two sanitary areas ought to be joined. Furthermore, when fire broke out at Long Benton Newcastle fire brigade had to be sent for.

To get rid of these weak points in their defence against Newcastle, Long Benton offered part of their area to Wallsend in exchange for: (a) sufficient sewer " way leave " through new pipes to be laid by Wallsend to their boundary; and (b) Wallsend keeping a strong fire brigade to be at the call of Long Benton when required.

Wallsend agreed to an arrangement of this nature, and Wallsend's first proposal was that they should take in Bigges Main, the Rising Sun Colliery, and Willington High Row. Benton demurred to this as they did not want to give up the Rising Sun Colliery, and they offered Bigges Main, Little Benton, the Red and the White Halls, and the land running west to the Newcastle boundary. There was much negotiation, and Willington Quay held out to the last day before they came to terms with Wallsend.

The Local Government Board Enquiry was held in the Moot Hall, and it lasted from 23rd February, 1910, until

2nd March, and the result was that Newcastle failed to get any part of either Wallsend or Benton, and Wallsend received substantially what it first asked for. Willington got preferential rating: the total rates not to exceed 5s. 5d. in the £ for ten years, and Willington Quay district rate, apart from Poor Rate, was to be 3s. 8d. for five years and 3s. 9d. for five years more.

At this time the areas (excluding the river) and their rateable values were:

	Acres	Rateable Value
Wallsend Urban District Council	1,096	£131,046
Willington Parish Council	1,127	7,642
Willington Quay Urban District Council	310	37,578

The total rates over the three years ending 31st March, 1909, averaged: Willington 5s. 2¼d. per annum, Willington Quay 5s. 9½d., and Wallsend 5s. 8¼d. Apart from the debts owing to the Guardians, Education Authority, County Council, and Burial Board, which fell upon all three areas alike, and apart from the Wallsend debt upon the public park, the hopper and wharf and the municipal buildings which were good assets, the ordinary debts of Wallsend represented 2s. 3d. in the £ upon their rateable value, those of Willington Quay 3s. 6d. in the £, and those of Willington 1s. 9d. in the £. The cost of administration for clerks, surveyors, accountants, inspectors, doctors, auditors, and assistants cost Wallsend 2¾d. in the £, Willington Quay 3d. in the £, and Willington 1¾d. in the £.

It was arranged that the enlarged Borough should consist of nine wards and should come into existence on 9th November, 1910.

The names of the wards in the original Wallsend Borough were retained, but the old Buddle ward was divided between Carville and Hadrian wards, and the name Buddle was transferred to a new ward taken off the west side of the original Holy Cross ward, which had grown greatly within the past ten years.

Willington ward comprised the rural portion of Willington township, and the Willington Quay and Howdon urban area was divided so as to give, as nearly as possible, an equal proportion of voters to each ward.

The first meeting of the new Council was held on the 9th November, 1910. Mark W. Swinburne was elected Mayor, and the following were elected Aldermen: For Wallsend—James Allan, Matt. Murray, John O'Hanlon, Samuel T. Harrison, Chris. Stephenson, Robt. H. Jackson. For Willington ward—Jas. G. McIlvenna (previously chairman of the Parish Council). For Willington Quay ward—Benjamin Swan. For Howdon ward—John T. Watson.

Thus the retiring Wallsend Aldermen were re-elected except that Mr Jackson filled the vacancy caused by the retirement of Mr G. B. Hunter.

The Mayors of the Borough

The following are those who have been Mayors of the Borough, and a biographical note relating to each will be found in Chapter IX:

		Year		Enlarged Borough	Year
1	Wm. Boyd	1901-2	10	M. W. Swinburne	1910-12
2	Geo. B. Hunter	1902-3	11	Geo. Elliott	1912-13
3	Geo. A. Allan	1903-4	12	John O'Hanlon	1913-14
4	Samuel T. Harrison	1904-5	13	Jas. G. McIlvenna	1914-15
5	Matthew Murray	1905-7	14	Wm. H. Thompson	1915-19
6	Chris. Stephenson	1907-8	15	Benj. Swan	1919-20
7	Robt. I. Dees	1908-9	16	Wm. Forrest	1920-21
8	Jos. Duffy	1909-10	17	Joseph Mullen	1921-22
9	James Allan	1910	18	Geo. M. Fitzsimmons	1922-23

Education

The earliest record of schools at Wallsend is that relating to the village school, which opened about 1748. The next school we hear of is that of Mr George Arnison, who began teaching at Wallsend about 1800 and gave a higher type of education which included the classics.

Then in speaking about St Peter's Church we mention that the " National " school was opened in 1833.

Doubtless at Howdon Panns there would be a school prior to that at Wallsend Village, but the first of which we have definite memo is that of Wm. Martindale, who was a schoolmaster here early in the nineteenth century. The school-room was near the south end of Glass House Lane, and it was also used by the Primitive Methodists as their meeting-place. He was succeeded by Mr Cumming, who began his school duties at Howdon Panns about the end of 1838. He taught reading, orthography, arithmetic, and geography.

In the following October he was fined 40s. for using a leather strap on the shoulders of a lad named Morrison, the son of a pilot, and the *Gateshead Observer* of 19th October, 1839, comments on the case as follows :

> The inhabitants of Howdon, who ought to be the best judges in the affair, are so surprised at the " conviction," and displeased with the conduct of Morrison, that they have not only subscribed the full amount of the schoolmaster's expenses, but have also purchased from Messrs Lister & Son, of Newcastle, a valuable silver snuff box, which, with a suitable inscription, will this week be presented to Mr Cumming as a memorial of the high esteem in which he is held by the parents of his pupils. Such a demonstration of public feeling is highly flattering to the schoolmaster.

From a report of the first annual examination, it would appear that this was the only school at Howdon Panns, as the chairman, the Rev. R. Caldwell (the first Independent minister), spoke of " the rapid improvement made by the youth of the place under Mr Cumming."

Then an additional school was started by Daniel Robinson in the large room at the west end of East Terrace, now Church Street.

After this several schools were opened. Mr Robert Patterson, who began teaching at Bigge pit, built a residence (Rose Cottage) and a school-room at Rose Hill. He retired and closed his school in 1873, and died in 1877 at the age of sixty-eight. He was a well-known dominie, as was also Mr Charles Adams of the Colliery School at Wallsend.

We have mentioned elsewhere the Ropery Schools opened in 1849, and the Stephenson Schools opened in 1860.

One of the Willington Quay schoolmasters, Wm. Dickson, went to Newcastle about 1870 as editor of Ward's *North of England Advertiser*, and when that paper was bought by the *Weekly Chronicle*, he became a member of the staff and remained so until his death on 29th April, 1886. He wrote in dialect as a "Retiort Keelman."

Prior to 1870 education only touched a mere fraction of the masses, for the schools available had generally a low standard and made little impression.

Directly the Parliament, elected under the great Reform Act of 1832, settled down to work, it made, in 1833, the first parliamentary grant for education, and £20,000 was given to aid the British (non-sectarian) and the National (Church of England) school societies to build more schools. Twenty years later this yearly grant had increased to nearly a £1,000,000.

Generally speaking, the Government gave half the cost of building a school, provided the other half was raised by local effort. Under these grants both a "National" and a "British" school was aided in our district. But W. E. Forster's Elementary Education Act of 1870 was an immense stride forward. It established a School Board in every district, whose duty it was to provide and maintain efficient schools where required.

In 1870 great hopes were entertained by those interested in the welfare of the masses as to the result of educating the rising generation. Vice and wrong-doing would, they expected, be greatly lessened, and slums and poverty rare events. England was to live on a higher plane, and the best men in every district were ready to help forward this new era of enlightenment. Our parish formed one area, as the Wallsend School Board district, and when the election of the new authority took place a healthy active interest was taken in securing what was thought the best men to carry out the duties of the School Board.

The members elected were as follows: Addison Potter, Wm. Cleland, Rev. John McNerney, Rev. David Wilson, Andrew Leslie, Geo. Clavering, and Rev. Richard Jenkyns.

The first meeting was held in St Peter's Vestry on Thursday, 28th January, 1875, and all the members were present, as was also the Returning Officer for the election, Mr Christopher Scott, clerk to the Tynemouth Guardians.

Mr Addison Potter was chosen chairman, Mr Andrew Leslie vice-chairman, and Mr Chris. Scott was appointed as clerk at a subsequent meeting, at a salary of £30.

Mr Leslie arranged with the Wallsend Local Board for the meetings to be held in their board-room on payment of £5 a year, the School Board to pay for their own fire and lights.

Immediately the question arose as to what new accommodation for school children was needed. The United Methodist Free Church of Willington Quay offered to rent their school-room; or as an alternative they offered to sell both their school-room and church, which was leasehold, for £4,000, " all costs to be borne by the school authority." This offer was promptly declined.

The Wallsend Co-operative Society offered to transfer their school in the Temperance Hall, Blenkinsop Street, as did also the trustees of the Stephenson Memorial Schools. The School Board accepted the Stephenson Schools, and agreed to build two new schools, each for six hundred children, one at Wallsend and one at Willington. An acre and a half of land, belonging to Mr Robert R. Dees, was purchased for £800 per acre, and on 6th March, 1876, the contract for the building of the Buddle Schools was accepted. The contract price was £8,400.

2C

This, with the cost of the site, fittings, etc., made the total estimated cost of £11,000. Two months later it was agreed to pay £224 14s. 6d. to the trustees of the Stephenson Schools for the furniture and fittings, and on Monday, the 18th September, 1876, the Board took over the management. Mr Geo. Turnbull was the head-master, at a salary of £150, the caretaker had £14, and a staff of ten assistants had £193 2s. 1d. amongst them. The numbers on the books were 186 seniors and 166 infants. The average attendance was 236, and the fees received from the scholars averaged £3 13s. 2d. per week.

After a futile attempt to secure a site for Willington at what is now the east end of Burn Terrace, two acres were purchased a little further east on the south side of the Turnpike from Calverley Bewicke at £450 per acre. The building contract was £8,710, and the total estimated cost was the same as for the Buddle Schools.

The Buddle Schools were opened on the 30th July, 1877, and the Bewicke Schools on 5th August, 1878. Mr James Tocher, of Allonby, Maryport, was appointed master of the former, and Mr John Robinson, master of the Methodist Free Church Schools at Wallsend, was appointed head of the latter.

The School Board for twenty-eight years did excellent work. A very much higher standard of education became universal, and gradually the illiterates of the district disappeared.

When the Conservatives introduced the Education Bill of 1902, which proposed to sweep away the School Boards, Wallsend district tried to prevent this being done. At a Board Meeting held on the 29th April, 1902, the Rev. E. H. Steel proposed, and Mr Thos. Fries seconded, a resolution asking that the Bill should be withdrawn, as it would be detrimental to education. The fact that it was proposed to put education into the hands of an authority who were specially elected for sanitary and road purposes, was felt to be a retrograde movement.

School Board

Canon Henderson proposed, and Mr Jas. Fitzsimmons seconded, an amendment approving of the Bill generally. On the motion being put, only the proposer and seconder voted for the amendment, and the motion was carried.

However, the School Boards were doomed, and the new Act was to come into force on the 1st June, 1903, and the last meeting of the Wallsend School Board was held in the board-room at the Bewicke Schools on the 26th May, 1903.

At this meeting the following were present: Adam Rutherford (chairman), Canon Henderson (vice-chairman), Thos. Richardson, Robert Wallis (Slipway), David Moyes, Jas. Fitzsimmons, John O'Hanlon, Thos. Fries, Robt. Davidson, Rev. E. H. Steel, together with R. C. W. Newlands, clerk, and M. W. Graham, assistant clerk.

After the routine business, there were the usual votes of thanks, but a special vote was passed to Mr Adam Rutherford, who had been chairman from 14th January, 1896, and he was also presented with a silver tea and coffee service.

Of the original staff, only Mr Geo. Turnbull, Miss Frances Selby, and Mr Jos. Hope remained.

The Borough Council of Wallsend took over the Buddle, Carville, and the Richardson Dees Schools, and the responsibility for elementary education in Wallsend township. The County Council took the Stephenson, Bewicke, and Addison Potter Schools, which were in Willington and Willington Quay areas, which were then outside the Borough.

Under the new Education Act the Wallsend Education Committee consisted of sixteen town councillors, with the following co-opted members who were specially interested in education: Rev. Canon Henderson, Dr P. P. Bedson of Durham College of Science, Newcastle, Messrs Jos. W. Tocher, Robert Wallis, and E. Griffiths, all of the Wallsend Slipway, representing the technical side; Mr Jos. Hope, representing the teachers; Mrs M. Laverick, formerly an elementary school teacher, and Mrs Wm. Richardson, who had been teacher of the methods of education at the Durham College of Science, Newcastle. Alderman George A. Allan was elected chairman, Alderman John Giles vice-chairman, and Mr Martin W. Graham, who had been assistant clerk under the School Board since 30th January, 1894, was appointed clerk to this new committee. Alderman G. A. Allan died in January, 1910, and Mr Robt. I. Dees was elected chairman of the committee on 17th February. He resigned in October, 1912, and Alderman George Elliott was elected chairman on 21st November.

The local members of the County Council Education Committee who were responsible for education in Willington and Willington Quay were Mr Arthur J. Haggie and Mrs Wm. Richardson.

However, when these two areas were incorporated with the Borough in 1910, the responsibility for their elementary education became vested in the enlarged Borough Council, and the Stephenson Memorial, Bewicke, and Addison Potter Schools became Borough Council Schools.

The County Council were still responsible for secondary education over the whole of the parish, and they continued the evening classes and opened a pupil teachers' centre in the Wallsend Congregational Church buildings on the 9th January, 1905, with Miss Eleanor Giles, B.Sc. (Durham), at the head. The present Secondary School and Technical Institute buildings, near St Peter's Church, were officially opened on 23rd September, 1914, by Sir Francis Blake, with Mr Walter McBretney and Miss Giles as the principals. On opening they enrolled fifty-three boys and ninety-one girls. The school was intended to accommodate pupils from Wallsend and Gosforth.

The first governors were Messrs P. P. Bedson, D.Sc., chairman, Robert I. Dees, G. C. Robinson, Benjamin Swan, Charles C. Swinburne, R. J. Walker, and Mrs Wm. Richardson, appointed by the County Council; Messrs

George Elliott, R. H. Jackson, John Scorer, John O'Hanlon, Robert Wallis, and Mrs Laverick, appointed by the Borough Council.

Before leaving the subject of education we must revert to Mr G. B. Hunter's early plans for the improvement of the education of the young men of Wallsend. He was ably assisted by a few educational enthusiasts, who had high standards and who started classes in the Café in 1883. As a result, Wallsend stood for many years in the forefront of technical education on Tyneside.

The first secretary of the Café classes was Mr F. I. Trewent. He left the district in 1887, and had a most successful career in London. On 3rd September, 1887, Mr Alfred Harrison, chief draughtsman at the North-Eastern Marine Engineering works, succeeded Mr Trewent, and continued until he left Wallsend to become manager at Mr Wm. Allan's Scotia works, Sunderland. Steam, theoretical and applied mechanics, and mechanical drawing were taken by Mr C. S. Metcalfe, now of Sunderland. Naval architecture was taken by Mr M. C. James, now of Jarrow. Other subjects were mathematics and languages. The classes were conducted under South Kensington Science and Art supervision, and the number of students grew as the soundness of the teaching became known, until in 1887 there were over three hundred regular attenders who came from all parts of the district.

Schools Built by Public Authorities
Buddle, opened 30th July, 1877.
Bewicke, opened 5th August, 1878.
Carville Infants, opened 12th September, 1892.
Carville Seniors, opened 5th February, 1895.
Addison Potter, Infants, opened 30th August, 1887.
Richardson Dees, opened 24th February, 1902.
Western, opened 8th January, 1906.
Central, opened 1st August, 1913.

THE COMMISSION OF THE PEACE

Until 1902 all Wallsend Petty Sessional matters had to be taken to the old " Correction House," Tynemouth, near the Blyth & Tyne North Shields Railway Station. Appointment of overseers, rate summons, "drunks," Jury Lists, as well as serious crimes, all had to be dealt with there.

As our town grew, the inconvenience and cost of this was realised, and strong local effort was made to have a Court of Petty Sessions held at the Café. The overseers called a public meeting in the Co-operative Society Hall for 2nd June, 1892. Mr John Giles took the chair. There was a large attendance, and urgent resolutions were passed which were brought before the Standing Joint Committee and the County Council without result.

However, after years of effort the County Authorities arranged to meet the needs of the district, and the first Court of Petty Sessions was held in the Café on 6th February, 1902, and the County Justices continued to hold the Court fortnightly until the Borough of Wallsend was incorporated.

In December, 1908, a separate Commission of the Peace for the Borough was issued, and those included were: Henry Hyslop Aitchison,* M.B., Park Villa; George Auburn Allan, Water Company's agent, Orchard House; James Allan, plater, Laburnum Avenue; Robert Casson, dock foreman, Camp House; John W. Clavering,* farmer, Howdon Farm; Robert Irwin Dees,* gentleman, Highfield; George Elliott, accountant, Burnside; William Giles, chemist, Western Villas; Arthur Jamieson Haggie,* rope manufacturer, Benton; Samuel Turner Harrison, cashier, The Green; Matthew Murray, Slipway Company's secretary, The Green; John O'Hanlon, plater, Woodbine Avenue; Christopher Stephenson, shipyard manager, The Green; Mark William Swinburne, brass founder, Newcastle.

Mr T. Y. Bramwell, who had been clerk to the Justices for the East Castle ward since 1889, was appointed to the

* Those marked with an asterisk were already County Magistrates.

same office for the Borough, and Mr C. J. Page continued to act as his assistant until 25th March, 1919, when he was appointed joint clerk to the Justices for the Borough with Mr Bramwell.

The first Borough Petty Sessions was held in the Town Hall on 6th April, 1909, and after the Court rose, Mr Robert I. Dees celebrated the event by giving a lunch to the Justices and officials.

Borough Magistrates on 31st December, 1922

The Mayor (ex-officio) : G. M. FITZSIMMONS

Robert S. Anderson
Henry H. Aitchison
Robert I. Dees
Wm. Forrest
Arthur J. Haggie
Samuel T. Harrison
Sir George Hunter
Robt. H. Jackson
Wm. S. Kirkley

James G. McIlvenna
Jos. Mullen
John O'Hanlon
John Reid
John Scorer
Wm. H. Thompson
Alex. B. Walker
John Thos. Watson

RATES AND RATING

Henry VIII. in 1531 passed an Act ordering the Justices of the Peace in every shire to tax every inhabitant for the repairing of bridges situated on highways. In 1572 Elizabeth authorised the Justices to rate every parish towards the relief of the prisoners in the common gaols. These assessments in the north are known as the "Old Book of Rates," and in it the local entries are:

	£	s.	d.
Wallsend	1	12	9
Wallsend Rectory	0	5	0
Willington	1	10	5
Willington Mill	0	2	3

A fresh assessment was made early in the seventeenth century, and in a County Rate levied in 1663 we find Willington Mill has disappeared and Howdon Panns,

Glass Houses and a Salt Pan at Wallsend added. The items are:

	£	s.	d.
Wallsend	... 1	12	9
Wallsend Rectory ...	... 0	5	0
Wallsend Panns ...	... 0	1	6
Willington	... 1	10	0
Holden Glass Houses	... 0	3	0
Holden Pans	... 0	3	0

After the great changes which the year 1541 saw in the ownership of the lands in our area, Wallsend township continued under the new Dean and Chapter of Durham, to be divided into seven " farms " or leaseholds of equal value and rentals, and Willington continued to be divided into eight farms, or tenancies, under the Crown, and these " farms " were used as the unit of local rating for generations.

This system continued long after " farms " ceased to be a seventh or an eighth part of the townships, and when trading and commercial concerns came into existence the number of " farms " were altered, in order to meet the altered conditions.

On 17th June, 1759, an important meeting was held in the Vestry resulting in—" A Protest of Separation of the Poor of the Township or village of Wallsend from the Township or villages of Willington and Holden Panns. Whereas the Parish of Wallsend in the County of Northumberland doth consist of three distinct Townships or villages, namely the Township, or village of Wallsend, the Township, or village of Willington, and the Township or village of Holden Panns." It was settled that each should " henceforth support and maintain " their own poor, but the poor who had no special claim upon any of the three villages were to be paid out of a general fund.

This arrangement was arrived at without any dispute or objection. The word " protest " used at this meeting stands only for the old meaning—pro (before) and testor (I bear witness); we would use the word declaration now.

Rating by "Farms"

Wallsend and Willington were each to keep their own poor and be separately rated for the cost, and although we can find no formal record of the arrangement, we know as a fact that the Andersons of the Salt Panns, and the Henzells of the Glass Houses, undertook to maintain the poor in the Howdon area.

The first account we have as to payments to the poor is under date of 23rd March, 1761. At this time in Wallsend the number of " farms " had risen to nine, which included the ministers' glebe land and tithes, accounted as one " farm." In Willington the " farms " numbered eight and one half.

There was then one man in Wallsend who received 1s. 6d. per week and four women who received 1s. per week. In Willington there was one man at 1s. 6d. and one woman at 1s., and there was also a man and a woman who were a joint charge upon the townships. Hence the total cost was £4 7s. 6d. per quarter. Therefore " The cess for Walsend and Partnership is nine shillings and nine pence per Farm quarterly wh. on 9 Farms is £4 7s. 9d.," and " for Winlington and Partnership is five shillings and 8d. per Farm quarterly wh. on 8 Farms and ½ and one shilling on Henzells House is £2 8s. 9d. The church cess agreed to by us of the four and twenty whose names are under written is Eight shillings and 1d. a Farm on 16 Farms and ½ amounting to £6 13s. 1d."

This minute is signed by E. Potter, minister, James Moncaster (The Hall), Edward Anderson (the Salt Panns), John Hemsley (Henzells), Thos. Hanch (a radical Howdonian), and by George Greene and Geo. Simpson, churchwardens.

Twenty years later the number of the poor had risen to seven in Wallsend and nine in Willington, and the rate is spread over the " farms " and 10d. for the Glass Houses.

On 2nd June, 1783, the whole question of rating the township of Wallsend was discussed by the Vestry, and the outcome was that Mr Potter, the curate, induced the

Vestry to reduce his glebe and tithes from one " farm " to half a " farm." The corn tithes, which had not been previously assessed, were brought into rating as a quarter farm, and the new Wallsend colliery was assessed as two farms. Hence the township of Wallsend was altered to nine and three-quarter " farms " instead of the previous eight.

On 17th April, 1786, Willington colliery was rated as equal to three farms, bringing this township up to eleven and a half farms.

In the year 1790 the ancient method of rating according to " farms " came to an end, at which time Wallsend was counted as having eleven and three-quarter farms and Willington eleven and a half, exclusive of the Glass Houses. The Wallsend Poor Rate for this year amounted to £88 8s. and for Willington £75 8s.

The following year the valuations are set out in pound sterling, the assessable value of Wallsend township being £1,680 and Willington township £1,580, but this was not agreed to as satisfactory, and an amended valuation was adopted for 1791-92, and Wallsend was assessed at £1,810 and Willington at £1,580. The details for Wallsend township were as follow:

Easter Monday, April 25th, 1791

	£
Wm. Russell & Co. for Wallsend Colliery	500
James Moncaster, Esq. (The Hall)	60
Mrs Waters for Rev. Mr Ridley and others	90
John Bigg, Esq. (Carville)	120
Rev. Mr Blackett for Tithes and Land	120
Mr John Langlands	30
Charles Atkinson, Esq., for himself and others	60
Matthew Smith	100
John Smith	60
Wm. Young	70
Robert and Wm. Swan, Farms	120
George Simpson	120
Robert Nesbitt	120
Thos. Mann	70
James Curry	70
John Winship	60
Wallsend Corn Tithes	40
	£1,810

First Valuation Lists

In 1809 the County assessments show:

Wallsend	£12,708
Willington	8,815
Howdon Panns	588
	£22,111

The earliest detailed valuations we have found for Willington and Howdon are dated 1814, so we give the assessments for the whole parish for that year as the values for Wallsend township had increased sevenfold since 1791 chiefly owing to the development of the colliery.

Township of Wallsend

	£
Wm. Russell, Esq., & Co. for Colliery	10,000
Lands	100
Farm	120
Matt. Bell, Esq., & Co. for Wayleave	200
John Wright, Esq. (The Hall), House and Land	130
Farm	105
John Walker, Esq. (The Red House)	100
Wm. Redhead, Esq. (Carville)	185
Nicholas Fenwick (The Grange and Land)	55
Miss Mary Peareth (Land and Villa)	62
Mr John Spark, Farm	160
Wm. and Elizabeth Swan (Farms)	362
Mr Thos. Whitfield	110
Messrs Buddle and Burnett, Land	130
Mr John Redhead	330
Mr Humphrey Curry (White House)	76
Mr Matt. Hutton	44
Mrs Sarah Thompson	40
Mr Thos. Swan	40
Thomas and Wm. Arkley	40
Mr James Addison	6
Wm. Losh, Esq. (Point Pleasant House, etc.)	90
Mr Robert Lownes	80
Mr John Reay	10
Mr John Hann	10
Owners of Kenton and Coxlodge, Staiths and Wayleaves	200
Owners of Fawdon, Staiths and Wayleaves	200
	£12,985

412 LOCAL GOVERNMENT

Township of Willington

	£
Matt. Bell Esq., & Co. Colliery and Wayleave	4,000
Willington Farm	662
Willington West Farm	325
Mr Watson's House	25
Corporation of Newcastle (Ballast Quays)	300
Assignees of Messrs Hurry, Mansion House	40
Dock Houses	66
Mr Charles Nixon (Corporation Farm)	90
Mr Wm. Hays	20
Mr Timothy Pollock (Rose Inn, etc.)	35
Jos. Lamb, Esq., & Co. (Copperas Works)	50
Messrs Wigham & Thouburn	167
Mr John Watson	175
Mr John Jopling	30
Mr James Charlton	320
Mr Wm. Hall	170
Sir J. H. Liddell, Bart., & Partners, Killingworth, Wayleaves and Staith rents	430
Chapmans, Wright, and Redhead	250
Jos. Unthank & Co. (Mill)	150
Mr Thos. Huntley (Prospect Place)	20
Mr Wm. Stewart	10
Mrs Ann Bowdon	10
John Walker, Esq., & Co. (Bewick & Craster Royalties)	3,000
Owners of Jarrow Colliery (Newcastle Corporation Royalties)	1,200
	£11,545

Howdon Township

	£
Assignees of J. & T. Hurry, Houses	162
Messrs Brunton & Crighton, Brewery	100
Houses	8
Mr Benj. Brunton, Houses	67
Mr John Ridley	20
Robert Huntley (Dr)	15
Mr John Cook	20
Mr Wm. Elliott	15
Mr Robt. Redford	8
Mr Wm. Wilson	12
Mr Edward Taylor	10
Mr Thos. Bruce	12
Mr Jas. Shotton	10
Mr Wm. Linsley	12
Mr John Mills	10
Mr James Miller	8
Mr George Turnbull	8
	£497

VALUATION LISTS

Summary in 1814:

Wallsend Township	£12,985
Willington Township	11,545
Howdon Township	497
	£25,027

The valuation lists and rate books for rates made in the parish between the years 1814 and 1850 had disappeared some time prior to 1891, at which date the writer began to make enquiries for them.

In 1850 the rateable value of the parish was:

Wallsend Township	£6,355
Willington Township, including Howdon	8,069
	£14,424

In 1860:

Wallsend Township	£6,962
Willington	6,709
Howdon	1,411
	£15,082

In 1870:

Wallsend Township	£14,708
Willington	13,949
Howdon	1,367
	£30,024

In 1880:

Wallsend Township	£29,701
Willington	2,958
Willington South	17,146
Howdon	1,435
	£51,240

In 1890:

Wallsend Township	...	...	... £49,989
Willington	... ...	...	... 4,288
Willington Quay U.D.	...	...	... 22,956
Howdon	... ...	...	... 1,364

£78,597

In 1900:

Wallsend Township	... ...	...	... £78,564
Willington	... ...	...	... 4,600
Willington Quay and Howdon	...	... 31,068

£114,232

In 1910, on November 9th, when the Borough was enlarged:

Wallsend Township	...	...	...	£125,375
Willington	...	...	...	6,835
Willington Quay	..	...	...	37,039
Bigges Main	...	...	...	4,462

£173,711

In 1920:

| Wallsend and Bigges Main | ... | £154,987 |
| Willington and Howdon | ... | ... | 49,553 |

£204,540

Up to 31st March, 1921, in the Valuation List of the parish and in the rate books, the rateable values of the old townships had been kept separate. Up to 1910 this had been done on account of the distinct local government areas, and even after these were united this division was continued, as the two districts, which together formed the old Willington township, had each preferential rating until November, 1920. In the spring of 1921 a new valuation was made of the Tynemouth Union, chiefly on account of the great rise in values since the war and the passing of the Rent Restriction Act. As there was no longer any necessity to keep our areas distinct in the new Valuation List, the railways, electric light mains, water pipes, collieries, etc., within our parish were each valued as one unit and not separated as heretofore, and the new rateable value total was:

Works, Buildings, etc.	£281,609
Agricultural Land	2,745
	£284,354

This was an increase of £80,004 7s. 6d.

Meanwhile bad trade had set in and a great number of objections to the valuations were entered. By 31st March, 1922, reductions amounting to £25,400 were made, chiefly allowed off the works, and the following is a summary of rateable property in the parish as on 31st March, 1922:

	£
Works, Factories, etc.	105,404
Licensed Premises	11,869
N.E. Railway Company	10,739
Coal Mines	11,688
Coal Staiths and Wagon-ways	1,494
Agricultural Land	2,717
Farm Houses and Buildings	622
Tithes	520
Theatres and Picture Houses	982
Houses forming part of Housing Scheme	750
Shops	11,765
Shops with Houses Attached	4,613
Dwelling Houses and Other Properties	95,790
Total Rateable Value	£258,953

CHAPTER IX

ADDITIONAL BIOGRAPHICAL NOTES

The ancient family of Durhams—The Surtees family—Billy Martin—George and Robert Stephenson and the Memorial Schools—The Weatherleys of Howdon—Dora Russell, novelist—Andrew Leslie—Wm. Thos. Stead—Dr Ernest Woodhouse—Wm. S. Daglish—Sir James Knott and others—The eighteen Mayors of the Borough.

THERE have been many men of note connected with our parish who were not especially connected with either works, churches, or estates, and hence we must needs give them a place in these records by themselves.

THE DURHAMS

By far the oldest Wallsend family who had their home within our area, for quite a phenomemal number of years, was that of the Durhams. Where they lived in the days when serfs were more numerous in Wallsend than free tenants, we cannot say. The first house we can locate them in is Howdon Hall, which up to 1866 was the oldest house in the whole parish. Tradition says this was owned by the monks of Jarrow and used by them as a rest house when pilgrims from the north were unable to cross the river in stormy weather. Of course this is only a tradition, but probably the monks had a hospice here. It was a large stone house near the south end of the Glass House Lane, on the east side (see plan, page 199). It had a large entrance hall with a wide staircase facing the door, and we may judge of the age and type of the building by the fact that there was a passage way on the first floor within the thickness of the walls. This passage was entered through cupboards.

It was for many generations the home of the Durhams, who for nearly five hundred years were residents in the parish. In 1368 John de Durham took a tenement in Wallsend, and the name of a Durham is mentioned four or five times as tenants in the Halmote Court Rolls within the next fifty years.

In 1539 the widow of John Durham was paying 5s. 4d. per annum to the Prior and Convent for a cottage in Wallsend. After this, the next mention of the family in local history is when "Robert Durham of Walshend, farmer," gave evidence in a case of witchcraft which we have already quoted.

In 1628 George Durham of Wallsend was one of the Grand Jurors of Northumberland.

In 1660 Robert Durham held one farm and fine under the Dean and Chapter of Durham assessed at £140.

In 1673, the Wallsend leasehold was in the name of Gawen Durham, and the assessment was £180. Five years prior to this Gawen had a son baptised in Holy Cross Church and named Henry.

In 1683 the church registers record "August 22nd, Mr Robert Durham buried."

About this time the family appear to have given up farming and become traders and shipowners and moved to Howdon. The first church cess which we have is one made on Easter Monday, 1719, and there, after making a rate of 6s. 8d. for each "farm," we have "and sixpence for Mr Durham's house at Howdon Panns."

In 1722 Thomas Durham, son of Robert Durham of Wallsend, gentleman, was admitted into the Newcastle Guild of Merchant Adventurers, and the following year another son, Robert, was also admitted. [It is to be

2D

remembered that these entries " of Wallsend " refer to the parish, not to the township.]

Three years after Robert Durham, junior, was admitted into his Guild, his father died, and we have in the Holy Cross Registers: " 1726, October 1st, Mr Robert Durham of Howdon Panns buried." There are several other entries relating to the family, but the last two are: " 1739, June 12th, Margaret, daughter of Robert Durham of Newcastle, Wine Merchant, was buried." " 1742, August 1st, George Durham of Howdon Panns was buried," and he appears to have been the last of the Durhams to reside in the parish. Robert Durham, from the entry concerning Margaret, had moved to Newcastle prior to 1739. The year 1746 was the last for which Mr Durham was rated for the house.

In a manuscript book in possession of Mr Robert I. Dees, there is a memo, probably by John Bell, the land surveyor. Commenting upon the long association of the Durhams with Wallsend, he adds the following notes :

Mr Roger Durham of Wallsend, a shipbuilder on the North Shore. 1736, his daughter, Heiress of Lands at Barress Bridge married Andrew Dick, Hoastman, Father of Sir John Dick, Consul at Leghorn, heir to Sir Wm. Dick of Braid, Bart.

1768. Thomas Durham Esq. late of Hanover Square, Newcastle, last male of above Durhams. He died owner of the Old Custom House, Newcastle, from the Burfields, etc., where was much painted glass visible to the Street before the late round turn was made at the angle on the Sandhill.

The Surtees Family

We have already seen that many of the men who occupied prominent positions in Newcastle had a country residence in Wallsend, and some of the well-known Surtees family is to be added to the number.

Auburn Surtees was a boothman, or corn-merchant, in Newcastle and was made a member of the Merchant Company on 28th September, 1737, and later he became a well-known banker. He was the Sheriff for the year

1744-45, and the Mayor for the years 1761-62 and 1770-71.

The tale is well known of how his daughter, Bessie, while living at the Sandhill, escaped through an upper window and eloped to Scotland with Jack Scott, the coal fitter's son, and how her father shut his door against the hasty lovers while the whole town, and probably Wallsend, rang with the romantic story. Presently the father forgave them—John Scott rose in the world and became Lord Chief Justice, and later Lord and Lady Eldon were of great assistance to the Surtees family when trouble overtook them.

Auburn Surtees, the father of Bessie, and his family resided for years in a house in the village which no longer exists. It belonged to the estate of Dame Allan's Charity, and he appears to have only paid 20s. per annum for it, but as he was a wealthy man and took an interest in the school and its accounts, possibly the rent paid did not greatly matter. He died on 30th September, 1800, aged eighty-nine years.

Before his death, his second son, John, was residing here, as we have the following entry in Holy Cross Registers of Baptisms, under the year 1800:

Jan. 3. Birth—April 19 Bapt.—Auborn John Surtees—1st son of John Surtees, Esq. son of Auborn Surtees Esq. of Hedley, County of North. Native of St Nicholas, Newc."

Another entry in 1803 records the " Birth on June 7th and the Baptism on Sept. 10th of Stevenson Villiers, 2nd son of John Surtees, Esq."

John Surtees was a partner in Surtees, Burdon & Co., bankers, and, of course, brother of the famed Bessie. He and his two brothers left the Newcastle Town Council when the eldest of them (William) was fined two hundred marks because he declined to accept an aldermanship. He and his brother Auburn were also partners in the Tyne Iron Co. at Lemington.

While John Surtees and his wife and family were

residing at Wallsend, financial disaster overtook them. The year 1803 was one of great commercial panic (one year after the signing of the Peace of Amiens), and the Surtees Bank was obliged to stop payment, and in the end the family retired to the continent and John Surtees died at Dinan in Brittany in 1849 at the age of ninety-two. Stevenson Villiers, doubtless with the assistance of Lord Eldon, was appointed a Judge in the Mauritius.

WM. MARTIN ("BILLY MARTIN")

He was the son of Fenwick Martin, a tanner, and was born at Twohouse in the parish of Haltwhistle on 21st June, 1772. His younger days were spent in Scotland with his grandfather. He was the eldest of a very remarkable family. Jonathan Martin, born in 1782, is chiefly known for having set fire to York Minster in 1829, thereby causing damage to the amount of £60,000, and John Martin, born in 1789, was the celebrated painter, who attained great honours.

In 1794 we find William Martin at Howdon dock working in Hurry's ropery. In the year following, he first joined the Northumberland Militia, where he distinguished himself as a swordsman and fencer, and at jumping competitions. He records a standing jump he made at Hornsey, of 12 feet 4 inches. The regiment was disbanded at Alnwick about 1802, and Martin returned to the Howdon rope works.

In 1814 he married, and began his housekeeping at the higher of two cottages half-way up Church Bank, Wallsend, opposite the cemetery gates. His wife was a dressmaker and continued her business, and did her part to maintain the household. This was very necessary, as her husband was much more interested in inventions and in bringing about "the downfall of all false writers" and the "defeat of learned humbugs" than he was in earning his daily bread in the ordinary way.

Without doubt his mind teemed with ideas. He made a "dandy horse," the forerunner of our bicycle, on which he sped to and from Newcastle, to the wonder of the neighbourhood. He spoke of ventilating coal mines by means of fans in the year 1806, only his idea was to force the air down the pit. He made a flying machine with wings on which he nearly broke his neck.

In 1794, while living at Howdon, he suggested iron tram rails instead of wooden ones. When George Stephenson and Sir Humphrey Davy were putting forward their safety lamps, he disapproved of both their designs, and made one of his own. This he had tried at Willington Colliery with the consent of Mr John Watson. Mr George Johnson, the under viewer, and the four waistmen who carefully tested it made a report to the coal owners, dated 19th April, 1819, certifying that Martin's lamp was in every way superior to both Stephenson's and that of Sir H. Davy.

Of his many inventions, the only one for which he received public recognition was for the spring balance with a circular index, which is now in common use. For this invention, in 1814, he received from the Society of Arts their silver medal and ten guineas.

During his residence in Wallsend of fifty years, he wrote many vigorous tracts and pamphlets defending his peculiar religious and philosophical views, and his claims to inventions patented by others. These are nearly all dated from Wallsend, and he published letters which are addressed to him at "Half-way Bank, Shields Road, Newcastle-upon-Tyne." He also delivered lectures and travelled up and down the north of England selling his literary effusions.

His wife died on 16th January, 1832, aged fifty-nine, and her only concern when on her death-bed was the future comfort of Billy. He stayed on in the Church Bank Cottage for some time by himself, but as a cook and housekeeper he was not a success, although he declared that boiled beans and salt contained all the nutriment necessary for man.

He remained in the district about fifteen years after the death of his devoted wife, and as he got older his eccentricities increased; instead of a hat he wore a tortoise shell bound in brass, and on his coat and breast a variety of medals, presented to him chiefly by those fond of practical jokes. Then his brother John invited him to London to reside with him, and thus the last two or three years of his life were spent in comfort and ease. He died in London on 8th February, 1851, in the eightieth year of his age.

Tradition says that John and Jonathan Martin also resided in Howdon and worked there, but we can find no evidence of this.

In "The Philosopher's Life from being a Child in Frocks to this Present Day, after the Defeat of all Impostors and False Philosophers since the Creation" Billy gives an account of his four brothers and one sister. Here he mentions that John and Richard paid him a visit at Howdon in 1805, but there is nothing about them ever living there. Furthermore, the biography of John Martin in "Men of Mark" practically disproves the tradition.

George and Robert Stephenson and the Memorial Schools and Institute

In the first years of the nineteenth century the Corporation of Newcastle were taking large quantities of gravel ballast from the ships which came to the Tyne to load coals, and they were piling it up in hills upon the ballast already laid down on the ancient shoreline of the river over one hundred years earlier, under the lease granted to Sir Francis Anderson in 1665. A ballast crane was at that time near what is now the north end of Tyne Street, and from there the loaded wagons were

STEPHENSON'S COTTAGE.

FROM A WATER COLOUR IN POSSESSION OF MR. CHARLES J. POTTER OF HEATON HALL, PAINTED IN 1838.
George Stephenson resided in the upper portion of the cottage on the left, at that time approached by outside stairs. [*Facing page 422.*

drawn up a steep incline to the top of the mound immediately to the north, by a stationary engine.

George Stephenson, then a young man not quite twenty-one years of age, became the brakesman or engineman of this hauling engine, early in 1802.

He had only recently learnt to read, but he was steady, observant, and of a decided mechanical turn of mind. When he came to Willington Quay, he was engaged to be married, and as soon as possible he secured the upper room at the west end of a small two-storied dwelling-house,[1] near the south-east end of the Ballast Hill, standing only a few yards from the river side, and on the 28th November, 1802, he and Miss Fanny Henderson were married at Newburn. Two farm horses brought the wedding party to Willington Quay.

To increase his income, he made shoes, and by chance he now acquired a more profitable occupation for his leisure. His house took fire, and his eight-day clock was clogged with soot and water. Hence George was obliged to try clock cleaning, and soon he became noted as a clock repairer over a wide district. This trade brought him such a welcome addition to his wages that by and bye it nearly prevented his removal to Westmoor, where his inventive genius had its full scope.

Fortunately, all Stephenson's spare time was not given to earning money; he spent much of it in making mechanical experiments and increasing his knowledge of engines. In 1803 his only son Robert was born, but there is some doubt concerning the date of this event.

In the Memorial Schools and Institute there is clearly cut upon the ornamental fireplace, " Robert Stephenson, born November 16th, 1803." The *Northern Daily Express* of 17th November, 1858, commenting upon the stone laying of the Stephenson Memorial, says: " Being the 16th of

---

[1] See illustration, which is reproduced from a water colour painting by G. F. Robinson, dated 1838, in possession of Mr Charles J. Potter of Heaton Hall.

November it was the birthday of Robert Stephenson," and one of the speakers mentions this also. Robert Stephenson himself had ample time to correct this report before it was carved in stone, but did not do so. The registers of Wallsend, however, give the date of birth as 16th of October, 1803. He was baptised in the school-room in Wallsend village, and the following entry is under the year 1804: " Robert Stephenson. (Birth) Oct. 16th. (Baptism) January 22nd. 1st son of George Stephenson of Willington Quay, Engine man, native of Ovingham by his wife Francis, late Henderson, native of the Par[h] of Bolam." Smiles' " Life " gives the date as it is in the registers.

In the early days of the eighteenth century the coals from Killingworth and West Moor collieries were shipped at Willington Quay, where the Killingworth Company had staiths near the site of Cleland's offices. Hence there was considerable intercourse between these places. The agent for the owners of the Killingworth colliery at Willington was Mr Chas. Weatherley of Low Willington House. In 1804 a brakesman was wanted at Killingworth, and Mr Weatherley, who knew Stephenson well, was able to offer him the post, but the engineman was not eager to accept it. His clock repairing was bringing him a fair addition to his wages, and he was reluctant to give this up. However, in the end he accepted the position, and he and his wife and infant son removed from Willington Quay.

His connection with our district did not quite cease in 1804. A few years afterwards he was engineman for several weeks at the Willington Ropery, as Mr Chapman arranged with the Killingworth owners for the " loan " of Stephenson during the illness of their man. Good working enginemen were few in these days, and George was not then occupying an important post at the colliery.

After he had been eleven years at Killingworth, the following is entered in the Minute Book of the partners, under date 18th March, 1815: " Resolved that the said

George Stephenson have his salary increased from 1st January, 1815, to £100 per annum."

When his spare time was largely given up to railroads and locomotives, he was a frequent visitor on Sundays at Point Pleasant House, where he and Mr Wm. Losh planned and perfected many improvements in matters connected with engines and railways. He died at Tapton on 12th August, 1848, aged sixty-six, and was buried at Chesterfield.

When the question arose of raising some special memorial to his memory on Tyneside, the place selected was the site of the house wherein he began his married life, and where his already famous son Robert was born, and this land was given by the Newcastle Corporation to the Memorial Committee.

The immense importance of education as exemplified in Stephenson's life decided the trustees to erect and endow a school for children and a Mechanics' Educational Institute for men.

The foundation stone of the Memorial was laid on 16th November, 1858, by Mrs Addison Potter, and among those present were Mr T. Sopwith of Allenheads, an intimate friend of both George Stephenson and his son, also the Mayors of Newcastle (Jos. Laycock) and Tynemouth (E. Potter), Mr and Mrs Chas. M. Palmer, the Rev. Dr Bruce, and Dr Moffatt of Howdon. After the speeches some of the visitors were entertained at Mr Addison Potter's house at Chirton and the others at a lunch in Mr Potter's works. One of the speakers voiced the general indignation at the unfriendly way the vicar, Rev. John Armstrong, had treated an invitation to the ceremony.

The trustees of the school were: Robert Stephenson, M.P., Jos. Whitwell Pease, Addison Potter, Geo. Robert Stephenson, W. Weallens, and Philip Holmes Stenton. The architect was Archibald Mathias Dunn. The building was not opened until 10th February, 1860, and again there was a distinguished company present. There was no formal opening of the doors, as the visitors filed into the large room as they arrived. Dr Bruce, however, asked the Divine Blessing upon the Institution, and Lord Ravensworth gave the first address delivered in the new buildings. Addison Potter, who had been the active trustee, reported that in response to an appeal for funds he had received promises for £675 and had so far only received in cash £85 and had spent £43 for expenses. This had delayed the work until Mr Robert Stephenson had offered to find the necessary balance, and then soon after this he decided to pay for the whole cost of the school, and the money collected might be used afterwards. The death of Mr Robert Stephenson on 12th October, 1859, before the schools were finished, had probably prevented him providing a good library and an endowment. Mr Potter also reported that Mr Alfred Goddard, the newly appointed master, came to Willington Quay with high testimonials. The Mayor of Newcastle moved a vote of thanks to Lord Ravensworth for his address, and Mr John Clayton seconded this. Tea was dispensed, and in the evening a soirée was held, the chair being occupied by Mr Jos. Cowan, junior, of Stella House.

The schools were excellent for their day; there was a suitable house for the schoolmaster, and the Institute, which occupied part of the east end of the building, was also well up to date.

The Institute was found to fill a useful place in the village of Howdon. After it had settled down to work, in 1863, there were two hundred books in the library. Five daily newspapers, one Newcastle weekly, and one London weekly paper were taken. Lectures were given during the winter, and the following is the list of lecturers for the season 1863-64: Addison Potter, Rev. Dr Bruce, Rev. T. E. Lord (vicar of Howdon), Dr Dodd (of North Shields), Mr Henry Shield (of Newcastle), Rev. Wm. Stead, Dr Dickinson, Rev. J. C. Weir (Jarrow), and Mr Henry Salkeld. This shows that the lectures were of a high level. There were sixty ordinary members; the subscription was

6s. 6d. per annum. In 1864 a Penny Savings Bank was opened. At a later date the lectures were given up and weekly "Penny Readings" were substituted.

About the year 1878 the Institute was required for teaching purposes, and the books, etc., were moved into the draughting offices of Palmer's Yard, then unused. It did not, however, flourish there, and the committee moved once more in 1882 into the old Primitive Methodist Chapel in Church Street, the lease of which was bought, and suitable alterations made.

When the School Board came into existence, they agreed to take over the schools. They paid £224 14s. 6d. to the trustees for the furniture and fittings, and on 16th September, 1876, the buildings passed into the hands of the new Board.

ALFRED GODDARD.—The first master of these schools was a man who made his mark on the educational policy of Tyneside, at an important period.

Alfred Goddard was born in Hampshire on 23rd February, 1836. He was trained at Battersea Training College. He was introduced by Thomas Sopwith to Robert Stephenson, with a view to his taking charge of the Memorial Schools. Satisfactory arrangements were the result, and Mr Goddard arrived at Willington Quay on 2nd February, 1860.

He worked hard with the evening classes, the reading-room, and the Artillery Volunteers, and in the summer was an active official in the Wallsend Cricket Club. After he had spent eleven useful years at Willington Quay, he was appointed first clerk to the Newcastle School Board on 1st May, 1871. He occupied this post during the whole period of the School Board's existence. His energy, care, and foresight in conjunction with the progressive and enlightened policy of the Board gave a lead in education to the whole district.

When the School Boards were abolished, and education

handed over to the sanitary authority, the Education Committee of Newcastle urged Mr Goddard to continue as their secretary. This he did until October, 1906, when he retired, at the age of seventy. He soon after left Newcastle for Hailsham, where he died on 28th September, 1916.

MARK R. WRIGHT.—Another name associated with these schools was a scholar and pupil teacher there who made his name in the educational field after he left our area. Professor Mark R. Wright, M.A., was born at Willington Quay and for some seven years was a scholar and for five years a pupil teacher at the Stephenson Memorial, then in January, 1872, he left for the Borough Road Training College. After having a tutorship in the College and headmasterships in Birmingham and Sheffield, he returned to Tyneside in 1884 to take the post of headmaster of the Gateshead Higher Grade School. Six years later he was selected Principal of the Teachers' Training Department at Armstrong College, Newcastle, and he remained here as Professor of Education for thirty years. During this time he became widely known as an authority on educational matters, and when he retired on 30th September, 1921, he was appointed by the Council of Armstrong College Emeritus Professor of Education.

He is a member of the Senate of Durham University, Chairman of the Higher Education Committee of Gateshead, Chairman of the Governors of the Whitley and Monkseaton High School, and Chairman of the Managers of Elementary Schools for Whitley and Monkseaton.

THE WEATHERLEYS

This is another family which deserves some mention in local history.

John Weatherley came to Low Willington House or to the " White House " prior to 1787, and he was the local agent and staithman for the Killingworth Colliery until his death on 26th June, 1809, at the age of seventy-five.

Three of his sons—John, Robert, and Charles—remained residents of the village all their lives; the others sought their fortunes elsewhere.

Of the latter, James Dent Weatherley joined the 60th Rifles when he was seventeen years old, served in Holland, Egypt, and through the Peninsular War. He retired from the Army in 1818 with the rank of Captain, and married Miss Sawyer. They were some years in Canada, and returning to Tyneside settled in Newcastle, and like many more Wallsenders he entered the Town Council, and rose to be Sheriff, Mayor, and Alderman. It was during his Mayoralty that the Queen, accompanied by the Prince Consort and the royal family, opened the High Level Bridge on 28th September, 1849. He left Tyneside in 1856 and died at St John's Wood, London, on 3rd January, 1864, aged eighty-seven.

Another son, Ilderton, became a shipowner, and lived in Northumberland Street, Newcastle. His son, Frederick Augustus Weatherley, born in 1830, followed the footsteps of his uncle and was one of the " noble six hundred." After the Crimean War he served through the Indian Mutiny. He left the Army in 1877 with the rank of Colonel. He was largely interested in the Transvaal and lived in Pretoria some years, and when the Zulu War broke out he raised a troop at his own expense. He took his son with him and led his men in the fateful battle on 28th March, 1879.

The following extract is from Welford's " Men of Mark " ;

In James Grant's " British Battles on Land and Sea," Major Ashe describes the closing scene of the Colonel's life in the following graphic narrative : " Nothing could be more sad than Weatherley's death. At the fatal hour when all save honour seemed lost, he placed his beloved boy upon his best horse, and, kissing him on the forehead, commended him to another Father's care, and implored him to overtake the nearest column of the

British horse, which seemed at that time to be cutting its way out. The boy clung to his father, and begged to be allowed to stay by his side, and share his life or death. The contrast was characteristic—the man, a bearded, bronzed, and hardy sabreur, with a father's tears upon his cheek, while the blue-eyed and fairhaired lad, with much of the beauty of a girl in his appearance, was calmly and with a smile of delight loading his father's favourite carbine. When the two noble hearts were last seen, the father, wounded to death with cruel assegais, was clasping his boy's hand with his left, while the right cut down the brawny savages who came to despoil him of his charge." A double-page engraving of this terrible scene is given in *The Pictorial World* for 24th May, 1879, and about the same time young Weatherley's determination to die with his father formed the subject of a poem entitled, "A Child Hero," which went the rounds of the metropolitan and provincial press.

Of the three sons who remained at home: (1) John Weatherley, born 30th September, 1774, was a wine merchant. He lived in the old portion of Low Willington House facing south-east. He died on 21st January, 1859, aged eighty-four. (2) Robert, born 29th April, 1777, was a shipowner and lived in the old house, with the porch supported by pillars, still standing in Church Street on the west side of the Coach open. The garden bordered the river shore.

This house with coach house and cottage was built by Mr Robert Weatherley in 1820, about which time Mr Wharton and he became occupiers of Howdon dockyard. In 1844, when other houses began to be erected on the opposite side of the road to Mr Weatherley's house, and which presently formed East Terrace, Mr Weatherley's view northward was threatened, therefore he leased the sites opposite and kept the land clear. He died at Howdon on 21st August, 1851, and his wife, Elizabeth, died three years later. Their daughter, Emma, married Wm. Adamson, of the Willington Slipways, the builder of Rose Hill House. His only son, John Jopling Weatherley, joined the Army and became Captain of the 6th Dragoon Guards and Northumberland Militia. He died on 6th May, 1872, at Whalton, aged forty-nine, but was buried in the family burying ground at St Peter's churchyard, Wallsend.

Charles, the third son of John Weatherley, senior, was born on 30th May, 1784, and succeeded to the post held by his father as local agent for the Killingworth Colliery. He lived first in the White House (opposite Cleland's yard) and then in the newer part of Low Willington House facing west. He died on 22nd July, 1865, aged eighty-one years.

The only member of the family now having any connection with Howdon, is Margaret, only daughter of John J. Weatherley. She married Major Maurice Harnet Stack, and she still holds part of the property in Church Street built by her grandfather Robert. All the family residing in the parish took an active part in local affairs, and a prominent tombstone in St Peter's churchyard marks the family burial ground.

Mr John Weatherley was one who sometimes puzzle those who search church registers for data, as the searchers do not find them where they expect it. We have been unable to trace in the church books the record of the births or baptism of some of his family. He did not have his children's births recorded from time to time as they occurred, but it appears as though he " saved them up " as it were. On 14th October, 1793, there are registered six births, beginning with Annie, born on 3rd October, 1770, and finishing with Charles, born 30th May, 1784. He may have forgotten the missing children were not registered.

Mr Weatherley is not quite exceptional in this; for example, Thomas Hanch had nine sons and daughters baptised all at once according to the entry in the registers. Matthew Knott of Howdon Panns had Margaret, John, and James all registered on 12th April, 1808, and there are several other instances.

Dora Russell

A family closely associated with Willington for many

years was the Russells, who were no connection of the Russells of Wallsend Colliery.

Peter Russell, who lived at Battle Hill Farm, was the agent and manager for the land and property of Messrs Bell & Brown. He died in 1831, and was succeeded at Battle Hill by his son Peter. Ten years prior to that, on 3rd January, 1821, another son, George Greenwell Russell, married Miss Dorothy Bulman, of Gosforth, and they took up their abode at the Willington Farm, and shortly afterwards he became the colliery agent.

On account of the closing of the pits Mr George G. Russell in 1857 took the farm on his own account and lost very considerably over it, and gave it up and moved in 1863 to Gosforth. He had three daughters, and the second, Dorothy, made for herself a considerable name in the novel reading world as Dora Russell. She wished to become a story-writer partly because she had ambitions in this direction, but chiefly in order to help the family fortunes.

Story after story was rejected by publishers, then by chance she met Mr Richard Welford, who was always ready to assist beginners. Her style fully accounted for the rejections she had met with. Mr Welford often found that one sentence took up a whole page. He spent a good deal of time advising her, and at last in 1870 one of her stories was published in the *Weekly Chronicle*, and a second one, "The Miner's Oath," in the Christmas number.

Mr George Rutledge, the publisher, was in this district on a visit to his relations, and Miss Russell was introduced to him. He published two of her stories, and from then onwards her success was assured. Her father died on 24th April, 1871, just as she was getting her foot on the ladder of fame, and she soon afterwards moved to London with her two sisters.

She was born at Willington on 21st July, 1829. After attaining middle age, she, by effort and study, made a name for herself, and she died in comfortable circumstances at Hampstead in 1905 at the age of seventy-six.

Over twenty of her novels were published, many of them week by week in the *Weekly Chronicle*; then in three volumes, then in the two-shilling yellow-backed book of thirty years ago. " Footprints in the Snow " (1876), " Beneath the Wave " (1878), and " Lady Sefton's Pride " were probably her most popular stories.

She has been classed with Mrs Henry Wood, but this is, we think, too high an estimate. Miss Braddon and Miss Lynn Linton would be nearer her standard.

Andrew Leslie

Andrew Leslie, the founder of the shipbuilding section of Hawthorn, Leslie & Co., took an active part in the life of Wallsend for many years.

He was born at Aberdeen on 1st September, 1818. After his school-days were over he started work as a rivet catcher, then served his apprenticeship as a boilermaker, and by the time he was thirty years of age he was practically acquainted with the art of iron shipbuilding from top to bottom. He made up his mind to be his own employer, and started in a very small way at Aberdeen.

He soon, however, realised the narrow limits of Aberdeen as a shipbuilding place, and he knew of two other Aberdonians who had migrated to Tyneside and reported that there were wider possibilities there.

John H. Coutts, the pioneer iron shipbuilder, had in 1840 begun at Low Walker, and in 1842 Charles Mitchell arrived at the same place to serve under Mr Coutts. In 1854 Mr Mitchell was shipbuilding on his own account, and in the same year Mr Leslie left the north and commenced his new shipbuilding yard at Hebburn Quay.

He began on a small scale and had an uphill fight for success. He had a very limited capital, but had also exceptional energy, perseverance, and shrewd business ideas, and Hebburn, its town, shipyard, and dry docks are the result.

While building up this huge concern, he resided at Wallsend, and was there an active worker. He lived in John Buddle's old house, which he occupied from 1859 for over twenty years. In 1877 Coxlodge Hall was destroyed by fire, and Mr Leslie bought the estate. He restored the Hall, and in 1880 he left Wallsend and took up his abode there.

He was one of the few who worked hard for the establishment of a Local Board of Health for Wallsend, and who failed to secure a seat at the election for members. However, on 1st February, 1869, he and his fellow-reformer, Dr James Aitchison, secured election. He was a member of the first Wallsend School Board and its first vice-chairman. It was due to his wide outlook that the Buddle and the Bewicke schools were built so substantially and were planned far in advance of other school buildings of forty years ago.

Generally his ideas were in advance of his day. For example, when he, as chief promoter of the building of a manse for the Wallsend Presbyterian minister, designed and contracted for Western Villa, the church members, when they saw the building, considered it altogether too large and too expensive, with the result he kept the proposed manse for himself, and a Church Committee erected a house for their minister on a smaller scale.

He retired from Andrew Leslie & Co. Ltd. in 1885.

We are only giving a few facts concerning Mr Leslie's connection with Wallsend, but much might be written concerning what he did for Hebburn. At his funeral it was truly said: " Hebburn would remain for ages a monument to Mr Leslie's toil and industry and good work."

He died at Coxlodge House on 27th January, 1894, aged seventy-five years.

WM. THOMAS STEAD.
Taken in 1908.

[*Facing page* 434.

WM. THOS. STEAD

Another family which stands out among the residents of Howdon is that of the Steads, and the most widely known of these was Wm. Thomas Stead, who was born at Embleton on 5th July, 1849, and came to Howdon when he was four months old.

He did not go to school until he was twelve years of age. His father was his tutor, and he and his sister began their lessons on school-days at six o'clock in the morning. He knew his Latin grammar before that of English, and he was soundly prepared for the Congregational School at Silcoates, where he went in 1861 for two years. When fourteen years of age he entered the office of Mr T. Y. Strachen, accountant, in Newcastle, but soon changed into that of Mr Charles Smith in the Broad Chare, a wine and spirit importer, and who was also the Russian Vice-Consul. Here he spent six years, and in the meanwhile often contributed articles to various newspapers.

However, the best work he did at Howdon was the influence he exerted upon the younger portion of Howdon community. Then, as afterwards, he did things after his own fashion without much regard to the orthodox way in which such things were usually done. For example, in the Sunday school, on " Speaking Sundays " every scholar sat enthralled by his graphic story of the adventures of two Hebrew children supposed to be living in Egypt during the Plagues, but those in authority would have no " fiction " palmed off upon the scholars, and hence the exciting biography of Korah and Ada was brought to an abrupt conclusion.

Later, he and his class were summarily turned out of the Sunday school because he would not give the lessons in the way the superintendent thought was the best way. After this expulsion his class met in their club-room, and he, among other things, trained his scholars to speak upon a given subject for so many minutes and allowed no wandering from the point.

Moreover, he did not look after his class on Sundays only. He thought it was no use training up a child in the way it should go one day of the week and letting it be trained up some other way the other six, hence long before the day of Institutional Churches, he organised for the summer-time a swimming club, a cricket club, and a garden club; in the latter there was a combination of horticulture and games, and a large summer-house built by his lads. In the winter the club-room was open, where there were newspapers, games, discussions, etc.

He had written many articles for the Darlington *Northern Echo*, and in 1871 was offered the editorship at £150 a year, and this he accepted. He stipulated that he was to do no work on Sundays, and he came home at the week-ends.

In our notes of the Congregational Church we have mentioned his marriage on 10th June, 1873, to Miss Emma Wilson, daughter of Mr Henry Wilson, provision merchant and shipowner, of Church Street.

He was not long editor of the Darlington *Northern Echo* before he made it a power in the north and widely known elsewhere. He left the *Echo* in September, 1880, to become assistant editor of the *Pall Mall Gazette* under John Morley. In 1883 he took full charge, and soon he revolutionised journalism by striking out on entirely new lines. His articles upon the " Truth about the Navy " literally drove the Government to reform our Navy. The Admiralty officials at first denied his statements, upon which he gave exact chapter and verse and heaped fresh facts upon their unhappy heads. Behind him were two of the Navy's best men, and they and he together threw such damaging daylight upon the rotten state of our ships that raised a public outcry which completely won the day.

This was only one of the many causes he took up. The most famous was when in 1885 there was before Parliament a Bill for the better protection of girls, and those reformers who had worked for years on behalf of this cause saw it was going to be once more defeated. When they appealed to Mr Stead for his help it was not surprising that he took up the Crusade and drove it forward and proved its need by unusual, but irresistible means, and the abandoned Bill was passed and even strengthened owing to the storm of popular opinion thus raised. He and Mr Bramwell Booth were said to have broken the law. The daily press were all against them, but they had men and women like Mrs Josephine Butler, the Archbishop of Canterbury, and Cardinal Manning on their side, and a fund of £6,000 was raised for their defence in a few days.

So far as Howdon was concerned, a crowded public meeting was held in the Main Street Chapel; the chief speakers were Colonel Addison Potter, C.B., Mr Albert Grey (afterwards Lord Grey), and the Rev. John Hughes, the vicar of Howdon, and a unanimous and enthusiastic resolution was passed protesting against his prosecution.

The trial was a strange one. Mr Bramwell was acquitted and a verdict of "Guilty" was given against Mr Stead, yet the jury added that they wished to put on record their high appreciation of the services he had rendered the nation by securing the passage of a much-needed law for the protection of young girls. He was sentenced to three months' imprisonment, and he entered Coldbath Fields prison with the special blessing of Cardinal Manning. He prohibited all agitations and petitions for his release; he said if the jurymen found he had broken the law he ought to pay the penalty, and he was absolutely content with the general result.

We need not trace his career in London in detail. No adequate "Life" has been published, but we refer our readers to "My Father," written by his daughter, Miss Estelle W. Stead. In this we think she over-emphasises the part which Spiritualism played in his life.

After the death of his mother he had a firm conviction

of the nearness of the spiritual world, and believed that the veil between it and our material life might be penetrated by exceptionally gifted persons. After his eldest son died in 1907 he became more and more anxious to bridge the gulf between the seen and the unseen world, and probably he was quite often deceived by charlatans, but he had some wonderful experiences, the truth of which there could be no question. As regards the famed "Julia," she was not a mere *nom de guerre*, but represented herself as the spirit of Miss Julia A. Ames, who was a level-headed Methodist and a temperance reformer and one of the editors of the *Union Signal*, Chicago. Mr Stead and his family became friends with her on one of her visits to London in 1890. She was not a Spiritualist, and she and Mr Stead never mentioned the subject to each other. She died in Boston of pneumonia at the age of about thirty, and re-introduced herself to Mr Stead by automatic writing very soon after her death.

Notwithstanding his interest in the spiritual world he remained, what he was at the beginning, a sane, common-sense man, a brilliant journalist, a fearless righter of wrongs, and an enthusiastic and devoted believer in the Fatherland of God and the Brotherhood of Mankind. When the end came and he went down, helpful and fearless, with the *Titanic* on 15th April, 1912, it was felt by all who knew him that one of the world's pathfinders and knight errants had gone from our midst.

A memorial to the memory of this widely known Howdonian will be found both on the Victoria Embankment, London (nearly opposite the gate to the Temple), and in the Central Park, New York (5th Avenue and 91st Street).

Dr Ernest E. Woodhouse

Dr Ernest Edward Woodhouse was the youngest son of the Rev. John Woodhouse, who was vicar of Byker for over sixteen years. He was born on 21st July, 1870, educated at the Newcastle Royal Grammar School, and took his M.B. degree at the Durham College of Medicine.

He came to Willington Quay as assistant to Dr Thos. Wilson in 1894, and a little later he arranged to take over the practice on his own account.

On 28th December, 1896, he married Miss May Younger, of Heaton. He was at his death the most popular man in the township. He was a careful and attentive doctor, and his cheery and attractive personality had a wonderful effect upon his patients, and won him the confidence and regard of all classes.

In 1898 he became a District Councillor, and was Chairman of the Council in 1901. He was an active member of the Wallsend Golf Club, and belonged to the Carville Lodge of Freemasons.

On Sunday, 16th October, 1910, he was in his usual health, and at midday on Friday, the 21st, he died of pneumonia at the age of forty. The whole district felt this loss, and to hundreds it was the loss of a personal friend and trusted adviser.

On the day of the funeral all the business premises were closed, and several of the works. County police acted as underbearers, and a great procession of officials, representatives of public bodies, and friends, assembled at the Wallsend cemetery.

He left a widow and four children, and his practice was continued by his brother-in-law, Dr Robt. Younger, who left Heaton and settled at Willington Quay.

A granite cross was erected by his friends in the cemetery to the doctor's memory. It was unveiled on the 10th November, 1911, by Archdeacon Henderson, who laid special emphasis upon the doctor's open, frank disposition, his wonderful sympathy, and his abounding generosity to the unfortunate and the poor. The Mayor, M. W. Swinburne, and Alderman John T. Watson, also added their tribute to Doctor Woodhouse's goodness and services to all.

W. S. DAGLISH

A leading part in the inauguration of Local Government in the mid-Tyne area was taken by Wm. Stephen Daglish. He was born in Newcastle in 1832, and was educated at the Royal Grammar School, Dr Bruce's Academy, the Grange School, Sunderland, and the London University. He was articled to Mr W. Lockey Harle, and was admitted a solicitor in 1853. He was for some time in the office of Mr R. P. Philipson, Town Clerk of Newcastle, for whom he acted as deputy. He was Under Sheriff in 1863, 1864, 1866, and 1867. In 1869 he was elected a member of the Newcastle Town Council for West All Saints' ward, a seat he held for eight years.

In 1863 he assisted Colonel Addison Potter to establish a Local Board of Health at Willington Quay, the first to be formed in the district. He was appointed clerk, and held the office during the whole existence of the Board, and of the succeeding Urban District Council until the amalgamation with Willington and Wallsend in 1910. In 1866 he was appointed clerk to the Walker Local Board, and to the Jarrow Local Board on its formation the same year. He became Town Clerk of Jarrow when it was incorporated in 1875, and he held this appointment until his death. He was also clerk to the Jarrow Borough Magistrates.

He was the first clerk to the Wallsend Local Board, when it came into existence in February, 1869, and he continued to hold the position until the 8th November, 1901, when the township was incorporated. He held the office of Town Clerk for the first year, and then resigned in favour of his partner, Mr W. V. Mulcaster.

He was clerk to the Justices of the West Castle Ward Division of Northumberland from 1873 until his death, and the other offices relating to Local Government and administration which he held were manifold.

On the 13th July, 1886, Mr Walter Villiers Mulcaster, second son of Mr John P. Mulcaster, Barrister-at-Law, of Benwell, joined him in partnership, and the firm became W. S. Daglish & Mulcaster.

In his early life Mr Daglish was a thorough-going, progressive member of the community, and his enthusiasm for progress often carried through improvements when a less eager man would have failed. He was a friend and ardent supporter of Mr Charles Mark Palmer, and also his political agent. With him he fought many strenuous battles in North Durham and Jarrow under the Liberal flag.

Few men were better known on Tyneside; and his genial outspokenness secured him friends on every side. In 1903 he was presented by his Wallsend admirers with his portrait in oils, painted by Ralph Hedley. This now hangs in the Wallsend Council Chambers. He took an active interest in the Newcastle Chamber of Commerce, the Wellesley Training Ship, the scheme for industrial dwellings, the Whitley Village Homes, and the affairs of the diocese of Newcastle.

His active and useful career closed at his residence, Collingwood Tower, Tynemouth, where he died on 7th April, 1911, aged seventy-nine, and he was buried at Jesmond old cemetery. His estate was valued at £8,016 1s. 8d., and by his will dated 10th February, 1905, all his property passed to his five nieces, in equal shares. Mrs Daglish was Adelaide Robson, the fourth daughter of William Robson, of Messrs Hoyle, Robson & Co., paint and colour manufacturers. Her death, on the 18th March, 1909, shadowed all the remainder of his life.

His business, and many of his activities, were continued by his partner, Mr Mulcaster.

Sir James Knott, Baronet

Another native of Howdon who attained to a prominent position in after life was Sir James Knott.

Some of the Knott family were settled in the village in the flourishing days of the Hurry dockyard, and in 1789 John Knott of Howdon Panns is described as a "ropemaker" in the Church Register, and after the failure of the Hurry firm in 1806 we find that their rope works, on the east side of the Howdon Burn, were taken over by John and Matthew Knott.

The Knott family came from Simonburn, and Matthew, the junior partner, was born there on 12th August, 1778, and he came to Howdon as a young man to join his elder brother (or uncle). He married a local lady, a Miss Ann Miller, on 8th November, 1802, and they had two daughters and six sons. The eldest daughter married and was the mother of Matthew Robson, the chemist and druggist in West Street, who was the only chemist in Willington township for many years; the other daughter died an infant. The fourth son, Samuel, born 7th June, 1814, was the father of Mr George Knott, the only one of the family still in Howdon. The fifth son, Isaac, born 5th July, 1819, succeeded to the Howdon Ropeworks. However, it is the family of the second son, James, born 1st August, 1807, that concerns us at the moment.

James married, and his eldest son was Matthew Knott, who began business as a grocer, biscuit baker, and ship chandler near the east end of Stephenson Street. On 31st January, 1855, while residing here, his eldest son, James, was born. Mr Matthew Knott and his family moved to North Shields in the following October, and James was a scholar there under Mr John Mavor, master of the Scotch school. In 1869 he began his business career on Newcastle Quay, and presently founded and built up the well-known "Prince" line of steamers and became a prominent man in the shipping world. He also studied for the Bar and was "called" at Gray's Inn in 1889. On the outbreak of the Great War his three sons enlisted. The youngest, Henry Basil, was killed in the trenches in front of Ypres on the 15th September, 1915, and the second, James Leadbitter, was killed on 1st July, 1916, on the Somme. The eldest son, Thomas Garbett, who had already fought in the South African War, went through the fighting in Gallipoli and Palestine and fortunately was spared. After the loss of his second son Mr James Knott sold his steamers and the " Prince " line to Messrs Furness Withy & Co. and retired from business and from public affairs generally. In 1917 he was created a baronet, and he now resides at Close House, Wylam-on-Tyne, and at Wylam Lodge, Torquay.

Mr CHARLES JOHN DENHAM CHRISTIE was a native of Dumbarton, but came to Tyneside to act as manager when Mr Wigham Richardson began shipbuilding on his own account at Walker in March, 1860. Mr Christie took up his residence in Wallsend at Hope Villas and resided here some years. After a successful career as a ship designer and shipbuilder, he died at Tynemouth on 13th May, 1905, aged seventy-four years.

Mr JOHN NIXON, of Blyth, was born at Wallsend in 1851, educated at Charles Adam's school, and began his business life in the office of Messrs Schlesinger, Davis & Co., where he presently became the head of the commercial department. He went to Blyth in April, 1883, to take the post of secretary to the Blyth Shipbuilding Co., which was then being formed to carry on the business of Messrs Hodgson & Soulsby, and the growth of this company, with John Nixon as general manager, belongs to the history of Blyth.

While at Wallsend his activities mainly centred round the Colliery Chapel and the Wallsend Cricket Club, but at Blyth he extended his work and interest over a wide field and he became one of the most prominent public men in that district. He died on 8th September, 1903, at the early age of fifty-two.

444 ADDITIONAL BIOGRAPHICAL NOTES

THE EIGHTEEN MAYORS OF THE BOROUGH

Wm. Boyd
Geo. B. Hunter
Geo. A. Allan
Samuel T. Harrison
Matthew Murray
Chris. Stephenson
Robt. Irwin Dees
Joseph Duffy
James Allan

M. W. Swinburne
Geo. Elliott
John O'Hanlon
Jas. G. McIlvenna
Wm. H. Thompson
Benjamin Swan
Wm. Forrest
Joseph Mullen
Geo. M. Fitzsimmons

Mr William Boyd[1]

Mr Boyd made his first acquaintance with Wallsend on 11th March, 1874, and some indication of his influence in the early days of Marine Engineering is given under the notes concerning the Wallsend Slipway and Engineering Company. However, not only is his name bound up with the history of that firm, but it is also inseparably associated for nearly thirty years with the civil government and social interests of the township.

Mr Boyd was born at Arncliffe in Yorkshire on 17th October, 1839, where his father, the Ven. Archdeacon Boyd, was Vicar. He received his early education at Rugby and King's College, London, after which he was apprenticed to engineering at the Atlas works, Manchester.

In 1863 he became a partner with Messrs William and Charles Thompson, and under the title of Thompson Boyd & Co., made marine engines at Spring Gardens works in the Barrack Road, Newcastle.

While in Newcastle, he served for six years on the Newcastle School Board, and from the years 1871 to 1879 was Colonel of the 1st Newcastle-on-Tyne Artillery Volunteers.

He was elected a member of the Wallsend Local Board of Health in place of Mr Andrew Leslie, and attended the

[1] See photograph on opposite page.

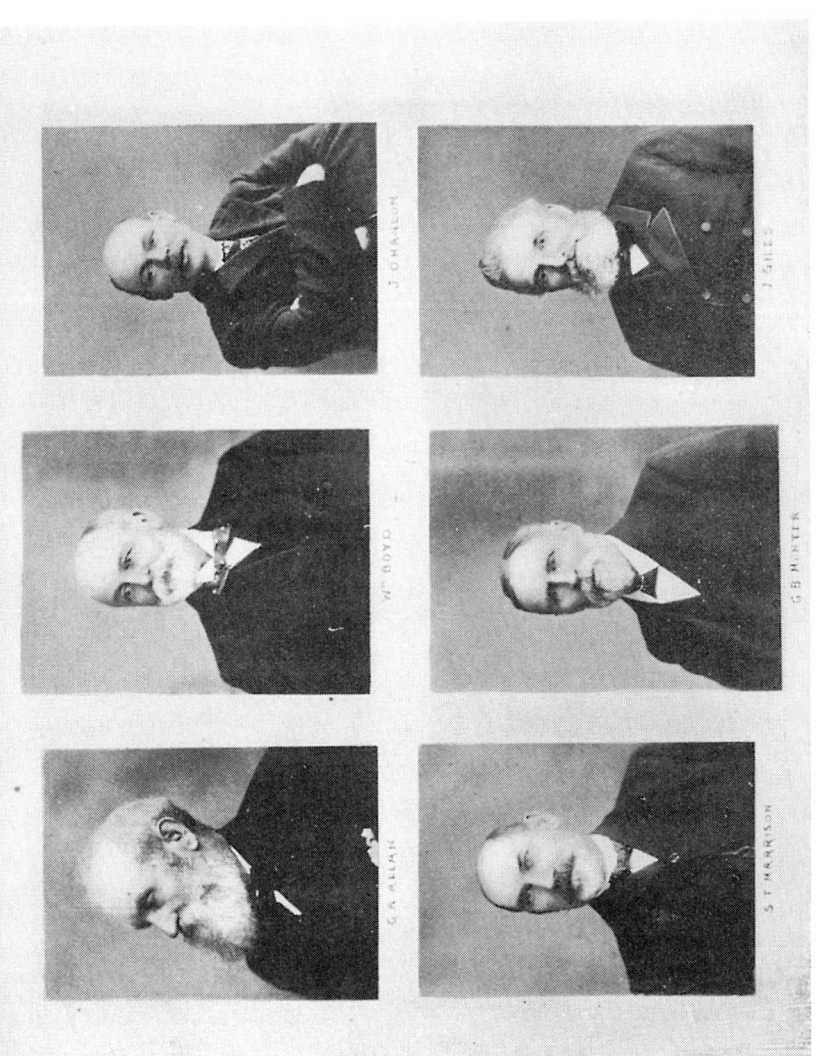

THE FIRST SIX ALDERMEN OF THE WALLSEND BOROUGH COUNCIL.

[*Facing page* 444.

Board meeting for the first time on 6th May, 1878. Only eleven months later his courtesy, his fairness to every section, and his grasp of affairs, were so appreciated that he was elected chairman of the Board to fill the vacancy caused by the death of Mr C. S. Swan, and year after year he was re-elected to that post until 1894, when the Local Boards were superseded by the District Councils.

At the opening of the District Council he was again chosen to preside. When Wallsend township was incorporated, at the first meeting of the Borough Council on 9th November, 1901, he was elected Mayor, and also an Alderman.

One of his many schemes which could not be carried out, and the failure of which must ever be a loss to the town, was his attempt to preserve the considerable remains of the Roman camp, which was literally the Wall's end.

In 1886 the site of Segedunum was an uneven grass field. The ruins were then partly bared, and Mr Boyd, realising the value of the remains to the town, endeavoured to save them from destruction. The area was about one and a half acres, and the land was owned by the Buddle Atkinson trustees. The Local Board undertook to have the walls and the old Roman streets cleared of soil, and to maintain the place in good order. Mr Boyd collected promises of subscriptions, but the terms of the owners were too high, and the invaluable possessions, except part of the foundations of the eastern gateway which were deeply buried, became the spoil of the housebuilders.

In 1903 the town presented Mr Boyd with his portrait painted in oils by Ralph Hedley, which is an excellent likeness.

In 1906 he resolved to retire from the Borough Council, and resigned his position as an Alderman on 2nd October. He then had thirty years of continuous, active, disinterested service in the public life of Wallsend behind him, and yet his retirement was universally felt to be a serious loss to the town.

When the Municipal Buildings were to be erected, Mr Boyd was invited to lay the foundation stone, which he did on 17th June, 1907, and the same day he was admitted as the first Freeman of the Borough. During Mr Boyd's connection with Wallsend, he resided first at North House, Long Benton, then at Prestwick Lodge, Ponteland, then in January, 1912, he moved to Benton House, Cheltenham, where he died on 19th May, 1919, aged eighty years.

Sir Geo. B. Hunter, D.Sc.[1]

George Burton Hunter was born at Sunderland on the 19th December, 1845, and is the third son of Mr Thomas Hunter, ship captain and shipowner of that town. He began his business career at the age of thirteen, as a pupil in the office of Mr Thomas Meek, C.E., engineer to the River Wear Commissioners. He afterwards went into the shipbuilding yard of Messrs W. Pile, Hay & Co., Monkwearmouth, Sunderland, and when under twenty years old, before the completion of his apprenticeship there, was appointed chief draughtsman and head foreman.

About the year 1868 he left Sunderland, and entered the works of Messrs R. Napier & Sons, Glasgow, but two years later he returned to his native town as the manager of Messrs W. Pile & Co.'s establishment.

In January, 1874, he entered into partnership with Mr S. P. Austin, who had an old-established wood shipbuilding and repairing yard on the Wear, and the firm began iron shipbuilding under the style of S. P. Austin & Hunter.

Six years later, in January, 1880, Mr Hunter left Wearside and became the managing partner of C. S. Swan & Hunter, as we have already noted.

In 1880 he moved his household to Western Villa, Wallsend, which he occupied for ten years, then he took up his residence at the Willows, Jesmond, Newcastle.

[1] For photograph see page 444.

From his first coming to Tyneside he was keenly interested in local affairs, and more especially in matters concerning temperance and education. One of his early efforts in this direction was the building of " The Wallsend Café " in 1883.

The establishment consisted of two departments, one devoted to meals and refreshments, with rooms for Clubs, Trade Union meetings, etc., and the other, the " Athenæum," a lecture hall, class-rooms, and games-room, devoted to the improvement of the mind and to recreation. There is also a large open space now used by boy scouts and others.

It was the first fine set of buildings erected in the High Street, and the first place in the village to be lit with electric light. It had a small library, and all sorts of indoor games were supplied. Membership of the library, the news-room, and the games-room was at the opening secured for one penny per week, and afterwards offered free.

It was opened on 19th December, 1883, by Mr Thos. Burt, M.P., and among those present were Messrs Benjamin C. Brown, Wm. Boyd, Alderman Philip A. Berkley, Jas. W. Dees, Wm. Glover, J. H. Holmes, and Robt. Knight.

The Café was an exceptional institution; it was the local centre for technical education, when technical education was in its infancy, and it was a bold experiment in the temperance movement and in popular education. Apart from capital charges, it cost Mr Hunter from £200 to £300 a year for very many years.

Mr Hunter for some time occupied a seat on the Wallsend School Board, and he was elected a member of the Local Board in May, 1880, and was one of the succeeding District Council.

In 1900 he, together with Mr Alex. Wilkie, contested Sunderland in the Liberal interest for the two seats. He was very late in announcing his intention to become a candidate, and there were local difficulties and dissensions in the Liberal party, so that he lost the election by 196 votes out of 10,000, Mr Wilkie, the fourth candidate, afterwards the M.P. for Dundee, polling 500 less. It was a matter of great regret to most people at Wallsend, as well as at Sunderland, that he was not elected as a Member of Parliament. He was urged to stand again for Sunderland, and also for Tyneside Division, before John M. Robertson was selected, but on account of business claims he declined.

When Wallsend township was incorporated, Mr Hunter was elected an Alderman, and one year afterwards he was elected Mayor for 1902-3. He was thus the second Mayor of the Borough. He continued his position as an Alderman until October, 1910, when, owing to increasing business claims, he resigned from the Council.

The Wallsend branch of the National Society for the Prevention of Cruelty to Children owes its inception to Mr Hunter, who offered £50 to cover the cost of forming a local branch. Mrs Wm. Boyd, the Mayoress, and he, called a meeting to inaugurate the movement on 23rd October, 1902, and it was his influence which induced Mr Chris. Stephenson to take the treasurership, and Mr Wm. Richardson the secretaryship, and which secured a specially strong General Committee, over which he became president.

In 1902 he, in conjunction with Mrs C. S. Swan, Messrs Wm. Boyd, Arthur J. Haggie, C. W. Mitchell, and John Wigham Richardson, his co-partners in the Wallsend and Willington Park and Building Land Syndicate, bought twenty acres of the Burn Closes from the owner of the Orde estate—an ideal playground or park—and offered it first to the Wallsend District Council, and on their declining the gift, it was offered to the Willington Quay authority with a like result.

Notwithstanding this, in 1909 he bought the Willington West Dene, consisting of seventeen acres, but this time he offered the land as a playground to trustees representative of the local churches and others, and with no hesitation the generous gift was accepted.

In 1909, when Willington Parish was invited to join the scheme to enlarge the Wallsend Borough, one of the conditions of the agreement made by the Willington Parish Council was that Mr Hunter be requested to renew his offer of the Burn Closes land, and that the renewed offer be accepted, and the land dedicated as a public park and recreation ground.

In 1914 Mr Robert I. Dees sold Wallsend Hall and grounds to Mr Hunter, in all about twelve acres, and of this Mr Hunter presented nine and three-quarter acres and the Hall to the Borough Council as an addition to the public park and the Burn Closes playground.

Of all the " employers of labour " in Wallsend during the present generation, Mr Hunter stands foremost in his practical and manifold good works and generosity to the community.

In 1906 the University of Durham bestowed upon him the degree of Doctor of Science, in recognition of his work in the shipbuilding world and the assistance he gave in placing the Durham College of Science, Newcastle, on a stronger and wider basis. In recognition of his work for the town, on 24th May, 1911, he was made a Freeman of the Borough of Wallsend, and in 1918, for his work during the war, he was created a Knight Commander of the British Empire.

In speaking of Sir G. B. Hunter's social work in Wallsend, we cannot omit mention of Mrs Hunter. She is the daughter of Mr Chas. Hudson of Whitby, and the niece of the late Mr Geo. Hudson, a former M.P. for Sunderland. Mr Hunter and Miss Annie Hudson were married on the 15th April, 1873. Mrs Hunter has always been at one with Mr Hunter in her sympathy with all movements for the good of the town. She was and remains the second President of the Wallsend Nursing Association, which she helped to form in 1894. She always took a very active interest in the local Society for the Prevention of Cruelty to Children, and in countless other ways she has given help to every deserving cause. No justifiable appeal is ever made to her in vain.

Mr George Auburn Allan[1]

Mr George Auburn Allan, the third Mayor of the Borough, came to Tyneside, as we have already recorded, in 1855. He first lived in Palmer's Terrace—then at Messrs Potter's works—then in Low Willington House (the house facing west). He was the second to be sworn in at Tynemouth when the First Corps of the Northumberland Artillery was formed.

He assisted Mr Addison Potter in extending the Volunteer movement at Willington Quay and in enlisting the Third Corps which had its headquarters for many years at the drill hall in Potter Street.

He and Mr Wm. Cleland began the movement to establish Presbyterianism at Willington, as noted.

Mr Allan was also one of the founders of the Tyne Lodge of Freemasons in 1863.

After he left Messrs Potter's works he became local agent for the Newcastle and Gateshead Water Company, which post he held until his death. He was also for many years secretary of the Newcastle Commercial Travellers' Association.

On 24th November, 1880, the Wallsend old Vicarage, at the south-east corner of the village green, with its gardens and orchard was put up for sale, and Mr Allan secured it for £455 and shortly afterwards took up his residence there.

Before coming to Tyneside he had seen a good deal of the world, and at one time undertook a missionary post in the deadly climate of Sierra Leone, yet up to his death

[1] For photograph see page 444.

was always an active, widely known public man, who at one time or other filled almost every public office open to him. In November, 1903, he was elected Mayor of the Borough, and Miss Annie Allan became Mayoress. He died at Orchard House (built on the site of the Vicarage garden) on 5th January, 1910, aged seventy-nine.

Mr Samuel Turner Harrison[1]

Mr Harrison came to Wallsend from Sunderland on 1st October, 1882, when the North Eastern Marine Engineering works were established here. He was the head of the commercial department, and his brother, Mr Alfred Harrison, came as chief draughtsman, and in 1884, when the Athenæum scheme for technical education was started, Mr Harrison was one of the small group who organised the classes. In 1885 he became a member of the Local Board, and his financial skill and foresight in meeting the needs of the rapidly growing town were soon recognised, and he was elected chairman of the Finance Committee. For two years, from March 1899 to March 1901, he was chairman of the succeeding authority—the Urban District Council.

At the first Borough election, 1st November, 1901, he was elected for Holy Cross ward, and received more votes than any other candidate in the election. He was chosen an Alderman at the first meeting of the Borough Council. He was the fourth Mayor of Wallsend, being elected on 9th November, 1904, and when the Borough Bench was formed in December, 1908, he was made a Justice of the Peace.

In addition to his municipal career, in 1894 he was chosen one of the first four overseers when Wallsend township became a separate parish, and he continued to hold this office until 30th March, 1912, being chairman during the last two years.

[1] For photograph see page 444.

He was also a Poor Law Guardian for many years. After thirty years of active and useful work in the town, he removed on 1st November, 1911, to Tynemouth. At the same time he resigned his aldermanship on the Town Council, and was presented with the Honorary Freedom of the Borough on 15th May, 1912.

Mr Matthew Murray

Mr Matthew Murray, the fifth Mayor, was elected to that position in November, 1905, and again in 1906. He was a native of Wallsend. His father, Matthew Murray, senior, came to Tyneside from Newcastleton in Liddlesdale, and after serving his apprenticeship with Alder Dunn, at that time the foremost draper in Newcastle, he came to Carville in 1845, started on his own account, and for thirty-seven years carried on business as a draper on the north side of what is now High Street West.

Mr Matthew Murray was born in 1857, and received his early education at the school of Charles Adams, Carville. In 1872 he entered the office of Messrs Wigham Richardson & Co., Low Walker, and steadily rose to the position of cashier. In November, 1891, he left this firm to take up the post of secretary to the Wallsend Slipway and Engineering Co. This post he held for twenty years, and retired in 1912 owing to ill health.

He entered the Town Council when it was incorporated in 1901, as a representative of the Hadrian ward. He was chosen Mayor on 9th November, 1905, and held the office for two years. He was made an Alderman in October, 1907, in succession to the late John Giles. He was elected a Poor Law Guardian for the parish in 1898, and was elected chairman of the Board of Guardians in June, 1910. On his removal from Wallsend, in order to retain his services he was co-opted a member of the Board, on which he remained until April, 1919, when he retired owing to his continued ill health. He was appointed a Justice of the

Peace for the Borough when the Borough Bench was formed.

He was an active worker in connection with the Colliery Chapel for many years, and afterwards at St Peter's Church, as a manager of the Church Bank schools, and as a churchwarden for 1895-97. He was one of the founders of the Carville Lodge of Freemasons in 1894, and of the Wallsend Golf Club in 1905.

In 1911 he moved from West Villa, The Green, to St Alban's, Tynemouth, and in November, 1912, he resigned his position on the Town Council. On 23rd September, 1919, in recognition of his services to the town he was enrolled an Honorary Freeman.

Throughout his residence in Wallsend, his breadth of outlook, his keen sense of fairness, and his impartiality made him a trusted adviser to all sections of the community.

In 1888 he married Kate, daughter of the late James Colbeck of Weetslade, and when he died at Tynemouth on 1st July, 1920, he left a widow, two sons, and two daughters.

Mr Christopher Stephenson

Mr Christopher Stephenson was born at Hartlepool and served his apprenticeship as a marine draughtsman with Sir Wm. Gray & Co. In 1882 he came to Messrs Swan & Hunter's Wallsend shipyard, and in 1891 became their yard manager. It was during the time of his management that the *Mauretania* was built. Apart from his work in the yard, his interests centred chiefly in St Peter's Church, the local branch of the Society for the Prevention of Cruelty to Children, the Borough Council, and the Wallsend Golf Club.

On the incorporation of the Borough in 1901 he was elected to represent the Buddle ward. In November, 1907, he was chosen Mayor, and on 1st February, 1910, he was elected an Alderman in place of the late George A. Allan.

He seemed a man of exceptionally fine physique, but died on 20th October, 1912, at the early age of fifty-three. A memorial window was placed in St Peter's Church by the directors, officials, and workmen of the Wallsend shipyard.

Mr Robert Irwin Dees

The seventh Mayor of the Borough was Mr Robert Irwin Dees, to whom reference will be found in the section dealing with Wallsend Hall.

Mr Joseph Duffy

Mr Joseph Duffy was born at Enniskeen, County of Monaghan, in 1848, where his father was a farmer. He first came to Wallsend when he was between eighteen and nineteen years of age, and worked at a chemical works.

In 1869 he went to America, and four years later returned and started in business at Jarrow as a grocer. His next enterprise was opening brick works at East Jarrow, and building houses there. About 1884 he came again to Wallsend, commenced brick making where the Carville schools now stand, and built over five hundred tenements in the same district. The Borough Theatre, opened on 4th October, 1909, was one of his enterprises. He extended his activities to Gateshead, where he also carried on brickmaking and the building of houses.

He was a member of the Wallsend Local Board, a Town Councillor for the old Buddle ward (south of the railway) from the incorporation of the Borough, and was elected Mayor of Wallsend on 9th November, 1909. He died during his term of office on 29th July, 1910, and was buried in Wallsend cemetery.

He left four daughters and two sons, Hugh and Patrick. Mr Hugh Duffy entered the Wallsend Borough Council in

1909 as the representative of Carville ward, but retired in November, 1919. Both brothers joined the Army in January, 1916, and Patrick, who was in the Royal Air Force, was killed in France at Happlaincourt Wood near Fremicourt on the 20th March, 1918.

Mr James Allan

Mr James Allan was born at Aberdeen on the 3rd December, 1851, and when he was only two years of age his parents removed to London. In 1869 his family came north to Walker, and he served five years apprenticeship as a boilermaker at Messrs Chas. Mitchell & Co.'s. In 1875 he joined the Boilermakers' Society, and then for many years his spare time was given to his trade society, and to open-air sports.

As regards his society, he rose to be its president in succession to the late George Baker of Sunderland, and as to out-of-door sports, although he was good in rowing, swimming, and running, he was widely known as a bicycle racer in the days of the old " ordinary " on both track and road.

He rode to London and back, and several times did the " Tyne to Edinbro' " ride in a day, which was considered a good test of endurance on a " boneshaker."

He entered the Urban District Council in April, 1906, and when the township was incorporated he was elected for the Northumberland ward.

He was Deputy-Mayor during the Mayoralty of Mr Jos. Duffy, and on the death of Mr Duffy, he took up the duties. He had, owing to Mr Duffy's protracted illness, been the Acting Mayor for some time, and he occupied the position during a trying period—trade depression, much distress, and a lock out of workmen.

After a term of office really lasting ten months, he declined to accept the post of Mayor for the year 1910-11, but when Mr M. W. Swinburne died during his Mayoralty, he again stepped into the breach. He was elected an Alderman when Mr Wm. Boyd retired from the Council.

Mr Mark Wm. Swinburne

The tenth Mayor was Mr Mark Wm. Swinburne, who resided at East Jesmond, and who was the senior partner in the firm of M. W. Swinburne & Sons. For a summary of his work in Wallsend see the memorandum concerning his firm. He was the first Mayor of the enlarged Borough.

Mr George Elliott

Mr George Elliott was a native of Walker, and started his business life in 1882 when he entered the office of Messrs Wigham Richardson's shipyard, Walker. He removed from Walker to Wallsend in 1891, and when the township of Wallsend was incorporated in 1901 he contested the Carville ward and became one of its three representatives.

His work on the Council mainly centred in the Finance Committee, of which he was chairman for many years, and in the Education Committee, of which he was chairman from 21st November, 1912, until his death.

He was one of the first Justices of the Peace to be appointed for the Borough, and was Mayor for the year 1912-13, Miss Thompson, his sister-in-law, acting as Mayoress. He was elected an Alderman on 2nd July, 1912, in succession to the late Alderman Mark W. Swinburne.

He was an active Wesleyan Methodist in connection with the High Street East Church, and also a local preacher.

While in the midst of a useful life, he died at Orchard House on 21st January, 1922, during an influenza epidemic, at the age of fifty-eight.

Mr John O'Hanlon[1]

Mr John O'Hanlon was born at Patterson Town, Washington, County of Durham, on 8th June, 1859. While born in England, his family belong to Armagh, and his interests and sympathies have always been on the side of Irish progress and Irish affairs. He began work at Jarrow rolling mills in 1871, and came to Wallsend in 1884 to work as a driller at the Wallsend shipyard.

When a young man he took an active interest in politics, and for many years he was the recognised leader of the Irish party in Wallsend, which he kept in a thoroughly effective state, and for three years he was the official organiser of the north of England.

He entered Wallsend District Council in 1894, and he was the first " working man " councillor in Wallsend district.

He was elected an Alderman when the township was incorporated in 1901, and chosen Mayor on 9th November, 1913. He was admitted a Freeman of the Borough on the 3rd October, 1917.

In July, 1907, he contested the parliamentary division of Jarrow as an Irish Nationalist. There were also candidates representing Liberals, Conservatives, and " Labour." The " Labour " candidate, Pete Curran, was at the head of the poll with 4,698 votes, and Alderman O'Hanlon was fourth with 2,122.

Mr James Graham McIlvenna

Mr James Graham McIlvenna was the fourth Mayor for the enlarged Borough. He was born at Glasgow and served an apprenticeship of nine years with Messrs R. Napier & Co. of that city under Mr Wm. Pierce (afterwards Sir Wm. Pierce).

[1] For photograph see page 444.

While there, he and Mr G. B. Hunter, who was also at Napier's, became known to each other, and hence as soon as his apprenticeship was over, having gone through every department, he went to Sunderland and, at the age of twenty-three, he became the yard manager for Messrs Austin & Hunter.

On 18th December, 1880, he became general manager at Messrs Edwards' dry docks at South Shields. While there orders were secured to build some hoppers for the River Tees Commissioners, and as the faculties for this kind of work was limited at South Shields, a lease of old foreshore recently covered with ballast at the west side of Howdon Dock was secured from the Duke of Northumberland by Mr Henry Edwards, and some of these barges were built there. This was the commencement of Messrs H. S. Edwards & Co.'s Howdon shipbuilding yard, which in 1898 became the Northumberland Shipbuilding Company.

In July, 1887, Mr McIlvenna became general manager at the Tyne Pontoons, Wallsend, and moved from South Shields, and after living about twelve months at The Grove, Walker, he became a resident in our parish, by buying and occupying Rose Hill House and grounds from Wm. Cleland's executors.

Soon after moving to Rose Hill he interested himself in local affairs, with the result that on 3rd March, 1895, he was elected upon the County Council as the representative for the Long Benton and Willington division after a sharp contest. This office he held until increasing business affairs compelled him to give it up in 1903.

His second representative office was that of Guardian for the parish of Willington, and from 1895 Rural District Councillor. When the Parish Councils were formed in all the rural areas, he was not only elected upon the Willington Council, but held the position of chairman during all the fifteen years of its existence.

In 1895 he bought West Chirton Hall from John

Hedley's executors, and took up his residence there, but his attendance at the meetings concerning local affairs was as regular, and his interest in the parish was as keen as ever.

He left the Tyne Pontoons and Dry Docks in 1906, and after a brief rest he began business in Newcastle on his own account in 1907 as a naval architect and marine surveyor.

Of the many local movements in which he took a conspicuous part, we need only mention the prolonged struggle for the public right of way up the Willington dene—the freeing of the north road to New York from tolls, and its conversion from a bridle road into a highway. When the Willington Parish Council area was included in the extended Borough of Wallsend, Mr McIlvenna was elected one of the first Aldermen. In November, 1914, he was chosen Mayor for the Borough, Miss Carrie McIlvenna being Mayoress. In December, 1912, he was added to the Commission of the Peace for the Borough.

Mr William Hamilton Thompson

Mr William Hamilton Thompson was elected Mayor of the Borough on 9th November, 1915, and was re-elected in the year following, and again in 1917 and 1918.

Mr Thompson, whose father was a native of Felton, was born in 1863 at Lishman's Houses, which stood near where Gainer's Terrace is now. In his younger days he was well known at local cycling sports as a racer. He began business life as a butcher, in partnership with Mr Robert Calvert in High Street, and when his father, who was a carting contractor, died, he took over his business. In 1893 he entered upon the occupation of Wallsend West Farm, and devoted most of his time to farming his land.

He married his cousin, Miss Susannah Hall, in September, 1899. He entered the Town Council in November,

1904, to represent the Northumberland ward. His name was inserted in the Commission of the Peace for the Borough in December, 1912, and he was elected an Alderman in January, 1913, on the resignation of Alderman M. Murray.

During his four years of office as Mayor, he and the Mayoress devoted a large part of their time to the promotion and assistance of war charities and of a Distinguished Service fund for recognising the efforts of the local sailors and soldiers who gained distinction. For these objects £3,276 was raised. On 1st October, 1919, he was made a Freeman of the Borough.

Mr Benjamin Swan

On 9th November, 1919, Mr Swan was elected Mayor of the Borough in succession to Alderman Wm. H. Thompson. He was a native of Willington Quay and lived all his life in the district. In his younger days he was attached to the Free Methodist Church, and later he became an active member at St Paul's Church, Howdon, where he was a churchwarden.

He was a member of the Willington Quay Local Board and of its successor, the Urban District Council. When this area was incorporated into the Borough of Wallsend he was elected upon the new Council for the Willington Quay ward and then chosen as an Alderman.

In April, 1910, he was elected County Councillor for Willington Quay and Howdon in place of Mr Haggie, who was made an Alderman.

During all his time of office in the different councils, his chief activities lay on the sanitary side of the work.

At the time of his death he had been over forty years at the shipyard of the Tyne Iron Ship Building Co., and had been for many years their foreman plumber.

When he undertook the office of Mayor his health was far from normal, and he did not live to complete his year of office. He died at Churchill Street on 30th June, 1920, aged sixty-eight years, and his deputy, Alderman Geo. Elliott, took over his official duties.

Mr William Forrest

The seventh Mayor of the enlarged Borough of Wallsend was Mr Wm. Forrest, J.P., who was elected on 9th November, 1920. His father was Mr Thomas Forrest, manager of the Walker and St Anthony's Gas Lighting Company, and Mr Wm. Forrest was born at Walker.

Owing to the amalgamation of the Walker, Wallsend, and Willington Gas Companies, the Forrests moved to Wallsend in 1874.

Mr Wm. Forrest commenced his apprenticeship with the Wallsend Industrial Co-operative Society Limited in 1878 and rose to be general manager in 1893.

In 1911 he was elected a Town Councillor for the Wallsend ward, and in 1912 a County Councillor for the Buddle ward. In 1920 he was added to the Commission of Borough Justices of the Peace, also by invitation from the Lord High Chancellor, a member of the Wallsend Borough Justices Advisory Committee, and later elected on the Licensing Bench.

He is a member of the Presbyterian Church, and was the first member of the " Labour Party " to be elected Mayor of the town.

Mr Joseph Mullen

Mr Joseph Mullen was born at Wallsend on 31st July, 1870, and in 1896 took over the business of Robert Bell, monumental sculptor, carried on at the top of the Church Bank.

He joined the Tyne Lodge of Freemasons over twenty years ago, and was one of the founders of the Buddle Lodge. The first public office he held was when he was elected upon the Willington Parish Council in April, 1907, and when the enlarged Borough Council was elected he headed the poll for Willington ward. In 1912 he was elected a member of the Tynemouth Board of Guardians, and on 6th November, 1917, he was elected an Alderman in place of Mr R. H. Jackson. In March, 1919, he secured a seat on the County Council as the Howdon representative.

In January, 1920, he was added to the Borough Commission of the Peace, and on 9th November, 1921, he was selected for the highest position in the gift of his native town by being installed as Mayor.

Mr George Mills Fitzsimmons

Mr George Mills Fitzsimmons was elected to be Mayor of the Borough on 9th November, 1922.

He was born at Walker on 13th April, 1882, and moved into the parish of Wallsend in his boyhood. He served his apprenticeship as a boilermaker at Wigham Richardson's shipyard, but as soon as this was completed in 1903 he entered the licensed victuallers' trade and acquired business interests in both Wallsend and the immediate neighbourhood. After he took up his residence at the "Northumberland Arms," Willington Quay, he began to take part in civic affairs, and on 1st November, 1911, he was elected upon the Town Council for the Willington ward, and in 1919 he was appointed an Overseer of the Poor. He is the eighteenth Mayor of the Borough.

CHAPTER X

MISCELLANEOUS

River, roads, railways and wagon-ways—Bigges Main—Freemasonry — Wallsend Nursing Association — Willington Quay and District Nursing Association—The Wallsend Golf Club—Subscriptions for French War (A.D. 1798)—In the days of the cholera (A.D. 1831)—The "booming" years of housebuilding (A.D. 1898-1902)—Wallsend newspapers—Various events—Population Statistics.

RIVER, ROADS, RAILWAYS, AND WAGON-WAYS

The River

FROM an early date the Corporation of Newcastle claimed the ownership of the whole bed of the river from Hedwin stream to the Bar, and also the right to control all the trade upon the Tyne. We need not go into the long struggle in which the Prior of Tynemouth, the Bishop of Durham, Ralph Gardner of Chirton, and others, resisted these claims.

One result of the river being considered as part of the parish of St Nicholas, and of the river trade as belonging to Newcastle, was that trade and shipping which really belonged to Howdon and other places on the banks of the Tyne are classed as belonging to Newcastle, and this sometimes misleads the historian.

In the beginning of the nineteenth century, the ships lay in the lower part of the river, and the coals were put into keels, estimated to hold twenty-one and a fifth tons.

They were loaded near high water mark, and then taken down to the ships. This employed an immense number of keels and keelmen.

Many of the keelmen employed by the Willington colliery lived in the Keelmen's Row; the shore immediately in front of the houses provided a convenient and safe ground where the keels could be " laid up " and at a small repairing yard near the east end of the Row repairs could be effected, or new craft built.

It was not until the early years of the nineteenth century that staiths were improved and were carried far enough into the river to enable ships to take in coals direct from the colliery wagons.

At Wallsend it was necessary to carry the coal staiths a considerable distance into the stream in order to adopt the new method of loading coals direct into the ships, and in 1824 Wm. Russell of the Wallsend colliery and others were indicted for obstructing the navigation. The case was tried at York on 11th August, and the hearing lasted thirteen hours; the verdict of " not guilty " was returned in three minutes. The matter was tried again on 14th and 15th August, 1825, at Carlisle; this time the jury took four hours to consider their decision, and then returned a verdict which both sides claimed was absolutely in their favour. It was: " We find that the navigable channel of the River Tyne opposite Wallsend has been straitened, narrowed, lessened, and obstructed by the gears described in the indictment, but we find nevertheless that the trade of the town of Newcastle and the harbour of the Tyne has at the same time greatly improved."

Without doubt the Newcastle Corporation neglected their duties as the river authority; sandbanks and shallows were found in every section of it, and in 1840 both Gateshead and North and South Shields began to press for a reform.

After a fierce fight the River Tyne Improvement Act was passed on 15th July, 1850, and the management of the river was taken out of the hands of Newcastle, and vested in a body of men representing Newcastle (6), Gateshead (2), Tynemouth (3), South Shields (3), with Wm. Rutherford Hunter, Joseph Cowen, Wm. Purdo, and James Cochran Stevenson as life members.

One of the first serious questions which the new body had to face was the injury done to the staiths at the Hayhole, east of the Howdon burn, by the Willington Quay groin, which projected 330 feet into the river, and which had diverted the current (see page 203). The result of this was the making of the Howdon (or Northumberland) docks.

The new Commissioners soon began work, and gradually effected improvements, although for lack of funds the progress at first was slow, and several times the writer, while crossing to Jarrow about the year 1866, was stranded in mid-stream. We have already explained how the works of the River Tyne Commissioners came to be located at Howdon.

So far as passenger traffic was concerned the chief means of travel between Newcastle and Tynemouth up to 1750 was the river. Notables, such as Charles I., who visited Tynemouth on 5th June, 1633, travelled in special barges which the Mayor and Corporation of Newcastle maintained for the purpose, but ordinary travellers used other means. Partly covered-in boats, called "Comfortables," and open rowing boats or "wherries," which took advantage of the wind sometimes, provided for most of the passenger and light goods traffic.

On "Barge day," 19th May, 1814, a great novelty appeared in the shape of a river passenger steamboat. With the tide it could do the journey between Newcastle and Tynemouth in an hour; against the tide it was able to "move at the rate of three or four miles an hour." It was built for passenger and goods traffic, and the fare for best cabin was a shilling, and second cabin sixpence. The first name of this steamboat was the *Tyne Packet*, soon changed to the *Perseverance*. This was the first river passenger steamboat in England.

For the next forty-five years the river facilities were unsatisfactory. The steamers were slow and the service intermittent. In 1859 Mr John Rogerson, of Newcastle and St Peter's, built special steamers, and established a line called the "Red Star" line, to distinguish it from the "Percy" or "Crescent" line, already plying on the river.

The Red Star steamers were a great improvement, and in the autumn of 1861 the owners promoted a Bill in Parliament to secure power to erect landing stages at various places on both sides of the river, and run steamers. This Bill received the Royal Assent in April, 1862. By virtue of this Act the Tyne General Ferry Company was formed with a capital of £60,000 in £10 shares. They absorbed the Red Star line, and among the landing stages fixed was one at Wallsend, where the west side of Parsons' yard now is, and one at Howdon at the foot of Tyne Street.

From very early days many direct ferries were in constant use, kept up by sculler men. One plied between the Benton spouts at Wallsend and Hebburn Quay. Another from the east side of the mouth of Willington Gut to High Jarrow, and another from Howdon Crane to East Jarrow, and after Palmers' yard started, Messrs C. M. Palmer & Company organised a steam ferry between Howdon and Jarrow, maintained by two small steamers, the *Punch* and the *Judy*.

The General Ferry Company's boats were speedy, comfortable, and cheap. They ran every half-hour and were a great convenience to the riverside public, and they soon superseded the direct ferries in our parish. But owing to the cheap workmen's tickets on the railways and the tramcars, the steamers were slowly superseded, and the Tyne General Ferry Company had to stop their boats on 5th December, 1908, and go into liquidation. The unsecured creditors received 2s. 11d. in the £, and the ordinary shareholders lost their capital.

Roads

The old road from Newcastle to North Shields did not follow the line of the present main road through Wallsend. Fifty yards west of our parish boundary, the old road turned north-east to West House, then eastward through the village. It was in use when a plan of " Sundry estates in the Township of Wallsend " was made on 7th January, 1781. A remnant of this may be seen in front of Western Villa, a piece of the old hedge, and the third milestone still exists in the field, a few yards to the north of present roadway.

The Willington Gut was crossed by a ford on the north side of the present bridge. When the water was deep, two simple plank bridges were available for foot passengers, one near the farm cottage, and another beyond spring tide high water mark three hundred yards higher up, approached by a footpath behind the cottages opposite the cemetery gates. The first stone bridge was barely above high water level, and in 1798 this was raised eight feet. This improvement eased the gradient from above the cemetery gate on one side, to above the old Rose Inn on the other. The old line of road was plainly seen when the twenty-four inch gas pipe was laid along the main road in 1907.

Although this was the main road to North Shields, it was reported in an official document, as late as 1747, as " so deep and ruinous that travellers cannot pass without great danger."

A Turnpike Act was passed in 1748. Road trustees were appointed, and tolls fixed to begin on 25th March, 1749. Two or three amending Acts were afterwards passed extending the time and increasing the tolls.

An important clause was incorporated in the third Act, enacting that " if any person raised or set any new hedge, wall or other fence whatsoever, at the side of the road, on or near any common or waste ground, within five yards from the outside ditch," the surveyor was to remove it at the owner's expense, after ten days' notice. The tolls at each toll gate were " let " by public auction.

As soon as wheeled conveyances could be used on the road, gigs holding six persons, and coaches, were started, and by 1827 there were ten coaches and twenty-eight gigs running. Trace horses were stabled at the Rose Inn to assist the conveyances up the Rose Hill and the Church Bank. In 1832 a new form of conveyance was put upon the Shields Road. Three years prior to this, omnibuses had been introduced into London, and on 12th November, 1832, these vehicles began to run between Newcastle and North Shields. There was an hourly service. The fare for the whole journey was 1s. 6d.

There was an ancient bridle road from the river quay at Willington, northward through Willington village. Thence, one branch went north-easterly to Greenchester (North Gate), crossed the Tynemouth Shire moor (which was enclosed by an Act passed in 1787) and joined the Great Lime Road near New York. Another road branched westward, passed the North Farm, then over Killingworth moor, crossed the Benton Road, and joined the Great Lime Road east of Killingworth. Another bridle road also went northward from the centre of the village green at Wallsend, passed the Rising Sun Farm, and joined the Willington north-west road on the moor. Bordering upon this lane on the west side were two rows of colliery houses, one Bridge Row, near the north end of the wagon-way bridge which conveyed the coals from the " E " and " F " pits across the stream towards what is now Park Road, and the other was Willington Low Row near the old George and Christer pits' wagon-way.

It will thus be seen that Willington had two public outlets to the north, and Wallsend one. With regard to the Willington road over the Tynemouth Shire moor, when the moor was enclosed this bridle road was not only set out, but made useable and kept in order and repair, as provided in the Enclosure Act. A toll was levied upon cart traffic until the Parish Council of Willington, as recorded elsewhere, arranged with Mr John H. Burn and the Tynemouth Rural District Council, to free this road from tolls, and for it to become a general highway.

The other road from Willington running north-westward, which was joined by the road from Wallsend village, largely dropped out of use after the Killingworth moor was enclosed.

The Act for enclosing and dividing this piece of land, 1,900 acres in area, was passed in 1790. It was divided between eleven gentlemen who promoted the Bill, and Balliol College, " who ownes certain lands in the parish " (Benton).

In the award, the Willington and Wallsend roads are appointed as public bridle roads, and it duly provides that these roads " shall forever hereafter be and continue of the breadth of 21 feet in the narrowest part and it shall be lawful for all Persons whomsoever, at all times and forever hereafter to pass and repass on foot and on horseback only, at their free will and pleasure."

The award also provides how the roads were to be maintained and kept in repair for ever hereafter. The encroachments, the obstruction of the road, and the lack of its maintenance, are matters of public knowledge.

Railways

The first movement towards making a railway between Newcastle and North Shields was made in 1830, and the history of various schemes can be traced in Tomlinson's exhaustive history of the North-Eastern Railway. The Act authorising the Newcastle and North Shields railway received the Royal assent on 21st June, 1836. There were fifteen directors, of whom Matthew Bell, Nathaniel Grace, John Jobling, and John Potts were connected with our parish. The foundation-stone of the Willington viaduct was laid on 13th January, 1837, by John Hodgson Hinde, M.P., chairman of the company. The bridge is 1,048 feet long and 82 feet high. The arches were of wood, each rib being composed of fourteen layers of three-inch planks bolted together. The longest span is 128 feet, four are 120 feet, and two 115 feet.

June 18th, 1839, was the opening day, and two trains conveyed the directors and their friends from Newcastle to Shields. The day was regarded as a fête day all along the route, bells were rung and cannons thundered. On the Howdon ballast hill the enterprising landlord of the " Black Bull " erected a large tent so that all and sundry could " refresh " continuously, without losing sight of the new railway. Here he also provided a hot dinner as well as his " well-selected stock of old Jamaica and double X." A deluge of rain in the afternoon spoiled the complete success of the day.

The line was fully opened for passenger traffic on Saturday, 22nd June, and well patronised. There were two stations in our area, " Carville for Wallsend " (changed to " Wallsend " about 1865) and " Howdon for Jarrow." It is to be remembered that all the south-west of our district, including High Street West, was then known as Carville, and that the Jarrow line was not opened until 1872. In order to facilitate the Jarrow traffic via Howdon, the Railway Company opened a foot road " cut athwart lane " from Howdon Lane through the fields to Palmer's Terrace, so as to greatly shorten the walk to the ferry.

In these early days, directors of a railway really directed. Here is a report published a month after the opening :

On a Saturday evening, crowds are rushing to the railway to enjoy a Sunday at Tynemouth; and too much praise cannot be bestowed on Mr Lowndes, and Mr Richard Spoor, the late Mayor of Sunderland, for the exertions they make, in their capacity of Managing Directors, to secure seats and safety for the numbers flocking to the station at Newcastle.[1]

[1] *Gateshead Observer*, 20th July, 1839.

In a week the number of passengers were 10,013 first class, 12,922 second, 15,069 third, and 13,248 fourth. The last train was at nine p.m. The early second class carriages on the Shields line had roofs, and some of them had curtains at the side; the third class had no doors and generally no roofs. In 1845 open and uncovered carriages were discontinued, but the second and third class carriages were not lighted at night, nor were they light for nearly ten years.

This seems very primitive, but even as late as 1871 railway management was very different from what it is to-day. In that year the train passing Howdon about eight a.m. only stopped if signalled to do so. Two or three lads travelled by the train to Newcastle. The stationmaster declined to trouble himself about mere " Quayside " boys, and they had to arrange between themselves which one would get to the station three or four minutes earlier in order to put up the signals to stop the train. For the engine-driver to wait for a belated lad was common; he knew a cigar (smuggled) would be forthcoming in return. Casual passengers by this train could get no ticket, but that was a very trivial matter in those days—they paid at their destination. The platform was raised only a few inches above the ground, and you mounted by two steps to the carriage, which had only a back rail between each of the five or six compartments. In 1871 there was one indifferent oil lamp to light the whole carriage.

The Newcastle and Shields Railway Company had been absorbed into the Newcastle and Berwick Railway Company in 1845, although the Tynemouth line was worked independently until the Berwick line was open for traffic. Two years later the Newcastle and Berwick Railway Company and the York and Newcastle Railway Company amalgamated under the title of the York, Newcastle, and Berwick Railway Company, and on 31st July, 1854, a further union was effected and the North-Eastern Railway Company came into being. At this time on the Tynemouth line there were sixteen trains running each way, and the fares for the whole journey were one shilling first class, ninepence second, sixpence third, and the fourth class had been abolished.

As the works on the north side of the river grew in importance the need was felt for connecting them with our railway system. Various schemes were suggested, all of which included the making of a line from Newcastle alongside the river to North Shields.

In 1871 the North-Eastern Railway Company countered all the proposals to set up an independent railway within their area by applying to Parliament for power to make the present riverside line. The Bill was duly passed, the railway constructed, and the line opened for traffic on 1st May, 1879. When this railway was opened there was a station at Willington Quay, but there was no station on the new line at Wallsend until 1st August, 1891, when "Carville" was opened.

In 1902 the Tyneside Tramways Company began operations, and at once diverted a large proportion of local traffic from the railways and steamboats. In order to meet this competition, the Railway Company installed electric motive power on the Tynemouth lines, and on 1st July, 1904, "electric" trains began to run from the Central Station, Newcastle, via Tynemouth to New Bridge Street Station.

Colliery Wagon-ways

As mentioned elsewhere, the first colliery wagon-way in our district was laid down by the Killingworth colliery owners in 1762. The route was via High Willington, and their coal spouts were erected on the site of Cleland's Slipway.

Then when the system of "inclined planes" came into use, the coals from the High Willington pits were conveyed to the river by a new inclined plane from Battle Hill

VIEWS OF WALLSEND, 1900. [*Facing page* 472.

to Willington Low pit, which crossed the dene on a timber bridge, the site of which is easily seen. From the " Low pit " another " plane " took the wagons down what is now Rosehill Road to the Willington spouts, part of which are still standing in the Tharsis Copper Co.'s yard.

The owners of the Killingworth collieries made their " plane " from the Rising Sun Farm to a bridge erected over the Burn Closes, and from the foot of this incline horses took the wagons to spouts close to those of the Wallsend pits. In 1850 the horses were superseded by " Puffing Billy," one of Stephenson's earliest engines, which worked this traffic until about 1875. This interesting example of an early locomotive is now preserved in the Central Station, Newcastle.

The Benton and Coxlodge wagon-way came through Bigges Main, and " Benton Way " is a reminder of the way to their spouts. The Heaton wagons came eastward and joined the Benton and Coxlodge wagon-ways at West Street, and the site of the line can still be traced between the Western Villas and West Street.

The coals from the Wallsend " A " and " B " pits went eastward along Hadrian Road to spouts near the east side of the site of Parsons' works. A wagon-way brought the coals from the " E " and " F " pits to the " C " pit, crossing the stream by a bridge. From the " C " pit, Park Road marks the wagon-way which joined the " A " and " B " coal line at the corving houses.

Bigges Main

This area of 819·625 acres, with a population of about 690, was added to the old parish of Wallsend on 9th November, 1910, when Willington, Willington Quay, and Wallsend were incorporated under the Wallsend Extension Order dated 21st June, 1910. The order, however, did not affect the ecclesiastical division of Wallsend and Long Benton.

In 1270 the Manor of Little Benton was held by Eustace de Benton, under the Barony of Heron, but there was no community of interests between Little Benton and Wallsend until the seventeenth century, when the larger part of the lands recently incorporated were in the possession of the Hindmarsh family, who were also largely interested in Willington and Wallsend.

These estates passed out of the possession of the Hindmarshs in 1706, on the marriage of Elizabeth Hindmarsh to Thomas Bigge, the son of Thomas Bigge, an attorney-at-law of Newcastle. His son, William Bigge, born at Benton on 25th March, 1707, who married Mary, daughter and sole heir of Charles Clarke of Ovingham, on 29th January, 1736, presently succeeded to the estates, and they remained in the Bigge family until 1862, when they were purchased from Matthew Robert Bigge and others by Mr David Burn.

This new owner had previously endeavoured with Wm. Archbold (the wealthy owner of the Queen's Head in Newcastle) and Geo. Clark of Walker to re-open Wallsend Colliery, and three years later he bought a large estate in Willington of 416 acres.

Mr David Burn resided and carried on a business at Busy Cottage, Jesmond. This area is now partly in the Jesmond Dene park, but one hundred years ago there were extensive iron works and railway wagon building sheds there, owned by Mr David Burn and his partner, Mr Robt. Rayne. His son and heir, Mr John Henry Burn, afterwards of Tynemouth, was born here on 15th April, 1827.

The Ouseburn valley became an out-of-the-way place for an iron foundry, and the business was given up, but the partnership was continued as iron merchants with a warehouse and offices at 20 Broad Chare, and Mr David Burn moved his residence to Ridley Villas.

He died on 17th March, 1873, and both his Little Benton and Willington estates passed to Mr John H.

Burn, who also became a part owner in West Stanley colliery. Mr John H. Burn was a great supporter of the church and the local Conservative party. When he died on 21st December, 1898, the two local estates passed to his sons, Mr John Henry Burn, junior, and Mr Frank Hawthorn Burn, under his will made 24th December, 1872.

Bigges Main colliery commenced in July, 1784, after the opening of the Willington and Wallsend coal seams. Messrs Bell & Brown of the Willington colliery, and Mr Johnson who was their agent, were in partnership as the owners of East and Little Benton colliery, and they arranged with Thomas Charles Bigge of Benton to lease his coal royalties.

They sank three shafts and built the miners' cottages which became known as Bigges Main, i.e., the colliery working Mr Bigge's Main coal seam.

The lease was for forty-one years from 12th May, 1785. The certain rent was 25s. per " ten " for the first three years, with an increasing minimum rent until it reached in the seventh year £600, in lieu of 480 " tens." A second lease covering the same period was made with Messrs Collingwood and partners, for the coal under their land in Benton, and a later dated agreement was made with the Dean and Chapter of Durham for a way-leave for a wagon-way over Threap Moor and their lands at Wallsend, at an annual rental of £200, with £2 2s. as a ground rent for houses built by the Colliery Company in Wallsend. One of these houses was what is now " West House," which was erected as a wagon-wright's shop. The highest yearly output was reached about ten years after the pit was opened, and we see that the vend for the twelve months ending 31st December, 1795, was 40,151 chaldrons. In 1805 it was 32,007 chaldrons.

The " experts " of one hundred years ago were no safer guides as to the future than those of to-day. A " calculation of the value of Bigges Main Colliery," undated, but made about 1800 or 1801, sets forth " the coal remaining is calculated to last eight years, and the total profits that may probably arise in the course of that time is calculated to amount to £93,000." It was worked fifty years after this, and then started afresh fifty years later.

The first chapter of the history of the Bigges Main colliery was closed in 1857, when it was " drowned out " by the general flood which overtook the mid-Tyne coal area. The engines were dismantled and the plant, etc., was sold off. The wagon-way was still used, as the coals from the Gosforth and Coxlodge pits continued to be shipped at Wallsend near the site of the present public quay until 1885.

In 1900 the Walker Coal Company were working their way northward through the coal seams under the land of the Newcastle Corporation, and they arranged with Mr John Henry Burn for the coal under the Little Benton estate. The lease is dated 31st December, 1903, and they began working the royalty in 1904. The " High Main " was practically exhausted prior to 1857, and it was the Bensham and the Beaumont seams which were worked by the Walker Company until they went into liquidation in 1918.

Included in the area taken over by the Wallsend Borough was Willington High Row, the remains of Willington Low Row, the farmstead of the Rising Sun Farm, the old mining village of Bigges Main, and the new Rising Sun colliery.

Willington High and Low Rows were built when the Bewicke pit and the Craster pit were opened. The Rising Sun colliery is part of the undertaking of the Wallsend and Hebburn Coal Company, and the only notable event in the history of the Rising Sun Farm took place on 28th January, 1742, when it was the centre of a thunderstorm such as rarely visits any place in England. As the early darkness set in, rain and lightning began all along Tyneside, but the centre of the electric disturbance seemed to gather round the Rising Sun Farm about eight o'clock. Killingworth moor was then unenclosed, and several persons crossing the moor seemed enveloped in blazing lightning. One gentleman had his whip twice struck, more than one had their clothes or horses singed, but the flashes seemed absolutely to rain down on the farm. The barn and byres were all fired, the stables were shattered, the dwelling-house was struck and wrecked, and the stackyard shared the fate of the buildings.

When the farmer and his terrified family, who took refuge behind a wall in an adjoining field, dared to examine the damage, they found that all the buildings were burnt out and in ruins; horses, oxen, and cows, to the number of twenty-two, were all killed; fifteen cornstacks were in ashes, and twenty-two bolls of corn and nearly one hundred bolls of oats were utterly destroyed. The devastation of the farmstead was complete—the darkness added to the terror of the scene—yet, strange to say, while a considerable number of persons were in the midst of this abnormal peril, no man, woman, or child was seriously hurt.

FREEMASONRY

On 24th September, 1863, a meeting of those in the district interested in Freemasonry was held in the Star Inn (near the Stephenson Schools). At this meeting George A. Allan, manager for Messrs Addison Potter, took the chair, and there was also present Nathaniel Colledge, the Howdon baker, Robert Bell, and Robert Richardson of the Star Inn. It was resolved to form a Lodge and to name it the Twizell Lodge, and it was also agreed that Bro. Wm. Twizell, North Shields, be requested to accept the Mastership of the Lodge.

The name was, however, altered to the Tyne Lodge No. 991, and the consecration took place in the Stephenson

Schools on 27th January, 1864, under the Mastership of the Rev. E. C. Ogle, Prov.G.M.

The master of the new Lodge was Bro. Twizell. The second W.M. for 1865 was John P. Simpson, and he continued for 1866 also.

In 1865 the Lodge meetings were moved from the " Star " to the " Red Lion," and in 1870 they were again moved to Mr Addison Potter's gas works, where they had a hall set apart which was furnished. The furniture was insured for £100, and when the question was raised as to whether " refreshments after labour " should be had in the Lodge room, or " whether the Brethren who held licences should still have the benefit," it was decided to have the refreshments in the Lodge room. It is always of interest to see what our forefathers took to " sustain the inner man," and we see in March, 1879, when the Lodge was honoured with a Provincial visit, the guests were hospitably entertained with bread, cheese, and beer.

Nothing very eventful occurred until 1890, when a proposal was started to move the Lodge to Wallsend, and as an outcome of this the foundation-stone of the present Masonic Hall in Station Road was laid on Monday, 1st April, 1891, by Sir Matthew White Ridley, R.W.Prov.G.M. of Northumberland. The architect was Bro. Wm. Hope, of North Shields, and the builder Bro. Wm. Thos. Weir, of Howdon.

The cost of the building, etc., was £2,500, and the necessary capital was found by organising a Wallsend Masonic Hall Co. Ltd., and issuing 2,500 shares of £1 each. The Tyne Lodge became part tenants at a rental of £20 for the first year and £25 a year afterwards. The other tenants were the Wallsend Local Board of Health and Messrs Hodgkin, Barnett, Pease & Spence.

The next thirty years saw the formation of no less than five new Lodges. On 25th July, 1894, the Carville Lodge No. 2497 was instituted, with Bro. Robert Hudson of Tynemouth (and the chief accountant at Messrs Swan & Hunter) as Master, Bro. Matthew Murray as S.W., and the Rev. W. M. O'Brady Jones, vicar of St Luke's, as J.W.

On 8th February, 1898, the Wallsend Lodge No. 2703 was instituted, with Mr Geo. Blair, of the Neptune Hotel, Low Walker, as Master, Bro. Dixon Cowie S.W., and Bro. Geo. Bell, stationmaster, J.W.

On 6th August, 1902, the Neptune Lodge No. 2908 was formed, with Bro. R. E. Womphrey, of Hadrian Road, as Master, Bro. John Saunders S.W., and Bro. Thos. Wm. Taylor J.W. This Lodge was promoted as a Temperance Brotherhood, and was the first temperance lodge in the district.

In 1909 the capital of the Masonic Hall Co. was increased to £3,700, and the building was increased by adding on the south side two shops and a kitchen on the ground floor and a supper-room on the upper floor.

On 11th August, 1913, the Holy Cross Lodge No. 3679 was formed. Bro. Geo. H. Cameron was Master, Bro. John Thornton S.W., and Bro. Surtees Wake Scott J.W. This was also a temperance lodge.

A third temperance lodge was formed on 1st September, 1919, when the Buddle Lodge No. 3937 was instituted, with Bro. Fred Robertson Master, Bro. John White S.W., and Bro. Robert Ayre J.W.

The last Lodge to be opened was that named Segedunum No. 4313, formed in August, 1921, with Bro. W. Jackson Clark Master, Bro. Geo. H. Cameron S.W., and Bro. George Hill J.W.

In 1921 the old Board room of the District Council and the two shops were incorporated into the bank premises of Messrs Lloyds Bank Ltd.

One remarkable fact is that while the sport of boat rowing was in its glory, and a rowing race on the Thames or Tyne drew its tens of thousands of adherents the four best rowers known were members of the Tyne Lodge.

In September, 1869, Stephen Renforth, the world's champion, was initiated; the following year Edward Winship was admitted. In 1871 his brother Thomas was initiated, and in 1873 Joseph Chambers became a member. At this time no four rowers could equal this quartette, and no single rower could beat Stephen Renforth.

While for nearly thirty years Freemasonry was confined to Willington Quay there are now six flourishing Lodges at Wallsend and none at the east end of the town.

The number of Lodge members in our district is at present about as follows:

Tyne Lodge	289
Carville Lodge	68
Wallsend Lodge	229
Neptune Lodge	226
Holy Cross Lodge	164
Buddle Lodge	63
Segedunum Lodge	44
	1,083

In 1914 Mr George Hill published a "History of the Tyne Lodge from 1863 to 1913." In this the chief events concerning the Lodge will be found.

Wallsend Nursing Association

This association was started in 1894 by the Women's Wallsend Co-operative Guild on the suggestion of Mrs M. Guthrie, 4 North View (now 50 High Street East), Wallsend. The Guild contributed £4 14s. as the nucleus of a fund. The Association was formally launched at a public meeting, presided over by Mr George Renwick. Mrs Henderson of the Rectory was elected president, Miss Harbit, High Street, treasurer, and Mrs M. Guthrie secretary. These ladies, assisted by the energetic part of the committee (which included Mrs T. P. Hill, Mrs Thos. Spence, Mrs Stuart, and Mrs Wiper) were able to present a very good report at the end of their year. The income was £147 10s. 5d., which included £10 10s. from the Co-operative Society, £10 from Messrs Swan & Hunter,

£5 from their workmen, £10 from Messrs Fisher, Renwick & Co., £5 from the Wallsend Slipway, and £64 from weekly and monthly collections. They finished their first year with £61 17s. 7d. in hand. The number of cases were 110, and their nurses had paid 1,778 visits.

The report for the year ending 31st October, 1899, shows Mrs Dees had become treasurer, two nurses were working, and the income had risen to £178 7s. 9d. Of this £115 was from donations, £63 from weekly subscriptions, and they closed the year with £210 os. 2d. in hand.

On the death of Mrs Henderson in January, 1906, Mrs Geo. B. Hunter became president, which office she still holds. At present (1923) Mr Henry W. Clothier is the vice-chairman of the committee, Mr Robert Scaife (London Joint City & Midland Bank) is the treasurer, and Mrs M. McBlain is the secretary.

WILLINGTON QUAY, HOWDON PANNS AND DISTRICT NURSING ASSOCIATION

A District Nursing Association had been found to meet a great need at Wallsend, and Mrs Arthur J. Haggie arranged a meeting at Low Willington Villa on 6th November, 1899, to consider the formation of an Association for Willington.

There were present the Rev. Henry Robinson and Mrs Robinson (Willington), Rev. John Hughes and Mrs Hughes (Howdon Panns), Rev. E. H. Steel and Mrs Steel (Stead Memorial Church), Father Savory, Messrs Wm. Bell, Jas. Churcher, Wm. Barritt, W. Blair, Nicholas Woodman, Mrs E. E. Woodhouse, Mrs Babst, Mrs M. Parker, Mrs Wm. Bell, Mrs W. C. Watson, and others. It was agreed to form a Nursing Association for the area of Willington, Willington Quay, and as far east as the "Bank Top" (East Howdon). Mr Arthur J. Haggie was elected president, Mrs Arthur J. Haggie, secretary, and Mrs Babst, treasurer.

2H

A public meeting and musical entertainment was held in the Co-operative Society's Hall on 28th November, at which a large committee was appointed.

On 15th December it was agreed that the Association join the Northumberland County Nursing Association.

On 21st December a nurse (Nurse Robinson) was engaged at £80 per annum, with uniform. She commenced her duties on 1st February, 1900, and Nurse Green started on 1st March—salary 16s. per week. In the first year the Association had 146 cases and the nurses paid 3,699 visits. Mrs Henry Robinson, Willington Vicarage, was elected president.

The second annual report showed—number of cases 163, number of visits 3,716, balance from first year £48 9s. 5d., subscriptions and donations £162 5s. 7d., salaries £131 3s. 4d., sundry expenses £10 2s. 1d., balance in hand £69 9s. 7d.

In April, 1902, a house of three rooms at the west end of Northumberland Terrace was taken for the two nurses, rent 5s. 6d. per week, including rates. This was furnished by a sub-committee consisting of Mrs H. Robinson, Mrs Wm. Richardson, and Mrs E. E. Woodhouse at a cost of £35 6s. 3d.

The men's committee collected £29 9s. towards this expense. In April, 1903, £70 10s. 6d. was raised by a fancy dress ball, and the year closed with a balance in hand of £121 10s. 4d.

At the annual meeting held on 14th February, 1905, Mr Geo. R. Baston was appointed assistant secretary. On 9th April, 1907, Mrs Wm. Richardson, who had taken an active share in committee work since she joined it on 19th February, 1901, was elected treasurer on the death of Mrs Babst. Between 1902 and 1912 the Nurses' Home was moved to Smeaton Street, then to Clavering Street, and then to Smeaton Street again, but this time to a house with a bathroom. In June, 1913, the first Alexandra Day in aid of local charities was organised, with the Mayoress, Miss

Thompson, at the head of the committee. £20 came to the Association as the result.

In 1916 Mrs Henry Robinson went to reside at Wylam. The year following she resigned her office as president and Mrs A. J. Haggie was elected to the post. Mrs D. Stephen undertook the secretaryship.

In 1919 the County Nursing Association, which supervises and assists the Local Associations, asked the Willington Committee if they would agree to a Training Centre for District Nurses being set up in their district, and that probationers might work in conjunction with Willington Quay Nurses, and thus receive practical training. A Matron would be appointed to give what other training was required. It was proposed that an army hut be obtained large enough to house not only those being trained but also the District Nurses. These proposals were agreed to on the understanding that the County Association was to meet all extra expense involved.

Army huts for the Training Centre were obtained in 1920. These were erected behind Tynemouth Road and fitted up at a cost of £2,320. They were finished and open to the public inspection on 25th and 26th May, 1921. This Training Centre has proved a success, and on 31st December, 1922, there were seven probationers being trained.

On 5th July, 1920, Mrs Wm. Richardson, who had been treasurer for thirteen years and an active member of the committee nearly twenty years, died, and Mrs Thos. R. Scott was appointed to the office, which she held until she moved to Edinburgh in 1922.

WALLSEND GOLF CLUB

The first to seriously take up the idea of forming a Golf Club for Wallsend were Messrs Matt. Murray, S. T. Harrison, James C. Henderson, Chris. Stephenson, N. E. Robson (North-Eastern Marine Engineering Co. Ltd.),

E. E. McClintock, Thos Wilkinson (Messrs Swan & Hunter), Joseph W. Tocher (Wallsend Slipway Co. Ltd.), James Edmond (Board of Trade Surveyor), Capt. Tindle (Howdon Dock Master), Dr E. E. Woodhouse, and Wm. Richardson.

Various sites were considered, including the Burn Closes, the land west of what is now King's Road, and the north end of Willington Dene. However, Wm. Y. Younger, who farmed the fields on the east side of Copperas Lane (Churchill Street), met the promoters in a very friendly spirit, and that land was chosen.

On 27th March, 1905, at a meeting held in the Café, promises to join were received from one hundred gentlemen, and the Wallsend Golf Club was formed, subscriptions to be 21s. for gentlemen, and 10s. 6d. for ladies. Messrs James C. Henderson and E. E. McClintock were appointed joint secretaries, Mr N. E. Robson treasurer, and Mr E. E. McClintock was elected captain. In order to meet the initial expenses of laying out the course and guaranteeing the rent, twenty of the original members formed a Guarantee Fund, and the guarantors elected half of the committee.

On 3rd June, 1905, a course of nine holes, and a club house, half the size of the present one, was formally opened. Mr Matthew Murray presided over the proceedings, and Alderman S. T. Harrison, the Mayor of Wallsend, presented a silver-headed cleek to Mr Crawford Smith, M.P. for the Tyneside Division, who drove off the first ball. He was partnered by Mr J. S. Caird of the Newcastle " City " club, who had planned out the course. Tea was served in a marquee to a large company.

The first year's subscriptions and entrance fees amounted to £232 1s., and the second year the membership numbered 182.

In November, 1907, Mr N. E. Robson left Wallsend and Mr Wm. Richardson was appointed treasurer.

The Race Field was acquired, and on 2nd June, 1912,

Mr Summers Hunter opened an extended course of eighteen holes. During the war the club gave up the Race Field at the instigation of the County Committee entrusted with the duty of increasing the supply of wheat, and the course was re-arranged into one of nine holes. The Government gave the club £100 compensation, but before this was received the club was nearly on the " rocks " owing to the great falling off of paying members. The president, Mr J. G. McIlvenna, however, saved the situation by canvassing the large firms in the district for assistance, and in this way he collected £186. The members subscribed £88 in addition. At Lady Day, 1921, Mr Wm. Richardson retired from the treasurership and Mr Wm. Pyle undertook the post. In 1922 Alderman J. G. McIlvenna resigned the office of president and Mr Wm. Richardson was elected to the position. The successive captains and secretaries have been :

Captains

E. E. McClintock	1905-1906-1907	O. P. Arton	1914-1915
Dr E. E. Woodhouse	1908	John A. Anderson	1916
James Edmond	1909	Joseph Hope	1917
Frank Lewins	1910-1911	James Cusworth	1918-1919
Dr R. J. Weidner	1912	Ed. Bomphrey	1920
Alex. B. Walker	1913	Lewis M. Douglas	1921
	Arthur G. Shearer	1922	

Secretaries

James C. Henderson and		James C. Henderson	1911
E. E. McClintock	1905-1907	Leslie Robson	1912-1913
James C. Henderson	1908	Edward Bomphrey	1914-1919
James C. Henderson and		J. C. McDougal	1920
Frank Baker	1909-1910	Thos. Mudie	1920-1921
	Jas. R. Maxwell	1922	

SUNDRY NOTES

SUBSCRIPTIONS FOR THE FRENCH WAR

On 5th March, 1798, a meeting was called in the Vestry. The war with France was raging, and the country was passing through a bad time, and many people were dreading defeat. England was without an ally and Bonaparte seemed winning all round. Furthermore, the public debt was rising by leaps and bounds, eighty millions had been added in three years, and though taxation was at a height undreamed of before, the Government thought that the people with money might help with voluntary subscriptions.

This was before the days of making garments for our fighting men, or the existence of Soldiers' and Sailors' Families' Associations to look after the widows and orphans, or help the families while their men were from home. The minutes of the meeting show:

1798, 5th March.—The Inhabitants present in Vestry this day finding that Parochial subscriptions for the defence of the Country are become general and being anxious at this alarming crisis to come forward themselves and to give an Opportunity to persons of every description to contribute according to their respective inclinations and abilities.

Resolved, that a Book be now opened, and a Committee appointed for this purpose of receiving subscriptions. Subscriptions of the Township of Wallsend to be paid to Mr Thos. Mann. Those of Willington to Mr Moses Pye. Those of Howdon Panns to Mr Pelham. Rev. Wm. Ridley to be general Treasurer and to forward the money to the Bank in London for the service of the Government.

Handbills were to be sent out and an appeal to be published in the three Newcastle papers.

We are afraid that there was not much money sent to London, as the only subscriptions we find recorded are: Henry Ridley, £1 1s.; Jos. Ireland, 10s. 6d.

THE CHOLERA

In 1831, the 8th of September was set apart for celebrating the Coronation of King William IV., and all over the district the day was spent in feasts and rejoicings. Guns were fired, bells were rung, and the festivities were kept up for three or four days. At Howdon five fat sheep, one hundred loaves, and a barrel of ale were distributed among the poorer inhabitants. But all unheeded a dread disease was making its way from Asia across Europe. In October it reached Sunderland, and the nearness of this scourge—Asiatic cholera—alarmed all Tyneside. A case was reported in Newcastle on 7th December, and at once everyone was on the alert.

All ships arriving were put into quarantine. Theatres were closed, and balls and public functions abandoned. Nearly three weeks elapsed before cholera reached the parish of Wallsend, for Christmas saw the first case. Between 25th December and 19th February there were forty-nine deaths in the whole area, and of these thirty died of cholera.

Then in the spring of 1832 there was a lull, as there was only one case in March, and people began their normal lives again, and Wednesday, 21st March, was kept as a day of fasting, humiliation, and thanksgiving that the plague " wherewith it had pleased Providence to afflict the country " was abated. Churches were filled, shops and industries stopped for the day.

Several large fancy dress balls were held, and there were great jubilations that at last the House of Lords had passed the Reform Bill (7th June). But presently panic once more spread, as cholera again appeared. The first death of this second visitation to Wallsend took place on 10th August, and in one month twenty-six persons died, and again ensued a period of fear and panic.

Growth of Wallsend

The years 1898 to 1902 were the " booming " years in the extension of Wallsend.

During the half-year ending September, 1898, 126 new houses were assessed, and during the six months ending March, 1899, the high water mark of building was reached, as 372 new houses and shops were added to the Valuation List. The following half-year, ending September, 1899,

268 shops and houses were added, and 225 more during the succeeding six months. In September, 1900, 213 new assessments were made, followed by 130 in March, 1902.

Hence in three years 1,334 new houses and new shops were added to the township, and the Poor Rate assessable value, which was £58,217 on the 29th March, 1898, was £84,765 in March, 1902, an increase of £26,548 in the rateable value of the works, houses, etc.

For the same period the assessable value of Willington Quay rose from £29,797 to £32,600, an increase of £2,803, and Willington from £3,447 to £4,784, an increase of £1,337.

Thus in these three years Wallsend valuation rose forty-five per cent., Willington thirty-nine per cent., and Willington Quay only nine per cent.

WALLSEND NEWSPAPERS

In November, 1901, a new local weekly newspaper, *The Wallsend Herald*, was started. It was printed at the Jarrow Guardian office, and was backed financially by Mr Geo. B. Hunter. It was a great addition to the amenities of the immediate district.

In July, 1909, a printer, Mr Wm. James Farrell, started business in High Street West, and also a rival newspaper, *The Wallsend Advertiser*. Needless to say, this adventure did not flourish, and the following December the newspaper and printing business was sold to Mr Hunter, and a new company, "The Tyneside Newspaper Company Ltd.," took it over, and it was amalgamated with the *Herald*. The price paid by Mr Hunter was £605 in cash and £250 in shares of the Newspaper Company, of which Mr Farrell was appointed manager and a director.

The printing of the *Herald* was transferred from Jarrow to Wallsend, but the concern was not a success, and Mr Farrell resigned on 13th February, 1911. The Tyneside Newspaper Company continued publishing the *Herald* and *Advertiser* until February, 1913, when it was stopped. It was a useful addition to the life of the town, but a continuous drain upon the pocket of the paymaster.

OTHER LOCAL EVENTS

1740. Horse races stopped at Willington and Benton owing to Act of Parliament which prohibited horse races unless the cup was worth £50. Race meetings in England had become a public scandal. The " Race Field," Willington, still marks the site of our local course.

1808. Monday, 6th June. Grand Volunteer Review on Newcastle town moor. The Wallsend Rifle Corps formed the advance guard of the right column. A great amount of rifle firing took place.

Joseph Lamb leased the Copperas works, immediately north of Willington House, for seventeen years. Hence the name of Copperas Lane (Churchill Street).

1814. 25th July. George Stephenson's first locomotive tried at Killingworth.

1815. 9th December. The Imperial Archdukes John and Lewis of Austria and suite visited the Wallsend colliery. Mr Buddle showed them round.

1816. 10th May. Dorothy Phillips died at Willington Low Row (Rising Sun), aged 110 years.

13th December. The Grand Duke Nicholas of Russia and his suite visited Wallsend colliery. He emphatically declined to go down the pit after looking down the shaft.

8th July. Dorothy Archer, of Howdon Panns, aged 101 years, buried.[1]

1822. Keelmen's strike for ten weeks.

1839. 7th January, Windy Monday. The hurricane was from the south-south-west, and its extreme violence

[1] St Peter's Church Registers.

raged between six a.m. and three p.m. Hexham, Tyneside, Darlington, and Alnwick alike visited.

1840. 28th November. Pipes having been laid from the " C " or Gas pit to Carville station (now Wallsend), the gas was supplied to several lamps. (At first this was a success, but the impure gas soon choked the pipes and the experiment failed.)

1844. 5th April. Second pitmen's strike, which lasted until August. On the Tyne, Blyth, and Wear thirty thousand men were out. As before, the men went back to work gradually.

1847. 12th September. Foundation-stone of Hayhole dock (Howdon) laid by Joseph Cowen, chairman of the River Commissioners.

3rd May. Railway from Blyth to Percy Main opened for passenger traffic.

1851. 1st September. Boat accident at Howdon. A Howdon picnic party was boarding a steamer bound for Marsden Rock. Seventeen were in the rowing boat, which collided with a ship at anchor. Six girls and one man were drowned. The proportion of girls lost was severely commented upon.

16th December. " Billy Purvis " died at Hartlepool, aged sixty-nine.

1853. An Act entitled " The Whittle Dene Water Works Amendment Act " was obtained by the then Whittle Dene Water Company, whereby the limits of supply were extended to the parish of Wallsend.

1857. 22nd October. Northumberland (Hayhole) Dock opened by the Duke of Northumberland.

1863. County Police Station erected at Tyne Street, Willington Quay.

1868. James Lavery, of 12 Potter Street, employed in the Cookson works, had a garden under the second arch from the east end of the railway viaduct. He had disputes about the hens kept by a neighbour. James Lynch took the part of the owner of the hens, and on 2nd May Lynch and Lavery renewed the quarrel. Lavery's unloaded gun was standing against his garden railings, and Lynch picked it up and smashed Lavery's head with the butt-end. He at once cleared off. The police were informed, and the whole district was roused. Police were called from other areas, and every place was searched, including the culvert between the Willington Dene and the Burn Closes. Lynch was found on 27th May in the County of Mayo. He was tried for wilful murder at the Northumberland Assizes on 16th July and sentenced for manslaughter to ten years' penal servitude.

1871. 16th May. Nine hours' strike commenced, which was settled on 6th October through the efforts of Joseph Cowen. The nine hours a day to begin on 1st January, 1872; wages to remain the same as before the strike.

2nd December. The hours of boys working in the pits reduced from twelve to eleven.

1871—1872—1873. Trade was on flood tide. 1874 was a year of declining trade and reduction in wages. 1875 marked low water.

1873. 26th December. The tug, *Gipsy Queen*, was bringing River Tyne Commissioners' workmen from North and South Shields to their work. A "hopper" lay sunk off the Howdon Dock wall, and although the wreck was properly lighted, the tug struck it and quickly settled down. In the darkness and confusion their small boat was overcrowded and sank. The Captain's dog took a man ashore and went back. Help was rendered from the Customs house and a dredger, and as the wreck was only a little distance from the quay over twenty-five men were saved, but eighteen were drowned, including the mate, the engineer, and the master, for whom the dog made a prolonged search.

1874. Locke Blackett & Co. (founded by Mr John Locke in Gallowgate, Newcastle, in 1797) purchased the Wallsend smelting works (Warwicks) at Wallsend Quay.

1882. 6th July. The Wallsend " Puffing Billy " placed at end of High Level Bridge.

1883. 16th July. Cart and horse ferry between Marshall Street, Willington Quay, and Jarrow commenced running.

1884. 10th July. The shipyard joiners came out on strike. Serious trade depression began this year and continued into 1887. In 1886 the total tonnage of the ships built on the Tyne was 83,320.

20th August. Prince and Princess of Wales passed down the river and opened the Albert Edward Dock.

1887. 27th January. Strike of Northumberland miners against a fifteen per cent. reduction of wages, which was settled on 21st May.

1890. 15th March. Engineers strike for fifty-three hours a week instead of fifty-four, and to stop at noon on Saturdays. This was agreed to on 24th March, the new arrangement to come into force on 10th May.

21st April. The first bank in Wallsend opened by Messrs Hodgkin, Barritt, Pease and Spence (now Lloyds Bank Ltd.). The bank was in the High Street, now High Street West, near where the post office is now. Mr Arthur Constable from the North Shields branch was the first manager.

1891. 22nd October. Sydney Old, of The Green, Wallsend, late secretary of the Pontoon and Dry Dock Company, after arrest in America, tried at the Quarter Sessions, Newcastle, and imprisoned twelve months.

1892. 30th January. Engineers' strike on Tyne and Wear began. Dispute was settled by referring it to arbitration, and work was resumed on 27th April. The

SUNDRY LOCAL EVENTS 493

award to which the men objected was held to be binding.

1900. 26th October. Great rain storm commenced during the evening and continued all night. The stream in the Burn Closes rose to within two feet of the top of the arch of the Turnpike bridge. The old culvert crossing Rose Hill Road below the railway arch, burst and left a hole in the roadway forty feet long and thirteen feet deep, and damaged the walls of the corner house. This culvert runs below Dr Woodhouse's old house, 11 Western Road, and the water rose to a height of four feet on the ground floor. In Howdon all the low-lying parts were flooded, and a widow, Mrs Ellen Shaughnessy, was drowned near the Wagon Inn. Her daughter was saved by breaking a hole through the floor above. Thos. Storey, who swam to the house through twelve feet of water at four o'clock in the morning, was unable to effect a rescue of the mother. To help the rescue work a boat was launched opposite the " Black Bull," and taken behind Main Street and the Brewery, and finally landed at the Shipwright's Arms.

1909. When the year opened, trade depression and distress was general on Tyneside, but the end of the year saw trade improving.

15th March. Robert Casson, foreman at the Tyne Pontoons and Dry Dock, killed by being knocked into the dry dock by a travelling crane. He resided at Camp House, was a quiet, thoughtful Town Councillor, a Liberal in politics, and an active member of the Co-operative Society's Committee.

4th October. The Borough Theatre, built by Mr Jos. Duffy, opened by Alderman John O'Hanlon.

1910. 3rd September. National lockout of boilermakers owing to sectional stoppage of work without notice, in breach of a national agreement made in 1908.

The immediate cause was a stoppage at Mitchell's yard at Walker and at Henderson's on the Clyde. 2,300 men were affected at Swan & Hunter's, 350 at Tyne Iron Shipbuilding Co. Ltd., and 450 at Northumberland Shipbuilding Co. Ltd.

1911. 23rd June. The Mayor and Mayoress, Mr and Mrs M. W. Swinburne, entertained the aged people of the Borough in celebration of the Coronation of King George V. and Queen Mary.

5th July. The Mayor presented a bronze medal in a case to many ladies and gentlemen connected with the Borough as a souvenir of the same event.

1912. 12th June. Public baths were opened by Alderman John O'Hanlon, J.P. Alderman John T. Watson, chairman of the committee, in the chair.

1913. 6th February. The old Rose Inn closed and the licence transferred to a new building at the foot of the hill. This inn gave the name to the hill and also to quite a large district. When Rosehill Terrace and Willington Terrace were built about 1865 both groups of houses were called Rose Hill. The Dobson family were the tenants longest associated with the Rose Inn.

1915. 15th August. National registration of boys and men between the ages of fifteen and sixty-five and of girls and women.

1916. May. First "Daylight Saving" Act passed. Period from 31st May to 1st October. In 1917 it was from 8th April to 17th September, and the following year from 24th March to 30th September.

1917. 4th January. Aeroplane flying from the south fell between Low Willington Farm-house and the Paddock Hall. The occupant was burnt. He had previously thrown out his pocket-book and papers. It was seen a few minutes before that something was wrong. He probably was endeavouring to effect a landing in the flat field, but the landing caused the machine to take fire.

9th May. Dr Craig died at Rosehill.

9th June. First meeting of Wallsend War Pensions Committee. Alderman John T. Watson appointed chairman. Mrs M. I. Richardson to " carry on " as hon. secretary until the committee get into working order.

1920. The coal mines were still under Government control, and on 18th October the miners went on strike for higher wages. They received part of their demands upon giving an undertaking to increase the output, and the pits re-started on 3rd November.

1921. The Government control of the coal mines was to cease on 31st March, and the owners gave notice to reduce the wages. A national coal strike began on 1st April. On 5th May a large contingent of miners from the Rising Sun pit forced their way into Burt Hall, Newcastle, and took possession for some hours. The strike failed and finished on 30th June.

Shipyard joiners strike. On 18th August men gave in after being " out " nine months.

17th December. On Saturday afternoon a high tide beyond any previously recorded. The water overflowed the Ropery Road, from Haggie's garden gate westward to within seventy-five or eighty yards of the Main Turnpike, and on the tramway lines it was two feet deep for most of this distance. The tramcars were stopped over three hours. A good deal of damage was done all along the riverside. A very strong west wind had been blowing for several days prior to this spring tide.

1922. 15th November. Wallsend parliamentary election. Result: Patrick Hastings, Labour (nominated by Rev. C. E. Osborne, M.A.), 14,248; Chris. W. Lowther, Conservative, 11,428; Thomas Geo.

Graham, Liberal (nominated by Dr Henry Aitchison), 2,908; Matthew T. Simm, Coalition (late member), 1,840.

31st December. The "Cost of Living" as calculated by the Board of Trade on this date was 78 per cent. above the pre-war cost. At the beginning of the year it was 92 per cent. The highest point reached was in October, 1920, when the prices were 176 per cent. above pre-war days.

POPULATION AND NUMBER OF INHABITED HOUSES IN THE PARISH OF WALLSEND

	Population	Houses
1801	3,120	230
1811	3,584	595
1821	5,103	560
1831	5,510	984
1841	4,758[1]	1,055
1851	5,721	864[1]
1861	6,715	1,079
1871	10,458	1,293
1881	13,737	1,430
1891	20,024	2,211
1901	30,537	3,669
1911	40,616	8,243
1921	42,900	8,941

Details as to Districts

In 1801 :
	Population	No. of Houses
Wallsend Township	1,312	
Willington	1,193	
Howdon Panns	615[1]	
	3,120	

In 1851 :
Wallsend Township	2,161	
Willington Township	2,284	
Howdon	1,276[2]	
	5,721	

[1] Wallsend Colliery almost at a standstill and in 1836 advertised to "let."

[2] Chapel Street, Brunton Street, and the north side of Main Street was built between these dates.

POPULATION

	Population	No. of Houses
Wallsend Urban District	11,211	1,348
Willington Quay District	6,340	576
Howdon	962	70
Willington Rural District	1,511	217
	20,024	2,211

In 1901:

Wallsend Township	20,647	2,655
Willington Rural District	1,999	283
Willington Quay and Howdon	7,891	731
	30,537	3,669

In 1911:

Wallsend and Bigges Main area	28,854	5,730
Willington	2,436	511
Willington Quay and Howdon	9,326	2,002
	40,616	8,243

In 1921:

Wallsend and Bigges Main area	30,421	6,269
Willington	2,945	612
Willington Quay and Howdon	9,534	2,060
	42,900	8,941

CENSUS 1921

	Males.	Females.	Total.	Dwelling Houses.	Rooms.
Wallsend and Bigges Main	15,483	14,938	30,421	6,269	22,800
Willington	1,495	1,450	2,945	612	2,166
Willington Quay and Howdon	4,787	4,747	9,534	2,060	5,941
Total for whole area	21,765	21,135	42,900	8,941	30,907

The Census was taken during the "Race Week" holiday and these are the actual figures, but the Registrar-General afterwards made an allowance for those on holiday and counted the population as 43,013.

NOTE.—The total number of families in the 8,941 houses were 9,809. The number of persons to each house averaged 4·99.

APPENDIX

Story of the Great Colliery Disaster in 1835—Epitaphs in the churchyard of Holy Cross Church—Extracts from deeds relating to Howdon Quay—Coal miners' wages in 1829.

The Story of the Wallsend Colliery Disaster

The 1835 Explosion

The most terrible day of woe and disaster which Wallsend ever saw or is likely to see was that of Thursday, 18th June, 1835.

As we have already said, several fragmentary accounts have been written—at the time of the accident the newspapers and broad sheets published from day to day details as they came to light, which were eagerly read all over the district. Some little time afterwards, Mr John Buddle gave to the mining world an account of the explosion, and since this, several brief accounts have appeared.

Mr Buddle's narrative is the most complete, but it was written largely for experts, and a detailed story of the great disaster, compiled after carefully examining information from every available source, will add an important and intensely interesting page in our local history.

In order to understand the story, some explanation of the working of the colliery is necessary, and to simplify matters we will refer to places underground as if they were on the surface.

" A " and " B " shafts, the first that were sunk (near the south end of Carville Road), were in 1835 used solely as "upcast" furnace shafts, for ventilating purposes. " C " shaft (near the park) was only used to draw the men, and at " G " shaft (the Church pit at present in use) all the coals were drawn, and it was sometimes used to draw men. " C " pit and " G " pit were both "downcast " shafts.

The seam which was being worked was the " Bensham." It is the second seam from the surface—the higher one, the " High main," had been worked out some years. There were in the " Bensham " seam at that time two worked out areas, from each of which a good deal of gas was given off. They were separately ventilated, although only to a small extent, and were both fully recognised as dangerous places. They were shut off from the working part of the mine, and only entered by the overmen by special doors. One of these closed up districts was an area of five acres under Richardson and Charlotte Streets. The gas from this was conveyed by a drift to the " C " shaft, then by a four-inch pipe up the shaft, and lit at the top, hence this was often called the Gas pit. The other worked out and gas-laden area lay to the south of a rolley-way which ran almost in a straight line from the " G " or Church pit to the " A " and " B " pits. This dangerous district was separated from the rolley-way by twelve yards of coal, except where a pair of manhole doors admitted the officials when necessary. What ventilation there was from this area was effected by a dumb furnace shaft at the " A " and " B " pits (a dumb furnace shaft is where gas-laden air is drawn out of the pit by means of heated air without it actually passing over the furnace, i.e., the gas-laden air only joins the shaft some distance higher up than where the fires are).

All told, about two hundred and twenty men and boys were employed in the pit, but on this disastrous day nearly all the hewers who went down at three a.m. returned about nine, leaving one hundred and seven men and boys below. These had gone down at half-past four o'clock, and their chief duty was to fill the wrought coal into the " corves," and get it sent to bank.

Most of them were working in three districts, either beneath the north end of Dene View, or under the land a little to the west of the Secondary School, or to the east of Point Pleasant Terrace. Out of the one hundred and seven at work, seventy-eight were under twenty-one years of age, and no less than thirty-two were mere children, whose ages were between seven and fourteen.

The first sign of disaster appeared at or about two o'clock in the afternoon. John Patterson, a banksman at the " G " pit (Church pit) was landing three " corves " of coal, and had just unhooked the middle one when he heard a heavy rumble, then a terrific gust of wind came up the shaft. It blew the bottom " corf," which had been emptied, completely out of the shaft, and carried his hat up into the air and over the top of the engine house. Patterson knew it was, to use a common expression of the day, " a blast," and he had the presence of mind to step back a few paces, to where he could see across to the " C " pit, and in a moment or two he saw issue from that shaft a puff of lightish smoke.

No smoke or vapour came from his own shaft. After that rush of air things appeared as usual, the air again was " down-cast," and the shaft looked clear. He called down again and again, but got no answering shout. He got the brakesman to start the engine gently, but the rope down the shaft was fast. On applying the full power of the engine, it came away with a jerk, and on coming up it was found that the piece of chain on to which the "corves" were hooked had broken, which showed that the "corves" were jammed near the bottom.

Patterson immediately sent for Mr John Atkinson, the resident viewer, and Mr John Reay, the colliery agent.

Before Mr Atkinson arrived, Mr Geo. Johnson, the viewer at Willington colliery, came upon the scene. He had been driving up the Turnpike Road, and must have been near the bottom of Church Bank when the pit exploded. He neither heard nor saw anything unusual, and this must have been because he was down in the valley, for the banksman at Willington Low pit, further off, but on the top of the hill, heard the noise distinctly.

On Mr Johnson arriving at the schools at the top of the hill, the schoolmaster was out looking round, and told him he was afraid something was wrong at the pit as he had heard the rumble. Mr Johnson hurried on, and found the men at the pit head in great distress. He had the winding ropes "chased," i.e., let down, then wound up slowly, over and over again, but without result. He then drove over to the "C" pit and found that nothing was disturbed there—everything appeared as usual. He told the men what was feared, and just then John Moor, a deputy overman, arrived, and he and a Geo. Watkin at once had Davy lamps lit, and without hesitation got lowered down.

Mr Johnson returned to the Church pit, and as he arrived Mr John Atkinson and Edward Comby, an overman, were just being hauled up the shaft after a vain attempt to get to the bottom— they had got down so far, but found the bottom part of the shaft choked by wreckage, which completely closed all access to the Bensham seam. Mr John Atkinson, Junior, the principal overman, now joined those present, and they all went over to the "C" pit, and were at once lowered down.

Here, let me say, a main rolley-way ran from "C" shaft eastward, close behind the north side of the village, and that from this main road another road branched off under the north end of the Burn Closes wagon-way bridge, at right angles to the south, and this led to where twenty-one men and boys were working near the north end of Dene View.

At the bottom of the shaft Mr Atkinson found John Moor and George Watkin, who reported that they had made their way towards the twenty-one men, but had been stopped by bad air, and they had only got back with great difficulty.

These two courageous men had got as far as the entrance into the district near Dene View.

Mr Atkinson and his party tried what they could do, but it was only with a considerable effort that they got as far as did Moor and Watkin—the stoppings were blown out, the air courses damaged, and the afterdamp so strong that their Davy lamps were filled with flames. They struggled back to the shaft and to daylight in despair, and some of them in a state of collapse.

Meanwhile, in another direction, one of the many heroic deeds which this disaster called forth, was being enacted. It will be remembered that " A " and " B " shafts near the Colliery Chapel were furnace and " upcast " shafts. When the explosion took place two men, Wm. Elliott and Thos. Kennedy, were at the furnaces. They heard no noise, and felt no concussion in the air, but found afterdamp rolling in from the workings like smoke. They realised that an explosion had occurred somewhere, and that they had better escape while there was yet time. They knew, however, that the ventilation of the working part of the mine depended upon their fires, so they spent some fifteen minutes of precious time in stirring up their furnaces and putting on fresh coal, then they hastened towards safety. They debated whether to go eastward towards the Church pit, or northward towards the " C " pit. Fortunately they decided to go north; certain death lay before them had they decided upon the other shaft. As it was, the time spent on their furnaces nearly cost them their lives. The deadly fumes were spreading, and Elliott dropped behind, but struggled on until he was within two hundred yards of the shaft. Kennedy, half unconscious, managed to get eighty or ninety yards nearer safety when he, too, fell, powerless to get further.

But they were destined to be saved. Another furnaceman, Anthony Hunter, heard that his " marrows " were among the missing, and he resolutely proclaimed his intention of going down himself to seek them. By great good luck this other hero found his two companions, and with a desperate effort got them out.

The news of the disaster seems to have spread over Tyneside with great rapidity, and in a few hours crowds assembled from all districts. Scores offered their services, including a group of experienced men from the other side of the Tyne.

Mr Buddle arrived on the scene about eight o'clock. After hearing a full account of the state of affairs, he thought that further immediate efforts would be attended with great risk and little or no hope of success, and he decided to make no more attempts to reach the men until two o'clock in the morning.

It was generally considered afterwards that this decision was an error of judgment on the part of Mr Buddle, but even if it were so, we must make the greatest possible allowances.

Let us recount what this great engineer had already done this day. Early in the forenoon he had arrived at Wallsend from Scotland, and travelling was no light undertaking then. He had an interview with Mr Atkinson, who had reported that the pit was all right—then started off for Seaham Harbour, and he arrived there between three and four o'clock. He remained inspecting the works until five o'clock, when he left for Penshaw House, his Durham home. On his way back he met a messenger sent to tell him " that the ' G ' pit had blasted and none of the men or boys had got to bank."

Needless to say, he returned with all speed to Wallsend, which he reached, as I have said, about eight o'clock. The first man he met in the village was Mr McIntyre, the surgeon, who had just left the pit mouth and had nothing but despairing tidings to impart.

Here we have a man without doubt physically exhausted with an extraordinarily heavy day's work. Most of his assistants were ill with afterdamp, and either in bed or ready for it. He dreaded that the large amount of gas in the ordinary air passages of the pit would be fired at the furnaces and a second explosion take place. Considering all this, we can understand that he thought the wisest and safest policy was a six hours' rest, which would also give the furnaces time to die out.

When the crowd of grief-stricken relatives and friends heard of Mr Buddle's decision they were very much distressed and absolutely refused to listen to any excuse for delay in exploring the mine.

Their sons or fathers or brothers were below and might be dying for lack of help. Furthermore, many experienced men had no fear that the gas would fire at the furnaces, and it was an indisputable fact that as long as the fires were burning the ventilation would be better than when the furnaces died out and the current of air stopped.

Scores of good men at once came forward, and a volunteer party was carefully selected.

It was divided into two sections. John Atkinson, junior, and George Hunter headed an advance party, and a reserve force under the direction of Mr John A. Forster, the viewer of the Jarrow colliery, composed largely of his own experienced men, followed.

The advance party were able to get much further than either of the previous explorers had done. They pushed on until they were utterly overcome, when the reserves came forward and carried or helped them back to the shaft. Mr Hunter was brought to bank and carried home insensible, and many of the others were very ill. Several dead bodies were seen, but no sign of life. Some of the reserves, however, were told off to repair the stoppings and thus improve the ventilation.

At two a.m. (Friday) Mr Buddle and his party went down as previously arranged—the air was better, but they could not get beyond the point Mr Hunter's volunteers had reached.

Meanwhile as many sinkers as possible were striving with might and main to get through the wreckage in the Church pit shaft.

During the day (Friday) the air courses were further repaired and the bodies of twenty-one men and boys recovered from the nearest district (north of Dene View). Among them was that of William Crister, "The Wallsend Miner," a humorous, eccentric and deeply religious local preacher, well known and much sought after by Methodist churches, even beyond Tyneside. He had started to earn his living down Bigges Main pit when he was only seven years of age. He moved to Wallsend colliery when he was eleven, and it took him until he was thirty years old to learn to read. His ready wit, intense earnestness, and cheery optimism endeared him to all who knew him, although his irrepressible eccentricities were often a sore trial to some of the regular ministers when they first came into the district.

On Saturday "a water fall" at the "C" pit was used to improve the ventilation. This was a somewhat antiquated method of setting up a current of air by letting a stream of water fall down the shaft. During the day thirty-five more bodies were found in the district beneath the allotment gardens west of the secondary school, and at nine o'clock at night the men working in the blocked shaft at the Church pit got a way cleared through the wreckage.

All hope of rescuing any men had been given up on the Friday, and a dumb, blank despair and sorrow had settled down upon the people affected. But late on Saturday a report spread like wildfire through the village that the "G" pit had been opened and a lot of men were being brought out alive. Despair turned to hope, and some went almost delirious with joy. Shouting the news to others, hundreds flocked to the Church pit head, only to learn that rumour had very sadly exaggerated the truth and that hopes had been raised in vain.

The truth was wonderful indeed, but only four lives were saved. At about nine o'clock, when the rescuers broke through the rubbish and got down to the seam they were positively startled by hearing the sound of voices. On shouting, three men—Robert Moralee, John Brown, and John Reid—were found close at hand. They were all weak and all burned—more or less—but sensible. One of Reid's legs was so dreadfully crushed by a fall of stone that he died a few days afterwards. One of the rescuers was named Middleton. He had a son in the mine and was overjoyed to learn that his lad was alive and somewhere near at hand. The father at once set out to seek him, and presently he heard a boyish voice singing " O, that will be joyful," a well-known Sunday School hymn. The father shouted once more, and the lad, although he recognised his father's voice, was found delirious, crouched under a rolley with his clothes off. The poor little chap was only thirteen years old, and as his father carefully carried him home, in a lucid interval he brought both tears and smiles to eyes and faces of those around by telling his father that if he took him safely home he would never play truant from Sunday School again—a promise, Mr Buddle tells us, the youngster failed to keep.

The story of the survivors as told by Moralee was that they were all near the shaft when they heard the rumble to the westward—the rush of air and flame left them burnt, bruised, and insensible. On regaining consciousness they got together, and as the roof was falling (one fall crushing Reid) they crept into a safe place. Somehow they had quite a fresh breeze of good air, which, however, made them cold. They were not in the least hungry, but very thirsty. The boy left them to go nearly half a mile to seek water when, fortunately, instead of walking into the deadly firedamp, he got frightened at the roof falls, and crept under a bogey while still in fresh air. None of them had any idea of how long they had been in the mine, and they were carefully conveyed to their homes, where they had been mourned for as dead.

During the night (Saturday) more bodies were got out, making a total of sixty. On the Sunday nine more were found, and operations were partly suspended for a few hours in order to pump out the water, and on account of the funerals; thirty-seven bodies being interred.

One pathetic incident was that on the Thursday before the explosion several of the womenkind had been engaged in baking " spice loaf " in the colliery ovens (one of which was behind where the Station Hotel now stands, and another at the south end of Long Row) because the coming Saturday was the annual Gala Day of the Sunday Schools. The bread which they expected to eat amid joy and festivities was used at the funerals on the Saturday and Sunday.

On the Monday the explorers got into the east district, which was that beyond Point Pleasant Terrace. When the searchers were opposite the east end of South Terrace they found a pathetic cluster of bodies. A well-known deputy overman, Joseph Lawson, and seventeen young men and boys were sleeping their last sleep. Disdaining to save only himself, which it is probable he could have done, Lawson had collected all the youngsters in his district and he was shepherding them towards the shaft. All under his care were there. Each had his linen cap stuffed into his mouth to protect him as much as possible from directly breathing the deadly afterdamp. They were all ahead of him. The stronger lads had pushed on and got within one hundred and eighty yards of the shaft. The younger ones were just in front of him, and the youngest of all, some only eleven years of age, were clinging to him on either side as they met death together.

He had left the district in order, and while cheering the frightened little chaps and helping along the weakest, he gave up his life.

Joseph Lawson lived in a small cottage at West Row, and he left a widow and ten children. He was a member of the Wesleyan Methodist Society, and appeared a quiet, unassuming, ordinary sort of man, but when this supreme crisis of his life faced him, he proved to be of the truest steel.

On this day (Monday) twenty-five more funerals took place. On the following day twelve more bodies were found in the district behind the "New Winning," and by the Thursday all had been recovered except that of a boy. Exploration went on until the Saturday, when the search was given up for the time being. On Sunday and the three following days work was entirely suspended in order that the officials might get a much needed rest.

It will be seen that on the Friday afternoon, the day after the explosion, twenty-one bodies had been recovered from the district nearest the "C" pit (near the village), and, therefore, a coroner's jury was at once collected and sworn in at Mr Buddle's office at eight o'clock that night. Mr Anthony Easterby, of Carville Hall, was foreman. There were also Mr John Wright, of The Hall, the Rev. John Armstrong, Curate of Wallsend, Mr Jos. Mordue, Parish Clerk, and recently village schoolmaster, Geo. Shanks, a farmer, Jos. Atkinson, of the "Coach and Horses," Wm. Jamison, a corf-maker, Patrick Pye, a chemist, and eight others.

After viewing the bodies then recovered, the jury adjourned until Monday, 20th, and at four o'clock they met at the church to view such other bodies as required immediate interment; they then went to the Wesleyan Chapel school-room, and evidence was taken. The proceedings were continued on the Tuesday and Thursday, and were concluded on Monday, the 29th of June. The record of the evidence is most interesting as showing by what dangerous methods a well-managed coal pit was worked one hundred years ago. Mr Buddle gave a long and clear account of the mine and how it was worked. In his evidence he said, " the Bensham seam, which is below the main coal, has always been particularly fiery. . . . The Bensham seam has always been known and considered as a dangerous seam, which required the utmost care in keeping in a working state."

Next, we are told by Mr J. Atkinson, underviewer, Mr Buddle's deputy, that, " at the face, the gas sometimes fired at the candle when they were driving their holes to blast the coal, but in such small quantities that it was easily doused out with a bag kept for the purpose. . . . In general, the jets of flames were easily put out, but if any difficulty arose in effecting this, a small cannon kept for the purpose was fired, and the concussion of the air thus caused had at once the desired effect."

John Atkinson, junior, an overman, said : " We allow men to smoke in the whole coal, but not in the broken (i.e., not in the pillars). We have open oil lamps placed on the rolley-way at different stations, but the nearest to the broken coal is about one hundred and forty feet."

This is the evidence of the officials, and the miners hint at still stranger things, and yet Wallsend was undoubtedly a well-managed pit in its day and generation. Matters are so different now that from a mine engineering point of view of to-day, such a method of working would be regarded as approaching lunacy.

Up to the close of the inquest no adequate explanation was forthcoming as to where or how the explosion had originated, but the general impression among the public was that the gas took fire at an oil lamp fixed in one of the rolley-ways.

The coroner's address to the jury was a wonderful effort (read in the light of twentieth century ideas), and was the subject of much adverse remark locally. He starts with the idea that no one was to blame. He assures the jury that " every care and caution has been studiously attended to." The whole cause and blame he puts upon Providence, and while he agrees that we cannot understand why Providence should go out of its way to bring this awful visitation upon Wallsend, he, in effect, implies that the people should be thankful that they escaped so long, that they got off so lightly, and that it was mainly the poor boys that were taken, who were not such bad men as their fathers. This is how he puts the matter : " Gentlemen, this unhappy occurrence which has taken place, might any day, any instant of time, for these last fourteen years past have taken place, and can it, therefore, be said that Providence has been unwatchful of the lives of the numerous individuals who have gained their bread in this perilous employment? For reasons of Infinite wisdom, inscrutable to the human mind, it has been suffered to take place. The fiat went forth, and one hundred human beings have instantly been swept away from the face of the earth.

"Perhaps this awful visitation could never have happened at a time when the consequences attending so great a waste of life could have been less serious and distressing to surviving friends. A small portion of men who had families depending upon them were down the pit; nor could there have been a class of sufferers, so suddenly removed, better fitted for being called into another state of being than those who have suffered, the most of them being children, having little to answer for."

The verdict was "accidental death," and the jury add their "full conviction that there has been no want of due care and precaution on the part of those who have the direction and management of the mine."

The disaster had profoundly moved the public interest and sympathy, and both the inquiry and the coroner's address were considered unsatisfactory. Dr Geo. Fife, a well-known Newcastle man, and the lecturer on medical jurisprudence in the Newcastle School of Medicine, published an outspoken "critical analysis of the evidence adduced at the inquest." In this he objects to the "majority, if not the whole of the evidence, being obtained from interested parties," and very plainly says there was a reluctance "to affix culpability to the persons who are, or ought to be, responsible."

When the whole of the workings could be examined it was found that this great disaster had originated at a spot a little to the south of where Fifth Street is now; in the main roadway which I have already mentioned, running between the "C" pit and the "A" and "B" pits. Two stonemen, William Thompson and William Johnson, were working in this with naked lights, and Thompson had either opened a door into the closed-up and gas-laden drift, which ran parallel to the roadway, in order to put his bait or tools just within, or he had been sitting close to the door and the gas leaked through. At any rate, his light fired the gas, and death and destruction was the dire result. The pit was got ready as soon as possible, and the missing body of John Hepple, a trapper, aged twelve, was found on 11th August under a fall of the roof.

When the furnaces were ready for starting there was some doubt as to the safest way of applying the light. The fear was that gas drawn in at first through the fire, might be strong enough to explode the pit again. Finally, a time-fuse was used, and all the workmen withdrawn, and by this means the furnaces were safely lit on 21st August, and work was resumed on 2nd September, 1835. We have before us a copy of the colliery accounts, showing the immediate cost of the explosion to the owners. It is dated 15th July, 1835, and is as follows :—Paid for shift work for recovering the bodies of the sufferers, £171 5s.; paid towards the funeral expenses, £107 2s.; paid deals and labour making coffins, say, £50; banksmen and others waiting on at bank, £25; subscriptions to sufferers, £210; total, £563 7s.

The magnitude of the disaster roused great sympathy far and wide.

A public meeting was held in the Vestry on 6th July, and a strong committee appointed to organise a relief fund, Mr Wm. R. Swan being the treasurer and Mr Wm. Jameson the secretary.

We give a few items on the subscription list : Wm. Russell, the owner, 200 guineas; John Buddle, 20 guineas. Church collections came from far and near, and included Wallsend Church, £20 15s.; Carville Wesleyan Chapel, £16 16s.; Wallsend Wesleyan Primitive Methodist Society, per the Rev. R. Chester and Mr B. Pyle, £2 6s. 3d.; Wesleyan Methodist Chapel, Shiney Row, £4; Independent Chapel, Howdon Panns, £5 5s.; Friends' Meeting House, Newcastle (after an interesting address by Jonathan Preastman), £37. The largest collection was from St Thomas' Chapel, Newcastle, £40 9s. 1d. The total amount subscribed was £2,010 9s. 9½d.

Compared with the need of the widows and orphans, and mothers dependent on their sons, this amount was all too small. Each family who had lost a son was allowed at once £2. Each widow was allowed 2s. 6d. weekly, and for each child under nine years of age, 1s. The fund only lasted a little over six years. The last balance sheet we have seen shows that on 18th June, 1840, the balance in hand was £398 19s. 11½d., little more than one more year's expenses, for £295 13s. was the cost of the previous twelve months' grants.

It was said that the sufferers came from every part of Wallsend except the Village, and in order that we may understand what the town then consisted of, we give the residences of those who were lost, and as it would probably puzzle middle-aged Wallsenders to point out even the site of some of these lost rows, we will add sufficient explanation : In Long Row (now Carville Road), twenty-eight lived; Shiney Row (North Road), fifteen; Colliery Row (near the Colliery Chapel), seventeen; West Row (facing south—opposite Industrial Terrace), ten; Swan's Row (on west side of Station Road, north of High Street), thirteen; Church Pit Row, six; Bog Row (above the Hall Farm, on west side of King's Road), five; Twice Baked Row (King's Road, opposite Mr Walker's House), four; Wallsend Pit Row (near park), three.

Among those who lost their lives were many whose descendants are in Wallsend to-day. To mention only a few, there were four Giles—of these Henry, John, and Andrew were brothers, and they were the uncles of the late Alderman John Giles; six Reavleys, between the ages of ten and forty-three; and four Rosebys, all boys, from ten upwards.

Altogether, the total deaths were one hundred and two, including John Reid, who died shortly after his rescue.

Holy Cross Churchyard

(a) *Epitaphs which can still be identified in addition to those mentioned in pp. 118 to 122.*

The stones lying flat on either side of the path between the gate and the church door are those which were moved in 1909 from the outlying part of the churchyard.

Mr Wm. H. Knowles, who supervised the preservation work, has deposited a plan with the churchwardens of St Peter's Church showing the original site of the moved stones.

(W) = on west side of the path. (E) = on east side.

ALDER.—In memory of John Alder of Willington Quay, who departed this life 17 November, 1792, aged 35 years. Margaret, wife of John Alder sen., who departed this life April the 11th, 1796, aged 73. (W)

ALDER.—The family burial place of John Alder of Howdon Pans, and Margaret his wife. John Alder their son died 17th of November, 1792, aged 35 years. Margaret, wife of John Alder sen., departed this life the 11th of April, 1796, aged 73 years. John Alder sen., died the 28th May, 1813, aged 91 years. (W)

BELL.—In memory of Thomas Bell, mason of Howdon Pans, who departed this life April 9th, 1781, aged 57 years. Also John, his son, who died in infancy. Henry, his son died December 29th, 1795, aged 26 years. (Flat—east of Bonners.)

BUNN.—Here lyeth ye body of Ambrose Bunn, who depted this Life May ye 12th, 1689.

COOK.—In memory of Alice, wife of William Cook of Willington who departed this life April 17, 1802, aged 57 years. Also John their son, who died May 27, 1802, aged 34 years. The above William Cook departed this life the 3ᵈ day of July, 1816, aged 73 years. (W)

DAVIDSON.—Memento Mori. The burial place of Robt Davidson, Master and Mariner, 1785.

ELLIOT.—In memory of Isabella Elliot, wife of Willm. Elliot of Howdon pans, who departed this life May 28, 1796, aged 35 years. Also lies here the body of Isable, wife of Robert Elliot, deceased, who departed this life February 27, 1797, aged 65 years.

ENGLISH.—The burial place of Matthew English, and Jane, his wife. Mary, their daughter, died May the 23, 1742, aged 13 years. Also the above Matthew died December the 21st, 1756, aged 68 years. Thomas, their son, died July 17th, 1775, aged 34 years. William English died March 5, 1786, aged 56 years.

HAILSON.—The burial place of John Hailson, and Mary, his wife. Michal, their Son, died January 19th, 1786, aged 30 years. Margaret, their daughter, died 28 of March, 1781, aged 38 years. Also the above named John Hailson departed January 16th, 1791, aged 60 years. (Upright.) (E)

HALL.—In memory of John Hall of Willington Colliery, blacksmith, who departed this life the 11th day of November, 1801, aged 73 years. He lived esteemed and died respected.

"Remember man as thou pass by,
As thou art now so was I,
As I am now so wilt thou be,
Prepare thyself to follow me." (E)

HEDLEY.—Sacred to the memory of John Hedley, late (mason) of Willington Colliery, who departed this life 31st of July, 1805, aged (60) years.

JAMSON.—In memory of Jane Jamson, wife of Jacob Jamson, master mariner of Howdon Pans, who departed this life October 7, 1795, aged 30 years. Also of their daughter, Elizabeth Jamson, who died in infancy. Also is interred here the body of the above Jacob Jamson who obt. July 6, 1802, on his passage home from Daviss Streights, aet 43 years.

Holy Cross Churchyard

William, son of the above, died at Monte Video in South America the 23 of June, 1826, aged 39 years. Also John, their eldest son, who died at Howdon Dock the 30th of April, 1827, aged 42 years.

JOPLING.—In memory of Elizabeth Jopling, wife of John Jopling of Howdon Dock. She died Aug. 30, 1781, aged 49 years. Also their children, William and Sarah, who died infants. Likewise their daughter, Elizabeth, who died April 15, 1785, aged 17 years. The above named John Jopling, who died November 13, 1788, aged 56 years. Isabella, their daughter, who died January 15, 1791, aged 17 years. Isabella Jopling, wife of John Jopling Junr., master mariner of Howdon Pans, obt. January 5, 1795, aged 37 years. The above John Jopling junr. died September 17, 1819, aged 61 years, universally respected and deservedly lamented.

And on the other side of the stone: Erected in memory of Margaret, relict of the late Robert Cavers, and sister to John Jopling. She died on the 9th December, 1841, in her 81st year.

MCKENNEY.—This stone was erected by Margaret, wife of William McKenny of Willington. Jane, their daughter, died April 28th, 1790, aged 27 years. Alice, their daughter, died August 1st, 1790, aged 18 years. William McKenny departed this life June 5, 1791, aged 55 years. (W)

MANN.—The burial place of John and Elizabeth Mann of Wallsend, Farmer. John Mann, son of the above, died May 9th, 1782, aged 11 years. Elizabeth Mann, wife of the above John Mann, died July 13th, 1783, aged 38. The above John Mann died October 15th, 1789, aged 58 years. Elizabeth Mann, daughter of the above John and Elizabeth Mann, died Feb. 7th, 1790, aged 21 years. Also two of their children died young. (Now flat with this inscription uppermost.)

On the other side: The burial place of John Man and Hannah his wife. Mary, their daughter, died February 10, 1732, aged 1 year. Thomas, their son, died (April) 8, 1743, aged 8 years. Also the above John Man died May 27, 1775, aged 69 years. Likewise Hannah, wife of the above John Man, died April 23, 1793, aged 77 years

MANN.—Thomas Mann of Wallsend, Farmer, died June 10th, 1806, aged 38. Also Maria, his daughter, who died in infancy.

METCALFE.—Here lieth the body of Joseph Metcalfe of Willington Quay, who died 28th March, 1770, aged 43 years. Also John and Joseph his sons, who died in the year 1769. May they rest in peace and rise in glory. (W)

MOFFITT.—In memory of James Moffitt of Willington Colliery who died the 11th of March, 1797, in the 64th year of his age. He lived esteemed, and died respected. Deborah Moffitt died January 30th, 1803, aged 70 years. (Close to east railings.)

NEWTON.—John Newton of Howdon pans, who died 17th April, 1778, aged 62. Elizabeth, his wife, died April 13th, 1795, aged 88 years. Barbara, daughter of John and Sarah Walker, died August 18th, 1780, aged 4 years. (Near west railings, barely decipherable.)

NESBIT.—In memory of Robert Nesbit of Wallsend, who departed this life the 9th day of February, 1795, aged 69 years. (W)

PARKER.—In memory of William Parker, late Tide Surveyor of Howdon Dock, who departed this life July 17th, 1793, aged 67. (Only a fragment left on east side of path.)

PATTISON.—In memory of Robert Pattison, vieuer of Bigges Main Colliery (viewer), who died (25 April), 1807, aged 53 years. Also Elizabeth, his wife, who died (12 December), 1811, aged 52 years. (W)

PYE.—The burial place of John Pye of Willington. Aaron, his son, departed this life the 22nd August, 1762, aged 21 years. Mary, wife of the above John Pye, departed this life the 14th day of January, 1796, aged 77 years. Also the above John Pye departed this life the 19th day of January, 1796, aged 87 years. Also Moses, son of the above John and Mary Pye, who died March 31st, 1810, aged 50 years.

REEDHEAD.—In memory of Elizabeth, wife of William Reedhead of Howdon Pans, who departed this life July 13th, 1758, aged 53. Also the above William departed 11th March, 1781, aged 76.

RENNISON.—In memory of Robert Rennison, Wallsend, who departed this life December 5th, 1813, aged 48 years.

> A faithful friend, a father dear,
> A loving husband lieth here,
> In love he lived, in peace he died,
> Life was required, but God denied.

HOLY CROSS CHURCHYARD

Also Mary, daughter to the above, died in infancy. Eleanor Rennison, wife of the above, died April 13th, 1820, aged 50 years. (Recently repainted.)

RICHARDSON.—George Richardson, of Willington Quay, died the 1st of September, 1781, aged 51 years. Elizabeth, his daughter, died the 12th of June, 1777, aged 5 years. George, his son, died the 1st of March, 1780, aged 6 years. Mary, his daughter, died the 6th of June, 1787, aged 17 years. Barbara, his daughter, died the 27th of August, 1790, aged 24 years. Margaret, wife of the above named George Richardson, who departed this life 17th June, 1799, aged 58 years. (W)

RICHARDSON.—The children of Ralph and Jane Richardson, of Winlinton Key. Dorothy died the 24th February, 1726. Jane died the 3rd May, 1731 William died the 27th March, 1736.

ROBINSON.—In memory of Mary, wife of John Robinson, Ship Wright of Howdon pans, also of their children, viz :—Joseph and Willm., who both died in infancy in 1791, and John, who died in infancy in 1793. The above named Mary Robinson departed this life May 10th, 1797, aged 28 years. Alice Robinson died March 15th, aged 4 years. Also the above John Robinson, died at Norfolk, in Virginia, Septr. 12th, 1801, aged 33 years. Also John Robinson, son of the above John Robinson, died Septr. 12th, 1803, aged 4 years.

SCOTT.—In memory of Mary, wife of Mark Scott of Willington, who died January 18th, 1806, aged 62 years. Mickle Scott, died April 12th, 1793, aged 5 years. Mark Scott junr., died September 9th, 1793, aged 17 years. Thomas Scott died November 23rd, 1795, aged 17 years. Mark Scott, Coal Viewer, died August 27th, 1808, in the 66th year of his age. He lived esteemed and died respected. (Stone broken in two places.) (W)

SHEPHERD.—In memory of William Sheppard who died April the 27th, 1754, aged 78. Also Ruth, his wife, died February 26th, 1758, aged 72.

SIMPSON.—The burial place of George Simpson and family. The above George Simpson departed this life December 23rd, 1802, aged 86 years. Isabella Simpson, his wife, died the 27th of April, 1817, aged 82 years.

SMITH.—The burial place of John Smith, master and mariner, of Howdon Pans. Sarah, his wife, departed this life January

27th, 1789, in the 47th year of her age. Mary Isab**ª**, daughtor of the said John and Mary Smith, his sec**d** wife, who died in infancy.

SPOURS.—Here lieth the body of Thomas Spours. He departed the 29th of March, 1675. (The oldest stone outside the Church.)

STORY.—Sacred to the memory of Joseph Story, late of Willington, who departed this life 2nd of May, 1802, aged 60 years. Dorothy, his daughter, died in infancy. Erected in grateful remembrance by his affectionate wife, Ann Story. (E)

SWAN.—The burial place of Thomas Swan, and Jane his wife. Their daughter, Ann, died September 10th, 1780, aged 9 years. William, their son, died the 6th of January, 1788, aged 10 years. Robert and Charles, their sons, died in infancy. The above Thomas Swan, innkeeper, departed this life the 5th of March, 1818, aged 75 years.

TAYLOR.—This stone was erected by Thomas James of Dentshole, in memory of his grandmother, Mary Taylor, who died January 29th, 1780, aged 80. (W)

THOMPSON.—Here lieth the body of Roger Thompson of Howdon dock, who departed this life March 23rd, 1775, aged 53 years. Also William, his son, died January 4th, 1783, aged 30 years. (W)

WADDELL.—In memory of James Waddell, late of Willington, who departed this life December 16th, 1808, aged 55 years. May he rest in peace and rise in glory. Also two children who died in infancy. (Only two small fragments remain.)

WATSON.—Here lieth the body of Robert Watson, husband of Dorothy Watson, who died November 1st, 1778, aged 57 years. Also the above Dorothy, who died 19 November, 1768, aged 74 years. (Only half of small stone left.)

WAUGH.—In memory of Mary, wife of William Waugh, of Howdon Pans. She died August 5th, 1786, aged 27 years. (With a text from Rev.) (E)

WILLINS.—Here lie the remains of Mark Willins of Howdon Dock, Shipowner, who died October 14th, 1803, aged 59 years. Also those of John Joseph, son of the above, who died March

2nd, 1790, aged 11 years. Also those of Catherine, daughter of the above, who died January 7th, 1796, aged 2 years.

WILSON.—Ann, wife of Joshua Wilson of Wallsend, carver, who died 16th May, 1803, aged 47.

YOUNG.—In memory of William Young, late of Wallsend, who died December 18th, 1802, aged 81. (Only a fragment left.) (E)

Stone now within Church—Lettering Complete

I. E. A.
1731.

(April 11th, 1731. John Aitchison of Willington was buried—Wallsend Registers.)

Fragments

Barbara the Wiffe ... S ... of ... May, ye 20 day, 1690. (There are no entries in the church registers for this year.)

" To the memory of Elizabeth Gotherie who depted ye 25th February Anno. ...."

(b) *Stones which can no longer be found*

BELL.—To the memory of Richard Bell, Master and Mariner, obt. June 15th, 1775, aged 75. Ann, widow of Richard Bell, died January 31st, 1797, aged 86 years.[1]

BEWICK.—Jonathan Bewick of Wallsend, who died November 17th, 1797, aged 3 years. Also of William Bewick, who died October 22nd ... aged 26 years.[1]

MARSHALL.—Ann, wife of James Marshall, of Howdon Pans, shipwright, who died July 29th, 1790, aged 30 years. Also six of their children who died in their infancy.[1]

PATE.—Near this place lies the body of Mrs Mary Pate, who died January the 26th, 1739, aged 80 years. Mr Christopher Barrow of Half-way House, died February the 26th, 1740, aged 88 years. Mrs Ann Barrow, his wife, died July the 12th, 1746, aged 85. (This was on a tablet on the west gable of

[1] In Mr Dees's MSS.

the church. In 1829 it was in a broken state standing in the porch.)[1] [2]

PELHAM.—Here lieth the body of Isaac and Sarah Pelham, who died August, 1763. Also Sally Pelham, who died the 12th of August, 1768, aged 4 years. Also Elizabeth Kerenhappuck, who died the 21st of March, 1771, aged 16 years. Albinus Pelham, father of the above children, obt. October 17th, 1780, aged 78.[1] [2]

ROUS.—John Rous, Mariner of South Cove in Suffolk, who died January 23rd, 1778, aged 20.[1]

SWAN.—Here lieth the body of Thomas Swan of Wallsend, who died the 23rd of November, 1744, aged 63. Robert his son died 23rd July, 1746, aged 24 years. Mary Swan, wife of the above Thomas Swan, who died June 20th, 1759, aged 78 years.[1] [2]

HOWDON PANNS QUAY

Extract from Deeds

30th Sept., 1788.—By Indenture of Release of this date made between Timothy Featherstonehaugh, Esq., and Jasper Harrison, Gent[n] (assignees of Edward Anderson) of the 1st part; Joseph Stevenson, David Hewson and Nathaniel Fenn, Grocers, of the 2nd part; the said Edward Anderson of the 3rd part; Sir Matthew White Ridley, Bart; George Lake, Esq; William Hargrave, Esq; Alex[r] Adams, Esq.; Paul Henzell, Gent[n]; Ann Shaftoe, Spinster; Ann Ord, Spinster; Hannah Ord, Spinster; Thomas Shadforth, Master mariner; Martha Rawlinson, widow; John Haye, Gent[n]; John Robson, Merchant; John Dunn, Esq; Jonathan Tyzack, Mariner; Sarah Tyzack, Spinster; and Anthony Hall, Esq; (the owners of Howdon Broad Glasshouses) of the 4th part, and Bernard Shaw, Esq., of the 5th part for the considerations therein ment[d]. (*Inter alia*.)

"The Quay or Wharf called Howdon Pans Quay from the East corner thereof including the crane thereon built towards the East boundary of the Dock Company containing in length 23 yards more or less" were (except as therein ment[d]) duly conveyed and assured unto and to the use of the said Bernard Shaw his heirs and assigns.

[1] In Mr Dees's MSS.
[2] In Mr Hodgson's copy.

Except and always reserved unto the said Timothy Featherstonehaugh and Jasper Harrison their heirs and assigns all that way or carriage road containing at least three yards in breadth leading from Newcastle to Howdon Pans and from thence to Wallsend pans lying on the North East side of the said Dockwall and passing through the first mentioned piece or parcel of ground. And also except unto the said Timothey Featherstonehaugh and Jasper Harrison their heirs and assigns all that other way or carriage road containing at least three yards in breadth leading from Newcastle Pans aforesaid to Howdon Pans and from thence to Wallsend Pans lying on the North side of the said Glasshouse and passing through the last mentioned piece or parcel of ground. And also except and always reserved unto the said Timothy Featherstonehaugh and Jasper Harrison their heirs and assigns and their tenants and all other persons Tenants of the Houses and premises late belonging to the said Edward Anderson at Howdon Pans and Wallsend Pans aforesaid liberty power and authority to pass and repass to from and upon the said Quay by themselves or any of them or by or with any of their Servants, Labourers, Horses, carts, wains and other carriages and to load and unload thereon and therefrom to or from any keel boat or Wherry, Coals, Merchandises, goods, chattels or effects, as the tenants of the said Edward Anderson have at all times hitherto done provided that none of the present or future tenants of the said premises do not suffer their goods to remain upon the said Quay above an hour at any one time.

Coal Miners' Wages in 1829

Extracted from the pay sheets of the Howdon Pit for the fortnight November 4th to 18th, 1829. The pay sheets were made up by Robert Jackson, Overman, and examined and signed by John Buddle, Viewer

The Fore-overman was paid 28s. per week, the Back-overman 26s., and the four Deputies 22s. per week each.

On Sunday mornings two Deputies went down the pit and were paid a further sum of 2s. 6d. each.

Hewers.—Only eighteen names are shown, and the number of marrows uncertain. The total wages paid was £117 10s. 1d.

Putters.—Number not known. Total wages £46 16s. Drivers.—

APPENDIX

Twenty boys paid 1s. 2d. per day. One boy had eleven shifts, but in no other case had any boy more than eight shifts for the fortnight. Total wages £8 6s. 10d. Trappers.—Ten boys—five paid 1s. per day, the other five paid 10d. per day. Total wages £2 18s. 10d. Four men or lads were paid "Smart Money" for being "lamed," one 10d. per shift and three 5d. per shift. The last item in the sheets is "For half a Barrel of ale £1 14s." The pit was a single shift pit.

Output—Hewed from the Whole ... ... 278 scores
    Hewed from the Pillars ... ... 167 ,,
    Small Coals ... ... 22¼ ,,

             Total 467¼ ,,

467¼ Scores = 9,345 Corves, 20 Pecks each = 186,900 Pecks
(144 Pecks = 1 Chaldron of 53 Cwts.)
186,900 Pecks = 1,297½ Chaldrons, or 3,439 Tons 10 Cwts.

Underground Labour Costs

	£	s.	d.	Per ton
Wages and Smart Money	270	6	11	= 1/6·86
Half Barrel of Ale	1	14	0	= 0·12
Total Underground Wages Sheet	£272	0	11	= 1/6·98

FINIS

SUMMARY OF SURVEY OF WALLSEND TOWNSHIP

Made by JOHN BELL for the Dean and Chapter of Durham in 1800

MANSION HOUSES.	OWNERS.	AREA OF ESTATE.
		a. r. p.
A. The Hall and Estate ...	Wm. Clark late Moncaster	146 0 15
B. Point Pleasant Estate ...	Wm. Clark late Mrs Stewart	127 0 22
C. St Nicholas Charity ...		131 1 33
D. Red House and Estate ...	John Walker late Waters	175 2 0
E. The Grange and Estate ...	J. M. Atkinson ...	124 1 2
F. White House	Wm. Cramlington late Hicks	129 0 32
G.	Mrs Harrison	66 3 7
H. Carville Hall	J. T. Bigge	67 0 16
I. Old Vicarage and Glebe Land		38 2 22
J. Threap Moor, Village Green and Lanes in Common		46 3 12
B.[1] Nicholas Thornton	late Stewart	4 1 11
F.[1] Mrs Peareth	late Hicks	0 2 8
		1057 3 20
Ground between high-water mark and mid-stream of river at low water		147 1 4
		1205 0 24

Capital letters indicate each Estate on the Plan opposite.

The first six letters, with **G** and **H** added together, undoubtedly denote the seven farmholds into which the township was divided in its very earliest days.

INDEX

ACT OF PARLIAMENT authorising new parish church, 126
Adams, Chas., schoolmaster, 145, 149, 400
——, Rev. Francis, 184
Adamson & Pringle, 293, 294
Adamson, Rev. Ed. H., curate, 132
——, Thomas, 310
——, ——, & Son, 293
——, Wm., Slipway, 293, 373
Additional biographical notes, 416-62
Aeroplane disaster, 494
Agricola, 21, 22
Aidan, Saint, 26
Ainslie, Rev. J. L., 176
Aitchison, Dr James, 367-71, 372, 390
——, Dr Henry H., 373, 381, 382, 383, 395, 407, 496
——, Dr Thos., 176, 386
Alan, priest of " Valeshead," 110
Alderson, George, of Wallsend, 178
Allan, Dame Eleanor (Dame Allan's School), 90, 91, 92, 274, 275
——, Francis, 90
——, George Auburn, 87, 137, 174, 176, 294, 332-4, 373, 382, 385, 393, 398, 450, 451
——, James, 398, 455, 456
——, John, 90
——, Sir William, M.P., 323, 324
Allen, John, chemical manufacturer, 89, 95, 99, 108, 166, 272-80
——, J. & W., chemical works, 305
——, Mary, 92, 95, 278
—— Memorial Church, 167
——, Rev. Thos. Wm., vicar, 181

Allen, William, 100, 274-80, 368, 371
Aluminium Co. Ltd., 346, 347
Amalgamation of shipbuilding and dock owning firms, 307
Anderson, Dr James Willington, 168, 366, 375
——, Edward, 192, 198, 206, 409, 517
——, ——, assignees of, 206, 208
——, Francis (1685), 197
——, George, 265, 266
——, Henry, 197
——, James Crosby, of Point Pleasant, 106
——, John A., 484
——, Joseph, 265
——, Robert S., mining engineer, 186, 267-70, 407
——, salt makers, 190
——, Sir Francis, fined, 48, 56, 62, 63, 195-7
Andrews, Edwin B., 338
Angles, The, 25
Angus, Geo., leather merchant, 89
Archbold, Wm., of Newcastle, 239
Area of districts, 17
" Arms " and Mottoes—of Hindmarsh, 72; Moncaster, 76; Cramlington, 94; Cosyns, 101; Hewbank, 119; Bonners, 121; Henzells and Tyzacks, 190; Borough, 392
Armstrong, Chas. H., 334
——, John H., 345, 355
——, Lord, 246, 350, 351, 352
——, Rev. John, curate and rector, 130-4, 246-368
——, Sir W. G., & Co., 329
——, Whitworth & Co. Ltd., 352, 353

521

Armstrong, Wm., solicitor (Sir W. G. Armstrong), 79
Arton, O. P., 485
Assessment in 1663 of Howdon and Willington, 56, 191, 407; Wallsend, 408
—— of Wallsend leaseholds, 68
Atkinson, Buddle, 246
——, Charles, of The Grange, Wallsend, 87, 88, 410
——, Frank Buddle, 181, 246
——, Jas. Moncaster, 76, 88
——, Robert Thos., 246
Ayton, Henry, viewer, 267

Babst, Dr C. T. U., 381
——, Mrs, 481
Backworth Coal Co., working in Willington, 270
Bainbridge & Wilson, 337
Bainbridge, Priscilla, 192
——, Rev. Geo. H., Wallsend, 178
——, Thos. H., 306
——, Wm., barrister, 95
Baker, Frank, 485
Balfour, Hon. G. W., 346, 348
Bank, first in Wallsend, 492
Baptists, Howdon and Wallsend, 184-5
Barclay, Curle & Co. Ltd., 309
Barnard, Robert, 329
Barritt, Wm., 487
Baston, Geo. R., 9, 482
Bates, Cadwallader, 60, 392, 393
Baths opened, 494
Battle Hill Estate Co., formation of, 270
—— purchases Milbank estate, 64; land from Orde, 61; from St Nicholas' Charity, 92
Batty, Francis, vicar, 49
Beattie, Walter, 325
Beaumont seam, 18
Beauty of the district, The. Two descriptions (Harry Haldane and Hamish Hendry), 281
Bede, Saint, 26
Bedson, Dr P. P., 403
Beilby, Sir G. T., 348
Bell, George, 479
——, John, surveys Wallsend in 1800 (map at end of vol.), 69
——, Matthew, 214, 215, 217, 223
——, Matthew (2), 215, 217, 221, 223
——, Matthew (4), 223, 224, 225
——, Matthew, & Co., 364

Bell, Matthew, of Woolsington, buys Milbank estate, 64; sells North Farm to Riddell Robson, 60
——, Rev. S. Ivan, 163
——, Richard, 217, 218, 221
——, Riddell Robson, 60
——, Thomas, salt pans (1539), 187
——, ——, of Whorlton, 60
——, ——, Slipway Co., 318
Bells & Brown, coal owners, 215-225, 252
Benedictine Monks, 28
Benton, vicar of, 45, 46, 49
Berkley, Philip A., 149, 168
Bernard, owner of Willington in 894, 26
Bewicke & Craster estate, 61, 62, 217
Bewicke, Calverley, 125, 142, 251
——, Sir Robert, 62
Bidder, George, 326
——, Sam, 326
Bigges Main, 396, 373, 476
Bigges of Carville and Willington—Charles Wm., 59, 223; John, 59, 103; John Thomas, 69, 104; Thomas, 57, 102, 124; Thos. Charles, 58, 59, 103, 216; William, 57
Bishops Palatine, 28
Black death, 32, 33
Black, Wm., North-Eastern Marine Engineering Co., 323
Blacket, Robert, curate (1789), 117, 138
Blackett, John Erasmus, resident, 71
Blackwell, John, 207
Blench, John, 9
Bolam, Thos., 379
Boland, Rev. Father L., 173
Bomphrey, Edward, 484
Bone, Wm. John, 310, 311, 312
Bonner, Joseph, family burial place, 121
Bonnin, Alfred, 318
Boom in house-building, 487
Borough Arms, 392, 393
Borough enlarged in 1910, 395-8
Borough formed 1901 (Wallsend Township), 391-5
Bottomley, Dr Jas. Francis, 350, 352
Bourn, John, 311
Bowes, Henry, 48

INDEX

Bowes, Sir Francis, fined, 48; rental value of land (1663), 68
Bowker, John, 338
Bowran, Thos., 218
——, Wm., 218
Boyd, Edward, 264
——, Wm, 318, 319, 320, 321, 355, 372, 373, 374, 381, 385, 392-5, 398, 444-6
Boyne, Viscount, 242
Bragiotti, F. M., 298, 372
Bramwell, T. Y., Clerk to the Justices, 406, 407
Brandlinge, Sir Robt., grant to, 52
Bridge cottages dismantled, 100
Bridle roads, 468
Brigantes, 21, 25
Briggs, Albert, Tyne Iron Shipbuilding Co., 312
——, Francis H., 356
Brigham, Thos. E., 338
Brighting, Rev. James, 161
Brooks, John Crosse, 86, 299
Broughton, J., 338
Brown, Dixon (Dixon Dixon), 64, 221
——, Sir Benjamin C., 246
——, Thos., dockowner, 293
——, Wm., coalowner, 214, 215, 217, 221, 223
Bruce, Rev. Dr Collingwood, 175, 426
Brunner, Mond & Co., 276, 349
Brunton, Ann, 207
——, Benjamin, of Newcastle and Howdon, 206
——, Mary, 207
Buddle Atkinson's estate and trustees, 24
Buddle, John, senior, 242
——, ——, junior, 94, 97, 124, 126, 205, 221, 225, 229, 230, 232, 233, 241-6, 267, 364, 501, 506, 517
——, ——, his heirs, 246
——, Miss, 244
Bulmer, Edward, (Queen's Commission 1580), 210
Burfield, Henry, rental value of leasehold (1663), 68, 90
——, Jacob (1700), 69
——, James, 90
Burial Board for district, 390, 391
Burn, David, buys estate, 64, 239
——, Frank H., 64

Burn, John Henry, 170
——, ——, junior, 9, 63, 170, 387

CAFÉ, the, building, 447
——, technical classes, 405, 447
Cail, Richard, 334
Caldwell, Rev. Robert, 155, 156, 157, 399
Calvert, Robert, 9
Cameron, Geo. H., 391, 479
Camp House, 24
Camps, outlying, 22
Carboniferous age, 18, 20
Carlisle, Lord, 222
Carr, Edward, 62
——, Frank, 334
——, John, 79, 297
——, Robert, buys Cosyn's house, 69; rebuilt it, etc., 102
Carville Chemical Co., 328
Carville Hall, owners and tenants, 101
Carville House, occupiers, etc., 109
Casson, Mrs Robert, 24, 25, 395
——, Robert, 406, 493
Castner, Hamilton Young, 345, 347
Castner Kellner Alkali Co., 345-349
Census returns, 396, 397
Chapman & Potts, 284
Chapman, Edward Walton, 282, 284
——, John, colliery, 228, 284
——, Marion (*née* Anderson), 189, 195
——, Wm., colliery, 228, 284
——, Wm., rope-maker, 282, 284
——, Oswald (1561), 187, 188, 189
Charlton, George D., of Dundee, 9
Chater, Thos., White House, 95; built " Villa," 95
Chemical period (alkali works), 271-81
——, decline and its cause, 276-7
——, the rise of the trade, 271, 272
Children in the coal mines, 251, 252
Cholera visitations, 487
Christie, Charles J. D., 183, 443, 355
——, John J., of Rose Hill, 354, 355

INDEX

Church land at Wallsend, price of enfranchising, 147
Church rates objected to and abolished, 133
Churchway to Holy Cross, 81, 116
Clapham, R. Calvert, 334
Clark, Atkinson. *See* Wm. Clark of North Shields
———, R. W., 350
Clarke, Charles of Ovingham, 58
———, George, of Walker, 239
———, Mary, 58
Clarks of North Shields and Wallsend—William, The Hall, 76, 106, 124; Mayor of township, 77; moves to Benton, 77; purchases Belford, 77; sells Benton estate, 95. Ann, 77, 139. Lydia, 77
Clavering, George, 169, 378, 379, 390
———, John W., 379, 381, 400
———, Wm. John, 380
Clayton & Gibson, 331
Clayton, George, 327
Clelands (shiprepairers) Limited, 293, 294, 295
Cleland, Wm. (Cleland's Slipway), 174, 176, 294, 300, 301, 401
Clements, Cornelius F., 335
Clothier, H. W., 137, 139, 481
Clough, George, 312
Coal measures, 18
Coal mine at Willington (A.D. 1581), 210, 211
Coal staiths, trial for obstructing river, 233, 464
Cobra, a tragic first voyage, 329
Coke, John, salt pans, 188
Cole, Henry Aylwin Bevan, 310
———, Robert Ernest, 310
Colliery Chapel, Wallsend, 144-6
Colliery explosion, 220, 221, 234, 235, 236
———, of 1835, detailed story, 498-509
Colliery, at Wallsend, 226-40
———, at Willington, 211-25
———, first modern shaft sunk, 215
——— pay sheet (A.D. 1829), 517
——— profits, 219, 230
——— valuation, 218

Colliery, the Wallsend & Hebburn Co., 264, 270
——— water drifts, 211, 215, 270
Collingwood, Edward, of Chirton, owner at Willington, 60, 71, 125
Comby, Edward, miner, 236
Commission of the Peace, 405-7; Borough Magistrates, 407
Common lands, enclosed, 85, 251, 252, 469
Concealment of Monastic property, 188
Congregationalism (Independents), at Howdon, 155-64; at Wallsend, 149-50, 183-4
Contents, Table of, 11-14
Cook, Thos. Aynsley, 99, 278
Cookson, Clive, 297
———, George John, 266, 296
———, Norman Chas., 266, 296, 297, 327
———, Wm., & Co., 275
Cookson's works, 203; family and partners, 295, 296, 297
Co-operative Societies—Wallsend Store, 96, 356-8; Willington Quay, 358; Laundries, 359
Copperas Works, 219, 489
Corder, Walter S., 9, 25, 395
Coronations—William IV., 486; George V., 494
Cosin, Bishop John, 49
Cosyn, John Carville, 47; rental value of leasehold, 68; built Hall, etc., 101
Coulson, Cooke & Co., 303, 304, 318
Coulson, John, 304
Coulterd, Thos., 273, 274
Council Chamber, 393, 394
County Council, The, elections and representation, 381-3
Coutts & Parkinson, 299
Coutts, John H., shipbuilder, 107, 246, 298, 317, 433
Couves, H. A., 352
Cowen, Malcolm, of Howdon and Tyne Dock, 159
Craddock, Jos., curate, 49, 118, 138
Craig, Dr Geo. B., 386, 495
Craig, Rev. James, 176
Cramlington, Henry, 94
———, Mrs Ann, will of, 94
———, Wm., 93, 285

INDEX

Craster of Craster, John, 62
Craster, Shafto, 125, 251
Crawford, Thos., 318, 333, 334
Crighton, Alex., 207
Cripples' Home (1889-97), 100
Crister, Wm., "the Wallsend miner," 149
Crowthers, John, 163
Cullen, Wm. Hart, 346, 348
Culley, F. J. (of Swan & Hunters), 306, 310
Cusworth, James, 345, 485
Cuthbert Jane Ann, née Cookson, 295
Cuthbert, Saint, Monastery of, 26, 27, 28, 51

DAGLISH & MULCASTER, 440, 441
Daglish, Wm. S., 292, 323, 367, 368, 369, 376-9, 395, 440, 441
Daimler Company established at Wallsend, 96
Dale, Elizabeth, of Howdon Panns, wife of James Moncaster, junior, marriage settlement, 76
Dame Allan's Charity land sold, 92
Danes, the, 26
Darknall, Robert, grant to, 52
Davidson, John, grocer, 168
——, Robert, of Rose Hill, 168, 178, 381, 386
——, Thomas, 168
——, ——, junior, 167, 249, 376
Davis, E. D., 302
——, Fred B., 302
Davison, Joseph, farmer, 373, 374, 383
——, Matthew, foundry, 338
——, Thomas, farmer, 367
——, ——, junior, 338
——, ——, mastmaker, 207, 338
Dean & Chapter of Durham Incorporated, 51, 61
——, leases, 66, 67, 69
Dean, Frank, 285, 288, 289, 290
——, Rosa, 289, 290
Dees & Thompson, solicitors, 80
Dees, James W., 80, 372, 390
——, list of Epitaphs in Holy Cross churchyard, 120
——, Ralph, 91
——, Robert Irwin, of Highfield, Wallsend Hall, 9, 80, 81, 181, 372, 382, 383, 398
——, Robert Richardson, of

Wallsend Hall, 79, 80, 87, 100, 129, 136, 368, 401
Delinquent, Wallsend Royalists, 47
Dendy, F. W., 9, 29
Dent, Isabel, 57, 60, 212,
——, Julian, 57, 60, 73, 212
——, Thomas, 57, 73
Denton, Wm. (of Palmers and Swan & Hunters), 306
Depression in trade after the Great War, 331, 332
De Russett, Edwin W., 185
Devane, Rev. Father, 173
Disasters at Heaton in 1815, 235; at Wallsend in 1835, 238, 498; to the Tyne Coal Basin in 1850, 247
Dissolution of the Monasteries, 50
District Bank failure, 59
Dixon-Dixon, 221
Dixon, George, 249
——, J. G., 316
——, Wm., 221
Dobson, Wm., 304
Dockwray, Thos., curate (1681), 115, 138
——, Thomas, junior, curate, (1718), 115, 138
Dodd, Michael, 381, 382
Donkin, Amorer, 246
——, Robt. S., 317
Douglas, Lewis M., 484
Douglass, Robert, 356, 357, 358, 374
Downey, Rev. Father, 174
Doxford, Wm., & Sons Ltd., 313
Draper, Clara, 246
Drury, Garforth, 382, 383, 384
——, John C. (Congregationalist), 183
Dudley, Robert (1581), grant to, 52, 54, 187, 211
Duffy, Hugh, 454
——, Joseph, 374, 454, 455
Duke of Northumberland, 251
Dunbar, Earl of, owner of Willington, 55
——, Lady Elizabeth, inherits Willington, 55
Dunn, Jos. (Clelands), 295
Durant, Wm., lecturer, 49
Durham and Northumberland Association of Congregational Churches, 150, 155
Durham, Alan, 47

INDEX

Durham, College of Science, 7
——— family (1368-1768), 416, 417, 418
———, John de, 34-36, 38, 40, 44, 45
——— Charter a forgery, 28
——— Monastery established, 28
——— Monastery surrendered, 51
———, Robert (1663), rental value of leasehold, 68
———, Valentine (1580) 67

EARLE'S SHIPBUILDING & ENGINEERING CO., 311
Easterby, Anthony (Carville), 104
Easton, James, mining engineer, 265
Ecclesiastical History, 110-186
Ecclesiastical parish divided into three, 133
Edmond, James, 485
Education—Schools and authorities, 398, 405; School Board, 400-3; Higher, 404-5; Science and Art classes, 405
Edward Withy & Co., 306
Edwards, H. S., South Shields, 313, 339
Edwin, King, 26
Elizabeth, Queen, grants lease (1580), 52, 53, 67, 68, 187-9, 226
Elliott, Edward, manager at the Mill, 157, 291, 292
———, George, 398, 405, 406, 444, 456
———, Sir George, 323, 326
———, ———, Hylton Philipson and others purchase Point Pleasant, 108
Ellis, James W., 312, 338
———, Robert, 338
Ellison, Mary, part owner of Howdon, 206
Elm Terrace, Wallsend, built, 100
Elphenston, James (Lord Balmermouth), grants to, 54, 55
Eltringhams Ltd. (Jos. T. Eltringham & Co.), 313-6
Eltringham, Harry, 315
Employment of children in mines, 251, 252
Encroachments—at Wallsend, 81, 85, 97; at Willington, 225, 387, 390
Enquiry as to Incorporation, 396
Eure, Sir Wm. de, grant to, 113

FAIRFIELD SHIPBUILDING & ENGINEERING CO., 313
Falconer, John Brunton, 207
———, John B, junior, 380
———, Mary, 207
———, Robert White, 380
———, William, 364
Farbridge R. (of Swan & Hunters), 306
Farmholds, 44, 45
"Farms" for rating, 408-10
"Farms," one eighth of Willington, 43
———, one seventh of Wallsend, 66, 69
Farrell, Rev. Father James, 173
———, Wm. James, 488
Fawdon staiths, 411
Featherstonhaugh, Timothy, 198, 206
Fenwick, Nicholas, of North Shields and the Grange, Wallsend, 88, 411
Feudal days, 28-42
First local manufacture (1539), 187
Fisher, Renwick & Co., 339
Fitzgerald, Arthur F., 315, 316
———, Durham W., junior, 315
———, ———, senior, 314, 315
Fitzsimmons, Geo. M., 398, 407, 444, 462
Fleck, Alexander (Castner Kellner Co.), 348
Fletcher, Alfred, 358
Forrest, Thos., 333, 334, 374, 385
———, Wm., 358, 359, 383, 384, 461
Forster, Geo. Baker, 266
———, Gideon S., 9
———, Robt. C., 140, 169
———, T. E., mining engineer, 240, 264
"Four and Twenty," the, 362-365
Frail, Ernest, 290
Franklin, Rev. Father R. J., 173
Fray in 1382, 40
Freemasonry, 477-80
———, Local lodges and officers, 477-480
French wars, 254, 285
Friendly Societies, the earliest, quaint rules, 260-3
Frigates, built at Howdon, 201

INDEX 527

GALLOWAY, W. R. (Baptist), 184, 185
Gauge for railway lines fixed, 213, 214
Geake, Rev. E. H. Augustine, first Willington vicar, 170
Geological, 18-21
Ghost, the haunted house, 291, 292
Gibson, Thomas George, 341
——, Wm., 266
——, ——, Town Clerk, 214, 215, 217
Giles, Eleanor, 404
——, Henry, 9
——, John, 148, 149, 165, 370, 372, 373, 384, 385, 404; portrait, 444
——, Wm., senior, and family, 148
Gillow, Rev. Thos., first Roman Catholic mission, 172
Gipsy Queen disaster at Howdon, 491
Glacial period, 20-1
Glass manufacturers settle at Howdon, 190
Glebe land area in 1765, 116
Glover Chemical Works, 275
Glover, John (Carville Chemical Co.), 108, 155, 275, 277, 279, 280, 368, 369, 370, 373
——, Wm., at Point Pleasant, 108
Goddard, Alfred, schoolmaster, 427, 428,
Golden age of Northumberland, 26
Golf Club, 483-5
——, founders of, 483-4
Gordon, Captain James (Carville), 104
Gossage, Wm., & Sons, 335
——, Fred H., 335
Gourdon, Alex., vicar (Nonconformist), 49
Grace, Ed., of Byker Hill and Wallsend, 78, 81, 82, 246
——, E. N., 79
——, Herbert Wm., 78
——, John (Carville), 78, 104, 106, 246
——, Nathaniel, 78
——, Wm., 78
Graham, Martin W., 403, 404
——, Thos., 353
Grange, The, Wallsend, 87-90

Gravestones in chancel of Holy Cross Church, 118, 119
Gravestones in churchyard, 120-2, 509-16
Graving dock, built in 1759, 199
Grayson, Henry M., of Liverpool, 315
Green, Rev. A. Glover, 184
Greenchesters, camp at, 23; North Gate, 65
Greenland Fisheries Inn, 164, 166
Greenland Fisheries ships, 200
Grey, Albert (Lord Grey), 394, 437
——, Sir Edward, lays stone, 152
——, Wm. J., 80
——, Wm., shipbuilder, 299
Griffiths, Sir J. P., 331
Guthrie, Mrs M., 480

HADRIAN, 22
Haggie & Son, 288, 292
Haggie, Arthur J., 285, 288, 289, 382, 383, 384
——, ——, Mrs, 9, 481
—— Bros., 285
——, David 285, 286
——, ——, junior, 285, 286
——, Peter, 285, 286
——, Robert Hood, 284, 285, 286, 287
——, ——, opposes his " ungodly minister," 157
——, ——, begins a mission, 158
——, ——, (2), 288, 289
——, Stanley S., 290
——, Stevenson, 288, 289
Haig, Thomas P., 315
Hailes, Wm. Anthony, Hebrew scholar, 143
Hall, C. M., 346
Hall Farm, The, Wallsend, built, 100
Hamilton, Gustavus, 242
Hammond, Sam., 49
Hann, Robert (Wallsend), 177
Harley, Lord, visit to Howdon in 1725, 197, 198
Harrison, Alfred, 405
——, Jasper, 198, 206
——, Mrs, owns land in 1800, 69
——, Samuel Turner, 325, 340, 373, 384, 398, 451, 452, 484
Harvey, John (Coal Co.), 267
——, H. C., 327

Hatry, Clarence C., 315
Havelock, Michael, 323
Hawthorn villas erected, 100
Hayes, Rev. Father, 173
Heatherington, Jos., coal owner, 109, 246
Hedderley, Thomas, 373
Hedley, Eliz. (wife of Robert Shafto), White House, 94
Hench, John, 259
Henderson, C. W. C., 266
——, Edward, of Newton-by-the-Sea, 99
——, ——, junior, 99
——, James C., 318, 484, 485
——, Mrs Jas., 480
——, Rev. James, rector, canon and archdeacon, 135-7, 139, 393
——, William, vicar (Nonconformist), 49
Henry VIII., 50, 51
Henzil family (Henzell), glassmakers, 121, 190, 192, 193, 409
Henzell, Edward, 198
Hetherington, Joseph, 205
Hewbanks—Arms of family, 102; George and his family, 69, 102; burials, 119
Hicks, Alice, 94
——, Lewis (White House), 93
High Church practices objected to, 132
High Main seam, 18, 215, 228, 247, 267
Hill, George, 9, 262, 479, 480
Hindmarsh gravestone, 118
Hindmarsh, Elizabeth, married Thos. Bigge, 73
Hodge, Sir Rowland, 313, 315, 316
Hodgkin, Barnett, Pease & Spence, 478, 492
Hodgson, G. (The Laundries), 359
——, J. C., list of epitaphs, 120
——, Rev. John, epitaphs in Holy Cross churchyard, 120
Hollings, George, surveyor, 373
Holt, Wm. T., 336
Holy Cross Church, building of, 29
——, history and illustrations, 110-22
Holy Cross churchyard epitaphs, 509-16

Holy Cross churchyard officially closed, 120
Home, Lord George, grants to, 55
Hood, Anthony, timber merchant, Mayor of township, 77, 78, 217
Hope, Joseph, schoolmaster, 403, 485
——, Wm., surveyor, 374
Hope Villas, Wallsend, 166
Hornsby, Wm. B., 310
Horse racing prohibited, 489
Houstoun, R. H., 352
Howard de Waldon, Lord, sells Willington, 55
Howdon, first mention of, 65
Howdon Colliery—owners, etc., 203, 205; pay sheet (A.D. 1829), 517
Howdon Hall and Quay, 68, 208, 209, 516
Howdon Panns, 187-209
——, ecclesiastical parish created, 133
——, origin of name, 187
—— quay, rights of tenants, etc., 516, 517
—— ratepayers in 1814, 412
Howdon village, owners in 1800, 206
——, older portion buried, 207
Hoyle, Robson & Co., 246
Huddart, Parker & Co., 306
Hudson, Robert (Swan & Hunters), memorial, 182, 306, 478
——, Thos., of Howdon, 153
Hughes, Rev. John, vicar, 161, 171, 172, 381
Huguenots at Howdon, 190
Humble, Riddell Robson. *See* Riddell Robson Bell
Hunter, Miss Barbara (Walker), 177
——, George, 95
——, Geo. B. (Sir George Hunter), 61, 81, 136, 180, 181, 182, 183, 304, 305, 355, 374, 385, 389, 392, 398, 407, 446-450
——, Mrs G. B. (Lady Hunter), 155, 167, 182, 449, 481, 488
——, Norman, 309
——, Summers, 325, 326, 355, 392, 484
——, William, Alderman, 323

INDEX

Hunting, Chas. S., 312
Huntley, Dr Robert, of Howdon, 157, 412
Hurry, Edward, 124
——— family of Howdon dockyard, 199
——— firm's failure, 205, 206
———, Francis, 125, 200, 202
———, Samuel, 88
———, Thomas, 200, 202, 259
———, trustees, 203
Hurry's dockyard, Howdon Panns, 256
Hyndmers (Hindmarsh), Ann, 60
——— "Arms," 72
——— burial place, 73
———, Edward (1553), 72
———, Gawan, 44, 72
———, John, 57, 60, 66, 68, 72, 73
———, Julian, 60
———, Richard, 68, 72
———, Thomas (1649), 60
———, "Widow" (1580), 67

IBBOTSON, HENRY, an ancestor of the Northbourne family, 122
Ida the Saxon, 25
Imperial Highnesses, Archdukes John and Louis of Austria, 233
Iron shipbuilding, pioneer vessels, 298, 299, 301
Irwin, J. H., 325

JACKSON, R. H., 398, 405, 407
———, Rev. Geo., 364
———, Rev. Wm. Hall, 157
———, Sir John, 317
———, Wm., 317
Jacobin Club at Howdon, 258, 259
James I., grants by, of Willington, 54
James, M. C. (Wallsend and Jarrow), 303, 405
Jarrow Colliery, 217, 412
Jarrow Guardian, 154, 488
Jarrow Parish, Wallsend and Willington attached thereto, 28, 111, 113, 141
Jenkyns, Rev. Richard, rector, 134, 135, 390
Jobling, Ald. George, killed at Howdon, 107
———, Thos. Edgar, afterwards of Bebside, 107

Jobling, Thos. Wm., mining engineer, 107, 108
Johnson, George, mining agent, 221, 222, 227, 229, 246
———, John, mining agent, 222, 264
———, John (Pochins), 338
———, ———, overman, 234
———, Robert, 205
———, Walter, 222
———, Wm., miner, 236
Jonassohn, John (N.E. Marine Engineering Co.), 323
Jones, Rev. Arthur, 162
———, Rev. W. M. O'Brady, vicar, 180, 479
Joplin, Hopper, 144, 183
———, John H., 153
"Jupiter Carlyle," visit to Wallsend 1769, 70

KAYE, REV. T. EMMETT, 164
Kellner, C., chemist, 347
Kelvin, Right Hon. Lord, 343
Kennedy, Sir Alexander, 313
Kenton and Coxlodge staiths, 411, 473
Kettle Inn, The, 167, 168
Kidman, F. C., 356
Killingworth Colliery, 213, 412, 424, 429
Kilvington, Wm., 325, 374
King v. Parliament, 47, 49
Kirkley, W. S., 185, 407
Knott family, 442
Knott, Isaac, ropeworks, 202
———, Sir James, 441, 442, 443
———, John, 202
———, Matthew, 202

LAING, ANDREW, 320, 321, 322
Lake, Anne, daughter, 93
———, Wm., of Long Benton, 93
Lamb, Humble, coal owner, 98, 205
———, Joseph (Copperas Works), 219, 412, 489
Lambton, J. D., 265
Land enclosures, 250, 251
Langdale, Sampson, 292
Laverick, Mrs Mary, 403, 405
Lawson, John, 251
———, Joseph, miner and hero, 149, 505
Lawsons of Carville—Ralph, 102; Rev. Wilfred, 103; Sir Wm., 102
Lead Works, Howdon, 205
———, Wallsend, 492

2L

530 INDEX

Lead Works, Willington, 295-7
Learmouth, Rev. John, 155
Lease from Newcastle Corporation to make new river shore line, 196
Leaseholders and rental value 1663, 68
Leaseholders and rents—in 1539, 44, 45; in 1580, 67, 68, 69; in 1585, 53; in 1700. *See* last page
Leases, terms for three lives (1564), 66
———, granted by Queen Elizabeth 1580, 67
Leatheart, Thos. H., 295
Leaver, Henry, lecturer, 49
Le Blanc process, 271, 272, 273, 276
Lee, Jos. E. (Red House), 100, 280, 372
———, Mrs Eliz. Jane, 92
Lemington new glass works (1780), 191, 193
———, partners in company, 192
Lennon, Rev. Father, 173
Leslie, Andrew, shipbuilder, 108, 151, 161, 367, 368, 370, 372, 390, 433, 434
———; ———, & Co. Ltd., 434
Lewins, Frank, 484
Leyland, Chris. J., 327, 331
Liddle, Edward, opens P.M. Church, 155
———, M., 264
Lisle, George, of Carvillé, 103
Little Benton, 43
" Little Chapel," The, Willington Quay, 167, 168
Little, John C., 356
Local Boards of Health—Wallsend 367-74; Willington Quay, 376-9; Howdon, 379-81
Local Boards—Willington Quay, members in 1893, 379; Howdon, members of, 380, 381; Wallsend, members in 1893, 374
Local Government, 360-415
Local Records, 360, 361
Lomas, chemical works, 275
———, John, & Co., 275, 280
London Coal Trade in 1813. Details as to expense and profit, 231
Lonergan, Rev. Father, 173
Long Benton, part taken by Wallsend, 17, 379

Lord, Rev. T. E., first vicar of Howdon Panns, 171
Loren (Lorraine), John, 46
———, Thomas, 46
Losh, Wilson & Bell, 240, 332
———, Wm., of Point Pleasant House, and family, 106, 246, 272, 273, 277, 411
Love, Joseph, Howdon and Brancepeth, 166, 204, 205
———, Mrs Joseph, 166
Lownds, Dr James R., 279
———, Robert, 411

MAGISTRATES for the Borough, 406, 407
" Malignants " in Willington, 47
Manor Court Extracts, 32-42
Manor Court Rolls, 31
Manor House at Westoe, 66
Manor of Westoe, within, 29
Marine Steam Turbine Co., 327, 330, 331
Marriages declared illegal, 125
Marshall Bros., 310
Marshall, Frank C., of Tynemouth, 161
———, Robert, 143, 310
———, Robert J., 310
———, Thos. Dunn, 310
Martin, Wm. (Billy Martin), 420-22
Mason & Barry, 328
Masonic Hall Co., 478
Matthey, Percy St Clair, 352
Mauretania built, 308
Mawer, Prof. Allen, on " Willington," 18
Maxwell, Jas. R., 484
———, Sir William, 156, 203
———, Sir Wm. Alex., 88, 203
Mayne, W. T. (Northumberland Press), 10
Mayors—of Township, 77, 78; of the Borough, 398; Biographical Notes, 444-62
McBlain, Mrs M., 481
McBretney, Walter, 404
McClintock, E. E., 484, 485
McCubbin, Rev. J. D. S., 176
McDougal, J. C., 484
McGaulay, Rev. John M., 163
McGillivray, Hugh, 334
McIlvenna, Jas. G., 339, 382, 386 388, 389, 398, 457-59, 484
———, Miss Carrie, 8
McIntyre, John, 300

Index

McLellan, W., 352
McLeod, Duncan, 259
McMillan, R. J., 334
McNerney, Rev. Father J., 173
Memorial windows, etc., in St Luke's Church, 182
Memorials within St Peter's Church, 139
Merz & McLellan, 345, 350
Merz, John T., 341, 345, 355
——, Norbert, 353
Metcalf, Elizabeth (a delinquent), 194
Metham, James, 56, 57
——, Mrs Julian, 56, 57
Methodism—Wallsend, 144-49; Willington Quay, 167-69; New Connexion, Wallsend, 164-67
Middle Farm, Wallsend, 96
Milbank, Baronetcy, 64
——, Edmund (1596), will of, 63
—— estate, 63, 64, 214
——, Marke (1638), 64
——, Sir Ralph Noel, 64, 214, 215, 219, 241
Milburn, Wm., 317
Miller, Wm. (miner), 235
Milne, Dr James, 367, 368
Mission at Willington Square, 185-6
Mitchell, C., & Co., 300, 302, 304, 316, 317, 318
Mitchell, Charles, 298, 302, 303, 304, 317, 318, 374
Moffitt, Dr Wm., of Howdon, 157
Moncaster (Muncaster) " Arms," 76
—— estates divided, 75
——, Mrs Isabel, 75
——, James, 74, 105, 125
——, ——, rector of Felton, 76
——, —— (the younger), 74, 76, 87, 105, 116, 410
——, ——, will of, 76
Money in A.D. 1300, 31
Monmouth Shipbuilding Co., 313
Montague, Mrs Elizabeth, at Carville, 103
Moor, Edward (Methodist), 148, 165
——, Edward, junior, 178
Moors, Willington, 22, 39, 57
Mordue, Francis, 83, 368
——, Isabella, 83
——, Joseph, three generations, 82-84, 139, 147, 366, 367, 371

Morton, Andrew, family burial place, etc., 122
——, Ann Ward, Crimean nurse, 122
——, Grace Ord, 122
——, Hugh, 323
Moyes, Geo. B., 164
Mudie, Thos., 484
Mulcaster, W. V., 440, 441
Mulherion, G. F., 311, 312
Mullen, Joseph, 383, 398, 461, 462
Muntsey & Jansen, 299
Murder at Willington Quay, 490
Murphy, Francis, 374
Murray, Matthew, 149, 318, 392, 398, 355, 452, 453, 479
Mussel, John H., 391

NATIONAL SOCIETY FOR P.C.C., 135, 448
Navy, high offers for volunteers, 255, 256
Navy Service hated, 254, 255
Neil, Rev. Robert, first Congregational and Presbyterian Minister, 150
Nelson, C. A., mining engineer, 268, 269
——, Donkin & Co., 316, 317
——, Henry, 317
——, Isabella, 86
——, John, 86
——, John, 368
——, Thos., 317
—— Villa, Edward Nelson, 85
Newcastle & District Electric Lighting Co., 341
Newcastle Corporation coal lease, 269
Newcastle Corporation estate, 62, 63
Newcastle Corporation lease to Sir Francis Anderson (1665), 196
Newcastle Gas Co., 333
Newcastle-upon-Tyne Electric Supply Co., history of, 341-5; 348, 350
——, original directors, 341
Newspapers, 488
Nichol, P. D., 323
——, Robert J. (Hood Haggie), 290
Nicholson, Rev. Ralph, vicar, 181
Nine hours' strike, 158, 159, 491
Nixon, John, of Blyth, 443, 444
Nonconformists in 1662, 49
Norman Conquest, 27, 28

532

INDEX

North-Eastern Marine Engineering Co., 322-6, 331, 373
North-Eastern Railway, 343, 344
North Farm Estate, 58
North Gate, Willington, 65
Northumberland, Duke of, 251, 394
Northumberland Glass Co., partners, 192, 193
Northumberland Press Ltd., The, 10
Northumberland Shipbuilding Co., 312, 313, 331, 494
Northumbrian Monks, 26, 27, 28
Nurses' Training Centre, 483
Nursing Associations—Wallsend, 480; Willington Quay and Howdon, 481-3

O'BRIAN, REV. FATHER, 173
Ogilvie, Joseph, 372
———, Rev. A. T., 152
O'Hanlan, John, 385, 398, 457, 494
Old Bank, The (Northumberland and Durham District Bank), 59
Old, Sydney, 339, 373, 492
Ord, Jemima, 58
———, Wm., of Fenham, 58
Orde, Ann, 192
———, Hannah, 192
———, John, 60
———, Leonard S. H. Charles, 60, 61, 391
———, Rev. Leonard Shafto, 60
———, Thos., 60
Organ for St Peter's, 131; for Howdon Wesleyans, 142; for Stead Memorial, 162
Ormston, John (Carville), 104
Osborne, Rev. C. E., rector, 9, 137-9, 495
Oswald, King, 26
Ottodini, 21
Overseers of the Poor, 384
Owners of Willington Colliery in 1837, 221
Oxley, George, 312

PADDOCK HALL, The, Willington, 168, 213, 494
Page, C. J. (Clerk to the Justices), 407
Paget, R. A. S. (Sir Richard Paget), 349, 350, 351, 352
Palmer & Co., Chas., Wallsend, 275

Palmer, C. M. & Co. (Shipyard), 175, 294, 298, 300, 301, 306, 314, 317
Parish Council, 385-90
———, Members of, 386
Park Villas, Wallsend, erected, 100
Parker, Michael, schoolmaster, 169, 379, 386
Parliamentary contest of 1826, 223, 224, 225
Parliamentary contest of 1922, 495
Parsons, Hon. G. L., 331
———, Sir Chas. Algernon, 327, 328, 329, 330
Parsons Marine Steam Turbine Co., The, 275, 327-30, 331
Passmore, Stanley J., 316
Patterson, Robert, schoolmaster, 399
Paulinus in the north, 26
Peacock, Francis, ropemaker, 98, 285
———, Francis Edward Werge, 99, 278
———, Mayor of township, 99
Peareth, Miss Mary, 411
Pelham-Clinton, H., 315
Pell, Bennett, 89
Perrin, Rev. Father W., 173
Philiphaugh, Altar found at, 23
Philipson, Hilton, 323
———, Hylton, 323, 325
———, Roland, 323, 325, 355
Picts, The, 25
Pilkingtone, Dr Leonard (1578), 115
Pilmour, W. H., 330, 331
Pilot Track dispute, 372, 373, 374
Pinkney, Alice M., memorial, 182
Pitmen made fugitives, 252
Pitmen, their harsh conditions, 253
Pitmen's bonds, 252, 253
Plummer, Sir Walter, 318
Pochin & Co., H. D., 203, 337, 338
Pochin, Henry Davis, 337
Point Pleasant House, owners and occupiers, 105-8
Pollard, Haggie & Co., 285
Ponchon (Punshon), Agnes, 44, 53
———, John (1369), 35, 44, 45, 52; (1671), 66, 68
———, Richard (1580), 67

INDEX 533

Ponchon (Punshon), Timothy (1717), 68
——, William (1539), 44
Poor Law Union, The, 365-7
Population and houses (A.D. 1801-1921), 496, 497
Potter, Addison, 175, 176, 275, 294, 332-4, 376-80, 395, 401
——, ——, & Son, 313, 314
——, Charles J., 313, 334, 355, 377
——, Emanuel, curate (1760), 116, 138
——, Mrs A., 171, 175, 425
Potter's Brick & Coke Works, 299
Potts, Captain John, 94, 95, 136
——, John, junior, 95
——, Washington, 284, 285, 367
Prebends, Tithes granted to, 114
Pre-conquest period, 25
Presbyterian Churches—Walker, 151; Wallsend, 149-52; Willington Quay, 174-6
Press gangs, 254-7
Price, John (of Swan & Hunter), 306
Prices, farming stock, etc., in 1549, 47
——, groceries, etc., in 1836, 366
Primitive Methodists at Howdon, 152-4; at Wallsend, 154-55
Pringle, Thos., 293
Prior and Convent of Durham, 28, 42, 43
Procter, Joseph, miller, 133, 286, 287, 291, 292
Proctor, Mrs Dorothy, of Carville, 103
Prospect Hill (or Place), Willington, 168, 412
"Puffing Billy" engine, 473, 492
Purvis, Billy, 225
Pyle, Wm., Borough Treasurer, 7, 137, 484

RAILWAY, 469
——, opened, 470
——, passenger traffic, 471
Rain storm, 293
Raincock, Henry, 302
Raine, George, curate (1620), 118, 138
Rates and Rating from A.D. 1572-1923, 407-15
——, "Farms," 409
——, Valuation Lists, 410-5

Rattray, Rev. Edwin Charles, 183, 184
Rawes Moor, Willington, 65
Raye, Richard, vicar (1577), 114, 138
Rayne, Charles (Carville), 104
——, George, minister (1620) married, 67
Reay, Henry Ulrick, 124, 223
——, John, 24, 109, 145, 246, 284, 367; his heirs, 148
Rector of Wallsend, 9
Rectory created, 130
Redhead, John, of Carville, 246
——, John (shipbuilder), 310
——, Wm. (corn merchant), 104
Red House, Wallsend, owners, etc., 96-100
"Red Lion" Inn, 172
Reid, John, 383, 407
Rents paid to Dean and Chapter, 69, 72, 73, 229
Renwick, George, M.P., 314, 315, 339, 480
Restoration, The, 49
Richardson, Anne Isabella, 9
——, George Gibson, 386
——, John, miller, 167
——, John Wigham, 61, 105, 183, 292, 355, 371, 372
——, Luke, of Rose Hill, 162
——, Maria Isabel (Mrs Wm.), 7, 404, 482, 495
——, Philip W., 183
——, Wigham, & Co., 303, 307, 318, 343
——, William, of Field Head, 137, 162, 163, 164
——, Wm. Leslie, 9
Ridley, Cookson, Widdrington, Bell & Co., bankers, 223
Ridley, Jane, 223
——, John, miller, 167
——, Richard, 223
——, Sir Matthew White, 59
Rifle Corps, Wallsend, 241, 489
——, Willington, 293
Riley, Rev. Father, 172
Rising Sun Colliery, 268, 269
Rising Sun Farm, 477
Ritchie, Nicholas, 374
River, 463
—— god Tyne, Mask of, 394
—— Improvement and new shore line started at Willington Quay, 203
— — passenger traffic, 465

River shore, ancient, 196, 199; later, 197
River Tyne Improvement Commissioners, 313
Roads, 467
" Robert Nicholson " Good Templar Lodge, 178
Robertson, Fred, 358
——, Rev. John, 151
Robinson, Frank, 170
——, ——, cement manufacturer, 109
——, Harry, 170
——, Joseph, shipowner, 312
——, Mrs Henry, 481
——, Rev. Henry, vicar, 170
Robson, Leslie, 485
——, Lionel, of Howdon, 201
——, Matthew, 380
——, N. E., 484
——, Riddell, 60
——, Robert (ropeworks), 202
——, Wm., 246
Rogers, Rev. A. S., 163
Roman Catholic Churches at Willington Quay and Wallsend, 172-4
Roman period, 21-5
Roman Wall, 17, 18, 22, 24, 25, 26
Rope making, important invention, 383
Ropery, Willington, 282-90
Rose Inn (Rose Hill), 213, 412, 494
Rosse, Earl of, 327
Russell, Allan & Wade, 227, 243
——, Dora, novelist, 431, 432
——, ——, her novels, 433
——, Emma Mary, 242
—— family, Wallsend Collieries, 240-4
——, John, The Grange, 89
——, Matthew, senior, Wallsend Collieries, 240
——, ——, junior, 241
——, William, senior, The Grange, 274
——, ——, junior, 274
——, ——, Wallsend Collieries, 124, 227, 232, 233, 238-42, 258, 410, 411
Rutherford, Adam, 154, 379, 381, 385
——, Peter, 359, 384, 385
——, Wm., 359
Rutter, John, 381
Rymer, Robert, 63

Ryrie, John A., 109
SALE and enfranchisement of Wallsend leaseholds (1851), 69, 70
Salkeld, Henry, of Howdon, 143, 377, 378, 380
——, Joseph, 152, 202, 380
Sally Gale sunk by Prussians in 1871; British outcry, 86
Salt panns as in the time of Queen Elizabeth, 188
Salt panns in 1539, 45, 52
Salt tax, 197
Salvation Army, 143
Sanderson, R. Burdon, 265, 266
Savory, Rev. Father, 173
Saxon times, 26
Scaife, Robert, 481
Schlesinger, Davis & Co., 301, 302, 303, 304, 306
——, Chas. Albert, 89, 301, 302, 368
——, Martin, 89, 301, 302
School opened by Wallsend Co-operative Society, 155
Schools and schoolmasters, 399-405, 427, 428
School Board, 400-3
——, first members, 401
Scorer, Geo. S., 305
——, John, 405, 407
Scott, James G. (of Eltringham's Ltd.), 316
——, Mrs Thos. R., 483
——, Walter, 280
Secondary schools, 9, 404, 405
——, Governors, 404, 405
Segedunum, 22, 24
Selby, Miss Frances, schoolmistress, 403
Select Vestry, The, 362-5
Senior, Rev. B. P., 161
Serfdom, 30, 33, 42
Shadforth, Elizabeth, 60
——, Thomas, 60, 125, 192
Shaftoe, Ann, 60, 192
——, Julian, 60
——, Rev. Leonard, 60
——, Sarah, 60
Sharples, Rev. Father Robert S., 173
Shaw, Wardle, 95
Shearer, Arthur G., 484
Shipmaster in 1360, 42
Shipyard, the first, 199
Short, Matthew, 345, 356
Shute, Chas. Ashley, 266

INDEX

Silica Syndicate Ltd., The, 351, 353
Silver plate at St Peter's Church, 140
Simpson, John B., 265, 266, 327, 331
——, John P., 359
Simpson's Hotel, 109
Sloan, Robert P., 345
Smith, B. Fenwick, 290
——, H. Crawford, M.P., 146, 484
——, John, 354, 356, 357, 368
——, ——, forgeman, 96, 354
——, Surtees, 354
——, Thomas, 354, 356, 357
——, Thompson (Slipway), 293, 366
Smith's Dock Co., 305
Smith's Wallsend Forge Co., Ltd., 354
Social conditions at end of 18th century, 249-64
Softley, John, 310
Soldiers' and Sailors' Families Association, 7, 8, 486
Sopwith, Thos., 246
Spence, Thos., of Howdon and Wallsend, 159
Spencer, John, 265, 280, 323
Spencers of Newburn, 266
Spivey, Maria Isabel, 7
St Aidan's Church, 173
St Aidan's Mission, 183
St Luke's Church, 180-3
St Luke's parish created, 135
St Mary's Church, Willington, 169-71, 354
St Patrick's proposed new parish in Wallsend, 183
St Paul's Church, Howdon Pans parish, 171-2
St Peter's Church, estimated cost, 124
——, actual cost, 130
——, building authorised, 126
——, consecration, 129
—— constituted a Rectory, 133
——, history, 123-41
Stallybrass, Chas. E., 302
Stead, F. Herbert, 159, 161
——, Mary Isabella, 161, 162
——, Mrs Wm., 159
——, Rev. Wm., 153, 158-61, 380
——, Wm. Thos., 96, 159, 160, 291, 435-8
Steel, Rev. Edward H., 162, 402, 481

Stephen, Mrs D., 483
Stephens, Ald. W. D., 294
Stephenson, Chris, 139, 305, 398, 453, 454
——, —— (2), M.C., 139
——, George and Robert, 422-6
——, George, engine maker, 203, 213, 214, 272, 489
——, Robt. B., M.C., 139, 140
——, Sylvia, 139, 393
Stephenson Memorial Schools and Institute, 425-7
——, trustees, 425
Stevenson, James C., 335
Stewart, Kate (Mrs A. J. Haggie), 289
——, Mrs, née Moncaster, 75, 76, 105
——, Thomas, 96
Stobart, Wm., 323
Stocks for non-churchgoers, 130
Stoney, Gerald, 327
Stout, Edward, 317
Stone, David (Wesleyan), 176, 177
Stot, Stott, or Stote. See Stote-Manby.
——, Hennie (1580), lease, 67
——, Edward (1638), 67
——, Richard, 67, 118
Stote, Bertram, 61
——, Dorothy, 61
——, Edward (1638), 67
——, Francis, 61
——, Margaret, 61
——, Richard, 56, 61; lease, 66, 67
Stote-Manby of Louth, 62
——, Wm., 62
Straker & Love, 202, 203, 204
Straker, John, Point Pleasant, 107
——, Joseph, 204, 205
Strakers of Hexham, 266
Strutt, Hon. R. (Lord Rayleigh), 349, 352
Stuart, Rev. Wm., 151, 152
Succession of Incumbents at Holy Cross and St Peter's Church from A.D. 1153, 138-9
Sun dial from Cosyn's house, 101
Surtees family—Auburn, Bessie, John, Stevenson V., 418-20
Surtees, John, Carville, 104
Survey of Wallsend township in 1800, Plan of, 520

Swallow, Ralph T., 266
Swan & Burnip, Swan & Arnott, Arnott, Swan & Walker, 91, 92
Swan, Benjamin, 379, 382, 383, 398, 404
——, Chas. S., 92, 108, 317, 318, 371, 372, 390
——, Chas. S., junior, 306
——, Henry C., 92
——, Henry Frederick, 304, 317, 318
——, Hunter, Wigham Richardson & Co. (C. S. Swan & Hunter), 274, 280, 303-10, 317, 321, 331, 494
——, Mrs C. S. (*née* Glover), 304
——, Thos., 262
——, Thos., of Howdon, 122
——, William, 91 94
——, Wm. Robert, 91, 92, 275, 278, 279, 366, 368, 508
——, Wm., 299, 364
Swinburne, Chas., 340, 341, 383
——, Mark W., 340, 398, 456
——, M. W., & Sons, 339, 340
Swinton, A. A. Campbell, 327, 331

TAYLOR, ALEX, 320, 339
——, Tom John, 264
Temperance Hall at Wallsend, 155; at Howdon, 88
Tempest, Robert, 62
——, Sir Nicholas, fined, 48; owner of Willington, 56, 63
Temple, Simon, of Jarrow, 217
Temples of Jarrow, 269
Tenants in feudal days, 29, 30
Tenants, leaseholders in 1539, 44, 45; in 1541, 52; in 1580, 67
Tenant rights acquired, 69
Tennant, Chas., 272, 335
Tharsis Sulphur and Copper Co. (Willington works), 216, 335, 336
Thermal Syndicate Ltd., 345, 349-53
Thompson & Co., 320
Thompson, Boyd & Co., 318
——, John C., 185, 186
——, Thos. Wm., 79
——, Wm. H., 407, 459, 460
Thomson, Alex., 312
Thornton, John, 479
——, Nicholas, 260
Thorp, T. A., MSS., 9, 65
Threap Moor, 43, 44

Tithes commuted into money values, 131
Tocher, Joseph W., 108, 403, 484
Todd, John, curate (1605), 118, 138
Tomlinson's History of N.E. Railway, 214
Toner, Rev. Father Wm., 174
Tontine to build St Peter's Church, particulars of, 127-9
Totten, Rev. Wm. D., vicar, 172
Town Hall, 393
Townsend, Mrs, of Hope Villas, 96, 166
Townships, 18, 29
Trench, Rev. Thos. S., 175
Turbinia, an epoch-making steamer, 328
Turnbull, Geo., schoolmaster, 403
Turner, John, 368
Turnpike Act, 467
Tweedy, John, 183, 355
Tyne Coal Co., 264, 265, 266, 269
Tyne Iron Shipbuilding Co., 303, 310-2, 331, 494
" Tyne " Masonic Lodge, 477, 478; History of, 480
Tyne Pontoons & Dry Dock Co., 307, 339
Tyne Steam Shipping Co., 294
Tyneside Newspaper Company Ltd., 488
Tyneside Tramways and Tramroads Co., 354-6
——, first subscribers and directors, 355
Tyzack, Elizabeth, 49
——, Jonathan, 192
——, Joshua, 192
——, Paul, 192
——, Sarah, 192
——, Timothy, 49, 193, 194, 208

UNIFORMITY, Act of, 49
Union Cement Co., 373
United Brassfounders & Engineers, Ltd., 316
Unthank, George, 291
——, Joseph, & Co. (mill), 412
——, Joseph, 283
Urban District Councils, 383, 384; names of councillors, 385

VALUATION LISTS for each district, 411-4
Valuation List of each class of property, 415

INDEX

Van Kippersluis, Rev. Father, 173
Vicarage, old, 85; sold, 87; new, 133
Village farm (St Nicholas' charity), 89-92

WAGONWAYS, 213, 472, 473
Walcher, Bishop, 27, 28
Walker and St Anthony's Gas Co., 332, 333
Walker and Wallsend Union Gas Co., 332-4, 342, 343
Walker, Alex. B., 333, 334, 407, 485
——, Bryan, of Willington (1596), 63
—— Copper Works, 89
——, John, of North Shields and Wallsend, 98, 205; Elizabeth, his heir, 98
——, John Duguid, 92
——, Oil and Coke Mills, 104, 356
——, Robt. J., 330, 404
Wallis, Robert, 108, 403, 405
Wallsend Advertiser, 488
Wallsend and Hebburn Coal Co., 60, 64, 266-70, 296
Wallsend parish at close of the eighteenth century, 249-64
Wallsend Blast Furnaces, 297
Wallsend Coke Ovens, 297
Wallsend Colliery, 226-40
Wallsend Colliery disaster of 1835, 498-509
Wallsend Golf Club, 483-5
Wallsend Hall, occupiers of, 72-81
Wallsend Herald, 154, 488
Wallsend Herald and *Advertiser*, 488, 489
Wallsend House, occupiers, etc., 108
Wallsend in the carboniferous age, 18-21
Wallsend in feudal days, 28-42
Wallsend Industrial Co-operative Society Ltd., 357
Wallsend leaseholders (1580) and rents, 67, 68; in 1700, 69
Wallsend parish not "ancient," 140-1
Wallsend parish, probable date of creation, 141
Wallsend Progressive Co-op. Soc. Ltd., 358
Wallsend Slipway & Engineering Co. (Wallsend Slipway Co.), 9, 304, 307, 308, 316-22, 331, 373

Wallsend township area, 17
Wallsend township granted to Dean and Chapter, 51
Wallsend township ratepayers in 1790, 410; in 1814, 411
Wallsend township under the monks and convent of St Cuthbert, 28-50
Wallsend township under the Dean and Chapter, 51, 66-109
Wallsend village, owners and tenants, 70-100
Walsh, Rev. Father, 174
Walters, Ralph, of the Grange, 88; Radical M.P., 89, 156
War Pensions Committee, 8, 495
Ward, Henry Jervis, 295
——, Joseph, 318, 386
Warwick, John, 368
Water drifts, 215, 270
Waters family, Red House—Arms, 98; Henry (1722), 97; Matthew (1766), 97; William (1749), 97; Thomas (1759), 97; Mrs, 410
Watson, John, mining engineer, 205, 219, 229, 364, 412
——, John Thos., 383, 398, 407, 439, 494, 495
——, Robert Spence, 341, 342
——, Rev. Wm. John, vicar, 170
Watts, E. H. (Slipway Co.), 317
——, Milburn & Co., 316, 317
Weatherleys, The, of Howdon—Emma, 293; John, 428; John Jobling, 430; James Dent, 429; Ilderton, 429; Frederick Augustus, 429; Robert, 374, 393, 430; Charles, 431
Weatherly, Charles, 364
Weidner, Dr R. J., 484
Weir, Wm. Thos., of Howdon, 157, 162, 163, 353, 354, 379, 381, 382, 383
——, John, 353, 380
——, William, 157, 353
Weld, Thomas, vicar, 49
Welford, Richard, 9, 294, 432
Wesley, John, at Howdon, 142
Wesleyanism at Howdon, 142-4; at Wallsend, 176-8; at Rose Hill, 178-80
West, David, 8
West Farm Estate, Willington, 58
Wharton & Weatherley, 202
Wheatley, Rev. Dr and Father, 174
White, Alex., vicar (Non-conformist), 49

INDEX

White House, Wallsend village, owners, etc., 92-6; sold, 96
William the chaplain (1379), 112
William, Clerk of Tynemouth, 38, 39, 42
William de St Carileph, 27, 28
William of Normandy, 26, 27
Williams, Rev. Father Antoninus, 173
Williamson, John, & Son, 336
Willington areas, 17, 57, 60, 61, 64
Willington boundaries, 65
Willington Colliery, owners in 1837, 221
Willington Colliery, the partners, 214, 217, 221, 223
Willington Ecclesiastical parish, 133, 169
Willington Foundry Co. (R. F. Brigham & Co., Davison Bros.), 338
Willington High Row Mission, 185
Willington Mill (Procters), 290, 291, 292
Willington New Close, 65
Willington Parish Council, 385-90
Willington Quay & Howdon Co-operative Society Ltd., 358
Willington Ropery, 282-90
Willington Slipway. See Clelands (Shiprepairers)
Willington Square, first church in, 185
Willington tenants in 1585, 53; in 1621, 56
Willington township, area, 17
———, ancient boundary, 64, 65
———, as before coal mining era, 212, 213

Willington, incorporated, 397
———, in private hands, 55
———, name, 18, 26
———, sold and divided, 56, 57, 61, 62
———, under the Crown, 51, 52
Wilson, Charles, of Howdon, 207, 208
———, Dr Thos., 109, 372, 373
———, Emma L. (Mrs W. T. Stead), 159
———, Henry, of Howdon, 96, 436
———, Rev. David, 151, 369, 390
Windsor, Dorothy, 61, 62
———, Hon. Dixie, 61
Winstanley, R. H. (of Wigham Richardson's), 310
Witchcraft, 45, 46
Wivling or Wiveling or Wyvel, 18
Womphrey, Robt. E., 479
Wood, Rev. George, 161
———, Sir Lindsay, Bart., 323
———, Skinner & Co., 303
Woodhouse, Dr E. E., 438, 439
———, Mrs, 482, 485
Woodman, Nicholas, 379, 385, 387
Workman Clark & Co., 313
Workman, R. A., 313
Wrenford, Rev., first vicar of St Luke's, 181
Wright, John, 364
———, John, of North Shields, 77, 411; leases Hall, 78; appointed Mayor of township, 78
———, Mark R., 428

YOUNGER, DR ROBERT, 439

ZION Chapel, Wallsend, 166, 167